De-Westernizing Media Studies

De-Westernizing Media Studies brings together leading media critics from around the world to address central questions in the study of the media. How do the media connect to power in society? Who and what influence the media? What is the nature of media power? How is globalization changing media and society?

In a series of case studies from Asia, Africa, North and South America, Europe, the Middle East and Australia, the contributors explore relationships between media, power and society. Their conclusions challenge the prevailing wisdom, on both left and right. Free markets can give rise not to consumer freedom but to new systems of power in which big business, media and state are closely allied. The nation continues to be dominant in contrast to cultural theories which celebrate the rise of the "global/local." Western "cultural imperialism" can be progressive when Hollywood feminism challenges third world patriarchy.

De-Westernizing Media Studies is essential reading because it draws upon the experience of countries throughout the world instead of generalizing from the experiences of a few rich nations in the West. Above all, it provides a comprehensive and challenging response to a key debate of our time: whether globalization is a force for bad, undermining democracy, imposing cultural uniformity and weakening popular movements based on organized labor, or a force for good, empowering minorities and promoting solidarity between people.

Contributors: Hussein Amin, W. Lance Bennett, Stuart Cunningham, James Curran, Peter Dahlgren, Terry Flew, Daniel C. Hallin, Chang-Nam Kim, Raymond Kuhn, Tawana Kupe, Chin-Chuan Lee, Colin Leys, Tamar Liebes, Eric Kit-wai Ma, Brian McNair, Paolo Mancini, Zaharom Nain, James Napoli, Myung-Jin Park, Arvind Rajagopal, Helge Rønning, Byung-Woo Sohn, Colin Sparks, Annabelle Sreberny, Mitsunobu Sugiyama, Keyan G. Tomaselli, Silvio Waisbord.

James Curran is Professor of Communications at Goldsmiths College, University of London. **Myung-Jin Park** is Professor of Communications at Seoul National University, Korea.

Communication and Society

Series Editor: James Curran

Professor of Communications, Goldsmiths College, University of London

Glasnost, Perestroika and the Soviet Media
Brian McNair

Pluralism, Politics and the Marketplace
The regulation of German broadcasting
Vincent Porter and Suzanne Hasselbach

Potboilers
Methods, concepts and case studies in popular
fiction
Jerry Palmer

Communication and Citizenship
Journalism and the public sphere
Edited by Peter Dahlgren and Colin Sparks

Seeing and Believing
The influence of television
Greg Philo

Critical Commmunication Studies
Communication, history and theory in America
Hanno Hardt

Media Moguls
Jeremy Tunstall and Michael Palmer

Fields in Vision
Television sport and cultural transformation
Garry Whannel

Getting the Message
News, truth and power
The Glasgow Media Group

Advertising, the Uneasy Persuasion
Its duboius impact on American society
Michael Schudson

Nation, Culture, Text
Australian cultural and media studies
Edited by Graeme Turner

Television Producers
Jeremy Tunstall

News and Journalism in the UK
A textbook, third edition
Brian McNair

Media Cultures
Reappraising transnational media
*Edited by Michael Stormand and Kim Christian
Schroder*

What News?
The market, politics and the local press
Bob Franklin and David Murphy

In Garageland
Rock, youth and modernity
Johan Fornäs, Ulf Lindberg and Ove Sernhede

The Crisis of Public Communication
Jay G. Blumler and Michael Gurevitch

Glasgow Media Group Reader, Volume 1
News Content, Language and Visuals
Edited by John Eldridge

Glasgow Media Group Reader, Volume 2
Industry, economy, war and politics
Edited by Greg Philo

The Global Jukebox
The international music industry
Robert Burnett

Inside Prime Time
Todd Gitlin

Talk on Television
Audience participation and public debate
Sonia Livingstone and Peter Lunt

An Introduction to Political Communication
Second edition
Brian McNair

Media Effects and Beyond
Culture, socialization and lifestyles
Edited by Karl Erik Rosengren

We Keep America on Top of the World
Television journalism and the public sphere
Daniel C. Hallin

A Journalism Reader
Edited by Michael Bromley and Tom O'Malley

Tabloid Television
Popular journalism and the 'other news'
John Langer

International Radio Journalism
History, theory and practice
Tim Crook

Media, Ritual and Identity
Edited by Tamar Liebes and James Curran

De-Westernizing Media Studies

Edited by James Curran and Myung-Jin Park

London and New York

First published 2000 by Routledge
11 New Fetter Lane, London EC4P 4EE

Simultaneously published in the USA and Canada
by Routledge
29 West 35th Street, New York, NY 10001

Routledge is an imprint of the Taylor & Francis Group

Typeset in Sabon by
Ponting-Green Publishing Services
Printed in Great Britain by
TJ International Ltd, Padstow, Cornwall

British Library Cataloguing in Publication Data
A catalogue record for this book is available from the British Library

Library of Congress Cataloging in Publication Data
A catalogue record for this book has been requested

ISBN 0–415–19394–X (hbk)
ISBN 0–415–19395–8 (pbk)

Contents

Notes on contributors   viii

INTRODUCTION   1

1   Beyond globalization theory   3
JAMES CURRAN AND MYUNG-JIN PARK

PART 1   Transitional and mixed societies   19

2   Rethinking media studies: The case of China   21
ERIC KIT-WAI MA

3   Media theory after the fall of European communism: Why the old models from East and West won't do any more   35
COLIN SPARKS

4   Media in South America: Between the rock of the state and the hard place of the market   50
SILVIO WAISBORD

5   Television, gender, and democratization in the Middle East   63
ANNABELLE SREBERNY

6   Power, profit, corruption, and lies: The Russian media in the 1990s   79
BRIAN MCNAIR

PART 2   Authoritarian neo-liberal societies   95

7   Media, political power, and democratization in Mexico   97
DANIEL C. HALLIN

8   Modernization, globalization, and the powerful state: The Korean media   111
MYUNG-JIN PARK, CHANG-NAM KIM AND BYUNG-WOO SOHN

9 State, capital, and media: The case of Taiwan 124
CHIN-CHUAN LEE

10 Globalized theories and national controls: The state, the market, and the Malaysian media 139
ZAHAROM NAIN

PART 3 Authoritarian regulated societies 155

11 The dual legacy of democracy and authoritarianism: The media and the state in Zimbabwe 157
HELGE RØNNING AND TAWANA KUPE

12 Media and power in Egypt 178
HUSSEIN AMIN AND JAMES NAPOLI

PART 4 Democratic neo-liberal societies 189

13 Media and power in Japan 191
MITSUNOBU SUGIYAMA

14 Media power in the United States 202
W. LANCE BENNETT

15 Media and the decline of liberal corporatism in Britain 221
JAMES CURRAN AND COLIN LEYS

16 De-Westernizing Australia? Media systems and cultural coordinates 237
STUART CUNNINGHAM AND TERRY FLEW

PART 5 Democratic regulated societies 249

17 Media and power transitions in a small country: Sweden 251
PETER DAHLGREN

18 Political complexity and alternative models of journalism: The Italian case 265
PAOLO MANCINI

19 South African media, 1994–7: Globalizing via political economy 279
KEYAN G. TOMASELLI

20 Mediating modernity: Theorizing reception in a non-Western society 293
ARVIND RAJAGOPAL

21 Performing a dream and its dissolution: A social history of broadcasting in Israel 305

TAMAR LIEBES

22 Squaring the circle? The reconciliation of economic liberalization and cultural values in French television 324

RAYMOND KUHN

Index 335

Notes on contributors

Hussein Amin, Professor, Adham Center for Television Journalism, American University in Cairo.

W. Lance Bennett, Professor, Department of Political Science, University of Washington.

Stuart Cunningham, Professor and Head, School of Media and Journalism, Queensland University of Technology.

James Curran, Professor of Communications, Goldsmiths College, University of London.

Peter Dahlgren, Professor of Communications, University of Lund.

Terry Flew, Lecturer in Media Studies, Queensland University of Technology.

Daniel C. Hallin, Professor of Communications, University of California, San Diego.

Chang-Nam Kim, Assistant Professor of Communication, Sungkonghoe University.

Raymond Kuhn, Senior Lecturer, Department of Politics, Queen Mary and Westfield College, University of London.

Tawana Kupe, Lecturer, Department of Journalism and Media Studies, Rhodes University.

Chin-Chuan Lee, Professor of Journalism and Mass Communication, University of Minnesota.

Colin Leys, Visiting Professor, Department of Media and Communications, Goldsmiths College, University of London.

Tamar Liebes, Director of the Smart Institute of Communication, Hebrew University of Jerusalem.

Eric Kit-wai Ma, Assistant Professor, School of Journalism and Communication, Chinese University of Hong Kong.

Brian McNair, Reader in Film and Media Studies, University of Stirling.

Paolo Mancini, Professor, Institute of Social Studies, University of Perugia.

Zaharom Nain, Researcher, Research and Education for Peace Unit, Universiti Sains Malaysia.

James Napoli, Professor, Adham Center for Television Journalism, American University in Cairo.

Myung-Jin Park, Professor of Communications, Seoul National University.

Arvind Rajagopal, Professor, Department of Culture and Communication, New York University.

Helge Rønning, Professor of Communication, University of Oslo.

Byung-Woo Sohn, Assistant Professor of Communication, Chungnam National University.

Colin Sparks, Professor, Centre for Communication and Information Studies, University of Westminister.

Annabelle Sreberny, Professor, Centre for Mass Communication Research, University of Leicester.

Mitsunobu Sugiyama, Professor, Institute of Socio-Information and Communication, University of Tokyo.

Keyan G. Tomaselli, Professor of Communications, University of Natal.

Silvio Waisbord, Assistant Professor of Communication, Rutgers University.

Introduction

1 Beyond globalization theory

James Curran and Myung-Jin Park

This book is part of a growing reaction against the self-absorbtion and parochialism of much Western media theory. It has become routine for universalistic observations about the media to be advanced in English-language books on the basis of evidence derived from a tiny handful of countries. Whether it be middle-range generalization about, for example, the influence of news sources on reporting, or grand theory about the media's relationship to postmodernity, the same few countries keep recurring as if they are a stand-in for the rest of the world. These are nearly always rich Western societies, and the occasional honorary "Western" country like Australia.

Yet, the universe is changing in a way that makes this narrowness transparently absurd. Globalization, the end of the Cold War, the rise of the Asian economy, the emergence of alternative centers of media production to Hollywood, and the worldwide growth of media studies are just some of the things that seem to invite a different approach.

Indeed, there are growing signs that US- and UK-based media academics are beginning to feel embarrassed about viewing the rest of the world as a forgotten understudy. A recent straw in the wind is the unhappy caveat that Michael Schudson inserted toward the end of an incisive, critical overview of the literature on news production. "All three approaches reviewed here," he laments, "tend to be indifferent to comparative … studies," weakening "their longer-term value as social science" (Schudson 1996: 156). Similarly, John Downing has recently poured scorn on attempts to universalize the experience of Britain and the United States, as if these affluent, stable democracies with their Protestant histories and imperial entanglements are representative of the world. Like Sparks (1998), he calls for "communication theorising to develop itself comparatively" (Downing 1996: xi).

However, the principal way unease about Western parochialism has been expressed has been through the recent boom of globalization theory. This is a welcome development, though it is also not without problems rooted in the past. Though most English-language media theory has been geographically confined, there has long been a minority tradition with a global orientation. What can be learned from it?

Geo-political perspective

In the 1950s, an enormously influential geo-political view of the world's media system was advanced in a book titled *Four Theories of the Press* (Siebert *et al.* 1956). This divided the world into three camps: the free world of liberal democracy (with competing libertarian and social responsibility models); the "Soviet-totalitarian" sphere; and authoritarian societies (a rag-bag category that included most of the developing world, the fascist experience, and the West in its pre-democratic phase).

Perhaps the most striking feature about this book, in retrospect, is how little its talented authors felt they needed to know. They display some knowledge of the American and Russian media,[1] and of the American Colonial and early English press, but little about any other media system. They got round their evident lack of comparative expertise by advancing a convenient, idealist argument. Media systems, they claimed, reflect the prevailing philosophy and political system of the society in which they operate. To understand the international media system, it is necessary merely to identify "the philosophical and political rationales or theories which lie behind the different kinds of press we have in the world today" (Siebert *et al.* 1956: 2). In their account, these rationales were written almost entirely by Western theorists. By implication, the world's communication system could be laid bare by studying their thought.

This analysis was viewed as a landmark study for the next forty years. It was summarized, and discussed, in key international textbooks during this period (e.g. McQuail 1983, 1987 and 1994, Wright 1959 and 1975). Why this book was taken quite so seriously is now something of a mystery. The explanation is probably that it drew upon a Cold War view of the world widely endorsed in the West, and seemed therefore authoritative. Whatever the reason for its success, it established a convention that has stayed with us: lack of knowledge about other media systems need not get in the way of confident global generalization.

Modernization perspective

If the 1950s "Four Theories" tradition saw the universe only through Western eyes, it was followed in the 1960s by a theory which assumed the developing world should imitate the West. It argued that good communication was the key to "the most challenging social problem of our time—the modernizing of most of the world" (Lerner 1963: 350). It was the crux of everything, from persuading Peruvian peasants to boil their water (Rogers and Shoemaker 1971) to encouraging Turks and Iranians to be more ambitious (McClelland 1961), to building a nation with a sense of cohesion and social purpose, willing to make collective sacrifices for the sake of progress (Schramm 1963). But if these and other goals were to be achieved, money had to be spent developing modern media systems in developing countries, something that American planners were roundly criticized for failing to recognize in contrast to their communist adversaries (Pool 1963).

Daniel Lerner offered the most coherent view of how a modern communication system supposedly contributes to the transition from "tradition" to modernity. He maintained that modern communications socialize people into wanting more out of life by extending their horizons. "The diffusion of new ideas and information," wrote Lerner (1963: 348), "stimulates the peasant to want to be a freeholding farmer, ... the farmer's wife to want to stop bearing children, the farmer's daughter to wear a dress and to do her hair." It also matures the political system so that it is able to respond and adapt to change. The media, he explained, inform people of things outside their village, encourage them to have opinions about public affairs, and convert them into a participant public. For this reason, he concluded, "the connection between mass media and political democracy is especially close" (Lerner 1963: 342).

This is not how "modernization" in fact took place in many pro-Western developing countries. The national development model was invoked to justify a repressive political system and the arbitrary exercise of political power. The media system was directed toward maintaining control rather than educating for democracy. In other words, modernization theory was used to restrict freedom of expression and to justify political indoctrination.

One reason why this theory was easy to suborn was because it paid so little attention to the development of a pluralistic media system. Indeed, "tradition" often featured in modernization theory as something to be defeated, not as a legitimate element of civil society. Communication was viewed as a trust-building exercise between leaders and led, rather than as an open-ended system of collective dialogue. Wilbur Schramm, a leading exponent of modernization theory, made what seems in retrospect to have been an especially revealing comment. "It is probably wrong for us," he wrote, "to expect a country which is trying to gather together its resources and mobilize its population for a greater transitional effort to permit the same kind of free, competitive, and sometimes confusing communication to which we have become accustomed in this country" (Schramm 1963: 55). He was not alone in thinking that "confusing" communication should be curtailed in certain circumstances. Another modernization luminary, Ithiel de Sola Pool, wrote rather chillingly, "no nation will indefinitely tolerate a freedom of the press that serves to divide the country and to open the floodgate of criticism against the freely chosen government that leads it" (Pool 1973 cited in McQuail 1994: 129).

Lack of local knowledge was another reason why questions of media access and pluralism were downplayed. The expertise of people like Schramm and Pool was in communications, not in "area studies." Had they been better informed, they might not have adopted so uncritical a view of Westernizing elites in developing countries.

Media imperialism

From the late 1960s onward, a determined and largely successful attempt was made to dethrone modernization theory. It was argued that American aid programs to developing countries, and the "free flow of information" policies promoted by the American state, assist the American media industry in its drive to achieve international dominion (Schiller 1969, 1976, and 1998). Far from promoting self-sufficiency, the "modernization" of developing countries merely fosters dependency within an exploitative system of global economic relations. It promotes American capitalist values and interests, and erodes local culture in a process of global homogenization. "Today," writes Herbert Schiller (1998: 17),"the United States exercises mastery of global communications and culture."

Like modernization theory, this was selectively exploited by autocratic regimes in newly industrializing societies. Indeed, the defense of "Asian values" and Eastern essentialism against Western imperialism is even now a standard pretext used by conservatives and communists alike to legitimate illiberal controls against their own people (see Chapters 2 and 10). As Hallin (1998) argues, this subversion of Western theory occurred partly because it was underdeveloped. It was sometimes naively assumed that, if Western influence receded, the vacuum would be filled by popular communication.

In the 1980s and 1990s, the media imperialism thesis in turn came under sustained attack. This was partly because the notion of a one-way flow of communication and influence from the West was challenged by the counter-argument that global flows are "multidirectional." Sreberny-Mohammadi (1996) points out that the simple image of Western dominion obscures the complex and reciprocal nature of interaction between different and increasingly hybridized cultures over centuries. Similarly, Giddens (1999), among others, points to "reverse colonization," exemplified by the export of Brazilian television programs to Portugal and the Mexicanization of southern California. More generally, it is argued, global media enterprises have been forced to adapt to local cultures, and to link up with local partners, in order to sustain their expansion (Croteau and Hoynes 1997). But perhaps the most telling exposition of this "multidirectionality" argument comes from Sinclair *et al.* (1996) who show that it is simplistic to think of the international television market as a single global entity dominated by Hollywood. Rapidly expanding regional or geolinguistic markets are giving rise to major centers of television production in Mexico, Brazil, India, Taiwan, and Hong Kong, each catering for different language groups.

The second main line of attack on the media imperialism thesis focuses on another weak link in its argument, its underestimation of local resistance to American domination. Critics point to consumer resistance to American television programs, with comparative research showing a preference for locally made programs (Silj 1988); political resistance, with a number of states supporting local media production through subsidies, investment quotas, import and ownership restrictions (Humphreys 1996, Raboy 1997); and cultural resistance, rooted in tenacious local traditions and social networks. Thus, *Dallas* may be transmitted around the world, but it means different things to different viewers, from Japan to Israel, who draw upon different belief systems and cultural references to make sense of it (Liebes and Katz 1990).

Critics also point to a certain fuzziness in the way in which three different categories—American, Western, and capitalist—can be used almost interchangeably in the media imperialism argument. To this and other complaints, defenders respond by saying in effect that complexity is being invoked to obfuscate the continuing reality of Western cultural preponderance. Media activity, in this view, may be multidirectional but it is still very unequal. Boyd-Barrett (1998) has recently argued that American or Western enterprises are dominant in certain key sectors, most notably film, news wholesaling, and computer operating systems. Similarly, Herman and McChesney (1997) and McChesney (1998) argue that a relatively small number of transnational media corporations, mostly owned or based in the United States, have recently emerged as dominant in the greatly expanded media export market.

The second counter-argument is that though there is global cultural diversity, it is being restructured by an underlying hegemonic dynamic. The dominant strain of global mass culture, according to Stuart Hall, "remains centerd in the West ... and it always speaks English." Though responding to cultural differences, "it is wanting to recognize and absorb those differences within the larger, overarching framework of what is essentially an American conception of the world" (Hall 1997: 33).

Cultural globalization

However, these reformulations seem to be falling on stony ground. A new orthodoxy emerged in the 1980s and 1990s, more in tune with the neo-liberal temper of the time. This new orthodoxy in effect synthesized critiques of media imperialism, and re-presented them as a coherent alternative perspective.

The central theme of this new orthodoxy is that, in the words of Anthony Giddens (1999: 31), "globalisation today is only partly westernisation. Globalisation is becoming increasingly decentered—not under the control of any group of nations, still less of the large corporations. Its effects are felt as much in Western countries as elsewhere." In other words, the focus of this perspective has shifted from the modernization or exploitation of developing societies to a view of globalization as a universal phenomenon that is transforming the entire world.

The other key claim of this view is that globalization is extending the basis of communication and cultural exchange. This argument is sometimes presented in a simple form, first suggested by McLuhan (1964). The rise of new communications technology, compressing time and space and transcending national frontiers, is bringing into being a "global village." This is reducing national division, and enhancing international understanding and empathy, because people are better connected to each other through international channels of communication.

However, a second, more qualified version of this view is increasingly being advanced. This argues that globalization is opening up new lines of communication between different groups, and constructing new spaces for the building of mutuality, without suggesting that the world is shrinking into a single, harmonious village. As Ien Ang (1990: 252) writes guardedly: "the transnational communication system … offers opportunities of new forms of bonding and solidarity, new ways of forging cultural communities."

New media crossing national frontiers are giving people access to information and ideas that those in authority, in national societies, have sought to suppress. For example, the audio-cassette recording of speeches phoned through by Islamic fundamentalists in Paris, and then amplified by loudspeaker in mosques in Iran, played a significant part in the successful revolt against the Shah (Sreberny-Mohammadi and Mohammadi 1994). Similarly, transnational broadcasting played a part in the erosion of the authority of communist states in the former Soviet bloc (see Chapters 3 and 6 in this book).

The supra-national is also supporting the sub-national in a new global–local connexion that is eroding the national. Globalization is promoting ethnic, cultural, religious, and linguistic diversity within nation-states (Robins *et al.* 1997). Thus, Korean-Americans can watch Korean TV on cable TV in California, just as Indian-British viewers can watch Indian films on cable in London. The identity of diasporic communities can now be sustained not through treasured postcards and the fading memories of grandparents, but through daily cultural feeds that sustain imperiled ethnic minority identities (Dayan 1998).

More generally, what Robins *et al.* (1997: 16) call "peripheral visions" can be transmitted center stage through the globalization of communications. Greenpeace transmitted video footage by satellite to fan international protest against nuclear testing in the Pacific, and the dumping of an oil rig in the Atlantic. Zapatista rebels in Mexico, and their supporters, used cyberspace to win international sympathy for their cause (Cleaver 1998). An especially well documented example of this general argument is provided by Sonia Serra, who shows that a local campaign against the killing of street children in Brazil had initially very little effect. It was only when local campaigners enlisted the help of international agencies like Amnesty International, and won a sympathetic hearing from media in the United States and Europe, that they made headway, securing a change in the law (Serra 1996 and 1999).

Some cultural theorists also claim that "globalization ... pluralizes the world by recognizing the value of cultural niches and local abilities" (Waters 1995: 136). Minorities too small to be catered for in national contexts are aggregated into viable global markets. Globalization also selects elements of neatly partitioned national cultures, and remixes them in new ways for an international public. As Kevin Robins argues, "audio-visual geographies are thus becoming detached from the symbolic spaces of national culture, and realigned on the basis of the more 'universal' principles of international consumer culture" (Robins 1995: 250). This global market system is also portrayed in some accounts as recruiting talent with impersonal efficiency. In the music business, according to Frith (1996: 172), "globally successful sounds may now come from anywhere."

These arguments now command the terms of debate. Indeed, textbook accounts sometimes narrate a linear development in which those mired in the error of media imperialism theory have been corrected by the sages of cultural globalization. However, waiting in the wings is a different, more critical account usefully condensed and developed by Panitch and Leys (1999).[2] This offers an understanding of economic power and of history that tends to be lacking in cultural globalization theory.

Global capitalism restored

What is exciting and pregnant with liberating possibilities, according to cultural postmodernism, marks a major reverse for humanity in the view of radical political economy. This latter tradition insists that globalization is not new. Unfettered global capitalism has merely been restored, and the power of people to curb its excesses has been diminished.

The decisive time when economic globalization remade the world was in the nineteenth and early twentieth centuries (Hobsbawm 1989 and 1975). Indeed, there is a heated debate among political economists about whether economic globalization is more advanced now than it was early in the twentieth century before the growth of protectionism, and whether the world economy is not, even now, better understood as being regionalised and national rather than globalized (Hirst and Thompson 1996, Radice 1999, Weiss 1998). In fact, the proportion of total output traded internationally was not much higher in the early 1990s than it was shortly before the First World War (Hirst and Thompson 1996).

But this appearance of historical continuity conceals important changes. The most important shift is in the relationship between democracy and the capitalist system. During the high tide of social liberalism (roughly from the 1870s to 1914), business came to be increasingly regulated, taxed, and rendered more socially accountable in advanced industrial societies. This was prompted by the rise of electoral democracy, and a popular reaction against "irresponsible" capitalism

(Rubinstein 1998). But it was also made possible by the fact that business could not readily relocate, and was still subject to effective national jurisdiction.

The second determined attempt to civilize capitalism occurred in the heyday of social democracy (roughly from the 1930s to the 1970s). This more ambitious project sought to insulate people from the insecurities of the economic system, from the cradle to the grave, through collective welfare services. It also tried to sustain the values of mutuality and community through policies based on social justice, in opposition to the individualizing, fragmenting, and morally callousing effects of the market (Hirsch 1999, McKibbin 1998). This tradition drew heavily on support from the industrial working class, and the fears egendered by the 1930s world slump. It was relatively successful because a global system of governance was developed that made national governments effective instruments of economic management.

During the Bretton Woods era, inaugurated in 1944, a system of international economic regulation designed to sustain global growth was put in place based on the control of cross-border movements of capital, fixed exchange rates, progressive tariff reduction, and the provision of credit to countries in trouble. This enabled the governments of developed economies to adopt full employment policies (the corner-stone of their social cohesion and welfare programs) and pursue, within defined limits, independent social and economic goals.

This system of global governance was gradually undermined and distorted from the 1960s onward (Helleiner 1994, Hobsbawm 1994). Transnational corporations be-came increasingly free to invest, produce, sell, and remit profit wherever they wanted. They also became more "mobile" as a consequence of technological change and the global redivision of labor, as well as more dominant in the global economy. Conse-quently, they were better able to play off governments against each other, evade tax and exert influence on public policy (Coates 1999, Mahnkopf 1999, Picciotto 1992).

Global deregulation also led to the spectacular growth of international financial markets, giving rise to capital movements between countries on an unprecedented scale. These movements were highly sensitive to the effect of national government decisions on short-term profitability, and curtailed what governments were able to do. Adverse market judgments could lead to rapid capital outflows, followed by currency depreciation, higher interest rates, and deflation. A fundamental loss of market confidence could result in economic crisis, and at best the provision of emergency credit from the International Monetary Fund (IMF) tied to "structural adjustment," a euphemism for externally imposed economic policies (Bernard 1999, Boron 1999).

In this new global context, national governments lost part of their sovereignty. There is now an active debate on the left about how the erosion of governments' "Keynesian capacity" came about, what should be done about it, and the extent to which the democratic state really is enfeebled. The answer seems to be that the dismantling of global controls was partly avoidable, and that right-wing govern-ments deliberately engineered their own eclipse. However, global deregulation is now extremely difficult to reverse, primarily for ideological rather than technical reasons (Helleiner 1994 and 1996, Weiss 1998). The global capitalist order enjoys elite and public consent, while its organized critics have lost influence partly as a consequence of economic change. This has given rise to four responses within social democracy: Clintonism (making individuals better equipped for the global market), the Rhineland or Nordic model (group-based approaches to sustaining both social justice and competitiveness in the global market), rebuilding government on a regional basis (radical Euro-federalism), and repairing global governance (for example, "Tobin tax") (Hutton 1997, Mahnkopf 1999, Weiss 1998).

The weakening of government is a particular problem for social democracy because it is a statist political philosophy. But globalization poses a problem for other political traditions as well. The Asian crisis in the late 1990s exposed the vulnerability of the state capitalist model, even when buttressed by covert protectionism. It revealed that years of working to achieve successful industrialization had still not rescued even middleweight economies from the sort of external "political" control formerly associated with poverty and economic depedency. In a globally deregulated world, all economies are subject to the pressure of market norms and behavior. The power to resist, and the power to support values and social arrangements that reflect the will of the people through the democratic system, have been diminished everywhere.

This account of the loss of democratic control over the economy has a counterpart in the history of communications. As with the economy, the globalization of communications is not a new phenomenon, and it has not been continuous. Globalization gathered momentum with the rise of the international news agencies in the nineteenth century, accelerated with the global rise of Hollywood in the 1920s, and then went into reverse when radio and, later, television were shaped into a national mold.

The motives for this extension of national control, though mixed, included strong altruistic elements in many liberal democracies. It was argued that public ownership or regulation of broadcasting was needed in order to promote an informed democracy, to which opposition parties as well as government had a right of access; to facilitate collective self-expression and national identity; and to ensure high standards and a planned diversity of programs. Underlying this approach was a conviction that the needs of society could not be equated automatically with those of the market, and that people should be able to express through the electoral system a preference for the kind of broadcasting system they want.

This approach is under attack, now that the drive toward the globalization of communications has been resumed. Cable, satellite, and digital technologies have facilitated the launch of new commercial TV channels that are eroding the audiences, revenue, and legitimacy of public service channels. The rise of communications giants as a political lobby and the spread of neo-liberal ideas have also led to deregulatory broadcasting policies. These have contributed to the marketization of some public service organizations, and a decline in their corporate sense of purpose. Increasingly, according to this argument, the forces of commercial globalization are encroaching upon and undermining publicly owned and regulated broadcasting media (Aldridge and Hewitt 1994, Avery 1993, Tracey 1998), although there is an unfashionable view which believes that this argument is in general overstated (Curran 1998).

New conventional wisdom

We are thus being invited to choose between two sharply contrasting views. Cultural theorists write with infectious enthusiasm about globalization as a process that is increasing international dialogue, empowering minorities, and building progressive solidarity. Political economists, on the other hand, write about globalization as a capitalist victory that is dispossessing democracies, imposing policy homogenization, and weakening progessive movements rooted in working-class and popular political organizations.

Informing this clash are often unstated (and undebated) differences of understanding. In the cultural globalization literature, the state and nation tend to be associated with hierarchy, monolithic structures, historically contingent identities, repressive cultures, spatial competition, and war. Indeed, cultural globalization is viewed as positive precisely because it is thought to weaken the nation. By contrast, the political economy literature has a less schooled approach, with one strand attacking the corrupting legacy of nationalism as the worm inside the apple of social democracy, and disputing liberal notions of state as illusory. But this tradition, in all its diversity, still tends to see the state as potentially the instrument of popular countervailing power and progressive redistribution, and views the nation as the place where democracy is mainly organized. In the absence of a developed alternative, the erosion of the national democratic state is viewed as a problem.

But if these two broad approaches diverge, they are agreed on one thing. The "nation" is in dire trouble. In despairing political economy, the nation has lost its ability to shape its own destiny. As Eric Hobsbawm (1994: 15) puts it, national economies have become mere "complications of transational corporations." In cultural theory, they are imagined communities that are losing their hold on the imagination. In the words of Anthony Giddens (1999: 31), the "era of the nation state is over."

When intellectual traditions as dissimilar as these start agreeing with each other, a new conventional wisdom has been born. It is at this point that an alarm bell should start ringing. The essays in this book suggest that this alarm should not be switched off.

Aims

The main aim of this book is to contribute to a broadening of media theory and understanding in a way that takes account of the experience of countries outside the Anglo-American orbit. It is also hoped that it will contribute to an informed response to rival globalization theories.

Indeed, this was originally conceived as a globalization book. What prompted us to switch direction was not only the thought that numerous other books about globalization are pouring off the presses (for example, Braman and Sreberny-Mohammadi 1996, Golding and Harris 1996, Hoskins *et al.* 1997, King 1997, Mohammadi 1997, Panitch and Leys 1999, Sreberny-Mohammadi *et al.* 1997, Taylor 1997, Thussu 1998, Tomlinson 1999, Van Ginneken 1998, Waters 1995) or are in the pipeline.[3] Our shift was prompted also by a suspicion that perhaps nations are still centrally important, and that their continuing significance tends to be underplayed by globalization theory.

Despite the internationalization of film, music, and news "wholesaling," and despite the rise of transational communications corporations and the growth of media export markets, communications systems are still in significant respects national. The most important medium of communication is television. Detailed comparative schedule analysis suggests that most television programs on mass channels are not imported, but produced nationally (Bens *et al.* 1992, Sepstrup and Goonasekera 1994). The popular notion that most people watch American television programs is also unsupported by the evidence (Sinclair *et al.* 1996). The press is also primarily a national medium, which has in many countries a continuing importance among national elites.

Secondly, national states are influential in shaping media systems. They are the licensing authority of national television and radio channels, an arrangement that is supported by international law. Since these national channels are still dominant, national states still largely determine who has control over television and radio. They also frame the laws and regulations within which national media operate. In addition, they have a range of informal ways of influencing the media, from information management to the provision of loans.

Thirdly, the nation is still a very important marker of difference. Different nations have different languages, political systems, power structures, cultural traditions, economies, international links, and histories. Indeed, one reason why a number of transnational television channels have failed to prosper is because their audiences are not truly transnational, but are subdivided by national cultural and linguistic differences (Collins 1994, Sinclair *et al.* 1996). But perhaps the key point to emphasize is that media systems are shaped not merely by national regulatory regimes and national audience preferences, but by a complex ensemble of social relations that have taken shape in national contexts. It is precisely the historically grounded density of these relationships that tends to be excluded from simplified global accounts, in which theorists survey the universe while never straying far from the international airport.

Rather than track particular aspects of media globalization, we decided to organize this book around national media systems. However, we have not followed convention in the way we have done this. There is a well worn formula, developed in American textbooks, that provides a summary of basic information about each country, and a succinct account of its media system (Gross 1995, Hilliard and Keith 1996). There is also another, more interesting tradition which adopts a national approach to tracking the crisis of public service broadcasting (Aldridge and Hewitt 1994, Raboy 1997) or which examines national media from a comparative social policy and administration perspective (Humphreys 1996, Ostergaard 1997). While all these books have their uses, we have opted for a more interpretive orientation, since our main concern is to extend communications theory.

We adopted, therefore, the device of setting a global exam paper, and inviting leading media academics around the world to sit it. To persuade them to take part, we agreed that they could answer as many or as few questions as they wished, and that they could be selective in how they responded. The four questions we asked, in relation to specific countries or regions, were:

1   How do the media relate to the power structure of society?
2   What influences the media, and where does control over the media lie?
3   How has the media influenced society?
4   What effect has media globalization and new media had on the media system and society?

These are all core questions that are addressed in theories of "media and society." The essays that follow provide a basis for answering them in a more broadly informed and less parochial way than in the standard media literature.

There are different ways of ordering or classifying countries. The conventional way in media studies seems to be either in terms of their geographical location (Gross 1995) or, despairingly, in terms of their alphabetical order (Ostergaard 1997). Sklair (1997) identifies five "standard" ways of classifying the world in comparative sociology. While all these are serviceable, we opted for an alternative scheme (see Figure 1.1). This divides the world into authoritarian and democratic political systems, each of which are further subdivided into neo-liberal and regulated economic systems. In addition, we have an extra category, transitional or mixed societies, that refers to countries that are being transformed or regions with mixed regimes. We begin with this last category, since it offers such arresting perspectives of the relationship of the media to power in society.

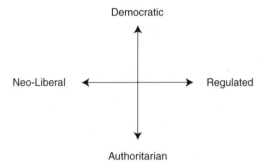

Figure 1.1 Classifying the global system

Comparative perspectives

This book is like a palette of paints from which readers can mix their own colors. Different hues, and different patterns, will suggest themselves to different people. It may be helpful, however, to indicate just some of the ways in which these essays seem to us to contribute to a wider media debate.

First, how do rival globalizing perspectives fare in the light of comparative evidence? While data can be culled from this book to support the cultural imperialism thesis, a number of essays clearly challenge its arguments. For example, Rajagopal highlights the continuing importance of local cultural tradition in shaping Indian media output (Chapter 20). Similarly, Waisbord argues in relation to South America that the notion of American cultural dominion fails to take adequate account of the formative influence of the national state in shaping media systems (Chapter 4). Furthermore, he argues that these states should not be seen merely as an extension of American domination. They were not neccessarily unified agencies, and they were responding in part to a range of local pressures and struggles. This reservation is implicitly echoed in a number of essays in this book.

What about the related radical account which argues that the global market is eroding popular sovereignty? This finds rather more support in this book. In particular, Dahgren argues that, in Sweden, power has shifted from elected representatives in favor of economic elites, and that the culture of citzenship has been eroded, partly as a consequence of global market influence (Chapter 17). Similarly, the Korean case study argues that external "reforms" imposed by the IMF reduced the play of popular influence. Their short-term effect was to strengthen political power located in the state, and to reinforce clientalist social relations corrupting the media system (Chapter 8). The influence exerted by major transnational communications conglomerates in different parts of the world can also be discerned in this book.

This said, the general tenor of this book goes against the global market disenfranchisement thesis. The book reveals in copious detail the continuing power of national political authority to regulate media systems through direct and indirect means. Though the macro-economic policy options of nation-states are being diminished by the impact of global financial markets, this does not seem to apply to domestic communications policy. The conditions of the IMF credit package to Korea, involving the enforced divestment of major newspapers from their conglomerate ("chaebol") owners, is one of the few exceptions to this generalization. Far from financial markets imposing a global norm of media policy, there continues to be very great variation in the communications policies of different countries.

What about the opposing claim that globalization is an engine of freedom, media diversity, and social emancipation? Again, this finds limited support. Foreign investment is portrayed as a source of pluralism in Zimbabwe (Chapter 11); Hollywood feminism is viewed as emancipatory in the Middle East (Chapter 5); and globalizing influences are viewed as progressive in their effects in China and Taiwan (Chapters 2 and 9). On the other hand, foreign investment is also portrayed as bolstering the control of established economic elites, and entrenching media oligarchy, in other countries (for example Chapters 3 and 6).

The one exception to this impression of variable and multifaceted truth, of global generalizations confounded and contradicted, of a tenacious and enduring national particularism, is a seemingly inexorable march toward media liberalization. While national states are still important in regulating the media, the general trend— documented in numerous chapters—is for state controls to be relinquished in favor of market controls. This should mean, according to classical liberal theory, that a new era of liberty is dawning. More and more media systems are becoming answerable to the sovereign consumer, and free to scrutinize critically the state. The fact that market liberalization seems to be coinciding with the rise of multiparty democracy merely reinforces the impression that the world is being "modernized."

This book offers only limited support for this contention. The market is viewed, in Mexico, China, and Taiwan, as being on balance an important agency contributing to the emergence of a more independent and critical media system (Chapters 2, 7 and 9). It is also featured as playing a positive role, at particular moments, elsewhere. Yet, in one country after another, the opposite argument is advanced, with the market emerging as a mechanism that fuses the circuits of freedom and critical disclosure. This is because, in many countries, the owners of private media are part of the system of power, and use their authority to muzzle criticism of the state. Commercial media were heavily involved in supporting military regimes in Latin America, and in general developed close relations to the regimes that replaced them (Chapter 4). Commercial media controllers are now part of a "media–political complex" that shapes public discourses in Russia, Eastern Europe, Korea, Malaysia, Japan, Egypt, and elsewhere. The dynamics of this process vary. In Russia, the flow of influence seems to originate in major economic interests which control major media enterprises, and also influence the direction of the state (Chapter 6). In Malaysia, Korea, Egypt, Zimbabwe, and former Korea and Taiwan, the flow of influence is reversed, with the political group dominating the state exerting influence over the media, and using state power to structure media markets (Chapters 8, 9, 10, 11, and 12). In other countries, such as Japan, Korea and in Eastern Europe, there seems rather to be an informal alliance between economic and political elites that shape the media system (Chapters 3 and 13). In many countries around the world, from China to Latin America, there is also a familiar pattern in which commercial media controllers keep their heads down, and avoid political retribution, by mixing tame journalism with profitable entertainment (Chapters 1, 8 and 13).

What emerges from this book is also a contingent and variable understanding of the place of the media in society. The nature of media power is a particular concern of chapters dealing with the United States and Israel (Chapters 14 and 21). But different ways of conceptualizing the role of the media also emerge from the general body of the book. In some societies, the media are sites of power struggle because fissures have developed within the dominant bloc, as in Mexico and Taiwan, or because there are class-based conflicts as in Britain and Italy (Chapters 7, 9, 15, and 18). In other societies, the media are agencies of social unity and integration. However, an important distinction needs to be made between those countries where consensus is achieved through corporatist power-sharing and compromise, as in Sweden, and where it takes the form of autocratic control imposed from above, as in Zimbabwe (Chapters 11 and 17). Furthermore, the building blocks of control vary considerably from class-based alliances to social formations built around ethnicity, gender or region.

In short, this book offers a greater sense of difference and variability than is usually registered in media theory. In making the case for de-Westernizing media studies, we are not suggesting that normative values have only a zonal application. On the contrary, the values of liberty, equality, and solidarity seem to us to have a universal validity. Our argument is that media studies will benefit from developing a wider comparative perspective. At the moment, ways of understanding the world's media system are unduly influenced by the experience of a few, untypical countries. These distort understanding not only of non-Western countries but also of a large part of the West as well.

This argument seems to us to be particularly powerfully marshalled by Silvio Waisbord and Paolo Mancini in this book (Chapters 4 and 18). Waisbord argues that some media people in South America concealed from themselves the reality of media collusion with authoritarian regimes by uncritically reproducing the Anglo-American concept of the media as a fourth estate. Similarly, Mancini argues that the same concept, with its assumption of dispassionate journalism informing indi-vidual members of the electorate, got in the way of Italian journalists correctly perceiving their place in the democratic system. They are agents of representation within a democratic public sphere that is made up of organized groups, and draw upon a literary and politicized tradition of journalism different from that of the United States. In brief, interpretive paradigms need to be tailored to local situations rather than imported uncritically and misapplied.

This reorientation calls also for a more questioning approach to globalization theory. This theory provides a fund of insight into trends that are reshaping the world. But it is also faddish, gaining momentum from mutual cross-referencing, and is often based on an aerial perspective that simplifies. In particular, it tends to understate the continuing importance of the nation. If there is one thing that emerges above all else from this book, it is that the nation—its history, cultural tradition, economic development, national configuration of power, and state policies—is still very important in shaping the media's global system. Rumors of the nation's death, to adapt Mark Twain, are much exaggerated.

Our thanks go to contributors from all over the world who responded so readily to this project, and to the Korean Research Council which helped to make it possible.

Notes

1 Their knowledge of the Soviet media, and of the thinking behind it, was in fact rather simplified. For an interesting insight into quasi-liberal elements within the Soviet theory of communications, see McNair (1991).
2 The next section owes a very great debt to Colin Leys's current research on markets, which he was kind enough to show us. We are also very grateful to him for his helpful suggestions for the comparative organization of the book.
3 Our thanks to Peter Golding who showed us an outline of his book, edited with Phil Harris, before it came out. It helped to prod us into a new direction.

References

Aldridge, A. and Hewitt, N. (1994) (eds.) *Controlling Broadcasting*, Manchester: Manchester University Press.

Ang, I. (1990) "Culture and communication: towards an ethnographic critique of media consumption in the transational media system," *European Journal of Communication*, 5(2–3).

Avery, R. (1993) (ed.) *Public Service Broadcasting in a Multichannel Environment*, White Plains, NJ: Longman.

Bens, E., Kelly, M. and Bakke, M. (1992) "Television content: Dallasification of culture?" in K. Siune and W. Truetzscher (eds.) *Dynamics of Media Politics*, London: Sage.

Bernard, M. (1999) "East Asia's tumbling dominoes: financial crises and the myth of the regional model," in L. Panitch and C. Leys (eds.) *Global Capitalism Versus Democracy*, Rendlesham: Merlin.

Boron, A. (1999) "State decay and democratic decadence in Latin America," in L. Panitch and C. Leys (eds.) *Global Capitalism Versus Democracy*, Rendlesham: Merlin.

Boyd-Barrett, O. (1998) "Media imperialism reformulated," in D. Thussu (ed.) *Electronic Empires*, London: Arnold.

Braman, S. and Sreberny-Mohammadi, A. (1996) (eds.) *Globalization, Communication and Transnational Civil Society*, Cresskill, NJ: Hampton Press.

Cleaver, H. (1998) "The Zapatistas and the electronic fabric of struggle," in J. Holloway and E. Pelaez (eds.) *Zapatista*, London: Pluto.

Coates, D. (1999) "Labour power and international competitiveness: a critique of ruling orthodoxies," in L. Panitch and C. Leys (eds.) *Global Capitalism Versus Democracy*: Rendlesham: Merlin.

Collins, R. (1994) *Broadcasting and Audio-Visual Policy in the European Single Market*, London: Libbey.

Croteau, D. and Hoynes, W. (1997) *Media/Society*, Thousand Oaks, CA: Pine Forge Press.

Curran, J. (1998) "Crisis of public communication: a reappraisal," in T. Liebes and J. Curran (eds.) *Media, Ritual and Identity*, London: Routledge.

Dayan, D. (1998) "Particularistic media and diasporic communication," in T. Liebes and J. Curran (eds.) *Media, Ritual and Identity*, London: Routledge.

Downing, J. (1996) *Internationalizing Media Theory*, London: Sage.

Frith, S. (1996) "Entertainment" in J. Curran and M. Gurevitch (eds.) *Mass Media and Society*, 2nd edn, London: Arnold.

Giddens, A. (1999) "Comment: the 1999 Reith lecture. New world without end," *Observer*, April 11.

Golding, P. and Harris, P. (eds.) (1996) *Beyond Cultural Imperialism*, London: Sage.

Gross, L. (1995) (ed.) *The International World of Electronic Media*, New York: McGraw-Hill.

Hall, S. (1997) "The local and the global," in A. King (ed.) *Culture, Globalization and the World-System*, London: Macmillan.

Hallin, D. (1998) "Broadcasting in the third world: from national development to civil society," in T. Liebes and J. Curran (eds.) *Media, Ritual and Identity*, London, Routledge.

Helleiner, E. (1994) *States and the Reemergence of Global Finance*, Ithaca: Cornell University Press.

Helleiner, E. (1996) "Post-globalisation: is the financial liberalisation trend likely to be reversed?" in R. Boyer and D. Drache (eds.) (1996) *States Against Markets: The Limits of Globalisation*, London: Routledge.

Herman, E. and R. McChesney (1997) *The Global Media*, London: Cassell.

Hilliard, R. and Keith, M. (1996) *Global Broadcasting Systems*, Boston: Focal Press.

Hirsch, J. (1999) "Globalisation, class and the question of democracy," in L. Panitch and C. Leys (eds.) *Global Capitalism Versus Democracy*, Rendlesham: Merlin.

Hirst, P. and Thompson, G. (1996) *Globalisation in Question*, Cambridge: Polity.

Hobsbawm, E. (1975) *The Age of Capital*, London: Weidenfeld and Nicholson.

Hobsbawm, E. (1989) *The Age of Empire*, London: Sphere.

Hobsbawm, E. (1994) *Age of Extremes*, London: Michael Joseph.

Hoskins, C., McFadyen, S. and Finn, A. (1997) *Global Television and Film*, Oxford: Clarendon.

Humphreys, P. (1996) *Mass Media and Media Policy in Western Europe*, Manchester: Manchester University Press.

Hutton, W. (1997) *The State to Come*, London: Vintage.

King, A. (1997) (ed.) *Culture, Globalisation and the World System*, London: Macmillan.

Lerner, D. (1963) "Toward a communication theory of modernization" in L. Pye (ed.) *Communications and Political Development*, Princeton, NJ: Princeton University Press.

Liebes, T. and Katz, E. (1990) *The Export of Meaning*, New York: Oxford Univesity Press.

McChesney, R. (1998) "Media convergence and globalisation," in D. Thussu (ed.) *Electronic Empires*, London: Arnold.

McClelland, D. (1961) *The Achieving Society*, Princeton, NJ: Van Nostrand.

McKibbin, R. (1998) *Classes and Culture*, Oxford: Oxford University Press.

McLuhan, M. (1964) *Understanding Media*, London: Routledge and Kegan Paul.

McNair, B. (1991) *Glasnost, Perestroika and the Soviet Union*, London: Routledge.

McQuail, D. (1983) *Mass Communication Theory*, 1st edn, London: Sage.

McQuail, D. (1987) *Mass Communication Theory*, 2nd edn, London: Sage.

McQuail, D. (1994) *Mass Communication Theory*, 3rd edn, London: Sage.

Mahnkopf, B. (1999) "Between the devil and the deep blue sea: the German model under pressure of globalisation," in L. Panitch and C. Leys (eds.) *Global Capitalism Versus Democracy*, Rendlesham: Merlin.

Mohammadi, A. (1997) (ed.) *International Communication and Globalization*, London: Sage.

Ostergaard, B. (1997) (ed.) *The Media in Western Europe* [The Euromedia Handbook], 2nd edn, London: Sage.

Panitch, L. and Leys, C. (1999) (eds.) *Global Capitalism Versus Democracy* [*Socialist Register* 1999], Rendlesham: Merlin.

Picciotto, S. (1992) *International Business Taxation*, Oxford: Clarendon.

Pool, I. de Sola (1963) "The mass media and politics in the development process," in L. Pye (ed.) *Communications and Political Development*, Princeton, NJ: Princeton University Press.

Raboy, M. (1997) (ed.) *Public Broadcasting for the 21st Century*, Luton: University of Luton Press.

Radice (1999) "Taking globalisation seriously," in L. Panitch and C. Leys (eds.) *Global Capitalism Versus Democracy*, Rendlesham: Merlin.

Robins, K. (1995) "The new spaces of global media," in R. J. Johnston, P. Taylor and M. Watts (eds.) *Geographies of Global Change*, Oxford: Blackwell.

Robins, K., Cornford, J. and Aksoy, A. (1997) "Overview: from cultural rights to cultural responsibilities," in K. Robins (ed.) *Programming for People*, Newcastle: Centre for Urban and Regional Development Studies, University of Newcastle and European Broadcasting Union.

Rogers, E. and Shoemaker, F. (1971) *Communication of Innovations*, New York: Free Press.

Schramm, W. (1963) "Communication development and the development process," in L. Pye (ed.) *Communications and Political Development*, Princeton, NJ: Princeton University Press.

Schudson, M. (1996) "The sociology of news production revisited," in J. Curran and M. Gurevitch (eds.) *Mass Media and Society*, 2nd edn, London: Arnold.

Schiller, H. (1969) *Mass Communication and American Empire*, New York: Kelly.

Schiller, H. (1976) *Communication and Cultural Dominance*, White Plains, NY: International Arts and Sciences Press.

Schiller, H. (1998) "Striving for communication dominance," in D. Thissu (ed.) *Electronic Empires*, London: Arnold.

Sepstrup, P. and Goonasekera (1994) (eds.) *TV Transnationalization: Europe and Asia*, Paris: UNESCO.

Serra, S. (1996) "Multinationals of solidarity: international civil society and the killing of street children in Brazil," in S. Braman and A. Sreberny-Mohammadi (eds.) *Globalization, Communication and Transnational Civil Society*, Cresskill, NJ: Hampton Press.

Serra, S. (1999) "The killing of Brazilian street children and the rise of the international public sphere," in J. Curran (ed.) *Media Organisations in Society*, London: Arnold.

Siebert, F., Peterson, T. and Schramm, W. (1956) *Four Theories of the Press*, Urbana, IL: University of Illinois Press.

Silj, A. (1988) *East of Dallas*, London: British Film Institute.

Sinclair, J., Jacka, E. and Cunningham, S. (1996) (eds.) *New Patterns in Global Vision*, Oxford: Oxford University Press.

Sklair, L. (1997) "Classifying the global system," in A. Sreberny-Mohammadi *et al.* (eds.) *Media in Global Context*, London: Arnold.

Sparks, C. (1998) *Communism, Capitalism and the Mass Media*, London: Sage.

Sreberny-Mohammadi, A. (1996) "Globalization, communication and transnational civil society: introduction," in S. Braman and A. Sreberny-Mohammadi (eds.) *Globalization, Communication and Transnational Civil Society*, Cresskill, NJ: Hampton Press.

Sreberny-Mohammadi, A. and Mohammadi, A. (1994) *Small Media, Big Revolution*, Minneapolis: University of Minnesota Press.

Sreberny-Mohammadi, A., Winseck, D., McKenna, J. and Boyd-Barret, O. (eds.) (1997) *Media in Global Context*, London: Arnold.

Taylor, P. (1997) *Global Communications, International Affairs and the Media Since 1945*, London: Routledge.

Thussu, D. (1998) *Electronic Empires*, London: Arnold.

Tomlinson, J. (1999) *Globalization and Culture*, Cambridge: Polity.

Tracey, M. (1998) *The Decline and Fall of Public Service Broadcasting*, New York: Oxford University Press.

Van Ginnekin, J. (1998) *Understanding Global News*, London: Sage.

Waters, M. (1995) *Globalization*, London: Routledge.

Weiss, L. (1998) *The Myth of the Powerless State*, Cambridge: Polity.

Wright, C. (1959) *Mass Communication*, 1st edn, New York: Random House.

Wright, C. (1975) *Mass Communication*, 2nd edn, New York: Random House.

Part 1
Transitional and mixed societies

2 Rethinking media studies
The case of China

Eric Kit-wai Ma[1]

China is undertaking economic reform of unprecedented proportions despite continued political control. The return of Hong Kong to China's sovereignty presents a unique impetus for change (Yahuda 1996). As part of China, Hong Kong is now politically subordinate to China's guidance. However, Hong Kong's brand of capitalism has become a dominant ideology underlining the open-door policies of mainland China. Whereas the transition from centralized socialism to a market economy has become an undisputed state policy, the role of the media has been an issue of continued debate. This is mainly due to the dual role of the media as commodities in the liberalized market and as ideological apparatuses of the Chinese Communist Party (CCP). Under the spell of this unresolved duality, the Chinese media in the 1990s are characterized by erratic reform, periodic repression, and a deep-seated contradiction between political control and market-driven changes. In China, the media are growing so rapidly that descriptive accounts usually lag behind the changes. Confronted with contradictory processes, structural complexity, and the rapidity of change of the Chinese media, grand academic discourses seem inadequate for theoretical generalizations. Instead of giving a comprehensive review, I will attempt to trace, in the first part, some of the most significant trends at play. In the second part, I will try to rethink some of the popular theoretical perspectives in Western media studies through the China/Hong Kong experiences. Since detailed accounts of various aspects of the media scene in China can be found elsewhere,[2] this chapter will focus more on the theoretical implications for media studies.

THE CASE OF CHINA

Media commercialization[3]

The most distinguishable characteristic of the Chinese media in the 1990s is the tension between rapid commercialization and continued ideological control. Strictly speaking, media operations in China are controlled and owned by the government. The Chinese government divides state-owned units into three types: administrative units, nonprofit units and profitable enterprises. Administrative units receive guaranteed funding, while profitable enterprises are allowed to generate profits. As ideological apparatuses of the state, media organizations are considered to be nonprofit units. These do not receive guaranteed funding, unlike those classified as administrative units. They are not classified as profitable enterprises since, in the past, they were not allowed to pursue commercial interests in the market. However, state-endorsed marketization has initiated significant changes in the financial structures of China's media system. Once dependent primarily on government subsidies, China's media operators have increasingly relied on advertising revenues. Since the economic reforms started in the late 1970s, state subsidies have been gradually reduced or terminated to media organizations except for a handful of party organs. Media managers have received a clear signal from the state that they have to generate revenues and be self-supportive in the long run.

The general pattern is that the media at the national level are closely censored, whereas local and provincial media enjoy a higher degree of autonomy. Controls over less official media and the dissemination of nonpolitical information are relaxed, whereas the state still maintains tight control over political news. But media organizations at all levels have been reoriented to include profit-making as one of their organizational goals. Profit-making channels accept advertising and sponsorship, publish "weekend supplements" with juicy infotainment, perform public relation functions for enterprises, and organize symposia, shows, and press conferences that promote their "clients." For a long time, CCP has been denouncing transnational conglomerates, considering them to be corrupting agents of imperialism. Despite this, however, the Ministry of Propaganda sanctioned the first newspaper conglomerate in 1996. The *Guanzhou Daily* conglomerate, a mere municipal paper, was handpicked by the central government to experiment with all forms of commercial ventures. These include investing in stock and property markets, setting up dozens of newspaper kiosks, publishing a series of minor papers, and managing a series of profitable media and non-media enterprises. In order to be cost-effective, some less profitable newspapers and periodicals have been advised by the government to merge and operate under the umbrella of major daily newspapers, while party papers have rushed to spin off mass-appeal papers and non-media businesses in order to generate profits. Groups and conglomerates, in the critical eye, are agents of exploitation. But in the Chinese context, their economic independence can weaken political control and enhance editorial autonomy. The irony is that the authority tolerates these conglomerates and groups because they can serve as the means to control chaotic free competition and limit the proliferation of minor papers. In the case of China, state control predominates, although the media is gaining some autonomy in dealing with nonpolitical affairs and business operations.

Improvising media practices[4]

The profound changes initiated by marketization can be felt at the organizational level. Operating within the administrative structure of the state, media workers are paid uniformly according to four professional ranks,[5] irrespective of whether they work for national or local media organizations. Promotions depend on political commitment and seniority. However, as the media become commercialized, the flow of cash into media organizations has encouraged new practices and reshaped journalistic culture. Despite the fact that all media organizations have institutional ties with the government, increased economic strength has given many media organizations operational freedom to hire freelancers, adjust pay scales, adopt new technologies, and restructure organizational practices. Previously, media workers received salaries and fringe benefits solely from the government. In the 1990s, bonuses have been regularized as "flexible wages" and distributed on the basis of individual merit. They have become the third component of the media workers' income and are distributed without reference to professional grades. Now media organizations can give aggressive journalists a wide range of incentives as part of their flexible wages. These incentives include story fees, editing fees, and good story cash awards, the amount of which varies greatly in different media organizations. In the past, when incomes were much more uniform, national media organizations were more prestigious. But now media organizations in coastal provinces are more attractive because they follow the laws of the market and have become financially thriving groups and conglomerates. They can offer much higher flexible wages and better housing for their employees and thus draw talent from all over the country (Chen and Lee 1998).

Market-related changes in journalistic practices are closely related to the development of advertising (He and Chen 1998, Yu 1991). Since advertising has not yet been institutionalized, advertising dollars enter the media through various informal and "innovative" channels. Journalists have suddenly found themselves in the prime nexus of exchanges. Public and commercial bodies pay journalists for political and economic favors. Paid journalism is now a systemic phenomenon with set prices for all sorts of favoritism. Under the current context of "no money, no reporting," even government officials have allegedly paid reporters for feature stories boosting their images and promoting official policies. Over the years, paid journalism has developed from the individual to the collective, from passive to active, and from commercial sectors to government bodies (Chen and Chan 1998).

The restructuring of reward systems within media organizations has created new career paths. In the past, media workers moved up the career ladder by political commitment. Political control could be exerted easily by direct bureaucratic measures. Now the market has contributed to the development of alternative career ladders. Media workers are rewarded directly by pay journalism. Within media organizations, the management also rewards staff who can produce good stories that boost circulation and ratings, which in turn increase profitability. Thus power exerted by both the state and the market can destabilize media practices. Because of the duality of political and commercial imperatives, organizational norms are fuzzy, but are nevertheless understood by practicing media workers. Paths of change are murky and contingent. Journalists constantly test the shifting boundaries of their organizations. Sometimes directives from above are ignored and non-routines become routines, thus providing gaps and spaces for political and commercial exploitation and sometimes spaces for unconventional media contents. However, improvising activities are characterized by their transient nature and could be subjected to abrupt repression and modifications (Pan in press). Here the dialectic of autonomy and control is evident at the heart of media production, and media workers deal with intense contradiction by improvising.

Uneven liberalization[6]

In principle, the state firmly adheres to the doctrine that the media are ideological apparatuses, but, due to marketization, the mediascape exhibits extreme forms of variations and discrepancies. For example, print media are more restrictive than electronic media. News media have a much lower degree of freedom than cultural media. Many periodicals, magazines, and books are loosely censored and can be filled with violence, pornography, and even politically incorrect ideologies. Television shows and phone-in programs can touch on many personal and social issues that were unthinkable in the past (Zha 1995).

Besides variations according to the types of media, there are obvious discrepancies between media in different regions. Party newspapers at the national, provincial, and municipal levels are closely watched. However, local papers, special interest journals, and evening papers in cities are more market-oriented and filled with more soft and sensational news. In fact, ideological differences can be found within the same medium. For instance, party presses can have their front pages filled with official news stories and policy speeches, but their other pages may be packed with advertisements and soft social news. On China Central Television (CCTV), the main evening news is said to carry very few negative or critical items, in contrast to the afternoon and late night news, which carry many more critical stories.[7]

This is not to say that there are some very special media spaces in which journalists can enjoy the kind of press freedom enjoyed in the West. Political control has remained tight after 1989. There have been only sporadic occasions on which media workers can cross the official ideological boundary. The expanded media spaces mentioned above are restricted to apolitical and consumerist contents. This uneven liberalization of the Chinese media can be related to Deng Xiao Ping's philosophy of pragmatism, which privileges improvization over dogmatism. It is also related to the policy of allowing special administrative zones to experiment with marketization. Market forces open up spaces and accumulate financial power, which can be translated into bargaining power. All these result in a very hybridized mediascape, in which very different types of media discourse coexist in the most conspicuous way.

The Hong Kong connection[8]

Added to the particularity of the Chinese case is the dialectic between mainland China and Hong Kong. Now part of China, Hong Kong's liberal media, operating in a full-blown capitalistic mode, should be seen as a sub-system of the Chinese media. Whereas in mainland China, the connection between the media and the political economy is more overt, powers are articulated across the Hong Kong/China border more by indirect and discursive means. Here a culturalist explanation of discursive control can make a strong case. The government of Hong Kong Special Administrative Region (HKSAR) is not legitimized by a full democratic election; it is a weak government which operates under the blessing of the Chinese government. However, the Chinese government grants Hong Kong a high level of media autonomy. Honoring the promise of "one country, two systems," China has refrained from explicitly intervening in the Hong Kong media. Despite this licensed autonomy, the Hong Kong media have skillfully navigated a return to the Chinese orbit by depoliticization and self-censorship.[9] The process of self-censorship does not involve direct administrative interference from the Chinese government, yet informal networking and subtle discursive formation have shaped a complying, secularized, apoliticized, and yet free media culture in Hong Kong.

Of more theoretical significance is the influence of the Hong Kong media in China. Although Hong Kong is at the political periphery, Hong Kong exerts a strong influence on the media environment of mainland China. For many years, Hong Kong has served as a template and window for China to relay to the media in Western liberal societies. Since the open-door policy starting in the late 1970s, Western culture has been an increasingly strong presence in the lives of the Chinese people. The most frequent exposure to outside programming is from the spillover of broadcasting signals from Hong Kong television, which can reach a large part of the Pearl River Delta, covering a mainland population of about 18 million. Audience reports show that Hong Kong programming, including local Hong Kong productions and foreign programs carried by Hong Kong channels, are very popular and usually attract a large audience share. Some local television stations in the area even insert their own advertisements while relaying Hong Kong programs. After several failed attempts to stop it, the provincial government tolerates this illegal but widespread practice. Another form of spillover is media piracy in the form of videos, laser discs and compact discs carrying such contents as popular songs and mainstream movies from Hong Kong and the United States. They are sold in shops and shown in small movie houses. This "illegal openness" is a result of the discrepancies between the central and local government and between stated policies and widespread routine practices (Chan 1996, 1994).

Another significant change started in 1991, when the Hong Kong-based regional satellite broadcaster STAR TV was launched to provide mostly Western and increasingly region-friendly programs. In 1996, Rupert Murdoch, the new owner of STAR TV, was allowed to work with Chinese investors to form the Phoenix Satellite Television Company in Hong Kong, offering entertainment and sports programming to China via STAR's channels. Exposure to foreign programming has created a demanding media audience and increased the pressure for media commercialization and liberalization. Coproductions, joint ventures, visits, international forums, television and film festivals and the sharing of expertise have become more frequent, especially with the media industries in Hong Kong. Here the influences are economic as well as "discursive." A materialist interpretation needs to be accompanied by a culturalist one. The culturalist argument stresses that dominant ideologies can provide the language, the "common sense," and the discursive context for media production. In the 1990s, Hong Kong and its international affiliations were the major "demonstrators," providing Chinese media with a new discursive context in which market capitalism is the name of the game.

RETHINKING MEDIA STUDIES

Benign market capitalism?

Against these general descriptions, I want to rethink some of the concepts in media studies and test their applicability to the changing media scene in China. In critical media theories, the media are seen as ideological agents reproducing dominant social relations. Critical culturalists stress the hegemonic articulation, despite active negotiation, between the media and dominant economic and especially ideological processes, whereas critical materialists stress the moments of determination of the media by the political economy. In contrast, liberalists argue that market competition promotes diversity and checks state power in a media forum where different social parties and agents are free to express themselves. I must admit my reservation concerning this liberal view of the market; I tend to concur with the critical view that the market limits social discourses and reinforces dominant ideologies. However, the multifaceted effects of the market on the media scene in China need careful theoretical interpretation.

Allowing the situation to speak for itself, the market does serve as a liberating force, no matter how exploitative it can sometimes be.

The commercialization of the Chinese media has carved new spaces of expression. Tight media controls have given way to policies seeking to stimulate competition, cut down subsidies, and streamline organizational structures. These changes have resulted in the decentralization, specialization, and multiplication of production and distribution processes, which in turn weaken ideological control and increase operational autonomy. Media organizations are now less dependent on government subsidies and can generate financial support directly from the market. This strengthens their bargaining power with state authorities and substantially increases the income and welfare of media workers. In fact the market helps breed a new generation of journalists, who are given mobile phones and sometimes even cars, and live an enviable lifestyle. Breaking the uniform reward system and installing diversified career paths, the market intensifies competition within and across the media. Producers and journalists improvise in the production of radio phone-in programs and investigative TV shows, bringing social, cultural, family, and personal issues into the mediascape. In some cases they can entice government officials out of their offices to engage in on-air dialogue with the audience (Zhao 1998). Armed with high circulation and rating figures, they can stretch the limit of ideological boundaries and justify their unorthodox innovations by invoking politically correct dogmas such as "serving the people" and "promoting market reform with Chinese characteristics." Of course it is not uncommon for market imperatives to clash with political considerations, but media workers seem capable of getting around the conflicting requirements of serving the state and satisfying their audience. The consequence is that the market has actually shifted the role of the media from that of a party organ of propaganda to a multiplicity of roles of entertaining, educating, and informing the audience. Right now, the sudden reconfiguration of the mediascape is confined to nonpolitical issues. The media take up the cultural role of providing some "breathing spaces" for the general public, who had been living in a society where the state "took care" of the details of everyday life. There is plenty of evidence that, in the 1990s, market forces in China provide more opportunity for freedom of expression than the authoritarian rule of past decades (Lee (ed.) 2000).

However, this is not to entertain a naive idea that market forces have initiated a process of peaceful evolution in China where the media have modeled themselves on the liberal media in Western capitalist societies. This liberalist claim is sometimes linked with the discourse of globalism, which harbors unqualified assumptions of inevitable global interactions and the final integration of Asian countries into a global village. In the case under consideration, media commercialization in China involves highly manipulative relations between political powers, economic interests, and pay journalism, which is in sharp contrast to a romanticized view of a democratic marketplace of ideas and values.

A critical perspective of the market is relevant here. Western critical media theory explains how a supposedly free market is responsible for producing a hegemonic media. This ranges from a strong version of the dominant ideology thesis to a soft version of discursive negotiation. But in the Chinese case, the articulation of power, money, and media is much more obvious and direct. There is no need to invoke the culturalist explanation of how the market subtly and discursively limits expressions and promotes the interests of the powerful. The state can punish a rebellious individual or media organization by direct order. Without institutional channels of advertising and without well established professional norms, there is only a very weak barrier between powerful interests and the media. In order to secure the support of the state and advertisers, the media tend to protect and promote the interests of big companies and sponsoring government units. In some media organizations, journalists are asked to check the list of advertising clients before releasing critical stories (Chen and Lee 1998). It is an accepted practice for enterprises to buy journalists to sing "hymns" in their favor. Besides direct interference, the market also has some other side effects: It privileges city dwellers and those with the ability to consume. In the past, the state-supported media ensured that the poor and those in remote villages had access to newspapers and broadcasting services. With the restructuring of distribution networks, low-density and low-consumption rural populations have become nonprofitable markets. The rapid growth in media contents and channels is sometimes restricted to large and wealthy cities. Cultural and artistic contents with limited commercial value are marginalized. Mostly, the media are opening up spaces for a work-and-spend culture. Whether the market will tighten and finally reveal its ugly face is an interesting issue for future observers. All these are compatible with the basic tenets of Western theories. But the unique character of the Chinese case is that some prominent features of liberal and critical theories are readily applicable at the same time. The Chinese media are gaining their relative autonomy in the midst of marketization and commercialization. But the state and the market, as the following section will elaborate, are transforming each other to become new sociopolitical powers. In this historical juncture of social transition, the Chinese media market is both restraining and enabling.

The bureaucratic–authoritarian state

As media scholars have noted, radical Marxist media theories in the Anglo-American literature focus mostly on economic power and take liberal democratic states for granted (Downing 1996, Lee 2000). In China, media analysts face a different type of political–economic situation, in which the Chinese state continues to play a constitutive role in media dynamics. In popular imagination in the West, the Chinese government is still the unchanging evil authoritarian state of 1989. However, this view ignores the transformative possibilities of the Chinese state. Since 1992, when Deng Xiao Ping visited the coastal provinces and endorsed market reform, the CCP has been recasting itself into a modern authority with a seemingly decreasing authoritarian character. This rehabilitated bureaucratic–authoritarian regime maintains its power more by legal and administrative means than by strong coercive apparatuses. I must stress that there is no hint that the Chinese state is peacefully evolving into a liberal state because of the "liberating force" of the market. But neither is there any hint of a second coming of authoritarian socialism.

Deploying the theoretical lens of either the liberal pluralist or the radical Marxist cannot put the Chinese state–market nexus into focus. As Wang (1998) observes, what we need is the dual recognition that neither the state nor the market is external to each other. The development of the market with the blessing of the state is constructing a hybrid of overt conflicts but structural coexistence between the two. In this state–market complex characterized by instability and struggle, the state is not weakening its control over or intervening in the media as a discrete body of governance.

Managers of media organizations are taking the roles of party members, journalists, and entrepreneurs at the same time. Mid-level and junior media workers receive their basic salary from the state and are rewarded by bonuses generated from the market. Government officials can exert power over the media either directly by political means or by the rule of the market. In fact, many big advertising clients are businesses run by government units or affiliated with government officials. The state is both an actor and a regulator of the market.

In the 1990s, political controls were implemented more and more by regulatory and administrative means. State control of the media has moved from expedient instructions to the formulation of laws, rules, and regulations. The state maintains tight control over major propaganda polices, but delegates routine operations to decentralized sites such as local bureaus and in-house management units. The state also develops and issues codes of conduct and sets up post-censoring groups which check and read major media of national influence (Chen and Chan 1998). It complies with the market in managing transnational capitals, but retains complete political control. For instance, STAR TV yielded to the Chinese government by dropping its BBC service. In order to "land" its Phoenix satellite channels to Chinese cable networks, STAR produces politically correct news and information similar to CCTV, the difference being that its programs are more entertaining and visually more attractive. Here the state continues to play a dominant role in deflecting transnational media flow. As Chen and Chan note: "The current effort to control the media is sustained and systematic. Also, a mixture of restrictive measures, including legal limitation, policy directives, administrative rules, mini campaigns and normative guidelines, are used" (1998: 656). The governance by administrative and regulatory technologies is flexible enough to contain strong commercial development within political control. This controlled decentralization sustains a negotiatory instead of a combative relationship between the political center and the regional media. The state sustains power by delegating power. It complies with the market to open up media space for a limited consumerist democracy. This complex interdependence satisfies media workers as well as lay consumers and at the same time consolidates the governance of the Chinese state.

This case is different from the Anglo-American contexts, where the media have relative autonomy and institutional separation from the state. Critical theorists in the West painstakingly search for the materialist/cultural link between the political economy and the media. In China, the state–market complex extends into the media. The links are explicit and much stronger. But it is not a birdcage in which the media are granted limited freedom within political confines.[10] In this oversimplified image, the existence of the birdcage seems independent of whether the bird is dead or alive. But in China, lively and commercially vibrant media are actually essential to the continued governance of the state. The state–market complex works in and through the media to form a contingent and shifting alliance for winning popular support. The state consolidates its power by promoting a consumer culture that fosters and satisfies social desire. In the Chinese case of the 1990s, we see the relevancy of Gramscian analysis in locating a moment of hegemony in which the state absorbs the power of the market and shores up popular support by the dialectic of occasional coercion and winning of general consent. Here we also see a Foucaultian bend: through the media, the state–market complex promotes regulatory discourses which are restraining and enabling, disciplinary and satisfying.

The active audience

There has recently been a strong emphasis on the idiosyncratic and subversive readings of media texts by active audiences. The claim of an active audience in the West is a reaction against theories of strong media influence; it developed under the umbrella of a combination of British cultural studies and American pluralism. The liberal faction celebrates semiotic democracy while the critical faction valorizes and empowers popular resistance. However, critics argue that the political effect of this celebration and valorization is the maintenance of existing power relations in capitalistic democracy.[11]

Nevertheless, the concept of the active audience, with a little adaptation, can be applied to the Chinese case with dramatic results. Under decades of strong ideological control, many among the Chinese audience within the country, and China watchers in the outside world, can skillfully read between the lines of censored media texts and come up with esoteric signals and subversive readings. It is "common sense" among Chinese that the real truth is probably closer to the opposite of what the official papers claim and that news sources from Hong Kong and overseas are more credible. After the June 4th Tiananmen Square incident in 1989, the Chinese government adopted restrictive media measures and engineered an official interpretation of the event. However, all sorts of oppositional encoding and decoding activities transgressed the official lines. At times journalists planted esoteric messages against the government. One poem in the overseas edition of *People's Daily* said "Down with Li Peng" if read diagonally. Another instance is a story about the symbol of the 1990 Asian Games hosted in China. People could find very strange ways of reading the symbol: looked at sideways, it was a 6 and on the left, it was a 4. It contained, as the story went, a commemoration to the democratic martyrs of June 4th (6/4). Another extraordinary instance occurred in a political prison in which prisoners were required to sing the national anthem. Surprisingly, they sang with gusto, "Arise! Refuse to be enslaved!" The authority sensed the irony and dropped the ritual (Friedman 1994).

These kinds of active decoding and recoding are becoming even more explicit under the recent trend of media commercialization. Since media producers serve two masters—the state and the public (sometimes interchangeable with the market)—they get around this by improvising and "double coding," creating textual and intertextual discrepancies.[12] There are discrepancies between the party mouthpieces and the local/liberal media. There are also ideological gaps between media texts of big factual news and soft infotainment. Local and entertainment media, which are more detached from the central government, can stretch ideological limits by loading latent and esoteric meanings beneath the apolitical textual surfaces. These competing imperatives translate themselves in the hybridized media texts, which exhibit strong polysemic tendencies.

Chinese audiences are now more likely to see through these textual cracks and spaces. In the 1990s, the Chinese mediascape was characterized by conspicuous discrepancies in different "reading zones." In everyday discourse, in the family, among friends, and in the workplace, Chinese people are free to criticize the government. Beijing taxi drivers are famous for talking about politics with their passengers. However, everyday discourse is quite different from media discourse, where politics is still taboo. Although it is an open secret that many party members and officials are engaged in widespread corruption, the media are very timid and only cover cases officially condemned by the party. But in everyday discourses, there are all sorts of jingles, rhymes, and poems which criticize the government and corrupt officials with biting sarcasm. These back-street rhymes have been collected and published as best sellers but are banned by the government once they become popular.[13]

Besides the discrepancies between mediated and social discourses, there is also a differentiation between the reading zones in offices and at home. In China, it is politically correct to read official newspapers during work hours. In the past, group reading and discussion sessions were treated as office routines and political duties. Even now, political imperative requires government units to subscribe to party papers. Stable subscription provides a broad readership base for the press to perform its ideological role. However, the rise of mass-appeal papers and magazines has eroded this readership base. New distribution networks, which include street sales and domestic subscription, have increased steadily since the late 1980s. The party press has been more and more restricted to offices. On the other hand, entertainment media, which include mass-appeal papers and magazines, television infotainment and radio phone-in programs, are becoming *the media* of the domestic sphere. Further differentiating the mediated domestic sphere is what has been called "weekend fever." In response to high levels of unemployment and the need to stimulate consumption, the Chinese state initiates a policy of five-day work weeks and a series of programs to promote a "civilized leisure culture" (Wang 1998). All these contribute to a proliferation of weekend papers, which specialize in promoting, educating, and catering for a collective desire to "consume" leisure. This weekend fever helps construct a private reading zone in which individuals can stay away from politics and cultivate their desire for personalized consumption. Thus it is common for an individual in China to move through these different reading zones, engage in different modes of reading, and adopt different reading strategies in different segments of his or her everyday life.

There is also a distinctive reading community connected with the Internet. Currently, researchers, academics, university students, and employees in large foreign companies can directly get online and receive uncensored news and foreign information. Those unable to read English can get access to the Chinese news provided by the newspapers in Hong Kong. Although Internet users are restricted to a limited number of intellectuals and professionals, they are the elite who can have significant influence in China. As some intellectuals and university students have pointed out, the Internet provides them with an effective and safe platform for discussing politically sensitive issues within and beyond the country border.

Having said all this, it should be noted that active audience activities in China should not be taken as a romanticized notion of audience power and autonomy. For instance, there are reports of investors and consumers buying into quasi-advertising stories in journalistic disguise and suffering from grave losses. The Chinese audience is more skeptical when reading political news, but more receptive when consuming entertainment contents. There are reports of high levels of emotional investment in watching soap operas, even to an extent that an intermitted broadcast of a drama serial leads to demonstrations in the street (Wang and Singhal 1992). What sense can media theorists make of this? Audience power or addictive consumption? These reading formations in the Chinese context can be more appropriately described as competing communities of discourse, which differ from those in liberal societies in that there are stronger discursive dynamics and more explicit boundaries of asymmetrical meanings. Of course my analysis here is a theoretical speculation. Further studies are needed to provide empirically grounded generalizations.

The sudden expansion in the domestic and entertainment media leads to another related theoretical question of whether popular communication has political consequences. In theories of popular culture, there has been a strong emphasis on the micropolitics of popular media texts, which are seen as powerful resources for individuals against dominant powers. It is in the particular context of China that this line of argument can have noteworthy applicability. The uneven liberalization of the Chinese media has created a large space for popular culture. The Chinese audience now shares the knowledge that big papers are dull and small papers are hot, the front page is boring whereas the entertainment or weekend sections are lively, and that flagship papers and official TV programs are numbing whereas spin-off publications and entertainment fares are stimulating (Pan 1996). Hong Kong, as a satellite metropolis of global capitalism, is "colonizing" the political center of China with popular media filled with consumerist and capitalistic ideologies. In China, the proliferation of Hong Kong popular culture, especially in the coastal provinces, has impacts at various levels. It lures audiences away from the Chinese media; it appears to have changed their frame of reference in their evaluation of Chinese media; it also exerts a strong impact on the institutional practices of coastal media organizations (Chan 2000, Gold 1993). Apolitical music television, soap operas, and weekend consumer reports carry values such as individualism, consumerism, and skepticism of authority. These popular texts have opened a modest, albeit tentative, space outside the power of the state, where the audience can explore their dreams and aspirations. This liberating potential is contingent and historical. The media become cultural intermediaries, introducing new ways of life and cultivating desire for individual freedom. Seen from a critical perspective, this can be interpreted as an ideological formation of market capitalism. As Sparks (1998) observes in the case of Central and Eastern Europe, the commercialization of the media in former communist countries in no way empowers the public for civic participation. This is even more true in China, because the state is policing the media and the media are empowering consumers, not citizens. But if we locate the present situation in decades of authoritarian rule, then the popular media in China really are widening personal spaces. They are democratizing access to a wide range of information and entertainment and also material and cultural goods. The 1990s seem to be the historical moment when Chinese popular media can operate as progressive resources, despite their connections to transnational capitalism. This brings us back to the "benign market capitalism thesis" discussed in the beginning of this theoretical section. But whether the reorientation toward the personal and the domestic of the Chinese media can foster political demands for a more participatory polity is a theoretically and politically significant issue for further empirical investigation.

Concluding remarks

The present book coins the term "de-Westernizing media studies," which suggests a self-critical awareness of the hegemonic nature of knowledge-building in Western countries. This echoes the sporadic call, among academics in Asia, for localizing social sciences and building theories which can better explain media and society in a context very different from that in the UK and the US. Many media scholars analyzing the Chinese media scene are ethnic Chinese trained in universities in the US or in the UK. As a member of this academic community, I think it is good to have a constant awareness of being inside the web of discursive formation originating in the West. However,

I doubt very much that Asia needs completely new media theories. Justifying the claims for new Asian media theories by essentializing and exoticizing the Asian experience in fact puts forward an unjustifiable claim that Asia is unique and isolated from the development of transnational capitalism. What we need, I believe, is to modify and adapt existing theories to suit the Chinese context. As Downing (1996) has pointed out, the major limitation of Western media theories is that they evolve from and are used to explain a relatively stable political economy. Western media theories seem to take for granted capitalistic democracy as a static backdrop for media dynamics. However, in other sociopolitical contexts, as in China, rapid and abrupt change seems to be a fact of life for many decades. This is not to say that in media dynamics the roles of the market and the state are completely different. The reconfiguration of the Chinese media contrasts sharply with the situation of the West, yet the characteristics of the Chinese case are commensurate with Western media theories. But the ways in which these theories may be used to articulate the Chinese case are unique, because no other country is moving from planned socialism to market socialism, not to mention other cultural differences. Here, the unique ways of articulating theoretical explanations are threefold. First, in the Chinese media scene, market forces are absorbed by the state. The tensions, contradictions, compliance, and partial resolution between the state and the market harbor great possibilities for theory building and testing. In this chapter, the conceptualization of the state–market complex is only a very tentative attempt, which calls for further theoretical investigation. Second, cross-cultural comparative studies will be very fruitful with regard to the recent theoretical turn toward the active audience. Patterns of esoteric and oppositional decoding and recoding activities can be generalized from the Chinese case and compared to other Asian cases where the media space is restrictive and sociopolitical powers are highly concentrated and unevenly distributed. Third, media analyses are mostly done within consistent theoretical approaches of either the liberal or critical perspective. But in the Chinese case, both perspectives can be applied creatively and flexibly. And sometimes this means transgressing the bounds of media analyses by cutting and pasting between liberal and critical perspectives in order to engage with the Chinese media in a context-sensitive and multiperspective approach.

Notes

1 The author would like to thank Professor Joseph Chan and Professor Myung-Jin Park for their insightful comments.
2 For a factual description of the Chinese media scene, see Huang 1998. For updated research reports, see Lee in press. Other book length studies are Lee 1994, 1990, He and Chen 1998, Zhao 1998. There is a comprehensive reference list in Goonasekera and Holaday 1998.
3 For a comprehensive review, see Chan 1993. Part of this section summarizes the accounts in Chen and Chan 1998, Chen and Lee 1998, Zhao 1998.
4 The concept of improvization in media organization is originated by Pan 2000. Part of this section summarizes from Pan 1996, Pan 2000, Liu 1998, Yu 1991, He and Chen 1998.
5 Senior reporter/editor, head reporter/editor, reporter/editor and assistant reporter/editor. See Chen and Lee 1998.
6 See He and Chen 1998.
7 See the content analysis done by Chen and Chan 1998.
8 For studies on the interaction between the media of Hong Kong and China, see Ma 1999, Lee 1997, Chan 1996, 1994.
9 See a report of self-censorship in Chan *et al*. 1995. There are some media critical toward the

Chinese government (e.g. *Apple Daily*, a Chinese newspaper published in Hong Kong). Here I am only describing a general pattern.

10 This is a popular metaphor used to describe China's state-controlled media and economy.

11 See a theoretical review in Ma 1998.

12 Textual producers coined the term "double coding" in an interview (Zha 1995: 74).

13 See report in *Apple Daily*, January 10, 1999.

References

Chan, J. (1993) "Commercialization without independence: media development in China," in J. Cheng and M. Brosseau (eds.) *China Review 1993*, Hong Kong: The Chinese University Press.

Chan, J. (1994) "National responses and accessibility to STAR TV in Asia," *Journal of Communication*, 44(3): 112–31.

Chan, J. (1996) "Television development in Greater China: structure, exports, and market formation," in John Sinclair *et al.* (eds.) *New Patterns in Global Television: Peripheral Vision*, Oxford: Oxford University Press.

Chan, J. (2000) "When capitalist and socialist TV clash: the impact of Hong Kong TV on Guangzhau residents," in Chin-Chuan Lee (ed.) *Money, Power and Media*, Evanston, IL: Northwestern University Press.

Chan, J. *et al.* (1995) *Hong Kong Journalists in Transition*, Hong Kong: The Chinese University Press.

Chen, Huailin and Chan, J.M. (1998) "Bird-caged press freedom in China," in J.Y.S. Chang (ed.) *China in the Post-Deng Era*, Hong Kong: The Chinese University Press.

Chen, Huailin and Lee, Chin-Chuan (1998) "Press finance and economic reform in China," in J. Cheng (ed.) *China Review 1998*, Hong Kong: The Chinese University Press.

Downing, J. (1996) *Internationalizing Media Theory*, London: Sage.

Friedman, E. (1994) "The oppositional decoding of China's Leninist media," in C. C. Lee (ed.) *China's Media, Media's China*, Boulder, CO: Westview.

Gold, T. (1993) "Go with your feelings: Hong Kong and Taiwan popular culture in Greater China," *China Quarterly*, 163: 907–25.

Goonasekera, A. and Holaday, D. (eds.) (1998) *Asian Communication Handbook 1998*, Singapore: Amic.

He, Zhou and Chen, Huailin (1998) *The Chinese Media: A New Perspective* (in Chinese), Hong Kong: Pacific Century Press Limited.

Huang, Changzhu (1998) "China," in A. Goonasekera and D. Holaday (eds.) *Asian Communication Handbook 1998*, Singapore: Amic.

Lee, Chin-Chuan (ed.) (1990) *Voices of China: The Interplay of Politics and Journalism*, New York: Guilford.

Lee, Chin-Chuan (ed.) (1994) *China's Media, Media's China*, Boulder, CO: Westview.

Lee, Chin-Chuan (1997) "Media structure and regime change in Hong Kong," in Ming K. Chan (ed.) *The Challenge of Hong Kong's Reintegration with China*, Hong Kong: Hong Kong University Press.

Lee, Chin-Chuan (2000) "Chinese communication: prisms, trajectories and modes of understanding" in Chin-Chuan Lee (ed.) *Money, Power and Media: Communication Patterns and Bureaucratic Control in Cultural China*, Evanston, IL: Northwestern University Press.

Lee, Chin-Chuan (ed.) (2000) *Money, Power and Media: Communication Patterns and Bureaucratic Control in Cultural China*, Evanston, IL: Northwestern University Press.

Liu, Hong (1998) "Profit or ideology? The Chinese press between party and market," *Media, Culture and Society*, 20: 31–41.

Ma, Kit-wai Eric (1998) *Television Theories* (in Chinese), Taiwan: Yan-Chih Book.

Ma, Kit-wai Eric (1999) *Culture, Politics and Television in Hong Kong*, London: Routledge.

Pan, Zhongdang (1996) "Television and spatial construction in popular phenomena" (in Chinese), *Journalism and Communication Research*, 4: 36–44.

Pan, Zhongdang (2000), "Improvising reform activities: the changing reality of journalistic practices in China," in Chin-Chuan Lee (ed.) *Money, Power and Media*, Evanston, IL: Northwestern University Press.

Sparks, C. (1998) *Communism, Capitalism and the Mass Media*, London: Sage.

Wang, Jing (1998) "Public culture and popular culture: metropolitan China at the turn of the new century," paper presented in the conference Modern and Contemporary Chinese Popular Culture, Duke University, May 8–9.

Wang, Min and Singhal, Arvind (1992) "Ke Wang, a Chinese television soap opera with a message," *Gazette*, 49: 177–92.

Yahuda, M. (1996) *Hong Kong: China's Challenge*, London: Routledge.

Yu, Xuejun (1991) "Government policies towards advertising in China (1979–1989)," *Gazette*, 48: 17–30.

Zha, Jianying (1995) *China Pop*, New York: The New Press.

Zhao, Yuezhi (1998) *Media, Market and Democracy in China Between the Party Line and the Bottom Line*, Urbana and Chicago: University of Illinois Press.

3 Media theory after the fall of European communism

Why the old models from East and West won't do any more

Colin Sparks

Introduction

The collapse of the communist regimes in Central and Eastern Europe was clearly an historic event of the first importance, both for the inhabitants of those countries and for the world at large. The political, economic, and social effects were real and immediate in the lives of millions of people, and since the fall of the Berlin Wall change has swept through every nook and cranny of social life. On the one hand, the populations of most of the states of the region won their first chance at anything like free elections. On the other hand, many of the indicators of material well-being, such as average living standards and life expectancy, dropped alarmingly. For some, it has been a decade of opportunity: of BMWs, mobile phones, and villas in select Mediterranean resorts. For others, it has meant unemployment, poverty, and increasing desperation. To the people who have lived through the changes, even to the regular visitor to the region, there can be no doubt that things are different now from what they were in 1989.

The mass media have, of course, been a central part of these changes. The formerly subsidized and controlled press is now dependent on subscription and advertising. Many more titles, some with only a very limited life-span, compete for the attention of the reader. The circulation of newspapers has fallen dramatically in some countries, and the sales of new magazines, addressing every special interest from computing to pornography, have risen sharply. Broadcasting, too, has changed. New radio and television stations, funded by sales of advertising space, are on the air in most countries. Sometimes they are locally owned, but more often they are partnerships between local businesses and foreign media companies. In Ronald Lauder's Bahamas-based, US-financed, Central European Media (CME), the region even had its very own transnational broadcasting corporation.

In this chapter, I want to try to show why the fall of communism represents a major challenge to the ways in which we think about the mass media. In doing this, I shall be concerned primarily not with the collapse of the "communist" view of the media, although that is discussed in passing, but rather with the impact on the dominant "Western" way of thinking. As I will show, these two views were in fact very similar indeed, and the crisis of the one is, by the same token, the crisis of the other. Considerations of space mean that I want here to address only three of the major issues that I believe arise from an analysis of these events. The first is the theoretical account of media systems and their trajectories with which Western scholars have hitherto operated, either consciously or unconsciously. The second and third follow very closely from the problems identified in that investigation: the ways in which we customarily think about the relationships between different kinds of social power and the mass media and, finally, lessons we can learn from the point of view of alternative, and more democratic, media structures.

The (still) dominant paradigm

The Cold War divided a continent, but there were many things that the propagandists of both sides were entirely in agreement about, and one of those was the nature of the communist media. The official communist view was enshrined in collections with titles like *Lenin: about the Press* (Lenin 1972). The almost equally official Western view was enshrined in a small book of startling power and longevity: Siebert, Petersen and Schramm's *Four Theories of the Press* (Siebert *et al.* 1963 [originally published 1956]). Both of these views relied on the same quotations from Lenin and other Russian leaders, and made the same claims for the consonance of "communist" reality with "Leninist" theory. The only real difference between what was believed in Prospect Marxa 20 and what was believed in the Armory Building was in the evaluations of the system in question. The Soviet ideologists thought that the media system they presided over was all a jolly good thing, whereas the US ideologists thought it was all a shockingly bad state of affairs.

Though the communist version has few friends today, the anticommunist version remains alive and robustly popular. *Four Theories of the Press* continues to sell and to win converts. It has survived numerous critiques, including a full-scale attempt at burial orchestrated by Schramm's successors at Illinois (Nerone 1992). Its conceptual influence is still pervasive, even in those textbooks whose authors have today retreated a little from their earlier explicit indebtedness (McQuail 1993). At least one group of very distinguished scholars is laboring, apparently interminably, to produce a new and better alternative. Meanwhile, the original book goes on and on: 1998 witnessed the publication of the first Russian translation, with an introduction by Professor Y. N. Zassoursky, long-time Dean of the Faculty of Journalism at Moscow State University. The fact is that, like it or not, the framework proposed by Schramm and his co-thinkers back in the depths of the Cold War has entered the collective unconscious of the profession, and it remains firmly lodged even in the minds of many of its sternest critics.

This is a remarkable achievement, and it should prompt the question: Why and how is it possible? The duplicity and gullibility of academic students of the media aside, any serious answer to that question must start from recognizing that the famous Four Theories actually possessed a degree of explanatory power, both at the pedagogic and at the investigative levels. It is often remarked that the book has a normative dimension (how media systems should be), and this is certainly present: the authors had no qualms in making it clear to their readers that the American way was better. What is less noticed, however, is that the book both proposed a methodology for analyzing media systems (how to understand media systems) and contained an account of then actually existing media systems (how the media in the USSR and the US really were). If the normative dimension explains the immediate appeal of the book, I think it is the effect of the latter two elements that has been more pervasive in the long term, and has made it such a deeply influential text.

The plain fact is that the account offered of the two main systems around which the book is organized, the "Soviet Communist" and the "Libertarian," is, in the scientific sense, beautiful. The opposition of free market and state direction has an elegance, a symmetry, a lack of redundancy, and a completeness that gives it paradigmatic status. What is more, this polarity tells us something true and important about the mass media: there really is a difference between the ways in which the market shapes the media and the ways in which the state shapes the media. Whatever other shortcomings it may have, the pattern proposed here is not just simply false.

The consequences of this basic insight are what has entered into the collective unconscious of the profession and which still structure the thinking even of those who wish to be extremely critical of the overt conclusions drawn by the original authors. We may summarize the three that are most important for our purposes here as follows:

1   The assumption that there is a fundamental distinction between economic effects on the media, derived from ownership patterns, and political effects, derived from the action of governmental or state structures. The influences derived from these two kinds of social power is assumed to be different in kind one from another.
2   The idea that media systems are coherent wholes, that in some way are derived from core value systems, and whose dynamic is traceable to a logic embodied in those core values.
3   A tendency to abstract "the media" from the real social relations of their production, and to consider them as servants of, or adjuncts to, systems of government, rather than as one of the primary mechanisms through which a particular way of ruling is organized.

Taken together, these three elements have, in my view, led to a largely sterile debate about the value or otherwise of state intervention in mass media, that has tended to obscure any real analysis of the ways in which the media actually do function with regard to social power.

What we did (not) know about the communist media

I want to argue that, in the light of the collapse of the communist media systems, and the struggles over the shape of their successors, it is no longer possible to hold to any of these propositions. The first, and apparently minor, problem with the model proposed jointly by Stalinists and Schrammists is that there never was a "Leninist theory of the press." One finds in Lenin's voluminous writings numerous references to the press, and some to other media such as cinema, but all of these are tactical responses, situated in particular historical conjunctures. In this, of course, they do not differ greatly from the bulk of Lenin's writing, which Lukács famously characterized as being centrally organized around "the actuality of the revolution"(Lukács 1970: 2–3). With regard to the press, there is a succession of positions in which the stresses lie in different, and often apparently contradictory, directions. So, for example, we find Lenin arguing, in clandestine conditions, for a press closely tied to the needs of the party apparatus, and, in conditions of mass upsurge, for a press closely tied to the expression of the experience of the proletariat. We find him arguing, in conditions of Tsarist persecution, for freedom of the press, and, in conditions of civil war, for the closure of newspapers advocating armed opposition to the Bolshevik government. It may be possible to construct a coherent theory of the media from these scattered remarks. Many writers have attempted to do exactly this with his more general theoretical propositions. So far as I can discover, however, there does not seem ever to have been such an undertaking in this special area of the media. Aspects of Lenin's theory of the press appropriate to political opposition in a capitalist society, particularly the idea of the press as party organizer, have indeed been taken up and developed. Attempts to combine those elements with an adequate account of the later views from the period of workers' power are, however, absent (Harman 1984).

What is present, both in the Schrammist and in the Stalinist commentaries, is not theory but selective quotation. This method produced a justification for a rigidly centralized, rigidly controlled, wholly politicized, and entirely propagandist media. The "Soviet Communist Theory of the Press" was said to justify the subordination of all media to the line of the party leadership. This was the case both where it was entirely justified according even to bourgeois theory (for example those newspapers that the party actually owned) and where it was obviously not justified (for example the state broadcaster). It is an entailment of the explicit methodology of *Four Theories of the Press* that the actual shape of any given media system be traceable to the "core values" of the society in which it exists, and of which it is, fundamentally, an expression. If the "Soviet Communist Theory of the Press" was indeed an articulation of the core values of the society, then we would expect the media system to embody it extremely clearly.

The problem with this view was that it did not correspond to reality. It may, once upon a time, in Moscow in 1936, say, have been a fairly accurate picture of what was published and what was broadcast, but come the 1980s, things were not at all like that in the communist countries of Central and Eastern Europe. For one thing, the media systems of various communist countries were widely different one from another. The Romanian system, according to its best-known Western interpreter at least, was in the 1980s an exact, direct, and faithful copy, down to the very last detail, of precisely the kind of system described by Schramm (Gross 1996). The Polish system, on the other hand, had gone through a long series of changes, starting in the 1950s, with different degrees of openness and closure, and had seldom, if ever, even approximated to the contours of the model suggested by theory (Goban-Klas 1994). By the mid-1980s, while party control of the official state media had been reestablished during martial law, the official media had to contend not only with a long-established, and moderately oppositional, Church media, but also with the flourishing, and extremely oppositional, underground media organized by Solidarity (Jakubowicz 1991). The Hungarian system had been undergoing a long process of liberalization that dated back to the failed revolution of 1956 (Kováts and Tölgeysi 1990). This evidence contradicts the notion, central to both sides of the Cold War, that there was one, single, communist type of media system that was reproduced, everywhere and at all times, in the same form.

Secondly, very far from being isolated and sealed against evil imperialist influences, the media systems of Central and Eastern Europe were, mostly, surprisingly open. Certainly, there was up to the end the jamming of some Western radio broadcasts, although never, apparently, of television. In general, however, the broadcasting systems of Central European communist countries took a very pragmatic view of Western media and Western programs. The extreme case was the former East Germany (the German Democratic Republic), where the majority of the population could receive the television signals of its Western, and aggressively capitalist, sister, the Federal Republic (Hanke 1990). Other systems had a greater natural insulation, through language or geography, although there was frequently some serious spillover: 30 percent of the population of Hungary could receive Austrian and Yugoslav signals, and this did not appear to alarm the communist authorities (Szekfü 1989). Regarding the domestic broadcasting of Western programs, the extent to which the regimes were prepared to allow imports varied widely. While, in 1986, 70 percent of the imported programs on Hungarian Television were from the West, only about 34 percent had the same origin in Czechoslovakia, where a whole TV channel was dedicated to rebroadcasting Russian programs (MTV 1991: 19, Tesar 1989: 138). More generally, though they might not actually have welcomed the uncontrolled and subversive materials new media technologies could potentially relay, the regimes did not fight any serious battles in the 1970s and 1980s to keep out either Western satellites or Western videos. There was very little evidence, at least for the last decade of their existence, of any systematic attempt to control the symbolic landscape in the way predicted by the dominant theory. In practice, the free market proved a much more effective censor of oppositional views than the state. By the 1980s, it was certainly much easier to see a capitalist TV program on prime time in Central Europe than it was to see a socialist TV program in prime time in the US.

Thirdly, the different media systems of the communist period had histories of substantial change. They were not the static articulation of central theories or values. The process of change in communist Europe was, and is, a protracted one. It did not begin the day the wall came down, and it did not end with the first free elections. The communist regimes of the region had already begun a process of internal and external decay at least a decade before the fall of the Berlin Wall. As with the media systems, the nature and extent of the decomposition varied from country to country.

The most important case was Poland, were there had been a long series of working-class struggles against the regime, that reached a high point with the growth of Solidarity in 1980–1. At its greatest extent, this union embraced the majority of society, including most people who worked in the media. It was able to force concessions on the conduct and content of the press and broadcasting from the government, and itself advanced very radical plans for reconstructing the media to make them much more open to the diverse voices within Polish society. Martial law, imposed in December 1981, drove Solidarity underground, and reestablished party control over the media, but it failed to break the opposition. By the mid-1980s, it was obvious to at least a wing of the communist leadership that there would have to be some sort of negotiated peace with Solidarity, otherwise there would certainly be another mass upsurge sooner or later. Given that Gorbachev's Russia was increasingly reluctant to play the role of the gendarme of Eastern Europe, the outcome of any such upheaval was highly unpredictable. As a consequence, the "reform communists" began a slow process of negotiation with the more moderate of their foes.

The experience of the Polish communists provided a lesson that was increasingly taken to heart by the more intelligent of their fellow thinkers throughout the region. At different speeds, in a number of countries, the "reform communists" started to cast around for opposition figures with whom they could do some sort of deal. As a consequence, all sorts of divisions and fissures opened up in the ruling elite, who had previously been unified, at least in public. These quarrels within the ranks of the "nomenklatura," who were that layer of communists who ran society, made it much easier for journalists to say what they thought and report what they saw as important. In fact, the period of the decline of the communist regimes was, in many countries, the golden age of freedom and independence for journalists.

A good example was the situation in what is now the independent state of Slovenia.

Prior to 1990, this was one of the constituent republics of the federal state of Yugoslavia. In common with the rest of the country, there had been a sharp crackdown in the 1970s, which had produced the so-called "leaden years," when any expression of independent thought was regarded as grounds for persecution. But during the 1980s, tensions developed between the bureaucrats who ran the different national units in the federal state. In particular, the leadership in Slovenia developed economic and political criticisms of the way the government in Belgrade was running the country. They saw the resources generated by their own, much more developed, economy being siphoned off for what they regarded as nonviable projects in the south, whose sole function was to secure the power base of the federal government. As part of their campaign against Belgrade, they began to allow, if not encourage, criticisms from below. All sorts of people, including journalists, now found that they had new freedoms to express their views of society. In particular, because of a special feature of the constitution, people found that they had a legal right to force newspapers to publish their opinions, and they used this right to widen the debate about the nature of society and the future. One indication of the depth of the crisis in the country was that most of the independently minded publications, for example the youth paper *Mladina*, were actually formally owned by the local Communist Party (Novak 1996). By the late 1980s, journalists in Slovenia were experiencing a golden age of freedom of expression.

This very considerable degree of freedom was not present everywhere in the region. In particular, in what was then Czechoslovakia, the Russian invasion of 1968 had meant that all of the potential reform communists were either in exile or relegated to minor positions in the provinces, and the opposition was very distant from, and hostile to, the regime. A similar position prevailed in East Germany. In Romania and Bulgaria, the situation was even more repressive. In those countries, the freedom of the journalists had to wait until after the collapse of one-party rule. Elsewhere, however, the declining years of the communist regimes were, contrary to the predictions of the dominant theory, experienced by journalists as an oasis of freedom and independence.

The inevitable conclusion that this brief review of the evidence suggests is that the account of the nature of the communist media offered by Schramm, or for that matter by his Stalinist opponents, was fundamentally incorrect. Contrary to the predictions of theory, there were very substantial variations between the media systems of different countries. Far from representing the articulation of the core values of the system, these differences are better explained by the exigencies of political and economic pressures upon the communist elite, and by the divisions that grew up between them as the terminal crisis of their system grew ever deeper. Very far from constituting tightly controlled, and propagandistically organized, symbolic systems, the media in at least some of the countries were heavily colonized by Western images, and allowed considerable freedom to their journalists to report on, and speculate about the possible future of, their society. It is high time the Manichean universe of Four Theories of the Press was abandoned as a starting point for media analysis.

What comes after communism?

If we are forced by the weight of evidence to abandon the approach favored by Schramm and his co-authors, then we need to think again about some of the ways in which the intellectual framework they deposited has influenced our thinking. One of the master oppositions present in that book was between the political role of government and the state with regard to the media and the economic role of private ownership and the market. As I remarked above, this is an important insight, but there are grounds for thinking that the original authors seriously overplayed it. Certainly, an examination of the aftermath of the fall of communism suggests a rather different interpretation.

It is entirely true to say that what comes after communism is capitalism, but the nature and form of the capitalism that has emerged in the former communist countries are distinctive. This invites a different perspective on the nature of the relationship between politics and economics from what one might derive from evidence drawn from the US in the 1950s. In country after country, there is very strong evidence, particularly with regard to the mass media, of the close interrelationship between political and economic power.

We may take as an example to illustrate these realities the Hungarian "media wars" that broke out shortly after the first democratic elections in that country, in 1990. Media conduct during the two rounds of elections had been regulated by an agreement between all of the political parties, including both the communists and their opponents (Körösényi 1992: 76). As part of the deal, it had been agreed that the President of the Republic had the power to appoint the heads of both Hungarian Radio and Hungarian Television, but that the candidates were nominated by the Prime Minister in order to maintain political balance (Kováts and Tölgyesi 1993: 40–4). The first director of Hungarian radio was a well known journalist, Gombár, and the first director of Hungarian Television (MTV) was a famous dissident sociologist, Elemer Hankiss, who was generally believed to be close to the new Prime Minister, Antall of the Hungarian Democratic Forum (MDF) (Cunningham 1994: 4).

Despite these close links, there was soon a sharp conflict between the MDF and the leaders of both radio and television. The basic charge was that they were attempting to pursue independent policies, and were thus not sympathetic enough to the policies, and in particular the strongly nationalist orientation, of the new government. The government mobilized their supporters, both inside and outside of parliament, against the two directors, in an attempt to force them to resign. A large part of the opposition came to the support of the men, and a full-scale political struggle developed. Eventually, after a long battle, the government won, and both men were forced out at the end of 1992. The overall effect of all of this was to make the direction of television and radio an intensely political issue. The MDF used its new control to sack any journalists suspected of political unreliability and to attempt to turn radio and television into reliable vehicles for their ideas. As it turned out, despite this control of broadcasting, the MDF lost the 1994 elections very heavily, and were followed by a government dominated by the Hungarian Socialist Party (the communist successor party), under the former Stalinist enthusiast Horn. He followed the precedent established by his immediate predecessors and intervened regularly in the appointment of senior broadcasters (Oltay 1995).

Although the Hungarian case is the best known and most protracted of the struggles to subordinate broadcasting to the government of the day, it is part of a more general pattern in the region. The Meciar-led nationalist governments in Slovakia waged a long campaign, between 1991 and 1998, to ensure that broadcasting followed the official line (Vojteck 1995). In the Czech Republic, there was a struggle between the Broadcasting Council and the government over the award of licenses for commercial radio and television and local cable systems (Korte 1994: 61, Šmíd 1994). In Poland, too, successive governments, as well as President Walesa, found themselves interfering in the appointments of people both to the leading posts in broadcasting and in the Broadcasting Council (Jakubowicz, n.d., Karpinski 1995). In all of these cases, the stabilization of capitalist democracy meant a reassertion of authority over journalists and media workers, and an ending of the anarchic freedom they had enjoyed during the decay of the old regimes and the actual process of changing regimes.

What all of this illustrates is the emergence of a close set of relations between politicians, businessmen, and the media that leads to a routine interchange between the different groups in post-communist countries. In this kind of society, there are no neat and clear divisions between what is "political" and what is "economic": the two are inextricably linked together. In point of fact, the situation could not be any different, since the process of transforming a collective ruling group, the old communist elite, into a mutually hostile private capitalist class could only possibly take place as the result of political decisions. Since the property to be disposed of was that of the state, it was only through state action that it could be transformed into private property. This emergence of political capital is a central feature of post-communist societies, but the fact that this phenomenon is present in extreme form here should not obscure the fact that it has very important consequences for media theory more generally.

The opposition constructed by the classical model of media theory poses separate and distinct spheres of action for political and economic agents. The political is concerned with the general interests of society as a whole. To the extent that it interferes with the economic sphere, it does so legitimately only when it sets ground rules, prevents abuses of market position, and so on. Thus, in the sphere of the media, political action is, or was, appropriate to regulate the use of scarce resources represented by those portions of the electromagnetic spectrum available for broadcasting, to prevent monopolies, and to provide the forum in which the reputations of individuals may be defended against calumny. All other forms of action are aberrations from this proper role. On the other hand, the economic concerns the private affairs of individuals, primarily the pursuit of self-enrichment. It only notices the political to the extent that it impacts upon these private activities, notably through taxation and various attempts to intervene in the economy. In the sphere of the media, there is a special interest in keeping as large a distance as possible from government, since the scrutiny of its activities, the exposure of its shortcomings, and the denunciation of its misdeeds, are the prime means by which the business can command customers.

This, of course, has always been a ludicrously idealized picture, even of the US in the 1950s, but it has derived part of its strength from its contrast with its Soviet opposite. There, normality was the complete unity between political and economic power, fused in the governing role of the elite of the Communist Party. The gap between the sphere of private activity and the sphere of government was completely absent, and this was one of the axes along which the "totalitarian" features of the regimes were organized. It was, incidentally, the erasure of this difference that led the political opponents of the communist regimes, in the 1980s, to speak so enthusiastically about the construction of civil society as an alternative to their totalitarian experiences. As we have argued, this was a ludicrously idealized (or demonized) picture of the social realities of Central and Eastern Europe in the last years of communism. It was, nevertheless, neatly complementary to the imaginary construction of the US as the land of an absolute distinction between politics and economics.

What the situation that has emerged after the end of communism suggests is that there is a third position, in which the relationship between politics and economics is one neither of identity nor of complete separation, but of interpenetration. The alignment of different sections of capital with various political forces can be seen at its extreme in what I. I. Zassoursky calls "political capital" in contemporary Russia. It can be understood as an effort by the political element to gain access to sources of funding, and by the economic element to secure a position of advantage in the competitive struggle (Zassoursky n.d.). The situation in Central and Eastern Europe is nowhere near as extreme as the case in the former Soviet Union. We can, nevertheless, see clear examples of the ways in which political and economic power are clearly linked, even in countries like the Czech Republic in which the transition to private capitalism has been much more peaceful and orderly.

The Czech Republic was the first of the former communist countries to settle a new legal framework for broadcasting, and the first to license a commercial broadcaster. We have already noted that the award of the franchise provoked political intervention in the running of the Broadcasting Council, but it is worth looking in slightly more detail at the arrangements that were put in place, and their outcomes. These provide a clear example of the new realities. The franchise was awarded to a group that consisted of three very different forces. On the one hand, there were a number of former dissidents, most prominently Vladimir Zelezny, who had been very close to the first post-communist government. (It was this proximity that caused the political row with the second, more rightist, post-communist government.) This group, organized as the dominant shareholder in "Central European Television for the 21st Century" (CET-21), was actually awarded the license to broadcast. Secondly, there was an institution descended directly and intact from the old regime, the Czech Savings Bank. Thirdly, there was the US-directed Central European Media Enterprises Group (CME), which has been active in many of the post-communist television and radio markets. The latter two elements formed a further company, Czech Independent Television (CNTS), that contracted to produce and broadcast the programming for the new station, called Nova TV. It was a combination of all of these elements, particularly the finance and expertise provided by the US partner and the political credibility provided by the locals, that ensured the award of the contract. Subsequent to winning the contract, Nova TV proved very successful in audience terms, and quickly became profitable. It also moved to repair its fences with the government, offering the Prime Minister a weekly spot to address the nation in the year before the elections. Because its operations infringed Czech law on a number of occasions, for example by advertising alcohol, Nova was in frequent conflict with the Broadcasting Council, and only survived intact because it was able to build important links with politicians. Using this influence, Nova was able to bring about detailed changes to broadcasting legislation which strengthened its commercial position (Kaplan and Šmíd 1995). By 1997, local observers calculated that it was so well integrated with the politicians that it was inconceivable that its operating license could be removed, even though there had been some extremely complicated, and perhaps dubious, changes in the ownership of the different companies involved. These resulted in CME becoming the effective owner of the whole operation (Kenety 1997, PSMLP 1996).

This pattern of an interpenetration of political and economic factors is clearly present in television throughout the region, governing the award of broadcasting franchises and the degree to which the successful bidders have subsequently been obliged to adhere to the conditions of their licenses. CME, before its takeover by Scandinavian Broadcasting Systems (SBS) in March 1999, applied the model successfully in Slovenia,

Romania, and the Ukraine. In each of these markets, it was able to secure an advantageous position because it managed to ally with influential local political figures who could ensure access to first-mover advantages in commercial broadcasting. In Poland and Hungary, where CME made the "wrong" alliances, other groups gained the first commercial licenses. CME was unable in both of those markets to overcome the disadvantages of a late start and was always very much a minority broadcaster. Its greatest strength originally was having good political contacts throughout the region, but one of the main reasons for its eventual failure and takeover by SBS was that it failed to turn political influence into commercial advantage in two of the biggest advertising markets in the region (Sparks 1999).

Newspapers, having operated in a much less regulated environment, do not everywhere display the same pattern of continuing close relations with politicians, but they do provide very clear evidence about the political nature of issues of ownership. The best known examples come from Hungary. In 1989–90, the staff of various papers managed effectively to seize them from their former owners and to treat them as their own property. Thus the staff of the regional papers owned by the Hungarian Socialist Workers' Party were, in 1989–90, effectively permitted to sell them to the Springer Company (Gálik and Dénes 1992). When, later, the former owners challenged this deal, Springer settled out of court for a substantial sum. The staff of major national newspapers was able to come to agreements with other foreign publishers, with the agreement of the departing leadership of the Communist Party (Jakab and Gálik 1991).

It should not be imagined that the readiness of businessmen to dabble in politics, and of politicians to court friendly relationships with particular business groups, is the product of "naive" politicians unused to democratic societies, or of "inexperienced" businessmen new to the idea of the market. In the whole region, there has been a very strong element of foreign ownership in both press and broadcasting. This was an important element in Czech broadcasting and in the Hungarian press, where they continue to have a major influence, particularly in the new tabloid market (Gulyas 1998). These foreign owners have been sophisticated enterprises, sometimes very large ones, with considerable experience in operating in conditions of capitalist democracy, but they also have been deeply involved in the alliances with local forces and have played the game of political capital without any apparent hesitation. The basis for the alliances that are so common in this field, and of which CME is such a prominent exponent, is precisely that the Western company brings expertise in programming and production, and sometimes the necessary financial resources, while the local company brings the political contacts needed for success. Such alliances, of course, are always strained and are often fragile. Sometimes, as in the case of Nova TV, the foreign owners have ended up in sole control. Sometimes, as in the case of the alliance between CME and the Polish company International Trading and Investment Holdings, the locals have come out on top (Dziadul and Drazek 1999: 1). What there is no evidence of, however, is that Western business, whether as partners or as sole owners, have refused to adopt the appropriate rules of societies in which capital and politics are closely intertwined.

There is a continuing and mutually supportive relationship between businessmen and politicians. This arises not from inexperience or ignorance, but from the nature of the transition itself. Not only did the politicians in the region help their friends to win important competitive positions in the new market economy, but they also continue to exert considerable influence over the media. The media, in turn, tend to rely on relationships with politicians to gain advantages in the competitive struggle for survival and profit.

A moment's reflection, however, suggests to us that this situation of close links between political and economic actors is very far from being some strange aberration unique to post-communist societies. On the contrary, it is much closer to being the global norm than is the allegedly sharp separation of the major social powers characteristic of the US. It is only the version of media theory that assumes that what it believes to be normal in the US is normal everywhere that registers this situation as unaccountable (Downing 1996: 229). Silvio Berlusconi is the name that springs to mind if one seeks to find other examples of the interpenetration of media ownership and political influence in the private capitalist world. So strong is this parallel that one of the main theorists of post-communist media calls it the "Italian" model of the mass media (Splichal 1994). The alignment of business and political interests, albeit in different constellations, is a commonplace throughout southern Europe. It is also strongly present in Central and South America (for example TV Globo in Brazil and Televisa in Mexico), and in much of Asia (for example Murdoch's relationship with the Chinese government). It seems more reasonable to regard this situation as the normal one, and to look upon the two polarities of the US and the USSR as the aberrations. In this light, political and economic power appear as facets of a single form of social domination, or class rule, as we orthodox Marxists would put it.

The advantage of such a position is that it enables us to understand a number of puzzling features about the mass media. For example, according to traditional theory, commercial media are necessarily better at presenting the political alternatives in any society than are state-controlled media. The way this is usually proved is by comparing the media in, say, the US with the media in, say, North Korea. Naturally, this comparison shows that the commercial media are better, in almost any conceivable respect, than the state media. On the other hand, from this standpoint, we would be at a loss to explain why it is that state-run television in Britain is clearly better at presenting political alternatives even-handedly than is the wholly commercial, and effectively unregulated, press. If, on the other hand, we look at concrete cases of the relationship between the media and politics in the light of the variable relations between businesses and political factions, we can begin to understand both of these situations much more easily.

In summary, one of the main lessons learned from the fall of communism is that the fundamental opposition, in terms of the mass media fulfilling a role of informing the citizens of a state about its government, is not between commercial media and political media. These two forces may relate to each other in a number of ways. Sometimes they are in conflict, sometimes in concert. They both follow a logic that places them on the side of power.

Outbreaks of (much more interesting) democracy

The final lesson learned from the fall of communism concerns the limitations of this logic of power. The media before the fall of communism were large-scale, hierarchically organized, bureaucratic establishments in which there were elaborate procedures for ensuring acquiescence to the will of the directorate. The media after the fall of communism are still large-scale, hierarchically organized, bureaucratic establishments in which there are elaborate procedures for ensuring acquiescence to the will of the directorate. Of course, there are very important differences. We may note particularly those arising from the fact that there are now competing sources of power that make for much more open conflict and public debate. These differences, however, should not be allowed to obscure the fact that in both cases most media workers, let alone the citizens who make up their audience, are systematically excluded from determining the policy and direction of the media.

This was not the necessary and inevitable outcome of the events of 1989, and indeed it was not the outcome that was desired by all of the opposition. As remarked above, many of the oppositional forces in communist regimes wanted to "create a civil society." This dream came in several different versions, but in many of them the idea was to extend the control that ordinary people had over the institutions that structured their social life. In these perspectives, there would be a much more radical revision of the structures of power, the mass media included, than simply the replacement of communist bureaucrat by capitalist entrepreneur.

In general, this third alternative never made much impact on the debates about the future of the media. The version of civil society that did emerge was the classical one envisaged by Hegel, who held that it was the realm of the pursuit of private economic interest. There were, however, a couple of exceptions to the normal rule of a negotiated transfer of power, in which the reform communists came to an agreement with the more moderate of the opposition. In the Czech Republic and in the German Democratic Republic the reform communist wing was weak or nonexistent. In both of these countries, it proved impossible to negotiate a transfer of power as smoothly as was done in Poland or Hungary. There was indeed a revolution, albeit a "velvet" one, in the narrow sense that there were mass popular mobilizations that forced the old regimes to surrender power.

A by-product of both of these upheavals was that the power structure in the media was briefly disrupted. In the Czechoslovak case, this was very brief indeed. Because the old leadership of television refused to broadcast any news of the mass demonstrations taking place daily in the center of Prague, a strike committee was formed by the broadcasting workers which negotiated with the old leaders, and eventually took over temporary control of broadcasting (Šmíd 1992). In East Germany, the disruption went on longer, and involved a much greater challenge to the hierarchical model of the media. The SED leadership believed, up until the end, that its relative economic success would isolate it from the worst effects of the crisis, and it took a series of mass demonstrations to force democratization. As a consequence of this, committees of media workers and citizens took over the running of newspapers and broadcasting outlets. There were, in the year that followed, attempts to put this kind of control over the media on a legal footing, but the terms of the unification treaty with West Germany included the acceptance of the Western model of the media. After the two countries came together, the West German model, and West German personnel, were imposed on the media of the East, completely extinguishing any vestiges of popular control (Boyle 1994).

There was thus, in the revolutions of 1989, as much as in any other great revolutionary upheaval, the promise of a more thoroughgoing and popular democracy than the one that prevails in capitalist countries. It is one of the marks of the limits of the events of 1989 that these shoots of citizen's power were crushed in the interests of the new capitalists and political elite. Certainly, Central and Eastern Europe are politically free today compared to their communist past, in the same way as Spain and Portugal are politically free today compared to their fascist past. But this is a democracy negotiated by elite groups, organized for the benefit of elite groups, and demarcated by the interests of those elite groups.

The lessons for media theory in all of this is that discussions of democracy and the media, however that relationship may be formulated, miss the point if they concentrate on the sterile debate between state and market, bureaucrat and entrepreneur. Those are real differences, but both terms in the debate are the enemies of popular expression and popular democracy. The attention of students of the media interested in finding ways in which they may be democratized would be better directed at the relationships between the media and their audiences, and the fault lines within media organizations between those who give orders and those who are forced to take them.

Conclusions

In this brief review, I have touched upon only three of the central lessons of what I believe to have been a rich, but not necessarily unique, historical experience. There are, of course, many other important consequences that can be drawn out, and I have addressed them in more detail elsewhere (Sparks 1997). The main points that I wish to emphasize here are:

1   Contrary to what was widely believed, there was no single, uniform, and monolithic communist media system. What there was, were different versions of the same basic template of a state-run media, but these varied depending on the concrete historical circumstances of the period and country in question. In particular, the decay of the communist system was accompanied by a breakdown of control over the political direction of the media. For a brief period of time, in a number of countries, journalists and other media workers enjoyed very great freedom to report and discuss their society and its future. This period ended with the transition to relatively stable capitalist democracies, where new owners and new bureaucracies reestablished control over their employees.

2   The experience of Central and Eastern Europe highlights the fact that, in most of the world, there is a close relationship, and often interpenetration, between capital and politics. The belief that these two terms are polarized into the states of (desirable) complete separation and (undesirable) complete fusion is to mistake extreme cases for the norm. The people who run politics and the people who run the media are not natural enemies, nor are they naturally the same people. Rather, they are normally different constituents of the same ruling class. They may squabble one with another, and make different alliances to achieve their ends, but they share the same universe of elite domination.

3   Discussions of democracy and the media need to shift their attention away from these debates about the relatively empowering virtues of the state and the market, and turn to the relations between the media and the mass of the population. In both the communist and the capitalist versions, the media were and are run by people very remote from the lives of the masses, and over whom the masses have no control whatsoever. Democratizing the media means breaking the control of those elites over what are necessarily the main means of public speech in large-scale societies.

The Cold War is over. It is time that we learned the lessons of that bitter epoch and addressed the problems of a world that is no longer naturally polarized into the supporters of Washington and the supporters of Moscow. That was never the only choice, and the fact that it no longer is any choice at all surely means that we need to start looking for an alternative way of thinking, about the mass media as much as about society as a whole.

Note

Since this article was written, developments in the Czech Republic have provided dramatic confirmation of the "political" nature of capital in the former communist countries. In the aftermath of the SBS bid, Vladimir Zelezny used the fact that he controls the actual broadcasting licence to cut off the CME signal to Nova TV and substitute his own. The current struggle over whether he can get away with this bold stroke is essentially a political one. The outcome is still (October 1999) uncertain. (For more details, *see* Sparks 1999.)

References

Boyle, M. (1994) "Building a communicative democracy: the birth and death of citizen politics in East Germany," *Media, Culture and Society*, 16(2): 183–215.

Cunnigham, J. (1994) "The 'media war' in Hungary," paper presented to the European Film and Television Studies Conference, London, July 3–6.

Downing, J. (1996) *Internationalizing Media Theory*, London: Sage.

Dziadul, C. and Drazel, E. (1999) "CME pulls out of Poland," *TV East Europe*, January 23: 1–2.

Gálik, M. and Dénes, F. (1992) *From Command Media to Media Market: The Role of Foreign Capital in the Transition of the Hungarian Media*, Budapest: Budapest University of Economics, Department of Business Economics.

Goban-Klas, T. (1994) *The Orchestration of the Media: The Politics of Mass Communication in Communist Poland and the Aftermath*, Boulder, CO: Westview.

Gross, P. (1996) *Mass Media in Revolution and National Development: The Romanian Laboratory*, Ames: Iowa State University Press.

Gulyas, A. (1998) "Tabloid newspapers in post-communist Hungary," *Javnost/The Public*, 5(3): 65–77.

Hanke, H. (1990) "Media culture in the GDR: characteristics, processes and problems," *Media, Culture and Society*, 12(2): 175–94.

Harman, C. (1984) *The Revolutionary Paper*, London: Socialist Workers' Party.

Jakab, Z. and Gálik, M. (1991) *Survival, Efficiency and Independence: The Presence of Foreign Capital in the Hungarian Media Market*, Manchester: European Institute for the Media.

Jakubowicz, K. (1991) "Musical chairs? The three public spheres in Poland," in P. Dahlgren and C. Sparks (eds.) *Communication and Citizenship*, London: Routledge.

Jakubowicz, K. (n.d.) "Poland: prospects for public and civic broadcasting," in M. Raboy (ed.) *Public Broadcasting for the 21st Century*, Luton: John Libbey Media. (Undated but probably 1996.)

Kaplan, F. and Šmíd, M. (1995) "Czech broadcasting after 1989: overhauling the system and its structures," *Javnost/The Public*, 2(3): 33–45.

Karpinski, J. (1995) "Information and entertainment in Poland," *Transition*, 1(18): 13–18.

Kenety, B. (1997) "Nova TV: new democracy or old-fashioned greed?," *Prague Post*, February 12–18: A1–A7.

Körïsényi, A. (1992) "The Hungarian parliamentary elections of 1990," in A. Dozóki, A. Körösényi and G. Schöpflin (eds.) *Post-Communist Transitions: Emerging Pluralism in Hungary*, London: Pinter.

Korte, D. (1994) "Speech," in Polish National Broadcasting Council (eds.) *The Mass Media in Central and Eastern Europe: Democratization and European Integration*, Proceedings of a conference held in Jadswin, Poland, June 3–5.

Kováts, I. and Tölgyesi, J. (1990) "The media—a change of model or continuity," paper presented to the August 1990 Conference of the International Association for Mass Communication Research, Bled, Yugoslavia (Slovenia).

Kováts, I. and Tölgyesi, J. (1993) "On the background of the Hungarian media changes," in S. Splichal and I. Kováts (eds.) *Media in Transition: An East–West Dialogue*, Budapest–Ljubljana: Communication and Culture Colloquia.

Lenin, V. I. (1972) *Lenin: About the Press*, Prague: International Organisation of Journalists. (Published in the UK by The Journeyman Press.)

Lukács, G. (1970) *Lenin: A Study in the Unity of his Thought*, London: New Left Books.

McQuail, D. (1993) *Mass Communication Theory*, 3rd edn, London: Sage.

MTV (1991) *Hungarian Television 1991: Facts and Figures*, Budapest: MTV.

Nerone, J. (1992) *Last Rites*, Urbana and Chicago: University of Illinois Press.

Novak, M. (1996) "The transition from a socialist to a market-led media system in Slovenia," unpublished Ph.D. dissertation, University of Westminster, London.

Oltay, E. (1995) "The return of the former communists," in *Transition: 1994 in Review Part One*, Prague: Open Media Research Institute.

PSMLP (1996) "Nova's success spurs attacks by potential competitors," *Post-Soviet Media Law and Policy Newsletter*, 27/28: 8–9.

Siebert, F., Peterson, T. and Schramm, W. (1963[1956]) *Four Theories of the Press*, Urbana and Chicago: University of Illinois Press.

Šmíd, M. (1992) "Television after the velvet revolution," paper presented to the symposium on Restructuring Television in East-Central Europe, University of Westminster, London, July 14.

Šmíd, M. (1994) "Broadcasting law in the Czech Republic," unpublished paper, December.

Sparks, C. (with A. Reading) (1997) *Communism, Capitalism and the Mass Media*, London: Sage.

Sparks, C. (1999) "CME and broadcasting in Central and Eastern Europe," in *Javnost/The Public*, 6(2): 25–44.

Splichal, S. (1994) *Media Beyond Socialism*, Boulder, CO: Westview.

Szekfü, A. (1989) "Intruders welcome? The beginnings of satellite television in Hungary," *European Journal of Communication*, 4(2): 161–71.

Tesar, I. (1989) "Television exchange of programmes and television co-operation between Czechoslovakia and Western Europe: experiences, problems, proposals," in J. Becker and T. Szecskö (eds.) *Europe Speaks to Europe*, Oxford: Pergamon.

Vojteck, J. (1995) "The media in Slovakia since 1989," *The Global Network/Le Reseau Global*, 3: 81–4.

Zassoursky, I. (n.d.) "From public sphere utopia to public scene reality: the first seven years of the new Russian press," unpublished paper.

4 Media in South America

Between the rock of the state and the hard place of the market

Silvio Waisbord

The evolution of South American media has been in constant dialogue with intellectual trends and policy debates in the wealthy West. The suitability of US and European models of media organization has concerned policymakers, media owners, intellectuals and others. The transplant of Western media models, however, was like fitting square pegs into round holes. Although US and European influences have left indelible traces in the historical development of broadcasting and the press, the resulting systems were not exact reproductions. Media systems combined various influences and were deeply shaped by a matrix of power relations that resulted from indigenous political and economic developments. Family resemblances were unmistakable, but differences were substantial.

My interest in this chapter is to explore this question by analyzing the articulation between power and media in the region. The analysis draws from experiences in a handful of countries in different historical periods. Reasons why media systems developed along different lines from US and European models are found in the different configuration of the relations among media, states, and markets. The media have been consistently situated in both states and markets. Even when commercial dynamics became ostensibly more important for newspapers and fundamental in broadcasting organization, there was not a strong movement to decouple the media from the state. The liberal ideology of the US press could not effectively serve as the organizing principle, given that newspaper owners were interested in cultivating close-knit relations with government officials and that press economics were anchored in the state. Nor did European-inspired ideals find a fertile soil. The spasmodic existence of democracy made difficult, if not impossible, the consolidation of party-based media or, for that matter, the incorporation of a myriad of civic organizations into media systems. Also, at no time did the idea of public service become the foundation for broadcasting systems that followed commercial guidelines and were continuously subjected to government control and intervention.

Liberal model in unliberal societies

The culture of South American journalism has long been influenced by trends in the European press. Since the mid-1800s, French, Italian, and Spanish dailies have historically gripped the imagination of publishers and journalists, being the sources for defining the identity and the role of the press as well as newsroom organization and graphic design and writing. The Anglo-Saxon model of the press gained increasing influence in the post-Second World War years. At that time, the liberal gospel of US news organizations didn't completely displace continental influences, but became widely present. Contacts between South American and North American publishers became more frequent in regional meetings and in visits to US newsrooms. The newly founded Inter-American Press Association, integrated by editors and publishers from both hemispheres, began to cast a powerful influence by delineating and promoting the ideals of classical liberalism. Press barons enthusiastically adopted the postulates of government autonomy and private property as the foundations of the press. In the name of market freedom, they condemned government intrusion and declared that state controls and restrictions undermined the basis for a truly free press (Lins da Silva 1990).

Even if we consider the liberal model in its own terms, without addressing the adequacy of its theoretical bases and prescriptions for the existence of a democratic press, it is obvious that its chances of becoming effective were at odds with South American politics. Its visibility in public discourse contrasted with the realities of press systems. Its prospects ran against conditions that differed glaringly from original contexts coupled with the questionable commitment of press barons. It was improbable that a liberal press would develop in antiliberal capitalist societies, considering that owners rhetorically exalted liberalism but ceaselessly courted states, supported military interventions, and only (and vociferously) criticized government intrusion that affected their own political and economic interests.

Crucial developments that nurtured the rise of a market-oriented press in the US never happened. Nowhere in the region do we find a commercial revolution similar to the one that US newspapers experienced, a process in which the economic bases of the press industry shifted from party coffers to the market. In South America, instead, press economics remained attached to both states and markets. The pursuit of commercial ambitions remained solidly tied to the state rather than just to the market. Also, newspapers were generally conceived as political enterprises rather than simply commercial ventures. The state retained control over important resources that greatly affected press finances. In economies with a sizable number of state-owned companies, government advertising remained a major source of revenue. Until the privatization of large industries in the 1990s, states directly owned large companies in key sectors of South American economies. Administrations also controlled decisions which determined the economic future of newspapers: Officials could manipulate the allocation of loans from state-owned banks, foreign exchange rates, taxes, and tariffs for the importation of newsprint and technology. The formidable economic power of the state worked as a powerful incentive for press organizations to keep the state at a short distance (De Lima 1998, Waisbord 1995).

Not surprisingly, newspaper owners were not extremely keen on burning the bridges to the state even though they frequently praised the liberal model. Instead, they courted the state with the expectation that goodies from the official *piñata* would fall in their hands. So if the press recoiled from printing inconvenient news or cheered official messages, governments corresponded by cancelling large debts with official financial institutions, offering special exchange rates to modernize newsrooms, and granting broadcasting licenses. Of course, relations did not always go so smoothly, and confrontations did emerge occasionally. Overall, however, the articulation between press and state was diametrically different from what the liberal model envisioned: Cooperation rather than adversarialism, mutual advantages rather than complete autonomy, were typical. These dynamics have been markedly evident in countless

cases of government officials who directly (or through family connections) participated in the ownership of media companies, particularly in the interior of South
American countries.

The fact that there hasn't been a strong cultural–political push to depoliticize the
press, to downplay partisan allegiances, and to follow the canon of objective reporting, also helps to explain why the liberal model didn't find appropriate conditions.
Newspapers continued to function as political tribunes identified with distinctive economic, political, and ideological interests. In a heavily politicized atmosphere, press
owners were uninterested in practicing "objective" journalism. Some newspapers openly
embraced partisan causes: in Colombia, for example, newspapers have been clearly
identified with political families and partisan factions (Santos Calderón 1989). In
countries where political parties have been weaker and intermittently came to life
amid democratic discontinuity, it was more likely that dominant dailies were aligned
with the interests of specific political and economic groups. Some newspapers revealed their partisan and ideological leanings; others did it by couching news in the
language of objectivity. In all cases, however, the idea of political dispassion and neutrality was contrary to the political turbulence of the region, the economic goals of
news organizations, and the intention of publishers to exercise visible influence on
political events. Under these circumstances, there was arid ground for the principles of
autonomy and professional journalism to take root.

In summary, if the push of commercial forces made possible the decoupling of the
media from the state, as some US scholars have argued, the tight connections between business and political interests impeded the formation of media systems along
the lines of the liberal model (Schiller 1981, Schudson 1978). Even though press
barons upheld the principles of private property and profit-making, the ideal of the
"fourth estate" was unattainable when the media was intertwined with the same
powers it was supposed to monitor, and owners sought to keep the state at a stone's
throw distance.

The "media dependency" critique

The media dependency paradigm, which profoundly shaped intellectual debates and
set the tone for the project of media reform in the region in the 1960s and 1970s,
offered an insightful critique of the liberal model (Beltrán and Fox 1980, Dorfman
and Mattelart 1970). Against the ideology of media owners and modernization theories, it argued that the export of Western models and content is neither desirable nor
appropriate in South America. It questioned liberalism for offering a limited analysis
of the question of power and media. The latter failed to address market constraints
and to analyze media developments within the historical evolution of international
power dynamics. As long as they are organized around capitalist principles, the media
constitute obstacles rather than conduits for democracy. The advancement of ruling
economic and political interests and the suppression of alternative views lie at the
heart of media operations interested in profit-making rather than public information.
Media systems represent unequal relations between the developed core and the underdeveloped periphery. They are not nonideological relayers of Western information but
Trojan horses that smuggle foreign ideas which benefit the interests of transnational
corporations and reactionary domestic classes. The media are a conveyor belt of foreign ideas and practices functional to the present power structure, namely, the intro-

duction of the culture of consumption and individualistic values that sap the strength of national cultures and lubricate the gears of foreign domination.

Media dependency arguments offered the state of Latin American media as irrefutable evidence of such conclusions. The principles of commercial broadcasting ruled uncontested and the reliance of local news organizations on international news services based in the developed world were symptomatic of dependent relations. The sway of the "American" media became more pronounced in the post-Second World War period, a time of the consolidation of US political, economic, and military hegemony in the hemisphere. Commercial principles anchored radio broadcasting, and television basically followed the same path. After its domestic market reached a point of saturation in the late 1950s, the US television industry found large and unexplored markets southward. Many studies have documented that the "big three" networks exported technology, expertise and programming to the newly developed television systems in the region (Fox 1997). The intensification of US investments and advertising growth also provided appropriate conditions for transplanting the commercial model of television.

In grasping the relations between media and power, the merits of the dependency paradigm are various. Above all, it perceptively brought power relations to the forefront, warning that little could be understood about media dynamics without confronting that question head-on. To understand the media, it is indispensable to understand how power functions, and to understand power it is necessary to analyze the historical legacy of economics and foreign interests in the organization of media systems. A *long durée* perspective was a much-needed antidote against ahistorical liberal interpretations that failed to acknowledge dissimilar historical trajectories between the core and the periphery (Schwoch 1990). Historical analysis meant, above all, exploring large-scale economic developments that fashioned inequalities that were tangible, among other social realms, in media systems. Dependency theory correctly indicated that the media have not been exempt from the processes that shaped economic relations and the general commodification of social relations. The media represented, and contributed to maintaining, a class structure whose historical development could only be understood as part of the evolution of a Wallersteinian world system. The emphasis on foreign interests also helped to explain the relations between media and power. In South America, the boundaries of media systems were not airtight, but deeply affected by larger international developments. Before globalization gained policy and intellectual currency in the post-Cold War era, the forces of internationalization had already influenced media systems in the region.

Notwithstanding its strengths, the premises of media imperialism offered difficulties for rendering nuanced interpretations of the relations between power and media. One of the problems was the scant attention paid to domestic politics and the state in shaping media systems. Politics inside "receiving societies" generally were understood as epiphenomena of global forces. The logic of domestic politics was intelligible only in terms of core–periphery relations. This explains why the state, a central actor in the evolution of media systems, was strikingly absent from most studies of South America (Waisbord 1995).

If liberal theorists overlooked how capitalist structures shaped media structures and the historical development of the government/media dyad in the region, dependency analysts minimized the role of the state. If addressed, the state was assumed to fit the Leninist model of the state as an instrument of bourgeois domination, the representative of ruling economic interests (Mattelart 1979). As an expression of the instrumentalism underlying dependency studies, politics was subsumed to capitalist interests. It is not my intention to rehearse well known critiques of the problems of economistic and instrumentalist views of media organization (Curran 1996, Sparks and Reading 1998). Doubtless, it would be shortsighted to underplay the web of interests linking markets and states. This relation, however, needs to be explained rather than assumed as being one of perfect symmetry. The main problem was that media dependency did not concede sufficient autonomy to the political, which is fundamental to recognizing and exploring divisions within states and markets, as well as differences across political regimes. The state has been an arena where competing media interests wage battles, rather than a unified agent that complies with the dictates of dominant elites in shaping the structure of the mass media.

Thus, media dependency has correctly signalled the importance of the market but has neglected the persistence and autonomy of politics, which cannot be assumed to perfectly mirror business intentions. For example, in countries such as Bolivia, Chile, and Peru, television originally was developed according to educational goals and UNESCO-sponsored plans. The introduction of television in Argentina, instead, obeyed the Perón administration's intention of building a media arsenal to strengthen its communication power. In Colombia, the Rojas Pinilla dictatorship found inspiration in Perón's government and imported television with similar goals. After it was replaced by an arrangement that assured the rotation of the Conservative and Liberal parties in government, television was reorganized around a mix of public and private criteria. The state was the sole owner of the frequencies and assigned licenses to private programmers. These companies paid a fee and scheduled their own productions and foreign programs. As another sign of the interwoven relations between politics and commerce, it was not unusual for prominent politicians, including presidents, to be members of the boards of those companies, or for companies that produced news programming to be integrated by conspicuous members of political factions. This order has remained basically unchanged despite the privatization of two channels in 1996 (Ruiz 1996).

Media under authoritarianism

The intertwined relations that media organizations maintained with both states and markets can also be seen in the context of the authoritarian regimes in the 1960s and 1970s. By the mid-1970s, all South American countries, with the exception of Colombia and Venezuela, were under military dictatorships. As many studies have amply demonstrated, dominant media organizations fervently supported military coups and applauded economic programs (Fox 1988, Peirano *et al.* 1978, Portales 1981). News media hushed up political matters such as human rights violations and the absence of press freedom. Chile's *El Mercurio* has often been cited as the prototypical case of a newspaper closely identified with authoritarianism, given its open support for the 1973 coup and the Pinochet dictatorship. Brazilian dailies generally accepted official censorship while the Globo network assumed the role of the government's main booster. The Argentine media kept silent on state-sponsored crimes and diligently served as government megaphone during the 1982 Malvinas/Falklands war.

It would be hard to make the argument that media control lay mainly in the hands of international and domestic capital. The military firmly believed that the media was a fundamental piece in the architecture of authoritarian governments and they were extremely concerned to keep the media on a short leash. The military's plans to achieve these goals had important yet varied consequences. They neither pursued identical goals nor equally benefited business interests. The Argentine military, for example, were not interested in sharing media power with private interests. They kept the four Buenos Aires-based television stations, which had been expropriated by the ousted Péronist administration in 1974, in their own hands. Political appointees ran the stations, supervised newscasts, and allocated time slots to private producers. Ownership was concentrated in the hands of the state (although it *de facto* was divided among the Army, the Air Force, and the Navy). Production remained fragmented among a dozen companies. There were no national networks: The main stations and producers churned out and nationally distributed local and foreign productions to independently owned stations. The fragmentation of Argentine television was rooted in two factors. First, unlike their Brazilian counterparts, the juntas did not carry out major technological transformations that could have laid the backbone for television networks. Second, they also feared that television networks might strengthen the power of private groups and thus become autonomous from the state. Different broadcasting laws, all passed during military governments, banned the formation of networks (Waisbord 1998a).

In Brazil, the 1964–85 authoritarian regime carried out a different plan. It championed a modernizing project of technological development to strengthen its own power and, more broadly, the role of the state. This goal certainly did not contradict the regime's economic policies favoring highly concentrated local and foreign capitals, as dependentistas rightly argued, but this project was not symmetrical with all media companies. The government was assigned great responsibilities in centralizing information flows and building a large communication infrastructure to reach all corners of a huge geography. These projects were linked visibly to some of the military's dearest ambitions: strengthening geo-political interests and military security, championing nationalistic causes, and cementing public acquiescence. Globo, then a small media company, greatly benefited from these policies. The availability of technology for national distribution of television signals coupled with the injection of capital and expertise from Time–Life laid the basis for Globo to become the media giant of today. It offered unconditional support for the military in return for having access to technology and being favored with valuable television and radio licenses (Amaral and Guimarães 1994).

In Peru, the 1968–80 period of military government merits attention for, perhaps like no other case in the region, it best illustrates the complexity of media/power relations. As a part of larger policy goals, the Velasco Alvarado government set out to accomplish ambitious changes in media organization. Its diagnosis was that the country, impoverished and with a high rate of illiteracy, had a media system that served the interests of privileged groups and foreign companies rather than the majority of the population. The media should serve social and cultural purposes, including national unification and education. To reform such conditions, the government elaborated a series of ambitious plans and put in action a number of measures. It expropriated the Lima-based newspapers and planned to turn them over to different social organizations. It established institutions to promote and produce educational programming. It passed legislation to strengthen the role of the state in both telecommunication and media industries and to limit the participation of private and foreign capital (Gargurevich 1991).

Whether these decisions responded to genuine interest in protecting indigenous cultures and fostering social participation or to Machiavellian intentions of manipulating and centralizing information is a question without simple answers. Original intentions were distant from actual accomplishments. The government actually never ceded the dailies to organized sectors of Peruvian society, as it promised, but instead kept them under its control. Similar plans to expropriate and transfer broadcast stations never materialized either, and television continued to follow commercial principles. The reinforcement of the state's ability to concentrate information in newly founded government institutions raised questions about its commitment to the promise of democratizing communications and bolstering popular participation. Aside from the conclusions from this experience, the coming to power of a military government imbued with a nationalistic ideology evidently indicated transformations in the relations between power and media. Although the Velasco Alvarado administration (and later the 1975–80 government of Gen. Francisco Morales Bermudez) only partially overhauled the existing media order, it certainly shook its foundations. The vocal opposition of traditional groups and changing support from others suggested that conflicts inside the "power bloc" were not inconsequential and, as in any other social realms, had the potential of crystallizing transformations in the organization of media systems.

The experiences of the Argentine, Brazilian, and Peruvian media under authoritarianism attest to the centrality of the state in strengthening the media power of the military and facilitating or preventing the building of media behemoths. The articulation between power and media in authoritarian regimes cannot be understood simply by explaining the existing media orders as the result of the influence of foreign interests in alliance with domestic capital. Nor is the media dependency model adequate to understand the position of the media during the downfall of military dictatorships. In Argentina, no media organization forcefully supported the move toward democracy. Broadcast stations remained until the end firmly in the hands of government directives; newspapers gradually followed, rather than led, the transition. In Brazil, instead, internal divisions inside the dominant bloc informed the different positions that media organizations adopted *vis-à-vis* democratic opening. *Folha de São Paulo* is commonly credited with having greatly contributed to the return of liberal democracy by pushing for direct elections at a time when other media, most notably Globo, remained mostly oblivious to mounting discontent and pro-democracy activities (Taschner 1992). In Peru, traditional newspapers largely supported the civilian administration of Fernando Belaunde. Media owners applauded the government for returning the expropriated newspapers and granting tax exemptions and cheap loans. The government, especially the Armed Forces, repeatedly clashed with left-wing media such as *El Diario de Marka* and *La República* regarding human rights abuses in the repression of guerrilla insurrection.

Media and liberal democracy

Important developments in the post-authoritarian era have brought new conditions that shape the articulation of power and media. Interestingly, these questions have receded from the forefront of media studies in the region. This is related partially to the critique of the dependency paradigm. Cultural and audience studies rightly have criticized the former for its media-centric perspective and its overdeterministic view of media effects (García Canclini 1995, Martin-Barbero 1993). To remedy these problems, they have suggested the autonomy of the cultural, its multiple relations to media structures and content, and the centrality of audiences in sense-making processes. For much of its merits in indicating the blind spots of media dependency, the shift in paradigms from the power of international and domestic capital to the power of audience and media consumers has resulted in decreasing attention to the question of how political and economic interests influence the organization of media systems (Fejes 1981). It is a matter neither of establishing intellectual priorities nor returning to old certainties, but of recognizing the relevance of that question to new conditions shaped by domestic and global processes. The question that needs to be addressed is, how do the seeming affirmation of liberal democracies and the whirlwind of media globalization affect the linkages between media and power in contexts of persistent and wide social disparities?

There has not been a return to the old cycle of democratic and authoritarian regimes that has long characterized the region. Even in Peru, civilian president Alberto Fujimori, who headed a 1992 self-coup with broad support from business organizations and the military, had to reinstate constitutional rights shortly thereafter in the face of domestic and international pressure. Against the background of continuous military interventions, the affirmation of polyarchical systems has been hailed as a watershed in South American history, which is certainly not insignificant considering the checkered record of liberal democracy.

Ideally, democratic continuity puts an end to the exercise of naked violence and censorship that authoritarian governments have inflicted on critical media organizations. Here I am referring to the observance of constitutional freedoms and rights that directly affect the functioning of media organizations and are fundamental for the prospects of democratic communication. The significance of freedoms of expression and speech cannot be overlooked. Unlike Western democracies, they cannot be taken for granted or dismissed as mere bourgeois rights that leave economic and social inequalities intact. There is no need to slip into romanticism to recognize that democratic liberties are potentially able to protect citizens and media organizations from official abuses. They don't overturn social inequalities, level the playing field, or eliminate less overt forms of government manipulation of media content. But, at least in formal terms, they abolish official censorship and persecution of dissident media in countries where the violation of all types of constitutional liberties has been the norm. Notwithstanding the overall improvement of the situation, serious doubts persist about the respect and enforcement of bourgeois rights of freedom. Considering countless episodes of violence against critical reporters and news organizations that directly or indirectly involve governments, there are sufficient reasons to be skeptical about the success of liberal democracy in upholding the rule of law (Conaghan 1998, Waisbord 1998b). The wielding of power by force certainly lacks the magnitude it had during the most brutal phases of authoritarianism, but it has not disappeared completely and still besets the prospects for democratic media.

Aside from the violent exercise of power, it is necessary to look at more subtle and common ways in which states continue to hold power in regard to media issues. Similar to what has been observed in Western democracies, government officials routinely exercise power through news management. Given the emphasis on official news, they enjoy privileged access and status in the news-gathering process. They are able to cultivate relations with news organizations by doling out exclusive information to loyal reporters and companies and to influence the news agenda through news frames and information leaks. Of particular importance to understanding media and power dynamics in liberal democracies is the fact that neither governments nor media organizations have unified political and economic interests. What Philip Elliott (1978) called "disaffection and disagreements between the different centers of power" have been crucial in generating new possibilities for critical reporting. In recent years, news organizations have occasionally confronted governments by dredging up cases of wrongdoing (Waisbord 1996). Rivalries among powerful interests and individuals have resulted in information leaks to news organizations interested in pulling the rug from under government officials. Internecine struggles among political and economic elites have coincided with the interests of some news media to bring wrongdoing into public view. The continuity of liberal democracy, a novel development in the region's political history, has opened room for reporting on subjects such as official corruption and human rights violations which were shunned in the past. Within the different boundaries of news organizations, journalists have cracked open cases that mainly involve officials in a vast array of cases of graft, influence-peddling, obstruction of justice, cover-up of crimes, and the like. Journalistic autonomy is still limited by editorial concerns but different media offer varying degrees of possibilities for reporting on sensitive issues within constraints determined by political and commercial interests. This does not mean that *all* news media have reported on *all* kinds of abuses. In each country, only some news media have practiced watchdog journalism that has focused overwhelmingly on matters related to the state rather than to corporate delinquency or social problems. Despite limitations, muckraking has contributed positively to democratic communication by reporting on state secrets and demanding responses from officials unaccustomed to being held accountable.

Intertwined government–media relations continue to set boundaries on critical reporting, however. Governments still rely on time-proven tactics of dangling economic carrots in front of media organizations, with the expectation of receiving favorable coverage (Machado Gonçalves 1995). The axing of a critical television report on the building of a multimillion-dollar airstrip inside President Menem's home property was interpreted as a result of government pressures. Suspicions seemed confirmed after Eduardo Eurnekian, the head of the multimedia conglomerate that owns the station where the report was scheduled for broadcast, was favored in the privatization of Argentina's main airports. In Colombia, critics concluded that media groups that defended President Ernesto Samper during the scandal about the funnelling of drug monies into his 1994 election campaign were rewarded in the privatization of two television channels and that news broadcasters that criticized the president didn't get their licenses renewed.

The ability of governments to allocate resources to reward complacent media organizations is particularly important in the context of the affirmation of market dynamics and media conglomerization. South American countries have not been exempt from the worldwide process of media concentration. Simultaneous to the growth of cable and satellite television, newspaper companies as well as businesses originally based outside media industries have diversified horizontally. In Argentina, Citicorp Equity Investments (CEI) owns two of the four main over-the-air television channels (Canal 9 and Canal 11), cable, and telecommunications. In addition to its flagship and highly influential daily *Clarín*, the Clarín Group controls interests in regional newspapers, radio, over-the-air and cable television, news agency, and newsprint production and participates with foreign groups in satellite television. Brazil's Globo has been likened to a parallel government. Not only is it a horizontally and vertically integrated media empire, but it also has interests in financing, banking, food, agriculture, mining, real estate, telecommunication, and insurance. Even though it hasn't reached the unmatched power of Globo, Editora Abril has turned into a media powerhouse in recent years. Traditionally a publishing group, it now owns one of the two dominant cable companies and has teamed up with regional groups in satellite television. Other powerful television networks, though with smaller audience and revenues than Globo, are SBT, Bandeirantes and Manchete. *Folha de São Paulo*, Brazil's leading daily, has recently diversified into telecommunications and other industries. In Colombia, the recent privatization of two television channels confirmed the power of the Santo Domingo and Arcilla Lulle groups. Both are multimedia giants with diversified interests ranging from food to airline industries. *El Tiempo* group controls the largest daily and has investments in over-the-air, cable and satellite television, recording industry, and film exhibition (Vizcaíno Gutierrez 1992). In Peru, media ownership is more fragmented than in the foregoing cases. Panamericana Television, with interests in radio, over-the-air and cable television, and cellular telephony, stands out in a field of companies that are based in different industrial sectors (mainly construction) and lately have expanded into the media (Catalán and Ramm 1997).

The multiple connections among domestic, regional and global companies suggest that the national/international dichotomy that was central to media studies in the region in the past needs to be reconceptualized. Different regulations about foreign ownership and sizes of media markets have stimulated dissimilar interests among global media corporations. Regional and global companies have arranged coproduction deals and participate in common cable and satellite ventures. Regardless of where their headquarters and primary markets are situated, a handful of media giants in the region is pursuing similar goals, namely, the consolidation of oligopolistic positions both at home and in a globalized media order. What remains to be seen and further explored is whether governments and "national champions" would collaborate in reaction to the penetration of mighty global and regional media corporations into new media industries. Would states favor local powers by raising protectionist measures or surrender to the forces of globalization by removing legal obstacles?

Conclusions

The recent affirmation of liberal democracy has not resulted in the democratization of media access. Quite the opposite. It has coincided with the further consolidation of market principles and media concentration. It would be wrong to interpret these developments as a fall from grace, considering the long-standing presence of business interests in media industries and the previous existence of conglomerates. A chain that included leading magazines, television and radio stations, and news and advertising agencies, Brazil's Diarios Associados was not that distant from contemporary media behemoths (Mattos 1990). The contemporary wave of concentration, however, has upped the ante, making impossible the existence of media relatively autonomous from market considerations and drastically reducing the possibilities for news organizations to critically examine issues that directly affect the wide-ranging interests of parent companies or that are relevant to large sectors of the population.

It would be incorrect to argue that the dynamics recently observed represent a radical shift from the past. The pre-1990s media order was not hermetically sealed, but was deeply intertwined with international developments. What has happened in the past decade, instead, was the deepening of preexisting trends. This process is different from "the private deluge" in Europe in the 1980s and 1990s, basically because the principles of public service have never been at the core of the organizations of media systems. In South America, the alternative to private ownership has often been formulated in terms of government, rather than public, control that mostly left the nuts and bolts of market media unchanged. The forces of commerce were already entrenched. It is clear, however, that privatization and deregulation have raised the barriers to entry and lowered the chance to survive. For small- and medium-sized media such as newspapers and magazines with modest economic goals, it is extremely difficult to survive in an environment ruled by media behemoths, especially in advertising-poor areas of the interior where media that don't rely on government monies and favors are prone to be bought off by economically solid companies based in the capital.

The ascendancy of market forces has not eclipsed the clout of governments in media matters: The latter still wield power in ways that are not essentially different from previous times. Both political and commercial logics are still present and closely linked. Today's governments do not directly control the media as in the past, but they aren't empty-handed in dealing with media groups. They concentrate economic resources and policy decisions that are vital for media companies and manipulate information that is highly prized in journalistic cultures closely tuned to official news.

Aside from the limitations posed by the multiple linkages between media groups and diverse economic interests, the liberal promise of market-strong media that engage in no-holds-barred criticism of states sounds particularly hollow in societies where the decisions that ultimately facilitate the expansionist ambitions of media companies lay in the power of government officials. Media organizations have made important denunciations about official wrongdoing but remain largely oblivious to issues of wealth concentration and social inequalities. Governments continue to apply the old-time formula of cronyism, news management and, in some cases, legal intimidation of news organizations and journalists who dare to take distance and cross the boundaries of expected behavior (Costa and Brenner 1997).

What is alarming is the virtual absence of efforts to incorporate the diversity of voices and to counterbalance the dealings of markets and governments. Assorted public and civic organizations have little, if any, influence, in the ongoing process by which substantial media resources change hands, officials reap sizable gains, and commercial interests become further entrenched. The return of liberal democracy has neither disturbed the steady march of companies to engulf substantial media resources nor overturned the intertwined relations between commerce and states. Admittedly, it has brought in opportunities for contestation and competition and general improvement of the conditions for journalistic work and citizens' participation. This is novel in societies used to military boots quashing any sign of dissent and to news organizations consistently bowing to official demands. The antidemocratic character of media structures tilted in favor of concentrated business and political elites, however, palpably reflects a legacy of power inequalities and the difficulties for even minimally redressing, let alone restructuring, wide disparities in access to the means of public expression.

References

Amaral, R. and Guimarães, C. (1994) "Media monopoly in Brazil," *Journal of Communication*, 44.

Beltrán, L. R. and Fox, E. (1980) *Comunicación Dominada: Los Estados Unidos en los Medios de América Latina*, Mexico City: ILET/Nueva Imagen.

Catalán, C. and Ramm, A. R. (1997) "Los cambios de la televisión chilena en los 90," *Diálogos de la Comunicación*, 48.

Conaghan, C. (1998) "Fear, loathing, and collusion: press and state in Fujimori's Peru," presented at the conference of the Latin American Studies Association, Chicago.

Costa, S. and Brener, J. (1997) "Coronelismo eletrônico: o governo Fernando Henrique e o novo capitulo de uma velha historia," *Comunicação & Politica*, 4.

Curran, J. (1996) "Mass media and democracy revisited," in J. Curran and Michael Gurevitch (eds.) *Mass Media and Society*, 2nd edn, London: Arnold.

De Lima, V. (1988) "The state, television, and political power in Brazil," *Critical Studies in Mass Communication*, 5.

Dorfman, A. and Mattelart, A. (1970) *Para Leer el Pato Donald: Comunicación De Masas y Colonialismo*, Buenos Aires: Siglo XXI.

Elliott, P. (1978) "Professional ideology and organisational change: the journalist since 1800," in G. Boyce, J. Curran and P. Wingate (eds.) *Newspaper History: From the Seventeenth Century to the Present Day*, London: Constable.

Fejes, F. (1981) "Media imperialism: an assessment," *Media, Culture and Society*, 3.

Fox, E. (ed.) (1988) *Media and Politics in Latin America: The Struggle for Democracy*, London: Sage.

Fox, E. (1997) *Latin American Broadcasting: From Tango to Telenovela*, Luton: University of Luton Press.

Garcia Canclini, N. (1995) *Hybrid Cultures: Strategies for Entering and Leaving Modernity*, Minneapolis: University of Minnesota Press.

Gargurevich, J. (1991) *Historia de la Prensa Peruana, 1594–1990*, Lima: La Voz.

Lins da Silva, C. (1990) *O Adiantado da Hora: A Influência Americana sobre o Jornalismo Brasileiro*, São Paulo: Summus.

Machado Gonçalves, E. (1995) "A noticias como capital politico no jornalismo baiano," *Pauta Geral*, 3.

Martin-Barbero, J. (1993) *Communication, Culture and Hegemony: From Media to Mediations*, London: Sage.

Mattelart, A. (1979) *Multinational Corporations and the Control of Culture: The Ideological Apparatuses of Imperialism*, Brighton: Harvester.

Mattos, S. M. (1990) *Um Perfil da TV Brasileira: 40 Anos de Historia, 1950–1990*, Salvador: ABAP.

Peirano, L. *et al.* (1978) *Prensa: Apertura y Límites*, Lima: DESCO.

Portales, D. (1981) *Poder Económico y Libertad de Expresión: La Industria de la Comunicación Chilena en la Democracia y el Autoritarismo*, Mexico: ILET/Nueva Imagen.

Ruiz, E. J. (1996) *Cuarto Poder: Como el Poder Económico se Inserta en los Medios de Comunicación Colombianos*, Bogotá: Rotativa.

Santos Calderón, E. (1989) "El periodismo en Colombia, 1886–1986," in *Nueva Historia de Colombia*, 6, Bogotá: Planeta.

Schiller, D. (1981) *Objectivity and the News*, Philadelphia: University of Pennsylvania Press.

Schudson, M. (1978) *Discovering the News*, New York: Basic Books.

Schwoch, J. (1990) *The American Radio Industry and its Latin American Activities, 1920–1939*, Champaign–Urbana: University of Illiniois.

Sparks, C. with Reading, A. (1998) *Communism, Capitalism and the Mass Media*, London: Sage.

Taschner, G. (1992) *Folhas ao Vento*, Rio: Paz e Terra.

Vizcaíno Gutierrez, M. (1992) *Los Falsos Dilemas de Nuestra Televisión*, Bogotá: CEREC.

Waisbord, S. (1995) "Leviathan dreams: state and broadcasting in South America," *The Communication Review*, 1.

Waisbord, S. (1996) "Investigative journalism and political accountability in South American democracies," *Critical Studies in Mass Communication*, 13.

Waisbord, S. (1998a) "Argentina," in A. Albarrán and S. M. Chan-Olmsted (eds.) *Global Media Economics: Commercialization, Concentration and Integration of World Media Markets*, Ames: Iowa State University Press.

Waisbord, S. (1998b) "Bad news: violence against the press in Latin America," presented at the conference of the Association for Education of Journalism and Mass Communication, Baltimore.

5 Television, gender, and democratization in the Middle East[1]

Annabelle Sreberny

Media studies, like all the social sciences, are embedded in the historical experiences of Western industrial capitalism, liberal democracy, and bounded nation-states. Even the sub-field of international communications has looked out with a scopic gaze from the West toward the rest of the world, proffering a set of paradigms about media dynamics in political, economic, and cultural contexts that are usually totally foreign to the authors.

Approaches rooted in political economy map the dynamics of increasing conglomeratization in the global media industries and rue the passing of a variegated range of mediated voices in conversation. Yet what if such a range of voices does not—and has not—existed within a polity? What if, after perceiving the globalizing power of Western cultural product, local entrepreneurs start to produce their own and regional competition begins to grow? What if expanding cultural industries actually build institutional capacity, help to construct a salariat of creative people, provide structures in which talent can grow and novel forms of cultural production can be imagined?

Analysis building on the Habermasian notion of the "public sphere" often manifests an inauthentic nostalgia for the heyday of the public sphere as a freely operating and protected zone of public debate, nostalgia now challenged by feminist critique of the patriarchal limitations of the public sphere as well as by class and race critiques of the control of access to participation in the public sphere. What if a public sphere is weakly developed because of overweening state power? What if the public sphere is also male-dominated social space? Can the development of media channels help to construct or enlarge a national public sphere?

Analyses rooted in a "cultural studies" approach can over-enthusiastically celebrate the postmodern bricolage of images and ideas that circulate in the contemporary global media environment, as all of equal value, worth, and significance. But is something made at home of equal or greater value than something made abroad? Is the answer to such a question derived from nationalistic, moral, or empirical grounds? What does happen when Mickey Mouse, the Spice Girls and the Koran collide? What kind of and whose imaginary prevails?

Each of these media paradigms can ask some useful questions, while each alone overdetermines the causal logic of impact it desires or predicts. Only an encounter across paradigms can pose new questions, even new methods for accessing the answers. Empirical work takes place within paradigmatic structures, but when the latter become so rigidified that only normal science endlessly repeats itself, then the demand is established for a new paradigmatic moment. So how are we to approach the analysis of the media in non-Western locations in a manner that not simply provides rich description but also generates analytic concepts and models that help to understand the processes and configurations of media?

My argument would be that it is not so much that media-centric models that operate within international communications are wrong, or ask inappropriate questions, but that they have tended to assume dynamics operating from without the national social system, the latter being a passive recipient of external forces. In such models, therefore, specific histories, congeries of social, political, and cultural forces—the dynamics of the "inside"—are obscured or forgotten in the assumption of pressures from the "outside."

These models are also too insistently media-centric, a problematic but understandable tendency in contexts with long histories of media institutionalization, with a wide variety of media channels, differentiated patterns of ownership and control, and a colossal output of media product. In many non-Western contexts, the particular histories of media development, their intersections with political and economic power, and their contribution to and impact upon cultural values are still poorly understood; here media studies remains an emergent kind of analysis, and only makes sense as a serious analytic enterprise if conducted within broader sociopolitical contexts.

We need historical specificity as well as sociological modeling; we need thick description of internal processes as well as analysis of external forces. Yet the aim of a more holistic and analytic approach to media issues in the South should neither simply privilege the "indigenous" as some kind of naturalized, unproblematic voice or position, nor simply abandon theoretical frameworks developed elsewhere as inappropriate, hegemonic, bad. A rich analysis would examine the conjunction and effects of global processes within specific, localized settings, exploring the dynamics of external forces combined with internal processes. Deep theory would interrogate the adequacy of existing concepts and models within new and different settings, being open to the challenge of the new "real" as well as offering novel frameworks for interpreting that reality; as usual, a dialogue between theory and its objects of study is needed. And sometimes media-centered analysis can indeed fill out the parts that other disciplines cannot always reach.

Media in the Middle East

The media environment in the Middle East has attracted only intermittent attention; the area is more usually analyzed in terms of its geographically strategic significance, the economics of oil, or the cultural traditions of Islam. Yet one of the most powerful models of modernization, the paradigm of "communications and development," emerged out of empirical research conducted in Turkey, Syria, Iraq and Iran during the late 1950s by Daniel Lerner, which resulted in his contentious volume *The Passing of Traditional Society* (1958). The model was deeply flawed: triumphalist, unilinear, stagist. It was also probably forty years premature, assuming certain modernizing dynamics of which media were both index and catalyst, but which are really only now becoming a possibility as television becomes a truly accessible medium across the region. This work prompted a recent "rebuttal" in an argument about the "passing of modernity" in the region (Mowlana and Wilson 1990), an equally ludicrous charge in a period of intense regional incorporation into global markets, the expansion of investment, institution-building, and media growth. A more useful approach is to explore the tensions between pressures of conservatism, tradition, and cultural maintenance and pressures toward change and modernization which exist within every society and are pronounced across the region: Where are the tensions manifest, who are their protagonists, what are the likely short-term and long-term outcomes? The analysis of media systems in and of themselves may be of limited significance; but when analyzed as institutions that contribute to national and transnational processes of political liberalization and democratization; social transformation and the emergence of individuation and gender equality; economic globalization, market expansion, and rationalization of employment and labor relations, the contradictory and ambivalent roles of the media can become a significant focus for analysis.

In this chapter, I concentrate on the television environment in the Middle East and its implications for democratization, for a number of reasons. First, the televisual environment has changed rapidly and is continuing to do so, bringing externally produced materials to the region but also allowing transregional program flows and audience groupings. As Callard (1997a: 18) has argued, "over the last seven years the Middle East has moved from a situation of very limited access to television which was virtually all government controlled, to a market where there is a vast number of channels to choose between, often more than that of many European countries." Second, because in contexts of considerable illiteracy, audio-visual media can reach larger audiences than print and thus potentially serve to construct a national audience and create a shared cultural–political space for the first time. Third, in contexts where patriarchal culture remains dominant, supported by religious values and social tradition, and there is an often intense masculinization of public space, the penetrative reach of television into the family home may have profound consequences. Fourth, because while national and international radio broadcasting is well established and popular, its audience is being challenged by television (Boyd 1997). Fifth, because in a milieu where people are most often addressed as consumers or as audiences, rather than as citizens or political participants, mediated culture may play a more significant role than the typical instruments of formal politics in constructing and defining what counts as political debate. The press often faces difficult challenges within the Middle East as various forms of censorship are brought to bear on its overt political discourses. I want to show that the advent of television may be more seductive and subversive than the political press, because it encompasses more people, opens up more imaginary spaces, and invokes more complex desires.

The significance of the international context: Where is the "Middle East"

The very term "Middle East" is a geo-political label given to a region by European powers after the First World War; that it has stuck as a name and is used as a way of clustering certain countries should not lead to assumptions about similarities between these countries. The histories of Ottoman and colonial rule have left some shared legacies across the region, while the political boundaries of the region are the result of various "lines in the sand" drawn by Western powers, arrived at through international conflict and colonial settlements. The enduring struggles of Palestinians, not yet fully a state, Kurds, perhaps further than ever from statehood, and Armenians, a global diaspora, are part of the cruel historical legacies of the region.

The region reveals remarkable differentiation along almost any indicator one cares to choose. It has countries with among the highest GNP in the world (UAE, Kuwait, Israel) and the lowest (Yemen). Though Arabic is a key linguistic unifier, it is neither singular nor universal, since Turkish, Persian, and Hebrew are also important regional languages. Similarly, though Islam is the dominant religion, there are significant and varied communities of Christians and Jews, and confessionalism dominates the politics of some states, such as Lebanon. There is also differentiation *within* Islam, perhaps most significantly the Sunni/Shiite division, and highly divergent interpretations of the appropriate role of religion in politics. The Middle East is also a region that has experienced considerable population mobility. There is significant internal and inward migration: in the mid-1990s, Iran had the largest refugee population of any country in the world, made up of Afghani war refugees who have not returned, and Kurdish and Iraqi Shiite refugees on its western border; guest workers play an important economic role in many countries, bringing different cultural values with them. Some countries, particularly the Gulf states, have significant proportions of non-nationals. In Kuwait, for example, approximately 70 percent of the population in 1990 were non-nationals, with long and complex procedures for claiming citizenship; where citizenship remains an issue, participation and democratization are stalled. It is also a region that has exported people: Turkish "guest workers" to Germany and elsewhere; the global Lebanese, Palestinian and Armenian, and most recent Iranian diasporas; Saudi, Iraqi, and Algerian dissidents.

It is a region that has flirted with periods of constitutional reform, often based upon Western models, as in the Iranian Constitutional Revolution of 1905 and the period of Turkish modernization under Ataturk; though a number of states are long-standing republics, many of those are highly centralized mobilizing regimes, and the area still boasts many of the last autocratic monarchies in the world. One of the enduring problems for many states in the region is how to build a modern state infrastructure and administrative capacity, establishing modern political and civic institutions.

While crude neo-Orientalist argument has focused on Islam as an impediment to democracy, by now a well critiqued argument, far more significant structuring factors include foreign intervention in the region and oil. Many, but not all, of the states in the region owe their high GNP and economic development to oil extraction, and have been labeled "rentier states" (Deegan 1993, Mahdavy 1970). Under this peculiar mode of production, the state does not need to engage its workforce and raise revenue; hence there is less pressure for democratization. From the outside, Western concerns about the oil resources of the region have led to persistent military and political intervention, with support for clientist and undemocratic regimes against movements of self-determination. It has even been suggested that there exists "an historic incompatibility of oil and democracy" (MERIP 1992).

The Middle East is thus a highly complex region, and any attempt to describe processes of political change and democratization within it has to be mindful of the real historical and contingent differences and particular political economies that exist—no essentialist or culturalist models will suffice. Further, the region's insertion into the global political economy, indeed the differential roles of particular states within the global order and the varying impacts of markets, migration, and media, have to be considered. Hence, the pressures toward and dynamics of political change need to be examined both from outside and from inside the region.

Global pressures toward democratization

It is worth asking why the past decade has witnessed such growing concern about the institutionalization of democracy and processes of democratization in the Third World. Leftwich (1996) suggests four reasons, all political: one is the legitimacy of conditionality as an instrument of policy, whereby international institutions, but especially the IMF and the World Bank, have developed "structural adjustment" packages which aimed to curtail the power of the state and support deregulation, privatization, and the growth of market economies. Democratic electoral politics were seen as a way of controlling vested interests and limiting the power of states. A second is the ascendancy of neo-conservative or neo-liberal theories and ideologies of political economy in the West, which not only extol the virtues of individual personal freedoms, rights, and liberties, but also hold that political liberalization compels a government to be more accountable, less corrupt, and more efficient in terms of development. Third is that the collapse of communism provided evidential support for this general orientation, and led to the massive movement after 1991 to rebuild Eastern European economies as both market economies and as politically liberal and pluralist democracies. Last is the growth of real and popular democratic pressures inside many developing countries from the 1980s, including South Africa, Haiti, Thailand. This emerging orientation has had the effect of reversing the predominant argument of modernization theory: that socioeconomic development was a prior necessity for democracy. Now the logic is reversed: democracy can help development, a position increasingly articulated by the United Nations Development Programme (UNDP) and the World Bank.

Sklair (1996: 39) proposes a less totalizing notion of "developmental democracy" that steers between "the cruel choice of laissez-faire liberalism without social justice ... and dictatorial forms of state-centered development" and argues that elements can already be found "in all regions of the world, contrary to common assumptions that cultural, religious or social barriers obstruct the progress of democracy in 'non-Western' countries'." As he argues, "Democracy is a means to effectuate improvement in the overall quality of human life" and in all countries "democracy is manifested in diverse forms, or fragments, which reinforce one another in the production of developmental effects" (1996: 40). Among these "fragments" might be included freedom of the press and the autonomy of professional organizations as well as juridical independence; guaranteed health services and welfare benefits as well as equal protection of the laws; elements of industrial democracy as well as electoral democracy. Deegan (1993: 9) also, referring specifically to the Middle East, rejects any simplistic notions of political homogeneity or singular models of democracy:

> Distinct differences exist between the nation-states to the extent that a move toward democratization in one country may be symbolized by the removal of a ban on the formation of political parties, whilst in another, it might be characterized by the establishment of a more equitable parliamentary system.

While there is clearly much debate about definitions of democracy, there is increasing agreement about the need for greater participation, growth of civil society and development of human resources as part of the development process. The growing acceptance of measures of "human development" instead of simply economic development, and the importance of women's participation and activity in new measures of development, all imply a more inclusive and holistic notion of development with implications for political and cultural participation. As a recent *Human Development Report* (UNDP 1996: 59) argues:

> active democracy can aid economic growth in several ways. More open and transparent forms of governance can reduce corruption and arbitrary rule ... the real issue is whether growth helps democracy. Democracy, participation and empowerment are valued in themselves—whether they enhance growth or not.

The Middle East does not score well on such new indices. Of twenty countries taken to comprise the emerging political–cultural region of the Middle East and North Africa (MENA), all but two score lower in their human development ranking than in their GDP, with the largest discrepancies to be found in the oil-rich principalities of Qatar, Kuwait, and Oman. Nor do the oil states fare much better in indices of gender development or gender empowerment. The significance of these indices, which are increasingly used as indicators of social development, is that they separate pure economic power from state policy; the poor findings of the richer Arab states suggest a considerable policy lag, an outcome of the democracy deficit.

The World Bank's 1997 development report focused on the state and argues that states and markets need to work together and that states need to build capability, inform and respond to citizen needs, allow greater transparency in decision-making, foster executive recruitment, and so on. It argues that although in 1974 only 39 countries were democratic, by 1994 117 countries used elections to choose their national leadership, and it suggests that of all world regions, the Middle East and North Africa are the most resistant to formal democracy. Though the region does possess some of the most unreconstructed autocratic monarchies and weak state institutionalization, there are clearly significant moves to democracy in some countries and dissenting voices arguing for greater openness and political diversity in others.

Internal pressures: emerging democracy in the region

The end of the Cold War, increased—if still tenuous—developments in an Arab–Israeli peace process with a Palestinian state as its outcome, and a changing global order have weakened autocratic justifications for "national security states" and could result in considerable political and social pressures within Arab countries for a share of the "peace dividend." It could, however, be argued that this is far from being translated into actual practices, since recent evidence suggests that the Middle East accounts for 40 percent of a £25 billion global arms trade, with Saudi Arabia alone buying £5.5 billion's worth (Black and Fairhill 1997: 17).

Democratization takes a crab-like configuration in the region, with some steps forward and many steps back. More and more states have experienced multiparty electoral competitions (for example Algeria, Tunisia, Egypt, Morocco, Jordan, and Yemen). Elections were held in unified Yemen in 1993, although civil war from 1994 has undone much. Algeria, which nullified the 1992 election, tried again in Autumn 1997, although proscribing participation of the Islamic Front and some other political groupings. Iran convincingly elected a more liberal president who took office in August 1997, yet suffered severe censorship and political violence in 1998. In the most politically traditional regimes such as Bahrain, Oman, and Saudi Arabia, often under pressure from dissident groups, experiments in consultative councils are being tried, and Qatar held elections in Spring 1999.

Norton (1994: 3) suggests that

> there has long been little doubt that the regimes in the region are under increasing pressure from their citizens. Repression at the hands of the state has become a topic of public discussion, and human rights activists, though relatively few in number, have become increasingly vocal. In short, the regime's governments, especially the Arab ones, are facing persistent crises of governance ... the pressures for change are general and growing, although they are obviously not equally intense in all states.

Thus concerns for greater participation, freedom, and democracy press in from the outside and up from inside. In a global environment where talk of democratization, human rights, and participation have become staples of political rhetoric, and with Islamic Declarations on Human Rights promulgated by the Islamic Council and the League of Arab States, the authoritarian regimes in the region are increasingly pressed from within and without to democratize.

Research supports such a trajectory. A major project of comparative analysis of civil society in the Middle East aimed to examine "society in juxtaposition explicitly to the state, and implicitly to the fate of authoritarianism" (Norton 1995: viii) and identified a host of social spaces as constituting civil society, such as "co-operatives, unions, professional syndicates, women's movement, and a panoply of sporting clubs and informal circles," yet it paid almost no attention to any forms of media or the changing mediascape in the region. Slowly, some Middle Eastern scholars are recognizing that a focus on political institutions and the development of civil society can no longer afford to ignore the media as potential instruments of civil society, particularly in the global context (Esposito 1996). Recent work on the region by Brynen (1995) explores political democratization and liberalization, the latter including the expansion of public space and the ability of citizens to engage in free political discourse. Their analysis focuses on four clusters of issues, which include the democratization of political culture, the nature of civil society, the regional political economy, and the global context. The media play a role within each of these four problematics, in ways that I can only suggest in this chapter, but reinforcing my argument that attention to media dynamics in the region speaks to much wider processes at work.

Population movements in and out of and across the region, whether of labor migrants, business and professional peoples, or students, spread images of other lives and rhetorics of change. And so do the media. Appadurai (1996) has presciently argued that media and migration are the two most powerful forces for modernity at work in the world, although he downplays markets. Strange (1988) prioritizes states, markets, and technology as three key ingredients of globalization, and she explores the global competition and tensions between states and markets. Media operate within that space, and the function of media power, whether economic, ideological, or cultural, is truly worthy of interrogation: can the media act as instruments of democratization in authoritarian regimes? Can market forces be helpful in the establishment of media and cultural industries that open up new spaces of cultural exploration not controlled by the state?

The changing political economy of television: international pressures, regional rivalries, national strategies

It is clear that there has been rapid and dramatic change in the media environment in the Middle East, the effects of which are only beginning to make themselves felt. The corpus of work on media in the region remains empirically and theoretically thin, what research exists being predominantly descriptive and devoid of significant analytic framing (e.g. Kamalipour and Mowlana 1996).

In what follows, the focus is on the Arab states of MENA. Turkey, Iran, and Israel—for linguistic, cultural, and religious reasons—share some but not all of these configurations and need separate analytic attention.

Up until the 1990s the development of broadcasting in the region had been somewhat limited. From the 1950s, television was introduced into the region by the US military and the big oil companies such as ARAMCO, and many countries had a state-controlled broadcasting system by the late 1960s (Amin 1996). Regional cooperation supported the development of ARABSAT in the late 1970s with the launch of ARABSAT 1-A and 1-B in 1985. Because of the limitations of state-supported broadcasting provision, by the 1990s the region experienced remarkable video penetration, estimated at over 80 percent in the Gulf States, and the growing circulation of non-regional produced material. But the big push to a new stage of televisual development was prompted by the Gulf War.

The Gulf War of January–February 1991 brought 24-hour American news coverage to the region, which found eager audiences and created pressure for change in the regional media industries. The sudden significance of CNN, the Pentagon's role in constructing the news agenda, and the lack of alternative, distinctively Arab, voices provided impetus for media development, especially electronic media. These changes, supported by a post-war economic boom which has helped media access, have radically altered the government broadcasting monopolies and produced a more open media environment in the region. Ayish (1997: 475) sums up these changes:

> greater political liberalization, the expansion of national privatization programs and the diffusion of new communications technologies ... seem to have had a significant effect on the Arab broadcasting scene. They have contributed to the relaxation of government controls over broadcasting; to the creation of more autonomous radio and television corporations; to the abolition of some ministries of information; to the granting of more access to diverse political views; and to permitting broadcasters to solicit commercial advertising to supplement dwindling government financing.

Much change has been provoked by intense national competition. The Egyptian Space Channel (SpaceNet) produced by the Egyptian Radio–Television Union (ERTU) was one of the first to launch an international television service, having just negotiated a deal with ARABSAT at the start of the Gulf War. It provided military and public information broadcasts to Egyptian and other allied Arab forces, countering strong Iraqi propaganda, although its post-war programming is far more varied fare.

SpaceNet was followed closely in 1991 with the launch of MEBC, latterly MBC, television from London, supported by a range of Arab investors and headed by Saudi businessmen connected to the royal family. Its London headquarters reinforced the stations's physical and political detachment from Arab governments, although it sees "the world through Arabian eyes" (Ayish 1997). Since it broadcasts from outside the region, it enjoys a far greater political license than domestic channels, including the establishment of a correspondent's office in Jerusalem.

The mad rush into broadcasting saw the launch in 1994 of no fewer than twenty pan-regional satellite-delivered television channels. Orbit, a satellite television and radio network, carries sixteen television channels and four radio networks in Arabic and English. Headed by yet another Saudi Prince, and based in Rome, Orbit provides an encrypted system which requires a decoder to view the programming. Initially very expensive, there was widespread belief that such a process of delivery would not take off in the region, but decoders have come down in price (pressured by an active black market) and Orbit has built a subscription base. Its "bouquet," as the package of channels is fragrantly called, include US news channels, CNN, the Hollywood Channel, Discovery and the Music Channel. Initially, it also included the BBC World Arabic channel, one of the first commercially self-supporting channels of the new BBC World organization. However, increasing pressure from the Saudis, who objected particularly to the BBC showing programs on human rights issues such as *Death of a Principle* (the title echoing the much earlier documentary *Death of a Princess*), meant that the BBC channel was pulled off the air in 1996. A number of its professionals have been absorbed by the emerging Qatari broadcasting system, supported by a coup-born new Emir, and its Al-Jazeera Satellite Channel has rapidly increased its hours of broadcasting and stunned MENA viewers with unprecedentedly frank, wide-ranging political debates.

Arab Radio and Television (ART) is headed by one of the Saudi entrepreneurs who helped establish but then left MBC, and broadcasts from Rome, with major production centers in Cairo and Jeddah. It carries four specialized television channels, three of which broadcast twenty-four hours a day. In 1996, Showtime, supported by Viacom Inc. and Kuwaiti partners, was launched in competition with Orbit, and closely aligned with 1st Net, the region's other satellite package from Arab Radio and Television. Gulf DTH, which is the parent company of Showtime, is half-owned by Viacom, and half by Kuwaiti Investment Properties Co., KIPCO, a public company of which 8.5 percent is owned by the Kuwait government through its investment arm, the Kuwait Investment Authority.

Some of the experience of the long-standing and highly productive Egyptian film industry has been harnessed into television production, and the state Egypt Radio and Television Union (ERTU) is massively investing in building a new media production city, dubbed "Hollywood on the Nile," in order to maintain Egypt's historic position as provider of entertainment to the Arab World.

The Lebanese entered the fray after 1996 with two stations, LBC and Future, providing satellite delivery; their more informal and relaxed style, which has included quite uninhibited game shows, has attracted a regional audience. One advertising manager in the region has described this as "audiences voting with their remotes" (Camp in Sakr 1999).

These brief examples show the complex and rapidly changing political economy of the broadcast media environment in the region. There are national channels, regional distribution systems, transnational coproduction and distribution arrangements, and strategies to locate corporate headquarters outside the region to maximize autonomy and evade local political and regulatory controls. There are dynamics best described as political rivalry, over hegemony of the Arab world and the Arab media audience, although some of the largest military players in the region are notably absent from this perhaps more mundane but more enduring game—notably Iraq and Syria. There is, of course, also economic competition.

The number of satellite-delivered channels in the Middle East and North Africa nearly doubled in 1997; it is such a dynamic environment that the detail of descriptive material is guaranteed to be well out of date before publication.[2]

Doing the dishes: the return of paternalistic policies

The public uptake of such new provision was dramatic, but then so too has been state reaction. In some countries the dishes that mushroomed in 1990–1 were banned, as in Saudi Arabia in June 1994, because they constituted a "threat to traditional values," and any subscription offering of television packages was also proscribed, thus limiting the money to be made in the television market. Increasingly worried about the inroads made by satellite television channels in their audiences, Jordan and Qatar, which had allowed dishes, have both moved to MMDS (multichannel multipoint distribution system), a relatively cheap delivery system, and Saudi Arabia is following. MMDS allows a central (state) authority the power to filter out programming of which it does not approve, thus controlling the choices that its audience is allowed to make, but it also means that revenue is not lost to foreign conglomerates. Arab states have also attempted to block terrestrial retransmission of foreign programming at prime time, especially applied against MBC.

In 1996 the region had around 50 million television homes, and this figure is increasing rapidly. Satellite penetration is still limited: around 3.7 million homes in 1996, about 7 percent, but this is expected to triple to 10 million by 2005. Algeria, Kuwait, Israel, Oman and the UAE have satellite penetration of more than 20 percent and Saudi Arabia is not far behind with 17 percent, despite dishes being legally banned. Forrester (1995) claims that Cairo's skyline has probably altered more over the past year than in the past fifty, not because of high-rise building but because of the tens of thousands of satellite dishes that crowd the rooftops. In Palestine the flat roofs of poor housing in the old Qalandiya refugee camp on the outskirts of Jerusalem groan under the weight of the huge dishes perched on them, while the personnel of the Palestinian Authority in their newly built housing in Ramallah sport antennae that resemble not-so-miniature Eiffel Towers. Increasingly market attention is moving toward North Africa, which is less wealthy but more liberally disposed toward satellite reception. In 1997 there were over 1.2 million dishes in Morocco; the Tunisian government has lifted its ban against dishes, and Algeria is seen by some as the next big market.

Media diffusion and shifting patterns of production and consumption

Much of the initial concern about satellite television related to the large amounts of foreign, especially American, programming coming into the region; yet much of this was in English and reached only a small elite, many of whom are foreign-educated.

One media strategy, fuelled not only by fear of potential restraint but also by desire to reach a broader audience, is a regional strategy of making Arab-language programming suitable for the regional value system:

The Middle East has two unifying elements: whether you go from Casablanca to Kuwait the great majority of the population is Muslim so there's a common culture, and although there is variation with spoken Arabic, you can put a Moroccan together with a Kuwaiti and they will understand each other so the language and religion are common and given that religion plays a tremendous role in culture and the family structure, you have two tremendous unifying factors.

(Zilo, cited in Hawkes 1997: 24–5)

Yet the region is far from homogeneous, and programming appropriate in one national context might well not merely raise eyebrows but give offense in another. For example, Orbit is proud of a live discussion program called Al Oula, made in Lebanon:

We deal with sexuality, and issues such as why married men have affairs. These subjects have not been addressed before in the region. There is no censor in this building. The approach we have taken is that we've put the responsibility on everybody to ensure that what we're putting out is acceptable and morally sensitive. And that has nothing to do with whether you are a Muslim or a Christian. If you have a family and you have values for your children, the values are very similar if you are a Muslim or a Christian. What we try to put out is appropriate family programming.

(Zilo 1997: 25)

Its ability to attract a regional audience "voting with their remotes" suggests a population looking for more stimulation, in all senses, than offered by the fairly bland and heavily policed state systems.

A second strategy is thus to produce programming targeted to the national audience. Bahraini television production is consciously aimed at Bahrain nationals, says its chief executive officer, with a "focus on local areas of interest and the cultural values of the society" (Callard 1997b). Local production is expanding, pressured partly by the cultural penetration from the outside. It is not only popular culture that is a cause for concern. Lebanon, which has one of the most open and dynamic media environments in the region, also fears internal instability and fragmentation, as confessional groupings become consolidated into divided audiences. Al-Umran, once a member of the Ministry of Radio and Television in Bahrain but later taking up the directorship of MBC in London, has argued (1996: 19) that political content no longer provokes much concern in the region, since from the advent of shortwave radio, new technologies have made that battle impossible to wage; the current strategy is to provide competitive alternative news to the biases of Western content. Yet even cursory evidence suggests that is not quite the case. For example, the Lebanese Ministry of Information, known as one of the most progressive in the region, instituted a new broadcasting law in January 1997 that introduced pre-censorship of news bulletins and political programs intended for satellite transmission and is authorized to stop the transmission of any news or political item affecting state security, fomenting sectarian sedition, or undermining public order. The use of television to stage more open political debates in the programming from Qatar has provoked consternation in the region: it suggests a novel genre, allows a comparison with the "lack" of debate elsewhere, and provides an actual counterpoint to politically dominant positions. Political and cultural orthodoxy are hard to maintain when an alternative can be found by pressing the remote.

A wider issue is the growing concern with "culturally sensitive programming," an issue which it is claimed enjoys government and public agreement, at least in the conservative states of the Gulf: "the biggest concern from open access to highly attractive and superior quality programming from the outside world is fear of its effect on the national language and the values and traditions of the society" (Al-Umran 1996: 22). It is this concern which has justified the development of MMDS systems: in Bahrain, the system allows encryption of entire undesired channels; in Qatar they use delayed programming; and the new Saudi venture Saravision will provide "cleaned up" tailor-made programming for most channels.

At work within such approaches, yet often very weakly elaborated, are deeply embedded understandings of cultural propriety, of the nature of childhood and the dynamics of family life, and particular assumptions about the role of women, in the Gulf and wider society. Patriarchal policies seek to "protect" the national citizenry, conceived as being childlike, unable to choose for themselves and potentially subject to extreme influence, whereas processes of democratization imply an adult population that demands to be (en)trusted with responsibility. Though some formal political liberalization is growing, there is a far deeper subtext of gender and sexual politics.

In the Middle East, as many places elsewhere, citizenship has traditionally been defined as male and women are often used as symbolic markers of cultural purity and national honor (Yuval-Davis 1997). Correspondingly, women's associations and involvements in local activities are often ignored in a gender-biased understanding of civil society (Rabo 1996, White 1996). As patriarchy itself modernizes, shifting from patriarchal structures rooted in everyday, private, life to forms of neo-patriarchy (Sharabi 1988), the state's role in "defending" female honor becomes both more contradictory and more overt. The cultural and media strategies of many states are ultimately directed toward maintaining the prevailing gender hierarchy and mode of sexual hygiene, at a moment when both are increasingly subject to critique.

There is evidence from across the region of women's growing unease with their most basic economic and political rights such as access to formal education, employment, and political franchise, but also with possibly more minor yet significant cultural limitations. The arguably most famous challenge to incursions on women's personal freedom was the Saudi women's drive-in in the 1980s in order to gain the right to drive; in Spring 1999 this seemed to be finally on the verge of supportive legislation. In another case, after the 1998 Football World Cup, Iranian women invaded a Tehran football pitch to welcome home their World Cup team, penetrating a space that had been rendered male since the Revolution. Increasingly, Islamic women are reinterpreting the Koran and putting forward their own culturally sensitive yet feminist arguments. Thus a simple paternalism in national policymaking, that does not take onboard the internal pressures for change from many women in the region, could backfire. Those whom a political press excludes by literacy, language, and formal education, televisual media includes, and with much of its content being directed to dynamics and issues within the private sphere, the social effects are not easy to anticipate. There can be no development without women, and there can be no democracy without women. The gender politics in the region are volatile.

Public space in the region has been, and in many places remains, male space. Women are often required to enter it veiled, covered by the rubrics of religious decency and appropriate relations between the sexes, work and shop under a male ethos, and return to the female arena of the interior. In such a cultural context, the very fact that broadcast media recognize no boundaries and can pass through borders, means that within private space women can increasingly access a range of images and information, to be viewed together or alone, to be reacted to or acted upon. Sketchy indications of these dynamics come from the work of Abu-Lughod and Davies, women anthropologists who have each conducted ethnographic work in the region. Abu-Lughod (1995) locates television within "a complex jumble of life" in which modernizing pressures have already been encountered through state intervention in agricultural production, the military, tourists, migrant labor, and so on. She does, however, raise three possible "effects" of television (which need research to clarify further) (1995: 206): one is shifting patterns of social life with less visiting as people stay home and watch, so that "television may have increased the number of 'experiences' shared across generation and gender" although conflicts also arise by generation and gender as to which programs to watch; second, that television may alter the nature of experience itself; and third, and most relevant for this discussion, that television may facilitate "new identifications and affiliations" as "imagined communities of citizens or consumers."

Consumption versus citizenship?

The new television broadcasting is binding populations into "national" audiences in a way that no medium has truly done before. Enduring illiteracy, especially among women, and urban concentration have meant that in many states the press has not reached beyond an already highly politicized, heavily male, educated readership. Television is constructing a national public space that addresses men and women, old and young, educated and poorly educated, urban and rural.

At the same time, as already indicated, regional programming and alternative newscasts are available as well as English-language news and programming. Thus audiences are increasingly able to compare "lifestyles" across the region, which do differ markedly, as well as images from the US, the UK, and elsewhere. Civil society is usually seen as that space between state and market where public discussion can develop. Though much television in the region is imbued with both commercial and statist concerns, it may nonetheless bring new images into the family home and address ordinary people in a way they have never previously experienced. If democratization is to be understood in its widest form, as increasing participation in public life and public debate and encouraging cultural pluralism, it is here that the potential role of the media becomes so important.

A political–economic analysis of the current television environment in the region suggests a growing tendency toward privatization and commercialization; indeed, the evidence of low expenditure on advertising combined with youthful and often wealthy audiences, only suggests that a significant increase in advertising content and further commercialization will occur in the media sector. Ironically, in a region where the dynamics of civil society have been somewhat weak, commercial media might bring more news, information, and debate than many state systems have previously allowed. Ayish (1997: 491) suggests that the likely impact of commercial broadcasting operating alongside the state sector will be as a catalyst for the latter to improve its performance, and provide the public with alternative outlets of expression, making a contribution to critical debates on the issues facing Arab societies. Here, then, the pressure of the (global) market might actually offer something new and more open to the regional audience as well as exerting pressure upon states to reform; repressive states have been a more enduring obstacle to development in the region than the commercial imperatives of markets.

Concerns about Western-mediated cultural domination sound thin in a region where colonialism has left a deep imprint, not only in territorial boundaries but in languages, cultural orientations, and religious affiliations. That is to say, the West is not a new arrival here; the flows of students, businessmen, scientific and other experts suggest a healthy ability for discrimination and selectivity. It would also be naive to see television as the vanguard of materialism or consumption in the region, with its deep pockets of familial wealth, mercantilism, and trades in land and gold and weaponry. Television will undoubtedly help to diffuse more modern, capitalist forms of profit-making and consumerism. Though concerns about commercial pressures and Western product still raise provocative issues, they also miss much of the particularities and evocative dynamics of television development in the region. Almost for the first time, men, women, and children are being drawn into a national sociocultural space that offers news, entertainment, and discussion. On the same dial are available channels from other Arab countries as well as newsfeeds from Western news media; that is to say, comparisons are readily available, and the lack of coverage of a certain story on one channel is easily revealed by tuning to another. One forcefully articulated position can be seen to be challenged by an equal but opposing argument on another channel, disturbing the regimes of truth that have prevailed. This is not to suggest that Middle Eastern audiences are going to be particularly active viewers, or less channel-loyal than most audiences. It is to suggest, however, that the possible range of news imagery as well as cultural content is already quite large, making political and cultural censorship harder and harder to legitimate and to achieve. The interregional competition for audiences, markets and even political hegemony also undermines any too-easy assertion of an Arab "cultural discount" (Hoskins and Mirus 1988) or the emergence of a geo-regional media zone; such developments are clearly not without considerable internal conflict and rivalry. Indeed, there remains a significant tension between narrow, competitive, geo-political nationalisms configured by existing state formations and a regional pan-Arab nationalism which still exists as a politico–cultural project for some; only detailed empirical research could begin to identify which of these tendencies the expansion of television serves to reinforce. The increasingly wide variety of imagery being produced within the region also erodes a simple traditionalist, often religious critique about the negative impact of Western material; the boundaries of who constitutes "us" and "them" keep shifting, and is brought closer to home if producers in the region are themselves testing the accepted boundaries of media content and cultural taste.

Arguments about the nature of late modernity focus increasingly on self-reflexivity and the chosen life, as compared with life lived within the remit of unchallenged tradition. Television, especially with significant doses of foreign programming, displays the variety of lives in the world, including the far greater individualism, freedom, and emancipation of women in Western societies—as well as in some Arab societies in comparison to others.

Gender is a key marker of potential cultural instability and democratization. In contexts where women's lives are still heavily bounded by religious culture, patriarchal values, and sheer habit, the force of mediated culture, especially images, which travels through public space into private living-rooms may be far greater than elsewhere. It is precisely the family orientation of Arab/Middle Eastern life, with parents and children viewing and discussing together, that makes the family a potential cauldron of conflict between generations and between genders with pressures for greater individuation, autonomy, and self-determination. Much of television's content shows, and reflects upon, the private sphere, making that an acceptable focus of public debate. If democratization and liberalization are understood to focus not only on a delimited arena of formal politics but on wider issues of participation, debate, and voice, then the public problematizing of personal politics may well be television's central contribution to gender politics in the region.

The limited research that exists suggests a playful and creative appropriation by women of images and styles that appeal to them, and their use in challenging elements of privatized patriarchal culture. This is of course not to argue that Western media representation is free of patriarchal values; they are, however, more subtle, more varied, and do allow women greater range of movement. The impact of external, Western and other cultural production, is only minimally constrained by a "Cinema Paradiso" approach of cutting out the (mainly sexualized) "naughty bits" because the entire programming is suffused with assumptions and values about individual choice, freedom of action, gender equality, attitudes toward parenting and the nature of childhood. We know that media effects are not direct or one-directional; it does seem possible that a more open and diverse media environment will spur greater debate in Middle Eastern societies, with further pressures for both cultural and political democratization. There might be limits to the extent to which a population can be addressed solely as consumers without encouraging any other forms of participation in public life or decision-making processes.

The media are clearly instruments of modernity, although they can be harnessed for traditionalist purposes, used both to redefine and maintain tradition as well as to destabilize it. Quite what form of modernity works itself out in the Middle East remains to be seen.

Notes

1 Some of the material and argument in this chapter is drawn from an earlier article, "Media and democratization in the Middle East: the strange case of television," in Vicky Randall, (ed.) *Democratization and the Media* (Cass, 1998); a version of this chapter was also presented at the Article 19 conference on Satellite Broadcasting in the Middle East and North Africa: Regulations, Access and Impact, Cairo, February 1999.

2 It is noteworthy that at least three commercial publications, *Middle East Broadcast and Satellite*, *Middle East Communications* and *Middle East Satellite Today*, focus solely on tracking the developments in media regulation, delivery systems and new players in the region, in itself a powerful indicator of the strength of this regional market.

References

Abu-Lughod, L. (1995) "The objects of soap opera," in D. Miller (ed.) *Worlds Apart*, Routledge.

Al-Umran, Hala (1996) "MMDS—the cultural alternative to DTH," *Middle East Broadcast and Satellite*, September, p. 19.

Amin, Hossein (1996) "Egypt and the Arab world in the satellite age," in J. Sinclair, E. Jacka and S. Cunningham (eds.) *New Patterns in Global Television: Peripheral Vision*, Oxford: Oxford University Press.

Appadurai, Arjun (1996) *Modernity at Large*, Minneapolis: University of Minnesota Press.

Ayish, Muhammad (1997) "Arab television goes commercial: a case study of the Middle East Broadcasting Centre," *Gazette*, 59(6) (December): 473–94.

Beck, U., Giddens, A. and Lash, S. (1994) *Reflexive Modernization*, Cambridge: Polity.

Black, I. and Fairhall, D. (1997) "The profits of doom," *Guardian*, October 16, p. 17.

Boyd, D. (1997) "International radio broadcasting in Arabic," *Gazette*, 59(6): 445–72.

Brynen, R. (1995) *Political Liberalization and Democratization in the Arab World: Vol. 1, Theoretical Perspectives*, Boulder, CO: Lynne Riener.

Callard, S. (1997a) "Cross-cultural broadcasting," *Middle East Broadcast and Satellite*, March, p. 18.

Callard, S. (1997b) "Broadcasting in Bahrain: an interview with Khalil Ebrahim al-Thawasi," *Middle East Broadcast and Satellite*, March, p. 37.

Davies, H. (1989) "American magic in a Moroccan town," *Middle East Report*, 19(4): 12–18.

Deegan, H. (1993) *The Middle East and Problems of Democracy*, Buckingham: Open University Press.

Esposito, J. (1996) *Islam and Democracy*, Oxford: Oxford University Press.

Forrester, C. (1995) "Regional broadcasting update," *Middle East Broadcast and Satellite*, October, p. 370.

Hawkes, R. (1997) "The Zilo interview," *Middle East Broadcast and Satellite*, March, p. 27.

Hoskins, C. and Mirus, R. (1988) "Reasons for the US dominance of international trade in television programming," *Media, Culture and Society*, 10(4): pp 499–515.

Kamalipour, Y. and Mowlana, H. (eds.) (1996) *Mass Media in the Middle East*, London: Greenwood Press.

Leftwich, A. (ed.) (1996) *Democracy and Development*, Oxford: Polity Press.

Lerner, D. (1958) *The Passing of Traditional Society*, Harvard: Belknap Press.

Mahdavy, Hossein (1970) "Patterns and problems of economic development in rentier states," in M. A.Cook (ed.) *Studies in the Economic History of the Middle East*, Oxford: Oxford University Press.

MERIP (1992) "The democrracy agenda in the Arab world," MERIP Report, 174(22)(1) (January/February): 3–5.

Mowlana, H. and Wilson, L. (1990) *The Passing of Modernity*, London, Longman.

Norton, A. R. (1994) "Introduction," *Civil Society in the Middle East*, Vol. 1, Leiden: E. J. Brill.

Norton, A. R. (1995) "The future of civil society in the Middle East," in Jillian Schwedler (ed.) *Toward Civil Society in the Middle East? A Primer*, Boulder, CO: Lynne Reiner.

Rabo, A. (1996) "Gender, state and civil society in Jordan and Syria," in C. Hann and E. Dunn *Civil Society—Challenging Western Models*, London: Routledge.

Sakr, N. (1999) "The emergence and development of satellite broadcasting in the MENA region: structures and actors," paper presented to the Article 19 conference on Satellite Broadcasting in the Middle East and North Africa: Regulations, Access and Impact, Cairo, February.

Sharabi, Hisham (1988) *Neo-Patriarchy: A Theory of Distorted Change in Arab Society*, Oxford: Oxford University Press.

Sklair Richard, L. (1996) "Toward a theory of developmental democracy," in A. Leftwich (ed.) *Democracy and Development*, Oxford: Polity.

Strange, S. (1988) *States and Markets*, London: Routledge.

UNDP (1996) *Human Development Report 1996*, Oxford: Oxford University Press.

White, J. (1996) "Civic culture and Islam in Turkey," in C. Hann and E. Dunn *Civil Society—Challenging Western Models*, London: Routledge.

World Bank (1997) "The state in a changing world," *World Development Report 1997*, Oxford: Oxford University Press for the World Bank.

Yuval-Davis, N. (1997) *Gender and Nation*, London: Routledge.

6 Power, profit, corruption, and lies

The Russian media in the 1990s

Brian McNair

More than ten years have passed between this publication and that of my first academic essay on what was then the Soviet media (McNair 1989). They have been years of transition and turmoil, punctuated at frequent intervals by a succession of economic and political crises, up to and including the Russian stock market crash of August 1998. Through it all, those who work in the Russian media have struggled for survival in an environment characterized by chronic resource shortages, political instability, and the ever-present threat of criminal interference. There have been sackings, bankruptcies, hostile takeovers, and assassinations along the way. And yet, media professionals in Russia will tell you with some pride, they and their organizations *have* survived. The establishment of a free media—free, at least, from the close administrative control by party or state which was the hallmark of the Soviet era—has been one of the main achievements of the post-1991 period; their continuing existence an indicator that no matter how bad things may at times appear to be, all is not lost in the struggle for political and economic reform.

"Freedom," of course, is always relative, limited by the political, economic, and cultural conditions within which media organizations must operate. If Russian media workers are free from the impositions of an authoritarian political system, they now grapple with the sometimes equally inhibiting pressures and constraints of the market capitalism which replaced it, and the new media barons who have replaced the old party bosses.

This chapter reviews that decade of uneasy and uneven media development, identifying its driving forces, its successes, and its failures, and assessing the role of the reformed media in the transition from Soviet to post-Soviet society and culture. These processes are of interest in and of themselves, because of Russia's present and future geo-political significance for East and West, North and South alike. But for social scientists, and all those interested in the dynamics of societal evolution, the former Soviet Union is in some ways a laboratory. Changes which took a century of capitalist development in Europe or North America have unfolded in Russia in less time than it takes to research, write, and see published an academic monograph. For media scholars in particular, Russia is an important case because it allows us to witness what happens when the attempt is made to build a politically and economically independent media system from the ruins of a state-controlled, propaganda-oriented one, and to replace a Marxist–Leninist approach to media organization, virtually overnight, by the principles of liberal pluralism. We rarely, as social scientists, have the opportunity to be spectators of such a radical upheaval. This chapter is one spectator's account of what happened to the Russian media in the 1990s, and what it means for the post-Soviet transition process more broadly.

It is an account necessarily qualified by the knowledge that events in contemporary Russia are rarely as they seem on the surface. Secrecy and subterfuge have been the favored instruments of economic and political elites in recent years. Openness and transparency in matters of ownership and control of the media (and of capital in general) are elusive, a problem complicated by the fact that disinformation and propaganda are regularly used against opponents in the struggles for control of the media which have dominated the post-1991 years. Thus, when a government agency states that a media organization, or an individual manager, is guilty of corruption, or "serious financial mismanagement"[1] verging on the criminal, most observers assume on the basis of past experience that the accused is just as likely to be the victim of a "softening up" campaign, prior to dismissal or takeover, as to be guilty of the alleged offenses.

Moreover, as was the case when the transition process began in 1991, change in all sectors of the Russian economy, and the media more than most, is rapid and unpredictable, as evidenced by the onset of the economic crisis of August 1998. This event greatly worsened the environment faced by an already unstable Russian media system. One consequence, cited here to illustrate the absurdist atmosphere in which Russian media managers operate, was the main television channel ORT's warning in November 1998 that, despite introducing an emergency program schedule (including a drastically reduced news service), it was unable to pay back official loans and was nearing bankruptcy. This would have been less remarkable in the Russian context were it not for the fact that the government at this time owned 51 percent of ORT's shares, and was therefore in effect suing itself for nonpayment of its own money.

Chekhovian farce aside, and given that no assessment of the state of the Russian media can avoid these limitations, the following is an account of how it looked, *za granitsu* (from abroad), at the close of the decade. Following a brief review of events leading up to the demise of the USSR in 1991, and the role played by the media in shaping that outcome, I discuss the economic, political, and cultural dimensions of post-Soviet media development, in the context of the pluralistic and democratic objectives set for themselves by the Russian reformers.

Gorbachev's legacy

From this distance, and with the advantage of hindsight, one looks back with no less admiration at the scale of Mikhail Gorbachev's ambition, and the courage of his political altruism, in seeking to save the Soviet Union for socialism. Gorbachev recognized what no previous Soviet leader had: that a rapidly changing global media environment would make the maintenance of authoritarian Marxist–Leninist regimes like that of the USSR, in the absence of significant economic success (if compared with the experience of post-Second World War liberal capitalism), untenable. Globalization, though still then a little-used term (I use it here to mean the late twentieth century's communication technology-driven collapse of time–space barriers, and the associated decline in the ability of nation-states to police the flow of information across their borders) was already undermining Soviet society, and its culture of secrecy and prohibition, when Gorbachev took office in 1985. Externally, the Western powers led by Ronald Reagan and Margaret Thatcher were using the emerging global news media to win the Cold War propaganda battle of ideas and values (McNair 1988). Internally, "information contamination" from beyond Soviet borders, and new information technologies like video and fax, were making a highly regulated and controlled society increasingly "leaky," undermining the Communist Party's (CPSU) ideological hegemony.

Gorbachev's strategic gamble was to embrace rather than evade this changing media environment, before it destroyed his party and the country it had run since 1917; to *use* the media (in the *glasnost* campaign, for example) to reassert a version of socialist values at home (socialist pluralism, as he labelled it), and to conduct a sophisticated public relations effort abroad. By the Reykjavik summit in 1986 (McNair 1991), Gorbachev and not Reagan was consistently getting the best global news coverage, and serious commentators were speaking of the end of the Cold War. Gorbachev's reforms set in motion a benign "domino effect," making possible the "velvet revolutions"—so-called because of their largely nonviolent character (the bloody downfall of Ceausescu in Romania was an exception)—which swept through the Warsaw Pact countries of Central and Eastern Europe in the late 1980s.[2]

Other Marxist–Leninist-influenced regimes followed different paths. The Chinese, for example, while entering at the economic level into a much more successful compromise with capitalism than the reformist Soviets were able to achieve, combined marketization with the maintainence of authoritarian political and cultural practices, exemplified by the massacre of student demonstrators at Tienanmen Square in 1989 (ironically enough, just after a state visit to China by Gorbachev).[3] The North Korean regime reacted to the end of the Cold War, and to the democratic liberalization of its southern neighbor, by retreating into an even more extreme isolationism, becoming notorious for its tragi-surrealistic blend of mass starvation and mass adulation of the Great Leader. The more legitimate regimes of Castro's Cuba and Vietnam also resisted political change in the direction of democratization, relying on the deeply rooted anti-Americanism of their populations to hold the line, although for these countries, too, that position became ever more difficult to maintain. In Cuba and Vietnam, as in the Soviet Union before them, mass tourism, video, satellite TV and other carriers of global culture were bringing ever closer the day when democratic centralism of the Soviet type came into fatal contradiction with the experiences and desires of the people.

Gorbachev by contrast, and to his credit, volunteered the Soviet Union for progressive political and socioeconomic change, with the mass media positioned as the main instrument of persuasion. *Glasnost* loosened the shackles of party control and opened up first the press, then broadcasting to increasing intellectual diversity and "openness" of opinion. Through this distinctively Soviet "information revolution" Gorbachev and his supporters hoped to encourage the growth of a measure of pluralism and civic dynamism in Soviet society. These, he hoped, would unblock the individual and collective potential of the USSR (then, as Russia is now, the world's most resource-rich and potentially wealthiest country), reinvigorate its founding ideology, strengthen the party's "leading role," and allow it to enter the third millennium with the same optimism and revolutionary pride which had characterized the establishment of the Soviet state in 1917.

Things turned out differently, of course. *Glasnost* and *perestroika* may have improved the USSR's global image and made the world a safer place, but by exposing more and more of the truth behind official propaganda it weakened the (as it turned out) fragile unity of the Soviet state, and the hitherto unquestioned authority of the Communist Party. In August 1991, in an effort to halt and reverse the reform process, CPSU conservatives launched a coup attempt against Gorbachev, and the Soviet Union was pushed into making a choice between a return to neo-Stalinist authoritarianism, or a headlong dive into unbridled capitalism.

As with the reform process which provoked it, the media were crucial to the progress of these events. While the putchists moved with predictable speed to close down all those media institutions which were not loyal to their cause, fax, e-mail, and other means of communication allowed the supporters of reform to stay in touch with each other, and with the outside world. The cameras of global news organizations like CNN and the BBC were on hand to record the collapse of the coup, transmitting live coverage to both Soviet and international audiences. When the leader of the Russian federation, Boris Yeltsin, clambered onto a tank parked outside the parliament building and pronounced his determination to resist the coup he produced, with the media's help, a potent televisual rallying point for the reformers and their supporters abroad.

The media scholar can never know with certainty what effect these information dimensions of the coup had on its outcome, but two conclusions *can* reasonably be drawn from the August events: that for all their limitations, the Gorbachev reforms had, by 1991, produced a civil society strong enough, and with enough accumulated experience of intellectual freedom (albeit the restricted form associated with socialist pluralism) to be able *and* willing (both were necessary) to resist armed reaction from the old guard; and secondly, that the putchists were not able to carry out their attempted seizure of power in isolation from the global community, present as silent witnesses in the unfolding drama. These two factors acted as a restraint on the coup's political leaders, and even more so on those sections of the Soviet military on whom they relied for support.

But the defeat of the August putchists, welcome as it was for the reformers, was also in the end Gorbachev's, since it opened a path to what one might call the revolutionary dismantling of the Soviet state, and its replacement with an economic and political system uncritically modelled on free-market capitalism (a neat reversal in the order of change predicted by Marxist–Leninist theory). Gorbachev's attempt to organize a dignified retreat from a decaying Soviet ideology was rejected, not just by the coup plotters, but by the great majority of the reformers, who now moved ahead secure in the belief that Marxism–Leninism was redundant and discredited as an organizing principle of government; that there was nothing in Soviet theory or practice worth hanging onto. In a true expression of the dialectic in action, hatred and contempt for the old collectivism produced a reactive, zealous faith in bourgeois individualism and market economics (especially among the new elites who moved to occupy the positions of power vacated by the communists). The majority of the Russian people, and the young in particular, gladly renounced Marxism–Leninism to take their place in the MacDonald's queue in Moscow's Pushkin Square.

Events have shown many times in the intervening years that this transference of political faith from one utopian ideal to another was a mistake (if a forgivable one in the circumstances) which merely allowed the replacement of one tyranny (that of the bureaucratic party apparatus) with that of another (the market). The result was the creation of a hybrid (or hyper) capitalism which has staggered from one politico–economic crisis to another, at times threatening the stability of global capital itself (it would be ironic, and the cause of many last laughs among unreconstructed Marxist–Leninists, if the seemingly interminable crisis of born-again Russian capitalism brought down the international system once perceived by Soviet socialists as the epitome of exploitation and evil). Even if, as most of its inhabitants still believe, the new Russia is on balance better than the old, and even if Russia's current difficulties turn out to be the necessary prelude to its entry into the promised land of post-Cold War global capitalism (big "if's), it has been a traumatic and painful experience for its citizens, including those who work in the media and culture industries. The rest of this chapter explores how the harsh economics of a capitalism frequently described by Russians as "bandit," and the lingering political culture of the Soviet era, have contrived to produce a media system which, despite displaying many of the worst features of both worlds (Soviet-type socialism, free-market capitalism), may nevertheless still be regarded as one of the most important and precious achievements of the transition process.

A political economy of the Russian media 1991–8

The movement away from a centralized, state-controlled information economy which began in the *glasnost* years and accelerated sharply after the 1991 coup, was the necessary abandonment of an approach to media organization which had failed to meet the objectives claimed for it by its designers. It was widely welcomed by the supporters of reform, not least because in the wave of elation which immediately followed on the demise of the Soviet Union the media were major beneficiaries. The press in particular, which had been in the vanguard of the reform process to a much greater degree than television (like all governments everywhere, Gorbachev's administration regarded television as much too important to be left to its own devices, and obliged it, with some exceptions, to maintain a relatively conservative stance in its coverage of *glasnost* and *perestroika*) (McNair 1992), enjoyed an enhanced respect and status. While the pro-coup *Pravda* and other conservative titles lost their preeminent place as CPSU-approved "collective propagandists and agitators" and went into decline, staff on *Izvestia* and other pro-reform papers, many of whom had risked much to maintain a basic service during the coup, were lauded as cultural heroes. This was a time of idealistic optimism for the Russian press, in which they consolidated their pre-coup role by contributing to the establishment of multiparty political pluralism and a functioning public sphere. The adversarial journalism so prized in liberal press theory flourished as *Nyezavisimaya Gazeta* (*The Independent*, modelled on the British newspaper of the same name) and other titles vigorously applied "critical scrutiny" to the new elites in government and business, and encouraged lively public debate around the administration and future direction of the reform process.

Before long, however, the less welcome consequences of a too-rapid, insufficiently regulated transition to capitalism in Russia asserted themselves. The dismantling of the Soviet party and state apparatus not only freed newspapers from political control, but removed their traditional institutional sources of funds. A beleaguered Russian government, wrestling with hyper-inflation and economic recession, was unable to replace these funds with sufficient public subsidies. Production costs rose, as did cover prices, to "realistic" market levels, and circulations fell. Where Soviet newspapers regularly claimed circulations of 20 million copies, even the most successful titles of the late 1990s were selling no more than 5 million copies. The traditional source of income for print media in capitalist economies, advertising revenue, was scarce, and tended to flow toward publications targeted at the more affluent sectors of the population, such as the emerging business class, whose members were more likely to be able to buy the commodities being advertised. Though a few titles prospered, therefore, most entered a prolonged period of struggle for survival, and many went under.

Many of the most successful titles were taken over by private individuals and companies, losing their pre-coup editorial identities as radical, independent newspapers and becoming commercial properties subordinated to the business interests of their new proprietors. In the classic case of this process, and to cries of outrage from many Russians, the legendary *Izvestia* was taken over in 1997 by the Oneximbank group.

Such transactions and changes of fortune are routine in a free market, of course, and in the post-Soviet context, were part of the process of streamlining what was a bloated and inefficient print sector. Many of the Soviet-era newspapers existed not just because they were cheap, but because subscribing to them was viewed by the party as a civic duty, a badge of loyalty to the system. With the party gone, and the system overturned, newspapers had to find new bases of support, and readers willing to pay competitive prices. Many failed to make this leap, although the best of the pre-coup, pro-reform titles, like *Argumenty i Fakti* and *Komsomolskaya Pravda* survived, indeed prospered, even if they now achieved only a tenth of their pre-coup circulations.[4] Replacing them at the top of the circulation tables, a number of Western-style tabloid, consumer and lifestyle-oriented newspapers emerged, such as *Centre Plus*, *Speed*, and *Extra M* (approximate circulations of 5 million, 4 million and 3 million respectively). In a society where ideological and moral puritanism had been imposed for decades, sexual prurience and scandal proved popular themes on which to build circulation and profit for these new titles. Political sleaze also became a feature of Russian newspapers (*Izvestia*'s coverage of Victor Chernomyrdin's reputed $5 billion fortune, for example, or the "gift"/bribe allegedly made to Boris Yeltsin in 1994 of a 26 percent share in the country's biggest TV company, ORT). These trends in content were condemned in terms reminiscent of the "dumbing down" debates which have featured prominently elsewhere in the capitalist world in the late 1990s (Franklin 1997). Russian liberals questioned the extent to which a free media, with the market-driven growth in tabloid sleaze, sensationalism, and pornography which it encouraged, could be too free for a fragile democracy such as theirs.

The commercial restructuring of the Russian press, accompanied by what media studies scholars would call their *tabloidization*, was inevitable, and not on the face of it undesirable (in so far as it allowed newspapers for the first time to reflect and articulate popular tastes and demands), but took many supporters of reform by surprise nevertheless. Critics of media barons such as Rupert Murdoch and Silvio Berlusconi found their echo in those sections of the Russian intelligentsia who, having cheered the end of the Soviet, found that the independence and editorial autonomy of their newly liberated print media were subject to the brute force of the market. Responding to these concerns, some government support for the struggling press was forthcoming, but it was never enough to substitute for lack of success in the marketplace, and acceptance of state subsidy was always inhibited by the suspicion that it might come with political strings attached. Some editors who saw their titles as genuinely independent resisted state funding on principle.

Liberal opposition to what were perceived as the excesses of the market was further muted by the fact that the reactionary, anti-Semitic and xenophobic "national-patriots" in the parliament often seemed to agree with them. They too fought against media privatization, in the belief that it was another gateway for the penetration of the motherland by "foreign" ideas and values. Throughout the 1990s, Russia's conservatives called for greater state control of newspapers, including ownership, believing this to be, in the best traditions of the CPSU, a means of reasserting political control over unruly, "alien" voices in the press. The conservative-controlled parliament advanced a succession of pro-censorship bills aimed at restricting the ability of the press to act as a genuine "fourth estate" (similar attacks were made on politically suspect TV channels), and made proposals to restrict the concentration of media ownership. They also mounted a legislative campaign against forms of "moral degeneration" such as pornography.[5] Yeltsin was usually able to resist these pressures, not least because the voices advocating them most forcefully were identified with the Soviet past, reminding many Russians of what the defeat of the August coup had been about in the first place, and how vulnerable post-1991 press freedom still was.

Finding the appropriate balance, given recent Russian history and present conditions, between the excesses of a capitalist media market on the one hand, and state regulation of the press on the other, remains one of the most difficult challenges of the transition period. As of writing, the scales were undoubtedly balanced in favor of the market and the interests of business, but most Russians (including most media scholars and professionals) accepted that this was preferable to any system of press regulation and control which a Zhuganov or a Zhirinovsky[6] might introduce, were they in a position to do so. In Russia, as elsewhere in the world, liberal arguments for media censorship and regulation are rightly constrained by the knowledge of what authoritarian-minded conservatives might do with such powers, once granted.

Stylistic and content excesses notwithstanding, the Russian press by the late 1990s displayed a degree of editorial diversity not different in kind from that seen in more mature media markets. A few titles pursued a recognizably tabloid obsession with sex and scandal, and some were openly racist and reactionary. Most, however, fell into more or less conservative, more or less reformist camps, supporting their favored politicians in the manner of the "free" press in other countries. As with the free press in general, "freedom" in Russia chiefly meant that proprietors were free to dictate what the editorial line of a title would be. Given that this is a normal feature of media markets, it would not have been especially worrying in the Russian context, were it not for the distinctive character of the politics–media interface in Russia. As is discussed in more detail below, the proprietors of many Russian newspapers are members of what might be described as a *media–industrial complex*, an elite whose ownership allows them to exert a degree of influence on the political apparatus which is rarely seen in mature capitalist systems.

Broadcasting

For Russian broadcasters, like their counterparts in the print media, a period of radical restructuring was inevitable after the 1991 coup. The Soviet broadcasting system, controlled by the CPSU through a State Committee for Television and Radio (GOSTELRADIO—see Figure 6.1), reflected the organizational principles of Marxism–Leninism in its organization and content. Not only were these no longer appropriate to the changed political circumstances of Russia, but the GOSTELRADIO apparatus was clearly too big and cumbersome to survive in a market economy.

In a previous article I used the phrase "from monolith to mafia" (McNair 1996) to refer to the processes of privatization, commercialization, and criminalization which characterized the Russian broadcast sector after 1991. Between the failure of the coup and the presidential election of 1996, the state-run broadcasting monolith was starved of funds, broken up, and exposed to the vicissitudes of an anarchic media market dominated by an emerging power elite of bankers, industrialists, and entrepreneurs, many with links to organized crime. Several senior broadcasters paid for this exposure with

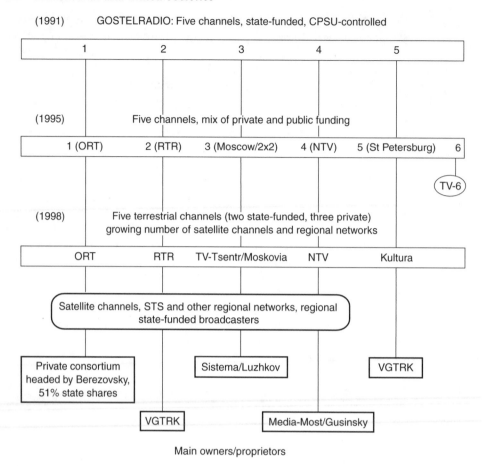

Figure 6.1   Russian television, 1991–8

their lives.[7] No effective regulation of the changing broadcast economy was put in place, and transparency in financial matters was absent. Program content was universally acknowledged to be in sharp decline, as resource pressures encouraged cheap foreign imports and low-cost domestic production. Civic-minded broadcasters in search of a coherent policy framework which might grant some stability and direction were caught in the constitutional battle between Yeltsin's reformist executive and the "national-patriotic" legislature which developed from 1992 onwards. There were exceptions to this story of decay and corruption—notably the establishment of the independent, journalism-oriented NTV in 1994, and the success of Eduard Sagalayev's TV-6 satellite channel in becoming Russia's first independent television network—but the perception, at home and abroad, of a general crisis in Russian television was entirely justified.

Then came the reelection of Boris Yeltsin in June 1996, with the more or less un-qualified support of Russian TV, and the start of another four-year phase of socioeconomic and media development, conducted within a pro-democracy, mixed-market frame-work in which political pluralism and media freedom would be protected. The broadcasters, having helped to secure their preferred electoral outcome, could look forward to a period of relative political stability and improving economic health as the backdrop to their operations.

And indeed, following the 1996 election the chaos and confusion of the first five years of post-Soviet broadcast development were replaced by greater stability, in which privatization was still the dominant trend, but producing a more cohesive and financially viable system than might have been thought possible a year or two earlier. The five television channels once owned and run by the state were reduced by 1997 to two (RTR or Rossiya, broadcasting on channel 2, and Kultura,[8] on channel 5), with the rest wholly or partially owned by private interests (Figure 6.1). This was a necessary divestment by a virtually bankrupt Russian state, permitting welcome investment by Russian and foreign capital in broadcasting production and infrastructure. In some cases the state retained a share of the privatized channel (51 percent of ORT, for example), and continued to exercize some control over its future development.

Freed from dependence on state funding, the privatized channels began to improve program quality, although some observers criticized what they perceived as a movement "downmarket" in programming, illustrated by the growing reliance of Russian broadcasters on game shows, talk shows and other cheap-to-make formats. These were international trends in televisual content, however, which Russia in its difficult economic circumstances could never have avoided. By the late 1990s Russian TV was judged by many observers to have achieved a higher standard of programming than might have been expected at the beginning of the decade. Despite resource constraints, the producers of news and current affairs, light entertainment, and TV for young people on the main channels were increasingly providing material which was just as innovative and well produced as that available in comparable countries.

The rise of the clans

If the privatization of Russian broadcasting was inevitable, it was accompanied, with equal inevitability, by the creation of private media empires, and media barons to lead them. As of writing, the key players were:

- Media-Most, headed by Vladimir Gusinsky, which owned NTV (channel 4) alongside substantial holdings in radio (including the highly respected Eko Moskvy, one of the first independent radio stations and an important focus of opposition to the 1991 coup), a regional satellite TV network, and print media (newspapers owned by Media-Most include the large circulation *Sevodnya*, *Syem Dnye* and *Itogi*);
- Logovaz, headed by Boris Berezovsky, which had the major private stake in ORT (channel 1), as well as several newspapers;
- Sistema, controlled by Moscow mayor and presidential contender Yuri Luzhkov, with controlling stakes in TV-Tsentr, cable and satellite channels, and newspapers such as *Rossiya*, *Kultura*, and *Metro*; and
- Premier-SV, controlled by Sergei Lisovsky, who dominated Russian TV advertising, and had an expanding cable and satellite interest in the regions.

There were other significant media owners, such as the Menatep and Oneximbank banking groups, and the relative importance of the interests listed here constantly changes as properties are bought and sold. Collectively, however, these individuals and organizations comprised a new power elite whose members have used capital accumulated in other sectors of industry (auto production, gas, financial services, for example) to break into media ownership on a strategic level. They have been described by the dean of Moscow University's journalism faculty as corporate "clans"(Zassoursky 1997), a term which accurately conveys their tightly knit, secretive networks, and their capacity to act in concert toward a common goal, as in their active support for Boris Yeltsin in the 1996 presidential election. Gusinsky, Berezovsky, Lisovsky and the rest were key behind-the-scene players in the Yeltsin reelection campaign while Igor Malashenko, the head of the once-independent NTV, joined the Yeltsin campaign team as an adviser. In return, they were rewarded with, in NTV's case, full access to channel 4, previously used for educational broadcasting, and in January 1998, privileged access to state-owned transmission facilities.[9] Gusinsky, Berezovsky, Luzhkov and Lisovsky won the continuation of a political environment broadly sympathetic to their long-term aims.

Some Russian observers have suggested, on this and other evidence, that political influence rather than economic gain was the prime motive for the buying up of Russian television by the new business elite (Vartanova 1997), and there is no doubt that media ownership has been a key factor in understanding the twists and turns of late 1990s Russian politics. When Yeltsin sacked one team of ministers and replaced them with another in the economic crisis of August–September 1998, many observers saw the hand of Boris Berezovsky stirring the pot. That said, political influence is rarely an end in itself for media entrepreneurs, in Russia or anywhere else, so much as a means to the achievement of a pro-business economic environment. Just as global media barons such as Conrad Black, Rupert Murdoch, and Axel Springer hope that their newspapers influence the political climate in the countries where they operate, in ways favorable to their media businesses as a whole, so TV has been identified as the key medium of influence by Russian capital, as well as a source of profit in the medium to long term. Through their ownership and control of television, and the influence this brings in dealings with the government, Berezovsky, Gusinsky and the others seek primarily to maintain and develop not just their media assets, but the pro-business, free-market culture of post-Soviet Russia as a whole. That their media interests are already, or will eventually become immensely profitable in a rapidly developing and potentially very lucrative consumer market is of course for them a further motivation for involvement.

In this respect, the Russian experience of broadcast privatization is consistent with the pattern of rational business behavior one observes in other free-market economies. Media ownership translates economic power into political and cultural power, which are key resources in the maintenance of economic power, and so on. Where Russia deviates from the situation in, say, Italy (where Silvio Berlusconi's ownership of print and broadcast media contributed substantially to the success of his *Forza Italia* movement) is in the lack of any real constraints on the abuse of media power, of the type built into most liberal capitalist systems, and the overt political interventionism of nearly all media owners. Add to that the lack of detail on the ownership and control of Russian media, and one can readily sympathize with the view that the takeover of Russian TV by the "clans" seriously threatens the democratic transition. (It could on the other hand be the case that Russia is becoming the world's first true *media-ocracy*, a form of capitalism in which politicians are dependent on—and sometimes indistinguishable from—economic power vested in the media and culture industries, and in which the traditional barriers separating political and cultural power dissolve. In this respect Russia, for all its robber-baron primitivism, may turn out to be a pioneer of the media-driven capitalism of the twenty-first century, in which the controllers of information in all its commodity-forms—journalism, entertainment, computer software, data services—are established as the key subsector of the capitalist owning class as a whole.)

As this chapter went to press, Russia's media–industrial complex was already positioning itself, and the media which it controls, for the first post-Yeltsin presidential election, scheduled for 2000. Moscow mayor and likely presidential candidate Yuri Luzhkov had secured control of substantial TV and press interests. Boris Berezovsky was believed to be playing the role of king-maker with respect to Alexander Lebed, and Vladimir Gusinsky had indicated his support for Victor Chernomyrdin. These allegiances were all conditional, of course, and subject to developments over which no media baron had control (such as the 1998 crash or the terror bombing campaign of September 1999), but the fact that they were known about by all, and accepted as part of the "democratic" process in Russia, reveal the uniquely close relationship between media power and politics in the country.

The public sector and public service

What, then, of the remaining state sector? After 1991, as we have seen, the bloated public sector broadcasting apparatus inherited from the Soviet period entered a period of near-terminal crisis, deprived of the revenue required to maintain services, over-manned and inefficiently run, forced to enter ill–considered and frequently corrupt deals with the private sector.[10] The post-Soviet Russian state was unable to maintain the old GOSTELRADIO system even if it had wanted to, and thus permitted its gradual transference to the private sector. But official support continued to be expressed for some public sector broadcasting to be retained, if only for the political control which some leaders assumed comes with such a system. Given this approach, and in the context of an expanded private sector of the type described above, the remaining public sector channel[11]—RTR, run by the All-Russia State Television and Radio Company (VGTRK)—might have expected greater financial support from the government after 1991. In the event, it entered a lengthy period during which it regularly received only 30 percent or so of its agreed annual state subsidy, and became dependent on advertising and sponsorship. In the face of this slow starvation (and *de facto* privatization) RTR, and its head Oleg Poptsov in particular, ran a principled campaign to retain public sector status, on the grounds that Russia needed at least one publicly owned TV channel, free of advertising if possible, and dedicated to the pursuit of public service goals in programming.[12]

The Russian government long paid lip service to this argument, but conspicuously failed to endorse it with resources, partly because of the emptiness of the public purse, but also, it seems clear, because the president's understanding of public service was rather different from Poptsov's. RTR took its commitment to public service values seriously, and began the election year of 1996 with a reputation as a critic of the government's policies in several key areas, including the management of the economy and the conduct of the military intervention in Chechnya. In dealing with this dissent the president revealed his, and the political system's, lingering preference for authoritarian media control. Poptsov, like any good journalist in a genuinely democratic political culture, understood the nature of the difference between political rhetoric and reality, and saw it as part of RTR's public service role to probe and expose this gap. He believed that "there is no such thing as objectivity. Objectivity is a sum total of subjectivities."[13] He believed, in other words, in pluralism, to which the president was also on record as subscribing. Yeltsin and his colleagues did not agree with Poptsov's definition of pluralism, however, accusing him and the journalists at RTR of being excessively doom-laden about Russia in general, and overly critical of the government in particular, in contrast to ORT, which had deservedly acquired a reputation as "the president's channel." As noted above, not just ORT and Berezovsky but the corporate clans as a group showed their willingness to lend themselves and their media to Boris Yeltsin's political program, and to his 1996 reelection campaign in particular. Why, Yeltsin appears to have thought, should his government pay for a public sector broadcaster to undermine that support?

In February 1996, as it became clear that Poptsov would not condone a wholly pro-Yeltsin approach by RTR staff in the run-up to the election, he was dismissed. As the newspaper *Moskovsky Komsomolets* put it in a disappointed commentary: "for all its talk of freedom of speech the Kremlin has now decided that the best method of dealing with journalists is suppression rather than persuasion, a time-honoured tactic echoing Communist strategy".[14] Yeltsin's chosen successor to Poptsov, Eduard Sagalayev, though a respected journalist and broadcast manager with impeccable reformist credentials, immediately announced that under his stewardship RTR would downplay the negative in its coverage of Russian society and politics, and accentuate the positive. Thus, RTR was made safe for Yeltsin's presidential reelection bid, joining an otherwise entirely pro-Yeltsin broadcast media.

The pattern of political interference in public sector broadcasting continued after the election, when Sagalayev, his job of supporting Yeltsin done, was removed. In the late spring of 1998, as another presidential election loomed into view, Yeltsin moved to consolidate his government's control over the state broadcaster, decreeing that VGTRK be turned into a "unified production and technological complex," centralizing control of the RTR and Kultura television channels, Radio Rossiya, and 113 regional TV and radio services. The strengthened VGTRK would also take over control of the state's monopoly of broadcast transmission facilities. A generous reading of these changes welcomed the enhanced support which they indicated for some form of public service broadcasting in Russia. Cynics on the other hand (and there were few in Russia by mid-1998 who were not cynical) saw the restructuring of VGTRK as an attempt to increase political control over the state-owned media, in anticipation of a presidential election which, whenever it took place, would be much more evenly contested than that of 1996.

Beyond that election, and depending to some extent on who wins it, the future of public sector, *public service* (the two are not the same thing, of course) broadcasting in Russia depends on the successful development of the economy as a whole, and improvements in revenue-raising systems, whether in the form of taxation, subsidy, or advertising. It will depend too on the extent to which VGTRK, with its Soviet-era legacy of bureaucracy and inefficiency, can reform its management structure and compete with a dynamic and innovative private sector. The appointment of Eduard Sagalayev to replace Oleg Poptsov as director in February 1996 began a period of management and financial reform designed to ensure, as Sagalayev put it, that RTR remained "the main pillar of state informational and cultural policy".[15] But some of his more radical proposals, and his management style, were reportedly too much for RTR employees. His forced resignation in February 1997, amid accusations (never proved) of corruption, was a sign of VGTRK's inherent conservatism as an organization. His successor, Nikolai Svanidze, experienced a similar fate in February 1998 when he and his colleagues were accused by the official auditor of "very serious mismanagement." As I noted earlier, it is difficult to assess the extent to which such charges are justified when they appear in the public domain, or whether they are political maneuvers designed to ease the removal of executives perceived as too independent by the authorities. Whatever the explanation for Sagalayev's failure at VGTRK, it is beyond dispute that those responsible for managing Russia's shrunken public sector broadcasting must undertake radical reform of their structures, and their organizational culture, if they are to survive in the new broadcast media environment of the twenty-first century.

Political culture and the Russian media

Yeltsin's restructuring of VGTRK, like his earlier removal of Poptsov, depressed many observers of the Russian media, but ought to be placed in proper perspective. All governments exert political pressure on the public sector broadcaster (where one exists), and play a key role (even if it is exercized behind the scenes) in the hiring and firing of senior management. In 1996, amidst the high political tension and excitement of preelection Russia, with a credible communist challenger in the race, directing threats at TV, the pressure placed on RTR was, if hardly welcome, at least understandable. Poptsov's dismissal certainly did not signify a return to CPSU methods of authoritarian control, and was widely criticized elsewhere in the Russian media. But Yeltsin's evident irritation at media criticism of his regime *was* evidence of the lingering authoritarianism and lack of democratic maturity which continue to characterize politician–media relationships in Russia. A political system which is unable to cope with justified (or indeed unjustified) media criticism of its governors is not yet fully democratic, and Russian broadcasters, particularly those in the remaining public sector, must continue to defend their existing media freedoms in the face of what Russian observers call, more than a decade after *perestroika*, "bolshevik psychology."

As for the private broadcasters who supported Yeltsin so unabashedly in the 1996 presidential campaign, they did so *voluntarily*, perceiving that the threat to their freedom (and their profits) posed by the communists justified their failure to provide objective coverage of the latter's platform. While understanding their motivation, however (and when we recall some of the abusive and threatening, often racist anti-media rhetoric of the communist–nationalist parties throughout the 1990s, who can blame the TV bosses for adopting a pro-reformist bias?), it should lead Russian media workers to examine their role in the fledgling democratic process. Journalistic objectivity has not yet emerged as the dominant professional ethic in Russia, which it will have to do if television is to contribute in the long run to the consolidation of liberal democratic norms in post-Soviet society. There is still relatively little accumulated experience of objective or independent journalism in Russia. The audience is used to, and still expects, journalists to be politically committed propagandists. The media in Russia continue to be associated with the manipulation of public opinion, rather than its formation, and with private interests, rather than public service.

These are problems of what I have referred to elsewhere as political culture (McNair 1996), rather than censorship;[16] of underdeveloped professionalism rather than dictatorial law. The existing media law is not especially illiberal (despite the best efforts of the state Duma), and guarantees editorial independence (state organizations may make representations about the content of programs, but editorial staff have the right to refuse them, under the terms of the Russian media law passed in November 1995), but it cannot prevent media personnel of a certain generation, schooled in the traditions of bolshevik press theory, from taking up inappropriately partisan, "committed" positions.

Recognizing this deficit in their professional culture, some Russian journalists have called for a code of ethical practice which will be applicable to all media organizations, and prevent (or at least stigmatize as unprofessional) a repeat of the wholesale pro-Yeltsin bias of the 1996 campaign. The assistance of foreign media organizations, aid agencies such as the British Know How Fund and the United States Information Agency, and NGOs like Internews has been welcomed. These agencies have provided training and, through projects such as Open Skies and the Marshall Plan of the Mind, supplied "public service" broadcasting of a type which the market is at present unable or unwilling to provide. External assistance is of marginal value, of course, and always risks attracting charges of "cultural imperialism" from the national-patriots. In the end, Russian professionals know that they must find their own paths to pluralistic, pro-democratic media practices; paths which reflect Russian history and conditions. If they can achieve this (and the growing influence of a new generation of young, innovative, and confident professionals gives some grounds for optimism in this respect) then the more pessimistic prognoses of Russian journalism's future may be proven wrong.

Postscript: the crash of 1998

The collapse of Russian stock markets and currency values in August–September 1998 was reported at the time as a pre-apocalyptic event, signalling not just the defeat of Russia's reform process, but the crisis of global capitalism itself (following as it did on the economic problems of Southeast Asia). This reaction, like those to previous crises, proved to be an exaggeration, and life carried on in Russia, as it had for the preceding decade, with the poor and the honest paying the price of reform, while the rich and the acquisitive reaped its benefits. The crash of 1998 did, however, reinforce many of the trends discussed in this chapter, forcing further streamlining of the media sector, and the closure of organizations which lacked the reserves to survive a period of low (or no) income. Even big companies with deep pockets like Premier SV were unable to remain solvent (in Premier's case, being taken over by ORT in November 1998). For some Russian media experts, however, such as Sergei Lisovsky, Premier's chairman, speaking before his own company's takeover, the crash could benefit the Russian economy if it reduced dependence on foreign imports. Television, he stated in an October 1998 interview, "will get healthier, and will seek out reserves. I know many channels where there is a lot of dead weight. The crisis will only make television stronger."[17] In the impoverished regions, however, small TV and radio companies faced a much greater threat, as their ability to attract advertising revenue, already weak, was further reduced (impoverished consumers cannot be sold to companies, even if the companies can afford to advertise to them).[18] As one media executive put it in October 1998, "their only chance is to forget about creative ambitions and concentrate on survival."[19] On the other hand, those who did survive would "become stronger" as the domestic economy, benefiting from a low ruble, was reinvigorated.

No-one, inside or outside of Russia, can predict with certainty what will happen to the country in the coming years, or what role the media will play in events. One can only hope that those principled professionals—journalists, producers, editors, managers—who have struggled not just for media freedom, but for a freedom worth having, will not have their ambitions thwarted by the force of unbridled commercialism on the one hand, or a return to authoritarianism on the other. In Russia, as the 1998 assassination of Galina Starovoitova showed, people die for their principles. Her murder was preceded by those of many media professionals, whose work puts them on the frontline of both economic and political struggle, pitted against cold and ruthless enemies. And yet, I hope to have shown here, their struggles have produced achievements to be proud of in the media sphere. The unsustainably large, centrally controlled ideological apparatus of the Soviet state has been replaced by a slimmer, more efficient media market which, despite its obvious failings, contains more editorial diversity, and is more responsive to popular tastes and demands, than what went before. In place of CPSU monopoly there is pluralism, in which even the communists are free to argue their case alongside the other parties. There is in Russia today a real *public sphere* through which ordinary people can learn about and participate in political debate. The current generation of Russian politicians may be largely incompetent and hugely corrupt, but their activities are frequently exposed to critical scrutiny in the public domain, where citizens can make their judgments. If they chose to vote for Boris Yeltsin in 1996, knowing what they did about him (and they, like the rest of the world, knew a lot that was unflattering), that is their democratic right, as it will be their right to vote for whomsoever they please in 2000. Despite the criticisms one may make of the Russian media, then, their continuing existence as *free media* (with all the limitations on that word which I have outlined) is a crucial support for democracy in the country, and a sign that things are still moving in the right direction.

Notes

1 In February 1998 this phrase was used by government officials to attack the state broadcasting organization VGTRK.
2 For a discussion of media development in post-reform Poland and Hungary (as well as the USSR and Russia), see Downing 1996. For more recent work on the media in east Central Europe, see Sparks and Reading 1998.
3 As recently as 1999, the Chinese government was still engaged in what one newspaper called "a titanic struggle to keep subversive material from seeping through the porous frontiers of cyberspace," prosecuting Internet service providers and setting up task forces to deal with the threat of information contamination by new technologies (J. Kynge, "'Subversive' on trial in China bid to stop news slipping through the Net," *Financial Times*, December 5/6, 1998).
4 As of March 1997, once multi-million sellers like *Argumenty i Fakti*, *Komsomolskaya Pravda* and *Trud* were achieving circulations of 3.4, 1.5 and 1.4 million respectively.
5 In January 1998 the State Duma approved on second reading a bill intended to restrict the circulation of "erotic materials" in Russia (reported in the *Moscow Times*, January 17, 1998).
6 Prominent conservatives, both on record as strong advocates of media censorship.
7 Most notably Vladislav Listyev and Oleg Slabynko. Although the perpetrators were never brought to justice, few Russian observers doubted that their murders were the consequence of their anti-corruption efforts in broadcasting.

8 Kultura was established in August 1997 in an attempt to strengthen public service broadcasting. The channel—the aim of which, as Yeltsin put it, was "to make culture enjoyable, accessible and understandable for millions and millions of television viewers"(from a speech delivered on August 29, 1997)—would broadcast programs of high educational and informational quality, albeit on a shoe-string. As of 1998, Kultura was attracting praise from the critics, who welcomed its novel use of "underemployed academics" and other intellectuals to make interesting and innovative programs.

9 In January 1998 NTV was officially recognized as an "all-Russian" broadcaster, alongside RTR and ORT, and given access to transmission facilities for the price of $13 million annually. Without all-Russian status, the cost would have been twice that figure, seriously threatening NTV's profitability and survival.

10 For example, RTR's budget shortfall after 1991 forced the channel to seek advertising revenue, effectively making its designation as a state sector company meaningless.

11 The Kultura channel joined RTR as a VGTRK broadcaster in 1997.

12 By "public service," in this context, was meant that combination of information, education and entertainment exemplified by the output of the BBC in Britain, to which VGTRK managers looked for their model in the immediate aftermath of the 1991 coup.

13 From comments made at a press conference in Moscow on February 16, 1996, and reported in the *Post-Soviet Media Law & Policy Newsletter*, 26, February 26, 1996.

14 Reported in the *Post-Soviet Media Law & Policy Newsletter*, 26, February 26, 1996.

15 From interviews and statements given to several media shortly after his appointment.

16 Frances F. Foster describes in detail the functioning of post-Soviet institutions set up to encourage a "developed legal culture" in the sphere of media and information (1997).

17 From comments made on the program *Chetvertaya Vlast* (Fourth Estate), October 11, 1998.

18 For a discussion of the difficulties and challenges facing post-Soviet regional media organizations, see Davis *et al.* 1997.

19 From an interview with Roman Petrenko, director general of the STS regional television network, published in *Teleskop*, 130, October 7, 1998.

References

Davis, H., Hammond, P. and Nizamova, L. (1997) "Changing identities and practices in post-Soviet journalism," *European Journal of Communication*, 13(1): 77–97.

Downing, J. (1996) *Internationalizing Media Theory*, London: Sage.

Foster, F. (1997) "Parental law, harmful speech, and the development of legal culture: Russian judicial chamber discourse and narrative," *Washington and Lee Law Review*, 54(3): 923–92.

Franklin, B. (1997) *Newszak and News Media*, London: Arnold.

Habermas, J. (1989) *The Structural Transformation of the Public Sphere*, Cambridge: Polity.

McNair, B. (1988) *Images of the Enemy*, London: Routledge.

McNair, B. (1989) "Glasnost and restructuring in the Soviet media," *Media, Culture and Society*, 11: pp. 327–49

McNair, B. (1991) *Glasnost, Perestroika and the Soviet Media*, London: Routledge.

McNair, B. (1992) "Television in a post-Soviet union," *Screen*, 33(3) (Autumn): 300–20.

McNair, B. (1996) "Television in post-Soviet Russia: from monolith to mafia," *Media, Culture and Society*, 18: 489–99.

Price, M. (1995) *Television, the Public Sphere and National Identity*, Oxford: Clarendon.

Sparks, C. with Reading, A. (1998) *Communism, Capitalism and the Media*, London: Sage.

Vartanova, E. (1997) "The Russian financial elites as media moguls," *Post-Soviet Media Law and Policy Newsletter*, 35: 18–23.

Zassoursky, Y. (1997) "Media and politics in transition: three models," *Post-Soviet Media Law and Policy Newsletter*, 35: 11–15.

Part 2
Authoritarian neo-liberal societies

7 Media, political power, and democratization in Mexico

Daniel C. Hallin

The Mexican political system has to be counted as one of the most effective systems of power of the twentieth century. With the fall of the Communist Party of the Soviet Union, Mexico's Partido Revolucionario Institutional (PRI) became the longest-ruling party in the world. Organized in 1929, it held an effective monopoly on political power until the late 1980s, and in 1999 still held the lion's share, including the powerful presidency. In recent years, however, a significant move toward a pluralist political system has taken place: opposition parties began winning state governorships and important mayoral elections in the late 1980s, and in 1997 the PRI lost its majority in the Chamber of Deputies. The PRI itself is increasingly subject to internal conflicts and is moving toward internal democracy. In the year 2000 it will for the first time select a presidential candidate through some sort of primary election, rather than by the designation of the outgoing president.

Mexico's media system is in many ways equally unique. Like the rest of Latin America, and like most of Latin Europe, the newspaper industry is poorly developed, at least in terms of mass readership. The television industry is another matter. Mexico introduced television in 1950, the sixth country in the world to do so. By the 1970s, its dominant television company, Televisa, had emerged as one of the most important transnational media conglomerates, exporting its signature "*telenovelas*" first to the rest of Latin America and then around the world. It also controls the most important Spanish-language television network in the United States. Within Mexico, Televisa's dominance was not unlike that of the PRI; with three and eventually four networks, it claimed the attention of 90 percent of Mexico's vast television audience. It is probably correct to say that there is no country comparable in size to Mexico in which a single private company so dominates the airwaves.

During the many years of PRI hegemony, the media were, for the most part, fully integrated into the structure of power. Today, with that structure in crisis, the media system has entered a period of significant and probably irreversible change. This chapter will explore the relationship between the Mexican media and the state and their role in the current process of democratization. It will, in particular, consider the adequacy of two dominant perspectives in media theory—liberalism, and the critical political economy perspective—to the understanding of the media, political power, and democratization in Mexico.

This focus requires setting aside several other issues, which are worth underlining before we move on. I will focus, for one thing, on the political realm in the narrow sense of the term. The media of course play a role in systems of power at many other levels. Mexican *telenovelas*, for example, clearly play a role in the reproduction and evolution of the traditional patriarchal system of gender relations, as well as in the development of racial ideology. These and other elements of social power may be affected in some ways by the current process of political democratization, but they also clearly have their own logic.

I will also be setting aside issues related to media imperialism, dependency, and nationalism. Mexico's development has of course been deeply affected by the influence both of its powerful neighbor to the north and of the global economy more generally. It accepted the North American model of a commercial media system, and its media have always been to a large extent vehicles for advertising of North American products; Mexican newspapers were selectively subsidized by the US government during the Second World War, and the Mexican film industry—like that in most countries—has been largely marginalized by competition from Hollywood. At the same time, the Mexican media have been far from appendages of North American media industries (Sinclair 1986, 1990). The Mexican radio industry, to take one example, played a decisive role in the development of distinctively Mexican forms of popular music (Hayes 1993, 1996). Most Mexican scholarship (e.g. Fernández 1982) points to the influence of outside forces, but places the emphasis on power relations within Mexico.

"The perfect dictatorship"

The political history of Latin America is generally characterized by an alternation between dictatorship and democracy. Mexico, on the other hand, has had an essentially stable system since the revolution (1910–17) was "institutionalized," a process which was complete by about 1929. That system stood somewhere between democracy and dictatorship. As Néstor García Canclini (1988) suggests, Mexican political elites were probably alone in Latin America in achieving hegemony in the Gramscian sense. The system was widely accepted as legitimate, and virtually all sectors of society were in some way integrated and given a stake in its persistence. There was no need for the kind of widespread repression practiced by the dictatorships that ruled many other Latin American countries through the 1970s.

Yet the "one-party dominant" regime the PRI created was far from being a real democracy (Cornelius 1996). Subordinate groups had little independent voice, and when softer means of control failed to keep political opposition within bounds, electoral fraud and coercion always stood in reserve. It was, as Peruvian novelist and politician Mario Vargas Llosa put it, "the perfect dictatorship," monopolizing power with great effectiveness but without open authoritarianism.

At the heart of this system is a set of corporatist organizations which tie various segments—workers, farmers, small businessmen, residents of urban neighborhoods—to the ruling party. These organizations deliver benefits to specific sectors of society, channel the political demands of those groups through the ruling party, and mobilize their support in elections in times of political conflict. They involve "clientelist" relationships (Fox 1994, Roniger 1990) in which material benefits and opportunities for participation and mobility are provided by elites in return for political loyalty and subordination.

The PRI is diverse ideologically, and has managed to incorporate a wide range of political tendencies under its umbrella. Often Mexican political history is recounted in terms of a series of shifts of political direction, usually coinciding with the transition from one president to the next, by which the PRI has maintained the loyalty of its various political currents. This political maneuverability in part explains how the PRI has succeeded in identifying itself with the populist and nationalist symbols of the Mexican revolution, even as it has drawn close to big business, both national and international.

The Mexican media as "ideological state apparatus"

The mass media have been an important part of this system of political power. Journalism is traditionally *oficialista*—passive and self-censored, with most political coverage based on official press releases, and with many areas of controversy being off limits. Ilya Adler (1993b), in a study of ten Mexico City dailies in 1984 found 123 stories favorable to the unnamed ministry in which he conducted his study, and 14 unfavorable. The sample also contained 211 stories favorable to the president of the Republic, and not one unfavorable: the Mexican president, elected for a single six-year term, exercizes vast power and has been treated as beyond public criticism. Adler argues, moreover, that when critical stories did appear, most could be explained either by conflicts among factions of the ruling party, or by a process of negotiation between newspapers and the political patrons they served. The press in Mexico has very limited circulation and, as in other regions without a mass circulation press—Southern Europe, for example—serves primarily as a means of communication among political elites and activists. The difference between Mexico and, say, Italy, is of course that in Mexico these elites have all belonged to the single, dominant party.

As far as the mass public is concerned, television is overwhelmingly the most important medium of political communication. Polls typically show about 50–75 percent of the Mexican public listing television as their principal source of political information, while 10–15 percent list newspapers, a similar percent radio, and the rest either multiple sources or none (e.g. de la Peña and Toledo 1992a, 1992b). And television is the least open of Mexico's media (Fernández 1982, González Molina 1987, 1990, Miller and Darling 1997, Trejo 1985, 1988). Televisa's news division, which until recently was the only significant producer of television news, has served essentially as an organ of publicity for the state and the PRI—as an "ideological state apparatus," to borrow the old Althusserian phrase.

The political character of Televisa's news has been particularly obvious during election campaigns. In 1988, for example, the ruling party faced its toughest electoral challenge in decades. Cuautémoc Cárdenas Solorzano, son of Mexico's most popular president, Lázaro Cárdenas, broke away from the ruling party, along with a faction known as the Democratic Current, and joined with various small leftist parties to run for president. The PRI was sufficiently worried about the challenge that it resorted to substantial electoral fraud to ensure victory. Televisa that year devoted more than 80 percent of its election coverage to the ruling party, 2 percent to Cárdenas's FDN, and 3 percent to the other principal opposition party, the conservative PAN (Adler 1993a, Arredondo, Fregoso and Trejo 1991).

In the next presidential election, in 1994, for reasons we will explore presently, Televisa gave substantially more coverage to the opposition. Still, its stories on the ruling party's campaign were full of color and enthusiasm, while those on the opposition were at best colorless (Aguayo and Acosta 1997, Hallin 1997, Trejo 1994a, 1994b). In part this was because the ruling party had far more money and organizational know-how to produce campaign events. But Televisa's manipulation of information clearly contributed. One example is particularly obvious. Shortly before the election the Cárdenas campaign held a vast rally at the National Autonomous University in Mexico City, which served to kick off the final phase of its campaign. Televisa's report was edited to show nothing but tight shots of Cárdenas at the microphone, with the hundreds of thousands of cheering supporters entirely invisible to the television audience.

Beyond elections, and beyond the question of access to television on the part of opposition parties, the authoritarian political culture of Mexico has been deeply embedded in Televisa's conventions of news presentation (Hallin 1997). Officials, and particularly the president, are treated with extreme deference, with reporters summarizing their words and the anchor praising their wisdom in frequent unlabelled commentaries. Negative news—about unemployment, corruption, disasters—was kept to a minimum. Ordinary citizens, meanwhile, traditionally appeared in the news in subservient roles, most of the time to receive clientelist benefits from political patrons. One of the most common visual images in Televisa's news was of the appreciative poor waiting to receive benefits from the president.

Media theory and the case of Mexico: liberalism

How well do the standard theoretical approaches in media studies apply to Mexico? Let's begin with the liberal, or what might be called for the Latin American case the IAPA perspective. The Inter-American Press Association, a Miami-based organization of publishers and editors from around the Americas, has played a particularly important role in promoting the liberal ideal of press freedom in the continent. The IAPA is committed to a privately owned commercial mass media, and sees the problems of Latin American journalism as rooted in state intervention. For many years, most North American scholarship on Latin American media reflected this point of view. Alisky (1981), for example, divided the countries in the region into three categories based on the degree and type of government control of the media: nations with censorship, those with media freedom, and, in between, nations with media guidance. For Alisky, Mexico belonged to the "media guidance" category.

There is obviously a good deal of truth in this point of view. Mexico, like other parts of Latin America, is characterized by a strong, relatively autonomous state and a much more weakly developed private sector and civil society. Indeed, the autonomy of the state is particularly strong in Mexico in many ways; because of the legacy of the Mexican revolution, for example, there is less direct participation by business in the ruling party than in many Latin American countries (Camp 1989). The media are deferential to the state, and in many ways are highly dependent on it. The newspaper industry, in particular, is integrated into the clientelist system much as other sectors of society are, receiving benefits from the state in return for political loyalty.

In 1990 Mexico city had twenty-five newspapers. One study estimated their combined circulation at 731,000 (Riva Palacio 1997; Lawson 1999 gives a lower estimate). How can so many newspapers survive with so few readers? To a large extent, they survive by selling advertising to government agencies and government-owned enterprises, including *gacetillas*, paid articles which look like news content and go for higher rates than ordinary advertising. PIPSA, the state-owned newsprint supplier (now privatized), provided Mexican newspapers with newsprint at bargain rates and had a monopoly on the import of that key commodity. Individual journalists, meanwhile, have typically been poorly paid, but able to supplement their incomes through payments from politicians and bureaucrats whose activities they cover—and whose protégés they become.

The state has also at times owned stock in newspaper companies and been involved in arranging financing for newspaper sales. And it has many means of pressure at its disposal when newspapers get out of line. In the 1970s, for example, when the important Mexico City newspaper *Excélsior* began moving toward a more independent, socially critical form of journalism and angered President Echeverría, the latter engineered a takeover of the cooperative which owned the paper, using organizations of urban slum-dwellers, who occupied land owned by *Excélsior*, and client labor organizations which packed a meeting of the cooperative's board. Violence has also been used against troublesome journalists, though more by local political bosses than by the central government.

Yet the liberal perspective is hardly adequate by itself to capture the complexity of media power in Mexico. One key weakness of the liberal perspective is that it fails to consider media owners as part of a system of power. As in the rest of Latin America, Mexico's media are overwhelmingly commercial and privately owned. One Mexico City newspaper, *El Nacional*, was government owned (it has since been closed) and the government has run various broadcast properties over the years. But the state sector has always been a small part of Mexico's media.

Even for the relatively dependent newspaper industry, it is probably too simple to treat the state as the only important actor. Mexican newspapers are typically owned by wealthy individuals, many with political connections, and reflect the views of those individuals (Camp 1989). In Mexican media scholarship, the most common approach to studying the media and political power is what might be called instrumentalist political economy, which involves "clarifying *who are* the groups and individuals who have established and developed the press, as well as their ties with other groups, especially in business or politics" (Fregoso Peralta and Sánchez Ruiz 1993: 23 [emphasis in original]; Fernández 1982, Valero, n.d.). From this point of view, the officialist character of the Mexican press results not simply from government pressure, but from collusion between economic and political elites based on social ties and shared interests.

The limitations of the liberal perspective become particularly obvious when we turn from newspapers to television—by far the most important medium. The state does, of course, have means of pressure that it could use against Televisa, and Televisa certainly has an incentive to maintain good relations with the state. Broadcasting is a regulated industry. In principle the state could revoke Televisa's broadcast licenses, or encourage the development of competitors, or enforce regulations on advertising or other media content that would hurt Televisa's business. But Televisa is hardly in the position of a newspaper with 10,000 readers and a dozen competitors. It is a highly successful business which dominates its principal market. Emilio Azcárraga, Jr. who owned the company until his death in 1997, was one of the handful of world-class Mexican capitalists who stand outside the clientelist organizations of the PRI, and can deal with the government as independent actors. Mejía Barquera (1989: 14) says of broadcasting, generally:

> The owners of radio and television have accumulated considerable political strength which permits them to maintain ... an attitude which varies from unrestricted

support for government actions which accord with their business interests to cen-
sure and denunciation of actions which affect their business or class interests ...
the government maintains a cautious attitude ... not only because within the
hegemonic faction of the government there exists a clear identification with business interests, but also because this sector of the political bureaucracy prefers to
govern with the support of private radio and television and not come into conflict
with the business group which controls them.

For a while, during the relatively leftist Echeverría administration of the 1970s,
there was widespread discussion in Mexico about whether commercial television served
the needs of a developing country, and calls for a stronger role by the state in enforc-
ing public service obligations on broadcasters. Little came of this, however. On many
occasions Mexico's media policy seems driven by Televisa's needs; this, for example,
is how Mexican scholars have interpreted the launching of the Morelos satellite in the
1980s (Esteinou 1988, Fernández 1982). In general, the state has played a more passive role in broadcast regulation in Mexico than in the United States, Europe or Asia.

Azcárraga, to be sure, was a loyalist of the PRI, something he declared openly on a
number of occasions—though, as Mejía Barquera suggests, he also broke with the
leadership of the PRI over certain issues, including the nationalization of the banks in
the 1980s, and the civil war in Central America in the same decade, on which Televisa
took an anti-communist position that conflicted with Mexican policy. Two other families
which were among the principal investors, the O'Farrill and Alemán families, also had
close ties to the PRI. In the 1940s it was President Miguel Alemán who rejected the
recommendation of an advisory commission that television be set up according to a
public service model, approved the introduction of commercial television, and when
he left office invested in one of the networks that eventually became part of Televisa.
But Televisa's relationship to the Mexican state is not comprehensible in terms of state
censorship or "guidance." It reflects interpenetration of political and economic elites
and convergence of interests between them. And it reflects a very great concentration
of relatively independent power in private hands.

Another limitation of the liberal perspective is that it dismisses the possibility that
the state might play a positive role in the democratization of the media. As we have
seen, Televisa's election coverage became substantially more open between the 1988
and 1994 elections, moving from a 25 to 1 ratio between coverage of the PRI and
coverage of the main opposition parties to a 1.5 to 1 ratio. The story of that change is
rooted in the aftermath of the 1988 election. The vote count was interrupted by a
mysterious "crash" of the electoral computer system. The opposition charged fraud,
and the phrase used to announce the "crash" of the computer system, "*el sistema se
cayó*," came to symbolize the collapse of the legitimacy of the political system itself.

Concerned to avoid further dangerous erosion of that legitimacy in subsequent elections, the government opened discussions with opposition parties on electoral reform.
One of the most important issues was access to the media. Free time for party broadcasts, provided by commercial broadcasters to the state and distributed among political
parties by the Instituto Federal Electoral (IFE), was expanded (Trejo 1997). The government also pressed the broadcasting industry to accept guidelines for news coverage of
the campaign. The IFE, which had itself been reorganized to reduce government control
and to operate more like an independent public agency, was given the task of monitoring
compliance, and produces detailed content analyses of broadcast coverage of each elec-

tion (Instituto Federal Electoral 1997). As we shall see, other factors also pushed Televisa in the direction of greater political openness. But state pressure played an early and important role. Azcárraga was aligned with the hard-line faction of the PRI which resisted democratization: the commercial broadcaster, far from leading the charge to pluralism, had to be dragged kicking and screaming by the state.[1] Here, Mexico provides a good illustration of Schudson's (1994) argument that the state and the democratic public sphere are by no means entirely separate or antagonistic.

Critical political economy

The critical political economy perspective emerged in the 1970s as a critique of then-dominant liberal media theory. Liberalism saw the development of market-based mass media industries as conducive to democracy: the development of media markets, according to the liberal view, freed the media from dependence on the state and on political parties, allowing them to play an independent role as a "watchdog" of the government and forum for debate. The critical political economy perspective tends to portray the market and political democracy as essentially antagonistic. The development of media markets, from this perspective, concentrates control of the media in the hands of business (both media owners and advertisers), limiting the range of points of view represented. It also, in some variants of the argument, tends to drive political content out of the media, replacing it with entertainment-oriented content that makes money for media corporations but does not contribute to the development of political democracy (Curran and Seaton 1997, Curran, Douglas and Whannel 1980, Hallin 1994).

In many ways, the critical political economy perspective applies well to the Mexican case. We have already seen that Mexican researchers tend to employ a variant of this perspective, which sees the media as instruments of private owners with political ties. In the case of television, the critical political economy perspective might be said to apply even more fully to Mexico than to the developed capitalist societies to which it originally referred, since many forces which moderate the effects of private ownership and of market logic are absent, including limits on media concentration, a tradition of public service broadcasting, regulatory agencies answering to a pluralistic political system, and journalistic professionalism (Televisa's journalists are very strictly servants of the company, without a conflicting sense of loyalty to the profession or the public [González Molina 1987, 1990]). Televisa's entertainment programming follows a strictly commercial logic, while its news broadcasts serve as a mouthpiece for the company's political views, as well as a promotional vehicle for its other corporate interests.

In other ways, however, the critical political economy perspective, as it has been developed primarily in Britain and in the US, fails to account for the complexity of the Mexican case. Certainly, for one thing, the economic dependence of the newspaper industry on the state is an important difference. In order to understand the process of democratization, moreover, a more nuanced view of the relation between market and political democracy is required.

Here it will be useful to step back and take an overview of the shift in the Mexican media toward greater openness and pluralism. The beginning of that shift can be dated to the late 1960s, when certain Mexican media, particularly the then very prestigious newspaper *Excélsior*, began to move toward a bolder, more sophisticated form of journalism, with greater focus on social problems. Why this shift began is something little explored in media research. Mexicans often say that society—presumably meaning the urban middle class, which reads newspapers—became more sophisticated and demanding. The change may be related to economic growth, which was robust in the 1960s, and to increases in education. At any rate, the change in journalism accelerated following the student rebellion and its brutal repression in the streets of Mexico City in 1968. (It was also in this period that Televisa organized its Directorate of News, breaking with an old practice of having sponsors produce news programs, and giving the corporation a political voice of its own.)

In 1976, as we have learned, the government engineered the ousting of *Excélsior's* editor, Julio Scherer García, who was joined in exile from the paper by many more of its journalists. The same year Scherer and other members of the old *Excélsior* staff founded the weekly magazine *Proceso*, which became the first of a series of new publications which would establish an independent media sector alongside the traditional officialist one. In 1982, the government cut *Proceso* off from government advertising, but the magazine managed to stay afloat with commercial advertising. Former *Excélsior* journalists also formed the newspapers *unomásuno* and *La Jornada*, and the latter became the principal paper of the Mexican left.[2] *El Financiero* was founded in 1981, incorporating some former *Excélsior* staff members, and also became part of the growing independent press.

Finally, in the 1990s, two additional independent newspapers were formed, *Siglo 21*, later replaced by *Público*, in Guadalajara, and *Reforma*, in Mexico City. *Reforma* was established by Alejandro Junco de la Vega, publisher of the Monterrey newspaper *El Norte* (Alves 1997). Published since 1972, *El Norte* was modelled on North American newspapers, and had always been far more independent of the PRI than Mexico City newspapers. (Monterrey is known for a business sector that is more independent of the state than the business sector of Mexico city, and more oriented toward the US. With a few exceptions, it should be noted, regional newspapers have been *more* deferential toward ruling elites than the Mexico City press.) *Reforma's* journalists, like *El Norte's*, are better educated than most Mexican journalists—meaning that they can approach government officials on a more equal basis, and better paid. They are forbidden to accept gratuities from government officials.

Since 1993, the independent papers have generally been more successful at competing for readers than the traditional officialist press, and certain of the latter have begun to move in the direction of greater independence (Lawson 1999). Their shift may also have been motivated in part by the realization that government support could not be counted on in the future. The last two Mexican presidents, Salinas and Zedillo, have pursued neo-liberal economic policies which have involved shrinking the state sector. PIPSA has been privatized, as have many state enterprises which once supported newspapers with their advertising; and the public relations budgets of government agencies—an important source of payments to newspapers—are being cut.

In the case of radio, the devastating Mexico City earthquake of 1985 played an important role. In general, the earthquake accelerated the process of political change in Mexico. The government was unable to respond adequately to the magnitude of the disaster, and citizen groups organized to coordinate relief and rebuilding from the bottom up. Many of these groups continued to function after the disaster, expanding the civic sector of Mexican society. The growth of a stronger civil society, as we shall see, has affected the development of independent media in many ways. For example, the Mexican Academy of Human Rights, an NGO, has carried out its own monitoring of media coverage of elections, and has played an important role in putting the issue of media access on the agenda (Aguayo and Acosta 1997).

In the aftermath of the earthquake, Televisa followed its usual habits, covering the disaster through comments of government officials. But a number of radio stations responded with more popularly oriented coverage, giving a voice to ordinary citizens and the neighborhood groups they had formed. This produced a jump in radio listenership, and in subsequent years radio talk shows, often much more open politically than anything that had existed in the electronic media previously, became highly popular. With popularity came success as an advertising medium, and radio news in general, which had little presence at the beginning of the 1980s, experienced a boom (Lawson 1999, Sarmiento 1997).

Televisa, as we have seen, faced political pressures which became acute by the 1994 election. It also faced market pressure beginning in 1993. President Carlos Salinas de Gortari had made the privatization of government-owned enterprises a centerpiece of his neo-liberal policies. Among the last to be privatized was Imevisión, a government television network, which became Televisa's first commercial competition since it had absorbed a rival network in 1972. The buyer was Ricardo Benjamín Salinas Pliego (not a family relation of Salinas, though it is widely believed that the president's family had a covert financial stake in the new enterprise), and the new enterprise was named Televisión Azteca. Salinas Pliego had no experience in media, and apparently was chosen in part because he was seen as having little interest in political activism. Asked by *Proceso* what role the new network would play in the democratization of Mexico, he said it would play none at all: "television is a medium of entertainment and relaxation" (Ortega Pizarro 1993: 6).

Nevertheless, the political role of Mexican television following the launching of Televisión Azteca did change rapidly. In 1996, for example, Televisa, then embroiled in a bitter internal conflict over the direction of its news division, aired a leaked videotape of a massacre of peasants by the army in the state of Guerrero—something which would have been inconceivable in an earlier period. In March 1997, Emilio Azcárraga, Jr. died, his son took over, and the internal conflicts within the organization intensified.

In the 1997 federal elections, the three major political parties for the first time received essentially equal coverage from both Televisa and Televisión Azteca, with slightly more coverage for the leftist Cárdenas, who ran successfully for the new office of Mexico City mayor. The attention to Cárdenas reflects a triumph of media logic over political logic: Cárdenas got more coverage because he was a better story. Research by Chappell Lawson (1999) provides strong evidence that the shift in Televisa's coverage had enough impact on Mexico's currently volatile electorate to have been decisive in the outcome of the election, in which the PRI for the first time lost its majority in the Chamber of Deputies. Finally, in January 1998, Jacobo Zabludovsky, who had been Televisa's principal news anchor since the 1950s and head of its Directorate of News since its organization in the early 1970s, was dumped and his flagship news broadcast renamed, reorganized, and oriented much more toward ordinary viewers (Hallin in press).

How large a role did the emergence of commercial competition play in changing the political character of Mexican television? It is difficult to untangle the forces that were at work, just as it is in general difficult to separate the effects of economic liberalization and political democratization in Mexico, as the two overlap historically. As we have seen, the changes in election coverage were in part the result of government pressure. It is also possible that the broader changes at Televisa resulted as much from a political calculation as from a concern specifically with commercial competition. That is, Televisa's management may have concluded that in a changing political environment the benefits of alliance with the PRI were rapidly diminishing and the costs or potential costs increasing, and chosen to distance itself from the ruling party—a choice which could have been made even in the absence of commercial competition. Televisa had become the subject of street demonstrations and protests by opposition politicians and citizen groups—the increasingly active civil society mentioned above; it was increasingly held in contempt, particularly among the educated and politically active, and if there were a shift in political power it could conceivably lose more than just prestige.[3] As one of Televisa's top executives said, shortly after the death of Azcárraga, "as far as politics is concerned, the company historically has had the capacity and the flexibility to read the times and to adapt to them" (Mayolo López 1997).

Still, it seems certain that the emergence of competition did play a significant role in the political change. Televisión Azteca was not particularly bold in pushing the political boundaries of Mexican television, though it did make some innovations. One of its early successes was a *telenovela*, *Nada Personal*, which dealt with questions of official corruption previously untouched in Mexican entertainment television. Its news broadcasts were modestly more lively—introducing puppet caricatures of political figures, for example, which were used extensively in its 1997 election coverage.

But the mere existence of competition may have pushed Televisa to make different decisions—the massacre videotape, after all, might have been aired by Azteca if Televisa hadn't done so—and eventually to rethink the whole character of the news broadcast. Televisa did suffer considerable losses of audience share from its news broadcast. These seem to have been politically motivated in part; that is, people who supported opposition parties abandoned the hated Televisa for Azteca. And the losses were significant because opposition supporters tend to be younger, better-educated and wealthier than PRI supporters—and hence more valuable to advertisers. The truth is that Televisa's news was always a bizarre product for a commercial television company—dreadfully boring, full of long-winded speeches by political functionaries, official press releases read word for word as the text scrolled on the screen, and interviews with wealthy cronies of the owner. Surely it could not have survived competition for long.

Conclusion

Neither the liberal nor the critical political economy perspective is fully adequate to the analysis of Mexico's unusual system of power or the process of political change now under way. This should not be surprising: both are broad-brush approaches which are likely to fall short in the analysis of any concrete historical case, particularly once they are removed from the particular contexts—for example post-war Britain—for which they were developed in their most detailed forms. The value of the kind of comparative enterprise undertaken in this book is to force us to think in more subtle ways about the variety of relationships which can exist among the state, commercial media, civil society, the profession of journalism, and other key elements of the system of public communication.

For the Mexican case, the liberal perspective is correct in pointing to the state as a key component of the system of power—though the triumph of neo-liberalism means that this will be considerably less relevant to understanding Mexican media in the future. It is also correct in its argument that the development of media markets can play a role in the process of democratization, both by providing the media with an economic base apart from the state, and by providing incentives for responsiveness to popular tastes and opinions. Its key failing is that it does not take into account the interdependence of state power and private capital.

The critical political economy perspective was developed primarily to provide a critique of the media system in liberal democracy. It has, for that reason, tended to take liberal media institutions—including both commercial media and journalistic professionalism—as given, and has never put a priority on theorizing the process by which they come into being to begin with. It falls short of understanding the old regime in Mexico, in which liberal institutions were never fully developed. It also falls short of understanding many aspects of the political transition now under way. It is clear, in particular, that the assumption that market forces inevitably push toward depoliticization and a narrowed spectrum of debate is too simple. Under certain historical conditions market forces may undermine existing structures of power, providing incentives for the media to respond to an activated civil society.

The role of civil society is worth underscoring here as something not adequately theorized in either perspective. Liberal media theory tends to assume an identity between commercial media and civil society. Critical political economy has shown greater interest in civil society in recent years, but its traditional concern is with the power of private media owners and the constraints of the market, and it is fair to say that it has not fully theorized the way these interact with developments in civil society. In the case of Mexican scholarship, the critical political economy school traditionally looked to the state as the source of reform in media institutions, but there has been a significant shift in recent years toward a concern with initiatives "from below" (Sánchez Ruiz 1994). As Mexico's political system becomes more pluralistic, one of the key issues will be how widely different sectors of civil society are served and represented by the emerging media system.

It is possible that with the passing of the transitional period in Mexico, many of the dynamics pointed to by research in the critical political economy tradition in the US and Britain may eventually assert themselves more fully. In the case of the press, for example, it is clear that the logic of commercial media production is not at this point fully dominant. The new independent papers were for the most part started as journalistic more than business enterprises. *Proceso* and *La Jornada* were founded by journalists who scraped together enough financing to survive; their motivation was to have a public voice and to democratize Mexico's press, not to build commercial media empires. *Siglo 21* was started jointly by a businessman and a group of journalists; the two later parted ways, the journalists founded *Público*, and *Siglo 21* closed. Only *Reforma* was started primarily on the initiative of a capitalist, but Junco de la Vega is something of a special case, a print media specialist who identifies strongly with journalism as a profession.

It is certainly possible, however, that as the newspaper market develops more fully in Mexico, right-of-center commercial papers will eventually drive out of the market not only the old officialist press, but also the independent papers started by journalists, which may be able to survive only in a period of political transition when interest in politics is high and the commercial press not yet fully developed. And it is possible that with the receding of this period of relatively high politicization, television news will eventually move strongly in the direction of apolitical sensationalism. As neo-liberalism triumphs, the role of the state recedes and that of the market expands, critical political economy may become more rather than less relevant to understanding the Mexican media—along with related perspectives centered on the notion of journalistic routines, which analyze the power of the state, for example, not in terms of censorship or pressure, but in terms of its role as a "primary definer" in the professional production of news.

Acknowledgments

I would like to thank Virginia Escalante, Andres Villarreal and Cynthia Lozano for research assistance. Enrique Sánchez Ruiz and Chappell Lawson provided extremely helpful comments on an earlier draft of this chapter, and Raúl Trejo provided valuable help in understanding the Mexican media. Miguel Acosta, Jeffrey Weldon and Margarita Moreno provided access to important research materials. Thanks also to my colleagues in the Binational Association of Schools of Communication of the Californias; my conversations with them over a period of many years have been invaluable in understanding Mexico and its media system.

Notes

1 According to Sánchez Ruiz (1994), Televisa's coverage of the 1994 election shifted substantially one day after the Interior Minister (Secretario de Gobernación) met privately with Azcárraga.
2 *La Jornada*, the most important leftist paper, has continued to receive some government subsidies; the Mexican government has always seen the continuation of some oppositional papers as important to maintaining legitimacy, and sees a newspaper that circulates among intellectuals as a relatively small threat to its political hegemony.
3 Research by Porto (1998) suggests that Brazil's TV Globo made a similar shift, without any clear change in its market situation or any reason to expect immediate gains in ratings.

References

Adler, I. (1993a) "The Mexican case: the media in the 1988 presidential election," in T. Skidmore (ed.) *Television Politics and the Transition to Democracy in Latin America*, Baltimore, MD: Johns Hopkins University Press.

Adler, I. (1993b) "Press–Government relations in Mexico: a study of freedom of the Mexican press and press criticism of government institutions," *Studies in Latin American Popular Culture*, 12: 1–30.

Aguayo Quezada, S. and Acosta, M. (1997) *Urnas y Pantallas: La Batalla por la Información*, Mexico, DF: Oceano.

Alisky, M. (1981) *Latin American Media: Guidance and Censorship*, Ames, Iowa: Iowa State University Press.

Alves, R. C. (1997) "The newly democratized media in Latin America: a review of the progress and constraints in five cases of 'democracy's vanguard newspapers,'" paper presented at the annual meeting of the Latin American Studies Association, Guadalajara.

Arredondo Ramírez, P., Fregoso Peralta, G. and Trejo Delarbre, R. (1991) *Así se calló el sistema: Comunicación y eleciones en 1988*, Guadalajara: Universidad de Guadalajara.

Camp, R. (1989) *Entrepreneurs and Politics in Twentieth-Century Mexico*, New York: Oxford University Press.

Conger, L. (1997) "From intimidation to assasination: silencing the press," in W. A. Orme, Jr. (ed.) *A Culture of Collusion: An Inside Look at the Mexican Press*, Boulder, CO: Lynne Rienner.

Cornelius, W. A. (1996) *Mexican Politics in Transition: The Breakdown of a One-Party Dominant Regime*, La Jolla, CA: Center for U.S./Mexican Studies.

Curran, J. and Seaton, J. (1997) *Power without Responsibility: The Press and Broadcasting in Britain*, London: Routledge.

Curran, J., Douglas, A. and Whannel, G. (1980) "The political economy of the human interest story," in A. Smith (ed.) *Newspapers and Democracy: International Essays on a Changing Medium*, Cambridge, MA: MIT Press.

Esteinou Madrid, J. (1988) "The Morelos satellite system and its impact on Mexican society," *Media, Culture and Society*, 10(4): 419–46.

Fernández Christlieb, F. (1982) *Los Medios de Difusion Masivo en Mexico*, Mexico, DF: Juan Pablos Editor.

Fox, J. (1994). "The difficult transition from clientelism to citizenship: lessons from Mexico," *World Politics*, 46(2): 151–84.

Fregoso Peralta, G. and Sánchez Ruiz, E. E. (1993) *Prensa y Poder en Guadalajara*, Guadalajara: Universidad de Guadalajara.

García Canclini, N. (1988) "Culture and power: the state of research," *Media, Culture and Society*, 10(4): 467–98.

González Molina, G. (1987) "Mexican television news: the imperatives of corporate rationale," *Media, Culture and Society*, 9: 159–87.

González Molina, G. (1990). "The production of Mexican television news: the supremacy of corporate rationale," Ph.D. dissertation, Centre for Mass Communication Research, University of Leicester.

Hallin, D. C. (1994) *"We Keep America on Top of the World": Television News and the Public Sphere*, London: Routledge.

Hallin, D. C. (1997) *"Dos Instituciones, Un Camino*: television and the state in the 1994 Mexican election," paper presented at the annual meeting of the Latin American Studies Association, Guadalajara.

Hallin, D. C. (in press) *"La Nota Roja*: popular journalism and the transition to democracy in Mexico," in C. Sparks and J. Tulloch (eds.) *Tabloid Tales*, Boulder, CO: Rowman and Littlefield.

Hayes, J. (1993) "Early Mexican radio broadcasting: media imperialism, state paternalism or Mexican nationalism?", *Studies in Latin American Popular Culture*, 12: 31–55.

Hayes, J. (1996) "'Touching the sentiments of everyone': nationalism and state broadcasting in thirties Mexico," *The Communication Review*, 1: 4.

Instituto Federal Electoral, Dirección Ejecutiva de Prerogativas y Partidos Políticos, Comisión de Radiodifusión (1997) *Monitoreo de las campañas de los partidos políticos en noticiarios de radio y televisión*, Mexico, DF: Instituto Federal Electoral.

Lawson, C. (1999) "Building the Fourth Estate: Democratization and the Emergence of Independent Media Opening in Mexico," Ph.D. dissertation, Stanford University.

Leñero, V. (1990) *Los Periodistas*, Mexico, DF: J. Moritz.

Mayolo López, F. (1997) "Televisa, asegura Cañedo White, sabe leer los tiempos y será más plural," *Proceso*, March 9, pp. 26–30.

Mejía Barquera, F. (1989) *La Industria de la Radio y la Televisión y la Política del Estado Mexicano (1920–1960)*, Mexico: Fundación Manuel Buendía.

Miller, M. and Darling, J. (1997) "The eye of the tiger: Emilio Azcárraga and the Televisa Empire," in W. A. Orme, Jr. (ed.) *A Culture of Collusion: An Inside Look at the Mexican Press*, Boulder, CO: Lynne Rienner.

Ortega Pizaro, F. (1993) "'En la democratización, la televisión nada tiene que ver': Salinas Pliego; 'nuestro proyecto, entretener': Suárez Vázquez," *Proceso*, July 26 , pp. 6–13.

de la Peña, R. and Toledo, L. R. (1992a). "Consumo Televisivo en el Valle de México," *Intermedios*, 3 (Agosto/Sept.): 48–57.

de la Peña, R. and Toledo, L. R. (1992b) "Hábitos de Lectura de Periódicos in el Valle de México," *Intermedios*, 4 (Oct./Nov.): 60–9.

Porto, M. (1998) "Globo's Evening News and the representation of politics in Brazil 1995–96," paper presented at the annual meeting of the International Communication Association, Jerusalem.

Riva Palacio, R. (1997) "A culture of collusion: the ties that bind the press and the PRI," in W. A. Orme, Jr. (ed.) *A Culture of Collusion: An Inside Look at the Mexican Press*, Boulder, CO: Lynne Rienner.

Roniger, L. (1990) *Hierarchy and Trust in Modern Mexico and Brazil*, New York: Praeger.

Sánchez-Ruiz, E. (1994) "Medios y Democracia en América Latina," *Comunicación y Sociedad*, 20: 153–79.

Saragoza, A. (1997) "Television," in M. S. Werner (ed.) *Encyclopedia of Mexico: History, Society and Culture*, Chicago: Fitzroy Dearborn.

Sarmiento, S. (1997) "Trial by fire: the Chiapas Revolt, the Colosio assasination and the Mexican press in 1994," in W. A. Orme, Jr. (ed.) *A Culture of Collusion: An Inside Look at the Mexican Press*, Boulder, CO: Lynne Rienner.

Schudson, M. (1994) "The 'public sphere' and its problems: bringing the state (back) in," *Notre Dame Journal of Law, Ethics and Public Policy*, 8(2): 529–46.

Sinclair, J. (1986) "Dependent development and broadcasting: 'the Mexican formula,'" *Media, Culture and Society*, 8(1).

Sinclair, J. (1990) "Neither West nor Third World: the Mexican television industry within the NWICO debate," *Media, Culture and Society*, 12: 343–60.

Trejo Delarbre, R. (coordinator) (1985) *Televisa: El Quinto Poder*, Mexico, DF: Claves Latinoamericanas.

Trejo Delarbre, R., (coordinator) (1988) *Las Redes de Televisa*, Mexico, DF: Claves Latinoamericanas.

Trejo Delarbre, R. (1994a) "1994: El voto de la prensa," *Nexos*, 204: 16–24.

Trejo Delarbre, R. (1994b) "Equidad, calidad y competencia electoral: Las campañas de 1994 en la televisión mexicana," Mexico, DF: Instituto de Estudios Para la Transicion Democrática.

Trejo Delarbre, R. (1997) "Medios y política en México: Una panorama frente a las elecciones federales de 1997," paper presented at the annual meeting of the Latin American Studies Association, Guadalajara.

Valero Berrospe, R. (coordinator) (n.d.) "Redes Empresariales, Medios y Sus Efectos Durante la Gestion Salinista," Mexicali, BC: Universidad Autónoma de Baja California, Facultad de Ciencias Humanas.

8 Modernization, globalization, and the powerful state

The Korean media

Myung-Jin Park, Chang-Nam Kim and Byung-Woo Sohn

Korea has an advanced media industry and its history of media education and research is more than forty years old. Western models and theories about media had long been accepted as the ideal with hardly any doubt. These models were applied and accommodated to local media education and research.

But since the 1980s, there have been continuous discussions among Korean media scholars about whether the concepts and theories developed in a Western context are proper for Korea. Some attempted "creative application" of Western theories to overcome the problems, but they largely failed to obtain satisfactory results. Scholars have continued to discuss how to complement and revise Western theories to properly address Korean realities but have yet to find any answers. This chapter is basically an extension of that ongoing search.

The Korean media began to acquire the features of an industry during the 1960s when a military regime which came to power through a coup d'état began to actively mobilize media for national development. In this chapter, we try to locate the unique aspects of the Korean media by focusing on media development from the 1960s. We will also address problems in applying Western theories and methodology to the Korean situation. The main focus will be on the relationship between media and the power structure; i.e. how the top–down political power, which has been the most powerful force in Korean society, has controlled the media; in what way the media have influenced society and how the audiences, in response, have established grassroots bottom–up power to counter them.

Political power structure and the media in Korea

One of the most distinctive features of Korean society after its liberation from Japanese colonial rule in 1945 was the dominance of political power. The new state, established in 1948, inherited the repressive ruling system of the Japanese colonial government. Therefore, Korean state power implied the possibility of relative superiority from the beginning. The power of the state was further reinforced by a military regime which came to power through a coup d'état in 1961 through the policy of state-run rapid industrial development. The division of the Korean Peninsula between South and North Korea also provided the basic conditions for nurturing the superior position of the state. The division which had made it possible to organize society for wartime mobilization, justified dictatorial rule by the state and enlarged the military sector. Based on these conditions, the state enjoyed enormous power, repressing and controlling not only the political and economic forces but also the daily lives of people and their culture.

The state's modernization policy in the 1960s was essentially a project to create compressed economic growth. It was characterized by the policy of nurturing the monopoly capital and repressing the people. The policy enabled the fast growth of capital power but suppressed the development of a civil society in Korea. Capital power was also subordinate to political power.

In the background of the long dominance of state power was also the tradition of Confucian ideology, which ruled Korean society for centuries. The development of capitalism in Korea was a top–down process led by the state. It was not accompanied, as was the case in Western countries, with development of a civil society. Instead, traditional Confucian ideology still prevailed. In Confucianism, the autonomy of society vis-à-vis the state is not recognized. Accordingly, the concept of civil society could not exist. As the premodern Confucian ideology still ruled society, the state was able to keep its paternal status in society and lead the social development process.

The state also adroitly fanned regional animosities, which historically date back for centuries in Korea, to sustain and strengthen its power. In particular, the Chung-Hee Park regime and its successors tried to maintain their power base by openly discriminating against people from the Honam region (southwestern part of Korea). Regional antagonism, as a result, has remained an important element of conflict in Korean society.

Another feature of state power in Korea is its lack of political legitimacy. The First Republic under the rule of President Syngman Rhee was based on a colonial power structure. Park, who ruled Korea from 1961 to 1979, was a former general and so were two of his immediate successors. Therefore, none of their regimes, which were essentially military, were mandated by the Korean citizenry. These military governments pursued economic growth to make up for their lack of a mandate. They also repressed all dissension and manipulated ideology in order to maintain their power.

The absolute power of the state started to weaken in the 1980s when political liberalization became a pressing social task and when the monopolistic capital power grew to such an extent that it could no longer be ignored. Since then, the statuses of the state and monopolistic capital in society have gradually changed. But this does not mean that capital has completely overcome its subordinate status.

The relationship between the power structure and media in Korea grew out of this background. Since the establishment of the government in 1948, politics has always been the main concern of Korean society. Since the media was viewed as a tool for social integration and control of the people, the state power actively used it for solving political problems and justifying its legitimacy. The media was also used as a tool for achieving rapid modernization and economic growth. The Korean press at times did put up a resistance. But it would be closer to the truth to say that the media has traditionally maintained a close relationship with political power, has largely represented its interests, and has contributed to maintaining the existing ruling structure.

Political power and its control on media

The history of the Korean media has been a history of continuous tensions and compromise with political power. Throughout history, the Korean media and political power have maintained a close relationship, which is sometimes criticized for being collusive. Collusive ties refer to the relationship where the media desert their function as social critics and form illicit ties with power. The media, in the relationship, attempt to cover up the truth about the power rather than expose it (Paeng 1993). This collusive relationship began under the rule of President Chung-Hee Park in the early 1960s. Unlike the previous regime of Syngman Rhee which resorted mainly to suppression of the press, the governments of Park and his immediate successor Doo-Hwan Chun adopted the policy of both repression and appeasement.

Types of repression (sticks)

Three major repressive measures were used on media. The first was the forceful reorganization of the media companies. The Park regime reorganized the media industry in 1961. It cancelled the license of the media which were found to fall short of its production machinery and facility. The number of dailies, as a result, decreased to thirty-three the next year. The Chun regime, which came to power through a coup in 1980, legislated the Basic Press Act and forcefully merged the newspaper and broadcasting companies. It allowed only one newspaper for each province, except in the Seoul area.

Secondly, the government forced journalists who were critical of its rule to resign. In 1974, 134 journalists had to leave the *Dong-A Ilbo* and 33 had to leave the *Chosun Ilbo*, both of which were leading newspapers at the time. A total of 933 journalists were forced to quit in 1980.

Thirdly, the state dispatched intelligence officials to mass media companies to monitor journalists and even to exercise influence on news reporting. Unofficial and secret methods were also used to control the media. The so-called "guidelines for reporting" which existed from 1980 to 1987 were an example. The Media Policy Office of the Ministry of Culture and Information issued the guidelines to media companies to control news reporting. The guidelines detailed not only what should be reported and what should not on the day. They also decided the priority of the news, pictures, and even the size of headlines for certain stories. The press faithfully followed the guidelines. Statistics show that the dailies published in Seoul observed 70–80 percent of the guidelines (Yeo 1989: 52).

As the society underwent a democratization process, direct control of the media by the state through censorship, manipulation, and other means were eased. But it was replaced by a mechanism of indirect control.

Types of conciliatory measures (carrots)

In the meantime, political power tried to tame the mass media by providing media companies and journalists with various benefits. First, it gave tax favor to media companies and their employees. The government revised a provision of the Customs Law in late 1981 to reduce the customs tax rate for the rotary press from 20 percent to 4 percent during 1982. A total of twelve newspaper companies bought some thirty machines during the period, enjoying a considerable tax cut. The government of Doo-hwan Chun also reduced the income tax for journalists.

The second measure concerned the public fund set up by the Korea Broadcasting Advertising Corporation (KOBACO). The fund, formed with a part of the commissions

KOBACO received from broadcasting companies for arranging advertisements, was officially aimed at returning some of the profits of broadcasting companies to society for their use of airwaves, which are a public asset. The public fund supported programs for training journalists (overseas training and overseas observation trips) and promoting their welfare (loans for housing and the education of children) (Joo, Kim *et al.* 1997, Kang 1998).

The Park and Chun regimes controlled the media in broader and more fundamental ways through changes in the system, which brought about mixed results. By abolishing media companies which were critical of it, the state was able to weaken the critical functions of the media and control it in a more efficient way. On the other hand, the closure of critical media firms guaranteed a monopoly on the industry by other firms and helped them to expand businesses. Without competitors, these media companies saw a considerable increase in their revenue from advertisement, whose market was rapidly expanding with the growth of the national economy.

Thirdly, cash or gifts were given to journalists as a means of media control. As was shown in a 1991 scandal involving the correspondents to the Ministry of Health and Social Affairs, journalists received a considerable amount of cash and gifts from government organizations or the businesses they covered. It was a deep-rooted custom in Korean society to provide cash or entertainment to reporters. Political power bought off journalists and bribed journalists became subject to political power. Journalists were unable to go beyond a certain line in political reporting because of their weak position deriving from this relationship. When they tried to break the line, they were threatened for their misdeeds. One example may be the Suso corruption scandal during the administration of President Tae-woo Roh. The prosecution leaked the news that it would investigate journalists who had received money from the businessman involved in the scandal when some newspapers started to print in-depth investigative stories about the scandal. Lawmakers and others in leading positions in society like doctors were often punished for bribery. But it was rare for journalists to face legal action for wrongdoing, possibly because the government didn't want to break its cooperative relations with the media.

The most outstanding carrot provided to the media might have been the recruitment of journalists as politicians and bureaucrats. The posts of the minister and vice minister at the Ministry of Culture and Information often went to journalists. Many journalists also served as officials in other ministries, information officials in overseas missions, presidential secretaries or assistants and spokesmen. There was also quite a large number of ex-journalists among lawmakers. The number was thirty-five during the eleventh National Assembly, twenty-seven during the twelfth Assembly, twenty-six during the thirteenth Assembly and forty during the fourteenth Assembly. The positions were often given to the journalists as rewards for cooperating with the government. But it ultimately served to open channels of dialogue with media companies. Media companies also welcomed the advancement of their employees to government offices and political circles, as they might provide them the links to politicians and officials, which would help them obtain high-class information and therefore more chances to get the inside scoop. The journalists recruited as politicians and government officials served both the government and media companies.

This mechanism had deeper implications. It gave media companies political power. A network of power was formed through these journalist-turned-politicians or bureaucrats, which functioned effectively during periods when there was a transition of power such as during presidential elections. Media companies often played an important role in "making a president" in order to extend their power to the next administration.

Clientelism based on regionalism

In the background to this relationship is the regional antagonism which has been a major source of social conflict and a central characteristic of the power structure in Korea. In Korean society, blood ties have long been regarded as of great importance. This informal relationship has been expanded to the relations based on the same educational or regional backgrounds. The phenomenon might be related to the long authoritarian rule in Korea. People often lose mutual confidence in each other when they live through long periods of authoritarian rule. Informal networks might have been formed as a way to compensate for the insecurity. Private ties also make up for the limits official social relations have. Regionalism, in particular, was openly promoted during the presidential election campaign of 1971 and has since then been a major factor in defining political practices. Ruling groups are often formed by people from the region where the president comes from (Korea Politics Association 1996, Seo 1988).

The media are no exception. It has long been a tradition that media companies fill their top posts with people from the region where the power of the ruling camp is based. Therefore, it is not regarded as unusual when the media companies replace their senior staff with figures from the hometown of the president. This tendency is not limited to the appointment of the media on which the government can exercise influence. Commercial media often do the same to have better access to the ruling party and the government. Journalists who entered political and official sectors from the Third to Sixth Republics (from the 1960s to the 1980s) were mostly from the Yongnam region (37.6 percent), which refers to the southeastern North and South Kyongsang Provinces, where the hometowns of Presidents Park, Chun and Roh are located (Ki-Sun Park 1994).

In fact, after the government of President Dae-Jung Kim was inaugurated in February 1998, major newspaper and broadcasting organizations rushed to appoint figures from North and South Cholla Provinces, the political bastion of Kim, to their top posts. This implies a feudalistic feature of the relationship between the government and media in Korea.

The political system of Korea has a Western appearance, but its operation has been more dependent on informal and premodern methods than official and reasonable procedures. The state has controlled media both officially and unofficially, but informal intervention has been more notable, providing a basis for collusive relations between the power and media. Of course, the state has led the media in this collusive relationship. Media, in the process, has become another political power which can decide the outcome of presidential elections. In this respect, the relationship between state power and the press in Korea contains the elements of a patron–client relationship. That is, the state–press relationship wears the features of the liberal system of Western countries on the surface, but it has strong characteristics of clientelism on the inside. Clientelism is based on the feudalistic feature of Korean society, which depends on regional networking.

This type of state–media relationship is quite different from those of many Western countries, in which media support certain parties based on their political leanings. In Korea, the relationship is based more on private and secret connections than on agreements in ideology or support for party platforms. Therefore, Korean media support the state more in unofficial ways than in official ones. This relationship has caused dysfunction of the media system in general, as evidenced in the loss of journalistic ethics, distorted news reporting, dependence on private relations, and negligence in tracking down the truth (Seung-Kwan Park 1994, Kim 1993).

Media control by capital and growth of media industry

Unlike in many Western countries where media control by big capital is the most pressing problem, the Korean media is controlled mainly by political power. But rapid industrialization and economic growth have expanded the power of big capital, allowing it to gain an influence on the media. Some large businesses own and operate media firms. Others exercise power over media through the provision of advertisement revenues. Revenues from advertisement have grown rapidly since the 1960s and account for more than 70 percent of the total revenues of media firms.

The power businesses have over the media as advertisers has been a main factor behind the conservatism in Korean media. This was well manifested during the conflict between *Dong-A Ilbo* daily and some advertisers in 1974. Even the *Hankyoreh*, which is said to represent the progressive forces in Korea, is not totally free from influence of the advertisers. The power of businesses over media has increased since the late 1980s when monopolistic businesses became stronger while the power of the state decreased. Monopolistic capital also began to rapidly advance into the media industry at the time.

The turning-point came in 1988 when President Tae-Woo Roh came to power. Since then, the government control over the media has changed from a direct to an indirect one. As the government lifted regulations on the establishment of periodicals, the number of dailies increased from twenty-eight in 1987 to sixty-five in 1988. The existing papers which had enjoyed monopolies on the industry finally abolished their cartel in 1988 and decided to liberalize subscription fees. In the wake of that disbandment, competition among newspapers to increase the number of pages started to take hold.

However, the competition failed to bring about diversification of editorial policy. It simply developed more competition for obtaining advertisements. This means that media companies started to pay more attention to gaining profits. The competition, accordingly, showed many aspects of unfair rivalry. Newspaper companies often delivered papers to people free of charge to increase their circulation. The government intervened in this process, but its attempts to stop the practice largely failed. The monopolistic character of the Korean media, which was briefly threatened during the rule of President Roh, has remained in place.

Changes in media industry

Since 1994, newspaper companies have extended their business into new electronic media. Three major newspapers, *Chosun, Joongang* and *Dong-A*, set up new media sections in their companies in 1994, providing a basis for full-scale competition in the area. To accommodate new communication technologies and overcome the limits of print media, they started such business as electronic bulletins and electronic newspapers. They also attempted to enter the cable TV and satellite broadcasting markets. But their efforts did not bear fruit because of regulations banning cross-ownership of print and broadcasting media.

Changes also occurred in the broadcasting industry. The government, which had allowed only two public channels for a long time, started to license commercial television companies. In 1991, SBS, a commercial TV channel covering the Seoul metropolitan area, began its service. Eight other commercial TV companies were launched throughout the nation from 1995 to 1997. Cable TV service was inaugurated in 1995, providing services on twenty-nine channels.

The government announced a five-year development plan for the broadcasting industry in 1995, which, for the first time, stressed the importance of competitiveness in the broadcasting media (Ministry of Information 1995: 66). This revealed that government officials who had regarded the broadcasting media only as a tool of maintaining power started to realize that broadcasting is an industry.

It is true that government influence over media has weakened since the late 1980s, while the power of capital has strengthened. But the economic crisis which hit Korea late in 1997 seems to have reversed the trend to some extent. A sudden drop in advertisement has left many cable and regional commercial television channels in financial difficulties. Newspapers which used to be owned by business conglomerates have also experienced financial hardship since the conglomerates gave up their ownership. Many of these media companies are apparently seeking government support, including the arrangement of loans, in order to survive.

Power of media

Monopoly of information and its echoing effects

To many Koreans, newspapers sometimes represented intellectuals suppressed by the government. People provided tremendous support to the *Dong-A Ilbo* in 1974–5 when it fought against the state and capital power for this reason. The respect and confidence the public had in newspapers largely disappeared during the 1970s and 1980s, but the Korean media have still sustained their power thanks to the oligopolistic feature of the media industry. A small number of media which were in collusion with political power dominated information flow. As the Korean economy grew, they gained more political and economic power under the protection of the state.

In Korea, the media was considered to have quite a significant political value because of its function of leading public opinion. Several unique factors may indicate the power of newspapers in leading public opinion in Korea. First, the proportion of home-delivery subscription was, and still is, overwhelmingly higher than that of newsstand sales. Therefore, people tend to remain loyal to their newspapers for a long time. But not many Koreans subscribed to more than two dailies. Another feature of the Korean newspaper market was that national papers published in Seoul dominate the entire national market. Five or so nationally circulated dailies shared the national market. This oligopolistic feature guaranteed the established papers secure advertising revenue but made it difficult for newcomers to enter the market. As a result, diversity in press discourse was restricted. The public did not trust newspapers and sometimes pursued alternatives. But in the end they had no choice but to rely on the existing media to get information.

Diversity in press discourse emerged, though in a limited degree, as the newcomers in the media industry started to break up the existing oligopolistic structure of the media in the 1980s. The existing media, in response, started to produce even more conservative discourses, which seemed to exert a significant influence on Korean society at large.

Ironically, the Korean media has gained more social power thanks to media control by authoritarian political powers and instability related to the division of South and North Korea. Media companies waged fierce commercial competition because national security and authoritarian rule did not allow them diversity in editorial policy. This resulted in a powerful echoing effect. The sarcastic expression of "pan journalism," which refers to the tendency of the media to become easily hot and cool soon after, is a product of the unique situation in Korea.

Cultural homogenization

Among the social impacts of the Korean media, especially the broadcasting media, are the homogenization and standardization of culture in general. Korean broadcasting was maintained by just a small number of nationwide networks. This made it difficult for Koreans to develop diverse local and class cultures. The intense competition for ratings and absence of distinctive features between channels produced a supply of similar programs, which ultimately caused the overall homogenization of culture. The influence of broadcasting on mass culture is immense in Korea. It often decides the markets of popular cultural products like pop songs. The homogenization of culture also affected the people's way of thinking and lifestyle. Rather than respecting and expressing individuality and creativity, people desired to be like others in consumption and lifestyle. For example, furniture and accessories featured in TV dramas often become an instant hit.

Active audience: from reading between the lines to creation of alternative media

The concept of active audience is somewhat different from the audience practicing a kind of "semiotic democracy" in John Fiske's terms. It means the audience who fights, in various ways, against the politico–economic power oppressing the freedom of the press and against the abusive media power itself.

During the period of authoritarian dictatorship and domesticated media in the 1960s and 1970s, the Korean audience did not remain passive recipients of the media. The audience already supported the journalists' fights for freedom and conducted a campaign against the abusive power of the media. This means that the Korean audience had an ability to read between the lines of messages offered by the state-controlled media and was able to grasp social realities despite being deliberately misinformed.

Many journalists resisted political control of the media and fought for freedom of the press in the past. Their struggles, however, were only possible with the assistance of the silent audience who supported and encouraged them. This is clearly illustrated during the incident at *Dong-A Ilbo* in 1974–5, which caused a mass dismissal of journalists.

In October 1974, journalists at *Dong-A Ilbo* adopted a "Declaration on Practicing Freedom of the Press," in which they rejected outside intervention in press organizations and protested the illegal arrests of journalists by the authorities. At the time, the media had already become a target of public criticism and distrust for failing to fulfill their social responsibilities. The declaration was an expression of the frustrations and crisis felt by journalists.

Declarations by college students, religious groups, writers, and professors followed soon after to support the *Dong-A* journalists and many readers made phone calls to the company to encourage them. Encouraged by the support, *Dong-A* journalists continued to fight for more responsible journalistic practices and to recover the original functions of the newspaper. Eventually, the government intervened. The state forced the advertisers to cancel the advertisement placements in the paper and its two sister media firms, the monthly *Shin Dong A* and Dong-A Broadcasting System (DBS). But the government measure triggered an unprecedented number of personal advertisements in the paper. Countless readers placed personal advertisements in the paper to encourage the journalists. This incident clearly demonstrated that the Korean public did not remain as passive audience at the time (Han *et al.* 1984).

The unprecedented movement for freedom of the press, however, ended when the company finally yielded to the financial pinch caused by advertisers' boycott and dismissed 150 reporters and producers. The incident, however, confirmed the existence of an active audience in Korea. People since then have persistently criticized the unfair practices of the media throughout the authoritarian rule of the country.

This public power enabled more organized audience movements in the 1980s. The environment of the media in the 1980s was much different from that of the 1970s. The forced restructuring of the media industry drastically reduced the number of mass media firms, and television companies started color broadcasting. Audience movements at the time took the form of campaigns for critical understanding of the broadcasting media, which was completely controlled by the state. Catholic churches and some civic groups led the movement to educate the audience in the early 1980s and contributed much to raising public awareness of the problem. This movement finally provided the basis for an active civic campaign against the Korea Broadcasting System (KBS) in the late 1980s.

Civic groups led the campaign to boycott subscription fees, which gained wide support from the public, which already had become discontented with KBS for openly patronizing authoritarian political power through biased newscasts and commentaries. The campaign not only succeeded in changing KBS policy on subscription fees and advertisements, but also contributed to the formation of solidarity among the grassroots movements during the nationwide democratization movement in June 1987.

The power of an active audience formed through the campaign against KBS later gave birth to various forms of media surveillance and educational programs. These programs included systematic media watch programs conducted during the 1987, 1992, and 1997 presidential elections, and general and local elections. Civic groups have also continuously protested against sensationalism and obscenity in sports dailies and have conducted campaigns against media harmful to young people.

Audiences have also created a variety of alternative media. During the 1970s and 1980s when many official media became servants of the government, alternative media in diverse forms were produced and circulated by university students, laborers and religious groups. Illegal copies of the publications which had been banned from sale were systematically produced without official permits. So were underground publications, discs, and videotapes. Distribution systems for these products were often formed among progressive social groups. The producers of these illegal discs and videotapes have now grown as independent productions to lead the alternative media movements. Development in technology has also allowed these progressive groups to produce a higher-quality medium at a lower cost. Fax newspapers, newsletters, and other publications by labor and civic groups are much more refined than in the past.

The most dramatic incident in the development of alternative media was the establishment of the *Hankyoreh* daily. Facing intensifying public resistance over media repression and a growing demand for freer expression, the government eased its restrictions on the establishment of new media in the 1980s. The measure finally gave birth to a paper owned by the public. The *Hankyoreh* was founded in 1988 mostly by journalists dismissed from some established papers for political reasons in the 1970s and 1980s. The money needed to start the paper was collected from the public. The paper has mainly functioned as a spokesman for progressive groups.

The emergence of the *Hankyoreh* contributed to diversifying media discourse to cover ideologies in a broader spectrum. A number of relatively small media representing alternative progressive ideologies have emerged since then. They include *Media Today* published by the Association of Media Labour Unions and the *Labourers' Newspaper* by labor groups. The success of the *Hankyoreh* has encouraged people to discuss a plan to launch a new broadcasting company financed with voluntary contributions by the public.

The state, diversity of media discourse and future prospects

The Korean media have developed in settings different from those in Western countries in many ways and therefore have several distinctive features. The most important aspect of the Korean media is that it developed under the strong guidance of the state. Media owe their growth and accumulation of wealth chiefly to the protective policies and preferential treatment they receive from the government. In order to achieve rapid industrialization and modernization and to complement its frail legitimacy, the state power maintained tight control over media, trying to use them as a tool to promote its policies. The state is still a major force in media control in Korea, although its power has somewhat decreased with the increasing dependence of media companies on income from advertisements.

The state is now regaining its muscle over the media in the face of unprecedented economic challenges represented by Korea's bail-out from the International Monetary Fund (IMF). Accommodating the IMF demands for economic and social reforms, the government has been implementing a sweeping restructuring campaign under the slogan of globalization. The state, as a result, exercises enormous power over society in general, including the media sector. It seems that political power in Korea is becoming stronger in this age of globalization, which usually is characterized by the weakening of the nation-state and the according reduction in political power.

State control and intervention in the media have been made in various ways, both official and unofficial, which caused a lack of diversity in social discourse. The established media in Korea are not much different from each other in their ideological leanings and represent, by and large, a conservative stance. This implies that the media do not adequately represent the voices of various groups and their ideologies. The discourse to counter the conservative ruling ideology is mainly made in the media outside the establishment. The inauguration of the *Hankyoreh*, therefore, bears significant meaning in the history of Korean media. The emergence of such a daily is evidence of democratization taking place in Korean society and changes in the power structure. But alternative media are still weak and insufficient in number.

The most important variable for future media development in Korea is the audience. True reform will be possible only when it is demanded strongly enough from the bottom up to counter the top down forces. One of the most significant changes about the media since the 1980s was the development of audience movements. The audience has been transforming into a more active and independent force in society. The increasing demands for media reform from civic groups clearly illustrate these changes.

It is difficult to predict where the current changes will lead the Korean media in the future. However, many of the changes will depend on how the new political power in Korea handles the ongoing restructuring of the media and how effectively the public will lead their campaign for reforms.

Some theoretical considerations

The Korean media and society are still standing at the threshold of changes, making it difficult to present a theoretical axis to penetrate them. Some liberal and critical political–economic theories provide useful explanations to some degree, but contain inconsistencies when being applied. The mistake seems to be in applying Western perspectives to Korean cases with wholly un-Western conditions. Much caution is also needed in applying some globalization theories to Korea in view of the fact that Korea is being forced to accelerate the globalization process by the ongoing economic crisis.

The media structure in Korea was based upon Western models and theories, particularly the Anglo-American free press model. But journalistic practice and content in Korea are far from Western rationalism. This makes it difficult to apply the liberalist approach to Korea. Strong and effective political power and various premodern elements still dominate media management and practice. The clientelistic networking based on school and regional ties still exists inside and outside media organizations. Conservative ideologies, which are the product of the Cold War era, still dominate the mainstream media in Korea.

Application of the liberalist approach has been questioned in Korea since the mid-1980s when criticism of the collusive relations between power and the press started to emerge. Media scholars paid attention to critical approaches based on Marxist political economy (Myung-Jin Park 1989). But the development in Korea in the 1990s, especially after the first transfer of power between the ruling and opposition parties in 1998, requires a revision of the critical approach. During the campaign for the presidential election in 1997, an opposition candidate advocated the transfer of power. The transfer may be interpreted, in the perspective of the political economists, as the transfer of power initiated by the middle and lower middle class. But in fact, the force behind the change in the government was based on regional alliances, rather than class. It should not be ignored that a number of factors contributed to the power shift. They included continued support from the urban, highly educated, white-collar groups and medium- and small-size entrepreneurs and laborers who had been largely left out by the authoritarian state. In addition, widespread public discontent and the public's demand for the punishment of the incumbent administration for the failure of economic policy also affected the election result. But the most fundamental and strongest factor in the election was the alliance of people based on regional backgrounds, as in previous elections. Critics say that, for this reason, it is difficult to adopt Marxist political economic approaches in explaining the Korean case.

The issue of changes in state power in the globalization thesis may also need review in view of the Korean experience. The administration of President Dae-Jung Kim which was born in February 1998 through the first transfer of power in Korea is actively pursuing a policy to join the neo-liberal world order. Facing the unprecedented and worst-ever economic crisis represented by the IMF bail-out, the administration adopted the policy for market opening and socioeconomic restructuring, saying it is the only way for the country to survive. It is generally believed that globalization brings about the weakening of state power in the long run (Morley and Robins 1995, Featherstone 1990, Grossberg 1998). But in the case of Korea, state power is being reinforced. Since there is no alternative power to replace the state which will work to cope with the tendency for globalization, the government is wielding the strongest hegemony in the process of restructuring.

Restructuring managed by the government has also brought about changes in the media industry. The separation of several dailies from their mother business groups was the most distinctive example. Government pressure has been a critical factor forcing the separation of *Joongang*, *Munhwa* and *Kyunghyang* dailies from the Samsung, Hyundai and Hanwha groups, respectively.

It is not easy to say that this is a temporary phenomenon or will last for some time. There is a prediction that political power will again weaken and capital power will increase once the globalization process proceeds and the economic crisis is overcome. However, a reverse prediction is also possible, considering that globalization is a process. Since the restructuring required by globalization and the establishment of global standards demand radical changes to the social structure, the way of life, and the value system of Koreans, it is difficult to discuss the time limit and the final phase in the process. As long as the government plays a central role in the process of globalization, it is difficult to view the strengthening of state power as temporary.

In her article "Globalization and Myth of the Powerless State," an Australian economist Linda Weiss shows why the recent debate on the powerless state is fundamentally misleading. Her arguments, mainly based on the cases of Japan, Korea, Taiwan, and Singapore, theoretically elucidate the degree of the adaptability of each state, their different capacity, and the problem of enhanced importance of state power in the new international environment.

> In failing to differentiate state capacities, global enthusiasts have been blinded to an important possibility: that far from being victims, (strong) states may well be facilitators (at times perhaps perpetrators) of so-called 'globalization.' Although those researching in the field have yet to explore this possibility, there is sufficient evidence to suggest that this would be a promising line of enquiry. Such evidence as exists for Japan, Singapore, Korea, and Taiwan indicates that these states are acting increasingly as catalysts for the 'internationalization' strategies of corporate actors. As 'catalytic' states, Japan and the NICs are taking the bull by the horns, providing a wide array of incentives to finance overseas investment, promote technology alliances between national and foreign firms, and encourage regional relocation of production networks.
>
> (Weiss 1998: 20)

As pointed out by Linda Weiss, globalization of the economy has been taking place under the strong initiative of the government. The same is true in the media sector. The restructuring of the media system, the rules of market competition, and the functions and operation of media are mainly decided by the government under the flag of socioeconomic reform. Through the process, the clientelistic practices of political power and media are reemerging. It is difficult to say whether this is a temporary phenomenon or not. But what is apparent at this stage is that the orthodox globalization thesis does not easily apply to Korea.

References

Featherstone, M. (ed.) (1990) *Global Culture: Nationalism, Globalization and Modernity*, London: Sage.

Grossberg, L. (1998) "Globalization, media and agency," unpublished paper, prepared for Seoul and Tokyo Seminar 1997, *Media and Society*, 18, Seoul: Nanam.

Han, Seung-Hun *et al.* (1984) *President Park's 'Yushin' Regime and Democratic Movement* (in Korean), Seoul: Chunchu Sa.

Joo, Dong-Hwang, Kim, Hae-Sik and Park, Yong-Gyu (1997) *Understanding the History of the Korean Press* (in Korean), Seoul: Korean Federation of the Press Unions.

Kang, Jun-Man (1998) *Chameleon and Hyena* (in Korean), Seoul: Inmul and Sasang Sa.

Kim, Hyon-Ju (1993) "Korean's ties communication," in Korean Society for Journalism and Communication Studies (ed.) *Research of Korean Communication Model*, Seoul: KSJCS.

Korea Politics Association (ed.) (1996) *Reflection on the Korean Politics* (in Korean), Seoul: Hanul.

Ministry of Information (1995) *5 Years Plan for Advanced Broadcasting 1995–1999* (in Korean), Seoul.

Morley, D. and Robins, K. (1995) *Spaces of Identity: Global Media, Electronic Landscapes and Cultural Boundaries*, London: Routledge.

Paeng, Won-Sun (1993) *Study on News Reporting in Modern Newspapers and Broadcasting* (in Korean), Seoul: Bum-Wo.

Park, Ki-Sun (1994) "Study on the relationship between the government and media under the authoritarian political system," in Chie-woon Kim (ed.) *Critical Reflection on the Media Culture*, Seoul: Nanam.

Park, Myung-Jin (1989) *The Issues of Critical Communication Studies* (in Korean), Seoul: Nanam.

Park, Seung-Kwan (1994) *Visible Face and Invisible Hand: The Communication Structure of Korean Society* (in Korean), Seoul: Jon Ye Won.

Seo, Jae-Jin (1988) "Study on social and political network of Korean capitalist class," *Korean Sociology* (in Korean), 22: 47–67.

Weiss, L. (1998) "Globalization and myth of the powerless state," *New Left Review*, 225: 3–26.

Yeo, Yong-Mu (1989) "Status of Korean media in the 80s: restructuring of media structure and incumbent media," *Press and Broadcasting*, October, Seoul: KPI.

9 State, capital, and media

The case of Taiwan

Chin-Chuan Lee

James Curran (1991), in a seminal essay on media and democracy, calls for giving liberal conceptions "a decent funeral" because the legacy of old saws "bears little relationship to contemporary reality." However, this would be a premature rather than decent funeral. It is widely agreed that many dominant Western assumptions in media studies lose their relevance beyond the "heartland nations" (the United States and Britain), partly on account of their failure to adequately explain either the authoritarian model in a comparative context (Schudson 1991) or media role in the process of regime change and democratic consolidation (Downing 1996a). It is my opinion that liberal conceptions will be viable to media studies for as long as authoritarian control in many Third World states remains obstinate against popular resistance.

The political economy of communication must, by definition, cope with both the larger "political" and "economic" conditions of the media as well as their dialectical influences on the media's structure, operation, content, and ideology. If political economy is indeed "the study of the social relations, particularly the power relations" and "the study of control and survival in social life" (Mosco 1996: 25–6), then the repository of power regulating such control and survival has been conceptualized very differently by "economistic" (radical Marxist) political economists and "political" (liberal-pluralist) political economists.[1] Three major points should be briefly noted. First, Western Marxists, in constructing at the margin of liberal or social democracies their "third ways" different from capitalist and Leninist alternatives, have concentrated their critique on capitalism and market conditions as distorting public communication through such processes as concentrated ownership control and the commodification of culture. Liberal-pluralists have regarded market competition as promoting media diversity and countervailing arbitrary state power. Second, while Western Marxists have criticized media professionalism as reifying the established power, liberal-pluralists have upheld it as a "creed of credibility" that empowers media workers to create an ideological space for fighting against naked authoritarian power. Third, Golding and Murdock (1979) and Garnham (1990: 30) complained that too much attention had been paid to the state–media relationship but not enough to the impact of privatized capitalism on the means of communication. But the coin can also be overturned: most Marxist "economistic" media studies have either glossed over the state as a source of threat to media freedom or assumed it to be an inherent consequence of the economic base.[2] This neglect is particularly untenable when it comes to analyzing the authoritarian regime.[3]

This chapter seeks to illustrate the paradoxical implications of liberal-pluralist and radical Marxist approaches to the political economy of Taiwan's media. Simply put, the radical Marxist perspective may have little light to throw on Taiwan's media struggle against the rough and tough state control imposed under martial law from 1949 to1987. Liberalization since then, however, has allowed the fostering of a new alliance between state power and market capital, making the radical Marxist perspective increasingly (yet only partially) credible in explaining how capital concentration restrains media diversity. Instead of privileging either of the two approaches on an ontological basis, I prefer to treat them as different concrete historical conditions of modern social life.[4] Not only may one approach obtain greater explanatory power than the other approach in a specific social context at a given moment. Both approaches may exist side by side paradoxically and even struggle against each other in the same social context at that given moment. It should be noted that this comparison is also of broader generality to Greater China and beyond.[5]

The patron–client relationship

Taiwan's state encompassed a "triple alliance" of the government, the ruling Nationalist Party (KMT), and the military. When Chiang Kai-shek imposed "hard authoritarianism" and his son Chiang Ching-kuo imposed "soft authoritarianism" on the island from 1949 to 1987 (Winkler 1984), the quasi-Leninist KMT not only assumed a central role in the state structure but was almost synonymous with it. Resembling "bureaucratic-authoritarian regimes" in Latin America (O'Donnell 1978), the KMT regime of Taiwan tried to maintain its effective control of civil society through a combination of coercion and cooptation, as manifested in the development of a "patron–client relationship" (Eisenstadt and Roniger 1981, Wang 1994, Wu 1987) between the state and the media. This was necessitated by the need for the KMT to maintain its legitimacy which had been called into question soon after Taiwan returned from Japan to China in 1945 and aggravated by the KMT's retreat from mainland China to the island after being defeated by the communists in 1949.[6] Immediate threats to the regime's legitimacy came from three sources: a potentially insurgent local population resenting the KMT's discriminatory policy, the communist regime vowing to take Taiwan by force, and the United States whose sponsorship was uncertain (Lee 1993). Martial law justified media control that was essential to consolidating the regime's legitimacy based on mainlander minority rule and selective incorporation of local-born Taiwanese elite. In single-mindedly pursuing a policy of "dependent development" (Gold 1985), the regime showed no hesitation in using the "state repressive apparatuses" to suppress popular participation and in using the "state ideological apparatuses" (the media and the educational system) to "depoliticize and demobilize the public sphere" (Lee 1992). Constitutional rights, including freedom of speech and the press, were suspended on the grounds that political stability was a prerequisite to economic growth and anti-Communism required unified leadership. The media not only accepted authoritarian rule but also helped to rationalize it.

Similar to South Korea (Yoon 1989), the state in Taiwan sought to maintain this patron–client relationship with the media through a policy of *incorporation* marked by a simultaneous and intermittent interplay of repression and cooptation.[7] Taiwan's party-state owned its own mouthpieces; as part of elite integration, other privately owned media were kept as a weak, auxiliary, and dependent organ of the state but not strictly as its mouthpiece. The authoritarian party-state tolerated what Linz (1974) calls "limited pluralism," in which the media were made politically subservient but had considerable autonomy in nonpolitical areas. Those who willingly acceded to state inducements relished vast economic benefits and political status, while those who contested the power structure were suppressed (Lee 1993). Unlike advanced capitalist countries where state power may be embedded within the economic system, Taiwan typifies "state corporatism" (Schmitter 1974) of late-developing countries in which the state plays a dominant role in shaping power distribution and deciding economic policies. Staniland (1985: 75) argues, "In domestic politics, state corporatist regimes are authoritarian, but not necessarily totalitarian: they presume to organize political expression, not to determine its content in any detailed and pervasive way."

The Press

In the early 1950s there was relative tolerance of dissent, as Chiang Kai-shek had not consolidated his total control. But US support of Taiwan in the wake of the Korean War strengthened Chiang's external legitimacy and domestic suppression. *Free China*, a leading liberal journal, was closed down in 1960; its publisher, who was actively organizing an opposition party, was given a ten-year prison term on charges of treason. The regime installed a complex web of regulations that prohibited the media from supporting Communism, advocating Taiwan's secession from China, or attacking the KMT and the Chiang family (Berman 1992). Meanwhile, the regime bestowed vast and arbitrary power on overlapping censorship agencies made up of the KMT's Cultural Committee, the Taiwan Garrison Command, and the Government Information Office. In the following decades hundreds of reporters, writers, and editorialists were detained, interrogated, harassed or jailed for stepping outside the bounds of the permissible.

The media enjoyed preferential tax treatment and many other benefits. Combined use of rewards and punishments was more effective than punitive measures alone. Better yet, the ideological effect was at its maximum when the state sought to condition the worldview of its media patrons so that their submission to authority and state-defined goals was unrecognized or assumed (Boulding 1990, Galbraith 1983, Lukes 1974). To this end, the KMT opened media resources to a small circle of favored clients through formal declaration of a press ban policy and through an array of behind-the-scene maneuvers that cemented their ideological solidarity and promoted their interest integration.[8] The KMT saw to it that mainlander loyalists largely retained media ownership, even though local Taiwanese were relatively free to pursue wealth in non-media sectors. The state exchanged its privileges for the media's allegiance as a whole package rather than a piecemeal deal. Despite the unequal power relationship, they struck a set of tacit understandings—oiled by *guanxi* (personal ties) and informal arrangements—to sustain mutual trust and responsibility. To protect its exclusive control, the state strictly forbade the media to forge any horizontal alliance or linkages with labor unions, social groups, or other media outlets (Lee 1992).

The state declared the press ban policy in 1951, foreclosing the issuance of press licenses while allowing the already held certificates to be traded. This ban froze the total number of newspapers at thirty-one. Inheriting Japanese colonial legacy and Sun Yat-sen's statist economic doctrines, the regime monopolized the control of Taiwan's state capital including a wide range of key nationalized industries, banks and other financial institutions (Wu 1987). Based on this control, the KMT was able to amass a magnificent sum of assets, properties, and investments. It also had free access to the national treasury by virtue of its monopolistic control in the parliament, where the budgets it submitted invariably sailed through without storms. Determined to forestall acquisition of newspaper licenses by potential power challengers, the party-state came to collect a half of Taiwan's thirty-one press licenses. Headed by party officials, most of these ideological loudspeakers would have long disappeared had it not been for a constant supply of public funds. Even other pro-KMT papers could "borrow" money from a KMT-controlled revolving fund to prolong their lives.

The *United Daily News* and the *China Times*, started in the early 1950s by two mainlanders close to the KMT, were at first of marginal importance relative to the party–state organ. But as the party–state organ suffered from tightened control, these two papers rose to prominence in the 1970s by offering a preponderance of sensational crime stories to attract readers. Moreover, profiting from Taiwan's "economic miracle," they reaped immense advertising profits. Under the press ban policy, the license eventually became a scare commodity affordable only to the party-state and to these two papers. Through progressive consolidation of press licenses, the *United Daily News* and the *China Times* evolved as conglomerates, known as the Big Two, eventually controlling two-thirds of Taiwan's newspaper circulation and advertising. (The third tier—besides the party-state organ and the Big Two—was a group of fringe local papers scattered around the island, sharing the limited leftover space.) In its midst, the state was poignantly obtrusive. In 1972, for example, no sooner had a local-born industrialist, Wang Yongqing, acquired two-thirds' controlling interests in the *United Daily News* than it began to criticize the government's economic policy (Zhang 1997). As a Taiwanese who owned an influential newspaper and then broke the tacit patron–client codes, he was suspected of using the press to promote self-serving policies and was curtly ordered to relinquish his shares to Wang Tiwu as a twenty-year low-interest loan. A former security guard to Chiang Kai-shek, Wang Tiwu went on to build the largest press conglomerate in Taiwan and made it a citadel of conservative state ideology. In 1979 the publishers of both conglomerates were recruited to serve as members of the KMT's standing committee whereas the publisher of the party organ, *Central Daily News*, was excluded from the inner circle of power. The *United Daily News* sided with the KMT's conservative wing, whereas the *China Times* leaned toward its reformist wing (Berman 1992, Lee 1993).

Broadcasting

Japanese colonial rule (1894–1945) did not produce a strong imprint on the development of Taiwan's broadcasting system. Since 1949 the KMT party-state has dominated much of the radio frequency in the name of national security (Zheng 1993: 109). Of the thirty-three stations, the KMT-controlled Broadcasting Corporation of China (BCC) alone accounted for 32 percent of total transmitters and 43 percent of radio power on the island. Then came the six military stations, which controlled 41 percent of the transmitters and 52 percent of radio power. A large number of small private stations (twenty)—owned by protégés of the security apparatuses, religious groups, and wealthy families—could only share the remainder (15 percent of the transmitters and less than 2 percent of radio power).

While the Japanese failed to transplant a radio model, Taiwan patterned its television after the Japanese commercial system in the early 1960s, which had been inspired by the Americans. Alternative models were never contemplated. National economy was too impoverished to finance a noncommercial system. Moreover, the state was eager to harness television to showcase its commitment to free enterprise *vis-à-vis* communist anti-capitalism before the Cold War international community whose support it sorely needed (Lee 1980). But Taiwan's capitalism being state capitalism, its three television stations did not have to meet free-market competition. As a product of the bureaucratic–business complex, they were owned by the government (TTV), the KMT (CTV), and the military (CTS). All members of the appointed board of directors bore conspicuous political credentials: retired generals or ministerial officials, current high-ranking politicians, and major businessmen well linked to the political elite (Lee 1980, Zheng 1993). As an expedient and powerful vehicle of state subordination, television avoided politically sensitive subjects and disparaged dissenting views. As a mass medium it had appealed to predominantly local Taiwanese tastes, but the party-state, imbued with Chinese nationalism, forced the three stations to purge their programming of local dialect in favor of Mandarin (Lee 1980: 157). This blatant suppression of cultural and linguistic localism was to develop into a focal point of relentless protests in the next decades. Chinese nationalism also served to limit imported fares to 30 percent.

These state-controlled television oligopolies were among the most significant profit-makers in an environment protected from free-market competition.[9] By catering to an audience with low cultural taste, they came to garner one-third of Taiwan's flourishing advertising revenues (the Big Two took another one-third of the total). The gap between the medium's professed cultural goals and actual performance was so glaring as to court public criticisms. Even both paramount leaders lashed out at television stations for not fulfilling their anti-communist and other cultural goals, insisting that television programs should not exaggerate the "dark side" of society or corrode public morality (Lee 1992). Scared by such criticisms, the state-appointed managers one by one vowed to curtail the amount of violence and vulgarity, but to no avail—the market logic dictated that they meet the cutthroat commercial competition head-on. Even paramount leaders could not completely impose their iron-fisted wills on (or against) market forces.

Capital concentration and power struggle

Democratic change means a gradual disintegration of the strife-ridden ruling regime, incorporation of the opposition, and media realignment with the power structure. Donohue, Tichenor *et al.*'s "guard dog" hypothesis (1995) argues that the media perform as a sentry not for the community as a whole, but for groups "having sufficient power and influence to create and control their own security systems." Moving from "authoritarian-clientelism" to "semi-clientelism" (Benson 1996, Fox 1994, Yoon 1989), the state attempts to induce media compliance more by the threat of the withdrawal of favors than by the use of punishments. Restrictive press laws have been lifted or relaxed, while censorship agencies have lost their functions. The changing political economy binds the once suppressed business capital to the state structure in a new coalition. I shall deal with the press in this section and return later to discuss post-martial law changes in broadcasting.

The first victim of liberalization was the party-state press, due to weakened ability of the KMT to "pork-barrel" government appropriations as press subsidies. Two of the KMT-owned papers were closed down and the military-owned *Taiwan Daily News* was sold to individual capitalists. The party-owned Central News Agency (CNA) and BCC became state-run; to seek parliamentary funding, they now must appear to be "fair and balanced." As the KMT's *Central Daily News* is further marginalized, neither has the DPP press organ taken root (Wei 1996). For the sake of its own legitimacy, the mainstream press must fairly "index" legitimate voices according to the range of views expressed by prominent officials and members of institutional power blocs in the new political landscape (Bennett 1990). The opposition voices, now included within the official range of debate, were to be admitted with growing visibility, albeit in accordance with respective press interests and ideology (Tao 1995, Lo *et al.* 1998). In 1992, the conservative *United Daily News* lost 90,000 copies in circulation as a result of a boycott campaign led by pro-DPP figures.

Nonetheless, the Big Two had left little room for the more than 200 newspapers that have appeared since 1987. In total, only twenty-five dailies are being published. In economic terms, the two oligopolies have far greater potential power as "price makers" in affecting economic parameters, including output levels, technology, and even tastes (Caporaso and Levine 1992: 167). Each of them invested an additional NT$200 million (US$1 = NT$27 then) into upgrading facilities and recruiting talent, while introducing evening papers. No one could match them in quality and quantity. They expanded from sixteen to twenty-four, thirty-two, forty-eight, even sixty pages, half of which were devoted to advertising. They have further installed full-fledged editorial offices and sophisticated printing facilities in central and south Taiwan, thus threatening the survival of fringe local papers (Yen 1998).

Symbolizing this new alliance of money and power, the *Liberty Times* is the only paper able to gain a significant foothold and to threaten the Big Two's market supremacy. As a cultural enterprise, the newspaper could provide burgeoning capitalists and political forces with opportunities to enhance their influence. The owner of the obscure *Liberty Times*, Lin Rongsan, was a real-estate tycoon. Having been humiliated by party functionaries in their attempts to prevent him from being nominated for a high political office, and ridiculed by the Big Two as a "cash cow" trying to buy political influence (Diao and You 1997), he decided to micromanage his own paper. He took on the Big Two by launching a NT$120 million promotion campaign in 1992, followed two years later by another NT$500 million giveaway with offers of extravagant prizes (Teng 1997).[10] A series of marketing campaigns sent the paper's circulation to 600,000 copies in 1994. Furthermore, in early 1996 the Big Two unexpectedly lost 20 percent of their circulation to the *Liberty Times* because the latter refused to raise the cartel-set newspaper price. Capable of withstanding further losses, the *Liberty Times* distributed as many as 300,000 copies at no cost to readers, prompting the Big Two each to give away 100,000 copies (Diao and You 1997). To raid on the Big Two's circulation networks, it offered the same newspaper carriers 10 percent more compensation. In some locales, it even delivered free companion copies to households subscribing to either of the Big Two, thus pulling in many new converts after the trial period was over. In 1996 the paper was able to raise its advertising price by 40 percent. Even though this paper's growth in revenues was matched by even greater losses,[11] the Big Two have seen little growth in revenue or profit. With the old patron–client relationship losing its potency, the trio—the Big Two plus the Johnny-comes-lately *Liberty Times*—must now join a fierce three-way battle. But together they still enjoy immense direct and indirect power over others, even setting and disrupting the rules of the game (Golding and Murdock 1991).

Their financial might intimidates potential challengers from entering into the market and elbows weaker competitors out of it.

Since no one was in full control of the KMT leadership fights from 1987 to 1995, the media did not have to play up to a single force (Teng 1997). Li Denghui, the first local-born president, never concealed his contempt of the Chinese Communist regime for seeking to bring Taiwan back to its fold. The opposing faction led by Premier Hao Bocun, a mainlander military strongman, criticized Li's separatist tendency. The *Central Daily News* briefly mounted a subtle attack on the military press for endorsing Hao. Most other papers did not explicitly take sides. The power and ideological struggle came to a head during the 1996 presidential election amidst China's missile intimidation off Taiwan's coast. Institutional conflict and leadership struggle of this kind fall into what Hallin (1986) calls the sphere of "legitimate controversy," and, as expected, the press devoted roughly equal and balanced attention to the three presidential hopefuls (Tao 1995). Political orthodoxy was resettled after Li's landslide victory, reshaping the media's spheres of "consensus" and "dissent" (Hallin 1986), especially on such explosive issues as ethnic identity and the China–Taiwan relations.

Though greatly broadened, media discourse in the post-martial law era has been narrowly oriented toward electoral politics and factional fights (Feng 1995). The *Liberty Times* in particular has fervently exploited ethnic politics and anti-China sentiments. As a self-designated defender of local Taiwanese interests, it supports President Li without reservation and regularly assails his political opponents and the Big Two's Chinese nationalism. Its staunch loyalty to President Li has made the KMT's party organs seem irrelevant. As if fringe local papers in south and central Taiwan (such as *Minzhong Daily* and the *Taiwan Times*) had not suffered enough from the Big Two's pressure, the *Liberty Times* further encroached on their small and ideologically overlapping readership bases (Diao and You 1997, Yen 1998).

Media impact on society

Like most authoritarian regimes, Taiwan's party-state harbored what I call an "illusion of high technology" that assumes technological sophistication as a direct measure, if not the main source, of its ideological power and social impact (Lee 1999). The party-state concentrated its control on the "big media" of the day (newspapers and television) with little appreciation for the potential power of the "little media" (primitive cable services and political magazines). Contrary to this exaggerated "developmentalist" view of technological prowess (Schramm 1977), Taiwan's movement groups used the little media to wage their guerrilla wars that finally changed the political contour. There was a natural marriage between the resource-poor movement groups deprived of access to the big media, and the little media that were financially and technologically less constraining.[12]

In Taiwan a succession of political magazines, which were not included in the press ban, operated as centers of organized intelligence for the opposition movement (Lee 1993). In the 1950s, liberal mainlander intellectuals surrounded *Free China* as a forum to advocate democratic reform, only to be aborted when they were on the verge of organizing an opposition party. The 1960s marked a decade of hushed silence. By the mid-1970s, oppositional magazines revived by indigenous Taiwanese politicians were not limited to urban intellectuals, but reached downward to attract a sizable middle-class and grass-roots following that yearned for more equitable power sharing and greater political participation. Oriented toward elections held almost annually, these magazines became synonymous with the *Dangwai* (opposition) movement. They contested the official "truth" and openly negotiated new rules of the game with the authorities. They also educated the public, mobilized their support during the elections, and nurtured collective oppositional consciousness among the *Dangwai* members. When the regime decided to harshly clamp down on the *Dangwai* magazines, they were already too strong to be uprooted and defiantly played a "hide and seek" game with official censors (Lee 1993). Toward the mid-1980s some of these magazines began to absorb market pressure by producing ethically dubious accounts that unveiled the mystery of the Chiang family.

Operating within "limited pluralism" (Linz 1974) under a market system, mass media must fulfill the dual goals of political legitimation and profit-making, thus creating certain ideological ambiguities on the boundaries of the expressible. Gouldner (1976: 157) notes that the imperatives of profitability contribute in part to the fostering of diverse media accounts that complement and check one another. The Big Two being allies of the official policies, competition for readership and market share gave them grounds to adopt a more independent journalistic approach than the party-state organs. As Tien (1989) contends, since business goals sometimes ran counter to party interests, the press frequently deviated from the official position and criticized government policies. Chiang Ching-kuo expressed occasional appreciation when he read to his liking some editorial criticisms of an administrative but not political nature. Under pressure from oppositional magazines, the Big Two were also instrumental in diffusing abstract democratic ideas by inviting respected scholars at home and abroad to write columns daily, whose stature "put them in a position to mildly and subtly criticize the KMT's continued imposition of martial law and its press ban" (Lee 1993).

Most journalists in Taiwan, whether from the mainstream press or from oppositional magazines, uncritically embraced the norms of professionalism and the "watch dog" rhetoric imported from the United States. Many idealistic reporters in the mainstream press, against their publishers' orders or wishes, contributed to poorly staffed *Dangwai* magazines the bulk of inside stories and biting criticisms of the KMT that were denied publication by their own papers. The regime never abandoned the abstract goals of democracy and press freedom, only arguing that they should be temporarily abrogated in the interest of anti-communism. The oppositional forces challenged the extra-legal character of the state–media clientelistic relationship as anti-constitutional. The gap between the regime's words and deeds provided for a fertile battleground against state censorship of the press and for the renewal of civil society (Lee 1993). The *Dangwai* magazines were living in symbiosis with the mainstream press as strange bedfellows for fifteen years until democratic change deprived them of their *raison d'être*. In this regard, exception must be taken to Rampal (1994) for crediting Taiwan's increasing openness mainly to the legacy of Confucian humanism. Confucian ethos may have constrained the authoritarian rulers in a general way, but Taiwan's liberal struggle for democracy and press freedom had come primarily from the US influence. Media professionalism has been favorably regarded in Taiwan. This contrasts with radical Western critique of media professionalism said to "reproduce a vision of social reality which refuses to examine the basic structures of power and privilege" and "represent collusion with institutions whose legitimacy was in dispute" (Schudson 1978:160).

Technology and globalization

In contrast to press liberalization, the party-state continued to hold a tight rein on broadcasting after 1987 for fear of losing its advantage to the DPP in electoral support. The pro-DPP *Capital Daily* having failed to survive, the DPP applied for a radio license in vain. After many organized protest rallies, the DPP decided to sabotage state monopoly by waging another electronic guerrilla war.[13]

Because of Taiwan's mountainous terrain, common antennas first appeared in 1969 to improve television reception in some remote areas. In 1976, cable operators began to offer illegal services by installing VCRs, cheap coaxial cable, and crude transmission equipment. Before long, similar stations sprouted up throughout the island, collectively known as "Channel Four." Despite occasional crackdowns, the party-state did not regard it as a serious threat to power. By 1985 total cable viewership reached 1.2 million people on the island and 40 percent of the population in Taipei. In 1990, however, the DPP used microwave technology to establish its first "democracy television station," followed by a loosely organized "democracy network" consisting of twenty-one small and unsophisticated stations, all attacking the KMT without mercy. Another DPP member even sought to jam the military-controlled network (CTS) with equipment smuggled in from the Philippines.

The agitated Premier Hao ordered full-scale crackdowns, which produced only skirmishes but not solutions. The party-state was at a loss to defend its continued television monopoly. State censors often found it difficult to locate the inexpensive and highly mobile cable transmitters that could be hidden away. Cable subscription was rising very rapidly when it could receive spillover signals from overseas satellites including the Japanese BS-3a and BS-3b, the AsiaSat 1, and the Indonesian Palapa-B2P. The Hong Kong-based Star TV, via AsiaSat 1, was particularly significant (Chan 1994); China's signals (including the CCTV), other satellite broadcasters, and American pay channels have made their way into Taiwan's livingrooms.

What finally forced the government in Taiwan to bring the chaotic cable industry into an institutional framework was pressure from the United States. Impatient with the trade imbalance, Washington threatened to apply sanctions if Taiwan did not stop cable operators and others from infringing American film copyright. Taiwan therefore in 1992 extended its copyright law from printed words to cover films, music records on laser disc, computer software and databases. Taiwan objected in vain to what it saw as unfair and hypocritical demands by the United States to allow airing of (largely US) tobacco and liquor commercials on cable channels. When the Cable TV Act was ratified in 1993 to avert US trade sanctions, it was twenty-four years after cable had existed on the island. Penetrating 75 percent of Taiwan's households, the cable industry remains weak in audience and advertising compared with the three television networks.[14] Some cable channels have covered elections more fairly than official television networks (Lo *et al.* 1998).

Under cross-pressure from various interest groups (including the KMT and the DPP), the state acquiesced to the *status quo* by legalizing all previously illegal operations in the Cable TV Act. The Act divided Taiwan into fifty-two regions, each with five multi-channel cable systems—too many for a small island nation. Only a few large industrial conglomerates, affiliated with foreign interests, possess the economy of scale to meet investment needs for the costly infrastructure and a voracious amount of (foreign) programs (Zheng 1993). The industry is going through the process of mergers and takeovers, with Liba and Hexin—two conglomerates close to the KMT—emerging to dominate the market; in Taipei, Liba alone controls three-fourths of the cable operators. The KMT-owned Boxin Entertainment Inc. has not measured up to its own ambition. As part of the global trend toward broadcasting deregulation, Taiwan's cable industry has brought the coalition between political groups and financial interests to another height, and the cable itself may serve as a conduit for international capital (Feng 1995).

In a naked display of power politics, the party-state finally opened up one more television channel to the pro-DPP forces in order to coopt dissent, defuse public pressure, and protect its own continued monopoly. In response to public outcry, the state had also set out to establish a public television under the supervision of a rubber-stamp committee. The state had no intention to abandon its habit and power to control public television, which was supposed to be insulated from political meddling and market competition. Sadly, having got its coveted television station, the DPP did not display any genuine interest in safeguarding this "public sphere" either (Xu 1997, Feng 1995 1998).

The implications for globalization are ambiguous. Globalization implies a decline of the nation-state, while the realist paradigm tends to gloss over the internal dimension of state sovereignty (Featherstone and Lash 1995, Hamelink 1995: 387). In the case of Taiwan, the origin of cable politics stemmed primarily from internal inequity whereas external forces played a subsidiary and catalyst role. The state structure, though weakened, remains powerful enough to make major decisions and allocate resources in alliance with the capital; power and capital have developed a new dialectical relationship. Large numbers of small merchants (for reasons of profit) and some opposition politicians (for reasons of power) found a strange bedfellow in external satellite signals (new technology) to fill their cable channels. The authoritarian state, having previously been aloof to domestic challenge, yielded to technological pressure and to the overwhelming politico–economic pressure of an external hegemonic power. Featherstone (1990) argues for conceptualizing a global culture more in terms of "the diversity, variety and richness of popular and local discourses, codes and practices which resist and play-back systemicity and order" rather than its "alleged homogenizing processes." The intersection of "global" and local media, however, seems to have created an amalgam of cultural diversity and homogenization in Taiwan. Cultural and linguistic localism has been revived, yet channel abundance is filled with "junk food" content. The Cable Act also greatly relaxed quota restrictions on imported programs, presumably under US pressure. This will link local capital more closely to "global" actors—multinational corporations and the US government—in their common goal to cash in on the affluent Taiwan market by providing standardized, deliberately bland and apolitical entertainment. The inflow of foreign capital is still small but will grow. All these contradictory developments have led Feng (1995) among others to condemn this technological diffusion as a process of "colonization" rather than "globalization."

Concluding remarks

The critical political economy of communication is more "economistic," whereas the liberal political economy of communication is more "political." The former is a "top–down" approach in the sense that its proponents critique the status quo—the "incomplete emancipation," resource inequity, and cultural distortion posed by *economic* dynamics in advanced capitalism—from the high plateaus of various radical Marxist humanist formulations, invariably committed to some form of socialism (Garnham 1990, Golding and Murdock 1991, 1997, Keane 1991, Mosco 1996).[15] These writers tend to take the state for granted precisely because state control of the media is more invisible and benign in advanced capitalism. However, the liberal political economy perspective seems to fit late-developing, most Third World and former communist countries, where the state takes a dominant role in "shaping the distribution of power within society and the direction of economic policy" (Staniland 1985: 75). In many of these countries, economic and media resources are significantly controlled by the state and its agents. Hence, the proponents of this "bottom–up" approach struggle against the low and rough ground of naked state media repression and are inspired by the liberal images of "checks and balances" in "the marketplace of ideas." After all, a freer market order, not abused by the state, offers an emancipatory alternative to aristocratic, oligarchic or authoritarian dictatorship.

It is clear that in Taiwan the liberal political economy perspective has greater power in explaining the martial-law media, whereas the critical political economy perspective has gained increasing relevance for the post-martial law media but *not* to the exclusion of the former perspective. Both perspectives, rooted in different conceptions of society and power, are *not* to be taken simply as two linear stages of "development." More important is the fact that in post-martial law Taiwan, both perspectives coexist side by side uneasily and paradoxically. The state—weakened but still dominant—negotiates with, seeks to coopt, and struggles against the market forces in a newly emerging relationship that is intermeshed, fluid, dialectical, and even blurred—with profound implications to media ownership and autonomy. The struggle is an ongoing process, neither an end state nor a settled terrain. Though this theoretical point is of broader generality to the media in many newly democratizing countries, its complexity obviously invites more vigorous scholarly debates and empirical inquires. How media technology impinges on or is impinged on by the state–capital relationship in the globalization process should also cry out for further articulation.

Notes

1 My use of the "liberal-pluralist" and "radical Marxist" labels partly follows Curran *et al.*'s (1982) "pluralist" versus "Marxist" and corresponds to Murdock's (1982) "theory of industrial society" versus "theory of capitalism."

2 To the extent that critical political economists (informed by different social theories) analyze the state, they differ in opinions. Herman and Chomsky (1988), Schiller (1992) and Smythe (1994) see the state as serving transnational media corporate interest. Golding and Murdock (1991), on the other hand, also single out "the changing role of the state and government intervention" as a guardian of public interest to ward off corporate assault on media diversity in Britain.

3 For an extensive comparison of these two approaches, see Lee (2000b).

4 In the light of Burrell and Morgan's (1979: 1–37) exposition, these two perspectives do not differ on ontological, epistemological or methodological grounds as much as they differ in the political dimension.

5 The liberal-pluralist view seems acutely applicable to the "authoritarian conditions" of today's mainland China and yesterday's Taiwan under martial law (Lee 1994, 2000a). What's more, as Hong Kong's media ownership is being conglomerated into the hands of those with substantial business interest in mainland China, market vibrancy and liberal claims of media professionalism have served to counterbalance the perceived political pressure from

Beijing (Lee 1997, 1998, 2000c). The South Korean case (Yoon 1989) also seems comparable to Taiwan.

6 Upon descending on the island, the KMT regime tried to squeeze resources from the war-torn Taiwan to mainland China for fighting a bitter civil war against the communists. The regime followed its economic plundering with political repression, igniting a major ethnic conflict in 1947 killing thousands of local Taiwanese. In 1949 after losing mainland China to the communists, the KMT imposed an authoritarian control on the island of Taiwan, calling itself the Republic of China. The civilian and military refugees who migrated with the KMT to Taiwan were superimposed on the local population, controlling political power and major media resources.

7 The policy of incorporation is different from the communist system of "repression without inducements," the liberal-democratic system of laissez-faire policy, or the policy of cooptation marked by high inducements and low punishments (as was the case in colonial Hong Kong, see Chan and Lee 1991).

8 In 1977, the pro-opposition *Taiwan Daily News* was taken over by the military for NT$100 million. In 1982 the KMT bought a press license for NT$60 million, and renamed it the *Modern Daily*, but the paper failed to survive. In the name of "publicizing government policy," the Provincial Government of Taiwan appropriated NT$300 million per year for village leaders to subscribe to any of the five party-controlled newspapers. The Ministry of Education covertly financed the overseas edition of the *Central Daily News* (NT$100 million in 1987), the CNA and the BCC, all owned by the KMT. Other funding sources were unknown to the public; CNA's former president (Huang 1996) disclosed that the agency had been subsidized by the Ministry of Foreign Affairs for eight years before nationalization.

9 Television ranked first in profit among other monopoly enterprises. In 1990, the three networks had a combined capital of NT$2.5 billion and the profit reached NT$1.8 billion, with a 73 percent rate of profit. By comparison, seven other monopoly enterprises in the service sector have a 47 percent rate of profit in 1991 (quoted in Feng 1995: 50).

10 The Big Two had been making claims and counter-claims about their circulation figures. In the early 1990s the *China Times* led the way with a drawing for 1,000 taels of gold, followed by the *United Daily News*'s giveaway of NT$20 million to "thank our readers." In 1992, the *Liberty Times* offered lucky draw winners big prizes, ranging from 6,000 taels of gold to 20 Mercedes Benz automobiles, 100 jeeps, and 1,000 motorcycles. The first prize in the 1994 promotion was a suburban home worth NT$30 million (Teng 1997).

11 Its revenue grew from NT$2 billion in 1994 to NT$2.9 billion in 1995, but its loss also increased from NT$250 million to NT$390 million.

12 This point has also found empirical support in, for example, Sreberny-Mohammadi and Mohammadi (1994), Downing (1996b), Hoffman and Duggan (1988) and Tomaselli (1989).

13 This section is adapted from Lee (1999).

14 In 1996, cable TV accounted for 13 percent of Taiwan's total advertising dollars, three television networks retained 30 percent (a slight drop from the previous year), newspapers and magazines controlled 46 percent and 12 percent respectively (News Council 1997: 300). The fact that so many cable operators have to share only 13 percent of the advertising revenues suggests that many operators are financially strained and may be gobbled up by conglomerates.

15 In the face of the seemingly public acceptance of the *status quo*, critical scholars in the "heartland" countries keep asking: "Why do people not rebel more often than they do?" (Downing 1996a: 230).

References

Bennett, L. (1990) "Toward a theory of press–state relations in the United States," *Journal of Communication*, 40(2): 103–25.

Benson, J. (1996) "Clientelism before and after 1987: consistency and change within the press–state relationship in Taiwan," unpublished term paper, University of Minnesota.

Berman, D. (1992) *Words Like Colored Glass: The Role of the Press in Taiwan's Democratization Process*, Boulder, CO: Westview.

Boulding, K. (1990) *Three Faces of Power*, Newburry, CA: Sage.

Burrell, G. and Morgan, G. (1979) *Sociological Paradigms and Organizational Analysis*, London: Heinemann.

Caproraso, J. and Levine, D. P. (1992) *Theories of Political Economy*, New York: Cambridge University Press.

Chan, J. M. (1994) "National responses and accessibility to Star TV in Asia," *Journal of Communication*, 44(3): 112–31.

Chan, J. M. and Lee, Chin-Chuan (1991) *Mass Media and Political Transition: The Hong Kong's Press in China's Orbit*, New York: Guilford.

Chinese Journalism Association (1996) *Media Yearbook of the Republic of China, 1996* (in Chinese), Taipei: Fengyun.

Curran, J. (1991), "Mass media and democracy: a reappraisal," in J. Curran and M. Gurevitch (eds.) *Mass Media and Society*, London: Arnold.

Curran, J., Gurevitch, M. and Woollacott, J. (1982) "The study of the media: theoretical approaches," in M. Gurevitch, T. Bennett, J. Curran and J. Woollacott (eds.) *Culture, Society, and the Media*, New York: Methuen.

Diao, Manpeng and You, Changshan (1997) "Is the 'largest' newspaper built by gold?" (in Chinese), *Commonwealth*, July issue.

Donohue, G. A., Tichenor, P. and Olien, C. (1995) "A guard dog perspective on the role of media," *Journal of Communication*, 45(2): 115–32.

Downing, J. (1996a) *Internationalizing Media Theory*, London: Sage.

Downing, J. (1996b) *Alternative Media and Political Movements*, Thousand Oaks, CA: Sage.

Eisenstadt, S. N. and Roniger, L. (1981) "The study of patron–client relations and recent development in sociological theory," in S. N. Eisenstadt and R. Lernarchand (eds.) *Political Clientelism, Patronage and Development*, Beverly Hills, CA: Sage.

Featherstone, M. (ed.) (1990) *Global Culture*, Newburry Park, CA: Sage.

Featherstone, M. and Lash, S. (1995) "Globalization, modernity and the spatialization of social theory: an introduction," in M. Featherstone, S. Lash and R. Robertson (eds.) *Global Identities*, London: Sage.

Feng, Jiansan (1995) *The Political Economy of the Broadcast Capital Movement: On the Changes of Taiwan's Broadcast Media in the 1990s* (in Chinese), Taipei: Tangshan.

Feng, Jiansan (1998) *Big Media* (in Chinese), Taipei: Yuanliu.

Fox, J. (1994) "The difficult transition from clientelism to citizenship," *World Politics*, 46(2): 151–84.

Galbraith, J. K. (1983) *The Anatomy of Power*, Boston: Houghton Mifflin.

Garnham, N. (1990) *Capitalism and Communication*, London: Sage.

Gold, T. (1985) *State and Society in the Taiwan Miracle*, Armonk, NY: Sharpe.

Golding, P. and Murdock, G. (1979) "Ideology and the mass media," in M. Barrett (ed.) *Ideology and Cultural Production*, New York: St. Martin's.

Golding, P. and Murdock, G. (1991) "Culture, communications, and political economy," in J. Curran and M. Gurevitch (eds.) *Mass Media and Society*, London: Arnold.

Golding, P. and Murdock, G. (eds.) (1997) *The Political Economy of the Media*, Brookfield, VT: Elgar.

Gouldner, A. W. (1976) *The Dialectic of Ideology and Technology*, New York: Oxford University Press.

Hallin, D. (1986) *The "Uncensored" War*, New York: Oxford University Press.

Hamelink, C. (1995) "Globalism and national sovereignty," in K. Nordenstreng and H. I. Schiller (eds.) *Beyond National Sovereignty*, Norwood, NJ: Ablex.

Herman, E. and Chomsky, N. (1988) *Manufacturing Consent*, New York: Pantheon.

Hoffman, D. and Duggan, W. (1988) *Guerrilla Media: A Citizen's Guide to Using Electronic Media for Social Change, The Inside Story From Tony Schwartz*, video program produced by Varied Directions, Inc.

Huang, Tiancai (1996) "New Agencies" (in Chinese), *The 1996 ROC News Media Yearbook*, Taipei: Fengyun.

Keane, J. (1991) *The Media and Democracy*, Cambridge: Polity Press.

Lee, Chin-Chuan (1980) *Media Imperialism Reconsidered*, Beverly Hills, CA: Sage.

Lee, Chin-Chuan (1992) "Emancipated from authoritarian rule: the political economy of the press in Taiwan" (in Chinese), in L. Chu and J. M. Chan (eds.) *Mass Communication and Social Change*, Hong Kong: Chinese University, Department of Journalism and Communication.

Lee, Chin-Chuan (1993) "Sparking a fire: the press and the ferment of democratic change in Taiwan," *Journalism Monographs*, No. 138.

Lee, Chin-Chuan (1994) "Ambiguities and contradictions: issues in China's changing political communication," in Chin-Chuan Lee (ed.) *China's Media, Media's China*, Boulder, CO: Westview.

Lee, Chin-Chuan (1997) "Media structure and regime change in Hong Kong," in Ming K. Chan (ed.) *The Challenge of Hong Kong's Reintegration with China*, Hong Kong: Hong Kong University Press.

Lee, Chin-Chuan (1998) "Press self-censorship and political transition in Hong Kong," *Harvard International Journal of Press/Politics*, 3(2): 55–73.

Lee, Chin-Chuan (1999) "State control, technology, and cultural concerns: the politics of cable television in Taiwan," *Studies of Broadcasting*, No. 34: 127–51.

Lee, Chin-Chuan (ed.) (2000a) *Money, Power and Media: Communication Patterns and Bureaucratic Control in Cultural China*, Evanston, IL: Northwestern University Press.

Lee, Chin-Chuan (2000b) "Chinese communication: prisms, trajectories, and modes of understanding," in Chin-Chuan Lee (ed.) *Money, Power and Media: Communication Patterns and Bureaucratic Control in Cultural China*, Evanston, IL: Northwestern University Press.

Lee, Chin-Chuan (2000c) "The paradox of political economy: media structure, press freedom, and regime change in Hong Kong," in Chin-Chuan Lee (ed.) *Money, Power and Media: Communication Patterns and Bureaucratic Control in Cultural China*, Evanston, IL: Northwestern University Press.

Linz, J. (1974), "Totalitarian and authoritarian regimes,"in F. Greenstein and N. Polsby (eds.) *Handbook of Political Science*, vol. 3, Reading, MA: Addison-Wesley.

Lo, Ven-hwei, Neilan, E. and King, Pu-tsung (1998) "Television coverage of the 1995 legislative election in Taiwan: rise of cable television as a force for balance in media coverage," *Journal of Broadcasting and Electronic Media*, 42(3): 340–55.

Lukes, S. (1974) *Power: A Radical View*, London: Macmillan.

Mosco, V. (1996) *The Political Economy of Communication*, London: Sage.

Murdock, G. (1982) "Large corporations and the control of the communications industries," in M. Gurevitch, T. Bennett, J. Curran, and J. Woollacott (eds.) *Culture, Society, and the Media*, New York: Methuen.

News Council of the Republic of China (1997) *Strategies of Television Management at the Turn of the Century* (in Chinese), Taipei: News Council.

O'Donnell, G. A. (1978) "Reflections on the pattern of change in the bureaucratic–authoritarian state," *Latin American Studies*, 8: 3–38.

Rampal, J. C. (1994) "Post-martial law media boom in Taiwan," *Gazette*, 53: 73–92.

Schiller, H. I. (1992) *Mass Media and American Empire*, 2nd edn, Boulder, CO: Westview.

Schmitter, P. (1974) "Still the century of corporatism?" *Review of Politics*, 36(1): 85–131.

Schramm, W. (1977) *Big Media, Little Media*, Beverly Hills, CA: Sage.

Schudson, M. (1978) *Discovering the News*, New York: Basic.

Schudson, M. (1991) "The sociology of news production revisited," in J. Curran and M. Gurevitch (eds.) *Mass Media and Society*, London: Arnold.

Smythe, D. (1994) *Clockwise: Perspectives on Communication*, ed. Thomas Guback, Boulder, CO: Westview.

Sreberny-Mohammadi, A. and Mohammadi, A. (1994) *Small Media, Big Revolution: Communication, Culture, and the Iranian Revolution*, Minneapolis: University of Minnesota Press.

Staniland, M. (1985) *What Is Political Economy?*, New Haven: Yale University Press.

Tao, Sheng-ping (1995) "The role of the press in the transitional Taiwan: an investigation of the 'guard dog' conception of the media," unpublished M.A. thesis, University of Minnesota.

Teng, Shufen (1997) "Hard-pressed Taiwan's newspapers battle for readers," *Sinorama*, August, pp. 6–15.

Tien, Hung-mao (1989) *The Great Transition: Political and Social Change in the Republic of China*, Stanford, CA: Hoover Institution Press.

Tomaselli, K. (1989) "Transferring video skills to the community: the problem of power," *Media Development*, 25(4): 11–15.

Tuchman, G. (1978) *Making News*, New York: Free Press.

Wang, Fang (1994) "The political economy of authoritarian clientelism in Taiwan," in L. Roniger and A. Gunes-Ayata (eds.) *Democracy, Clientelism, and Civil Society*, Boulder, CO: Lynne Rienner.

Wei, Ran (1996) "Coping with the challenge of a changing market: strategies from Taiwan's press," *Gazette*, 58: 117–29.

Winkler, E. A. (1984) "Institutionalization and participation in Taiwan: from hard to soft authoritarianism?" *China Quarterly*, 99: 481–99.

Wu, Nai-teh (1987) "The politics of a regime patronage system: mobilization and control within an authoritarian regime," unpublished Ph.D. dissertation, University of Chicago.

Xu, Jiashi (1997) "Public media in Taiwan" (in Chinese), *News Mirror Weekly*, 436 (March 17): 6–9.

Yen, Bohe (1998) "Price war in southern Taiwan" (in Chinese), *News Mirror Weekly*, 514 (September 14): 42–5.

Yoon, Youngchul (1989) "Political transition and press ideology in South Korea 1980–1989," unpublished Ph.D. dissertation, University of Minnesota.

Zhang, Zuojin (1997) "If Wang Yongqing had run the *United Daily News*" (in Chinese), *Global View Monthly*, October.

Zheng Zhuicheng (ed.) (1993) *Deconstructing the Broadcast Media* (in Chinese), Taipei: Yunchen.

10 Globalized theories and national controls

The state, the market, and the Malaysian media

Zaharom Nain

To the casual observer, the contemporary Malaysian media[1] scene is one which is rapidly changing and expanding. Over the past two decades, both the mainstream print and broadcast media in Malaysia have undergone a major period of transition, coinciding with the period in which Mahathir Mohamad has been prime minister. New newspapers and radio and television stations have emerged during this period, signifying to many a liberalization of media policies, a relaxation of control. However, casual observations often tend to be very misleading. In the Malaysian context, as I attempt to illustrate in the second part of this three-part chapter, the seemingly rapid expansion of the media indeed needs to be located at least within the larger framework of increasing commercialization and ongoing state control. In the third part, I attempt a critical evaluation of the major strands of Western media studies which have impacted, continue to impact, and have the potential to impact on not only Malaysian media studies but also on Malaysian media policy. I conclude by providing some observations regarding the supposed need to rethink media studies in Malaysia.

CONTEMPORARY MALAYSIA: A BRIEF BACKGROUND

The Malaysian population is multiethnic and multireligious, with three major ethnic groups—Malay, Chinese, and Indian—and numerous other ethnic minorities (including Iban, Kadazan, Bajau, and Murut), particularly located in East Malaysia. According to 1997 estimates (Bank Negara Malaysia 1996), Malaysia has a total population of 21.7 million. Of these, more than 17 million (78.3 percent of the total population) are located in Peninsular Malaysia. The ethnic composition of this 17 million is as follows: 9.8 million (57.7 percent) are Bumiputera (Malay and certain other indigenous groups), 4.6 million (27.1 percent) are Chinese, and 1.5 million (8.8 percent) are Indian.

Given its multiethnic nature, not surprisingly, Malaysia's history[2] has been dominated by ethnic-based parties and ethnic politics since it attained independence. The three major political parties that form the basis of the ruling Barisan Nasional (BN) coalition government, for instance, are ethnic-based.[3] Indeed, it would be no exaggeration to suggest that ethnic preoccupations continue to dominate Malaysian society, where there is a deep sense of being part of specific ethnic and cultural communities.

The BN coalition, headed by Mahathir Mohamad since 1981, came into being in 1974 as an expansion of the Alliance Party (also a coalition of major ethnic parties). Since Independence in 1957 until it became the BN in 1974, the Alliance had won every single general election held. And the story has remained virtually the same since, with the BN coalition having won more than two-thirds of the seats in the Malaysian parliament during each of the four general elections (1982 1987 1990 1995) held since Mahathir first became Malaysian prime minister. I would argue that in any attempt to understand why the BN government often easily seems to get its way with legislations and policy decisions which to an outsider may appear repressive, this massive majority which the BN enjoys in parliament needs to be borne in mind.

For more than a decade, until the Asian "meltdown" of 1997, the Malaysian economy had been growing rapidly. The average annual growth rate over this period stood at 6.5 percent. During the recession period between 1980 and 1985, it slowed down to 5.4 percent per year, but rose to 9.7 percent in 1990, 8.7 percent in 1991 and 8.5 percent in 1995. Indeed, since 1987, annual growth rates have topped 8 percent. Real GDP per capita grew from US$1,110 in 1960 to US$5,649 in 1990 (see Kahn 1996: 49–75 and Jomo 1997: 89). By September 1993, when the World Bank published *The East Asian Miracle: Economic Growth and Public Policy*, Malaysia had become one of the eight "high performing" Asian economies which had achieved the highest growth rates in the world between 1965 and 1990. Malaysia's "miracle"—until the 1997 meltdown, that is—has largely been attributed to the Mahathir administration's supposedly prudent policies and the accompanying liberalization of the Malaysian economy.

Before Mahathir became Prime Minister in 1981, Malaysia's development had been guided by the New Economic Policy (NEP). Formulated soon after the ethnic riots of May 1969, the NEP has a two-pronged objective of eradicating poverty and eliminating racial imbalances in the Malaysian economy.[4] The Mahathir administration, in turn, using the NEP as the basic guideline, introduced a variety of policies and strategies, the most notable of which were the Look East[5] policy, Malaysia Incorporated,[6] and the Privatization[7] policy, ostensibly to make the Malaysian economy more competitive in the global marketplace. A decade later, in 1991, Mahathir introduced his vision, "Vision 2020",[8] which, together with the earlier policies, has impacted on the development of the media, and the nation as a whole. Indeed, we can deduce a variety of similarities and continuities from Look East to Vision 2020.

First, we can deduce an emphasis on attitudinal change in these statements and strategies. From the need to adopt a new work ethic, as embodied in the Look East policy, to creating a "psychologically liberated" Malaysian society, as outlined in the nine challenges of the Vision, it is clear that psychological states of mind and changes in individual behavior are deemed crucial for change to come about, for Malaysian society—assumed here, to all intents and purposes, to be homogeneous—to move forward, to progress to becoming a developed society. Indeed, this change in attitudes, especially among the poor, has been consistently proposed, certainly by Mahathir. In 1984, for example, he asserted (*New Straits Times*, May 2, 1984):

> There must be a change of attitude among the less well-to-do if poverty eradication is to be realized ... The poor must face up to the fact that their fate lies in their own hands.

Three years later, Mahathir again called for a change in the people's attitude, arguing that "without such a change in attitude and philosophy the country would not progress further in trying to wipe out poverty" (*New Sunday Times*, September 13, 1987). Pointing to the success of the industrialized countries and urging Malaysians to use them as role models, Mahathir, using rhetoric reminiscent of modernists such as McClelland (1961), reiterated the oversimplistic and historically naive view that these countries had prospered "due to the industriousness and willingness of their people to face challenges" (*ibid.*).

The second common theme running through these policies and strategies is, of course, conformity towards—if not celebration of—the market. Until Mahathir's ascendancy, Malaysia's open economy—a legacy of British colonialism—had been one dominated by the state. This was made more obvious under the NEP, when the state began to introduce strategies to restructure the economy and played an interventionist role. As a consequence, state-financed bodies, such as state economic development corporations (SEDCs) played a key role in attempting to develop the economy and ostensibly ensuring that the economic cake, as it were, was more equitably distributed. However, as if following global trends and, arguably, aware of the lumbering bureaucracy that had emerged from this interventionist policy, the waste that had accumulated, and the increased costs to the government, the Mahathir administration turned toward the market soon after it came to power. Many previous state monopolies and services were either privatized or monopolized. The practice continues up until today, with education and health being the new targets. As Mahathir (1983: 277) himself puts it:

> the government may be able to obtain substantial revenue from telecommunications, ports, radio and television, railways, etc. … In view of this possibility, there is a need to transfer several public services and government owned business to the private sector.

Thirdly, what can be gleaned from these strategies is the state's almost unconditional support for the private sector managers, the capitalists. This, when we consider Malaysia's political economy, is to be expected. Indeed, anyone with a basic understanding of the contemporary Malaysian economy would be aware of the heavy corporate involvement of the major parties in the ruling BN coalition. Although allegations of "cronyism" and "nepotism" have only recently surfaced in the mainstream Malaysian media, more academic accounts (see Gomez 1990, 1991, 1994, Lim 1981) have detailed the extensive links between the leading political parties and the Malaysian corporate sector. The Malaysian labor movement, such as it is, thus plays second fiddle, having little say in the overall scheme of things.

Fourthly, these strategies also imply an administration that seems hellbent on making Malaysia into a major global player. Whatever his posturings and (continuing) rhetoric against the rich, industrialized nations, or "the West," Mahathir has never been an anti-capitalist. As Khoo (1995: 64) aptly puts it in his excellent intellectual biography of Mahathir:

> Mahathir's anti-Westernism did not derive from earlier radical critiques of the capitalist origins, impulses and structures of Western imperialism and the global pattern of dominance and dependence. He was not an anti-capitalist but a capitalist. He was only against "imperialism" as protectionism but would hardly have conceived of imperialism in the form of "foreign investments." He defended transnational corporations against "vilification" by the "old protagonists of the superior race [and] also … the working class in the developed countries" … He accepted that the transnationals had to take advantage of cheap labor which he continued to prohibit from unionizing in the Free Trade Zones of Malaysia.

Indeed, despite Mahathir's antipathy to the rich industrialized nations, his—and his administration's—strategy is not to break away from the world economic system, but to compete tooth and nail within the established order. This is clearly reflected in the following passage from his recent publication (Mahathir 1998: 17, emphasis added):

> Vision 2020 has given the focus and direction to Malaysians, especially the private sector, to set bigger goals for greater achievement. Collaboration between the private and public sectors will ensure the sustenance of the nation's comparative advantage and *promote its competitive edge in the global market.*

With this wider backdrop of Malaysian development policies very much in mind—a backdrop which, I would insist, is crucial for understanding the development and future direction of the media in Malaysia—we now turn to the development of the contemporary Malaysian media.

MALAYSIA'S CONTEMPORARY MEDIA: STATE CONTROL AND COMMERCIAL MOTIVATIONS

Television

State control over Malaysia's media, particularly television, has been evident right from the beginning. When television was first introduced into the country in 1963, it comprised a single channel national network, under the control of the Department of Broadcasting (RTM) which, in turn, was one of three departments under the control of the Ministry of Information. In October 1969, a second channel was launched, also under the direct control of the Ministry of Information, and guided by the same directives as those which governed the operations of the first channel (Karthigesu 1991). These directives—which have remained virtually unchanged and which have informed broadcasting policy, at least for what are now called TV1 and TV2—are:

- to explain in depth and with the widest possible coverage the policies and the programs of the government in order to ensure maximum understanding by the public;
- to stimulate public interest and opinion in order to achieve changes in line with the requirement of the government;
- to assist in promoting civic consciousness and fostering the development of Malaysian arts and culture;
- to provide suitable elements of popular education, general information and entertainment; and
- to aid national integration efforts in a multiethnic society through the use of the national language (Ministry of Information 1983).

Both the RTM channels were established not through an Act of Parliament or by a Royal Charter, but via decisions made by the then Alliance coalition government which, in turn, formulated the policies that would determine the role television will play. The latter practice continues, certainly with the RTM channels, to the present day. After almost two decades of virtual state monopoly of the television airwaves, a commercial television station, TV3, was permitted by the government to begin operating in 1984. There is indeed no doubt that, in quantitative terms, television in Malaysia has undergone profound changes since, particularly during the latter part of the 1990s. In 1993, for example, there were only three television stations, two of which were under direct government control. Five years later, by mid-1998, there were five television stations, three of which were commercial entities, one local cable company, MegaTV, providing five subscription channels, and a local satellite broadcasting company, Astro, providing fifteen subscription television channels.

Despite this increase in channel offerings and broadcast hours, however, questions still remain regarding concentration of ownership and the continuing links between media owners and ruling political parties, particularly UMNO. Indeed, ongoing developments illustrate the continuing concentration of media ownership. In early 1994, a local media giant closely aligned to UMNO, the Utusan Group, became part of a consortium of four companies that was awarded a tender by the government to operate Malaysia's second commercial television station, MetroVision (Zaharom 1994). Yet another company in the consortium is Melewar Corporation, controlled by Tunku Abdullah of the Negeri Sembilan royal house and a longtime close associate of Prime Minister Mahathir.

Malaysia's first pay-TV or subscription service, Mega TV, which began operating in the third quarter of 1995, is also run by a consortium using the company name Cableview Services Sdn. Bhd. The largest shareholder in the consortium, with a 40 percent stake, is Sistem Television Malaysia Berhad or TV3. The Malaysian Ministry of Finance has a 30 percent stake, while Sri Utara Sdn. Bhd., a wholly owned subsidiary of Maika Holdings Bhd. (the investment arm of the Malaysian Indian Congress [MIC], another component of the BN coalition), has a 5 percent stake. In the three-and-a-half-year period since it began operation, Mega TV has been able to extend its reach to virtually all the states in Peninsular Malaysia (Zaharom and Mustafa 1998).

As for satellite broadcasting, on January 13, 1996, Malaysia's first communications satellite, the Malaysia East Asia satellite, Measat-1, was launched from Kourou, French Guyana. Measat-1 is owned by Binariang Sdn. Bhd. which, in turn, is owned by trusts associated with three Malaysians, the most prominent of whom is manufacturing and horse-racing tycoon, T. Ananda Krishnan. Ananda has been politely referred to by one Malaysian daily as "a businessman who enjoys the confidence of Prime Minister Datuk Seri Dr Mahathir Mohamad" (*Star*, January 9, 1996). In other words, he is a Mahathir crony. And the chairman of Binariang's board of directors is a former Inspector-General of the Malaysian police force, Hanif Mohamad Omar. Hence, as far as television— including satellite television—is concerned, what we have in Malaysia is a situation where the selective[9] privatization exercise by the Malaysian government continues to extend the tentacles of the ruling coalition and its cronies even wider across the Malaysian economy, adding economic and cultural domination to what is already virtual political domination.

The press

Malaysia's press has had a longer and more diverse history than broadcasting. The earliest recorded newspaper, the English language *Prince of Wales Island Gazette* was a commercial newspaper aimed at the colonial administrators and traders. Others that emerged soon after were either missionary newspapers or vernacular ones serving particular ethnic groups. As the nationalist, anti-colonial movement grew, so was the press, especially the Malay press, utilized to galvanize support for the movement. The independent nature of the press was dramatically transformed, however, under the New Economic Policy (NEP), instituted in 1971. Under the NEP, the government designed a five-year development master plan that emphasized economic growth as well as redistribution of economic opportunities to the Malays.

This spirit of the NEP, and also the desire to increase Malaysian participation in the national economy, provided dominant political partners in the ruling coalition with the convenient excuses to invest in the country's major newspapers and other media. The NEP thus helped to justify their corporate maneuvers, and enabled them to exert control and influence over the media they owned. The government-owned trading company, Pernas, for example, acquired 80 percent control of the *Straits Times* (Means 1991: 136), which was originally held by investors from Singapore. Later a majority of the shares were transferred to Fleet Holdings, an investment arm of the dominant partner in the BN coalition, UMNO. The transfer of ownership was then followed by a change of name to the New Straits Times Press (NSTP). Fleet Holdings subsequently set up an investment company called Fleet Group that oversaw its subsidiaries such as the NSTP. This corporate move was of great political significance because the take-over involved major mainstream newspapers under the NSTP stable. Effectively, then, UMNO currently has control over NSTP, the largest media conglomerate in Malaysia which, in turn, controls the English language broadsheet, *New Straits Times*, the Malay language daily, *Berita Harian*, TV3 and a variety of other newspapers and magazines.

Further, in this drive to purportedly Malaysianize media ownership, UMNO now has direct ownership of the other big local media conglomerate, the Utusan Melayu newspaper group. The group has an array of major newspapers in its stable, such as the *Utusan Malaysia*, the most widely circulated Malay language daily in the country, which has a wide appeal among the Malay-speaking readership, in particular UMNO constituencies. Further Malaysian participation in the private sector in this period also witnessed the involvement of another partner in the ruling coalition, the Malaysian Chinese Association (MCA), in the newspaper industry. It now has a major stake in the popular English language tabloid, *Star*, a business rival of the established *New Straits Times*.

Legal controls

Despite constant assertions about being democratic, the Malaysian government has a slew of laws at its disposal which are anything but democratic. And these are laws which it has not hesitated to enforce. At the top of the pile, most certainly, is the Internal Security Act (ISA), a draconian piece of legislation, introduced during the colonial era to counter communist terrorism in the country during the Emergency period. The ISA allows for indefinite detention without trial and was used repeatedly in the 1980s—and even as recently as 1998—to detain political dissidents, religious cult figures, opposition members of parliament and, most recently, a sacked deputy prime minister.

More specifically for the media, there are the Printing Presses and Publications Act (1987) and what was until recently called the Broadcasting Act (1988). Under the Printing Presses and Publications Act, all mass circulation newspapers in Malaysia need to have a printing permit, granted by the Ministry of Home Affairs, before they can be published. A new permit needs to be applied for every year. Section 13A of the amended Act totally empowers the Home Minister to reject applications for a printing license (popularly known as the "KDN") and to revoke or suspend a permit. The Minister's decision is final and cannot be challenged in a court of law. As stated under Section 13, Subsection (1) of the Act (emphasis added):

> Without prejudice to the powers of the Minister to revoke or suspend a licence or permit under any other provisions of this Act, *if the Minister is satisfied* that any printing press in respect of which the licence has been issued is used for printing of any publication which is prejudicial to public order or national security or that any newspaper in respect of which a permit has been issued contains anything which is prejudicial to public order or national security, he may revoke such licence or permit.

Added to this, Section 7 of the amended Act empowers the Minister to prohibit the printing, sale, import, distribution or possession of any publication. Thus, we have a situation where the decisions of one Minister are binding and, strictly speaking, the Minister is under no obligation to explain these decisions. And up until very recently, the Home Minister was none other than the Prime Minister, Mahathir.

The 1988 Broadcasting Act which was superseded by the Multimedia and Telecommunications Act in 1998 provides similar powers to the Minister of Information. Under the Act, any potential broadcaster would need to apply for a license from the Minister beforehand. Further, Part III, Section 10, Subsection (1) of the Act states:

> It shall be the duty of the licencee to ensure that the broadcasting matter by him complies with the direction given, from time to time, by the Minister.

It is certainly evident that there are two clear trends in the Malaysian media. These developments may seem contradictory at first glance but, upon closer scrutiny, are not exactly at odds with each other, given the nature of politics and control in Malaysia. First, there is little doubt that the government's privatization policy has resulted in greater commercialization of the media which, in turn, has resulted in more being offered. This has happened not by accident, but as part of the government's strategy. Secondly, this supposed liberalization has not really resulted in a loosening of government control over the media, contrary to the initial beliefs of many. The reverse in fact has happened. Over the past two decades, the main forms of control over the media—legal, political and economic—have certainly been tightened.

Within this type of environment, it is not surprising that although Malaysians appear to be getting more from the media, what they are really getting is, essentially, more of the same. Invariably where the ownership and control of the media are in the hands of a few who are closely aligned to the government and who wish to profit from the situation, there is increasing emphasis on the production and importation of "safe," often trivial, artifacts. From the endless talk shows on television to the crossword competitions in the press, the emphasis continues to be on non-contentious and easily marketable material—that will not question, examine or challenge the official discourse (Zaharom 1996).

IMPORTED THEORIES, DOMESTIC CONTRADICTIONS

Any discussion or proposal on the need to *de-Westernize* media studies in the context of Malaysia, I believe, would need to take into account at least three factors which are discussed in some detail here.

The first is an awareness of how media policies and official media strategies have been—and continue to be—informed by specific assumptions about the role the media should play in Malaysia. These assumptions are by no means Malaysian in origin or Malaysian by design. As I have indicated elsewhere (Zaharom 1996), the origins are essentially Western. Indeed, on the basis of media policy frameworks informed and heavily influenced by a paradigm of development epitomized by the works of, for example, Lerner (1958) and Schramm (1964), the media in Malaysia, particularly television and broadcasting and, more generally, the print media, have been—and continue to be—promoted as valuable, indeed central, agents required for the so-called development of the country. Malaysian policymakers perpetually assert the vital role played by the media in changing Malaysian society. As far back as 1964, when television was first introduced into Northern Malaysia, the then Minister of Information spoke of its so-called revolutionary potential. According to him (*Malaysian Times*, October 2, 1964):

> television will be an important instrument of our social revolution. It will be a means of informing the people about the progress in various sectors of our national life. It will also enable them to know of the progress outside Malaysia.

Conforming to the orthodoxy that the media are powerful agents for change enables the Malaysian government to insist that they are too important for the development of the country and its peoples to be allowed free rein. It helps to legitimize the state's strategy of maintaining strict and tight political control over the media, for the supposed "good" of the nation and in the "national interest," vague and undefined though these terms may be, while at the same time seemingly complying with the needs of a "free" market. As I have indicated in the previous section, it enables the state to embark on a strategy of, if you will pardon the oxymoron, "regulated deregulation," where, predictably, the powers to regulate do not lie in the hands of independent bodies but, as with many other countries in the region, come directly from the government. It allows no less than Mahathir (1981: 19) to constantly reiterate warnings such as the following:

> So long as the press is conscious of itself being a potential threat to democracy and conscientiously limits the exercise of its rights, it should be allowed to function without government interference. But when the press obviously abuses its rights by agitating the people, then democratic governments have a right to control it.

Any attempt to critically assess this orthodoxy would need to be aware that it continues to be perpetuated, indeed further reinforced, in the majority of the media studies programs in Malaysia's academic institutions, because the country has a profoundly conservative education system which, in the main, preaches conformity and compliance (Zaharom *et al.* 1995).

The second factor that needs to be accounted for, if we wish to locate the structures and policies of the Malaysian media within the wider political economy, would be the central role played by state actors—particularly political parties within the ruling coalition—in the Malaysian economy generally and in the media industries specifically. The majority of critical studies on media structures and policies in industrialized countries take it as read at the outset that the media are institutionally separate and are indeed relatively autonomous from the state. These studies then attempt to illustrate how markets—and the capitalist system generally—impinge on the operations of the media.

In Malaysia, on the other hand, the role of the state, as I have indicated, is central. Granted, the deliberate and rapid opening of the Malaysian economy to the global market in the 1980s, particularly when Mahathir took over as prime minister, in turn led to greater commercialization of the Malaysian media. Nonetheless, increasing commercialization, far from loosening state control, has, in fact, enabled control to be extended further in the economic sphere, with dominant Malaysian political parties having investment arms which own business concerns and are active players on the corporate scene (Gomez 1990, 1991, 1994). This, of course, is not common only to Malaysia. However, the nature and extent to which the leading political parties in the ruling BN coalition are involved in business are details which need to be vigorously investigated in order to help us understand why the Malaysian media operate as they do and how their operations may, indeed, not only legitimize or shore up support for a "free market" system but also for particular, dominant groups in Malaysian society and the regime as a whole.

Before discussing the third factor, namely studies on Malaysian media audiences, it will suffice to say at this juncture that media research in Malaysia generally is very much in its infancy. The bulk of media research that has been conducted thus far in Malaysian academia may be categorized as being: (a) positivist and quantitative in nature; (b) policy oriented—insofar as the aim is to examine the effectiveness of policy implementation, primarily by the state; (c) least concerned about the development of theory and largely concerned about the refinement of methods; and (d) blissfully unaware of the ideological nature of media artifacts (see respectively Bukhory 1992, Mustafa 1992, Samsudin 1992, and Md. Salleh 1992).

As for academic research into the media–audience relationship—the little that has been done—it would be no exaggeration to suggest that such research in Malaysia appears to have been very much caught up in a time warp, resembling the 1940s and 1950s in the United States. The primary concern has been with looking at the "effects" of the media (principally film and television)—in its narrowest, behaviorist sense—on the audience (principally the generalized categories of "children" and "youth"—the supposed "impressionable" groups). The research methods employed for analyzing media texts have been predominantly quantitative content analysis, while the analyses of audiences have been conducted principally through social surveys. In the rare instances when the complexity of what constitutes "audiences" is acknowledged, these audiences are assumed to belong to particular social categories, invariably defined by what Ang (1990: 272–3) terms "the institutional point of view."

Underlying these local research and concerns is the belief that the media are (or should be) reflective or expressive of an already achieved consensus. The *status quo* orientation of this research is all too obvious. However, more recent, critical developments in mainly Western media audience research, especially the work broadly called "reception studies,"[10] have raised new questions which I believe need to be addressed in relation to Malaysia.

Important though reception studies may be for a more thorough understanding of media–audience relationships, what is equally important—certainly within the context of this discussion—is that such studies, and the underlying assumptions, are not all the same. As Curran (1990: 153–4) points out, there are at least two main variants of reception studies: "one ... continues to situate cultural consumption in the broader context of social struggle ... [and another] ... is grounded in a less radical conception of society ... engaged in analysing cultural consumption and identity formation almost as an end in itself."

It is this second variant, with its optimistic, virtually celebratory, embracing of the "power" of the "active audience" and the seemingly infinite variety of meanings the audience can "read off" from the text, that poses a number of problems for an understanding of the media–audience relationship in the context of Malaysia. Within this variant, there are three principal tendencies (Morley 1992). First, there is the tendency for the researchers to "read" media texts, often very cleverly, with the implicit assumption that all media audiences are equally capable of doing so. This tendency is inextricably linked to the second tendency, that of assuming that all audiences have virtually unrestricted access to a vocabulary of meanings, alternative forms of knowledge outside that provided by the dominant discourse of the media, thus enabling all to interpret media texts equally. Third, is the tendency to assume these supposedly "active" audience members to then be "powerful" in a very real sense.

As Morley (1992: 31) puts it, these researchers "often make overblown claims that their perspective, in itself, involves an empowering of the audience, a privileging of the reader which is in fact quite illusory ... the researcher is often presented as no longer a critical outsider but, rather, a fellow participant, a conscious fan, giving voice to and celebrating consumer cultural democracy." There are certainly fundamental flaws with this view, not least of which is the fact, as Ang (1990: 274) puts it, that though "audiences may be active, in myriad ways, in using and interpreting media ... it would be utterly out of perspective to cheerfully equate 'active' with 'powerful.'" Here, following Morley (1992: 31), what must indeed be recognized is "the difference between having power over a text and having power over the agenda within which the text is constructed and presented."

This complexity of the process of audience–text interaction is often conveniently sidestepped by those espousing "semiotic democracy" (Fiske 1987), assuming as they do that "people drawn from a vast shifting range of subcultures and groups construct their own meanings within an *autonomous* cultural economy" (Morley 1992: 26, emphasis added). By assuming thus, works of this nature not only overrate the decoding power of all audiences but, more dangerously, tend to underemphasize questions of (media) institutional ownership and control. Following Morley (1992: 26), these studies are "readily subsumable within a conservative ideology of sovereign consumer pluralism."

By the same token, such a concern also runs the risk of validating the domination and control of domestic media industries by the state or economic interests. Indeed, there are at least two related problems with this variant of reception studies, if utilized to study the media–audience relationship in Malaysia. First, it will ignore the very real question of differential access to alternative forms of explanation and knowledge needed to empower audience members, to make them "active." In an environment where the education system preaches conformity, where alternative explanations are constantly being curbed, and where the dominant religious/value system is profoundly conservative, assumptions of a generalized "active" media audience would be rather premature, if not downright naive.

The second problem, of course, is that of shifting attention away from what seems to be more crucial issues of institutional power, control, and exploitation, at best leaving these issues outside the frame of reference and analysis and at worst dismissing them as inconsequential. The preceding discussion on the central role played by the state in terms of control over Malaysian media institutions has attempted to illustrate that ignoring these issues pertaining to power risks missing out altogether more fundamental problems regarding the availability of choices in Malaysia and how the range of choices produced may be predetermined. As Murdock (quoted in Morley 1992: 32) aptly put it:

> People playing adventure games on a home computer, ordering goods from a television shopping show, or responding to an electronic opinion poll certainly have choices, but they are carefully managed. Once again the crucial question to ask is not simply "What kinds of pleasure do these technologies offer?" but "Who has the power to control the terms on which interaction takes place?"

De-westernizing, demonizing and democratic space

There have been numerous attempts—more often than not with dubious results—among media academics and practitioners in Asia to "redefine" media studies for the region and assert the need for "Asian" theories of communication and the media. Not surprisingly, these attempts have been buoyed in recent years—certainly before the "Asian meltdown" of 1997–8—by declarations made by heads of government, such as Malaysia's Mahathir and Singapore's Lee Kuan Yew and Goh Chok Tong, about the need for Asian societies to seriously consider "Asian values," Confucianism, and Islam as viable alternatives to so-called "Western values" and Western civilization.[11]

I would argue that, unfortunately, albeit predictably, many of these attempts have been conservative, jingoistic, even "anti-West," time and again asserting the uniqueness of the Asian political economy. In arguing for the need to discover "new" media theories and research strategies, often they end up helping to legitimize repressive regimes, undemocratic practices and tightly controlled media systems whose *raison d'être* is to uphold and help perpetuate these regimes. Hence, in demonizing an overgeneralized "West"—its values, its systems, its media—this view at the same time elevates the equally over-generalized "East," more particularly the regimes in control, to a higher level.

As far as Malaysia is concerned, what is evident is that it is a country inextricably linked to transnational capital, indeed is a cog in the wheel of global capitalism. Inasmuch as it is, it would be unfruitful and certainly erroneous to entertain romantic notions of an authentic, isolated, unique Malaysian media—or other—experience which requires explaining based on a separate, "Malaysianized" set of theories and models. Indeed, it would appear for me that it is not a question of whether media studies are "Western" or "Eastern," or even which "set" is "better." Rather, I would argue that it is a question of what role we assign media studies, be it in a "Western" or an "Eastern" context. If, based on our ideological stand, we insist that the media are predominantly an ideological apparatus of the state or the market, as they evidently are in the context of Malaysia, then the role of media studies, I believe, would be threefold. First, to analyze critically how that apparatus operates and how the power of the state and/or market is translated in the media and possibly reinforced by the media. Second, to argue in turn, and in a convincing fashion how this would be detrimental to the development of ideas and, invariably, detrimental to different segments of society. Third, to strategically locate ways in which alternative policies and structures could be realized to make the media—systems, organizations, practices—more representative, more egalitarian, more liberating.

Notes

1 The term "media," unless otherwise stated, is used throughout this chapter to denote the Malaysian mainstream media of the press and television.
2 When the country attained political independence from the British on August 31, 1957, it was then called "Malaya." In 1963, "Malaysia" was formed, comprising Malaya (now Peninsular Malaysia), Sabah and Sarawak (formerly British Borneo, now East Malaysia) and Singapore. Two years later, Singapore left Malaysia to form an independent state.
3 The largest component party is the United Malays National Organisation (UMNO), followed by the Malaysian Chinese Association (MCA) and the Malaysian Indian Congress (MIC). The names of the parties themselves reflect their ethnic bias.
4 The NEP remains the key reference point for Malaysia's economic development policies. Its objective is summed up in the Third Malaysia Plan 1976–1980 (government of Malaysia 1976: 7): "The NEP seeks to eradicate poverty among all Malaysians and to restructure Malaysian society so that the identification of race with economic function and geographical location is reduced and eventually eliminated, both objectives being realised through rapid expansion of the economy over time ... the present compartmentalisation of racial groups by economic function, with the Malaysia and other indigenous people concentrated in the traditional sectors of the economy, is the core of the problem."
5 The Look East policy was introduced soon after Mahathir became Prime Minister, initially to boost productivity by promoting more effective modes of labor discipline and emphasizing hard work, emulating the Japanese and South Korean models. As Mahathir (1983: 305) himself puts it, Look East "means emulating the rapidly developing countries of the East in the effort to develop Malaysia." New work ethics, labor discipline and productivity are the key terms embodied in the policy. Soon after it was introduced, Look East also appeared to mean favoring Japanese and South Korean businessmen in the awarding of contracts, but after some bad business experiences and criticisms from those disfavored by these arrangements, the earlier definition has been emphasized (Jomo 1990: 202–5).
6 Adapted from the originally pejorative term, "Japan Incorporated," Malaysia Incorporated represents an attempt by the Malaysian government to improve state–business relationships, to ensure that the state and its bureaucracies serve rather than hinder private capitalist interests. As Mahathir (1983: 306) puts it, "Malaysia Incorporated can therefore be defined as the concept of cooperation between the government and the private sector for the latter to succeed, thus make greater contributions to national development."
7 Officially, privatization in Malaysia began in 1983, two years after Mahathir became prime minister. It also occurred at a time when, globally, Thatcherism and Reagonomics were setting the trends while, domestically, the poor performance of the Malaysian public sector, particularly many Malaysian public enterprises, was being questioned and addressed. As outlined by the Malaysian government (EPU 1985):

> Privatisation has a number of major objectives. First, it is aimed at relieving the financial and administrative burden of the government in undertaking and maintaining a vast and constantly expanding network of services and investments in infrastructure. Second, privatisation is expected to promote competition, improve efficiency and increase the productivity of the services. Third, privatisation, by stimulating private entrepreneurship and investment, is expected to accelerate the rate of growth of the economy. Fourth, privatisation is expected to assist in reducing the size and presence of the public sector, with its monopolistic tendencies and bureaucratic support, in the economy. Fifth, priva-

tisation is also expected to contribute towards meeting the objectives of the New Economic Policy (NEP), especially since Bumiputera entrepreneurship and presence have improved greatly since the early days of the NEP and they are therefore capable of taking up their share of the privatised services.

8 Vision 2020, to all intents and purposes, is a master plan for transforming Malaysia into a developed country by the early twenty-first century. As Mahathir (1991: 1) himself put it when he unveiled the Vision: "The ultimate objective that we should aim for is a Malaysia that is fully developed by the year 2020." Nine challenges facing the nation in its attempt to attain fully developed status have been outlined by Mahathir and these continue to be the driving force behind the Vision. These challenges (Mahathir 1991: 2–4) may be summarized as follows:

1 establishing a united Malaysian nation with a sense of common and shared destiny ... at peace with itself ... (and) ... made up of one "Bangsa Malaysia."
2 creating a psychologically liberated, secure and developed Malaysian society with faith and confidence in itself ... psychologically subservient to none and respected by the peoples of other nations.
3 fostering and developing a mature democratic society, practising a form of mature consensual, community-oriented Malaysian democracy that can be a model for many developing countries.
4 establishing a fully moral and ethical society ... strong in religious and spiritual values and imbued with the highest of ethical standards.
5 establishing a mature, liberal and tolerant Malaysian society.
6 establishing a scientific and progressive society ... innovative and forward-looking.
7 establishing a fully caring society and a caring culture, a social system in which society will come before self.
8 ensuring an economically just society ... in which there is fair and equitable distribution of the wealth of the nation.
9 establishing a prosperous society, with an economy that is fully competitive, dynamic, robust and resilient.

9 There is, for example, no competitive, open tender system when bids are made for projects which the government is privatizing. The decision to award tenders often lies in the hands of the minister whose ministry is privatizing a project.

10 Instead of dealing with questions of whether the media has "effects" in a narrow, behavioristic sense, reception studies begin with a couple of fundamental assumptions. First, that there is no homogeneous "media audience," but that there are, instead, "media audiences" belonging to different social groupings—including gender and class. Their location within this social structure, in turn, tends to determine the discourses available to them in their interaction with the media. That is to say, the range of "readings" audiences may derive from media texts depends, to a large extent, on where they are situated within the social structure. Second, it is argued that media texts are seldom wholly open to an infinite variety of interpretations but, as Morley (1980) puts it, take the form of "structured polysemy." Media texts, in other words, are constructed in ways that will guide audience interpretations or "readings" in certain preferred ways, although in some cases these may be rejected or negotiated.

11 Mahathir, for one, for a long time in the 1990s had been boasting about the superiority of Asian values in attempting to explain the tremendous economic success stories among Asian countries from the mid-1980s to the 1997–8 meltdown.

References

Ang, I. (1990) "Culture and communication," *European Journal of Communication*, 5(2–3).
Bank Negara Malaysia (1996) *Annual Report 1996*, Kuala Lumpur: Bank Negara.
Bukhory Hj. Ismail (1992) "Penyelidikan komunikasi dari Kajian Sebaran Am, Institut Teknologi

Mara," in Mohd. Dhari Othman *et al.* (eds.) *Pasca Sidang Seminar Penyelidikan Komunikasi*, Bangi: UKM.

Curran, J. (1990) "The new revisionism in mass communications research," *European Journal of Communication*, 5(2–3).

EPU (Economic Planning Unit, Prime Minister's Department) (1985) *Guidelines on Privatization*, Kuala Lumpur: Government Printer.

Fiske, J. (1987) *Television Culture*, London: Routledge.

Gomez, E. T. (1990) *Politics in Business: UMNO's Corporate Investments*, Kuala Lumpur: Forum.

Gomez, E. T. (1991) *Money Politics in the Barisan Nasional*, Kuala Lumpur: Forum.

Gomez, E. T. (1994) *Political Business: Corporate Involvement of Malaysian Political Parties*, Queensland: James Cook University of North Queensland.

Government of Malaysia (1984) *Printing Presses and Publications Act 1984*, Kuala Lumpur.

Government of Malaysia (1988) *Broadcasting Act 1988*, Kuala Lumpur.

Jomo, K. S. (1990) *Growth and Structural Change in the Malaysian Economy*, London: Macmillan.

Jomo, K. S. (1997) *Southeast Asia's Misunderstood Miracle*, Boulder, CO: Westview.

Kahn, J. (1996) "Growth, economic transformation, culture and the middle class in Malaysia," in R. Robison and D. S. G. Goodman (eds.) *The New Rich in Asia: Mobile Phones, McDonalds and the Middle Class Revolution*, London: Routledge.

Karthigesu, R. (1991) "Two decades of growth and development of Malaysian television and an assessment of its role in nation building," unpublished Ph.D. thesis, University of Leicester, England.

Khoo, B. T. (1995) *Paradoxes of Mahathirism*, Kuala Lumpur: Oxford University Press.

Lerner, D. (1958) *The Passing of Traditional Society: Modernizing the Middle East*, New York: Free Press.

Lim, M. H. (1981) *Ownership and Control of the One Hundred Largest Corporations in Malaysia*, Kuala Lumpur: Oxford University Press.

McClelland, D. (1961) *The Achieving Society*, Princeton: Van Nostrand.

Mahathir Mohamad (1981) "Freedom of the press: fact and fallacy," *New Straits Times*, July 9.

Mahathir Mohamad (1983) "New government policies," in K. S. Jomo (ed.) *The Sun Also Sets: Lessons in Looking East*, Kuala Lumpur: Insan.

Mahathir Mohamad (1991) *Malaysia: The Way Forward*, Kuala Lumpur: Malaysian Business Council.

Mahathir Mohamad (1998) *Mahathir Mohamad on the Multimedia Super Corridor*, Subang Jaya: Pelanduk Publications.

Malaysian Movement (1976) *Third Malaysia Plan, 1976–1980*, Kuala Lumpur: Government of Malaysia.

Md. Salleh Hj. Hassan (1992) "Aktiviti Penyelidikan Jabatan Komunikasi Pembangunan, Universiti Pertanian Malaysia," in Mohd. Dhari Othman *et al.* (eds.) *Pasca Sidang Seminar Penyelidikan Komunikasi*, Bangi: UKM.

Means, Gordon P. (1991) *Malaysian Politics: The Second Generation*, Singapore: Oxford University Press.

Ministry of Information (Malaysia) (1983) *Radio and Television Malaysia Handbook*, Kuala Lumpur.

Mohd. Dhari Othman *et al.* (eds.) (1992) *Pasca Sidang Seminar Penyelidikan Komunikasi*, Bangi, Malaysia: UKM.

Morley, D. (1992) *Television, Audiences and Cultural Studies*, London: Routledge.

Morley, D. (1980) *The Nationwide Audience*, London: BFI.

Mustafa K. Anuar (1992) "Perkembangan penyelidikan komunikasi dan Rancangan

Komunikasi," in Mohd. Dhari Othman *et al.* (eds.) *Pasca Sidang Seminar Penyelidikan Komunikasi*, Bangi: UKM.

Samsudin A. Rahim (1992) "Perkembangan penyelidikan komunikasi di Jabatan Komunikasi," in Mohd. Dhari Othman *et al.* (eds.) *Pasca Sidang Seminar Penyelidikan Komunikasi*, Bangi: UKM.

Schramm, W. (1964) *Mass Media and National Development*, Stanford: Stanford University Press.

World Bank (1993) *The East Asian Miracle: Economic Growth and Public Policy*, New York: Oxford University Press.

Zaharom Nain (1994). "Commercialization and control in a 'caring society': Malaysian media 'Towards 2020,'" *Sojourn*, 9(2): 178–99.

Zaharom Nain (1996) "The impact of the international marketplace on the organisation of Malaysian television," in D. French and M. Richards (eds.) *Contemporary Television: Eastern Perspectives*, New Delhi: Sage.

Zaharom Nain and Mustafa K. Anuar (1998) "Ownership and control of the Malaysian media," *Media Development*, 45(4): 9–17.

Zaharom Nain *et al.* (1995) "Communications, curricula and conformity: of national needs and market forces," *Pendidik dan Pendidikan*, 14: 103–24.

Part 3

Authoritarian regulated societies

11 The dual legacy of democracy and authoritarianism

The media and the state in Zimbabwe[1]

Helge Rønning and Tawana Kupe

The African media carry contradictions which have roots in the colonial period, when newspapers and broadcasting mainly served the needs of the colonial administrators. These media, together with other colonial social and cultural institutions, constituted a colonial public sphere. In opposition to this, the anti-colonial movements developed their counter public spheres, with an alternative media structure, which in many cases operated from exile. This was particularly the case in situations of armed struggle, as were the circumstances in Zimbabwe. At independence, the media then were linked either to the inheritance of an authoritarian colonial state or to a liberation movement with a political agenda that often implied a contradictory attitude to fundamental democratic values. On the one hand the movements professed and had fought for liberation and independence and egalitarian and democratic ideals, but on the other they had often done this on the basis of at least partly authoritarian marxist ideologies uncritically inspired by Eastern Europe, China or North Korea. In few places was this contradiction clearer than in Zimbabwe.

The democratic agenda of the liberation movements was to be found in the demands for majority rule, but the democratic implications of this demand were often contradicted by an authoritarian ideology which often comprised a mixture of Soviet-type Marxist ideology and Africanist one-party statism. This contradiction only became clear, also to the northern sympathizers of the liberation movements and the African "progressive one-party states," at the end of the Cold War. In very many instances the media policies implemented by the new post-colonial regimes expressed this contradiction.

The media policies pursued by the new governments that grew out of the liberation movements after independence may be interpreted as a reflection of this discrepancy between a democratic and an authoritarian impetus. In some of the so-called progressive or developmental one-party states, the authoritarian longing became particularly strong and as a consequence the media were placed under government control in a variety of institutional arrangements. Examples of this are the situations in Tanzania under Nyerere, in Zambia under Kaunda, and in Mozambique from independence in 1975 till the multiparty elections in 1994. One aspect of this was that newspapers that previously had been run by either British, Portuguese or in some cases South African, or local colonial capital were bought by the government, and reestablished as state-linked companies. In other cases as in Zambia, one of the dailies was government-controlled, while the other was controlled by the party. This was, however, little more than a formality, as the country under Kaunda was a one-party state. The broadcasting corporations, which to a lesser or greater degree had been the voices of the government under colonialism, changed editorial policies and personnel, but for all practical purposes continued the organizational forms and structures established under colonialism. The consequence of these developments was that the news media developed into praise-singers for the party and the leader in the name of national unity, and their agenda consisted of an emphasis on development journalism in its most uncritical form. These were hardly circumstances that promoted critical and independent media practices.

The situation in Zimbabwe after independence in 1980, with the fall of Ian Smith's Rhodesian Front regime under the Unilateral Declaration of Independence (UDI), and the coming to power of ZANU(PF) and Robert Mugabe, bears the marks of the contradictions outlined above, and the media policies pursued by the new independent ZANU(PF) government resemble those of neighboring countries. But the situation in Zimbabwe also differs significantly from that which existed in countries like Zambia, Tanzania, and Mozambique, countries which ideologically were close to the new nationalist government. The reasons for these differences are complex, but we will try to identify some of them. In spite of the authoritarian character and increasingly oppressive nature of the Rhodesian regime, there existed a semblance of pluralism and openness under UDI. It was to a large degree confined to white society, but it constituted a form of civil society with a public sphere. Zimbabwe had a considerable industrialized sector with a tradition of militant unionism, African organizational structures of a variety of types, and a concomitant and more than an embryonic African public sphere consisting of a variety of magazines, papers and so on—partly linked to unionism, partly linked to churches, and partly linked to the nationalist movements. Even if these organizations' publications often were banned under UDI, there nevertheless had evolved civil society structures in Zimbabwe before independence.

Thus the media policies and media situation in Zimbabwe are more complex than in other Southern African countries, and the contradictions between the authoritarian and democratic impulses are more conspicuous than elsewhere. In this context the history of the Zimbabwe Mass Media Trust (ZMMT) is an interesting "Lehrstücke" for interpreting the relationship between the government and the press in Africa (Saunders 1991). The Zimbabwe Mass Media Trust was created by the government in January 1981 as an articulation of the new independent government's media policy. It was created against a background of dissatisfaction with the situation in the national press, which was part of the South African Argus company's chain of newspapers. The ZMMT was intended to serve not just as a vehicle for changing staff and editorial policy, but also to oversee the transition in the management and operation of the public print media from white minority control to serving the interests of the broad section of Zimbabwean society. It was emphasized by the government that the press should be a free press responsible to the national interest and should in principle be mass-oriented, nationally accessible, and nonpartisan in content.

The creation of the ZMMT solved an initial policy dilemma for the ZANU(PF) government when it came to acquiring the Argus shares and finding a new structure to replace the previous ownership model. The dilemma was how to decolonize the foreign-owned media while maintaining some national stake in them without the direct intervention of the state. If the media were "indigenized" the question remained as to which local interests should be allowed to control them? On the one hand it was not in line with ZANU(PF) policies to privatize the press, and there were powerful sectors of the party that wished to nationalize the press. On the other hand the government was reluctant to expose itself to charges of exerting undue influence over the media, particularly as ZANU(PF) had criticized the Argus press for being at the service of the UDI regime. If the Ministry of Information were to have controlling influence in the management of the restructured Zimpapers, this could have cast doubt on ZANU(PF)'s commitment to traditional democratic freedoms, which they had promised to adhere to during the Lancaster House negotiations with Britain. In January 1981 the 43.2 percent of Zimpapers stock held by South African investors was bought at a cost of Zim $ 2.7 million (US $5 million) and placed by the government under the new Trust's control. The money to buy the shares was put up by the Nigerian government, but it is unclear whether all the money was ever transferred to Zimbabwe.

The ZMMT was supposed to serve two interests at the same time, that is to manage a press which was formally tied to the development aspirations of the government. But it was also committed to the independence of the press. The ZMMT was thus constituted as a nongovernmental, nonparty, not-for-profit-making trust, with a constitutionally prescribed nonpartisan board of trustees. It was to have administrative and financial autonomy and the government would not interfere in the running and management of its affairs. Subsequently the Trust entered into a business relationship with other Zimbabwean private investors, who to a large extent consisted of fractions of domestic white capital which had figured as the commercial stalwarts of white Rhodesia. This was the situation until 1986 when the Trust obtained 51 percent of the shares in the company. In addition, the Trust was given control of the new national news agency ZIANA and the new school of journalism (later transferred to Harare Polytechnic as a department), and later it acquired the national bookselling chain Kingston's, and set up the Community Newspapers Group. ZMMT is thus in principle the central media institution in Zimbabwe, together with the Zimbabwe Broadcasting Corporation (ZBC).

The structure of the ZMMT was (and is) unique in the world of the press in developing countries. The Trust is neither a state-linked nor a private enterprise. It is a creation of the state as it is duty bound to report to and liaise with government, but it also acts as the most important shareholder in the country's largest "private" media enterprise—Zimpapers—and thus interacts with other shareholders and investors in a private enterprise whose major decisions are made by an "independent" Board of Directors, whose members among others include government and party representatives. Initially the trustees (a maximum of seven and a minimum of three) were appointed by the government: thereafter the Board was designed to be self-perpetuating, naming on its own any new members to replace former members who ceased because of resignation, death or other reasons to sit on the Board. Regulations prohibited the inclusion of members of parliament, the uniformed services or the Public Service on the Board. An administrative secretariat headed by an executive secretary vested with responsibility for running the day-to-day affairs of the Trust was set up. From the very beginning the structure of ZMMT had inherent contradictions in relation to the Trust's autonomy, as the Deed of Donation was made by the government and is subject to amendment by the government. As long as the government retains that monopoly to amend the deed, there is very little that can be done by other actors to secure the independence of the Trust. It appears to be legally free, but it is in practice bound to the government, and its legal autonomy can be changed anytime whenever it is unfavorable to the government. The requirement that the Trust has to furnish the government with reports of its annual accounts and other details of its operations also potentially compromises its autonomy.

At its inception ZMMT may be interpreted as being, together with the restructuring of ZBC, the most important practical expression of ZANU(PF)'s line of decolonizing, nationalizing and democratizing the media. However, as the party's project of acquiring total hegemonic control over the political sphere, the state, and civil society with the explicit aim of introducing the one-party state unfolded in the 1980s, the ZMMT and its component media became increasingly submerged in political struggles for leadership in the state and civil society. The Trust's appearance as a neutral buffer between the state and the ruling party on the one hand and an independent public press and civil society on the other became more and more hollow. A number of factors were at play here, but among them were ZMMT's growing structural dependence on the state for financial planning, and economic and political support. The most important factor in the relegation of the Trust to a secondary function in the running of the public press was its financial insecurity, which at times bordered on severe crises.

Very early in its existence the Trust was to encounter problems on several fronts because of its internal financial and political weaknesses, which were linked to the growing presence of the Ministry of Information in the direct supervision of the public media and the Trust itself. Correspondingly the ZMMT was increasingly distanced from real control of the media placed under its authority. This may be illustrated by the relationship between the Trust and Zimpapers. After the creation of the Trust, a tripartite decision-making structure emerged at Zimpapers consisting of the Trust, the Ministry, and the new black senior management at Zimpapers, who, there is no doubt, was closely allied to the ZANU(PF) leadership, and to a large degree acted to secure the interests of the ruling party in controlling the national press (Rusike 1990, Saunders 1991).

The conflict between the principle of editorial and journalistic independence on the one hand, and the urge to put the press under state and party control on the other, came to the forefront in a number of *causes célèbres* in the 1980s which led to the dismissal and removal of editors and journalists in Zimpapers. In addition there is the clear partisan coverage that Zimpapers to a lesser or greater degree gave (and give) to political events in Zimbabwe, including blatantly skewed, or scant and nonexisting, reporting of opposition to, grievances with, and demonstrations and strikes against, the government and the ruling party, as well as uncritical praise of the party and its leadership. The effective subjection of the ZMMT to the state and ruling party must be seen as perhaps the most important casualty of the ruling party's invasion of nominally autonomous public institutions. This, in light of the dominance that Zimpapers have in the newspaper market and among the readership for the print media in Zimbabwe, raises serious doubts about the degree of media democracy in the country.

The other strictly government-controlled media institution in Zimbabwe is the Zimbabwe Broadcasting Corporation (ZBC), whose history and organizational structure have their roots in the colonial era. In Zimbabwe, as elsewhere in Africa, broadcasting, in this case the radio, initially served to provide the "colonies" with links to the metropolis. Later radio services in Africa, especially in the British settler colonies, were partly developed along the lines of the BBC public service ideals (Wedell 1986). It is, however, important not to forget that the laudable British noncommercial, public service institution has two sides. On the one hand we have the idea that broadcasting should be independent of political authorities or semiautonomous. On the other there are the emergency clauses that allow the government to take direct power over the BBC in situations of national crisis, and the question of what is a national crisis is not decided by the broadcasting institution. This flip side of broadcasting history is often forgotten when speaking of the BBC heritage, and it is this side of the history which has dominated the way broadcasting was conducted in Rhodesia/Zimbabwe. The public service broadcasting that emerged in Africa represented reflections of the cleavages in colonial society. In Rhodesia, for example, this had as a consequence the establishment of separate publics for different radio stations—a general African service for African listeners and a specific service for white listeners (Zaffiro 1984).

The Zimbabwean broadcasting system resembles what has been the norm in most of Africa since independence. There is a national broadcaster, based in the capital, which transmits from one to four national programs with different profiles and audiences in mind. This system has historical advantages, it conforms to the need for nation building, and it facilitates control of the media. Centralizing radio operations, however, brings about many problems. It compromises the quality of service provided to the rural population, which has been disadvantaged educationally, politically, and informationally in comparison with the urban centers. The practice of promoting a uniformity of values, and reinforcing nationalism as opposed to diversity, in reality implies the dominance of the urban elites over the majority rural population. In this regard, the powerless rural population always find its needs and interests ignored. An illustration of this is that in most African countries, Zimbabwe included, the tendency has been to utilize high-quality VHF/FM transmission mainly to serve the urban centers. Shortwave transmission has been used to cover rural areas, because it has greater coverage at relatively low capital and operational costs. However, it is a poor-quality signal which often suffers from interference. The rural and peripheral populations are thus disadvantaged in terms of the quality of radio signals (Article XIX 1995).

Radio is mainly used for two purposes—as an entertainment medium, and as an educational medium. The entertainment consists mostly of music programs. The relatively large proportion of African music transmitted may be seen as being representative of experiences and lives led by the broad sectors of society in a form which appeals to fantasy and imagination. But other forms of entertainment and artistic presentation have not been developed fully. The educational programs cover a range of material from formal to informal forms of education, from relatively advanced courses to elementary informational programs on practical problems. Otherwise broadcasting companies offer a variety of programs ranging from information and discussions of current affairs to entertainment.

However, newscasts and discussions on national social and political affairs have a tendency to shun controversy and investigative reporting. It is not characterized by journalism but by readings of statements. It seems as if conscious use of radio as a pure developmental medium is very difficult, and that it is not easy to reach an audience without including clear entertainment aspects. This also may have some implications for the strong emphasis which has been given to so-called grassroots developmental forms of communication in international communication policies and research (Melkote 1991). Some of the most tightly controlled broadcasting companies such as ZBC have subscribed to the radio and development paradigm for their radio policies. Broadcasting in Zimbabwe was and is used to consolidate regime power, smother opposition, and legitimate the ruling party's policy agenda, by defining political reality on its own terms, behind the shield of developmental journalism.

There is still a colonial legacy to ZBC. The legal basis of the corporation is still the Rhodesian Broadcasting Act of 1957 as amended in 1974. In part II (14 a) it says: "The functions of the corporation shall be ... to carry on broadcasting services for the information, education and entertainment of listeners in Rhodesia." The law further gives ZBC a monopoly and places the authority over broadcasting firmly in the hands of the political authorities. Under the Act, ZBC is assigned a monopoly status and accountability to the Minister of Information, Posts and Telecommunication (MOI). This minister is also responsible for advising the President whom to appoint to the Board of Governors. The Board of Governors are responsible for mapping broad policy decisions. ZBC is financed through a combination of license fees, advertisements, and government grants. This Act restructured the broadcasting arrangement that was in existence during the so-called Central African Federation. A British royal commission recommended a new broadcasting authority along BBC lines with explicit autonomy. But the act placed the final authority, politically and financially, in the hands of government, and left the autonomy—so to speak—to the good will of practical policies, or to political culture. Consequently during the Rhodesian Front (RF) and UDI years the Rhodesia Broadcasting Corporation (RBC) developed into an institution very much like the South African Broadcasting Corporation under apartheid, and during the liberation war it became an outright racist propaganda machine for the Ian Smith regime. Top posts were filled by parliamentary appointment, which again were subject to approval of the Prime Minister. This procedure meant that all important staff at RBC were loyal to RF. This in practical terms resulted in the responsibility for the daily news production shifting from the RBC broadcasters to the government Department of Information. During the liberation war RBC "news selection criteria stipulated that the lead story on all newscasts must be any Prime Ministerial message" (Zaffiro 1984: 75).

At independence in 1980 a BBC task force was commissioned to examine the existing television and radio services and to assess the likely future requirements of broadcasting in an independent Zimbabwe. Particular reference was made to the feasibility of expanding the broadcasting services to reach the whole population and all parts of the country. The report indicated that one of the main problems was that the RBC had institutionalized a form of control which was outdated and insensitive to the interests of the majority of Zimbabweans. The report argued that the ZBC should be strengthened in such a way that it would fully reflect the interests and cultural diversity of the totality of the people of Zimbabwe and would serve the nation as a unifying force. Following these general principles the BBC task force made the following basic recommendations, for the use and development of radio: that the then existing radio services be renamed, reorganized, and relaunched as three national networks transmitting from Harare; that one of these should be an around-the-clock FM station, broadcasting primarily music but also news and topical affairs of special interest to the young; that an FM channel be used to provide a new national educational service; and that once developments of greater priority had been achieved ZBC and the government may wish to consider the possibility of establishing local, or community radio stations in certain centers of the country. (This last suggestion was never realized.) In addition, the creation of a new centralized board of management was recommended, and finally it was suggested that the corporation needed sweeping and expensive capital and technical expansion. The government accepted most of the recommendations and the result was that ZBC became financially and politically dependent upon the government.

Shortly after independence most of the white staff left ZBC and new people loyal to the new regime were appointed. Many of them had their background in the radio stations operated by the liberation movements in Zambia and Mozambique. The content of the broadcasting changed. But the fundamental style of the institution was more or less the same, and has remained so ever since. As under UDI, broadcast policy plays a central role in the management of political change and legitimation efforts. Professional and political attitudes and loyalties at ZBC appear inseparable. Politicians approach the corporation with their own interests in mind. ZBC must respond to official interests, even at the price of being reduced at times to a sycophant of the regime (Zaffiro 1984: 217). Thus there exists a basic continuity between broadcasting before independence and after. But this is not to say that there are no differences between then and now.

In 1997 a British consultant—Peter Ibbotson—was asked to assess the situation of broadcasting in Zimbabwe, and also to look into the commercial viability of ZBC. In his report it was stated that for all practical purposes the corporation was bankrupt. There was an accumulated backlog of Zim $100 million, which the corporation said was due from government and was needed to save the ZBC in spite of its monopoly (Ibbotson 1996, *Africa. Film & TV. News Flash* 1997). The government seemed, however, very reluctant to pay. It was furthermore pointed out that ZBC seemed to be an inefficient and costly organization to run, for example debt servicing and administrative overhead absorbed 62.7 percent of the corporation's earned income. A conclusion which may be drawn from the report, is that the state is no longer willing, or able, to put its financial muscle behind ZBC. As a consequence the institution is left in a financial squeeze which can only be solved through more commercials. But commercials presuppose listeners and viewers, and therefore ZBC has to put up a schedule which can function as a nice environment for ads. In the long term this market logic will affect the programming of the corporation. In general terms this is the condition of most public service broadcasters all over the world after the breakdown of a broadcasting monopoly. ZBC is in a difficult position, not between dependence on the state and the political establishment and freedom, but between degrees and various types of dependence.

In Zimbabwe, TV is both a commercial and a strictly government controlled medium (Andersen 1997, Manhando 1997). It is subject to the controls of both the market and the state. A consequence is that news and current affairs reporting are characterized by an absence of controversial and investigative journalism. After independence in 1980 there were plans for a two-channel system, where TV1 was supposed to be the vibrant entertainment channel for the whole country, while TV2, which was set up in 1986, was to be developed into the serious educational and informative channel, with no commercial breaks. However, this policy did not work well, and TV2 became a "repeater" channel, repeating programs aired on TV1. The weakest point was that TV2 was accessible only to a small urban population in Harare and surrounding areas. TV2 became an absorber of scarce financial resources.

Only around 25 percent of Zimbabwean households have their own television set, and, as one would expect, high education and income groups own a high percentage of the total number of sets. Between 60 and 70 percent of the population in the big cities watch television more than five days a week. A common way of watching is with neighbors and friends. A set is shared by many people in private homes or at beer-halls, bars and so on. The core viewer, however, lives in a big city, is relatively young, well educated, and has a good income, and thus may be characterized as "middle class." What is here referred to as the "middle class" is—or has the potential of being—the central political agent in the process of development or change in Zimbabwe. It is from this "class" that the "political class" of the ruling party is recruited, and it is through groups within the same "class" that the present formalities of a multiparty system in theory, but not in practice, may be changed, and attain real democratic political substance. From this social grouping initiatives that may constitute a challenge to the hegemonic position of the ruling party will come, and in this possible struggle the prime medium of the "middle class"—television—is of some importance. Consequently the government is wary of relinquishing control over it.

Since mid-January 1999 the official Zimbabwean print and broadcast media have been monitored under a project supported by Article XIX, MISA, and the Catholic Commision for Justice and Peace in Zimbabwe (CCJPC). Its weekly reports conclude that an average only 6 percent of stories in ZBC TV newscasts can be said to be fair and balanced; between 68 and 80 percent of the stories are based on only one source; and roughly half the stories are characterized as "the voice of ZANU(PF)." The struggle over the control with the total programming of ZBC is continuous. In a court ruling early in 1999 it was decided that ZBC TV was obliged to show ads for alternative political forces. The case was brought by a new political initiative—the National Constitutional Assembly—which aims to challenge ZANU(PF) in the elections in 2000. The court ruled that the sole public TV channel has no right to dictate content or ban views that differ from the government's.

The "Ibbotson report" recommended that the airwaves should be opened to competition, that private broadcasting should be introduced, and that a separate regulatory authority should be set up which should have the task of drawing up, advertising and allocating detailed licenses to broadcast. By 1999, however, the recommendations have not yet been implemented. It is indicative of the role of ZBC and particularly its contradictory position as regards commercialism and state control, that the only recommendation from the report that was implemented was that ZTV2 was made available to three private broadcasters, of which only one remains, and important interests in this channel have close links with the ruling party. The process of granting franchise to the remaining company JoyTV apparently involved corruption implicating, among others, Vice-President Simon Muzenda, according to *Zimbabwe Independent*. There have been no concrete initiatives for opening up independent radio.

The first important contribution to the opening up of the Zimbabwean media after independence was the so-called "Willowgate" scandal in 1988. This exposure of corruption may serve as an exemplary tale of how professional journalism may contribute both to the democratic process and to an increased awareness of professional standards among journalists. First it is a case of how one courageous editor, Geoffrey Nyarota, and his colleagues, partly through having good contacts with, and legitimacy within, a number of circles with access to information on corrupt practices, managed through professional journalistic work to expose serious corruption high up in government. Secondly it is an indication of how dissatisfaction with such practices created an alliance between the press, honest civil servants, and the public, which may be seen as an example of how this in itself may serve as a safeguard against governmental malpractice. Furthermore the case is interesting because the newspaper of which Geoffrey Nyarota was then editor, the *Chronicle* in Bulawayo, belongs to the government-controlled part of the Zimbabwean press, and it is thus also a case that illustrates what limits exist to independent and professional journalism in a press that is part of an authoritarian political structure.

There are several reasons why it was the *Chronicle* that exposed how ministers and other high officials abused their right to buy cars from the assembly plant at Willowvale, and in a situation of strict regulations on the sale of cars, resold them for high profit. One reason is that the *Chronicle* is published in Bulawayo where dissatisfaction with the ZANU(PF) government had been strong almost all through the 1980s. This was linked to a number of factors, of which two interrelated aspects were of particular importance. In the elections of 1980 and 1985 Matabeleland had voted heavily for (PF)ZAPU which became the opposition party. Partly because of that, but also because Matabeleland in the early 1980s was subjected to gross repression and as many as 20,000 people were killed in massacres performed by the notorious 5th Brigade in cleansing operations against so-called dissidents, who were thought to be old members of the ZAPU army (ZIPRA). Well known ZAPU politicians had also been jailed under emergency laws. Secondly, at the time there was a hesitant atmosphere in the Zimbabwean political sphere in general because of the unity accord signed between ZANU(PF) and (PF)ZAPU in December 1987. This had led to a certain opening of the debate, particularly around the issue of the one-party state. Third, the general disillusionment with the politics of the government was growing in many circles. Thus the Willowvale case showed how a broader political situation led to the testing of the limits of government control within the official press.

The public outcry, the pressure by independently minded politicians within the ruling party and from wide circles in Zimbabwean civil society, led to President Mugabe setting up a commission of inquiry under the leadership of Justice Sandura in January 1989. The commission's findings resulted in the resignation of five ministers and civil servants, and Nyarota and his journalists were praised for their investigation. This is an example of the importance of an independent judiciary for the democratic process. However, Geoffrey Nyarota had at the time already been relieved of his editorship and moved to an administrative position at the headquarters of Zimpapers in Harare. He had tested the limits of the official press, and overstepped them. The Willowvale scandal showed that there was a definite need for a strong and independent press dedicated to critical and investigative journalism.

Geoffrey Nyarota was not the first, nor the last, editor in Zimpapers to be removed from his position because he exercised editorial independence. In 1983 the legendary Zimbabwean journalist the late Willie Musarurwa was sacked as editor of the *Sunday Mail* for giving prominent coverage to what was called the opposition, that is ZAPU. In 1987 Henry Muradzikwa, then editor of the *Sunday Mail*, later editor-in-chief of the national news agency ZIANA, published an article that was critical of the treatment of Zimbabwean students in Cuba at a time the then Cuban foreign minister was visiting Zimbabwe. He was punished by being "promoted" to group projects manager at head office. In early 1998 the editor of the *Herald*, Tommy Sithole, was removed from his post and "promoted" to director of business projects and public relations at the Zimpapers head office. The Sithole case was remarkable for many reasons, as he generally was known to be a staunch ZANU(PF) supporter who during his fifteen years at the helm of the flagship publication of Zimpapers defended and espoused government policy.

The events that brought about his removal were the protests and riots against the government in January 1998, which were preceded by unrest, strikes, and demonstrations in 1997. This also had the effect that the *Herald* became somewhat critical of government policy and also published independent reports on issues such as police brutality in quelling demonstrations, government's mismanagement of the economy, and the wastage of public funds. This development of editorial attitudes at the *Herald* finally led to sharp editorial comments of January 20 and 21 following violent food price riots. The background to the editorials was partly that Mugabe and government ministers had accused the labor movement and whites for the unrest. The editorials stated that to accuse ZCTU or "ethnic groupings" was a form of delusion. Scapegoating was not the solution to the problem, and the government should face the existing crisis in the country head-on. The editorials accused the government of inaction and of not being "truly concerned" with "what might be potentially the most serious problem our country has faced to date." It was time for Zimbabwe to start reacting to crises, in a different manner from what the government had done in the past. It was necessary to start reflecting soberly on where the country was going, because "things cannot go on the way they are. ... Yesterday was the end of the era of business as usual. Today we must start fixing the underlying problems facing our country or watch disaster unfold." The Sithole affair is indicative of, on the one hand, the strong government control of Zimpapers, but also, on the other hand, that even such a faithful government supporter as Sithole may be swayed by the general opening up of Zimbabwean society, and the increasingly powerful struggle between government and civil society institutions.

An interesting illustration of the opening up of Zimbabwean media is the changing styles and content of the monthly magazines *Parade* and *Horizon*, which in the 1980s and early 1990s under the editorship of Andrew Moyse developed a hard-hitting investigative political style of journalism, which exposed and criticized a number of political and economic scandals in Zimbabwe (Kupe 1997). In place of color pin-up pictures and pop music gossip, *Parade*'s content came to be characterized by a mixture of topical investigative journalism on the one hand, and on the other by popular features on music, sports, and entertainment. This form of journalism went down well with the readership, and the circulation peaked at more than 110,000 copies per month in 1989. The magazine was owned by a big publishing company by Zimbabwean standards, Thomson Publications. In 1991 Andrew Moyse was sacked as editor, and the rest of the editorial staff left with him.

The reasons for Moyse's sacking are not clear and have been the subject of much speculation. Moyse himself believes he was fired for asking the management to allocate more resources for the production and improvement of the magazine. In dismissing Moyse, Alex Thomson claimed that the editor was failing to adhere to production schedules and therefore the magazine was missing publication dates. The rest of the journalists and advertising staff then resigned in sympathy with their former editor and regrouped to start their own monthly magazine *Horizon*.

Horizon was established from a combination of a grant by a local nongovernmental organization, Zimbabwe Projects, and a grant from the Swedish International Development Association (SIDA). A local businessman, David Smith, who runs a music retailing business, Music Express, provided temporary office space. Initially the journalists used Moyse's house as offices, a not untypical set-up for journalist owned and controlled publications in Zimbabwe. Beyond their highly recognized journalistic skills, the new owners had no capital to invest into the new venture.

The SIDA grant, while substantial then (ZWD $450,000),[2] was not sufficient to launch the magazine on a fully capitalized basis. Since the journalists were not and had never been business managers, they asked for what they thought was sufficient at the time of application for funds. Even if they had asked for more, it does not mean that they would have secured all they needed, since SIDA would obviously have a limit on how much they could fund a single project. *Horizon* was therefore launched on a weak financial basis which has not improved and over time has worsened.

The SIDA grant also attracted the ire of some members of the ruling party and as a result was debated in parliament. The government protested to SIDA, alleging that they were supporting opposition newspapers and therefore interfering in the internal politics of the country. SIDA justified the grant by saying their intention was to support the creation of a pluralistic media system necessary for democracy in Zimbabwe. The reaction of the government to the grant probably had the effect of discouraging donors from supporting the commercially owned media in Zimbabwe. Indeed SIDA was interested in further grants in Zimbabwe but the head office in Sweden was not in favor because of this adverse governmental reaction.

After Andrew Moyse left, *Parade* changed its style for a much less controversial form of reporting under the new editorial leadership. *Parade* is now a magazine devoted to a form of journalism which might best be described as Zimbabwean tabloidism, while *Horizon* has continued the form of investigative and critical journalism. *Horizon*, however, faces a precarious economic existence and a number of libel cases, and often difficulties in acquiring support for its special projects from among international donors otherwise dedicated to the promotion of democracy and free and critical press. Before the Zimbabwean elections in 1995 *Horizon* approached the Norwegian donor agency NORAD with a request for support for a voter education supplement, which was to be run over three issues in conjunction with a voter education project. They did not receive the grant, and no reason was given. On the other hand, in 1995 the Dutch Communications Assistance Foundation (CAF) gave a grant of nearly Zim $2 million to the journalists' cooperative for the purchase of computer and print originator equipment.[3]

On Christmas Day 1994 the last issue of Zimbabwe's first independent daily appeared. The saga of the *Daily Gazette* is of great significance for the understanding of the relationship between state-controlled newspapers and the private press, and the role of the market in relation to the press in Southern Africa. The *Daily Gazette* had then existed for a little over two years. The first issue appeared on Monday October 5, 1992. In his publisher's statement, Elias Rusike declared that the new newspaper was dedicated to national unity, a mixed economy, and democratic rights. But more than anything else, there was an emphasis on the independence of the new paper, and on its right in the interest of the nation to criticize the government, individual ministers, political parties, business interests, and private individuals. The newspaper did not see itself as an oppositional paper, but as an alternative to what was called the government-controlled press. The paper would concentrate on issues, not persons, and pursue an objective, balanced, and fair form of journalism, in the interest of bringing truth to the public.

The *Daily Gazette* aimed at becoming a modern hard-hitting popular newspaper, mixing political news and comments with typical tabloid material in the form of sensationalism and particularly crime stories. While the *Herald* in its staidness and avoidance of popular and critical journalism may be seen as a poor copy of British or rather South African quality newspapers, the *Daily Gazette* might be likened to a British tabloid in the *Daily Mirror* tradition. In its first weeks of existence the paper carried a number of stories revealing abuse of power and corruption in public institutions. Many Zimbabweans interpreted this as a sign of the appearance of a more open society, and that it would be possible to gain more insight into the goings-on behind the closed doors of power. On the other hand it became clear very early on that the paper lacked sufficient resources to undertake the kind of investigative journalism that it had set out to do. Much of the material in the paper were stories from news agencies, and poorly researched reports, of an often sensationalist kind, and also a form of snooping journalism which showed little respect for the privacy of individuals, based on very weak sources.

From the very beginning, the *Daily Gazette* had severe logistical problems such as lack of telephone lines and equipment, not enough vehicles and so on. It also had problems with distribution, acquiring enough advertising, in short with establishing a sufficiently strong basis for the continuation of the paper. It also became clear after the paper had folded, that the financial basis for the launch was weak. The proprietors probably did not have enough capital to sustain the paper for more than a year. The experiment with the *Daily Gazette* thus tapped the publishing company—Modus—for most of its resources and left it more or less bankrupt when the paper ceased publication. At its launch, the print run was 40,000, it peaked at 55,000, and was at the time of its folding probably around 20,000. Contributing to the fall of the paper were high interest rates, soaring production costs, and restricted consumer demand, which led to shrinking margins. Furthermore there is no doubt that the *Daily Gazette* in trying to break the Zimpapers monopoly was confronted by a government jealous of its privileged access to the national press. In consequence its existence was made as difficult as possible. Potential advertisers were probably discouraged from advertising in the paper. Although evidence is scant, there are indications that both state-linked and private businesses were wary of placing ads in the *Gazette* for fear of antagonizing the government. It should be borne in mind that the liberalization of the Zimbabwean economy had not developed as far as it has toward the end of the 1990s.

The financial difficulties which became clear very early in the paper's existence also influenced the editorial line of the paper, which all through its existence may be said to have been a bit "schizophrenic." On the one hand it had as its implied audience a relatively broad urban section of the Zimbabwean population, something which was reflected in its tabloid style of journalism, but on the other it also hoped to appeal to the affluent white sections of society from whom it hoped to acquire advertising. The editorial line of the paper under its first editor—Mike Hamilton—may be described as mildly left-wing and pro-Zimbabwean, but it also carried columns with what may be called a quite conservative and also anti-Africanist attitude, primarily written by the man who was to take over from Hamilton as editor in 1993, Brian Latham. The paper also had a third editor, the veteran journalist Bill Saidi, at the end of its existence, but his job consisted of little more than overseeing the demise of the paper.

The checkered background history of the *Daily Gazette* is in many ways central to the history of the independent press in Zimbabwe. The paper grew out of Modus publications, whose history goes back to 1959. Its main publication before the start of the *Daily Gazette* was the weekly *Financial Gazette* whose roots go back to 1956. During UDI it was called the *Rhodesian Financial Gazette* and was in many ways a mouthpiece for The Rhodesian Front. In 1979 it was bought by a group of liberal white investors—Clive Murphy and Nigel and Rhett Butler. In 1982 they hired a very capable and liberal conservative journalist Clive Wilson as editor, and started upgrading the paper with new staff and equipment. In the course of a few years the paper became not only the most important voice of the mainly white business community, but also came to be regarded as the paper for alternative opinion in general, in spite of the fact that it never pursued a popular form of journalism. It increased its circulation in the course of five years from around 4,000 to 20,000, and it was an economic goldmine which attracted a lot of advertising.

In 1989 Modus publications and the *Financial Gazette* were bought by a group of three black investors under the leadership of Elias Rusike, who until then had been Group Managing Director of Zimpapers. They hired Geoffrey Nyarota as editor of the *Financial Gazette*, and he started changing the paper's profile to be more involved in political news reporting, and started the *Weekend Gazette* as a special supplement, which later became a separate publication and formed the basis for the *Daily Gazette*. In 1991 Nyarota was fired as editor, for reasons never established, but he later won compensation in a court case for being unfairly dismissed. At about the same time Modus bought a new printing press, and the preparations for starting the daily had begun. The publication of the *Financial Gazette*, however, continued all the time, its editorial independence gradually coming under pressure from Modus's owners, who were under pressure from their creditors at the government-controlled Zimbank. Staff and infrastructure was pared back sharply, in a desperate attempt to cut costs and stay afloat. In the wake of this and the management's increasing admonition to ease up on criticism of the government and ruling party, the editor Trevor Ncube and several other senior editorial staff left the paper in 1996. However, the *Financial Gazette* continues to be an important voice, especially of the black business community, and it maintains its independent editorial line under a new editorial leadership.

What, then, did the *Daily Gazette* achieve during its short life? Probably the most important result was that the paper proved that it was possible to challenge the monopoly of Zimpapers, and that it was feasible to create alternative more open forms of journalism. Thus the paper together with other alternative media developed a form of critical journalism which at its best definitely has contributed to the opening up of Zimbabwean society. There is also little doubt that the *Herald* during the years that the *Daily Gazette* existed, changed its journalistic style and became more adventurous and open. Journalists working for the *Herald* maintained that they would be much more set on getting a story first. The paper became more oriented to being first with the news, and to prioritizing real news stories rather than pure minister journalism (Andersen and Olsen 1997).

In May 1996 a new weekly newspaper hit the streets in Harare. It was called the *Zimbabwe Independent* and it came in the wake of the crisis in the independent press after the collapse of the *Daily Gazette* and the *Sunday Gazette*. The paper was an attempt to revive the private sector press which had been severely eroded, and to widen the scope and national reach of published opinion. The *Independent* was set up with the backing of solid capital, management, and editorial resources (including a translocated senior editorial team from Modus, headed by former *Financial Gazette* editor Trevor Ncube). The *Independent*'s leading investors were Clive Murphy and Clive Wilson.[4] Since they sold their controlling interest in Modus, they consolidated a new publishing company and developed a national distribution agency which was used to support the *Independent*. The editorial line included support for meaningful "black empowerment" measures, and for the government's economic reform program ESAP, but also a consistent criticism and exposure of government mismanagement, corruption, and abuse of power. The newspaper proved to be a success, and reached a circulation of 25,000 after little more than a year. The publishers bought a second-hand press, and also started a Sunday paper, the *Sunday Standard*, in April 1997. The editorial line of this paper may be characterized as a form of up-market populist entertainment journalism—an attempt to emulate the *Parade* formula in a weekly newspaper format, and its editor was Mark Chavunduka, who had taken over from Andrew Moyse as editor of *Parade*.

The market for both the "Independent" papers is the professional urban sector, but their impact is doubtlessly larger than their circulation indicates. However, there is also little doubt that the papers are susceptible to populist attacks from government and an increasingly militant black business indigenization lobby, concerning both their editorial line and their economic background. The independent press in Zimbabwe in 1999 may be said to be quite vibrant. In addition to the *Financial Gazette* and the two "Independent" papers, it also consists of the weekly *Zimbabwe Mirror* which started publication in December 1997. This had its background in an intellectual and academic trust built up around the monthly magazine *Southern African Political and Economic Monthly (SAPEM)*. In the beginning it bore the marks of its background in intellectual circles and lacked a journalistic style, but it has developed and may now be characterized as an informed, analytical paper with sharp articles. Its editorial line is radical and quite different from the business-based attitude of its competitors. Its political message, which may be characterized as critical of, but with an affinity to ZANU(PF), also gives it access to information about what goes on inside the party in a way that none of its competitors can. The paper's greatest challenge and problems probably lie in an insufficiently developed infrastructure and distribution network. It is said to have printed around 30,000 copies in July 1998.

The independent press poses a challenge to the Zimpapers, even if the latter dominate the newspaper market with their four weeklies and two dailies. But the existence of the *Daily Gazette* and the subsequent development of both magazine and newspaper publishing has given Zimbabweans a taste of a free press, and space has been opened up. The independent weeklies together have a print run of almost 100,000 and the broad readership has become more sophisticated. There are strong indications that Zimbabweans do not as easily accept news which is hidden, distorted, or massaged. Zimpapers have lost legitimacy.

These tendencies were reinforced in July 1998 when plans for establishing both a new daily newspaper and a chain of local newspapers in Zimbabwe were announced. The company behind the initiative, Associated Newspapers of Zimbabwe (ANZ (Pvt) Ltd), intended to spend Zim $65 million to launch a new national daily newspaper —the *Daily News*—to be printed simultaneously in Harare and Bulawayo, and five local weeklies in urban centers around the country, employing about 100 journalists in addition to technical and advertising personnel. Behind these ambitious plans were local journalists and editors such as Geoffrey Nyarota with a background as an editor of, among others the *Chronicle* and *Financial Gazette* and Wilf Mbanga, who for many years ran the project of establishing local/rural newspapers in the country under The Mass Media Trust. By March 30, 1999 all the papers had been launched, and it is going to be very interesting to see whether they are able wrest the market from Zimpapers and survive in the very difficult economic climate that Zimbabwe faces in 1999.

One of the most interesting aspects of the project is the economic background to it. Behind it is a consortium of Zimbabwean institutional, corporate, and private investors, backed by companies and individuals with publishing interests in the United Kingdom, New Zealand, and South Africa. ANZ was capitalized through Zim $39 million[5] raised by the company's foreign partners and channelled to Zimbabwe through Africa Media Investments (Zimbabwe) Ltd (AMI), a company which is registered in the United Kingdom and controls 60 percent of ANZ. Zimbabwean investors, meanwhile, have put up Zim $26 million in capital and control 40 percent of the new publishing house. The rest of the capital has been put up by foreign shareholders who have equal stakes in the projects. The outside investors, who make up the AMI group, are the Bank of Scotland; Tindle Newspapers, one of Britain largest publishers of local and regional papers; Cross Graphics, a British supplier of printing and associated equipment; Allied Press, New Zealand's largest private media group; Commonwealth Publishing Ltd, which publishes a range of publications in several Commonwealth nations; and Michael Stent, who has wide experience in South Africa and internationally with journalism and media management. Stent maintained that Zimbabwe's newspaper market is under-tapped, and that the project was just the beginning for AMI to set up similar partnerships with media investors in the SADC region. It has been speculated that the project is in the forefront for a South African based media incursion into the region as a whole. Originally the South African newspaper group Independent Newspapers controlled by the Irish magnate Tony O'Reilly was supposed to be among the investors, but in early 1999 it was announced that the group withdrew from the project. The reasons for the withdrawal are not clear, but there have been speculations that it may be due to two main factors: that the difficult situation in the Zimbabwean economy with deteriorating living conditions makes newspaper investment extremely risky, and that the increasingly hostile climate between government and the independent press is not conducive to South African investment in the private press in Zimbabwe.[6]

In a short-term perspective this initiative may be seen as an example of how the market can further media diversity. Particularly interesting is the fact that it is foreign media capital that provides the impetus for greater media pluralism in Zimbabwe. This aspect, however, also provoked the most worrying response from the government; both the Minister of Information Chen Chimutengwende, and the Minister of Industry and Commerce Nathan Shamuayirira, criticized the project for being foreign dominated and for having the potential of destabilizing the political order and of furthering oppositional political agendas. In early 1999 Chimutengwende also stated that he was considering introducing rules against foreign investments in Zimbabwean media and restrictions on the right of international donors to support media in the country.

If the *Daily News* and its sister local papers succeed—though it will take up to five years to find that out—then the monopoly of Zimpapers will be broken, and this will undoubtedly have important political consequences for the country. The ANZ initiative suggests that in the interest of media pluralism it is necessary to adopt a pragmatic position to what often may be seen as fundamental doctrines in relation to restrictions on foreign ownership and media concentration. Such principles must be applied in relation to historical circumstances and contexts, and it is to a large degree true that in Africa it is the market media that are independent.

It is characteristic of the relationship between the government and the press in monolithic systems that representatives of the rulers tend to attack the independent press regularly on the basis of two sorts of arguments: either that they represent a divisional threat to national unity and cohesion, or that they purvey slander and lies.

An example of the first attitude is to be found in regular attacks on the independent press in Zimbabwe from both the ZANU(PF) press and ministers. This is a process which started in the early 1990s. An early example is an editorial in the October/November 1992 issue of *Zimbabwe News*, which is the official organ of the party. It consisted of an attack on the *Financial Gazette* which stated that the paper's criticism was "destructive, negative and even subversive," and went on to argue that the type of incitement of the people against the police, the army, the CIO, and hostility to the government could not be tolerated in any society. "If it is tolerated it will certainly lead to the type of violence which all responsible Zimbabweans want to avoid." An example of the other is an attack by President Mugabe on the *Zimbabwe Independent* in July 1998, when he accused what he called "the opposition press" of trying "to sell their papers on the basis of manufactured lies" and claimed that it was thriving on these lies. He ended up by threatening that the "gutter press" should "take heed because we are not going to have this kind of journalism in this country" (Electronic Mail and Guardian, July 15, 1998). It is furthermore significant that this attack occurred at the same time as the President took the opportunity to attack MPs who refused to toe the party line.[7] And in January 1999 the most serious attack on the independent press occurred, the implications of which are much more far-reaching than being only a conflict between the press and the government.

It started when the *Standard* on January 10 claimed that there had been an attempted military coup in the army and that twenty-three officers had been arrested. The newspaper reported that the plans for the coup had their background in widespread dissatisfaction in the army and in Zimbabwean society over the country's involvement in the civil war in the Democratic Republic of Congo. Some days after the publication of the story, military police stormed the offices of the *Standard*, and subsequently arrested the editor—Mark Chavunduka—and the reporter Raymond Choto who had written the story. They were tortured during the nine days they were in military detention. During the torture and interrogation the military police wanted to know who the military sources were and especially the alleged link with South African military intelligence. The police furthermore wanted to know the source of funding of the two papers and the military police and air-force sources used by the *Standard*, and they also threatened to arrest other senior people in the Independent newspapers company, as well as the people behind *Zimbabwe Mirror*.

The two journalists were transferred to civil police and formally charged only after a judge had ruled that their arrest was unconstitutional and that they should be released forthwith. That did not take place till some days later, and after the Minister of Defence Moven Mahachi had been threatened with being taken to court for contempt, because he had stated that his ministry did not take orders from courts. When they appeared in court, the journalists were charged under the Law and Order (Maintenance) Act, a law introduced by the Smith regime and aimed at suppressing African nationalism before independence. Its terms cover the publication of "false news" and "spreading alarm and despondency." The state alleged that the story was not verified and was meant to tarnish the image of the Zimbabwe Defence Forces and cause public disorder. However, Chavunduka and Choto in their statements to the police denied that their story was bound to cause "alarm, despondency and public disorder" since the alleged coup was quelled. They also said they took reasonable steps to verify the story with the Defence ministry without success. Two days later Clive Wilson was also arrested, only to be released after a weekend in custody without being charged.

Whatever the true version of the coup story, the events are yet another example of the conflict between the Zimbabwean government and the independent media. This was also clearly borne out by the statements made by the government in relation to the events: Moven Mahachi, Zimbabwe's Defence Minister, said that the independent media had a well calculated program to destroy the country and the ZANU(PF) government. He said that while the government fully recognized the freedom of the press as enshrined in the constitution of Zimbabwe, it also had responsibility to protect the nation from malicious misinformation deliberately intended by some newspapers to create instability because of their financial greed, and that the independent press had a hidden agenda. Chen Chimutengwende, the Minister of Information, said that he wished that Chavunduka could stay in detention for good, because "If you read his newspaper every Sunday, there is a big lie. Their aim is to show Zimbabwe as unstable and that nobody should come here and invest." Like Mahachi, Chimutengwende accused the independent media of tarnishing the image of the government. "Yes that is the position that we as Ministry of Information have taken because the independent media goes as far as deliberately telling lies which tarnish, sabotage the economy. To us what they are doing is tantamount to treason." He said that his ministry would "do something" about the "lies" in the independent media. "We will not sit idly while some people try to sabotage the country," he said.

The struggle between the government and the independent press in Zimbabwe over how to interpret the crisis-ridden situation in the country, particularly in relation to the country's heavy engagement in the civil war in the Congo, did not end with this. Three weeks later the editor and three journalists from the *Zimbabwe Mirror* were also arrested for having written about the dissatisfaction within the army with the military engagement in the Congo. The editor-in-chief, Ibbo Mandaza, and the journalist behind the story, Grace Kwinjeh, were both charged with "publishing false information likely to cause alarm, fear and despondency" (reported in the *Independent*, the *Standard*, the *Financial Gazette*, *Mail and Guardian*, Harare IPS office). A particularly interesting aspect of the latest arrest is that Ibbo Mandaza is not typical of Zimbabwean editors, and he does not share a political background with the owners and journalists of the Independent group. His background is in ZANU(PF), being in exile during the war, and he served in senior civil servant and political positions in the 1980s. He is primarily an intellectual and a high-profile social scientist, who took the initiative to set up one of the most important independent social science research institutions in Africa—The SAPES Trust. His increasing critical position in relation to government policy, and principled defense of democratic principles, must be seen as indicative of the widening split in the party over the role of the leadership's increasing dictatorial policies. The Ministry of Information is considering whether to introduce censorship of stories dealing with military matters, which ironically was the reason behind the introduction of censorhip in Ian Smith's Rhodesia. Furthermore the setting up of an official press council and licensing arrangements for the press have also been hinted at. The government's arguments in relation to this confrontation with the press may be summed up by the following quotation from a letter in the Johannesburg paper the *Star* (March 19, 1999) by the Zimbabwean High Commissioner to South Africa:

> The fact of the matter is that the arrest of the journalists followed persistent, false and malicious reports aimed at destabilizing the army. Some of the stories included the following:

- That a soldier died in battle in the Democratic Republic of Congo and only his head was brought home for burial;
- That there was mutiny by soldiers in the DRC;
- That 23 officers in the Zimbabwe National Army had been arrested for planning a coup.

On the first allegation, the soldier in question died of malaria while on duty in the DRC and his body had to be exhumed in order to prove that the story was without foundation. That there was mutiny by the Zimbabwe Army in the DRC proved to be a complete fabrication as the soldiers continue to serve with the unquestionable loyalty expected of a disciplined and well trained army.

The coup plot story was without foundation, and yet it cost the country's image abroad dearly.

Regarding the alleged torture of journalists we wish to state that the Zimbabwe Government does not condone the use of torture. It is for this reason that this matter is being taken up with the courts. The logical thing for the press in general therefore is for it to be patient enough to wait for the law to take its course instead of rushing to unsubstantiated conclusions.

The facts of the cases may be disputable, but the problem is nevertheless the legal apparatus used by the government in its struggle to control which issues are to be debated.

The seriousness of the situation was furthermore borne out when President Mugabe went on television accusing the white population of the country of fermenting unrest, the judges of sabotaging the government and asking them to resign or be fired, and the independent press of behaving dishonestly and unethically, saying that it did not deserve the protection of the law. Mugabe's speech and Mahachi's and Chimutengwende's statements confirm what the independent media and human rights organizations have alleged since the early 1990s, namely that the government treats all nonofficial media like an opposition party, and as enemies of the state. It is a conflict which illustrates how a power-conscious and increasingly corrupt authoritarian government feels threatened by open media, particularly over issues which involve struggle within the governing party.

In such a political atmosphere there are good reasons why a principled liberal media ideology easily finds proponents, particularly in circles wanting to further a democratic policy and defend the free and independent press. The question of media independence is at the heart of debates about the establishment of democratic media, not only in Southern Africa, but also in other societies that have undergone the change from authoritarian state formations to more open and liberal free-market societies. The issue is complex because it involves more than a simple counterpoising of state media on the one hand and private media on the other. For historical and understandable reasons, however, the debate about what is entailed by media independence has been centered on the state. Thus all private media enterprises have been regarded as independent. This attitude is clearly related to a liberal way of thinking that argues that the primary democratic function of the media is to act as a public watchdog, checking the state and revealing abuse of state authority. The watchdog role is regarded as more important than all other media functions (Curran 1991).

Particularly in societies where government practices are not transparent, where there exist gross abuses of political power, and where the independent press is weak, it is easy to argue that critical surveillance of government and the state is the most important aspect of the democratic functions of the media and that it is essential in order to build public confidence in the news media. The history of investigative reporting and the uncovering of public scandals and corrupt practices by the independent press and courageous journalists in the official media in Southern Africa exemplifies how the media perform a public service by investigating and stopping malpractice by public officials. This often entails considerable risk to individual journalists and editors, because the powers that be would rather have a docile press. No wonder there have been many attacks on the independent press in countries such as Zambia and Zimbabwe over the years, and many veiled attempts to prevent the press from uncovering abuses of power. The threats to introduce measures to curb the freedom of the press and repress the right to freedom of expression and information, which repeatedly have come from Presidents Chiluba of Zambia and Mugabe, and lately also from Namibian government sources, are signs that governments are wary of public exposure. The independent press that has emerged in Southern Africa in the 1990s faces challenges which may be a threat to the growing media independence in the region (Sandbrook 1996).

These attacks indicate that freedoms of expression and information are precarious, and that they are dependent on an awareness of the need to maintain and extend them. The watchdog role of the press is particularly important in societies where political parties or organizations have failed to provide an effective opposition to the ruling party, whether through fragmentation or inexperience—such as is the case in Zimbabwe. In such situations it is doubly important that the press examine the conduct of the rulers and question how public resources are managed. An important prerequisite for a developed democracy is that there exist institutions which can defend public interests and question government acts and decisions in a public manner on behalf of a variety of cultural and social interests and opinions. This is one of the functions of the parliament and particularly of parliamentary oppositions. When parliaments do nothing but toe the party line, and when parliamentarians who try to raise critical voices, are taken to task for not following the party line, then one of the most important safeguards of the freedom of expression is severely weakened.

In such a situation the independent press more or less automatically will take the place of the absent parliamentary opposition, and together with other civil society institutions defend the interests of the public. In Southern Africa the watchdog role has been linked to another essential function of protecting citizen's rights, namely that of testing the constitutionality of undemocratic laws. This has been an important part of the opening up of space for democratic action, and in this context the activities of the Media Institute of Southern Africa (MISA) with its information and solidarity network of media alerts have been of great importance.

This has in many ways been the case in Zimbabwe in the 1990s, where an organized political opposition is virtually nonexistent in what may be characterized as a *de facto* one-party state. This is the authoritarian legacy of the independence struggle which President Mugabe increasingly has come to embody. At independence the ZANU(PF) government pursued a policy of reconciliation, embarked on ambitious health and education programs, and was by all standards relatively incorrupt. There were limitations to full democratic freedoms, not least due to emergency laws inherited from UDI, and kept in force because of the threat from apartheid South Africa. However, already in 1983 the brutal oppression and large-scale massacres in Matabeleland were largely kept out of international media, which indicated a strong dictatorial tendency (The Catholic Commission for Justice and Peace in Zimbabwe 1997). This was underlined by the expressed policy of wanting to turn Zimbabwe into a one-party state, and increased corruption and lust for power among leading party cadres. In the 1990s the crisis in both the economy and politics has created increasing dissatisfaction with the government, which has answered protests against the erosion of welfare and corruption with brutal suppression. The symbol of this conflict is the deployment of Zimbabwean troops to the Congo, which cost the country dearly and the reasons for which are to be found in two sets of intertwining motives. One is the rivalry between Zimbabwe and South Africa, and Mugabe and Mandela, which is linked to old competition over economic and political interests in the Congo area. The other has to do with Zimbabwean capital interests in mining and mineral exploitation in the Congo, and the role of the international arms trade for the whole region by shady Zimbabwean interests. Hence the concern in ZANU(PF) over critical press reports about the war and dissatisfaction in the army.

The conflict between ZANU(PF)'s and Mugabe's authoritarian tendencies and the democratic legacy of the struggle against the Rhodesian regime, has always been a factor in Zimbabwean political life. The formal political opposition has been weak, but with its center in the courageous independent member of parliament Margaret Dongo, a new political party is now being built—the National Constitutional Assembly (NCA)—which may pose a challenge to ZANU(PF) in the parliamentary elections in 2000, and the presidential election in 2001. The democratic impulse in Zimbabwean society has mainly been expressed by the numerous civic organizations in the country, a vocal intellectual community, churches, and human rights organizations, and a small, but vocal independent press. In addition, the judiciary has been independent and principled in its defense of the constitution. This in spite of everything has kept Zimbabwean society relatively open. And it is the struggle over maintaining this open space and extending it, which is currently a factor in the conflict between President Mugabe and the ZANU(PF) leadership on the one hand and the independent press on the other. An authoritarian state ideology is posed against the democratic agenda of a multifaceted civil society.

Notes

1 This article is based on research undertaken under the program of cooperation between the Department of Media and Communication at the University of Oslo, and the Media Program in the English Department at the University of Zimbabwe through the research project Media and Democracy—Cultural and Political Change in Southern Africa funded by the Norwegian Research Council and the NUFU program for cooperation between Norwegian universities and unversities in the South funded by the Norwegian Ministry of Affairs. The present text has mainly been written by Helge Rønning, but is the result of a long period of cooperation between the two authors.

2 The Zimbabwe dollar has suffered severe depreciation since the country achieved independence in 1980. Then 1 ZWD was worth approximately 1.2 US$, in early 1999 there are approximately 40 ZWD to the US$. The currency crisis was particualarly severe in 1998.

3 In August 1999 *Horizon* stopped being published due to financial difficulties linked to the economic problems of Associated Newspapers of Zimbabwe (ANZ) (see note 5) to which it linked itself in 1998.

4 Clive Murphy withdrew from the company in early 1999.

5 The figures reflect the value of the Zim dollar in July 1998 before the last serious drop in the currency July/August 1998.
6 In August/September 1999 it was reported that ANZ was in serious financial difficulties. It had to shut down three of its regional newspapers, and it had to retrench many of its staff. Several of the central staff of the company were also leaving. ANZ was said to owe a total of Zim$ 88 million and was at the time seeking a Zim$ 114 million rescue package. A financial summary of the situation reported in *The Financial Gazette* pointed out that ANZ had been undercapitalized from the beginning. (*The Financial Gazette Electronic Edition*, 2 September 1999.)
7 The seriousness of the President's attack should not be underestimated, but the background to the attack is also interesting. The *Zimbabwe Independent* on July 10 had published a story where it was alleged that the First Lady had acquired a costly property in her home town Chivhu. The newspaper had, however, not been able to verify the story, nor had it checked its sources properly. In its July 31 issue the paper retracted the story and excused itself. Thus this form of unethical journalism gave the President the excuse for his more general threats to press freedom. Furthermore it is not the first time that there has been a conflict between the editor of the newspaper and the President. When Trevor Ncube was the editor of the *Financial Gazettte* he published an unverified and untrue story of the alleged marriage of the President. This also provoked threats to the principle of a free press, and both Trevor Ncube and the proprietor of the *Financial Gazette* were arrested. Thus unethical journalism may play into the hands of authoritarian forces.

References

Africa. Film & TV. News Flash (1997) Edition 1, May 30.

Andersen, E. W. and Olsen, R. K. (1996) "Press freedom and democracy in Zimbabwe," M.Phil. thesis, Department of Media and Communication, University of Oslo.

Andersen, M. B. (1997) "The Janus face of television in small countries. The case of Zimbabwe," *Critical Arts*, 2, Durban.

Article XIX and Index on Censorship (1995) *Who Rules the Airwaves? Broadcasting in Africa*, London.

Catholic Commission for Justice and Peace in Zimbabwe (1997) *Breaking the Silence*, Harare: CCJPZ, The Legal Resources Centre.

Curran, J. (1991) "Mass media and democracy. A reappraisal," in J. Curran and M. Gurevitch (eds.) *Mass Media and Society*, London: Edward Arnold.

Ibbotson, P. (1996) Report, delivered in Oxford, December 18.

Kupe, T. (1997) "Voices of the voiceless. Popular magazines in a changing Zimbabwe 1990–1996," unpublished Ph.D. thesis, Department of Media and Communication, University of Oslo.

Manhando, S. (1997) *Broadcasting in a Deregulated Southern Africa. Zimbabwe's Efforts to Engage with Technological Changes in Electronic Media*, Department of Media and Communication, University of Oslo.

Melkote, S. R. (1991) *Communication for Development in The Third World. Theory and Practice*, New Delhi, Newbury Park and London: Sage.

Rusike, E. T. M. (1990) *The Politics of the Mass Media. A Personal Experience*, Harare: Roblaw Publisher.

Sandbrook, R. (1996) "Transitions without consolidation: democratization in six African cases," *Third World Quarterly*, 17(1).

Saunders, R. G. (1991) "Information in the interregnum: the press, state and civil society in struggles for hegemony, Zimbabwe 1980–1990, unpublished Ph.D. thesis, Carleton University.

Wedell, G. (ed.) (1986) *Making Broadcasting Useful: The African Experience. The Development of Radio and Television in Africa in the 1980s*, Manchester: Manchester University Press.

Zaffiro, J. J. (1984) "Broadcasting and political change in Zimbabwe 1931–1984," unpublished Ph.D. thesis, University of Wisconsin, Madison.

12 Media and power in Egypt

Hussein Amin and James Napoli

Egypt is located in the northeast of Africa facing the Mediterranean Sea on the north, bounded on the south by Sudan, on the west by Libya, and on the east by the Red Sea, Israel, and Palestine. Cairo is the capital city and also the largest city. There are numerous smaller cities and villages scattered along both sides of the Nile river and in the Nile delta. A population explosion is a serious threat to Egypt. The population is almost 60 million and growing, with most of the population engaged in agriculture (Europa 1998).

The official language in Egypt is Arabic. Islam is the religion of the state, which also has a large religious minority of Coptic Christians. King Farouk was the last of the kings to rule Egypt. General Mohammed Naguib, who was the first Egyptian to rule Egypt since the time of the pharaohs, headed the Egyptian revolution in 1952 which ended British rule over Egypt. Naguib remained in power for almost two years, until Gamal Abdel Nasser seized control of the country in 1954. Nasser continued in power until his natural death in 1971. Nasser's successor, Anwar el Sadat, was assassinated in 1981 and was followed by Egypt's current president, Hosni Mubarak (Amin 1986).

The political system of the state is that of a presidential republic, under the Permanent Constitution of 1971, which declared a democratic socialist state based on the alliance of the people's working forces and guaranteeing the rights of individuals. The constitution defines the structure and functions of the state, the basic components of society, public liberties, rights and obligations, the supremacy of the law, and the system of government (Napoli *et al.* 1995).

Egypt has made steady progress toward becoming a multiparty democracy. The legislature is bicameral, consisting of the Shura Council and the People's Assembly. The People's Assembly incorporates a minimum of 350 members. While the president determines the main policy of the state, the cabinet of ministers supervises its implementation, and ministerial responsibility to the legislature is constitutionally established. The Shura Council is an advisory council established in 1980 and consisting of 210 members. The four main political parties are the ruling National Democratic Party, the Socialist Workers Party, the Liberal Socialist Party, and the Unionist Progressive Party (Napoli and Amin 1997).

The legal system has been influenced not only by Islamic teaching, but also by the Napoleonic Code. Sharia, or Islamic law, is the main source of legislation. The Egyptian constitution guarantees the independence of the judiciary, and legal decisions are the mandate of the judges, as there is no jury system. The Supreme Council, presided over by the president, supervises the affairs of the judicial organizations, although the highest judicial authority, with the power to determine the constitutionality of laws and regulations, is the Supreme Constitutional Court or the Court of Cassation (Amin 1986).

The development of modern mass media in Egypt was shaped by three men. The first was Gamal Abdel Nasser, president of Egypt from 1954 to 1970; the second was Anwar el Sadat, president of Egypt from 1970 to 1981; and the third is Egypt's current president, Hosni Mubarak. Nasser realized from his first days as a ruler of Egypt that the press was controlled by political parties, and most publishing houses were owned by non-Egyptians (Nasser 1990). It was not until 1960 that Nasser made his move—realizing the power of the press in mobilizing the public—and nationalized the Egyptian press, including all privately owned press organizations. These organizations had to surrender their ownership to the country's only legal political organization, the National Union, later renamed the Arab Socialist Union. Nasser's successor, Anwar el Sadat, theoretically adopted an open attitude toward the press, but in practice, his policies with regard to the press were ambivalent (Amin and Napoli 1995). Sadat removed censorship but retained the government's control of the media. President Hosni Mubarak—unlike his two predecessors—moved toward more press freedom and lifted many of the restrictions and censorship. The Egyptian press under Mubarak operates far more freely than under the two previous regimes and more freely than in the majority of Arab and African countries (Amin and Napoli1997a).

The organization of the entire press underwent drastic revision just a few years after the revolution. Egypt was the first of the revolutionary Arab regimes, which included Algeria, Libya, and the Sudan, to take publishing out of the hands of private owners and make it the property of their political support system. In 1960, an Egyptian law was passed stipulating that no newspapers could be published without the permission of the National Union. The ownership of the nation's four large private publishing houses—Dar el-Ahram, Dar Akhbar el-Yom, Dar el-Hilal and Dar Rose el-Yusuf—was transferred to the National Union, which already owned Dar el-Tahrir publishing house (Rugh 1989). Other major changes were designed by Nasser to permit the government to mobilize the press behind his socialist policies, as was already the case with the state broadcasting system (Nasser 1990).

The mobilization of the press for supporting the government and for promoting the goals of national development was accompanied by an increased centralization of publishing in Cairo. The vestiges of that policy are particularly evident today in the newspaper press. Magazines and other periodicals were generally politicized. The monthly *al-Tali-ah* became a Marxist organ and *Rose al-Yusuf* became a strident, extreme voice of anti-imperialism—roles they maintained until their excesses incurred the wrath of President Sadat in 1977. On the right of the spectrum during the Sadat era, religious conservatives had their own magazines, *al-Da'wah* and *I'tisam*, which had been suspended under President Nasser.

President Sadat was responsible for shaping the conditions that have resulted in what has become a publishing boom in Egypt. In the course of moving the country away from its political dependence on the Soviet Union and toward democratization, he also instituted policy reforms that began to open up the economy to domestic entrepreneurs and the West. Further, Sadat ended the formal system of censorship and restored the right to establish political parties, which also were given the right to issue newspapers. The major opposition parties in Egypt are el Ahrar, the socialist party; el Wafd, the rightist party; el Tagamo'a el Watani, a leftist party. They all have their own newspapers. The most important and the only daily opposition newspaper is *el Wafd*. Other small party newspapers are published on an irregular basis (Napoli and Amin 1997).

The restoration of the capitalist impetus under Sadat helps to account for the later proliferation of book publishers under Hosni Mubarak. In 1992, it was observed that a good number and a wider range of private and energetic publishers of English-language magazine were establishing an industry in Cairo (Tresilian 1992).

Egyptian newspapers and magazines since the turn of the century provided a clamorous and lively forum for the nation's conservative and modernist tendencies. Numerous periodicals arose that helped propagate ideas and movements for economic and political reforms, feminism, secular liberalism, religious conservatism, trade unionism and so on (Vatikiotis 1991). The relaxation of censorship and the partial opening up of the economy after years of socialist controls also cleared the way for a revitalization of the magazine press. That revitalization picked up considerable energy under the pro-Western government of President Mubarak. Since the 1980s, however, more than 300 publications of all types have been licensed, including many magazines for hospitals, airports, companies, the military, and various trades. But special interest consumer magazines have also begun to create a market for themselves on Egyptian newsstands. The biggest category of new special interest magazines is devoted to religion (Amin and Napoli 1997a).

Today, despite the fairly high illiteracy rate in the country, the press is continuing to develop, and there is a new trend toward privately owned newspapers. Cairo is considered to be the publishing center in the Arab world and Africa. The most important national newspapers, *Al-Ahram* (The Pyramids) with a circulation of 900,000 and *Al Akhbar* (The News) with a circulation of 980,000, are popular outside the state as well. There are many newspapers that represent the government, the different political parties, and the private sector as well as many English and French language newspapers. The main source of news in Egypt is the national news agency that was founded in 1956, Wakalat Anba' alSharq alAwsat (The Middle East News Agency, MENA) (Europa 1998).

The Egyptian government has been committed to economic structural adjustment since 1991 but it was not until 1996 that the government demonstrated a sense of urgency about the implementation of economic reform. This policy was also reflected in the press, and the Egyptian newspaper market is slightly shifting. New private newspapers entered the Egyptian market in the past two years such as the dailies *Al Isbo'a* (The Week) and *AlDostour* (The Constitution) as well as the daily business newspaper *A'lam AlYoum* (The World Today). The newly introduced private newspapers are very small in terms of circulation and influence in comparison to the power and authority of the ruling political party and the National Democratic party and national newspapers but try very hard to present balanced and objective journalism (Korff 1998).

After a long period of quiescence under the rigidities of socialism, the magazine press in Egypt appears to be evolving in the same direction as it did decades ago in the United States and elsewhere. Specialized consumer magazines are being produced to meet what is perceived by editors as audience demand. They are doing so just as Egyptian television—a medium which in the United States had helped turn general interest magazine giants into dinosaurs—is also beginning to thrash about for new ways to raise revenues in an increasingly competitive media environment.

The availability of the Internet through new private service providers (ISPs), as well as through a government provider, gives Egyptian publishers the chance to reach Egyptian labor working outside the country and they started publishing newspapers on the Internet, including the main newspaper *Al-Ahram*.

The story of electronic media is different. Broadcasting systems in Egypt are absolute monopolies, under direct government supervision. As in most Arab countries, Egypt owns and operates its broadcasting institutions, radio as well as television. Egypt has a centralized model of broadcasting system for radio and television that was introduced after the Egyptian revolution in 1952 and is hosted by Cairo, the capital city. The predominant reason for centralizing broadcasting in Egypt is the desire of the ruling power to preserve national unity. Other reasons include the centralization of governmental administration and the high cost of establishing a television system in terms of technology and resources. Although the state has begun to decentralize the system by launching a series of local television channels in addition to the two main networks, the control remains the same. Moreover, Egypt embraces the broadcast media as a political tool and is keenly interested in keeping these technologies out of hostile hands. One more reason for centralized control of electronic media is the low literacy rate in Egypt. Since radio and television have the ability to overcome or bypass the problem of illiteracy, they are frequently used as an arm of the government to guide and mobilize the public (Amin and Boyd 1993).

Egypt has the most extensive and powerful as well as influential radio broadcasting system in the Arab region. Radio broadcasting started in Egypt in the early 1920s, but did not officially begin until May 1934. The system is under direct control of the government and operates under the mobilization type of broadcasting which views broadcasting as primarily a means of economic and political motivation (Rugh 1989). Radio as a medium comes second in terms of popularity after television. There are an estimated 18 million radio sets in the country (Amin 1996). In 1981, the radio broadcasting services were divided into seven radio networks: the Main Radio network (the general program), Voice of the Arabs network (Sout AlArab), the Cultural Radio network, the Commercial Radio network, The Qur'an network, the Local Radio network, and the Overseas network (ERTU 1997).

The Voice of the Arabs network consists of three radio services: Voice of the Arabs broadcasting service, the Palestine radio service, and the Nile Valley (Wady Al Nile) radio service. The Cultural Radio network consists of three services: these are the European service, the Second Program service, and the Music Program (Boyd 1993). The Commercial Radio network mainly includes the Middle East radio service and the Koran Radio service. The Local Radio network consists of ten radio services covering local areas. Examples of these services are the Alexandria radio program, established in 1954 to serve the country's second largest city; the Youth and Sports radio service that was introduced in 1975; the Middle Delta radio service that was established in 1982; the Upper Egypt radio service that was started in 1983; the North Sinai radio service that was established in 1984; and the South Sinai radio service that was introduced in 1985. The latter two radio services were introduced to encourage Egyptians to inhabit the Sinai and also as a service for tourists. The Canal radio service was established in 1988, and the New Valley and the Educational radio services were started in 1990. The Overseas network started in 1953 and includes forty-two radio services in thirty-two languages (ERTU 1997).

Radio broadcasting in Egypt is intensive. Egyptian radio networks produce a huge number of broadcast hours every year. Other international radio networks that are popular in Egypt include: the BBC Arabic radio service, the Voice of America Arabic service, and the Monte Carlo Arabic service. The Egyptian government's plan for comprehensive development calls for the expansion of radio as a primary means for communication and information services in various fields, especially in the education, health, sanitation, social, economic, and cultural domains. The state therefore needed to find an effective and popular medium to enable transmissions to reach all parts of the country and the Arab region as soon as possible and at minimum expense. In 1998, Egypt signed an agreement with WorldSpace Communication to be a user of their latest digital radio satellite, Afristar (ERTU 1998).

Egypt established its television system in 1960. This system was considered one of the most extensive and effective television systems among all the underdeveloped countries of Asia and Africa and particularly the Arab world. Unlike other Arab countries, Egypt was able to start television production without importing engineering equipment from abroad. This was due to the well financed radio services and film industry which were in existence at the time (Amin 1995). Egyptian Television started its first broadcast with verses from the Holy Koran followed by a speech from Nasser, and it was obvious from that time that the medium was going to be used as a propaganda tool for the government (Napoli *et al.* 1995).

Television initially began broadcasting its programs on two channels. A third channel that was added soon after was banned after the 1967 war. It was revived to cover greater Cairo in 1984. Within the last decade, Egyptian Television has begun implementing a plan to decentralize the system by introducing local television channels. Channel 4 was introduced in October 1988 to cover Ismailia, Suez, and Port Said; the first official broadcast was at the end of May 1989. Channel 5, covering Alexandria and surrounding areas, was introduced in December 1990. Channel 6, also known as the Delta channel, began broadcasting in May 1994. It is currently covering the Delta and the surrounding territories. Channel 7, covering Minia and some parts of southern Egypt, was introduced in October 1994 . A new local channel is operating on an experimental basis in Aswan and covers the far southern areas of the state. Most of the local television channels carry American programs on their broadcast schedule (Amin 1996).

Egypt's cultural products are by far the most popular in the Arab world, particularly in a culture that gets most of its entertainment in the home with an estimated 6.5 million television sets. Egyptian culture is still considered the most influential Arabic culture in the region. Egyptian Television has a powerful hold over the people of Egypt, providing them with entertainment, information, and culture.

The most important sources of programming for Egyptian television were films, including romance, slapstick comedy, and political films. News was broadcast initially only in Arabic, but later English and French news programs were added. Foreign programs, including British and American programs, were also telecast by Egyptian Television until the 1967 war. After Egypt's defeat in the war, the number of foreign programs, particularly American programs, broadcast over Egyptian Television decreased substantially. This was due mainly to the breakdown of diplomatic relations between Egypt and the United States and Great Britain and reflects the political nature of Egyptian television. American programming in Egypt was replaced by television programs from the Soviet Union. This situation lasted until the 1973 war. During President Sadat's rule, Egyptian Television reoriented itself toward the West, specifically the United States, and was a direct reflection of the Egyptian government's change of international political orientation. This situation has continued throughout Mubarak's regime, where foreign programs continue to appear on the Egyptian television schedule (Amin 1998).

As is the case with both print media and radio, it is important to state that Mubarak's regime undoubtedly provides the television media in general far more freedom than either of the two previous Egyptian regimes as well as most regimes elsewhere in the Arab world (Amin and Napoli 1995).

The Egyptian government made it clear from the beginning that it was going to adopt an "open window" policy to allow Egyptians to purchase or rent satellite dishes. A satellite dish allows Egyptians access to satellite broadcasting services from European countries as well as Turkey and Israel. There are currently about 800,000 satellite dishes in Egypt. Different patterns of obtaining a satellite dish range from full purchase to finance and lease-to-own arrangements. The main motivation behind the purchase of the satellite dishes is to watch Western programs. The Egyptian market has been stimulated by the drop in the price of television receiving only (TVROs) and direct broadcast satellite (DBS) receiving devices. Whereas a 2.4m dish might have cost LE 22,000 (US $6,400) back in 1990, now it costs LE 7,000 (US $2,000) (Omar 1995). Some Egyptian experts predict that the future will witness a growing market for direct-to-home broadcasting as a means for home entertainment. Also, the cost of pay television has been dropping. It is expected that Egypt will witness continued growth in the popularity of satellite dishes and a wider variety of television satellite services as well as more selective viewer bases (Omar 1995).

Islamic society in general and Egyptian society in particular is culturally defensive. It is proud of its enduring cultural legacy preserved through the use of the Arabic language. The Egyptian individual identifies himself or herself first with the family and second with the religious community. Egyptian people share social values derived from religious traditions, such as kindness, charity, virtue, and hospitality. The availability of foreign programming has raised concerns which are broadly cultural, specifically religious and inescapably political. These concerns have existed for quite a long time, but the sudden visual impact of popular Western culture courtesy of television, coupled with radical changes in Western mores as projected in much television programming over the past three decades, intensified these defenses (Schleifer 1995).

In the past decade, direct broadcast satellite as a service made a strong entry into Egypt. Although Egypt's economy has its weaknesses, its diplomatic contacts, rich television tradition and long-time involvement in program exchange set the stage for the development of the Egyptian Satellite Channel when Egypt returned to the Arab League in 1988. In the 1990s, just before the Gulf War, the Egyptian government moved into satellite broadcasting.

In a counter-effort to balance the flow of information coming from the West, Egypt has acted as a leader of a new wave of international pan-Arab television transmission for Arab viewers in the region with the introduction of the Egyptian Satellite Channel, followed by an English-language network named Nile TV International.

Realizing the importance of transnational broadcasting in the new millennium and the utilization of digital satellite broadcasting technology, Egypt launched their new NileSat satellite from Kourou, French Guyana on April 28, 1998 (ERTU 1997). NileSat-101 is a state-of-the-art digital satellite. Although the cost of the NileSat project is estimated at US $158 million, the country is looking forward to gaining maximum benefits from it in many different areas. NileSat-101 carries twleve transponders, each with a capability of transmitting a minimum of eight television channels. Transmitting across North Africa and the Arabian Peninsula, NileSat beams downs more than 100 digital television channels. Egyptian Radio and Television Union (ERTU) make use of at least twelve of NileSat's channels; this gives Egypt the chance to produce and broadcast its own specialized channels for the first time. ERTU currently broadcasts the Nile TV specialized package from the satellite. This package includes Nile Drama (TV movies, soap operas, and drama), Nile News, Nile Sports, Nile Culture and Nile Children, as well as educational channels. On the planning board is a new art channel coproduced by ERTU and the Ministry of Culture.

In addition to these packages, Showtime, which initially broadcast from PAS-4, has recently added NileSat to its capacity, and it has developed (in conjunction with Samsung/Galaxis) a decoder box capable of receiving digital signals from more than one satellite. The Showtime Movie Channel package will include Networks such as Discovery, Hall Mark, Bloomberg and Nickelodeon (MultiChoice Chart 1998). ART/1st Net and Showtime were originally established with the intention of satisfying both linguistic groups, Arabic speakers and international/English-speaking viewers. It would be fair to say that initially not all went well for 1st Net and Showtime, but 1998 has seen squabbles repaired and good relations restored. If this cooperation continues there can only be added benefits for viewers and platform owners alike (Amin 1998). It is expected that NileSat as a national satellite will save Egypt a great deal of money, estimated at US $3.5 million, which is spent annually to transmit the Egyptian Satellite Channel (ESC). The project is being supervised by a newly established joint stock company, the Egyptian Company for Satellites (NileSat); at least 40 percent of the shares of this company belong to ERTU and the rest are shared by Egyptian banks and foreign investors (ERTU files 1998).

Cable television made an entry to Egypt in October 1990 when the Egyptian government approved the establishment of Cable News Egypt (CNE) in a cooperative arrangement with CNN to last for twenty-five years. The main purpose of CNE was to retransmit Cable News Network International (CNNI) in Egypt. The initial investment was LE 1.6 million, later increased to LE 25 million (US $7 million). This co-venture represented a historic change, in that the chairman of the Egyptian Radio and Television Union (ERTU), Egyptian television's governing body, was also chairman of CNE. CNE, a subscription television system, operates over an ultra high frequency channel (UHF) controlled by ERTU and has a satellite receiving station and transmitter that covers greater Cairo (Foote and Amin 1993).

At the end of 1994, CNE underwent a major change. Cable News Egypt, the name of the original company, was changed to Cable Network Egypt. The renamed company then made an agreement with a South African-based company (MultiChoice Africa) to market CNE in Egypt. Within the framework of this agreement, MultiChoice began selling a new decoder and introduced new services such as CNNI; music television (MTV); the Showtime channel; MNet, a movie channel that carries mostly American movies and was rated first among the other networks in terms of popularity from CNE subscribers; KTV, a children's channel carrying mostly American children's television programs as well as movies; and Super Sports (Amin and Napoli 1995).

The introduction of CNN International services in Egypt had a tremendous impact on the Egyptian news media. Egyptian print and broadcast journalists were heavily dependent on CNNI as a source of news during the Gulf War (Amin and Napoli 1997b). Egyptian Television also changed the technique, format, and presentation of its news programs in an attempt to match CNNI's performance.

It is obvious that Egypt is trying very hard to prepare itself for the age of information; however, it faces tremendous problems, economic and political as well as cultural.

It has always been the case that the gatekeepers of Egyptian culture are fiercely defensive when they talk about concepts of cultural identities. Over the past three decades, this concept has been intensified because of the availability of direct-to-home television broadcast services. In the age of information the tremendous and incredible flow of information and cultural products, especially from the West, is going to challenge Egyptian culture. It has been documented in statements from guardians of culture and information that in many cases foreign cultural products reverse traditional rules, for example where representatives of law and order are treated as villains while the outlaws and other criminal characters are portrayed as misunderstood, romantic, lovable heroes. These are shocking to Egyptian culture, especially from the religious point of view. One of the most important points that will reflect on Egyptian culture is the speed-up of two processes; one is the process of democratization and the second is the process of privatization. Egypt and its cultural industries must seize the opportunity that these two processes represent to maintain its dominance in the cultural fields.

It is still being debated in Egypt whether or not globalization threatens Egyptian culture. The fear of cultural invasion is affecting Egyptian minds to an almost hysterical degree. Generally speaking, gatekeepers, especially in late age groups, cannot recognize and realize the importance of moving into the information age in order to close the gap between the North and the South. The world is changing, and Egypt must change as well. Although Egypt came late into the industrial era, now is a golden opportunity to use the new technologies to leapfrog stages of development into the information age.

The political concerns that affect culture are freedom of expression as well as government sensitivity to unfavorable news reporting, negative stereotypes, and damaging images of the state. The government is concerned about the possibility of direct-to-home broadcasting of biased information from a hostile country. These concerns keep government censors on the alert all the time. However, the advent of the information age and the era of globalization have collapsed the role of censorship, and political experts are debating the kind of reactions that can be expected to take place. Egyptian cultural experts are not sure what kind of route they should choose because of their fear of losing the country's cultural identity. Communications as they know it started to change to "computercations," where multimedia, interactive systems are going to be available to the public.

Over the past decade, the global information revolution, represented by satellites, the Internet, computers, and inexpensive printing technology, has broadened the range of available information and entertainment. It puts people in closer touch with economic, political, and social trends occurring elsewhere in the world, and sometimes within their own country. It has the capacity to magnify awareness and, at least potentially, to involve the public in more informed debate on public issues. It can be viewed as an element in, or perhaps a precursor to, democratization and economic liberalization. Its diffuseness discourages centralization; its ubiquity discourages control. In short, it implies everything that any government marked by rigidity and hierarchy is poorly disposed to incorporate.

Though the media in Egypt have seemingly adapted to and even thrived in the changing global communications environment, the country's political and legal structure has not significantly changed to accommodate it. In fact, efforts have been directed toward maintaining long-standing policies of centralization and control incongruous with economic and technological developments.

The impulse to maintain control in the face of a decentralizing technology is most evident in the government's continual rewriting of the national press law, usually with repressive consequences. The press operates under the Egyptian constitution, which prohibits censorship, and law 148, which states that the press is "an independent popular authority performing its mission freely in the service of the community." In theory, there is no press censorship, but in fact censorship permeates every aspect of expression in Egypt—not just newspapers, but broadcasting, theater, movies, magazines, and books. The principal censoring organization is the office of censorship in the ministry of culture, but other organizations that exercise censoring authority include the ministry of the interior, ministry of information, Al Azhar University, the state information service, the office of the president, and even the Egyptian post office.

The inherent contradiction between government protestations that there is no censorship and the fact of its implementation by government officials cannot be lost on the Egyptian public. And, while every technological innovation urges toward a more open information system, government updates of press law have tended to tighten the screws. In May 1995, for example, amendments to the penal code were peremptorily passed by parliament imposing what were arguably the most repressive controls on the press in its 200 years of history. The law, which was immediately signed by the president, would impose heavy fines and prison sentences from five to fifteen years for journalists for a range of vaguely worded crimes. These included publishing false or malicious information, inflammatory propaganda or anything that disturbs the public peace. Later, a new press law was ratified by the Shura council reaffirming earlier bills proscribing criticism of public officials, especially the head of state. It outlawed, for example, news stories that "abuse public officials," "insult the parliament, army courts, authorities, or public agencies," "vilify foreign heads of state," "damage the nation's reputation," or "insult the president." The bill also allowed for journalists to be tried in military courts and for newspapers and magazines to be banned without any form of due process. After protests from the journalists' syndicate and even the usually compliant government press, president Mubarak rescinded some onerous provisions, but left many others in place, including criminal penalties for insulting the president, his family and foreign heads of state.

Since then, the Egyptian public has been entertained by the spectacle of running battles between the press, particularly *Al-Shaab*, and top officials and personages, particularly the president's two sons. When *Al-Shall* was barred for publishing for two weeks, it went ahead and published anyway—on the inside pages of a sympathetic rival.

In sum, even as the number of newspapers and magazines grows, as access to foreign media becomes more common, as the availability of alternative sources of communication and information, such as the Internet, becomes more widespread, the government's instinct continues to be to find ways to stop the flow of information. In so doing, it is not only running against the tide of media globalization, economic liberalization, and democratization, but damaging, in a very public way, its credibility with the Egyptian public. The government may still be able to inhibit the dissemination of some information within the country—but not for long, and not without making a public display of censorship that it claims does not exist. Further, government does not seem to be acting in a way consistent with some ideological position that might, for example, be associated with Nasserism. Instead, it is reacting reflexively to various political pressures of the moment, such as the perceived need to protect the high, the mighty, and their relatives, or to protect something as nebulous as Egypt's international image.

Contradictions and inconsistencies also mark government broadcasting policy. Although that policy is committed to centralized state ownership and control of broadcasting because of the presumed power of radio and television to unify and mobilize the public, the private sector has gotten a foothold in the Egyptian broadcasting system through its share in CNE, which of course provides competitors to the Egyptian media themselves. In addition, both TV and radio networks now allow for privately sponsored programs, as do the satellite broadcasting networks. These and other early indications of privatization across the media suggest at least that the state system is beginning to take cognizance of the competition and perhaps that there is even the beginning of a change in the media ownership pattern. That would be consistent with the global trend.

When there is some obvious alteration in the static tradition of the news format on Egyptian television, that may be the signal that media officials have finally taken to heart the challenge emerging from the private sector. If Egyptian television cannot compete successfully against outside private media, particularly well financed Saudi broadcast enterprises, it could find itself playing to an empty house, increasingly marginalized and isolated. Its market share will slowly but inevitably erode as more interesting sources of television become more widely accessible to the Egyptian public.

References

Amin, H. Y. (1986) "An Egypt-based model for the use of television in national development," unpublished dissertation, Ohio State University, Columbus, Ohio.

Amin, H. Y. (1995) "Satellites and direct broadcast television services in the Arab world," paper presented at the Broadcast Education Association Convention (BEA), Las Vegas, Nevada, April 7–11.

Amin, H. Y. (1996) "Broadcasting in the Arab world and the Middle East," in A. Wells (ed.) *World Broadcasting*, Norwood: NJ: Ablex Publishing Corporation.

Amin, H. Y. (1998) "American programs on Egyptian television," in Y. Kamalipour (ed.) *US Image Around the World*, SUNY Press.

Amin, H. Y. and Boyd, D. A. (1993) "The impact of home video cassette recorders on the Egyptian film and television consumption patterns," *European Journal of Communications*, 18(1): 2–7.

Amin, H. Y. and Napoli, J. (1995) *Clash of Communication Culture, CNN in Egypt*, proceedings of the Twelfth Annual International Intercultural Communication Conference, Miami, Florida, February 2–4.

Amin, H. Y. and Napoli, J. J. (1997a) "'De-Westernizing' of media studies: the Middle East experience," paper presented at the Workshop on De-Westernizing Media Studies, Seoul, Korea, November 16–20.

Amin, H. Y. and Napoli, J. (1997b) "The politics of accommodation: CNN in Egypt," *Journal of African Communication*, 2(2).

Boyd, D. (1993) *Broadcasting in the Arab World, A Survey of Electronic Media in the Middle East*, 2nd edn, Ames: Iowa State University Press.

ERTU (Egyptian Radio and Television Union) (1997) printout, Ministry of Information, Cairo.

ERTU (Egyptian Radio and Television Union) (1998) printout, Ministry of Information, Cairo.

Europa Publications Limited (1998) *Europa Yearbook*, London: Martins Printing Group.

Foote, J. and Amin, H. (1993) "Global TV news in developing countries: CNN's expansion to Egypt," *Ecquid Novi, Journal of Journalism in Southern Africa*, 14(2): 153–78.

Korff, Y. Von (1998) "Egyptian press journalists' professional standards and challenge of privatization," paper presented at the Third Annual International Conference of the Arab–US Association for Communication Educators, Cairo, Egypt, September 7–10.

Merrill, J., Lee, J. and Friedlander, E. J. (1990) *Modern Mass Media*, New York: Harper & Row.

MultiChoice Chart (1998) printout, MultiChoice Egypt.

Napoli, J. and Amin H. (1997) "Press freedom in Egypt," in F. Eribo and W. Jong-Ebot (eds.) *Press and Communication in Africa*, Trenton, NJ and Asmara, Eritrea: Africa World Press.

Napoli, J. *et al.* (1995) *Assessment of Egyptian Print and Electronic Media*, submission to the United States Agency for International Development.

Nasser, M. K. (1990) "Egyptian mass media under Nasser and Sadat," *Journalism Monographs*, No. 124, December.

Ochs, M. (1991) *The African Press*, Cairo: The American University in Cairo Press.

Omar, N. (1995) *Business Monthly* 11(6) (July).

Rugh, W. A. (1989) *The Arab Press*, Syracuse: Syracuse University Press.

Schleifer, S. A. (1995) "MMDS in the Arab world," paper presented at the Broadcast Education Association Conference, Las Vegas, Nevada, April 7–11.

Tresilian, D. (1992) "Egypt's publishing industry is very far from gathering dust," *Cairo Today*, January, pp. 66–70, 118–20.

Vatikiotis, P. J. (1991) *The History of Modern Egypt*, London: Weidenfeld and Nicolson.

Part 4
Democratic neo-liberal societies

13 Media and power in Japan

Mitsunobu Sugiyama

Are the Japanese media similar in nature to the European and American media or do they have more in common with the media in developing countries where they are rigidly controlled by the state?

Japanese media researchers have struggled for some time to offer clear answers to this question. After its defeat in the Second World War, Japan adopted a democratic constitution and rapidly grew into a wealthy society. Although Japan became the second-largest economic power after the United States by the early 1980s, the development of the Japanese media did not necessarily follow in the footsteps of the European and American media. The thirty-seven-year domination by the conservative Liberal-Democratic Party (LDP) significantly influenced the post-Second World War development of the Japanese media and as a result the media, particularly broadcasting, never gained complete freedom from the LDP, the leading political party. Needless to say, Japanese society has changed in the past fifteen years. Labor movements have been restructured toward a labor–management coalition and many Thatcher–Reagan-like neo-liberal policies were adopted in the mid-1980s. Following the collapse of the East–West Cold War in the late 1980s, Japan's conventional political dispositions also began changing. How, then, has the Japanese media been affected by these circumstances and what kind of influence have they had?

In the past, only limited research was conducted on the Japanese media and it focused on the structure and roles of the mass media as a whole. Much research tended to separate newspapers from broadcasting, treating them as independent entities. In addition, research tended to overlook the mutual relationship between the providers of information, the newspapers and broadcasters, the receivers, the readers, and the audience. Researchers pointed out the ambiguous or unsound aspects of Japanese media coverage in comparison to American newspapers and television and called incessantly for improvements. It was precisely for this reason that there were no sociological studies that examined the Japanese media including newspapers and televisions. This chapter attempts to do just that. Before expanding on the subject, I will give an overall summary of the Japanese media, placing special emphasis on television and newspapers.

Television and newspapers: the current situation

In television broadcasting, there are two satellite channels sponsored by NHK and a private satellite broadcasting station, WOWOW. Although cable satellite (CS) channels are also available, CATV has been slow in expanding, barely reaching 2 million households by 1997. Though Japanese audiences watch an average of 3 hours and 46 minutes of television on weekdays and 4 hours and 25 minutes on Sundays, most of the time is spent watching ground broadcasts made up of NHK and private broadcast stations.

NHK is a public enterprise comprising two channels, a generalist channel and a special educational channel, whose operation is supported by subscription fees collected from the public. In addition to the main broadcasting center in Tokyo, it has fifty-four broadcasting stations across the nation including fourteen branch stations and its comprehensive broadcast network extends to every prefecture. Private broadcasts are offered by four nationwide networks headed by Tokyo-based commercial broadcasting stations that serve as key stations. Although the Ministry of Posts and Telecommunications has plans to place four commercial broadcast stations in each prefecture in order to ensure fairness, it has yet to achieve this goal completely.

In reality, however, more than four channels can be watched in most parts of the country. Moreover, in Tokyo and neighboring prefectures, another commercial broadcasting station, TV Tokyo, as well as UHF and VHF stations are made available to the public. These commercial broadcast stations serve as key stations for nationwide networks and are all so-called general channels. While it is mandatory for a generalist channel to broadcast news programs in addition to a certain percentage of educational programs, most of the Japanese audience has shown a preference for entertainment programs (music programs, soap dramas, variety shows, professional baseball games, and so on) during prime time and therefore commercial stations have traditionally emphasized such programs. An allocation of roles is recognizable to a certain degree. NHK, for example, is more inclined to broadcast news and educational programs.

What is particularly interesting concerning Japan's television broadcasts is that all four of the Tokyo-based key stations enjoy close relationships with Japan's prominent national newspapers: TBS with the *Mainichi*, Nippon Television (NTV) with *Yomiuri*, Fuji Television (CX) with the *Sankei*, and TV Asahi (ANN) with *Asahi*. Even *Nikkei* is tied-up with Tokyo's local station, TV Tokyo (TN). Japanese newspaper companies have consistently shown an interest in new developments in media. They were quick to make their entry into the broadcasting industry when the media shifted its primary emphasis from radio to television. Even today, these commercial stations prefer to use news dispatches provided to them by their affiliated newspaper companies rather than set up their own news departments. Although newspapers exercised greater influence when television broadcasts began in the 1950s, they now operate wholly independently. In Japan, there is also an FM staion, "Hoso Daigaku (University of the Air)".

In radio broadcasting, there is NHK with two medium-wave channels and a music-oriented FM station, two nationwide commercial networks, JRN (thirty-three stations including Tokyo Radio Broadcast) and NRN (thirty-eight stations including Bunka Radio Broadcast), forty-seven music-oriented FM stations and one shortwave station. During the height of radio broadcasts in the 1950s, countless radio drama programs were produced, some of which were extremely popular at the time and are still remembered and talked about today. In line with the rapid growth in television ownership in the 1960s, however, radio popularity began declining. Though a segment of programs, such as music programs, late-night programs for teenagers, and informative programs for car owners, have been promoted and are regaining some popularity, with so few educational programs and no resurgence of radio dramas, radio remains a secondary form of media.

One distinct characteristic of Japanese newspapers is that national newspapers based in Tokyo wield overwhelming influence. While Japanese newspapers can be classified into national newspapers (papers having a head office in Tokyo and circulated across the country), regional papers (papers circulated to more than one prefecture), and prefectural papers (papers primarily read within a single prefecture), the five national papers account for approximately half the total daily circulation (53,550,000 copies, an average of 1.2 copies per household). Circulation figures for these five newspapers as of February 1997 were as follows:

Yomiuri	10,171,968
Asahi	8,375,986
Mainichi	3,948,714
Nikkei	2,981,749
Sankei	1,941,438

(*Source*: *The Japanese Press 1997*, The Japan Newspaper Publishers and Editors Association, pp. 92–6)

Japanese newspapers are characterized by several factors foreign to European and American newspapers. Most Japanese newspapers publish both morning and evening editions on a daily basis, as well as Sunday editions. Readers subscribe to all three editions as a set, on a monthly basis in the case of the five national papers, and almost 93 percent of the copies sold are personally delivered directly to the households of subscribers. The distribution channel of a newspaper runs from the publisher to the sales agent to home delivery. Under this marketing system, neither the opinion of a particular publisher nor the quality of any given issue has any direct influence on the actual number of papers sold. Whatever articles a particular newspaper may carry, its circulation figure is wholly dependent on the marketing efforts of individual sales agents.

The classification of Japanese newspapers into national papers, regional papers, and prefectural papers, as mentioned earlier, is only a perfunctory classification based solely on the range of circulation. Another distinctive characteristic is that Japanese newspapers cannot be categorized either as tabloid or as broadsheet newspapers. Though some tabloid newspapers are sold on the streets of Tokyo and Osaka, they comprise a small percentage of the gross circulation and, therefore, do not exert much influence. This demonstrates that national newspapers have been successful in offering columns that please both readers who are interested in public issues such as politics and economics, and readers who seek articles related to television programs, entertainment, human interest, and sports. With the exception of *Nikkei*, which specializes in economic news, the four remaining national newspapers all devote the same amount of space to columns on sports, culture, and family-related articles. As for *Asahi*, *Mainichi* and *Yomiuri*, these three newspapers are frequently criticized for being very similar in content. Newspaper publishers, as is true with other businesses in other industries, pay close attention to the developments of their rivals and are very careful about carrying the same news and issues as other newspapers. Consequently, not only are the contents similar, but they also end up with similar plans for expansion and development into other media fields.

As for magazines, while the economic boost from the late 1980s to early the 1990s saw a dramatic increase followed by a decrease in the total number of publications, magazines specializing in fields like microcomputers, automobiles, and sports are increasing. As with other countries around the world, magazines geared toward female readers, and magazines on fashion and lifestyle, occupy a significant percentage of Japanese publications. But what must be noted is that there is also a market for 4 million copies of comics. Readers of comic magazines are not limited only to teenagers and often, popular comics are turned into animated programs aired on TV. In contrast, magazines on politics and international affairs have been decreasing in both number of titles and circulation, and the Japanese edition of *The Times* can hardly be called a financial success. But I will show later, although these magazines are few in number, the influential power of opinion magazines cannot be denied.

LDP dominance in television

Within the general structure of Japanese broadcasters and newspapers as outlined above, what roles do the media play? Although Japan has become a rich economic nation under a democratic political system, the Japanese media, particularly broadcasters, still remain extremely sensitive to politically biased issues. They have consistently taken care to avoid any expression of political opinion. Under the Broadcasting Codes, a broadcaster must obtain broadcasting licenses from the Japanese government. Because the Broadcasting Codes allocate bandwidth, a limited resource, they stipulate that broadcasting is a form of public service and is expected to contribute to the development of democracy by relaying the truth from an unbiased standpoint. These codes, however, are probably no different from those found in any other developed country. How, then, did Japanese broadcasting come to possess a distinct nature unlike that of other countries? During the Occupation period following Japan's defeat in the Second World War, an administrative committee (the Radio Regulatory Committee) was formed in accordance with the US system, independent from the Cabinet. All broadcasting organizations including NHK and private broadcasters were placed under its jurisdiction. After the occupation in 1952, this system was abolished and authority over commercial broadcasting was transferred to the Ministry of Posts and Telecommunications. The Ministry of Posts and Telecommunications was granted authority to decide whether or not the principles of fairness and impartiality were reflected in program contents if an issue was deemed politically controversial or troublesome.

This authority exerted a profound effect on the political context of post-war Japan. The year following Japan's defeat in 1945, executives of various publishing companies who were considered to have cooperated with the military in promoting the war, were purged. It was a time of heightened labor movements in the media industry. Newspaper company workers engaged in such labor strikes as the famous the Yomiuri Strike and the West Japan Newspapers Strike and began to take control of their own companies and publish newspapers without seeking outside help. Though labor union movements included broadcasters and newspapers in support of their actions, the US Occupying Forces intervened in support of management and the entire saga came to an end with the defeat of the labor unions. At that point, it was confirmed that the decisive power to overrule newspaper editing and program productions lay in the hands of management. Clearly, "fairness and impartiality of the press" meant that media workers did not violate the editorial authority of the management. The LDP was able to influence the media because the authority of the media's management had been consolidated.

In addition, the thirty-seven-year-long one-party rule by the conservative LDP was influential in the development of Japanese media. Post-war Japanese politics was marked by the conflict between the LDP, which represented the interests of the industrial elite, middle-class managing officers, traders, technicians, and farmers, and the Socialist Party (along with the minority Communist Party), which supported organized workers and progressive intellectuals. This dichotomy corresponds with the East–West conflict during the Cold War era. During this period, the LDP occupied an overwhelming majority of the Diet and hardly ever had to compromise with the progressive parties. Rather, the intensity of the ideological differences between the conservative and progressive parties was related directly to the issue of whether television programs were broadcast from a fair and neutral standpoint on political issues. During the Vietnam War, in 1960, the LDP government severely criticized commercial broadcasters for broadcasting programs that were politically biased. Although they contained no false reports, programs such as those featuring commercial newscasters visiting Hanoi and forecasting the defeat of US troops or documentary footage on the U.S. Marine Corps in Vietnam, were attacked by the Japanese government as being politically biased. Programs that dealt with such subjects as farmer's protest movements against the construction of Narita airport, and discussions on the national sentiment regarding the Rising-Sun flag (which was not the national flag at the time) were similarly criticized by the government. The government and the LDP labelled all programs they deemed inappropriate or disadvantageous as "biased." By using their influence as a licensing authority, they inhibited the independence of broadcasters and exercised control over program contents. Broadcasters had no choice but to become sensitive when dealing with political issues and current events.

The LDP further exerted influence upon NHK in two ways. The first concerns the selection of the NHK chairman. From among the candidates nominated by the members of the NHK management committee, the chairman of NHK is selected and appointed by the Prime Minister. Consequently, the selection of the NHK chairman never escapes the influence of the majority party, the LDP. The second is the manner of determining NHK's sole source of income, subscription rates. Since NHK has managed to contact practically every household in Japan, the only way it can increase income is to raise subscription rates, or reduce the number of employees and out-sourced program productions. The raising of subscription rates, however, requires approval from the Diet. And every time Dietary approval is received for a rate increase, NHK has to answer to the complaints and requests of the LDP. Among other criticism, the LDP charged that NHK's coverage of nuclear power generation was overly negative; that NHK's coverage of the Tokyo gubernatorial election favored opposition candidates; that when NHK invited politicians to its studios for debates, there were too many opposition MPs and the LDP was not given sufficient time to elaborate on its positions.

When discussing Japanese television broadcasts, in addition to the LDP's intervention concerning program contents, the effects of the fierce competition for higher audience rating cannot be denied. For commercial broadcasters, their source of income is comprised of revenue received from sponsors for programs and spot commercials. For sponsors, audience rates are a benchmark for measuring the effects of their advertisements. Since audience rates decide the price of any particular program or spot commercial, they have a direct influence on the broadcaster's income. Thus, competition for higher audience rates is bound to become intense. Recently, broadcasters have shifted the weight put on audience rates for individual program popularity to the station's popularity as a whole. Consequently, even if a particular program is outstanding in terms of its informative and cultural content, if it is not considered to contribute to an increase in the station's average audience rates, then the program is cancelled. In the Japanese broadcasting business, both the pressure of competing for audience rates and the pressure to remain noncommittal *vis-à-vis* politics, weigh heavily.

Objective reporting or self-censorship

It frequently has been pointed out that Japan's national papers, which have an enormous circulation, are very similar in contents and lack aggressiveness in putting forward their opinions. Why is that the case? Any newspaper with an enormous circulation has a wide variety of readers hailing from various organizations and classes, ranging from the industrial elite and company managers to organized laborers and owners of independent enterprises. One explanation for this similarity is that the values and standpoints of newspapers must be uniform in order to maintain the interests of readers who come from varied backgrounds. Diversification of article contents invariably means that newspaper publishers refrain from aggressively expressing opinions. This results in the affinity of content and "neutralization." But since many European and American newspapers print factional views while having an enormous circulation at the same time, this explanation hardly suffices.

The explanation may relate to the history of the development of Japanese newspapers. Until the 1880s, Japanese newspapers were diverse. They were generally divided into political party papers (*osinbun*), which printed articles that reflected the views of a particular political party, and papers known as "small newspapers" (*kosinbun*), which carried predominantly scandalous articles related to incidents in daily life and gossip. Political party papers could not, however, compete with the emergence of industrial papers (*shogyo shinbun*) that were aimed at providing news reports, and they soon disappeared along with the "small newspapers" that were absorbed into the industrial papers. Hikoichi Motoyama, a publisher of an industrial paper in the 1900s, commented on the "neutral stand" that his paper would take:

> The company shall not comment on whether or not the company supports the bill currently being proposed to the Diet or whether Japan will actually suffer if this bill were to be passed. Even if this bill is rejected and the current Cabinet is overthrown this year, Japan, as a nation, will still remain. If this bill truly answers the needs of society, then it will most likely be adopted either next year or the year after. Even if this administration does not implement this bill, future administrations will surely do so. Thus, the newspaper can neither support nor oppose the bill.

This principle was later shared by the developing industrial papers like *Asahi*, *Mainichi* and *Yomiuri*. Indeed, during the era of "Taisho Democracy" in the 1910s and in the post-war period immediately after 1945, Japanese newspapers refrained from making aggressive comments. These periods, however, were followed by a tightening of control over freedom of speech by military dictatorship and the political domination by the LDP forced an ideological recession, returning to the times of the industrial newspapers. Behind the "neutral stance" that Japanese newspapers prefer to take is the journalists' position on "objective coverage" in the post-war era. During the Second World War, Japanese newspapers cooperated with the government and the military in promoting the war, and provided extremely biased news coverage. In reflecting on these facts, Japanese journalists have come to advocate a need for newspapers to remain independent from the government. This is the idea behind "objective coverage." In the post-war era marked by severe conflict between the conservative parties and the progressive parties, however, the longer political domination by the LDP lasted, the more this ideology of "objective coverage" came to serve as justification for the politically opportunistic stance of Japanese newspapers.

When the LDP government pushed the revision bill for the US–Japan Mutual Cooperation and Security Treaty through the Diet in 1960 against the strong opposition of minority parties, the Japanese press unanimously criticized the actions of the LDP and called out to "protect democracy." This was the only incidence of any clear demonstration of opposition by the Japanese press against the LDP government in the post-war era. Indeed, there were several instances in which newspapers chose to support minority parties concerning antipollution measures and welfare policies, but, for the most part, the "neutrality" and "objectivity" of Japanese newspapers merely confirmed the stance of the LDP government.

Though newspapers, unlike broadcasters, are commercial enterprises, independent from the government, there are no legal regulations that bind them. The LDP government nevertheless exercises great power over them. One reason for this, and one which is often compared to those of American newspapers, lies in the method which newspaper reporters use to gather information. The LDP, as a whole, is a conservative political party supported by an industrial elite, company administrators, self-managed enterprise owners, farmers, and conservative laborers. Internally, however, it is divided into five factions. Although the five factions have some ideological differences, such as being right-wing or liberal, they are fundamentally groups formed by personal relationships with influential politicians. The factional leaders are influential politicians who have the ability to secure the funds needed when fellow faction members run for elections, and to appoint ministers when new cabinets are formed. In the years of the LDP's one-party dictatorship, key decisions in Japanese politics were made through negotiations and bargaining among factions. Hence, faction leaders and influential politicians became particularly important sources of information for political reporters of newspapers and NHK. Japanese newspapers assign specific reporters to cover individual faction leaders and influential figures. The reporter assigned to a specific politician follows him or her all day long, from the time he or she leaves the house early in the morning until he or she returns home late at night. Since politicians do not divulge to reporters everything they want to know, the only way to get information is by winning the trust of politicians. In order to do so, the reporter must commit himself to becoming a co-conspirator of sorts, involving himself in all activities that the politician partakes of including the factional politics within the LDP. This method of political information-gathering prevents Japanese reporters from keeping a safe distance from politicians in order to write objective articles. Thus, Japanese articles frequently represent the positions of influential politicians or are intentionally used by them for their own purposes. Needless to say, individual newspapers do offer some insights into the claims and opinions of other political parties, as well, but on the whole, they have generally been supportive of the LDP government.

New trends for opinion media

In response to the radical changes taking place in Japanese society in the early 1990s and the fall of the LDP from its one-party rule, the conventional method of Japanese broadcasting and newspaper publishing began undergoing a change. The most significant of all political changes during this period was that the Socialist Party, the definitive figure among non-government parties, virtually ceased to exist. The Japan Socialist Party collapsed because of the transformation occurring among organized labor, the backbone of the party. Labor movements in post-war Japan were comprised of two sections: laborers in the public sector who sought out socialist policies and were opposed to increased productivity, and labor unions in large commercial businesses. These labor unions hoped for a stronger voice in society commensurate with their role in Japan's leading industries and companies, and their contribution to increased productivity under the leadership of businesses. The Japan Socialist Party has historically supported the left-wing labor movements of pubic sector laborers. While public sector laborers sought ways to withdraw from social isolation after the defeat of labor movements seeking strike rights, the labor unions of big businesses began establishing connections by sending their members to the powerful Administrative Reform Committee, so they could exert a direct influence over the LDP government. Thus, Japanese labor movements were united and restructured under the leadership of commercial big business labor unions in the direction of a more right-wing or labor–management coalition. The emergence of a wealthy society as a result of economic growth and the successive changes in the awareness of Japanese laborers helped promote these political changes. The Japan Socialist Party lost its backbone as a result of these changes. During the period in which the LDP enjoyed a one-party dictatorship, the Japan Socialist Party occupied roughly one-third of the Diet seats, and it served as a check on any excessive measures by the LDP. The only thing that remained after the collapse of the leftist opposition party was the conservative party. But precisely at this moment, when it seemed as if there were no other actors besides the conservative party on Japan's political stage, that the conservative party split into various groups. The disintegration was the result of differences in opinion regarding conflicting interests and the emergence of new political issues such as the problem of protecting domestic industries as opposed to deregulating the market in the face of globalization, or maintaining the current structure as a welfare state instead of giving priority to financial restructuring. The eight-party coalition, comprised of several groups that had seceded from the LDP and other long-time opposition parties, took over the administration in 1992.

It was not until 1994 that the LDP, in coalition with other political parties such as the Socialist Democratic Party, returned to power. Instead, a changing of alignment of factions within the conservative party occurred. There are some conflicts between the ruling party and opposition parties. These parties are, nonetheless, both conservative parties with right-wing as well as liberal factions. While they do have their differences, these differences are not ideological, but rather, conflicts of interest or personal differences, all of which can be settled. Under these new circumstances, the relationship between the media and the political powers is beginning to undergo change. One example worth mentioning is the come-back of news programs.

It has been said that the broadcasting of full news programs during prime time posed a difficult problem in Japan. ANN, however, managed to succeed doing precisely this in 1985. Because it broadcast a full extended program, the station had sufficient time to elaborate on certain new items, explaining the necessary background information concerning various incidents. In addition, they skillfully took an inside look into the LDP's factional conflicts, explaining the situation using building blocks. Partly due to the popularity of its anchor person, who was not afraid to speak his mind clearly, the program managed to get a rating of 20 percent. This popularity allowed ANN to reject any claims by the LDP concerning comments made by the anchorman. Since then, various broadcasters, including NHK, have been competing fiercely for higher ratings from night prime time news programs.

Since the years of LDP's dictatorship, when legal interventions were common, we not only see a decrease in government intervention, but also signs of growing independence among broadcasters. In 1993, the head of ANN's news department was unofficially quoted as saying that ANN was discussing the possibility of covering the coming Dietary election in favor of the eight-party coalition rather than supporting the LDP. The LDP naturally made an issue over this. Needless to say, ANN's position regarding news coverage was inappropriate, but this incident clearly showed the kind of effect political changes in the 1990s had on television broadcasting.

Though it is true that Japanese newspapers are frequently criticized for being identical, there are some differences in the disposition from one newspaper to the other. *Yomiuri*, which has the largest circulation, supported the LDP government when they implemented such neo-liberal policies as the privatization of several public institutions including the Japanese National Railways and the proposed review of the current welfare system. In turn, *Asahi* showed sympathy for the LDP when they announced liberal policies, and, in some cases, even for the progressive parties. *Nikkei*, a technical newspaper devoted to economics, reflects on the opinions of industrial businesses and supports increased deregulation of the market and stability of politics without any confusion. The positions of individual newspapers, however, were demonstrated in a euphemistic way. The political changes of the 1990s in which the definitive opposition party, the Japan Socialist Party, collapsed, and the conservative party was divided into small factions, allowed individual newspapers to express their opinions more freely. This was best demonstrated in the editorials of individual papers printed in 1994, when two of the eight parties that made up the coalition administration seceded to establish a new coalition with the LDP. Although the Socialist Democratic Party had become a more right-wing party, *Yomiuri* was very much opposed to the LDP's coalition with the Socialist Democratic Party. *Nikkei* and *Asahi*, on the other hand, welcomed this development. They noted that it was hardly necessary to be hampered by tradition at times of political restructuring and that it was a coordinated effort to try to settle the existing conflict between the hawks and the doves inside the new coalition. Although the executive office of the LDP was liberal at the time, *Mainichi* ran a critical editorial, calling the new cabinet the result of an easy compromise.

From 1994 to 1995, newspapers increasingly grew more willing to express their opinions outright and clearly. In the November 3, 1994 edition, *Yomiuri* ran an eight-page special article on suggestions for reforming the Japanese constitution. In this article, *Yomiuri* drafted a proposal for a Constitution Reform Act along with commentaries. Japan's current constitution goes back to 1946 when Japan was under the occupation of the allied forces. It includes provisions for renouncing war and staying demilitarized. As opposition between the East and the West grew more intense in Cold War politics in the 1980s and with the request for the participation of

Japan's Self-Defense Forces—fundamentally militaristic institutions—in the Gulf War and Cambodian peace talks as part of the UN Joint Force, discrepancies between this idealistic constitution and the reality became too great to ignore. Factions within the LDP have yet to come to a consensus over the issue of whether to leave the Constitution as is and to change its interpretation, or to amend the constitution in accordance with changing times. While the latter is closer to the position *Yomiuri* is taking, *Yomiuri*'s proposal is more moderate than proposals made by others. *Yomiuri*'s proposal includes such clauses as calling for more detailed provisions on the protection of human rights and the right of privacy, as well as special consideration toward the environment. On the other hand, two conflicting positions exist within Japan's progressive parties regarding the discrepancies between the constitution and reality. One is a position that the Japan Socialist Party had maintained for many years, in which it advocated a strict defense of the current Constitution and an immediate dismissal of Japan's Self-Defense Forces. The other was to accept the existence of the Self-Defense Forces as a fact and to allow for their contribution to international peace as members of the UN Joint Force by legalizing them under a Fundamental Peace Act.

This latter position, which called for a restructuring of Japan's Self-Defense Forces under fundamental principles of idealism, is the position assumed by a group of intellectuals who were once very close to the Japan Socialist Party. This idea was introduced in 1994 in a monthly magazine titled *Sekai* (The World). Although this magazine today has a circulation of only approximately 60,000 issues per month, it was once highly influential and a leading magazine in introducing progressive ideas, affecting many intellectuals significantly in the post-war era. Once the concept was introduced by *Sekai*, *Asahi* was quick to follow suit. In *Asahi*'s May 3, 1995 Constitution Day edition, it further elaborated on this concept. Thus the number one and number two newspapers in Japan with the largest circulation not only printed conflicting perspectives on Japan's constitution but each introduced its own proposals. This was something never seen before in Japanese history. The political changes in Japan in the 1990s have made way for more independence in news coverage by Japanese television and bolder and clearer demonstrations of opinion by the newspapers. It is also important to pay special attention to the increased enthusiasm within the media in the wake of the disintegration of a conventional left-wing opposition party and the change in the scope of public opinion from the most conservative to the most liberal. Public opinion at this juncture is supported by a consensus between the industrial elite and the labor unions that have been progressively restructured. More observation is required before commenting on how society will open its doors to new social movements such as environmental protection and feminism.

Problems in media theory

From the defeat of 1945 to the beginning of the 1970s, among the Japanese researchers on journalism and mass communication studies, the influence of Marxist theories was very grand. Marxist theories achieved a great success in the analysis of the economic and social structure of pre-war Japan. Their analysis demonstrated that, though Japanese society was constructed as a modern capitalist one, it contained many semi-feudal factors not only in the land ownership system in rural districts, but also in social relations in the industrial world. The democratic reforms which the occupied power had undertaken seemed to confirm the accuracy of their analysis. At the same time, the liberals also criticized the backwardness of Japanese society and its media according to the model of Western countries. Marxist researchers understood the long dominance of LDP and its strong influence on the media to be a result of class relations. And the liberalists considered the Japanese media to be like that of developing countries where they were rigidly controlled by local authorities.

Following the economic growth from the end of the 1950s to 1973, the affluent society came to Japan and economic growth drastically changed Japanese society. The Japanese media could not escape from this movement. The themes which I mentioned in this chapter belong to this process of transformation. All through the post-war period, Japanese journalists asserted that objectivity was required in political reporting. But, this aim was not always achieved because activities of Japanese journalists were bound by press companies whose influence on journalists increased in the period of economic growth. It was also due to the fact that the training system of professional journalists was not completed. In the academic world in Japan, there was no tradition of journalism schools. In the newspsaper companies or broadcasting stations, people usually consider that a journalist is formed on the job. In this situation, even if the reporters become good company men, journalism does not thereby become a profession. And there are also the problems such as the distribution system of the newspapers and the competition in the market developed by the press companies in the post-war period, resulting in a similarity in the content of newspapers and television programs. To analyze this new situation of Japanese media, it is not sufficient to apply Western media theories to it. We have to try to make clear the concrete cases one by one with a new framework and new concepts. And in advancing this sort of study, we can develop the work of de-Westernizing media theory.

Bibliography

Arai, Naoyuki and Inaba, Michio (eds.) (1988) *Shinbun gaku* (The Science of Newspapers, new edition), Nihon-hyoron-sha.

Arai, Naoyuki and Uchikawa, Yoshimi (eds.) (1983), *Nihon no janarizumu* (Journalism of Japan), Yuhi-kaku.

Fujita, Hiroshi (1991) *Amerika no shinbun* (Newspapers in the United States), Iwanami shoten.

Hara, Toshio (1997) *Janarizumu no shiso* (Journalism Thought), Iwanami shoten.

Katsura, Kei-ichi (1990) *Gendai no shinbun* (Newspapers of Modern Japan), Iwanami shoten.

Kawasaki, Yasushi (1997) *NHK to seiji* (NHK and Political Power), Asahi shinbun sha.

MacCormack G. (1996) *The Emptiness of Japanese Affluence*, New York, M. E. Sharpe.

Oka, Mitsuo, Yamaguchi, Koji and Watanabe, Taketatsu (eds.) (1994) *Media gaku no genzai* (The Present State of Media Studies), Sekai shiso sha.

Okamura, Reimei (1993) *Terebi no Asu* (The Future of Television), Iwanami shoten.

Special Issue of "Journalism drifting on the sea," *Mado*, Autumn 1994.

14 Media power in the United States

W. Lance Bennett

There has been a great deal of discussion of the "Americanization" and, more recently, the transnational corporate invasion, or simply the "Westernization" of other societies through the export of media formats, cultural products, and the replacement of public broadcasting systems with deregulated commercial markets (Herman and McChesney 1997, Schiller 1992, Tunstall and Palmer 1991). There are good democratic arguments for preserving and promoting national media systems with diverse contents and public service norms (Keane 1991). However, there equally good, practical reasons to better understand the local political effects of the global trend toward more commercialized media systems. Just as democracies differ, so do media systems. And the interactions among particular cultures, governmental institutions, and media establishments must be understood if comparisons among nations are to be meaningful.

Even in nations that qualify as prototypes of highly deregulated commercial broadcasting such as the United States, the interaction between media systems and distinctive cultural formations and governmental institutions needs to be carefully analyzed before hazarding guesses about the effects of similar media models in other societies. Another point in favor of developing both global and local frameworks for understanding mediated politics is the evidence that individuals in different societies interact with global cultural exports in often critical and local ways (Katz and Liebes 1990). A similar story emerges if we track the diffusion of American, and more generally "Western," models for news production, public relations, election campaign communication, and political advertising through various national contexts. The list of converging international trends proposed by Blumler and Kavanaugh (in press) in mediated politics includes:

- professionalization of political communication (polling, marketing, image management, and spindoctors);
- transformation of mass publics into differently targeted markets for messages;
- test-marketed appeals to private emotions rather than collective interests; and
- decline of the ideological and party mechanisms that have structured power and participation in many nations over extended periods of time.

All of these global media trends interact with local factors that distinguish different political systems. These factors include government institutions, parties, participation patterns, communication technology infrastructure, the organization and regulation of the press, cultural norms about information and citizenship, corruption levels, and other elements that define the calculus of political power (Asard and Bennett 1997, Blumler and Gurevitch 1998).

In short, it is tantalizing to hear about the "war room" mentality behind contemporary European election campaigns, and to learn of preoccupations with audience research and tight news budgets in formerly insulated state broadcast systems. However, it is unclear how to assess the local political significance of such trends. For example, are these developments symptomatic of Western cultural imperialism facilitated by governmental trade agreements and implemented by global conglomerates? (And even if they are, what are the local political effects?) Or, are convergent international media regimes, as characterized by standardized technologies and overlapping production values in news and entertainment, driven equally by audience demands? And, speaking of popular demand, how do we think about the acceptance of consumerism and market competition which have become the "default" ideologies in many nations in the wake of the collapse of communism?

Even those who point to declining collective political identifications (e.g. party and national loyalties) must establish better evidence for their concerns. Why, as Inglehart (1997) proposes, should we worry at all about the decline of nationalism in many countries? Or should we, instead, recall the horrors of nationalistic moments in human history, and celebrate the opening up of global electronic identifications associated with world music, sports, international political activism, and greater awareness of suffering and human rights (Bennett 1998)?

The big questions about media, society, and politics are further complicated by the choices media scholars make in defining the effects of media technology and content. For example, is media power in society limited mainly to voter and citizen responses to electronically rendered political candidates and public policy campaigns? Or, as Slater (1997) suggests, is media power perhaps better understood as the saturation of public life with promotions for consumer values and commodified interpersonal relationships that drive out concerns about other human needs, environmental degradation, and common fates?

Perhaps the prudent response is to develop comparative frameworks that enable us to understand the effects within nations of increasingly mediated political and social experience. Without clear understandings about how media content is filtered by institutions and processed by individuals within different societies, all the talk about globalization remains scary, but speculative and unanchored. I take the spirit of this book to be concerned with understanding media within diverse societies in terms of the fundamental relations of power through which individuals effectively express and obtain (or suppress and sacrifice) their life preferences. Understanding national, social, and cultural differences is just as important for building communication theory as is documenting common cross-national adaptations of media technologies and content.

The subject of this chapter is media and power in the United States. This short tour introduces some generalizations about media in the American context that may help explain what must seem to outsiders as a truly bizarre place. American society is at once filled with wondrous fantasy, unfathomable political structures, wacky religious and moralistic cults, political access that is openly (i.e. legally) sold to those with cash, consumerism taken to absurd extremes (e.g. Mall of America), and near anarchic levels of everyday violence and despair plaguing large numbers of unfortunate outcasts in a land of plenty. While attending to such distinctive aspects of the American media spectacle, I will also adopt a simple framework for thinking about power that provides a basis for comparing media power in different societies.

THE MEDIA AND POLITICAL POWER

There are, of course, many ways in which to understand and compare the impact of media on societies, but the relationship to power is among the most compelling grounds for comparison. It is power that encourages or discourages people from acting, taking risks, forming human associations, feeling secure or insecure, and promoting various visions of private and public interest. But what, exactly, is power? A simple view of power involves having access to and using resources (from nuclear weapons to advertising) to get people to do things that they would not otherwise do without the intervention of those resources in their lives.

This simple way of thinking about power quickly takes on greater complexity when we think about real examples. In some cases, power is naked coercion tailored to particular situations: "Invade us and we will nuke you." Another level of power is more institutionalized and procedural: "If you want us to stop dumping toxic waste in the river from which your town draws its drinking water, you will have to take us to court and get the government to stop us." There is yet another aspect of power that exists primarily in the form of human consciousness. To an important extent, the workings of power in society depends on how people think about political actions that affect them: whether they accept them as legitimate, whether they resist them, or whether they resign themselves to being powerless about them. All three forms of power often combine to determine the outcomes of human events, from elections to decisions about going to war, to personal decisions about whether to resist injustices or to avoid thinking about social problems at all.

The three aspects of power outlined above are derived from Lukes's (1974) typology of power in society. The first example corresponds to Lukes' most basic level of power as organized coercion through which various agents (government officials, businesses, interest groups, individuals) force others to do things. The second level is the level of the established regimes, rituals, and institutions that shape public decisions. This level of power is where the agenda of publicly decidable issues is routinely set by institutionalized systems of rules, incentives, and political access that ultimately define *whose concerns about what issues* matter, and whose do not. The third level is the distribution of consciousness in society about the acceptability or naturalness of the first two levels.[1] In other words, patterns of popular political support, opposition, and withdrawal can be understood as indicators of political consciousness, expressed through observable patterns of language and social behavior. In her important work on why so many Americans avoid politics, Eliasoph (1998) shows that considerable personal work goes into being apolitical. For example, members of a local volunteer anti-drug group denied that their actions were political by mutually constructing drug usage as a personal, apolitical, "close to home" problem about which ordinary individuals can do something. At the same time, these anti-drug activists saw toxic contamination of local air or water supplies as distant political issues over which they had little control. Such perceptions of what is political and what can be done about it are shaped by various factors including institutional structuring of the public policy agenda, media representations of citizens and the effectiveness of their actions, and the ways in which individuals key into social discourses about government, politics, and individual agency. Gamson (1992) shows how different media representations affect individual political engagement.

When power is viewed from this three-level perspective it is easy to see in how many ways the media are involved in the production and reproduction of power:

- framing coercive power within societies in ways that can encourage, discourage, hide, or expose it;
- selecting and representing actors and policy problems in formal political settings (e.g. emphasizing some actors and activities within government institutions and de-emphasizing others); and
- transmitting values, problem definitions, and images of people in society that provide resources for people in thinking about their lives and their relations to government, politics, and society.

POWER I: MEDIA PORTRAYALS OF COERCION

Since the United States is among the oldest, most stable democracies, it is easy to think that most, if not all, of its politics occurs within the second level of power, the network of finely rule-governed institutions such as local school boards, courts, legislative bodies, executives, and the like. While much of politics is played out in these settings, much is still handled the old-fashioned way: through coercion. Factories hold communities hostage to pollution by threatening to close and take their jobs elsewhere. Investors squeeze profits from corporations by rewarding worker layoffs (called "downsizing"), lower payrolls, and cost-cutting that may harm consumers. At the interpersonal level, startling numbers of Americans pull guns on each other to extract money, upgrade their mode of transportation (called "carjacking"), or to pay back various emotional losses.

More generally, the US leads the world in many categories that suggest violence and coercion as everyday facts of life: numbers of citizens in prison, numbers of troops in uniform, the numbers and types of law enforcement personnel, and the millions of guns on the streets and in night tables next to beds. The ways in which media frame (emphasize and categorize) the uses of these resources of coercion are important to the functioning of society and politics. For example, a widely publicized incident of large-scale violence occurred in Los Angeles in 1992 following the jury verdict that acquitted a group of white policemen who had been recorded on videotape administering a severe beating to a black motorist (Rodney King) following a traffic stop. The video received wide media play on news and talk programs. Few Americans were neutral in their thinking about the episode by the time the all-white jury reached its verdict in a suburban court far removed from the inner city context in which the arrest and the charges of racism and police brutality had been played out. Following the verdict, the central area of Los Angeles became the scene of a fiery uprising in which stores were looted and burned and, in one highly publicized incident, a white truck driver was pulled from his truck and beaten.

What was the nature of this violent episode? Was it a political event? If so, what kind of politics and power relationships were involved? News coverage in prominent mass media outlets such as the *Los Angeles Times* quickly framed the event as a "riot," and the *New York Times* headlined the episode as "random violence." Such news stories were filled with various official sources who denounced the situation as lawless and illegal. By contrast, the black press in Los Angeles was far more likely to frame the event using terms such as "rebellion," and "insurrection," and to tell a story of blacks whose frustration at being excluded from the American justice system finally boiled over in angry political protest.[2] These stark differences in media coverage reflected equally stark differences in opinion polls about race and justice in America. The depoliticization and simultaneous criminalization of the event in the mainstream media suggest that the very question of where politics actually and properly occurs in society (on brute force terms of Level I power? or in the legal and political institutions of Level II?) is a matter of considerable difference of opinion among different publics (Bennett 1993). Moreover, the differing public perceptions of political reality are selectively endorsed or ignored by different media.

The question of what is and what is not included in representations of Level I power has obvious implications for power at levels II and III as well. For example, the ways in which mass or mainstream media define coercive power relations in society may affect whether different groups perceive institutions at the second level of power as legitimate. These public perceptions of power, in turn, may affect whether institutional failings (at Level II) are corrected or not. Whether democracy's failings in the eyes of different groups are addressed or ignored also affects the consciousness (at Level III) that people have about the legitimacy of the political system as well as levels of social and political support for each other.

In short, the very question of "What is political?" is hotly contested. Whether people reinforce their biases or learn from each other's differences depends in part on how the media frame commonly occurring features of everyday life. Following the work on England of Hall *et al.* (1978), an important collection of cases that illustrate the relationships between media and power in American society involve the many forms of street-level interpersonal violence, particularly crime. Both the nightly news and the movies are filled with stories about armed gang wars, home invasions by criminals in once safe suburbs, hostage situations, assassinations of abortion clinic workers, bombings of churches, violent beatings of gays, and on and on. The ways in which the media handle these forms of violence—and the ways in which other forms are deemphasized— are instructive about power in society. I consider below several ways in which media treatment of brute force in American society may encourage or reinforce particular popular understandings and discourage others.

Mediated crime

Crime is portrayed overwhelmingly as street-level violence that is lawless and that requires punishment. At the same time, blacks are disproportionately portrayed as the criminals, and they are shown in news and "reality-based" "cops" programs as sinister and predatory threats (Entman 1994). There are many consequences of these portrayals, including:

- The more television people watch, the more likely they are to overestimate their chances of being crime victims (Gerbner and Gross 1976).
- The more people watch "cops" programs that dramatize "real-life" crime incidents, the more likely they are to overestimate the proportion of crimes committed by blacks (Oliver and Armstrong 1998).
- For the past quarter century, crime has been among the most important public problems cited in opinion polls. Getting ever tougher on criminals is among the

few problems in American public life on which majorities actually favor spending tax dollars, and call for more active government involvement (Bennett 1998).

These media portrayals, and the public responses to them, have several important correlates, including the overrepresentation of blacks in prison populations. Not surprisingly, there are big racial differences in respect for the US legal system. For example, polls following the acquittal of sports and TV star O. J. Simpson on charges of brutally murdering his former wife and a friend of hers, indicate that many blacks and whites were worlds apart in their reactions to the trial. The majority of whites could not believe that Simpson was let off after all the evidence that was presented against him. The majority of blacks felt that the justice system itself was on trial as an oppressive and illegitimate extension of white and upper-class power in a racist society. Such reality gaps do not promote universal belief in justice, or respect for the legal institutions on which democracy depends.

Understanding the culture business

But what is the alternative to these media portrayals of crime if American society is truly violent, and people are genuinely fearful because of it? First, recall that fear, a sense of personal threat, and a desire to punish particular kinds of people are all related to—though surely not caused solely by—exposure to media portrayals. Under these circumstances it is tempting to ask why more prominent media coverage is not devoted, say, to industrial polluters who arguably pose more serious threats to larger populations than do crack-smoking muggers. The answer to this question would occupy a chapter in itself. However, at least three factors explain media patterns in which transgressions of poor minorities are far more likely to be featured than are the corresponding social transgressions of more powerful actors.

- First, dominant cultural beliefs lead audiences to accept familiar themes in news and entertainment fare, and to complain loudly of "bias" when alternative frames do appear. For example, racism remains perhaps the greatest American cultural divide, and racial framing is a subtle but pervasive element in media content (Entman 1994). At the same time, all but the "alternative" or fringe media respect strong cultural taboos against systematic critiques of business power that might challenge the virtues of free-market capitalism.
- Second, the American media are owned predominantly by large business interests who do not support systematic reframing of the terms of power in society. There are, of course, occasional news stories about bad behavior by big business (generally occasioned by oil spills, and the like), and audiences may flock to the periodic Hollywood send-up of Wall Street. However, there is no corporate interest to expanding sinister portrayals of big business, or airing them nightly on the local news or in TV drama series. There are already enough public relations problems presented by the undercurrent of negative personal experiences on the part of individual consumers, residents, and employees who have had bad reactions to their dealings with the corporate world. Crime is far safer media fare.
- Third, and speaking of public relations, it is no accident that media are far more saturated by public relations campaigns promoting free enterprise and the virtues

of business and industry, than by campaigns sponsored by poor people who might frame violence in their lives as more of an economic than a moral failing.

These generalizations help to explain media representations of everyday coercion. In particular, they help us understand why various categories of street-level violence are framed as crime, as opposed, for example, to being represented as political acts or linked to economic conditions. Although it may seem strange to even think about seemingly random acts of violence in political or economic terms, there are plenty of reasons to do so—if only mass mediated discourse in society were organized differently. For example, not only does violent "crime" rise and fall (almost as a leading economic indicator) with economic cycles, but many of the patterns of violence that most elicit public demands for legal crackdowns are associated with poverty, unemployment, and low economic mobility. Yet instead of framing falling crime rates in economic terms, they are generally reported as the results of successful crime control, prison, and policing policies. When crime rates rise, they are generally represented as indicators of the need for spending even more money on crime control.

The point here is not that society should ignore crime or pretend that it is not a problem. My criticism is with simplistic "media-ready" thinking that goes something like this: Since crime is a bad thing, it is each individual's social responsibility not to behave badly, and, therefore, more police and prisons are the best responses to bad people. The only problem is that the widely publicized policies for crime control that flow from this logic simply do not work as advertised, either to make individuals more responsible or to reduce the levels of crime over extended periods of time (i.e. longer than the business cycle). It would appear that a key contribution of the media to culture is the promotion of important kinds of dysfunctional behavior and thought.[3]

An important point here is that mediated politics begin well outside the institutions of government, with the introduction of implicit organizing logics for the personal world. These implicit categorizations for everyday life experiences have important links to the workings of the other levels of power. For example, media representations of power and politics at street level can help or hinder politicians and activist groups in their political activities at the next level of power, where we encounter formal crime legislation, public battles over controlling individual rights to own and use guns, and the like. And, at the third level of power (political consciousness), most Americans do not challenge the institution-level result that more public money is spent each year in the United States on prisons and incarceration, than on schools and education. Similarly, few citizens, and even fewer politicians, challenge practices that have raised charges of human rights violations in international circles, as reflected, for example, in an Amnesty International report questioning the treatment of juvenile prisoners in a number of American states.[4] The point is not that everyone thinks the same way or that media messages affect everyone equally, but that enough people think enough alike to support (or at least not to challenge) the basic regime of policing that creates the first level of political order in society.

POWER II: MEDIATED GOVERNMENT

Media representations of the next level of power—the formal workings of government and related political institutions—are necessarily complicated in the United States by the nearly unfathomable numbers and layers of government institutions. Legislative, executive, and judicial bodies can become involved with the same issue or policy problem at national, state, and local levels. This means that new policy initiatives can emerge from any of these institutional points, and work their way, often slowly, through the rest of the political system. Moreover, making political decisions and implementing them can entail many different levels and units of government acting in opaque ways. Even if news organizations become aware of political trends or issues developing within this complex governing system, it is challenging to tell the stories in ways that information-overloaded and often politically disinterested audiences can follow.

Further complicating the challenge of representing the activities of government in a comprehensive or comprehensible way are the two parties that dominate American politics. Compared to most European parties, the Republicans and Democrats are loosely organized associations of entrepreneurial politicians characterized as much by factional fighting and internal fragmentation, as by organizational discipline and regular position-taking. Not only are state and national party organizations often at odds in their issue positions, but party discipline at all levels is so weak that official party positions seldom emerge on more than a few high-profile issues.[5] When the press seeks views on both sides of an issue, reporters more often go to prominent, personable, high-profile individual members of the parties who have influence over different policy areas, rather than to clearly designated party leaders or spokespersons.

These layers of complexity stand in sharp contrast to other political systems with more centralized (non-federal or unitary) institutional structures. Indeed, the more typical democratic state is characterized by parliamentary dominance of government, more disciplined parties, and less involvement from different branches and levels of government in making political decisions. Such governing systems make it easier to report about political agendas, issue positions, policy debates and the logic of government decisions. The American case is further complicated by an overwhelmingly private or commercial media system that emphasizes drama, simplicity, and emotional storytelling, rather than information-rich, complex, running analysis.

How a commercial press reports on a complex government

One way in which the American press has responded to governmental complexity is to organize itself in terms of work routines that yield fairly predictable amounts of daily news from certain locations in government. Thus, news organizations have typically assigned reporters to "beats," which correspond to locations in the government that are typically regarded as likely arenas of political action. Traditional beats include Congress, White House, Supreme Court, Defense Department, State Department, and other prominent executive departments at the national level, state legislatures and governors' offices at the state level, and city councils and police departments at the local level. Cook (1994) examined how the beat system interacts with cultural frames to construct a political story. He contrasted American and French accounts of diplomatic initiatives prior to the opening of the Gulf War in 1991, beginning with French national television's account in which "the world was first globally constructed, then ideologically constructed. By contrast, for this American broadcast, the world was first domestically constructed, then institutionally constructed" (Cook 1994: 105).

This beat system is beginning to erode, but the changes do not result in improved political information flows. To the contrary, beats—particularly at the local level—are being replaced by daily assignment decisions that reflect the shrinking space devoted to political news. News decisions are increasingly driven by audience research and profit calculations, resulting in less detailed coverage of routine politics, and more human-interest features involving health, personal investments, weather, and horrible crimes. Meanwhile, political coverage increasingly emphasizes crises, scandals, and the most dramatic, shocking, or entertaining angles on politics.

Because reporters and news crews are expensive to maintain, the geographic distribution of news bureaus is further calculated according to the expected yield of daily news. One result is that more news-gathering goes on, and more news flows from, places like Washington, New York, Los Angeles, and Chicago, than from Seattle, Atlanta, Denver, or San Diego (Epstein 1973). The world is covered in similar fashion, with many more stories flowing from London, Tokyo, Tel Aviv, and Moscow, than from Cairo, Nairobi, Brasilia, or Jakarta. American images of these lesser-known world capitals are shaped almost exclusively by occasional dramatic news of natural, political, and economic disasters.

These strategic choices over what to report, and where to report it from, make sense largely in organizational and business terms, given the challenges of how to represent the politics and commerce of a large and complex society. However, the resulting news content is characterized by several qualities that may affect the distribution of power in both society and democratic institutions in important ways. For example, the more complex the issues in a story, the more abruptly the story is likely to jump from one institution to another, with reporters telling how the issue touches that institution, rather than how the issue, crisis, or event has evolved in more coherent historical or political terms. As a result, there is almost no reporting about how issues get onto the agendas of government institutions in the first place. In a society where most citizens believe that money (usually in the form of documented contributions to politicians' political campaign funds) buys influence, it would seem appropriate for journalists to routinely track the money trails on the policy decisions made by government officials. Instead, news coverage of policy decisions, if there is any at all, tends to report who made what decisions, and what political accusations they threw at each other in the process.

Since few news organizations have regular beats for "lobbying" or "money," stories about these elements of the governing process occur only rarely. When money and influence stories do appear, they generally involve corruption or high-profile issues, rather than routine aspects of power in government. Moreover, the media are owned increasingly by large conglomerates that take full political advantage of their lobbying and financial resources. As such, it would become awkward to focus too much media attention on these subjects. Though they are probably the most commercialized in the world, the American media thrive on the myth that public interest and public demand, and not business interests, alone drive editorial and programming decisions.

The overall result of this system for representing formal politics is often a fragmented portrayal of confusing institutional activities. Such news accounts make it hard to grasp the reasons for legislation, the causes of government failures, or the impact of new policies on society. Iyengar (1991) has termed this pattern "episodic" news, in which isolated narratives provide a close-up on how featured politicians are handling, or how people with problems are affected by, the latest issue or crisis *du jour*. Seldom do national news organizations identify their own agenda of important issues and report them with more independent journalistic assessments of the origins of problems, the politics behind the often puzzling movement through various institutional arenas, or the reasons for the alternative policy outcomes that officials are considering.[6] Such "thematic" reporting, when it occurs, makes a significant difference in how people understand political situations and what they imagine doing about them. Research by Gamson (1992) demonstrates broad variation in the representation of different policy issues, and corresponding differences in the ways in which individuals engage in thinking about them.

Origins of news agendas and sources of political information

In the often-confusing journey from institution to institution, and up and down the federal levels that characterize the complex decision processes of American government, the most prominent sources of information available to strategically stationed reporters are the government officials who reside at the various beats. In the modern press era spanning the past fifty years, government officials have provided the vast majority of information about political issues in the media (Sigal 1973). In many ways it seems natural that officials in a representative democracy should dominate news about government that is beamed back to citizens and voters. However, critics have raised various questions about this relatively closed information circuit.

Perhaps the most enduring concern about this media system is that relatively little independent check is provided by the press on the good judgment or the representative quality of official views and actions. There are, of course, scandals and character attacks that may surround isolated policies or decisions, but such stories seldom arise from investigative reporting; they are far more often the result of successful public relations strategies originated by political opponents. Routine coverage of politics has little in the way of critical journalistic edge. In an era in which elected representatives are widely suspected of being as obligated to the financial backers who helped them get elected as they are to the voters who elected them, the absence of much background research on the origins of officials' issue positions and decisions is particularly troublesome. Moreover, the strange two-party system of American government makes it difficult for smaller segments of the public—at least those who cannot afford to hire public relations services—to have their views represented in the pronouncements of government officials.

The press preoccupation with officials (and with their personal power struggles) means that many alternative sources of information about complex public decisions seldom appear in press reports. Put another way, most major news organizations are guided primarily by the trail of official power as decisions move through the institutional maze of government. As a result, grassroots and citizen opposition groups tend to be featured prominently in news reports only when there are serious splits and divisions within the ranks of official decision-makers. The press tendency in such cases is to "index" the range of possible news sources and viewpoints according to the range and duration of public conflict among key officials (and occasionally entire political parties) who control decision points in the governmental process (Bennett 1990). Accordingly, there tends to be fairly wide-ranging and detailed presentation of information on hotly contested issues such as abortion and taxation that divide officials openly and enduringly. However, other important issues, from many foreign policy decisions, to what to do about toxic waste management, tend to receive relatively little grassroots input or sustained news coverage unless crises occur and key decision-makers express public differences.

The rise of scandals and tabloid journalism

Those who have watched the scandals that routinely rock American politics in recent times may counter that officials do not always have such an easy time of it with the press. While this is true, the ways in which officials are criticized in news, talk shows, tabloids, and late-night comedy programs may not be all that helpful either to citizens or to the quality of democratic deliberation. Indeed, the tone of American public discourse has become harsh, moralistic, and corrosive in the view of many observers.

For example, much of the world watched with some combination of shock, amusement, and incomprehension, as American headlines and airwaves in 1998 were filled with lurid details of sex between the President, Bill Clinton, and a young White House intern, Monica Lewinsky. The political "hook" used to excuse the prestige press from sounding like the tabloids was that Congress (driven by an election-and-publicity-minded Republican majority) was considering whether Clinton's lying about the affair in an earlier personal court case constituted grounds for removal from office.

The reasons for such personalization of politics may have as much to do with the evolution of media–government relations, as with any deeper shift in cultural attitudes about privacy or morality. In recent years, media consultants increasingly manage not just politicians' careers, but the relations between politicians, press, institutions, and publics. In this era of managed, strategic news, what passes for press scrutiny is often just putting the spotlight on exchanges of negative and personal attacks between political opponents. Such attacks often have less to do with the merits of an issue or policy than with strategic concerns about publicity and political image.

Those who reported (and many of those who watched) the endless presidential sex scandal were aware that much of its momentum came from the organized efforts of Bill Clinton's personal and political opponents to discredit him through highly publicized lawsuits and placement of news stories. Perhaps the most distressing development has been the tendency of reporters to join the personalization of politics by playing up these squabbles and dramatizing the personal motives in many political situations. Even as they condemned themselves for publicizing the lurid details, reporters and media executives excused themselves on grounds that they simply could not drop a story with enough sex and power to light up a movie screen. Television ratings (numbers of viewers) for the periods following key events in the scandal were over twice as high as during normal news periods. Several gripping episodes of the scandal produced ratings that were considerably higher than the numbers who tuned in to hear the results of the important 1998 national election. The election-beating episodes of Bill and Monica included the first reports of the affair, Clinton's admission of the affair, release of a special prosecutor's report filled with explicit sexual detail, and broadcast of the president's testimony to the prosecutor's grand jury (*New York Times* 1998).

The irony of a free press

What is it about American journalism that leads to such uniformly unsatisfying representations of politics in American society? Here we move squarely to the interaction between a media system and political institutions. Some analysts trace the development of contemporary media politics to historical roots in the weakening of American political parties as agenda-setting and information-filtering institutions. It is ironic that too much democracy may be to blame here, in the form of increasing selection of party candidates directly by voters through complicated "primary" (candidate nominating) election reforms dating to the late 1960s. As a result of potential candidates bypassing party screening selection, and appealing directly to voters, already weak American parties became even weaker in terms of organizing, screening, and providing coherent information to the public. At the same time, politicians have faced ever-greater challenges in terms of raising money and communicating with voters in an increasingly chaotic information environment (Patterson 1993).

But why did the press fail to step into this chaos and organize a coherent political information system as party-based information structuring declined? Many observers conclude that the press—as constituted in America—has little independent capacity to evaluate the merits of issues, to explain the governmental process apart from the personal political battles of politicians, or to provide the kind of information that citizens say they want for thinking about public life. The answer involves the fact that the United States is among the least regulated and most commercialized press systems in the world. The irony is that despite the highly competitive appearance of this free market of ideas, the content is relatively limited and the consumers express extreme dissatisfaction with it. How can this free marketplace of ideas produce such restricted choice of content and such low consumer ratings?

The answer to this important question requires a somewhat deeper understanding of the organization of the media in the United States. At least two features distinguish American media in general, and the press in particular, from almost any other nation on the planet. First, the US does not just display a tendency toward private ownership of media and unregulated political content; it is likely the most extreme case in these regards among the industrial democracies. Most other media systems have large sectors devoted to public or state-funded broadcasting, with various regulatory solutions that provide broad social and political representation in the programming and editorial policies. Second, the overwhelming professional norm guiding political journalism in the US is somewhere between "objectivity" and "fairness." Most media systems are mixed not just in ownership, but in the political and professional biases of different news organizations.

Whereas party-affiliated, ideologically diverse papers and even broadcasting outlets are common in other societies, most US news organizations attempt to create a similar political "balance" in their reporting. There is little felt obligation to educate citizens, to introduce useful organizing schemes for political information, or to worry much about whether neglected issues or social viewpoints are being represented. In other words, fairness and balance in the American media system do not mean assessing all views and preferences on a given issue, but publicizing the dominant views that are most readily available to the press. This means that the most prominent politicians, the best-organized interests, and, above all, those players with good publicity and strategic communication operations shape the flow of information in society.

As noted earlier, the irony of this system is that even though it is arguably freer of government regulation and political constraints than any in the world, the result is greater conformity and uniformity of program content than in many systems that are more highly regulated. For example, a study of the press in five democracies (US, Britain, Italy, Sweden, and Germany) conducted by Patterson and Donsbach found that American journalists reported fewer pressures and limits on their professional judgments and reporting choices than their colleagues in other societies. Yet American journalists displayed by far the smallest differences in their decisions about how to report various hypothetical news events and political issues (Patterson 1992). The irony of the free press in America is that the convergence of private ownership and the historical evolution of norms of nonpartisanship and political neutrality generally restrict the range of ideas circulating among the mainstream audience.

Add to this picture the increasing pressures from media ownership for profitability, and the news shows few signs of getting more sophisticated. As large conglomerates buy out smaller media organizations (e.g. General Electric now owns the National Broadcasting Corporation, Disney owns the American Broadcasting Corporation, Time–Warner bought Turner Broadcasting, and so on), there are greater pressures to turn large profits. The buy-out, consolidation, and economic reorganization of the American media have resulted in closing news bureaus, eroding costly investigative journalism, and dramatizing news content to draw audiences.

Compared to entertainment, the news is more cheaply produced (i.e. easily gathered and presented) and relatively more profitable. One result of these trends is news that looks more like entertainment, with emphasis on drama, human emotion, personal threat, and consumer topics. TV news programs are proliferating during "prime time" evening viewing hours. To draw audiences, the programs feature dramatic themes of government waste, crime, health scares, and political scandal. The term for this evolution of information and entertainment is "infotainment." In these and the many ways described above, the commercialization of public information surely affects the third level of power: how citizens think about the political world and their place in it.

POWER III: MEDIATED CONSCIOUSNESS

It is tempting to think that increasingly sophisticated political communication and decreasingly informative media would leave citizens easy prey for manipulative politicians and governments. Yet, the American people, although notoriously ill informed, are also notoriously independent-minded, at least when it comes to evaluating political propaganda. Even when bombarded for months on end with something like the Clinton sex scandal, most people were quite resistant to joining the partisan attack on the President, or supporting his removal from office. Indeed, public support for Clinton actually rose to the highest levels of his presidency following the disclosure of the affair, and remained high throughout the year-long media spectacle of sex in the White House, images of presidential deceit, and impeachment activities in Congress (Zaller 1998).

When asked to make serious decisions about whether Clinton should be impeached and removed from office, or whether the government should be spending time on this case, strong majorities disengaged from the media blitz long enough to say "No." It is of course impossible to know how public opinion would have gone if the economy had not been prospering under Clinton's presidency, or if the circumstances surrounding his lying had been different. The point is that at least on some heavily publicized matters, people seem to think fairly critically and carefully. One conclusion is that when the airwaves are filled with information for long periods of time, people will deliberate seriously, and will make obvious distinctions between the jokes of late-night comedians and the smirking barbs of political opponents in Congress.

Yet there are other cases in which the quality of public thinking may be undermined by the political communication trends reported here. For example, what about the quality of public thinking when it is not clear who is behind an information campaign? (In the earlier example, it was clear to many from the beginning that the special prosecutor and the Republicans who magnified the Clinton scandal were partisans out to get the President.) Or, what about public consciousness when one side wins an election, or defeats a public policy initiative because it hit on a scarier, more deceptive set of commercials produced by a better ad agency? And what about the sheer absence of informed public opinion on the large percentage of issues and government activities that receive little or no publicity at all?

The latter cases may be more typical of American public life, suggesting a distinction about information and public opinion in the American case. Major, contested issues seem to generate reasoned public opinion even when media coverage seems unreasonable. Yet the quality of more routine public deliberation is more questionable because the national media system has no governing center, few regulations, and offers little opportunity for smaller parties or weaker interests to get their messages out, while presenting obvious advantages for the already organized and well funded (Cappella and Jamieson 1997).

Deeper problems of public consciousness

Perhaps the most important response to political manipulation and confusion does not occur on the level of public opinion about particular issues or election choices, but on a more general level of suspicion toward politics and government in general. American society is distinctive among world democracies in low levels of political participation and the degree to which individuals actively avoid politics. This avoidance of politics is not just a matter of hating government or politicians, but claiming to be apolitical even in areas such as drug activism and homelessness that could easily be embraced consciously as political. Thus, large numbers of Americans think of themselves as either nonpolitical beings or political only because moved by negative governmental forces to take action. In short, the bottom line on American politics in the recent era is one of finely constructed avoidance of politics (Eliasoph 1998).

The opinion trends reported in Figure 14.1 show a precipitous drop in confidence for the basic national democratic institutions of press, executive, and Congress (and growing support for a military that has not lost a war since the beginning of the measured period of time). The intriguing aspect of this figure is that the drops in confidence in institutions in the 1970s and early 1980s were balanced by increases in confidence in the press. This suggests a lively democratic communication system in which institutional failings (such as the executive branch Watergate scandal in 1974, and the paralyzing hostage crisis during the Iranian revolution of 1979–80) were reported in ways that large majorities found useful, even if distressing. In the recent decade, however, the confidence in both the conduct of government and in the national press as primary sources of information about politics, have both taken steep dives. Is it just a coincidence that the explosion of money in politics, the saturation of all levels of politics with strategic marketing-driven communication, and the corporate media merger mania all came into full development over this same period of time?

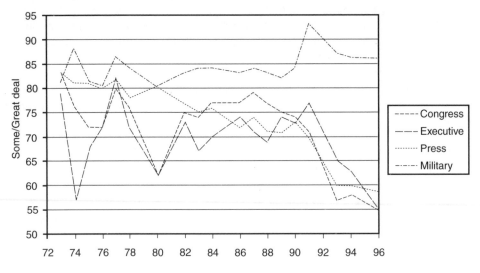

Figure 14.1   Confidence in leaders of national institutions 1973–96

CONCLUSION

Perhaps the most important question about American public life today is to understand the causes of the sweeping disaffection from politics that threatens the legitimacy of government itself. The media and American politics seem caught in a double bind. First, as noted above, the growing commercialization of news decisions results in emphasizing tabloid political melodrama and other low-cost, audience-attracting programming over more independent analyses of issues that are more costly to research and even more costly to present in interesting ways. Second, these evolving commercial media formats become tied to the transformation of governance itself through the increasing reliance of parties and politicians on media and image consultants. Indeed, Timothy Cook has argued that getting political messages into the news (and coordinating news, advertising, and other media content) has become so important both for the careers of politicians, and to the daily operations of institutions, that the news media have effectively become a co-equal institution of American government (Cook 1998).

This strange loop of government-by-media is completed by media representations of government as a calculated insider's game designed to win elections, damage opponents, manipulate public support, or repay debts to financial backers (Jamieson 1992, Patterson 1993). Critics argue that representing politics as an insider's power game does not provide audiences with a deeper sense of how the governmental process itself works, or how many dedicated officials are actually attempting to serve the public interest. To the contrary, media cynicism breeds public cynicism (Jamieson 1992, Patterson 1993). While it is clear that majorities of the public are turned off both to the media and to the government they see portrayed in the media, the solution would seem more complex than reporting more happy news. Indeed, the centrality of media strategies in the governing process makes it difficult to say that what the public sees and hears about politics is entirely distorted. It may make more sense to talk about the evolution of a dysfunctional communication system, in which the messages disgust those who receive them, but enough people continue to participate to reward those who create and send those messages.

Many difficult questions remain to be answered about the sources of political disaffection in America. Commercialized and antagonistic communication practices on the part of politicians and the media are surely not the only (or, perhaps, even the principal) factors driving people away from politics. For example, important changes in economy (employment instability and household debt), society (breakdowns in group structures and norms of conduct), and culture (weakening of common identifications) over recent decades have changed individual values in ways that make old government institutions seem irrelevant. If this is the case, much of the political communication in contemporary American politics may be off-putting simply because it is aimed at herding disaffected citizens back into institutions and behavior patterns that they find either repellant, or simply irrelevant to their life concerns.

If the formal institutions of government seem increasingly out of touch with individual concerns, the popular media are brimming with those concerns on a twenty-four-hour-a-day-basis. News reports tell of rises in drug addiction, depression, teen suicide, spree killings, and other alarming signs of social collapse. Of course, the actual state of society may be better, worse, or simply different than these media portrayals. This is precisely why the media become so central to understanding politics. As noted earlier, the representation of the brute conditions of life at the first level of power makes a difference for what government responses at Level II seem appropriate, and for how people think about the state of society and politics at Level III.

Indeed, one of the most remarkable aspects of contemporary American life is the degree to which social experience is at once highly personalized, yet freely shared with strangers, and often painstakingly removed from examination of deeper causes—particularly when those causes might touch upon political or economic taboos. Talk shows fill cable channels with bizarre tales of cheating husbands and wives. Mothers appeal to national audiences of strangers to save their teen daughters from careers of prostitution or exotic dancing. Research on changes in individual lifestyles conducted by a leading advertising company reveals that Americans are increasingly overworked, overstressed, burdened by debt, and unable to manage work, family, relationships, and social lives in satisfying ways (Bennett 1998).

It may seem quite a stretch to get from these symptoms of personal and social disorder to politics. Indeed, if we turn to the third level of power, we find that people tend to see these problems as personal struggles, and that they are offered as good reasons why there is little time or energy left over for getting involved in politics and government. Reinforcing such individual perceptions, both news and entertainment programs tend to present the epidemic of stress, addiction, dysfunction, and otherwise troubled lives as alternately heartwarming or tragic personal struggles.

At the same time, relatively few connections are drawn between these common individual experiences, and broad social changes that range from radical reorganization of the corporate world and the work experiences of the majority of employees, to the bombardment of individuals with advertisements for consumption and debt. Even rarer, still, are representations of broad social or economic trends in political terms that might generate thinking about governmental or collective solutions. Mainstream media and government officialdom are largely silent on how society, economy, and individual experiences might be linked by political problem definitions or solutions that might alter the patterns of economic or political power in society. As a result, it is hardly surprising that few initiatives have emerged in credible public forums for increasing the responsibility of employers to employees, or for regulating (or even educating citizens regarding) the temptations of easy debt and obsessive consumption patterns.

Neither the media nor politicians can be faulted directly for keeping many of the major problems facing Americans today outside of politics. Indeed, journalists, entertainment programmers, and elected officials all claim public support for their gatekeeping choices. Perhaps the proper level for the analysis of power and perception in society is at the level of corporate ownership where programming policies are set, and contributions are made to the politicians who decide whether to regulate businesses, and what to talk about in public information and education campaigns. At this level, too, claims are made about the people being the ultimate sovereigns in the democratic order. If the people are unhappy, so the logic goes, let them find other programming and let them elect other politicians.

These slippery issues that complicate our efforts to follow the trail of media power in even one society also show how much the analysis of power is affected by how the analyst thinks about power in the first place. Stripped of the proposed multidimensional framework for understanding power, this entire argument loses its critical edge. If we examine just the uses of force in society, we learn that the powers of the state are defined in most media treatments, and by most authorities, in sensible terms of crime, punishment, policing, taxation, and security. If we examine just the level of institutional procedures, we find that courts, legislatures, executives, and elections continue to function more or less according to plan. As for the level of consciousness about power, most polls show high levels of support for the most coercive functions of the state, except taxation. At the same time, most people also favor shrinking the routine, non-coercive institutions of politics as a reaction against perceived governmental intrusions in areas of social and economic regulation. Not surprisingly, most individuals take on the responsibility for their own problems. Indeed, large majorities also report that, despite all its travails, life is for the most part good. It is just government, society, politics, and the media that are bad.

Notes

1 This level of consciousness is wrapped in troublesome Gramscian issues of hegemony and consciousness. Some problems of understanding consciousness can be avoided by looking for publicly visible signs of whether those who wield coercive power are widely perceived as legitimate, whether there are observable levels of overt and covert resistance, and how individuals understand their own power within the institutional order. See, for example, James Scott's (1985) analysis of low-level resistance in Malaysian society.
2 I am indebted to Rachael Noguera for this example, and for educating me about media coverage of this case.
3 For a cogent analysis of why such dysfunction persists in the realm of power, see Edelman (1977).
4 Amnesty International report released November 18 1998.
5 When it comes to popular election issues such as crime, taxes or morality, party members may stand together as long as it is in their individual electoral interests to do so. However, on more volatile policy problems such as health care for those without it, party discipline on broad policy positions often crumbles.

6 Some news organizations, generally at the local level, claim to have some independent news agendas, but these members of the "civic journalism" movement are often accused of using marketing research to select issues that draw audiences—not to investigate issues that have some higher claim to political importance.

References

Asard, E. and Bennett, W. Lance (1997) *Democracy and the Marketplace of Ideas: Communication and Government in Sweden and the United States*, New York: Cambridge University Press.

Bennett, W. Lance (1990) "Toward a theory of press–state relations in the United States," *Journal of Communication*, 40: 103–25.

Bennett, W. Lance (1993) "Constructing publics and their opinions," *Political Communication*, 10 (April–June): 101–20.

Bennett, W. Lance (1998) "The uncivic culture: communication, identity, and the rise of lifestyle politics," *P.S.: Political Science and Politics*, 31 (December): 741–61.

Blumler, J. and Gurevitch, M. (1998) "Americanization reconsidered: US–UK campaign communication comparisons across time," paper presented at the Annenberg Policy Center Workshop on Mediated Politics: Communication in the Future of Democracy, University of Pennsylvania.

Blumler, J. and Kavanaugh, D. (in press) "A third age of political communication: where is it heading?" *Political Communication*.

Cappella, J. and Jamieson, K. (1997) *Spiral of Cynicism: The Press and the Public Good*, Oxford: Oxford University Press.

Cook, T. E. (1994) "Domesticating a crisis: Washington newsbeats and network news after the Iraqi invasion of Kuwait," in W. Lance Bennett and D. L. Paletz (eds.) *Taken by Storm: The Media, Public Opinion, and U. S. Foreign Policy in the Gulf War*, Chicago: University of Chicago Press.

Cook, T. (1998) *Governing with the News*, Chicago: University of Chicago Press.

Edelman, M. (1977) *Political Language: Words that Succeed and Policies that Fail*, New York: Academic Press.

Eliasoph, N. (1998) *Avoiding Politics: How Americans Produce Apathy in Everyday Life*, Cambridge: Cambridge University Press.

Entman, R. (1994) "Representation and reality in the portrayal of blacks on network television news," *Journalism Quarterly*, 71: 509–20.

Epstein, E. J. (1973) *News from Nowhere*, New York: Random House.

Gamson, W. A. (1992) *Talking Politics*, Cambridge: Cambridge University Press.

Gerbner, G. and Gross, L. (1976) "Living with television: the violence profile," *Journal of Communication*, 26: 173–99.

Hall, S., Crichter, C., Jefferson, T., Clarke, J. and Roberts, B. (1978) *Policing the Crisis: Mugging, the State and Law and Order*, New York: Holmes and Meier.

Herman, E. S. and McChesney, R. W. (1997) *The Global Media: The New Missionaries of Global Capitalism*, London: Cassell.

Inglehart, R. (1997) *Modernization and Postmodernization: Cultural, Economic, and Political Change in 43 Societies*, Princeton: Princeton University Press.

Iyengar, S. (1991) *Is Anyone Responsible?*, Chicago: University of Chicago Press.

Jamieson, K. H. (1992) *Dirty Politics*, Oxford: Oxford University Press.

Katz, E. and Liebes, T. (1990) *The Export of Meaning: Cross-Cultural Readings of Dallas*, New York: Oxford University Press.

Keane, J. (1991) *The Media and Democracy*, Cambridge: Polity Press.

Lukes, S. (1974) *Power: A Radical View*, London: Macmillan.

New York Times (1998) "Lewinsky: why news networks would miss her," November 9, p. c7.

Oliver, M. B. and Armstrong, G. B. (1998) "The color of crime: perceptions of Caucasians' and African Americans' involvement in crime," in M. Fishman and G. Cavendar *Entertaining Crime: Television Reality Programs*, New York: Walter de Gruyter.

Patterson, T. (1992) "Irony of a free press: professional journalism and news diversity," paper presented at the Annual Meeting of the American Political Science Association.

Patterson, T. (1993) *Out of Order*, New York: Knopf.

Schiller, H. I. (1992) *Mass Communications and American Empire*, 2nd edn, Boulder, CO: Westview.

Scott, J. (1985) *Weapons of the Weak: Everyday Forms of Peasant Resistance*, New Haven: Yale University Press.

Sigal, L. V. (1973) *Reporters and Officials: The Organization and Politics of Newsmaking*, Lexington, MA: D. C. Heath.

Slater, D. (1997) *Consumer Culture and Modernity*, Cambridge: Polity Press.

Tunstall, J. and Palmer, M. (1991) *Media Moguls*, London: Routledge.

Zaller, J. (1998) "Monica Lewinsky's contribution to political science," *PS: Political Science and Politics*, 31 (June): 182–9.

15 Media and the decline of liberal corporatism in Britain

James Curran and Colin Leys

Introduction

Some liberal accounts of the British media never go beyond a simple description of their structure and regulation. They do not look behind media façades to check their wiring and plumbing, their complex articulation to power in British society. If they do, it is usually to check only the circuits that run between media and government.

By contrast, there is a radical tradition which prides itself on offering a more penetrating account. But while it is more critical in tone, it shares with the liberal approach a basic weakness. It offers a media-centered analysis which sheds light on media organizations, while leaving in shadow the wider processes of society. Written by media specialists, it is "better" on the media than on the context which crucially shapes the media. This is why this chapter departs from convention by giving an account first of political power in Britain, before going on to consider the British media.

Power in Britain

Any attempt to characterize the structure and dynamics of political power in Britain at the end of the century must be more than usually cautious, since the period is so obviously one of transition. What is clear is the unravelling of the power relations of "liberal corporatism"; the ensuing flux is harder to specify.

"Liberal corporatism" is a convenient label for the political regime that resulted from the balance of power between capital and labor in much of Western Europe after 1945. *Laissez faire* had been discredited by the depression of the 1930s; full employment enormously strengthened the unions and the fear of communism made governments of all parties anxious to conciliate them. The Labour Party won a massive majority in the 1945 election and from then until 1974 never polled less than 40 percent of the vote. Because of the peculiarities of the British electoral system the Conservatives were able to return to office in 1951, but could do so only by accommodating themselves to the new balance of economic power that underpinned Labour's new-found electoral strength. The Conservatives accepted full employment as a prime goal of economic policy, and retained and even extended the Welfare State (Timmins 1995); and when, from the early 1960s onward, relatively slow economic growth, reflected in recurrent balance of payments crises, began to jeopardize the concordat between capital and labor, Conservative governments no less than Labour ones sought support from the Trades Union Congress for wage controls and policies of retrenchment (Middlemas 1980, Panitch 1976).

This was liberal corporatism. It was liberal, both economically, in that the economy was still "mixed," with only 20 percent of GDP produced in the publicly owned sector, most of it in the power, transport, and communications infrastructure; and politically, in that all the main political institutions of liberal democracy remained unchanged. It was corporatist, in that whichever party was in office, it ruled on terms more or less agreed by representatives of both labor and capital. And for twenty-five years it was remarkably stable, as the electorate divided its support rather evenly between the two main parties, each with a very firm base in the class system: "generally, about two thirds of working-class voters supported the Labour Party and four-fifths of the middle class voted Conservatives" (Denver 1989: 30). Over time, too, state and professional elites gradually adapted themselves to this new order: judges, bishops of the Church of England, university vice-chancellors, even senior police and military officers, and not least, senior producers and program controllers of the BBC—and in due course, independent television too—all came to take liberal corporatism for granted. The stability and homogeneity of this power structure were accentuated by the country's unitary constitution; local government ran on the same party lines as national government and, though there were local newspapers, throughout most of the era of liberal corporatism there was in effect no local radio or television.

From the late 1960s, however, liberal corporatism began to be undermined by a number of developments which in retrospect can be seen as resulting from contradictions inherent in it. Sustained economic growth and full employment further strengthened the position of organized labor, but British capital did not respond by undertaking extensive labor-saving investment. Productivity growth in British manufacturing, in particular, lagged behind that of competitors, and the share of profits in GDP fell from 16.5 percent in 1946 to 12.5 percent in 1976. As balance of payments difficulties from the late 1950s onward led successive governments to impose severe credit squeezes, employers called for a reversal of this shift which labor was in no mood to accept (Glyn and Sutcliffe 1972). The social consensus on which liberal corporatism was premised—the idea that labor should share in rising prosperity in return for industrial cooperation—began to dissolve in increasingly bitter industrial conflict.

But although industrial action continued to dominate the front pages throughout the 1970s and unionization rates continued to rise—union "density" peaked, at half of the total workforce, only in the late 1970s—a countercurrent was also in evidence. Full employment—unemployment remained well below 2 percent from 1947 to 1967—and sustained economic growth meant that for the first time almost all workers had some "discretionary" income. Individualism and consumerism steadily gained ground; class consciousness gradually succumbed to the "joyous ringing of capitalism's cash tills" (Blackwell and Seabrook 1985: 114). There was a loss of deference, a "desubordination," especially among younger workers who no longer feared unemployment, as well as among students; but it was expressed as much in the explosive growth of the hedonistic popular culture of the period as in strikes and political radicalism (Beer 1981). The two major parties' domination of the electoral scene began to crumble—their combined share of the vote fell from 88 percent in 1945 to 70 percent in 1983. This reflected a growing public disenchantment with their record as managers of the economy, but it was also due to the fact that the class contours of British life were beginning to erode.

As British capital did try, belatedly and not very effectively, to improve its competitive position by modernizing investment, and as manufacturing gave way to services, the proportion of semiskilled and unskilled jobs declined (to only 15 percent for men and 18 percent for women by 1990), and the share of women in the total workforce rose from 30 percent in 1954 to 42 percent (Lindley 1994: 24–25). The latter shift was reflected in trade union membership, especially in the public sector unions. Though in the long run this feminization of the unions was essential to their survival, in the short run it involved a difficult process of changing their traditionally masculine culture, which contributed, temporarily at least, to weakening the key institutions which defined and sustained working-class identity.

A further factor contributing to the collapse of liberal corporatism was the profound change in politics produced by developments in radio and television. In the early 1950s public meetings were still a major medium of political communication between politicians and voters. By the 1970s they were well on the way to being almost completely replaced by television. Television and radio were also fast eclipsing parliament as arenas of party-political debate, and entertainment was gaining ground over information and public affairs in both. These developments particularly affected the Labour Party, with its culture of vigorous internal debate and its leadership's by no means purely formal dependence on rank and file sentiment. It was doubtful if political competition focused on telegenic leaders and "news management" was compatible with genuine internal party democracy. But the new media also affected politics generally, in more indirect ways, perhaps most of all by reducing the length of the collective memory, as visual images increasingly displaced both print and the oral traditions of family, club, and neighborhood (Hoggart 1957, Hobsbawm in Jacques *et al.* 1981). To the extent that liberal corporatism had been a reaction to bitter memories of the depression years, the willingness of workers to let it go may well have been accelerated by this change.

Whatever the mix of causes, liberal corporatism came to a definitive end in the early 1980s with the abolition of its defining precondition—national controls over cross-border capital movements. The resulting loss of "Keynesian capacity" (Scharpf 1991) meant that most governments could no longer pursue any significant social or economic policy of which the bond markets disapproved, or impose much tougher regulatory or tax regimes than those of competing countries. Some economic sovereignty could be recovered by pooling it with other countries in the European Union, so as to create a united front *vis-à-vis* multinational corporations; but this involved political compromises and laid the government open to attack at home for "surrendering national interests to Brussels" (or to Germany, or France, or Spain, depending on the issue). And British governments were more constrained than most because, contrary to the claims of the Thatcherites, no economic miracle was wrought in the 1980s (Graham 1997), and Britain's competitive position depended very heavily on keeping wages and taxes low to attract foreign capital. This strategy also led to dramatic increases in inequality, poverty, drug addiction, and crime (Commission on Social Justice 1994), to which the Conservatives responded by increased policing and incarceration; and to heightened pressure for separation in Scotland and for devolution in Wales, to which the Labour Party responded with the establishment of a Scottish Parliament and a Welsh Assembly in 1999.

The less real power national politicians had, the more precarious their electoral position became and the more they sought to monopolize what control they still possessed. This was particularly obvious in the internal politics of the Labour and Conservative parties. After Labour lost its third successive general election in 1987 the party's "modernizers" concluded that it could not win again unless it unambiguously demonstrated its accommodation to the markets. This meant that left-wing "activists" in the constituencies, trade leaders and even potentially dissident senior party figures outside the Leader's inner circle of confidants had to be disempowered—though in the name of empowering all party members as individuals. Policy determination by annual conferences of trade union and constituency delegates was replaced by a system of centrally managed policy "consultations," by making MPs ineligible to be elected to the National Executive by the rank and file membership (thus denying any independent power base to prominent figures outside the Leader's inner circle), and by rule changes which converted the annual conference, and even the National Executive, from arenas of policy debate into instruments of centralized party management (Panitch and Leys 1997). The elimination of dissent was also achieved by the increasingly ruthless central vetting of party candidates for local government, the Welsh Assembly and the Scottish Parliament, and the European Parliament.

These changes entailed equally radical shifts in the party's sources of intellectual and financial support. Marketing, public relations, and management increasingly replaced academia as the intellectual fields from which advisers were drawn.[1] The New Labour leadership also moved as rapidly as possible away from reliance on trade union funding to donations from wealthy individuals; and several prominent businessmen, but no trade union leaders, were appointed to positions in the Labour Government formed in 1997.

The reforms instituted in the Conservative Party by its new leader William Hague after its disastrous electoral defeat in 1997 were no less dramatic. Here, the need was to appear to empower the Conservative rank and file—which by 1997 was a clearly endangered species, with an average age of 62—and really to disempower the party's MPs, too many of whom were ideologues recruited during the ascendancy of Mrs Thatcher and willing to sacrifice party unity to their contradictory passions for both unregulated markets and "national sovereignty" (i.e. bitter opposition to European integration). For the first time the constituency membership was given a role in the election of the Leader, making him far less subject to pressure from Conservative MPs. On the other hand, the reforms gave the membership no real role in policymaking.

While the party leaderships thus tried to protect themselves against the conflicting pressures and risks generated by the post-corporatist flux in the structures of political power, they could do little to control, or even anticipate, some of the "new social movements" which increasingly filled the vacuum (Dalton 1990). "Roads protesters" whose resistance to the Newbury bypass road added £20 million to the costs of a £100 million project, Greenpeace activists who forced the abandonment of plans to dispose of used oil rigs in the Atlantic, animal rights activists who forced major changes in the fur trade, the veal trade and the cosmetics industry—these and other new social movement activists who enjoyed some public sympathy showed a capacity to impose important policy changes in the new media-driven, focus group-dependent politics of the 1990s, and were not inclined to accept tutelage by any political party. (It seemed almost a sign of the times that one week in November 1998, while these kinds of activists were making almost daily appearances on the BBC's agenda-setting morning radio program *Today*, the General Secretary of the country's biggest trade union, Bill Morris, could only be heard talking about his private life and musical tastes on *Desert Island Discs*.)

Corresponding to the prevailing individualization of political life—and indeed partly intended to foster it—was the "hollowing out" of the state and parastatal institutions undertaken by the Conservative governments of the 1980s (Dunleavy 1997, Rhodes 1994). The aim was to shrink the state, to transfer decision-making to market actors, and to reshape public political culture in such a way as to reflect and reinforce this change.

Privatization of the public sector in the 1980s and 1990s not only restored to private ownership all the utilities taken into public ownership after 1945; it also transferred to private ownership many other state sectors and agencies previously regarded as quintessentially public, such as a growing number of hospitals prisons, government offices and even some schools, not to mention the phone system and much public housing. In this way vast areas of everyday life that used to connect people to the state now connected them to the private sector. In the process, moreover, shares in the privatized corporations were offered to the public at big discounts, permitting windfall profits to be taken the day after the issue. Though most of the shares ended up in the hands of institutional investors, the proportion of people owning some shares rose to 21 percent of all adults, including 10 percent of the manual working class (*General Household Survey* 1988). Even though the average shareholding of the latter group was very small, the shift in attitudes that the spread of shareholding implied was probably significant. It could no longer be presumed that most "ordinary people" regarded shareholders as having interests opposed to their own, as would have been true even twenty years earlier.

And what was not privatized was comprehensively remodelled on business lines. By the mid-1990s 60 percent of all civil servants were employed in Next Steps agencies, semiautonomous agencies with chief executives on short-term contracts with performance-related pay, committed to running them as far as possible on business lines. Government accounting practices were reorganized on private sector lines (Shaoul 1999), imposing intense pressures throughout the state and parastatal system to find "efficiency savings"—which all too often became a euphemism for cuts in the services provided. The National Health Service and personal social services were reorganized into so-called internal markets in which purchasers were separated from providers with a view to making providers compete with each other to reduce costs. Planning on the basis of social needs gave way to unplanned outcomes driven by the efforts of agencies to survive financially in these quasi-markets, which according to official rhetoric could alone be relied on to yield the "three Es" of "economy, efficiency and effectiveness." Cuts, "downsizing," asset-sales, "outsourcing," "income-generation," charity appeals and rationing became part of everyday life in the public sector.

Another dimension of these changes was a sharp decline in democratic accountability. Elected local government was stripped of its powers through the imposition of central limits on spending as well as drastic curtailment of local tax powers and the effective removal of most of its responsibilities for education and housing; while so-called quangos ("quasi-non-government" bodies), filled (by government appointment) largely with businessmen, proliferated, until by 1994/95 quangos were responsible for a third of all government expenditure, almost as much as elected local councils (Hall and Weir 1996: 7). Unlike local authorities, which are responsible to voters for the powers they still have, quangos are answerable only to ministers, and have very few duties to consult or even to make their deliberations public (Hall and Weir 1996: 9–16).

The counterpart to this de-democratization was a proliferation of *auditing*, that is, the use of business-derived concepts of independent supervision to measure and evaluate the performance of public agencies and public employees, from primary school teachers and university lecturers to social workers and doctors—"value for money" audits, management audits, forensic audits, data audits, intellectual property audits, teaching audits, technology audits, clinical audits—creating a society of individual auditees in place of a society of democratic citizens with collective responsibility for their own and others' use of public office (Power 1997). A punitive culture of naming and shaming individual teachers, schools, doctors, social workers and social work departments for allegedly poor performance replaced the idea of a nationally and locally shared responsibility for the problems public employees confront, and for ensuring that they have adequate resources.

The resulting demoralization of public employees—especially those designated as "providers"—in face of reduced resources, loss of independence and constant scapegoating, had its own political costs. It could no longer be assumed that public sector workers were attached to the state or served it from professional commitment (Mackintosh 1998, Rose 1993). At the same time there was widespread contempt for much of the privatized sector, especially the railways, the bus services, and the water companies, which were perceived as inefficient and profiteering at the expense of the public interest. By the mid-1990s opinion polls suggested that alienation from the political system was deeper and more widespread than at any time since the introduction of the mass franchise (Nolan 1995).

So long as economic growth continued, governments could ride this unstable and even somewhat febrile situation, especially through "image-management." This "realm of hyper-politics, where politics is exclusively concerned with itself"—a world in which "politics is a daily struggle to win the attention of a public which has its mind on other matters"—is familiar from North America: "the *software* of politics becomes decisive, its ability to adjust itself ... to the country's state of mind, to intercept and encourage its moods" (Polito 1998, quoted in Hobsbawm 1998: 5–6). In this realm power belongs increasingly to "special advisers" and "spin doctors"—attitude researchers, focus-group animators, information management specialists, and press officers.

Access to their world becomes extremely important. Old elite groups—doctors, academics, schoolteachers, churchmen, senior public service broadcasters and even judges and lawyers, lose access and status, insofar as their professional values, having become adapted to the values of liberal corporatism, make them unwilling to abandon "old-fashioned" conceptions of the public interest (such as clinical or judicial independence, academic freedom, the Catholic Church's "option for the poor," public service broadcasting, and so on), or their commitment to the institutions that embody these values (the jury system, the National Health Service, and so on).[2] In their place come new elite groups, attuned to and successful in the market—entrepreneurs (Lord Archer, Richard Branson, Lord Hollis) and chief executives (Sir Roy Griffiths, Lord Sainsbury), media stars (Glenda Jackson, Trevor Phillips), popular music groups (Oasis). Party leaders seek photo opportunities with celebrities, recruiting them to endorse their political products—for example Labour's plans (revealed after her death) to use Princess Diana as a sort of roving ambassador, and the later proposal by the minister responsible for women's issues to cast former Spice Girl Geri Halliwell as a "women's role model."

As these last examples suggest, the enhanced status of women was another notable, if still somewhat ambiguous, feature of the post-corporatist era. In the generation that benefited from the dramatic expansion of higher education in the 1950s and 1960s, and from full employment, women were educated alongside men and no longer saw home and domesticity as their natural destiny. Though the gap between women's and men's pay failed to narrow significantly (and even showed some signs of widening again as the 1990s drew to a close), women did advance steadily into higher-paid professional employment; by 1991 a third of all corporate managers and administrators and health professionals were women, as well as two thirds of all teaching professionals and nine out of ten health-associated professionals (Lindley 1994: 25); and women accounted for 18 percent of all MPs elected in 1997 (a total of 120, up from 60 in the previous parliament). There were still very few women at the top, for example as chief executive officers in banking and industry, but there were some; and many other indices of women's rising status and influence could be cited. Given the centrality of the media in the new order, the emergence of powerful women media figures—from the former BBC Radio 4 program controller Liz Forgan to the Express Newspapers editor Rosie Boycott—perhaps signified more clearly than anything else a shift—even if modest—away from the male-dominated social, political, and cultural agendas of the past. A parallel development that seemed to proceed in step with the advance of women was the reduction of discrimination against homosexuals, reflected both in a lowering of the legal age of consent and in public acceptance of gay men and women in public life.

All these diverse changes in the British power structure cannot as yet be subsumed under a simple analytic formula. The swirling currents released by the break-up of the corporatist logjam are significant as much for what they are—movement itself—as for where they may be tending. To call the changes of the last three decades the emergence of post-industrial, reflexive, individualized, society in Britain, with presidentialist, personalized, and mediatic politics, is not very helpful. What is clear is simply that the political system has slipped its class moorings and become to an unprecedented degree *market-driven*: a new system of political power whose essential and defining characteristics only the passage of time—and perhaps a period of testing by economic difficulty—will fully reveal.

Organization of television

If the future is uncertain, the nature of the immediate past is coming into clearer focus. The best way to make sense of the British television system is to see it as a relic of liberal corporatism which has survived into the post-corporatist era. This is the key to understanding both its strengths and limitations, its resilience and vulnerability.

But first, we give a brief account of its formal structure. The British television system has at its core five terrestial public service channels: BBC 1, BBC 2, Channels 3 (ITV), 4, and 5. Surrounding this core system are numerous cable and satellite TV channels of which the most successful are those controlled by Rupert Murdoch through the satellite-based organization, BSkyB. However, the public service system is still overwhelmingly dominant, and accounts for over 80 percent of total viewing time.

This core system is shaped by positive program requirements: in particular, to maintain quality, and offer variety (including informative programs). These objectives are advanced through public ownership (BBC and Channel 4), and through the regulation of commercial TV channels by the Independent Television Commission (ITC), which has the power to impose fines as well as shorten or revoke franchises.

This core system is constituted by different types of organization in order to foster program diversity. The BBC is one of the largest broadcasting organizations in the world, with over 20,000 employees, while Channel 4 is a shell organization that commissions but does not make programs. ITV is a regionally based network, while Channel 5 is London-based but transmits to most of the country. These organizations also have different sources of revenue in order to avoid head-to-head competition for the middle market. The BBC is financed by a license fee paid by all TV set owners. ITV and Channel 5 are funded by mass advertising, and Channel 4 by minority advertising.

When viewed in comparative perspective, British television has certain salient features. It is relatively independent of government. It is well resourced, with its revenues concentrated on two mass TV channels (BBC 1 and ITV). Its core system is heavily reliant on domestic production. Above all, its most distinctive characteristic is the relative freedom it allows its staff (Tunstall 1993). Program makers at the level of producer generally have more personal decision-making power than either their equivalents in the market-driven television of the United States or the more representative-directed public service systems in many European countries. The British approach plays down representation as an objective, and sees broadcasting as transcending both politics and social interest in a quasi-civil service model. In practice, this gives to professional broadcasters considerable leeway and freedom to interpret public guidelines.

Liberal corporatist inheritance

However, British broadcasting developed in the context of liberal corporatist power relationships, and has been shaped by these. Not only government, but also the main opposition party has an informal right of access to the microphone. The democratic authority of their views is respected within the conventions of broadcast reporting. From liberal corporatism has been derived also a recognizable broadcast rhetoric: a stress on reasonableness; a way of presenting political discourse as comprising different and legitimate points of view susceptible to agreement or compromise; and a tendency to define politics in terms of policy and problem-solving rather than as an expression of values and interests.

From this legacy has been created an independent sphere of communication that reports and debates the public direction of society. The public are viewed as citizens, with a right to be informed as well as entertained. In turn, the public views television as a more reliable and trustworthy source of news than the press.

Yet despite its strengths, British television is not in fact as removed from authority as its practitioners like to claim. British broadcasting is obliged by law to display "due impartiality." This is understood to mean that opposed interpetations should be foregrounded in reports of controversial issues. However, these opposed interpretations tend to reproduce the narrow arc of disagreement between the two competing parliamentary leaderships rather than the full range of disagreement in society. Moreover, the definition of what is controversial is strongly influenced by what is contentious between the political parties. If an issue does not come within an area of legitimated controversy, the conventions of balance tend to be downplayed or set aside.

This background helps to contextualize radical analyses of program bias. During the high tide of liberal corporatism from the 1940s to the 1970s, broadcasting responded to elite political consensus over a wide area of public life. Studies conducted by the Glasgow University Group, and others, reveal the way in which television journalism internalized assumptions hostile to trade unions in the 1970s; drew upon a limited repertoire of understandings when reporting issues relating to the economic management of Britain, also in the early 1970s; accepted Cold War categories relatively uncritically in making sense of the conflict between East and West over a long period; and provided a partisan account of the Falklands War in the early 1980s (Glasgow University Media Group 1976, 1980, 1985, McNair 1988). These ideological closures reflected a convergence between the official positions of the major parties over these issues.

But when the differences between the major political parties widened, and tensions in society grew in the 1980s, the discursive field of television expanded. Broadcasters gave airtime to voices that had been little heard before. For example, when all popular national newspapers were united for a time in attacking the allegedly Marxist-led Greater London Council, both television and radio opened up a debate. In addition to giving airtime to attacks, they also reported the view that the Council was doing positive things in the local community, and that its abolition—implemented in 1986 by the Thatcher government—was an attack on local democracy (Curran 1987 and 1990). Similarly television gave prominence in the late 1980s and early 1990s to the nation-wide campaign that was mounted against the "community charge," a regressive local tax opposed not only by Labour but also by organizations in the public, private and voluntary sectors, by demonstrators in the streets and ultimately by some senior Conservatives as well (Deacon and Golding 1994). What amounted almost to an anti-"law and order" campaign, focusing on miscarriages of justice, police violence, and penal reform, also received some sympathetic television coverage in the early 1990s (Schlesinger and Tumber 1994).

The election of a right-wing Labour government in 1997, and its acceptance of a large part of the Thatcherite legacy, seems to have reestablished an elite political consensus. Once again very little separates the major political parties, and the field of debate offered by broadcasting has narrowed. But the new movement toward closure is incomplete, and seems less secure than before. The new consensus is based more on populist manipulation than corporatist conciliation. It is sustained partly through increased pressure exerted by government publicists, which is generating a groundswell of resentment among broadcasters. The establishment in 1999 of elected assemblies in Scotland and Wales is also likely to produce a less unified state, and a more decentralized media system (Schlesinger 1998).

British broadcasting has also changed in a way that makes its incorporation more difficult. It has more channels; the BBC and ITV buy a quarter of their programs from the independent sector; and their staff are recruited from a wider social pool than before. Where once the BBC talked about serving the nation, it now stresses the need to respond to the diversity of a multicultural society (Scannell 1996).

Ambivalence

Moreover, this portrayal of broadcasting as, broadly, an extension of the leaderships of the main parliamentary parties, is a simplification that needs to be qualified on a number of counts. First, broadcast journalists are not entirely passive, and they work according to conventions that are not fully formalized. How they respond to the political environment is influenced by their own conceptions of what constitutes good journalism. One strand in the ideology of public service broadcasting emphasizes the imparting of knowledge, the disinterested briefing of the electorate. This routinely results in holders of accredited knowledge—such as doctors and scientists—gaining privileged access to the airwaves. Another strand emphasizes the importance of widening social access, of opening up debate to different voices and viewpoints. This is a subaltern tradition, but a significant one that has gained in influence within the broadcasting community. It has given rise to "access programs," new program formats allowing greater audience participation, and in some cases a new openness to a range of pressure groups and spokespersons representing ethnic, green, feminist, animal rights, and other new social movements outside the standard news beats (Curran 1997, Dowmunt 1997, Holland 1997, Livingstone and Lunt 1993). This reorientation to diverse pressure group sources is partly a response also to the decline of political parties as sources of loyalty, influence, and ideas. Finally, there is a well embedded element in broadcasters' professional culture that emphasizes their role in holding government to account. This can cut across political consensus, and lead broadcasters to initiate controversy. For example, in 1988 ITV broadcast the documentary *Death on the Rock*, which gave prominence to allegations that British troops had murdered an unarmed IRA active service unit in Gibraltar. The attempt by the government to suppress the program, and of newspapers to rubbish it, prompted ITV to retransmit the program, and encouraged the broadcasting industry to give it the top industry award. Both acts symbolized the broadcasting community's defiance of the government and the right-wing press.

The second qualification relates more broadly to the full output of television, including its entertainment. Broadcasters have responded to wider cultural changes in society, both as members of society and as communicators needing to relate to the changing concerns of audiences. For example, intergenerational shifts in the early 1960s gave rise to a new genre of satire programs attacking the moral conservatism of the older generation (Tracey 1982), and led in the later 1960s to a complete restructuring of radio music broadcasting (Chapman 1992). In the 1980s and 1990s, changing gender relations gradually penetrated broadcasting, most notably in soap opera and daytime chat shows, both with a predominantly female audience.

The third qualification has to do with the heterogeneity of the broadcasting system. While it is constrained in rather similar ways, it also exhibits some differences. Thus, Butler (1995) pointed out that the conflict in Northern Ireland was reported, to some extent, differently in Northern Ireland than in the rest of the United Kingdom. Similarly Schlesinger, Murdock and Elliott (1983) showed that radical TV drama offered understandings of Northern Ireland that broke with the political consensus. McNair (1988) found that perspectives contesting Cold War understandings occurred mainly in off-peak and minority programs, and Schlesinger and Tumber (1994) reported that Channel 4 sometimes framed news reporting differently from that of other channels.

Thus, broadcasting in Britain has been powerfully shaped by the consensus fashioned in Westminster, but has also been open to some extent to other influences. It is this which explains public service broadcasting's ambivalence. It is part of the political establishment without being wholly defined by it.

System under siege

The radical right mounted an assault on public service broadcasting in the 1980s and 1990s. The context seemed favorable. The Prime Minister, Margaret Thatcher, personally favored reform (Thatcher 1995). An influential section of the right-wing press was strongly critical of the BBC, while a media lobby pressed for greater deregulation of broadcasting (Goodwin 1999, O'Malley 1994). The ideological climate of the 1980s and 1990s seemed propitious. Free-market thinking was overwhelmingly dominant, yet the BBC had been conceived in a bygone era when public bureaucracies were viewed as agencies of progress and enlightenment (Scannell and Cardiff 1991). The rise of new communications technology had also undermined the traditional argument that regulation was needed in order to manage scarce airwave frequencies. "The original justification for public service broadcasting," declared a government White Paper, "no longer exists" (National Heritage 1992: 15).

In the event, the frontal assault on public service broadcasting failed because it did not secure the support of the Cabinet, the Conservative parliamentary party or the public. Public service broadcasting in Britain remains popular because it made, relatively early on, a strategic compromise between high culture and market values. It is respected because, despite compromises, it has retained a reputation for being independent of government. It is also valued for supporting quality and high standards, crucially on the right as well as on the left. But perhaps above all, it survived for much the same reason that other institutions of the welfare state weathered the rise of neoliberalism. There continues to be a collectivist political culture in Britain supporting public institutions that contribute to the general good (Curran 1998).

However, public service broadcasting was weakened in a variety of ways (Leys 1999). A key decision was taken to exempt cable and satellite TV from the need to provide variety, guarantee quality or, in the case of BSkyB, to originate programs. These partly deregulated channels generated a cumulative pressure on the entire broadcasting system to become more market-oriented. In the front line absorbing this pressure was the mass, public service–commercial Channel 3 (ITV). Its power to resist was weakened by the establishment of a "light touch" regulatory authority in 1990, and the "liberalization" that resulted in a series of Channel 3 company mergers. Its surrender to market values was symbolized in 1999 by its decision to dislodge its main evening news program in order to create an advertising-rich, news-free zone between 7 and 11 p.m. This was followed shortly afterwards by an announcement from Channel 4 that it was cutting back on minority programs.

This creeping marketization is eroding the autonomy of broadcasters in a new way. The effect of active regulation of commercial broadcasting before 1990 had been to create pockets of space in which some broadcast staff had considerable freedom to make important programs. These pockets are becoming smaller, and less insulated. At the same time, the BBC's survival strategy during the Thatcher era involved increased centralization and managerialism in ways that reduced staff autonomy (Barnett and Curry 1994, Curran and Seaton 1997). The mainspring of British broadcasting's quality, the relative freedom it allows to production teams, is being steadily depleted.

Press and corporate power

The British press differs from broadcasting in that it is unregulated, and almost entirely in private ownership. As a consequence, it connects to the power structure of British society in a different way.

Before considering this, brief reference should be made to the structure of the press. Unlike the press systems of most countries, the British press is predominantly national rather than local. Nationally distributed titles account for about two-thirds of total daily circulation. This dominant national press is made up of ten dailies and nine

Sunday papers. This multiplicity gives rise to two further characteristics. The national press is still very strongly influenced by competition, and it is polarized between minority newspapers for the "prestige" market (broadsheets) and newspapers for the mass market (tabloids).

The modern press in Britain grew out of the party system. By the 1940s and 1950s, there was still a relatively wide range of partisan newspapers whose allegiances were distributed between the major political parties. These papers' overall direction was strongly influenced by the liberal coporatist consensus of the period, and by the increase of journalistic autonomy and professional consciousness which reached its apogee in the 1960s. The press thus reflected approximately the balance of political opinion in the country, and became less partisan. Though privately owned, the press also retained close links to the democratic system (Curran and Seaton 1997, Koss 1984, Seymour-Ure 1996, Williams 1997).

However, the political complexion of the press shifted as a consequence of the closure of minority-popular newspapers, mainly on the left and center. From the 1960s onward, the press was largely bought up by or diversified into large conglomerate corporations. Editorial control also became more centralized, reversing the trend toward journalist autonomy. The implications of these changes became clear in the mid-1970s when the press became markedly more right-wing and partisan. It contributed to the Thatcherite mobilization of the late 1970s, culminating in the landmark general election of 1979. This inaugurated a period of unbroken Conservative rule for almost two decades, during much of which a large part of the national press adopted a cheerleading rather than adversarial stance. It endorsed enthusiastically a program of anti-union legislation, privatization, and low tax policies. In effect, a press owned by big business supported a party and political program receptive to the interests of big business.

That this rightward shift was due more to a change in the ownership and control of the press than to a change in the climate of opinion is indicated by the growing gap that developed between editorial and public opinion. The Conservative Party never obtained more than 44 percent of the vote in the four general elections between 1979 and 1992, but the Conservative press accounted for between 64 and 78 percent of national daily circulation (Seymour-Ure 1996: 217–18). The Conservative Party's share of circulation was some 50 percent greater than its share of the vote during this period.

How was this dealignment from public opinion possible in an intensely competitive market? One part of the answer is that tabloid newspapers put pleasure before politics. Indeed, the public affairs coverage of the popular press probably declined as a proportion of its total space. The tabloid press also refined a style of "attack journalism" which marries right-wing politics with entertainment. Tabloid jihads were directed at a succession of public enemies: squatters, football hooligans, union militants, scroungers, black muggers (and later rioters), Irish bombers, loony lefties, homosexuals, drug addicts, and paedophiles. Yet, tabloids shrewdly drew back from too explicit a form of evangelism. While editorials extolling the virtues of enterprise culture were published, these were not supported by attempts to glamorize business leaders.

Secondly, the newspaper market is not as competitive as it appears to be. Five groups controlled, in 1995, 96 percent of national newspaper circulation (National Heritage 1995). This oligopoly is protected by high entry costs. Even after the introduction of new print technology in the mid-1980s, it cost about £20 million to establish a new national daily. As a consequence, it has been difficult for groups without large capital and accumulated management expertise to break in. During the past fifty years, no national newspaper has been launched by an independent group, and stayed independent.

Thirdly, the British press is exposed to a range of influences other than its shareholders' commitments. It is shaped by external political developments, news source competition, journalists' sense of professionalism, perceptions of what readers want, and the wider cultural patterns of society (Curran 1998, Tunstall 1996). This gives rise to ideological tensions and differences of viewpoint within some newspapers, enabling them to reach out to different types of reader.

Globalization

Exposure to diverse influences also accounts for change in the press. The relationship between the national press and the Conservative Party soured during the 1990s. This was mainly a consequence of internal divisions within the Conservative hierarchy, principally over Europe. It was also fuelled by growing public disenchantment, and journalists' perception that "sleaze" had spread within the Conservative administration.

Yet, this souring had an unexpected denouement which perfectly illustrates the indirect rather than direct ways in which globalization is influencing both media and power in society. The conventional assumption that the "tendency is towards globalization, such that everybody, everywhere, will be viewing *Dallas* or *Dynasty* or the Olympics at the same time" (Katz 1996: 26) does not fit the British experience. British television remains largely national. ITV, Channel 4 and Channel 5 are required by ITC regulation to originate 65 percent of their programs in Europe, which largely means, in practice, Britain. This proportion of domestic production is more than matched by the BBC. These channels combined still account for the great bulk of TV viewing in Britain. The national press is even more British in its content and affiliation. International affairs accounts for a small and declining proportion of its content. The British press routinely makes the assumption that its readers are British; that they are mainly interested in what happens in Britain; and that they identify with other British people. Though part of the national press is owned by two transnational corporations based in Australia and Canada, they publish in fact the most nationalistic tabloid and broadsheet titles (*Sun* and *Daily Telegraph*) in Britain. Global media ownership should not be equated with internationalism.

Yet, globalization is influencing the British media by reshaping the political environment in which they operate. The development of global capitalism has weakened organized labor, and convinced the new Labour administration that labor flexibility and improved education are the best ways to adjust to the new realities of the global market. But it has also undermined organized Conservatism, revealing it to be "weak" in government, incapable of preventing currency depreciation in the face of adverse judgment by the international financial markets, and unable to protect its natural constituency. Globalization is, for reasons given earlier, weakening democratic power and helping to uncouple the political system from its class moorings.

Globalization is also destabilizing the institutional props of this old order. A key change took place in the 1997 general election when for the first time ever Labour secured more press support, in terms of circulation, than the Conservatives (Scammell and Harrop 1997). This was primarily a consequence of the mutual preelection courtship of Labour leader, Tony Blair, and the principal press magnate in Britain, Rupert

Murdoch. Blair signalled his sensitivity to Murdoch's interests when Labour unexpectedly attacked the Conservative government in 1996 for failing to go far enough in dismantling anti-monopoly media controls. Murdoch responded with fulsome praise for the promising, young Labour leader. These and other exchanges culminated in Britain's largest circulation newspaper, the *Sun*, shifting from its Conservative allegiance to back New Labour in the 1997 general election.

Murdoch is different from most of the dominant press barons who preceded him. An Australian, educated at Oxford University, and now an American citizen, at the head of a media empire girdling the globe, he is a citizen of the world. Unlike Lords Northcliffe, Cowdray, and Beaverbrook (all ex-government ministers) or archetypal press barons from the past like Lord Kemsley, Rupert Murdoch is not part of the Westminister scene. A global businessman with right-wing views, he has no emotional, family or social attachment to the Conservative Party in Britain. His tacit pact with Blair was simply a pragmatic arrangement between a corporate mercenary and a local, market-friendly politician that sidelined the public.

It was a defining moment, both for the media and for British politics. On the one hand it showed a major player in the global media market adapting to the reality of a national system of power which he could influence but not control. On the other hand, it revealed the transition of a leading political party of a nation-state from being the parliamentary wing of organized labor to becoming a professional machine of the North American type, eager to reach an understanding with corporate power. The speed of technological change in global communications, represented by the rise of Murdoch's media empire, was paralleled by the speed of political change at a national level, as politicians like Blair adjusted to the economic pressures and cultural shifts of increasing globalization. The interdependence of the media and politics had become unprecedentedly dynamic, and no longer analyzable within the framework of the nation-state alone; but it was still the essential starting-point for the understanding of either.

Notes

1 Even the economic journalist and *Observer* editor Will Hutton, who was highly sympathetic to the New Labour leadership, found that although they flirted briefly with his ideas about "stakeholder capitalism" (Hutton 1996) when they were still in opposition, they dropped them again unceremoniously when their unacceptability to the financial markets became obvious. It is true that the notoriously vacuous concept of "the third way," which Blair and his colleagues deployed extensively in 1998, was given a degree of philosophical respectability by Anthony Giddens, Director of the LSE (Giddens 1998). More symptomatic of New Labour thinking, however, was the contribution of Geoff Mulgan, founder and first director of the think-tank Demos, which specialized in "innovative" ways of talking about the epiphenomena of social life in a world whose comprehensive adaptation to the logic of corporate power it took for granted and even welcomed. In 1998 Mulgan resigned from Demos to become a full-time adviser to the government.

2 Indeed MPs themselves were casualties of the changed power system. The role of backbencher becomes still more thankless when even the power of frontbenchers is reduced, and when parliament has been displaced as a public forum by television and radio studios (the situation of Labour backbenchers was particularly pitiful in 1997–8, because of the huge size of the government's House of Commons majority; the party managers, well aware that the devil makes work for idle hands, took to sending MPs "home" in batches to do "constituency work"). To stand out of the crowd and secure some leverage *vis-à-vis* the party leadership an MP without private means now needed to find a way of raising his or her

income to something closer to parity with opposite numbers in business (in effect, to treble it). The circle was then complete—a successful career in politics required a successful career in the marketplace.

References

Barnett, S. and Curry, A. (1994) *The Battle for the BBC*, London: Aurum.

Beer, S. (1981) *Britain Against Itself: The Political Contradictions of Collectivism*, New York and London: Norton.

Blackwell, T. and Seabrook, J. (1985) *A World Still to Win: The Reconstruction of the Post-War Working Class*, London: Faber.

Butler, D. (1995) *The Trouble with Reporting Northern Ireland*, Aldershot: Avebury.

Chapman, R. (1992) *Selling the Sixties*, London: Routledge.

Commission on Social Justice (1994) *Social Justice*, London: IPPR.

Curran, J. (1987) "The boomerang effect: the press and the battle for London 1981–6," in J. Curran, A. Smith and P. Wingate (eds.) *Impacts and Influences*, London: Methuen.

Curran, J. (1990) "Culturalist perspectives of news organizations: reappraisal and case study," in M. Ferguson (ed.) *Public Communication*, London: Sage.

Curran, J. (1997) "Television journalism: theory and practice. The case of *Newsnight*," in P. Holland (ed.) *The Television Handbook*, London: Routledge.

Curran, J. (1998) "Crisis of public communication: a reappraisal," in T. Liebes and J. Curran (eds.) *Media, Ritual and Identity*, London: Routledge.

Curran, J. and Seaton, J. (1997) *Power Without Responsibility*, 5th edn, London: Routledge.

Dalton, R. (1990) *Challenging the Political Order: New Social and Political Movements in Western Democracies*, Cambridge: Polity.

Deacon, D. and Golding, P. (1994) *Taxation and Representation*, London: John Libbey.

Denver, D. (1989) *Elections and Voting Behaviour in Britain*, Deddington: Philip Allan.

Dowmunt, T. (1997) "Access: television at the margins," in P. Holland (ed.) *Television Handbook*, London: Routledge.

Dunleavy, P. (1997) "The globalization of public services production: can government be 'best in world'?," in A. Massey (ed.) *Globalization and Marketization of Government Services*, London: Macmillan.

General Household Survey (1988) London: Office of Population and Census Statistics.

Giddens, A. (1998) *The Third Way: The Renewal of Social Democracy*, Cambridge: Polity.

Glasgow University Media Group (1976) *Bad News*, London: Routledge and Kegan Paul.

Glasgow University Media Group (1980) *More Bad News*, London: Routledge and Kegan Paul.

Glasgow University Media Group (1985) *War and Peace News*, Milton Keynes: Open University Press.

Glyn, A. and Sutcliffe, B. (1972) *British Capitalism, Workers and the Profits Squeeze*, Harmondsworth: Penguin.

Goodwin, P. (1998) *Television Under the Tories*, London: British Film Institute.

Graham, A. (1997) "The UK 1979–95: Conservative capitalism," in C. Crouch and W. Streeck (eds.) *The Political Economy of Modern Capitalism*, London: Sage.

Hall, W. and Weir, S. (1996) *The Untouchables: Power and Accountability in the Quango State*, London: The Democratic Audit of the United Kingdom/The Scarman Trust.

Hobsbawm, E. (1998) "The death of neo-liberalism," *Marxism Today*, November–December, pp. 4–8.

Hoggart, R. (1957) *The Uses of Literacy*, London: Chatto and Windus.

Holland, P. (1997) *The Television Handbook*, London: Routledge.

Hutton, W. (1996) *The State We're In*, London: Quartet Books.

Jacques, M., Mulhern, F. and Hobsbawm, E. (1981) *The Forward March of Labour Halted?*, London: New Left Books.

Katz, E. (1996) "And deliver us from segmentation," *Annals of the Academy of Political and Social Science*, 546: 75–92.

Koss, S. (1984) *The Rise and Fall of the Political Press*, Vol. 2, London: Hamish Hamilton.

Leys, C. (1999) "The public sphere and the media: market supremacy versus democracy," in L. Panitch and C. Leys (eds.) *Global Capitalism Versus Democracy*, Rendlesham: Merlin Press.

Lindley, R. (ed.) (1994) *Labour Market Structures and Prospects for Women*, Manchester: Equal Opportunities Office.

Livingstone, S. and Lunt, P. (1993) *Talk on Television*, London: Routledge.

Mackintosh, M. and Hulme, D. (1998) "Public management for social inclusion," in M. Minogue, C. Polidano and D. Hulme (eds.) *Beyond the New Public Management*, London: Edward Elgar.

McNair, B. (1988) *Images of the Enemy*, London: Routledge.

Middlemas, K. (1980) *Politics in Industrial Society*, London: Deutsch.

National Heritage, Department of (1992) *Future of the BBC*, London: HMSO.

National Heritage, Department of (1995) *Media Ownership*, London: HMSO.

Nolan, Lord (1995) *First Report of the Committee on Standards in Public Life*, London: HMSO.

O'Malley, T. (1994) *Closedown?*, London: Pluto.

Panitch, L. (1976) *Social Democracy and Industrial Militancy: The Labour Party, the Trade Unions and Incomes Policy 1945–1974*, Cambridge: Cambridge University Press.

Panitch, L. and Leys, C. (1997) *The End of Parliamentary Socialism: From New Left to New Labour*, London: Verso.

Polito, A. (1998) *Cool Britannia: Gli Inglesi (E Gli Italiani) Visti da Londra*, Rome: Donzelli.

Power, M. (1997) *The Audit Society: Rituals of Verification*, Oxford: Oxford University Press.

Rhodes, R. A. W. (1994) "The hollowing out of the state: the changing nature of the public service in Britain," *Political Quarterly*, 65(2): 138–51.

Rose, N. (1993) "Government, authority and expertise in advanced liberalism," *Economy and Society*, 22(3), August: 283–99.

Scammell, M. and Harrop, M. (1997) "The press," in D. Butler and D. Kavanagh *The British General Election of 1997*, London: Macmillan.

Scannell, P. (1996) "Britain: public service broadcasting, from national culture to multiculturalism," in M. Raboy (ed.) *Public Broadcasting for the 21st Century*, Luton: University of Luton Press.

Scannell, P. and Cardiff, D. (1991) *Serving the Nation*, Oxford: Blackwell.

Scharpf, F. W. (1991) *Crisis and Choice in European Social Democracy*, Ithaca, NY: Cornell University Press.

Seymour-Ure, Colin 1997, *The British Press and Broadcasting Since 1945*, Oxford: Blackwell.

Schlesinger, P. (1998) "Scottish devolution and the media," in J. Seaton (ed.) *Politics and the Media*, Oxford: Blackwell.

Schlesinger, P. and Tumber, H. (1994) *Reporting Crime*, Oxford: Clarendon.

Schlesinger, P., Murdock, G. and Elliott, P. (1983) *Televising Terrorism*, London: Commedia.

Shaoul, J. (1999) "Economic and financial context: the shrinking state?" in S. Corby and G. White (eds.) *Employee Relations in the Public Services*, London: Routledge.

Thatcher, M. (1995) *The Downing Street Years*, London: HarperCollins.

Timmins, N. (1995) *The Five Giants: A Biography of the Welfare State*, London: HarperCollins.

Tracey, M. (1982) *A Variety of Lives*, London: Bodley Head.

Tunstall, J. (1993) *Television Producers*, London: Routledge.

Tunstall, J. (1996) *Newspaper Power*, Oxford: Clarendon Press.

Williams, K. (1997) *Get Me a Murder a Day*, London: Arnold.

16 De-Westernizing Australia?

Media systems and cultural coordinates

Stuart Cunningham and Terry Flew

Australian media demonstrate a hybrid quality, with its mainstream elements fashioned out of the intersection of British and American structures. A commitment to public service broadcasting and a "Fourth Estate" journalistic ethos exists alongside an unabashedly popular commercial sector, which has predominated in both broadcasting and print. To this established mainstream hybrid has been added significant new elements. The unique Special Broadcasting Service (SBS) arose as a result of contemporary progressive politics and policies of multiculturalism as a top–down strategy of governance, while there has also been support for bottom–up initiatives in the community broadcasting sector. These developments have occurred alongside further commercialization of mass media with the introduction of subscription broadcasting services and deregulation of related industries such as telecommunications.

The mix is distinctive and dynamic despite very high levels of media ownership concentration—particularly in print media, where Rupert Murdoch's News Corporation controls over 70 percent of the daily newspaper market—and evidence of further concentrations of power in response to convergence of technologies. It is also dynamic in spite of a tacit protocol of power-sharing in the modes of interaction between media power brokers and the state, which gives Australian media policy a strong corporatist flavor (also characteristic of other areas of policy, notably in the case of the Accord between the Federal Labor Government (1983–96) and the trade union movement) and elements of outright cronyism, or what Chadwick (1989) termed the "media mates" approach to policy formation. Australia is also increasingly self-identifying as part of the Asian region, in spite of its original status as a British convict and colonial outpost and the "European" orientation of much of its population. The extent to which its media performance and practices can and should be seen on a continuum with those of Eastern states and cultures can be treated as a case study in the project to de-Westernize media studies.

Cultural coordinates

It is possible to argue that "when Australia became modern, it ceased to be interesting"—interesting, that is, to an international cultural intelligentsia and anthropological audience (Miller 1994: 206). What made Australia "interesting" in the late nineteenth and early twentieth century was both the radically premodern cultural difference of its indigenous peoples set against a transplanted white settler colonial culture, and the utopian belief that the ideals of the European Enlightenment could be transplanted upon the *Terra Nullius* which, until the Australian High Court's Mabo judgment of

1992, Australia was held to be by its settler population under British Crown law. Equally, it is arguable that what may again trigger international interest in Australia, due in no small part to its media output, is its emerging profile as a postcolonial and multicultural society—a postmodern "recombinant" culture—well suited to playing a role in global cultural exchange.

Andrew Milner (1991) argues that social and cultural modernity was only ever partially realized in Australia, making it a society ripe for a rapid turning towards globalization and postmodernity:

> Australia has been catapulted towards post-industrialism at a speed possible only in a society that had never fully industrialized; towards consumerism in a fashion barely imaginable in historically less affluent societies; towards an aesthetic populism unresisted by any indigenous experience of a seriously adversarial high culture; towards an integration into multinational late capitalism easily facilitated by longstanding pre-existing patterns of economic dependence; towards a sense of being "after," and of being post-European, entirely apposite to a colony of European settlement suddenly set adrift, in intellectually and imaginatively uncharted Asian waters, by the precipitous decline of a distant Empire.
> (Milner 1991: 116)

Although Milner points to reasons why Australian media have a certain dynamism within globalizing and postmodern cultural exchange, his is a one-sided account. There have been strong modernist institutions and structures in Australia, and a reliance on an interventionist state with three ramified layers of government arising out of modernist projects of nation-building.

Australia's media, then, exhibit both modern and postmodern characteristics. The central public broadcaster, the Australian Broadcasting Corporation (ABC), seeks to fulfil its Charter functions as an instrument of national citizenship and "common culture" while also needing to exploit commercial and corporate opportunities in new markets in Asia through satellite television, new media, and strong ancillary marketing. The mega-budget "event" television of the 1980s, the historical mini-series, enjoyed great popular success on the commercial networks while also being imbued with the nation-building ethos of revivifying popular memory around defining moments in Australian history (Cunningham 1993). Film financing policy has also been influenced by the desire to combine critical and commercial success with occasions for mass popular reflection upon national identity, most notably with the period dramas of the late 1970s such as *Picnic at Hanging Rock* and *Breaker Morant* (Dermody and Jacka 1987; see also O'Regan 1997).

Ross Gibson (1992) depicts the ambivalent nature of Australia as an antipodal relay point between Europe and Asia, the local and the global, the old and the new in these evocative terms:

> For two hundred years the South Land has been a duplicitous object for the West. On the one hand, Australia is demonstrably "European society," with exhaustive documentation available concerning its colonial inception and development. Yet on the other hand, because the society and its habitat have also been understood (for much longer than two hundred years) in the West as fantastic and otherworldly, the image of Australia is oddly doubled. Westerners can recognize them-

selves there at the same time as they encounter an alluringly exotic and perverse entity, the phantasm called Australia. Westerners can look South and feel "at home," but, because the region has also served as a projective screen for European aspiration and anxiety, Australia also calls into question the assumptions and satisfactions by which any society or individual feels at home.

(Gibson 1992: x).

Discussing the wide international as well as domestic success of the 1986 film *Crocodile Dundee* (it is the all-time top grossing Australian film), Meaghan Morris (1988) points to the "positive unoriginality" of such a film in negotiating the tensions between cultural nationalism and global film industry economics. Morris shows how *Crocodile Dundee* exemplifies the dynamism of Australian culture in turning its derivativeness (as British colonial outpost and mendicant of the US) to its advantage, producing a "recombinant" cultural product well suited to the demands of the contemporary global film industry while also invoking a "sense of place" characteristic of national cinemas.

Australian film and television provide important case studies of the degree to which success in international media markets entails "playing at being American" (Caughie 1990). Tom O'Regan (1993) refers to the "double face" of Australian television, where cheap imported programs cross-subsidize local production under a policy regime of domestic content quotas, and where Australian television production and reception are profoundly moulded by the import/export dynamic of industries which benchmark against the most successful international models (the US and to a lesser extent the UK), but also where industry economics necessitate generic formats which can be exported as low-cost "filler" into the programming schedules of European, Asian, South Pacific and North American broadcasters (Cunningham and Jacka 1996).

The Australian television system has bred a talent for successful low-budget production, and has attracted a reputation (for good or ill) throughout the world for it. Concerns were expressed for a time about the possible "Australian" future of European television production in a more open globalized audiovisual system: "The question is whether the European programme industry has to follow the Australian recipe: imitation of American TV formulas, thus stimulating the globalisation and homogenisation of the international TV market" (de Bens *et al.* 1992: 94). In New Zealand, there is a view that Australian television is also a trojan horse for US culture: "Australian programmes are merely American programmes once-removed ... as a consequence of the internationalization of television, Australian television networks had readily adopted formats and styles 'born in the US'" (Lealand 1990: 102).

Populist engagement has been a characteristic Australian negotiation of tensions between the national and the international. Rupert Murdoch, head of News Corporation and Australia's singular contribution to the global pantheon of media moguls (even though he has been a United States citizen since 1985), sometimes has his status as the "ringmaster of the information circus" (Shawcross 1992) attributed to perceived "Australian" characteristics of sharp practice, anti-establishment commitments, and brash populist beliefs. This is particularly so in Britain, where he has been highly influential in newspapers and satellite television, but increasingly through Asia with his take-over of Star TV, and his lead in the expansion and commercialization of television in Asia, eastern Europe, and India. Lumby and O'Neil draw attention to News's Australian lineage when they point out that:

Tabloid television, as the term is generally understood, was born in the United States. But before anyone cries Yankee cultural imperialism, they should consider this: if the Americans nurtured the genre, Australians fathered it.

(Lumby and O'Neil 1994: 152)

Structure of Australian media

Australian media is characterized by the dominance of commercial, private sector interests and logics, albeit with a strong history of state subvention and regulation, and the structuring of markets by political as well as economic means. Australian broadcasting has a long history of a "dual system" of public service and commercial sectors which dates from the early 1930s, when the two sectors were termed the A and B class stations, with equivalent audience expectations of highbrow or lowbrow, or informative or entertaining program content (Johnson 1988). Television was introduced in 1956 on the basis of a similar dual system logic. To this structure has been added, in the early 1980s, a specialist multicultural public service broadcaster, the SBS, which has, since 1992, taken advertising to supplement its government appropriation, and during the 1990s both pay television—delivered through cable, satellite, and microwave mixtures—and community television delivered on the little remaining bandwidth for terrestrial television in the main metropolitan markets. The SBS has attracted much international attention as an innovative quality service and has been described as "the lean, hungry, efficient, postmodern TV of tomorrow" (Hartley 1992: 200), and by Canadian communications theorist Dallas Smythe as "creative in a way that I haven't encountered in television programming previously anywhere" (in More 1990: 57). In the late 1990s, a television broadcasting ecology exists which sees the ABC (12–15 percent) and the SBS (2–3 percent) occupying between 14 and 18 percent of the audience share, the three established commercial networks between them occupying around 80 percent of audience share. In addition, the penetration of Australian homes by the three pay television services (Foxtel, Optus Vision and Austar) is reaching 15 percent.

There is very high concentration in print media ownership, with News Corporation controlling over 70 percent of the daily newspaper market. News's competitors are much smaller and increasingly divided. The Fairfax interests own approximately 22 percent of the market and are strategically placed through ownership of two flagship quality broadsheets, the *Age* and the *Sydney Morning Herald* and the flagship business daily the *Australian Financial Review*. However, Fairfax is increasingly squeezed between the global leviathan of News and the local but aggressive cross-media interests of the Packer family, which controls Nine, the leading commercial television network, and is the dominant player in the lucrative magazine market (circulation is divided between Packer's company PBL at 46 percent and News Ltd at 26 percent). Packer has shown strong interest in buying into Fairfax when the politics of changing cross-media ownership rules are right. The malleability of cross-media and foreign ownership laws and regulations has regularly been and is an increasingly strategic issue for the major media players as technical and corporate convergence proceeds.

Cinema distribution and exhibition are highly concentrated. The four major distributors, three of whom are foreign owned and controlled—Village Roadshow Distributors, United International Pictures, Colombia Tristar, and Twentieth Century Fox—control over 90 percent of the market. In exhibition, the majors are majority Australian-owned, but the three largest, Greater Union, Village Roadshow and Hoyts, together control almost all metropolitan outlets and receive 70 percent of the cinema box office. The fourth largest company, Birch Carroll and Coyle, is regionally based and is a wholly owned subsidiary of Greater Union. Greater Union is a major shareholder in Village Roadshow, and Greater Union, Village Roadshow, and Warners (US) in a joint venture control a further large slice of the exhibition market.

There is a long history of anti-competitive practices in the distribution sector of the industry, with exhibitors claiming that the market power of US-owned distribution companies make it virtually impossible to operate outside the marketing strategies of the US majors and that they are able to extract extortionate conditions for film release because film distribution is more concentrated in Australia than in the US, Japan, and most European countries. This has meant that there has been a continuing theme throughout the century of local production being marginalized within the structures of distribution and exhibition in the country, and a history where governments, rather than take on the entrenched power of foreign-owned cinema interests, have positioned their interventions around production support rather than regulation of distribution.

Australian film production, then, is very much a creature of public policy and funding. Variations of the theme of cultural nationalism have always been the key rationale for such support, ranging over time from the view in the 1970s that Australian films could help Australians to "tell their own stories, [and] dream their own dreams" (Morphett, quoted in Appleton 1991), to the hopeful declarations of *Creative Nation*, the cultural policy statement of the Keating Labor Government released in 1994, that "so long as we are assured of our own heritage and talents, we have nothing to fear from being open to other cultural influences" (DoCA 1994: 6), and that "culture is one of our most intelligent exports" (Keating 1995: 6).

Media and power in Australia

Interest in the relationships between media and power has been a recurrent theme of Australian media studies. It has been strongly associated with the political economy tradition, as there is a strong historical association in Australia between political economy and cultural nationalism. It follows from the thesis that Australia has been a political and economic "client state" of Britain and, in the twentieth century, the United States, and hence unable to develop strong local industries outside of the agricultural, mining, and tourism sectors, and that this engenders an internalized sense of subordination (or cultural "cringe") among elites in Australia, who judge Australian culture to be inferior to the output of metropolitan centers (Buckridge 1988, Crough and Wheelwright 1983, Wheelwright and Buckley 1988). There has also been populist opposition to media barons such as Murdoch and Packer and their forebears, a cultural nationalist counter-tendency to the influence of American popular culture, and suspicion of the depth of links between Australia's political leaders and their "media mates" (Chadwick 1989, Pilger 1989). One of the ABC's most popular programs in the 1990s has been *Media Watch*, a program headed for most of the period by a prominent QC and barrister who was once a crusading broadcast journalist, which forensically advances allegations that news is managed, syndicated and, if necessary, suppressed in ways favorable to proprietors and other elites, alongside specific exposés of the declining standards of the Fourth Estate.

However, traditions of political economy analysis need to take account of concrete circumstances in a peripheral, Second World nation such as Australia. Its peripheral and subordinate position within the global system means that strategies for promoting alternatives to globalized and commodified capitalist circuits frequently involve the strengthening of nationally based institutions, in spite of the limits of such institutions, and the nation-state more generally, as a vehicle for realizing progressive and egalitarian political goals.

Public broadcasting is a case in point. Like many other such institutions, the ABC can be criticized for its integrationist approach to a broadly shared official culture, its association of quality with noncommercialism, and its lumbering bureaucratic nature. Nonetheless, the ABC remains a fundamental strut of the Australian information and cultural ecology, with a commitment to national news which simultaneously incorporates the range of local and regional perspectives with a distinctively Australian perspective on international issues. Its commitment to local content in all of its TV and radio services, and to the promotion of diversity and producer autonomy in its slate of local programming, marks it out sharply from commercial services whose programming strategies frequently involve the rebranding of imported material and a perpetual circulation of network stars rather than providing windows to new talent and new ideas. The wars of attrition and outright attack by powerful political opponents for many years of its history—and consistently during the 1990s—are evidence of its strategic and progressive place in the polity.

Equally, when critics from the political economy tradition argue, in the context of economic globalization and multiculturalism, that a progressive future in Australia entailed a need to "transcend the nation" (e.g. Castles *et al.* 1988), and attain a "community without nation," they ignore the extent to which the most durable and significant cultural formations which represent a "post-national" consciousness, such as the Special Broadcasting Service (SBS), are the direct outgrowth of national government policies which promoted multicultural and minoritarian concerns precisely because they were in the national interest.

> National rhetorics, which might appear transparently ideological to [these] social critics, are of recent vintage and are quite vulnerable to the stronger imperatives toward internationalization which have such a persuasive technological and economic cachet. Without a national cultural infrastructure, and a workable rhetoric to sustain it, the sources for enlivening community, local, regional or ethnic cultural activity would be impoverished.
>
> (Cunningham 1992: 43)

The political economy approach argues that changes to media arising from globalization or new media technologies largely mark a continuation of existing power structures rather than a modification or undermining of established sources of power (Garnham 1997, Mosco 1995). This opens up questions, which have been put with particular strength in cultural studies (Hall 1986, Hartley 1996), of whether it is adequate to understand power in top–down terms, or whether power needs to be thought of as more diffuse and, in Foucault's terms, capillary in its operations at multiple levels of social relations? After two decades of attention to the provenance of the audience in media and cultural studies, and the potential polysemy of media texts, if we are to think afresh about the media and power, it is worth at least considering relations of power between controlling interests, media producers, and audiences/consumers, with none of these three categories being homogeneous and predetermined in its forms of agency.

The power of the audience for Australian television outside the population hubs of Sydney and Melbourne (which account for approximately 45 percent of the Australian population) to influence programming or production has certainly shrunk over the past decade, with greater centralization of programming buttressed by more insistent rhetorics of regional sensitivity which mask the loss of actual programming responsive in the nonmetropolitan areas of the country. On the other hand, the clear tendency for younger demographic segments (particularly teenagers and the 18–24-year-old group) to watch less television and engage more widely in interactive computer-based entertainment—and what this may signify for the future of broadcast television, particularly when viewing patterns during the 1990s show significant declines in share for early evening information programming—signifies a shift of power which media owners and producers must respond to over time. Equally, the dramatic decline in the newspaper reading base—a pattern replicated in most developed countries of the world and which has been consistent over a forty-year period—has demanded radical changes to the nature of newspapers. In Australia, the tabloid segment of the newspaper market has moved almost entirely into the burgeoning field of magazines. Newspapers have consistently moved upmarket, in what is perceived as a rapidly segmenting market. Most newspapers have positioned themselves for a crossover of at least some significant portions of their activities into fully online formats with very active Web presences from the mid-1990s, while proprietors have had to move outside of print exclusively, with very variable corporate outcomes.

Of course, none of this has modified significantly the established sources of power at the ownership end of the media power continuum—within its own explanatory grids, political economy is right. Consistent with the experience of many countries of the world, established owners have positioned themselves in the new media markets in order to spread risk and take "first mover" advantage of breakthroughs in the commercialization potentials of the Internet. Murdoch's News has built on its dominant position in print with strategic shareholdings in the second most popular commercial television network (Network 7), and as one of two dominant shareholders in pay television company Foxtel (which is well positioned to emerge from the inevitable shake-out of the new pay television industry as the dominant if not the only player in subscription television). News has moved into highly strategic partnerships with the dominant telecommunications carrier, Telstra, for both subscription television and online services, while Packer's Nine Network has joined with Microsoft for delivery of Australian online services.

And, ironically, dominant players like News have not been slow in appropriating for their own purposes the rhetorics of the active audience and of consumer sovereignty. (For example, News's submission to the 1997 Review of Media Ownership Regulation and Law in Australia contained a study which purported to show that News was low on a list of media companies when measured in terms of the amount of time consumers spent with the products of those companies. This form of measurement is, of course, highly tendentious, as it conveniently skirts the influence which elite media, the metropolitan and national quality dailies such as New's *The Australian*, are able to exert on the national political agenda without commanding a large readership.) This is where media studies' championship of the active audience converges ominously with economic rationalism's championing of consumer sovereignty, and is vulnerable to a takeover by corporate interests.

Australian governments have shown themselves particularly partial to not earning the ire of powerful media owners, and this has taken a thoroughly bipartisan political color. Lobbying by commercial interests saw government endorse a dominant commercial TV system in the late 1940s, after intense debate about the importance of keeping such an influential medium in public hands (Curthoys 1986). Murdoch was advantaged by a conservative government in the early 1980s when he was allowed to "grandfather" his control of the Ten television network to avoid being required to sell down to new ownership-reach limits. The Hawke Labor Government's changes to media ownership laws in 1987 cemented the power of network control and its inevitable centralization in Sydney and Melbourne. And it was arguably only the inability to be able to potentially assist both of Australia's dominant media moguls, Packer and Murdoch—with their irreconcilable sets of expansionary strategies—which led the Howard conservative government in 1997 not to change the media ownership rules. Recent gala receptions of media moguls (such as Murdoch and Bill Gates) by Prime Ministers and Cabinets of both major political persuasions indicate an ongoing perception that a small power placed on the geographical and political margins of the world needs "powerful friends" (a phrase used to describe Australia's foreign policy posture towards first Britain and then the US during this century), not just and perhaps even more in the emerging information- and knowledge-based industries of the future.

De-Westernizing Australia

A much better grounding in the empirics of non-Western media systems is needed, using models which will allow us to make enlightening contemporary comparisons across regions and across the world. The outdatedness and inadequacy of models such as those developed many years ago by Siebert *et al.* (1956) and McQuail (1987) are glaring today. A categorization of East–West is also inadequate to encompass world regions today, as it treats the regions as relatively homogeneous and differentiated on an axis derived from normative Western models. A more powerful model may be to differentiate along colonial/imperial and postcolonial lines, such that the divisions would be the West, the postcolonial, the communist and the postcommunist. The region of East Asia would then be divided into the socialist and communist states of the PRC, North Korea, Burma/Myanmar, Laos, Cambodia, and Vietnam and the capitalist states of Japan, South Korea, Taiwan, Thailand, Indonesia, Singapore, Malaysia, Brunei and the Philippines. Many of these have had a distinctive history of colonization: the French in Vietnam, Laos, and Cambodia; the British in Burma, Brunei, Singapore, Malaysia, and Hong Kong; the Spanish and the Americans in the Philippines; the Dutch in Indonesia. There has been the powerful impact on the modern histories of many of these countries of Japanese occupation leading up to and during the Second World War. Those countries which had not experienced a sustained period of recent colonization—Japan, Mainland China, Taiwan, and Thailand—have, in most cases, been strongly influenced by Western models of economic development, and political and administrative organizations. The clear exception to this rule is the PRC.

Having set up this model of the countries of the region, what is the value of placing Australia within it? To attempt this may open up issues central to the methodologies of media studies, in case-study format. Given that Australia is the most Western nation in the Asian region, it is of interest to consider how the limits of a Western liberal pluralist model of press freedom and the fourth estate are played out in the region, with Australia considered in terms of regional practice. And Asian migration and refugee resettlement into Australia (the "Asia in Australia" side of the "Australia in Asia" theme), and the state policies and media responses to which such population movements give rise, offer examples of the loosening of the gross geopolitical categorization of East and West (with the introduction of a deterritorialized "fourth world," and relations between core, semiperipheral, and peripheral nations) and of the limits of, and genuine alternatives to, mainstream media.

The notion of "Asian values" in cultural and media systems may be questioned as the expression of political elites attempting to foster economic liberalization while maintaining strict limits on political and cultural liberalization. Nevertheless, the "Asian values" critique of a West which promotes adversarial media cultures for their own sake, and seems too sanguine about the spread of anti-social values, is a critique shared by broad sections of Western publics as well as by political elites in certain Asian countries. The argument that it is only the imperatives of nation-building in the developing regions of the world which justify "non-Western" communitarian values in news and the media is brought in to question if the solidly communitarian approaches to media practice in leading economies such as Japan, South Korea, and Singapore are taken into account.

It is not the case that there is an ideal Western practice of the media in a liberal democracy, which the majority of the other media systems of the world either failed to live up to or take as a model of aspiration. In many cases, the ideals of liberalism and pluralism are used to generate far more radical models of media reform than are found currently in the West. In other cases, there are sophisticated and sustainable arguments in defense of development communication, the critique of overly adversarial and oppositional journalistic styles, or the excessive emphasis on masculine individualism and violence in Western media. And, if even only elements of the analysis offered by Noam Chomsky on the ideological and propagandistic control exercised by Western media in its severely distorting coverage of global politics and economics are correct (Chomsky and Herman 1988), then the differences between Western and non-Western news production center on the nature and methods of controls on them, and potential for contesting that control, rather than purely on freedom versus control.

The extent to which it is possible to buy journalistic favors, and the methods used to elicit such favors, exist on a continuum in the region from direct bribes to the subtleties of the way the "envelope culture" of Indonesian journalism is an expression of Javanese gift-giving through to the spread of advertorial content in the lifestyle, motoring, wine, real estate, employment, and travel sections of many if not most Western newspapers. Similarly, the ethos of development journalism and communication is not the sole preserve of the "developing" world. It can be found in Western countries, precisely at those moments at which their strategic interests, particularly in international trade, are vested in their ability to project themselves symbolically and financially into international markets. The ABC's recent Australia Television satellite and cable regional channel (1993–7) was conducted as a form of "second track diplomacy" and its guidelines for news production reflected the values of development journalism (Cunningham and Jacka 1996: 205–13). To the extent that multiculturalism, as the official policy of the Australian state, is directly promoted within the representational and editorial practices of the SBS and to a lesser extent the ABC, and indirectly through affirmative action and equality of opportunity employment practices at those and other media companies, this strongly points to an ethos of developmental nation-building and promotion of civic tolerance which is on a continuum of socially engineered racial pluralism as practiced in Asian countries.

Taking a broader, social rather than media-centric view, it is notable that, despite the image of the Australian media (particularly in some countries in Asia) as having aggressive oppositionism, and adversarial relations with and independence from government, they exist in a country which is one of the only countries of the region—certainly of the Southeast Asian region—not to have experienced a major revolution or overt struggle for decolonization. This is of singular significance for the authors of a contemporary analysis of Australia's media in relation to the region's media systems:

> Surprisingly, for a country that prides itself on its adversarial nature, Australia provides very few examples of truly "resistant" or "oppositional" mainstream media. Despite it emphasis on debate and confrontation with politicians and other authority figures, Australia is one of the few countries in the region never to have had a genuine revolution or to have systematically rejected its colonial past. Behind the rhetoric of confrontation there seems to lie (for most of the population) an easy acceptance of the status quo.
>
> (Berry *et al.* 1996: 218–19)

Apart from the strong but recent agenda in the ABC of positive coverage and equal employment opportunity for Aboriginal and Torres Strait Islander citizens, and the role of the SBS in actively propagandizing multiculturalism in the Australian public sphere, most of the resistant or alternative agendas—those which relate to marginalized and deterritorialized populations—are found in community media and in the usually non-English-language video sectors. Consider, to conclude this chapter, the case of Asian communities' media in Australia.

Australia is one of the most multicultural nations on earth, and is, in proportional terms, the world's second largest immigrant nation next to Israel, with 40 percent of its population born elsewhere or at least one parent born elsewhere. In 1947, the Australian population was 7.6 million, of whom only 9.8 percent were overseas-born. Of these, 90 percent were from Great Britain and Ireland. By the mid-1980s, the proportion born overseas had grown to 21 percent, while another 20 percent had one or both parents born overseas. More than half of Australia's post-Second World War population growth was driven by immigration, with the proportions changing from overwhelmingly British and Irish to migrants from eastern and southern Europe and, since the 1970s, Asia, Africa, the Americas, and the Middle East. In response to this, Australian governments have constructed, from the late 1970s, an official policy of multiculturalism, and organized an impressive array of state support for this policy, including the Special Broadcasting Service (SBS), which is both a TV and radio broadcaster, one of the few major public broadcasters in the world dedicated to not only the reflection but also the propagation of multiculturalism.

However, the fact of the largest immigrant groups being historically Anglo-Irish; the sheer variety of immigrant and refugee/humanitarian communities (at present, over 150 ethnic groups speaking over 100 different languages); the fact that immigration has occurred in several distinct waves over a period of fifty years (some earlier groups successfully negotiated their resettlements more than a generation ago, while many Asian groupings have only begun the process); and the relatively low numbers of any individual group has meant that a critical mass of a few dominant NESB (non-English-speaking background) groupings has not made the impact that Spanish-speaking Hispanic cultures, for example, have made in the United States. Nor do Australians experience "strong" cultural diversity through policies of official multilingualism (such as in Canada); nor the considerable cultural intermixing caused by the sheer contiguity of the major imperial languages in Europe; nor the significant accommodation in the daily life, the polity, and in the public rhetorics of those societies with a critical mass of indigenous persons, such as New Zealand. Add to this a history of direct subvention to multicultural cultural forms from government arts bodies that has tended to focus on the folkloric and the literary rather than on the most popular cultural forms such as video and popular music, and you can get, with the exception of zones of "official" contact like the SBS, community radio and the like, a sort of mutual distance and official monolingual incomprehension in terms of cultural diversity in the media. As Jamrozik *et al.* (1995) put it, the bulwarks of monocultural power in Australia, which include the mainstream media, have yet to be challenged.

Asian communities have therefore constructed a media environment for purposes of cultural maintenance and negotiation with the dominant host culture that significantly displaces consumption of the mainstream (Cunningham 1997). This involves accessing the "global narrowcast" output of US-based small business entrepreneurs producing music video in the case of the Vietnamese diaspora. For Chinese communities, product is made available through specialist subscription channels providing both news and movie and television serials and series and through Chinese movie theatres. For other less numerous groups, the media environment is created through middleperson initiatives including flying in tapes of recent series drama on a weekly basis, film nights or concerts featuring community-based stars. The mainstream media environment has barely begun to take account of the million-plus Asian-Australians in the community.

References

Appleton, G. (1991) "How Australia sees itself: the role of commercial television," in Australian Broadcasting Tribunal, *Oz Content: An Inquiry into Australian Content on Commercial Television*, Vol. 3, Sydney: Australian Broadcasting Tribunal.

Berry, C., Birch, D., Dermody, S., Grant, J., Hamilton, A., Quilty, M. and Sen, K. (1996) "The media," in A. Milner and M. Quilty (eds.) *Australia in Asia: Comparing Cultures*, Melbourne: Oxford University Press.

Buckridge, P. (1988) "Intellectual authority and critical traditions in Australian literature 1945 to 1975," in B. Head and J. Walter (eds.) *Intellectual Movements and Australian Society*, Melbourne: Oxford University Press.

Castles, S., Kalantzis, M., Cope, B. and Morrissey, M. (1988) *Mistaken Identity: Multiculturalism and the Demise of Nationalism in Australia*, Sydney: Pluto Press.

Caughie, J. (1990) "Playing at being American: games and tactics," in P. Mellencamp (ed.) *Logics of Television: Essays in Cultural Criticism*, Bloomington and Indianapolis: Indiana University Press.

Chadwick, P. (1989) *Media Mates: Carving Up Australia's Media*, Melbourne: Sun Books.

Chomsky, N. and Herman, E. S. (1988) *Manufacturing Consent: The Political Economy of the Mass Media*, New York: Pantheon Books.

Crough, G. and Wheelwright, E. S. (1983) *Australia: A Client State*, Sydney: Allen and Unwin.

Cunningham, S. (1992) *Framing Culture: Criticism and Policy in Australia*, Sydney: Allen and Unwin.

Cunningham, S. (1993) "Style, form and content in the Australian mini-series," in J. Frow and M. Morris (eds.) *Australian Cultural Studies: A Reader*, Sydney: Allen and Unwin.

Cunningham, S. (1997), "Floating lives: multicultural broadcasting and diasporic video in Australia," in K. Robins (ed.) *Programming for People: From Cultural Rights to Cultural Responsibilities*, report presented by RAI–Radiotelevisione Italiana in association with the European Broadcasting Union.

Cunningham, S. and Jacka, E. (1996) *Australian Television and International Mediascapes*, Cambridge: Cambridge University Press.

Curthoys, A. (1986) "The getting of television: dilemmas in ownership, control and culture 1941–56," in A. Curthoys and J. Merritt *Better Dead than Red: Australia's First Cold War 1945–1959*, Vol. 2, Sydney: Allen and Unwin.

De Bens, E., Kelly, M. and Bakke, M. (1992) "Television content: dallasification of culture?," in K. Siune and W. Truetzschler (eds. for the Euromedia Research Group) *Dynamics of Media Politics: Broadcast and Electronic Media in Western Europe*, London: Sage.

Dermody, S. and Jacka. E. (1987) *The Screening of Australia, Vol. 1: Anatomy of a Film Industry*, Sydney: Currency Press.

DoCA (Department of Communications and the Arts) (1994) *Creative Nation: Commonwealth Cultural Policy*, Canberra: Australian Government Publishing Service.

Garnham, N. (1997) "Political economy and the practice of cultural studies," in P. Golding and M. Ferguson (eds.) *Cultural Studies in Question*, London: Sage.

Gibson, R. (1992) *South of the West: Postcolonialism and the Narrative Construction of Australia*, Bloomington: Indiana University Press.

Hall, S. (1986) "Cultural studies: two paradigms," in R. Collins, J. Curran, N. Garnham, P. Scannell, P. Schlesinger and C. Sparks (eds.) *Media, Culture and Society: A Critical Reader*, London: Sage.

Hartley, J. (1992) *Tele-ology: Studies in Television*, London: Routledge.

Hartley, J. (1996) *Popular Reality: Journalism, Modernity, Popular Culture*, London: Arnold.

Jamrozik, A., Boland, C. and Urquhart, R. (1995) *Social Change and Cultural Transformation in Australia*, Melbourne: Cambridge University Press

Johnson, L. (1988) *The Unseen Voice: A Cultural Study of Early Australian Radio*, London: Routledge.

Keating, P. (1995) "Exports from a creative nation," *Media International Australia*, 76, May.

Lealand, G. (1990) "'I'd just like to say how happy I am to be here in the seventh state of Australia': The Australianisation of New Zealand television," *Sites*, 21, Spring: 100–12.

Lumby, C. and O'Neil, J. (1994) "Tabloid television," in J. Schultz (ed.) *Not Just Another Business: Journalists, Citizens and the Media*, Sydney: Pluto Press.

McQuail, D. (1987) *Mass Communication Theory*, London: Sage.

Miller, T. (1994) "When Australia became modern" (Review of *National Fictions*, 2nd edn) *Continuum*, 8(2): 206–14.

Milner, A. (1991) *Contemporary Cultural Theory*, Sydney: Allen and Unwin.

More, E. (ed.) (1990) *TV 2000: Choices and Challenges*, Sydney: Australian Broadcasting Tribunal.

Morris, M. (1988) "Tooth and claw: tales of survival and *Crocodile Dundee*," in M. Morris *The Pirate's Fiancé: Feminism, Reading, Postmodernism*, London: Verso.

Mosco, V. (1995) *The Political Economy of Communications*, London: Sage.

O'Regan, T. (1993) *Australian Television Culture*, Sydney: Allen and Unwin.

O'Regan, T. (1997) *Australian National Cinema*, London: Routledge.

Pilger, J. (1989) *A Secret Country*, London: Jonathan Cape.

Seibert, F. S., Peterson, T. and Schramm, W. (1956) *Four Theories of the Press*, Urbana: University of Illinois Press.

Shawcross, W. (1992) *Rupert Murdoch: Ringmaster of the Information Circus*, Sydney: Random House.

Wheelwright, E. L. and Buckley, K. (1988) *Communications and the Media in Australia*, Melbourne: Macmillan.

Part 5
Democratic regulated societies

17 Media and power transitions in a small country
Sweden

Peter Dahlgren

Times change, and some of the features that once seemed so central or definitive of a society can transmute, altering its character. Sweden at the turn of the century looks different than it did two decades ago. At that point, the familiar stereotypes about, for example, a welfare state with a robust public sector, emphasizing material security for its population, was still pretty much in place. The ruling Social Democratic Party, allied with the unions and popular movements, could still claim to successfully repre-sent the interests of the working class *vis-à-vis* industry and capital. Class and labor relations under the Swedish "middle way" were characterized by relative harmony. A certain climate of self-satisfaction with a well engineered society with a promising future, still prevailed. Today, such features, as well as many others, have been deeply altered by historical developments. Some of these changes are unique to Sweden, but many of them reflect patterns common to most Western societies. What have also changed are some key dimensions of the Swedish media. In this chapter, I will be looking at the Swedish mass media, primarily with reference to journalism, against the backdrop of these larger societal changes. My angle of vision will emphasize power in relation to the media, with the theme of democracy as a basic horizon. The focus will be on the mass media; the newer interactive media have as yet not played a decisive role in the realignment of power. How this will be in the future is of course an open question.

Power is a concept often associated with the media, but in different ways, depend-ing on the perspective at hand. Some observers are quick to point to the power *of* the media, in shaping political agendas, in conveying and reproducing certain worldviews. Others will underscore the powers that impact *on* the media—for example political elites, private interests, audiences—influencing how the media operate and the kinds of representations of reality they provide. Yet others highlight how social power of various forms generate ambivalent force-fields in and around the media, resulting in contradictory consequences in terms of social power. All of these perspectives are valid, if not always simultaneously, and come into play in the discussion at hand. Moreover, we need to keep in mind that power relations are not fully static, but are to some degree in process of transition—not on a day-to-day basis, but certainly from the perspective of decades and years, where societal transitions more readily can come into view.

In recent years there has been an emphasis on power as a micro-phenomenon, as a ubiquitous dimension of all social relations, no matter how small the number of peo-ple concerned. Perspectives from cultural analysis as well as Foucault-inspired initiatives have invited us to see how power seeps into every nook and cranny of social life; it is found even at micro-levels of social interaction. This has been a useful development, not least in offering a more nuanced approach to earlier, more simplified accounts. For my purposes here, however, I will be sketching at the macro-level. Though social reality and power relations are of course endlessly complex, this does not invalidate basic, overarching patterns. We need to see and understand the forest, before we can grasp trees, branches, and leaves.

Schematically, in addition to looking at the media, I will be working with a triad of three sets of actors and their relationships to the media and to each other: economic elites, political elites, and the citizenry. I will first present a capsule summary of some of the major elements of the power arrangements in Sweden and their recent evolution. I then turn to the Swedish media system and the current major trends within it. From there I discuss the relationships between the media and the three sets of actors.

The corporatist "people's home"

Sweden has had since the 1930s a strong tradition of social democracy, which has involved, among other things, an activist state and an extensive welfare system. The ruling Social Democratic Party, the SAP, came to power in the 1930s and has remained in power with the exception of two periods in which a bourgeois coalition ruled the government: 1976–82 and 1991–4. The SAP began in the 1930s to implement what became known as the "folkhem," the people's home. This "folkhem" was predicated not only on socioeconomic viability, but also on a high degree of cultural homogeneity. The model was characterized by the goal of economic and social security for all citizens and, while it can be argued that this goal was never fully attained, Sweden had at one point the most extensive welfare system in the Western world. High taxes and social allocations helped reduce the more obvious manifestations of class differences, even if class structure as such was not dismantled. (For an interesting recent discussion of the rise and fall of the Swedish folkhem, and a comparison with the American New Deal, see Åsgard and Bennett 1997.)

In terms of power arrangements, this model was predicated on what has, since the 1970s been termed corporatism. This form of socio-political organization signifies the tendency toward a high degree of organization of—and coordination between—interest groups within a social formation. In particular, it points to a smooth interaction between the state, capital, and labor. In practice, corporatism involves the delegation of much decision-making to elites within the spheres of economics, politics, and labor. The efficacy of corporatist arrangements is an important part of its democratic legitimacy: group interests are synchronized on a society-wide basis. Corporatism is often contrasted with another ideal model of democracy, namely liberal-pluralist interest group competition, most obviously typified by the US. Both versions obviously have their strong and weak points as models of democracy.

Politically, corporatism in Sweden has been linked to a strong element of consensus; the political culture has emphasized cooperation and the resolution of conflicts. Swedish corporatist tendencies found their expression not least in the very orderly nature of organized yearly wage negotiations. The traditional capitalist class of Sweden was basically happy with the cooperative spirit of the SAP; also, the unions stood for a disciplined labor force. And as long as the economy expanded and workers saw their standard of living increasing, labor was largely satisfied. The SAP had a strong base in the unions; it could be argued that the SAP and the unions together constituted a unified political front which gave strong representation to the interests of wage earners. An accord was attained, and the Swedish model, the so-called "middle way," was established.

For citizens, the vast majority, around 90 percent, were union members. Moreover, beyond the unions, the other popular movements, as well as a myriad of associations also contributed to a highly organized civil society, where the culture of collectivist interest group democracy tended to prevail. The citizenry had a strong representation among the political elites and the state, while the political and economic elites cooperated with little friction. The citizens as wage earners had a solid representation via the unions and other movements *vis-à-vis* the economic elites. This high degree of organization around voluntary associations prevailed also among professional, industrial, and financial circles as well as among ordinary citizens.

The media of course strongly reinforced these arrangements, not just by their modes of representing reality, but also structurally. The press leaned strongly toward party affiliation, which helped foster a certain vitality in the public sphere, while public service radio, and later television, with a limited number of stations and programming, served to promote a strong sense of cultural unity and consensual politics. While the vision—and realities—of a "folkhem" have largely passed into history from the standpoint of politics and economics (I will return to this below), it lives on culturally to some extent in the media. The public culture of Sweden, as reflected in its media, can still symbolically convey an impression of a people's home—even if the gap between this image and social realities is widening.

Though geographically large, Sweden still has a population of less than 9 million, which makes it a small society in the modern world. This smallness has consequences for the country's mediated public culture: it is congruently small and held together by a limited pantheon of recurring figures in the media. The elected officials, scientific experts, popular celebrities, sports figures and others who populate the media sphere, especially television, the daily press, and weekly magazines, comprise a familiar population. In the case of the political elites, this visibility means that there is often one or more specific faces one can associate with a particular realm of social issues, for example cabinet ministers who have specific domains of responsibility. This visibility is strongest at the national level; local officials are less visible, since local television is not at all as developed and the public sphere at the local or municipal level is more anchored in the press and to some extent radio. The mediated familiarity at the national level gives a sense of public proximity to power, though it of course does not mean that power is always socially accessible or politically responsive.

Realigning the triad

If we look at the triad of political elites, economic elites, and citizenry in Sweden, we can see how the power constellations between them have evolved over the years. Within the economic realm, Sweden has been moving steadily away from the national entrepreneurship that characterized the early years of the Social Democratic regime. Economic activity has become increasingly transnational, with many Swedish firms moving abroad or being bought by multinational corporations. The recent sale of the Volvo automobile corporation—a veritable symbol of Swedish industry and technical competence—to Ford was more than just an economic transaction. Though it was on some level a blow to Swedish national identity (judging from the way it was framed in the media), on a long-term basis it signals the continual removal of key economic elements from the traditional corporatist framework of national interest group negotiations.

With the appearance of the leftist groups in the late 1960s, the Social Democrats began to feel outflanked. At about the same time, elite business interests were beginning to react against the constraints of the rather circumscribed limits to maneuverability within the established framework (Micheletti 1994). Bourgeois interests and associations were feeling stifled by the Social Democrats on the one hand, and the newer left on the other; much of the political and cultural climate was hostile to liberal-conservative values. A "rebellion" on the right was beginning to take form. Through book publishing, magazines, adult education courses, debate forums, and other means, a new ideological initiative was quietly launched. By the 1990s a new hegemony had emerged, which I will discuss shortly.

Also, a number of other elements which had defined Swedish civil society up until this period began to change. By the 1970s one could observe dissatisfaction among various segments of the population with the prevailing corporatist structures; growing pluralist/individualist discourses could be heard. Many previous SAP-supporters were now in more middle-class circumstances and found it harder to identify with the party. This growing discontent was increasingly fanned from the right. In fact, the discourse of the market was becoming very widespread by the mid-1980s. To compress quite a bit of history into a short synopsis, the growing fiscal crisis of the state led to increased taxes, against which the right could fuel discontent. Economic growth was sluggish; capital was flowing out of the country. The welfare state, faced with runaway expenditures it could not keep in check, began taking massive loans to keep its operations going. By the mid-1980s, Social Democratic fiscal policy increasingly began to follow a more bourgeois pattern, culminating in 1990 in the most pervasive change in the tax system to date, a change that tended to favor the well-to-do.

Yet these measures were not enough; in 1991 a bourgeois coalition won the national election, led by the Moderates (who, with a sense of the spirit of the times, had changed their name from the Conservatives in the late 1960s). The Moderates then began a radical program of privatization, decentralization and cut-backs in social spending. Much of the public sector suffered massive reductions. The mechanisms and ideology of the market—with, for example, the drive toward profitability, individual wage bargaining, and the view of citizen-clients as "customers," began to take root in many public sector services. The effects were devastating in many areas, and in 1994 the Social Democrats, playing on the discontent, were voted back in.

The economic situation, including unemployment levels not seen since the early 1930s, however, was worse than it had been three years earlier. The Social Democrats, politically and fiscally pressed, continue still today to oversee the dismantling of the public sector. With the ongoing economic crisis, a series of major scandals among public officials, as well as the divisive referendum that brought Sweden into the European Union, and other difficulties, the traditional class-based accords have dissipated to a great degree. The Social Democrats appear unable to provide any alternative ideological direction for the present problems. Any convincing degree of hope for future reconstruction of at least some of what has been lost, is largely absent. The economic elites are today in a more powerful position, and increasingly invoke the global arena to press for favorable conditions in the political realm. The citizenry is less organized and less empowered, collectively, in the face of the economic elites, and more distanced from the political elites. Among citizens, class differences are becoming more apparent, not least due to the decline in social services and the increasing prevalence of market mechanisms in the public sector (e.g. rising costs for social services) and the social domain more generally.

Politically we see in Sweden today patterns familiar to other countries, including a growing distancing—especially among the young—from the formal political system. Declining party affiliation and participation in elections, though by no means approaching US levels, is still noticeable. In the past, for example, voter turnout was about 95 percent; in the last election it was 80 percent, with younger citizens heavily overrepresented among the nonvoters. There is not only a diminished involvement with traditional civic associations and popular movements, but also with the newer movements. Greenpeace, for example, has seen its membership halved in recent years. All of these trends are part of the emerging post-corporatist situation. The formal political system is increasingly reactive, while finance, industry, and technology become all the more proactive, in shaping societal development. Remnants of the corporatist consensus are still very visible in Sweden, but much of the recent political history of the country can be seen as a decisive unravelling of this framework (Micheletti 1994). If the consensus continues to dissolve, the situation can further deteriorate into one of crass elitist interest group domination, deaf to the wills of a politically and culturally pluralist citizenry.

In this context it can also be noted that in Sweden today, 20 percent of the population has immigrant background. This is a diverse minority encompassing many different cultures, which mainstream Sweden tends to ideologically homogenize with the label "invandrare," meaning "immigrant." The word has come to signify not just cultural otherness, but also an implicit hierarchy: though this collective label is attached to most people who move to Sweden (and not infrequently even their subsequent generations), it tends not to be used to refer to people from the other Nordic countries, northern Europe, and the English-speaking world. In short, the term, as used in popular parlance, is not free of racial and class overtones. Immigrants in Sweden on the whole have been marginalized socially, culturally, economically, and politically.

Though educational and occupational backgrounds vary enormously among immigrants, systematic discrimination prevails in housing and in the job market. This has its counterpart in the media, where one can note a disproportionate lack of visibility, and a negative framing where there is visibility, for example, most news stories concerning immigrants and immigration accentuate problems of some kind. That the immigration of the 1990s—which has become much more restrictive than in the past—coincides with an economic crisis of course creates a volatile situation, and social tensions have grown. Sweden is in the midst of redefining itself; one can say that it is slowly moving from treating "Swedish" as an ethnic category—based on cultural origins, language, name, appearance, and so on—and moving toward a civic conception. But it's a long and slow process.

Sweden is not politically or economically worse off than many other Western countries—and is still very privileged in a global perspective—but the point is that the contrast between present circumstances and the first post-war decades is profound. The traditions that defined power relations and public culture in Sweden in the past have been altered over a relatively short time. Many citizens today are experiencing "culture shock": they do not recognize the current forces at play and have difficulty orienting themselves in a fundamentally altered political milieu. A number of revelations in recent years have served to further problematize many Swedes' notions of themselves and their society.

For example, it is now known that Sweden's international neutrality—virtually a sacred cow in terms of collective identity—was severely compromised during the Second World War and virtually a fraud during the Cold War.

Summing up the power realignments between political and economic elites and the citizenry, the power of the economic elites has unquestionably expanded at the expense of the other two collective actors. Citizens are situated further from the centers of economic decision-making, not just because the economy has become increasingly globalized, but also because the political elites, who ostensibly represent the citizenry, have lost power relative to the economic elites. Meanwhile, there is a declining confidence among the citizens in the formal political system's capacity to deal with contemporary problems. For their part, the citizenry's relative power has declined, as it has become increasingly fragmented by growing class divisions and cultural pluralism, including the relative nonintegration of immigrant populations.

Media transitions

I have of course simplified and compressed a lot of history in the preceding paragraphs, but they do convey a thumbnail sketch of the major developments relevant for this discussion. In these developments the media played a role, or rather, several roles, since their functions cannot be reduced to a simple, one-dimensional mechanism. Moreover, the media have also been part of these changes, both in their structural transitions and in their representations of reality. The changes in power relations emerging from the post-corporatist situation in Sweden are thus accompanied by key developments in the media landscape, which can be illuminated by looking at the altered relationships between the media and the three main collective actors I have discussed. This section looks briefly at the changes in media structures, and the following sections take up the relationships with the three actors.

Sweden is (still) a well run, well researched, and well documented society, and it also has a strong tradition of public access to information, not least about private individuals. With each citizen bearing a "person number" that is tagged to virtually every institutional encounter she or he has with the administrative state and increasingly with the market, it is difficult in Sweden to maintain any secrecy about, say, one's age, income, or taxes. These are available as public documents, and if Swedes may at times feel ambivalence about this particular aspect, they are proud of the overall openness fostered by the traditions of freedom of expression and access to public information that have characterized the citizens' relationships to the power structure. A long legacy of press freedom and the history of public broadcasting have underscored Sweden's perception of itself as an open society with a media system that has enhanced the democratic character of society. Of course all freedoms are relative, and media institutions are always in various ways conditioned by economic circumstances and relations of power.

If we begin with the press in Sweden, we observe a relative institutional stability over the past decades. There are just over one hundred papers that publish at least four days a week, and the total circulation is about 535 copies per thousand inhabitants, among the highest in the world. Three out of four blue-collar workers read a daily newspaper in Sweden. The Swedish press can be conveniently divided into three major elements: the metropolitan morning papers of the three major cities (Stockholm, Göteborg and Malmö), the evening tabloids of these cities, and the provincial press of the smaller towns. The two morning and two evening papers of Stockholm are the only ones that can be called "national" in their circulation. Sweden has had since the late 1960s a press subsidy system that has tried to compensate for the negative effects of the market and to help failing newspapers. This subsidy system constitutes about 5 percent of all newspaper revenue in the country.

Traditionally, the press has had a close affiliation with political parties. This remains largely the case even today, though the links are less tight. The move away from strong party affiliation and toward a "professional" model of journalism began after the Second World War. For example, the morning papers began to make explicit the distinction between news and leaders, and the evening tabloids subordinated party considerations to search for more sensationalism in the social field. The tabloids would often side with "the common man" against the power structure, but never call into question the basic power arrangements of society. In the turbulence of the past decade, the Social Democratic press has had severe economic troubles, and today the papers with a bourgeois political view overwhelmingly dominate the scene. Thus, in Sweden, the press is in a sense largely "oppositional" to the power of the Social Democratic government, although circumstances vary at the provincial level, where bourgeois parties often dominate municipal governments. Thus there is a problem of declining diversity in terms of political viewpoints available to readers.

Generally, the press's relationship to the power elite has been a subordinate one. The press can harshly attack an individual politician if they sense a scandal—and has even been instrumental in driving some officials out of office in recent years—but the press for the most part has had a cooperative relationship with the power structures. This is most noticeable at the provincial level, where the editors or owners often are part of the small town power elite; the big city press constitutes more of a critical public sphere. Most political journalism in the provincial press lets the politicians define the agenda, the information obtained is often relayed with a minimum of journalistic filtering, and investigative journalism is quite rare.

During the social changes of the past two decades, the most obvious structural transformation in the press has been the growing concentration of ownership. This is not dramatic in overall statistical terms, but rather in terms of some key paper acquisitions, particularly on the part of the Bonnier family, the single leading media group. However, the main change has been the intensification of the commercial imperatives: the press has been subjected to tougher conditions in the market. There are clear signs of commodification of journalism: as the economic situation tightens, commercial logic moves more to the fore. During the 1990s one can trace shifts in news values to the easier, the more popular, that is, a trend toward popularization (I will return to this point later).

Commodity logic is still more noticeable in terms of the employment patterns and working conditions of journalists. There are fewer solid positions, more part-timers, short-term contracts, freelance jobs. The professional identity of journalists is becoming less clear, not only as many more of them work in a variety of non-journalistic media jobs on a freelance basis, but also as the notion of "professional" becomes more contested. Increasingly, it means that loyalty to the organization and its economic criteria prevails over loyalty to journalistic ideals. This suggests a shift of power in the newsroom: as owners and managers apply tougher economic criteria, the professional power of journalists as representatives of the citizenry becomes reduced. This drift away by the press from its special role and responsibility toward increased emphasis on commodity logic is neatly exemplified by the recent economic takeover of the

Social Democratic evening tabloid *Aftonbladet* and the Moderate (conservative) morning *Svenska Dagbladet* by the Norwegian media outfit Schibstedt. That the two most idelogically polarized Stockholm/national newspapers now have the same (foreign) owner suggests that their publicist role will become still more subordinated to their commercial functions.

Turning to broadcasting, until about ten years ago, Sweden had two noncommercial television channels and three noncommercial radio channels, along with some community radio stations. The fundamental contours of public service broadcasting were fully homologous with the corporatist tradition, and Sweden was, with the exception of Albania, the last country in Europe to relinquish its noncommercial broadcasting monopoly—as the neo-liberal rhetoric was fond of pointing out. Today, broadcasting looks radically different. The crisis of public service broadcasting in Sweden in the 1980s followed similar paths as in other Western European countries, with fiscal shortages, a new competitive situation, and an uncertainty about its mission. Along with the two non-commercial TV channels, STV1 and STV2, which now cooperate instead of compete with each other, we now have a third terrestrial channel, the commercially financed TV4. There are also several Swedish-language channels on cable/satellite, as well as various packages of international channels to which one can subscribe. Satellite dishes are not widespread in Sweden, but about two-thirds of all households have cable TV. Viewing tilts strongly to Swedish-language channels, even if audiences for English-language channels are growing among younger viewers. The terrestrial channel TV4 has a slight edge in audience size over the two non-commercial channels. Its programming can be termed "popular public service." While lacking the diversity of the noncommercial stations, it has just as much news and current affairs, and its entertainment profile is not markedly different.

On the radio side, there are now four noncommercial channels, the fourth one being a network of regional channels, and an array of commercial stations. In the 1980s there was some activity and interest in noncommercial neighborhood radio, which was set up for information dissemination and opinion formation by nongovernmental (civic, political, and religious groups). The idea was that neighborhood radio would not be encumbered by the constraints of impartiality and factuality of the public service channels and would thus serve as a different, more provocative contribution to the public sphere. Neighbourhood radio declined dramatically when private local radio took off in 1993. The government held auctions, selling concessions to the highest bidders, with the result that they were bought up by a small number of actors, mainly media entrepreneurs, who have come to run them as networks, filling their stations in different areas with the same formats and programming. The formats are largely derived from US commercial broadcasting, with a dominance of pop music genres. This has resulted in a restructuring of radio broadcasting and its audiences. As the new arrangements in radio solidified, the bulk of news and current affairs became ghettoized to channel P1, which has a very small audience (between 5 and 10 percent) whose profile is middle-aged, urban and educated.

The economic elite and the media

The greater free reign given to market forces in society has thus had its corresponding impact on the media. It has also had a significant impact on the ideological climate in the media and in public culture more generally. In simplified terms, we can specify two major consequences here; they can feed off and reinforce each other, but it is useful to keep them analytically separate. On the one hand, there is the obvious trend toward popularization and tabloidization, as mentioned. On the other hand, and perhaps at a more subtle level, there has been an ideological development. The media, as sources of public knowledge and discussion, have increasingly given voice to views supporting market forces as the prime motor for more and more areas of social life. The realm of the political as defined in public culture has become diminished as issues and views relating to the democratic control and accountability of economic power increasingly fade from the political agenda. This is by no means a neat linear or uncontested development, but the pattern is clear. It must be understood that if the overall structural transition of Swedish society was a necessary precondition for this change in the media's ideological parameters, then this change in mediated public culture is not merely an automatic consequence. Rather, it should be seen as the result of concerted organized initiatives on the part of economic elites. Their interventions have contributed to shaping popular perceptions and opinions and have been instrumental in forming the current climate of public debate.

These initiatives have evolved and grown over the past three decades, but have intensified and borne fruit in the 1990s. Business interests, representing industry, trade and finance, responded in the late 1960s to the dominant Social Democratic union–leftist hegemony in politics and civil society by building up a vast consortium of well-funded organizations engaged in lobbying, opinion-building, information dissemination, and education. In the middle of this network is the Swedish Association of Employers (SAF), which until 1990 was the employers' main organ for collective wage negotiations. While that role is passed, SAF and two other major associations with strong links to the Moderate party, now promote and coordinate efforts aimed at enhancing business interests. Within the umbrella can be found funding agencies, as well as both commercial enterprises such as PR firms and advertising outfits, and nonprofit, privately funded organizations such as the City University in Stockholm and the Commerce Forum for the Future. Particular mention should be made of Timbro, a well developed think tank with publishing activities, that among other things helped transform the Moderates from an old-style conservative party into a modern neo-liberal one.

From the standpoint of the media, several organizations in this network are of particular relevance, such as a press service, a media research institute, and the educational outfit SNS, which is a major publisher and research sponsor. For example, it publishes an annual "democracy report," which has become an important contribution to debate in the public sphere. These and other organizations under the SAF umbrella provide the media with a steady flow of information and debate materials, and the SAF is proud of the impact its activities have had in fostering general opinion as well as lobbying for specific major legislation to support business interests. What is impressive about this development is the sheer scale of the operations and the money behind it. According to a recent study (Koch 1999), the SAF network altogether spends about 700 million kronor per year, which is over £60 million in a country of less than 9 million inhabitants. Certainly only a part of this is aimed explicitly at the media, but by comparison we can note that the Swedish federation of labor unions, LO (equivalent to the British TUC) has about 20 million kronor at its disposal each year to make its voice heard in the public sphere. It could well be argued that a new hegemony on the right has replaced the leftist hegemony of the "folkhem" era.

The power of economic elites to shape information and debates in the media via the SAF-network was facilitated by the general political direction of society, but also by circumstances in the media. With economics gaining as an area of journalistic coverage, and with journalists pressed for time and in need of material, journalists find it difficult to turn down ready-made informational "packages" offered by the corporate world. Most journalists covering economics come from business schools, not journalism schools, and tend to have fairly homogenous views about economic matters. Further, we have seen not only a growth but also changes in economic journalism. The economy sections expand, but also economy as a dominant theme is spreading into news journalism and feature journalism (Wolters 1998). The economic experts used as sources and for interviews tend increasingly to come from the business world, not from academia. Coverage of the economy during the 1990s has strongly emphasized the crisis, but less often discussed its origins or where responsibility lies. Ideologically, market forces become abstract powers, less amenable to political intervention. Such a climate is favorable for business definitions and initiatives in the political realm. In short, the power of the economic elite has steadily increased in relation to the media.

The political elite and journalistic practices

If the economic elite has witnessed a rise in its power relative to the media, the political elite's situation is more ambivalent in this regard. It is still the case of two sly foxes using the rules of the game to maximize their advantage; "symbiosis" still prevails between journalism and the political class, where there exists a mutual dependence. Political elites need easy access—and preferably favorable coverage—while journalists need good source contacts. However, the rules themselves have been evolving, and a different kind of journalism is emerging. This development can have long-term impact on the relative power of political elites.

Basically, what has been developing over the past decade or so is a gradual shift in the manner in which national politics is presented in the media. On the one hand, the imperatives of commercialization are serving to escalate the general level of drama associated with national politics, which in earlier decades had been characterized by more sedate forms of journalistic coverage, as well as the overarching mentality of consensus. On the other hand, much of the drive-shaft of politics today comes at least indirectly from the corporate sphere. The flow of power from the formal political system to the upper echelons of the private sector has, as I suggested earlier, resulted in a relative decline in the power of the political elites. These developments have given rise to a new dramaturgical framework for journalistic practices, a framework that builds on sensationalism in the context of contemporary media logic and power relations.

Traditional sensationalism has emphasized dramatization, the highlighting of conflict via a polarization of viewpoints and positions of political actors. In Sweden as in other places, sports metaphors become a key discursive device in presenting political issues and conflicts. Related to this is personification, which involves not just a focus on individual actors, but also an emphasis on psychological reasoning and emotionalism. Swedish politics is moving away from clear ideological differences between parties; for example, today one can vote for specific politicians in elections, not just for parties, a very recent addition to Swedish electoral procedures. As political discourse becomes ideologically less sharp, personification in journalism becomes more central. And in the media, well known people become constituted as a symbolic pantheon of celebrities, blurring the distinctions between political elites, entertainers, sports heroes, and other categories. Popular artists appear in political contexts; even more common, politicians appear in entertainment contexts in the media. They are interviewed as individual persons, their feelings and sentiments are elicited, and they of course make use of these occasions to promote themselves.

Further, media scandals (Lull and Hinerman 1997) are a dominant element of sensationalism: some moral or legal code is violated by a well known person. Here politicans have come to figure prominently in journalistic coverage in recent years.

In the past decade Sweden has witnessed a series of political scandals that have pivoted not around political issues or ideological themes, but around personal morality. Journalists have pointed out how specific politicians have abused their power for personal gain, or in some cases simply made a formal violation of morality, which, even if of minor economic consequence, have become moral scandals. In several cases, this has resulted in elected officials or ministers being forced to resign form their posts, which the media of course herald as an important event for the health of democracy.

In the new media logic that is emerging, speed is of the essence. The compression of time in and by the media means that political events are often made to accelerate their velocity in order to accommodate the tempo of the media, giving less time for reflection and planning among decision-makers, and less opportunity for contemplation among audiences. Another feature is the growing density of the "media-go-round": the tendency for news stories to be picked up by the various media in the course of a day, according to their publication and broadcast schedules. Each step involves a "media-add-on" to the story. The self-referential symbolic world of the media thus accelerates events, but also generates situations where the referential function of journalism—to describe and analyze events in society—becomes remote, as the "events" increasingly become intertextual media phenomena.

What has this to do with the relative power of the political elite and the media? Under circumstances where the political elite is losing relative power to the economic elite, and where the economic elite is available to the media largely under circumstances that these elites themselves decide, the media dramatize and personalize current affairs most readily by pouncing on the political elites whenever possible. What emerges is a dramaturgical framework that becomes not only a game-plan for a lot of journalism, but also an ideological construction offered to (but obviously not always accepted by) the citizenry, namely that society basically consists of the political elite, the media and the citizenry (Olsson 1996). At its worst, this framework suggests that the political elite is to be viewed with suspicion, as self-serving manipulators. The media present themselves as guardians of the public interest, while the economic elite basically gets edited out of discourses about power.

In recent years, there has been a good deal of complaint from the political elite that the media are fostering a popular contempt against them. This view of political elites has not been totally undeserved, but there is some justification to the claim. The media have taken a more active watchdog role, but they have been barking at too many shadows. The media have, in a sense, taken advantage of the political elite's relative decline in power, but at the same time not focused their critical eyes on the economic elite. It can also be argued that the media have gained a notch in power over the political elite in that contemporary media formats emphasize so much the forms, the modes of representation. Television cameras, sound bites, and so on compel the political elite to some extent to dance to a tune composed by the media. Yet we should be careful in not exaggerating the shift in power balance here: the political establishment have also become more sophisticated in dealing with the media.

Media for citizens—or consumers?

The question is to what extent this direction in media development helps citizens. We should not ignore the fact that popularization of journalism *per se* need not be negative. It can mean that more people have access to the public sphere, that they feel incorporated into society as citizens. In a diverse media landscape, popular forms address those segments of the population who may feel excluded by more highbrow formats. Popular forms often can engage, evoke response, provoke discussion. Even the blurring of the boundaries between journalism and popular culture (Dahlgren and Sparks 1992) need not always be a bad thing. It can open up for public discussion new areas of social experience that need to become a focus of political debate, as witnessed by certain versions of talk shows, where private, personal concerns have been able to link up with public issues. Yet, there are the obvious pitfalls. Popularization in the form of tabloidization generally entails a different set of journalistic values, ones that do not promote critical engagement with contemporary issues, but instead diverts, and positions its audiences as spectators or voyeurs.

The hardening commercial climate of the Swedish media has not produced a popularization or tabloidization that is exceptional in an international context. The popularization of journalism has become somewhat more pronounced in Sweden in the past decade, with the ambivalent consequences I just mentioned. And certainly the evening press in Sweden, for example, is no rival to the British tabloids in terms of sensationalism. Rather, to understand the significance of the media *vis-à-vis* the citizenry in terms of power realignments, we need to look beyond the specific practices of journalism toward the larger media landscape of which journalism is but a small part. In fact, it is this relative smallness of the journalistically based public sphere in relation to the overall media milieu that is significant. One can say that the power of traditional journalistic ideals has given way to other forces and goals within the media. In the increasingly mediatized life of late modern society, journalism, in its various forms, is wedged in between a vast sea of media culture that is explicitly nonjournalistic, even if we include all the genres of quasi-journalism. Here the circumstances of Sweden mirror international trends. Mediated public culture is increasingly a consumerist culture, pivoting on individual rather than collective action, and situated in the market rather than in civic or public contexts.

To say this is not to engage in a nostalgic lament about higher ideals being trashed by crass materialism. We of course need markets, we need consumption. The point, rather, is that in terms of power relations, these developments resonate very well with the interests of the economic elites and with the political right. However, we must understand that these trends are so encompassing, so complexly integrated, that they will be misunderstood if reduced to the instrumental strategies of any specific political actors. However, taken together, these developments within the media and in their interplay with other societal factors, are generating conditions which reduce the relative power of the citizens. The organized civil society of the "folkhem", which resulted in a strong relative power for the citizenry, is rapidly being replaced by the new constellations of social relations and engagement shaped by market mechanisms. Indeed, the central point of concern here can be expressed as follows: will the current media trends, backed up by the changes in political economy toward more free reign for market forces, generate a culture which is at all conducive for citizenship, or will citizenship, as a way of being and as a mode of thinking, be largely displaced by consumerist frames of reference?

Democracy has many aspects: legal, institutional, traditional/historical, but also cultural and subjective. We can schematically make a distinction between a formal democratic system, with its institutional structures, laws, parties, elections, media processes, and so on, and a complex, multidimensional civic culture, anchored in everyday life and horizons, which both reflects and makes possible this system. (My conception here should of course not be confused with the behaviorist and psychological use of the term in political science studies from the 1960s.) Both the political system and civic culture are mutually dependent; both evolve in relation to each other. The notion of civic culture points to those features of the sociocultural world which constitute everyday preconditions for democracy, for example values, norms, practices, procedures and, not least, identities that may promote or hinder democratic virtues (however understood), including forms of interaction among citizens (Dahlgren 1997).

If *citizenship* within the Swedish political context—and elsewhere—has traditionally been understood largely in terms of formal and legal sets of rights and obligations, today we witness a robust expansion in new ways to approach the analytic category of citizenship (Preston 1997, Turner 1993). What much of the new literature emphasizes is that citizenship must also be seen from the perspective of people's experiences within everyday life, as an integral feature of people's composite identities (Clarke 1996, Mouffe 1993). One of the hallmarks of late modern society is the pluralization of our "selves": in our daily lives we operate in a multitude of different "worlds" or realities. If democracy is to thrive, people must have "citizen" as one element of their multiple self-conception.

At the same time, there need not be—nor should we expect—a singular, unified understanding about what citizenship is: people are evolving a variety of ways of "being" citizens and "doing" citizenship. Today, structural, historical change is altering the character of Western democratic systems. At the same time, from an actor perspective, people are altering democracy by what they do (or not) and by what they envision (or not). Contemporary civic culture in Sweden is at a crossroads. The "folkhem" is gone, but the present still embodies potential for new politically relevant meanings, activities, and identities. The power triad of economic elites, political elites, and citizens has been realigned. It cannot be locked, but new realignments do not occur overnight.

Note

I am indebted to the work of colleagues in Sweden for much of the background information presented here. In particular, the following have been very useful:

Hadenius, S. and Weibull, L. (1999) *Massmedier*, 7th edn, Stockholm: Bonnier Alba.
Weibull, L. and Gustafsson, K. E. (1997) "The Swedish media landscape in transition," in U. Carlsson and E. Harrie (eds.) *Media Trends*, Göteborg: Nordicom.

References

Åsgard, E. and Bennett, L. (1997) *Democracy and the Marketplace of Ideas*, Cambridge: Cambridge University Press.

Clake, P. B. (1996) *Deep Citizenship*, London: Pluto.

Dahlgren, P. and Sparks, C. (eds.) (1992) *Journalism and Popular Culture*, London: Sage.

Dahlgren, P. (1997) "Enhancing the civic ideal in TV journalism," in K. Brants *et al.* (eds.) *The Media in Question*, London: Sage.

Koch, S. (1999) "Åsiktsjätten," *Ordfront*, 1–2.

Lull, J. and Hinerman, S. (1997) *Media Scandals*, Cambridge: Polity.

Michelettis, M. (1994) *Det civila samhället och staten*, Stockholm: Fritzes.

Mouffe, C. (1993) *The Return of the Political*, London: Verso.

Olsson, T. (1996) "Den politiska klassen i gungning," in K. Becker *et al.* (eds.) *Medierummet*, Stockholm: Carlsson.

Preston, P. W. (1997) *Political/Cultural Identity: Citizens and Nations in a Global Era*, London: Sage.

Turner, B. (ed.) (1993) *Citizenship and Social Theory*, London: Sage.

Wolters, S. (1998) "Journalistiken har blivit marknadsanapassad," *Journalisten*, 14.

18 Political complexity and alternative models of journalism

The Italian case

Paolo Mancini

The usual question: Is there a gap between theory and practice?

Journalism and, more generally, media structures do not grow up in a vacuum. They are born and develop within a network of interactions and negotiations with a number of other social systems and factors, most of all with economics and politics. This seems to be a simple, trite, almost stupid statement. And, nevertheless, if one looks at media and journalism theory, this statement is very often dismissed and contradicted and a single theory is elevated to the level of universal rule, putting aside the role and importance of the interacting factors, of historical, social, economic, and political context.

This point has to be associated with a more general tendency, which is very diffuse in media theory: its normative dimension. When dealing with the mass media, it is not easy to separate what is objective and factual from what "ought to be." Most of the time media studies do not just describe and interpret their subjects but rather try to define what is supposed to be the ideal model of reference (McQuail 1987).

Journalism theory seems to be a very good example of both, the unavoidableness of normativism and the "dominant bias" in media theory. One model, the so-called "professional model," has been raised to the point of becoming the unique, universal model for journalism practice and theory all around the world; it is addressed as the reference model even to measure distance and difference from. This model has been labelled in different ways: "liberal or social responsibility model" (Siebert *et al.* 1963, Curran 1991), "Anglo American model" (Chalaby 1996), "professional model" (Tunstall 1977). This is the only model which has been widely theorized, discussed, and diffused so that "classical liberal theories of the media have been advanced so often that their central arguments seem almost wearisomely familiar" (Curran 1991: 27). Curran gives a clear definition of the liberal model of journalism:

> in traditional liberal theory, the media are conceived primarily as vertical channels of communication between private citizens and government: they inform individual choice at election time, and they influence governments by articulating the collective view of private citizens ... the dominant strand in liberal thought celebrates the canon of professional objectivity, with its stress on disinterested detachment, the separation of fact from opinion, the balancing of claim and counterclaim. This stems from the value placed by contemporary liberalism on the role of the media as a channel of information between government and governed.
>
> (Curran 1991: 32)

Is this model applicable in all countries? Does it fit with contextual factors in different cultures, political environments, traditions? Is this model really applied even in those countries in which and for which it has been conceived? I shall not deal here with this last question; rather, I shall try to underline the reasons why in some countries, such as in Italy, where the "professional model" has been imported from abroad, there is a striking gap between theory and everyday journalism practices.

As a matter of fact, during interviews or discussions with Italian journalists (I imagine we could find the same problem in many other parts of the world) they continuously say that they act according to what is supposed to be the best model of journalism, a journalism which is neutral, objective, and independent of other social powers and which performs a watchdog function. In reality, journalists act in a different way: they follow a different model of journalism. This point clearly emerges from research carried out together with Tom Patterson:[1] when asked about their perception of their role, Italian journalists state, even if less than their colleagues in other countries, that they follow the neutral and objective model of journalism. They say that they are practictioners of factual reporting which is not involved in advocacy or partisan behavior. They claim to be strongly convinced that their profession is addressed substantially to keeping the public neutrally informed. In reality, Italian journalists are advocates, linked to political parties, and very close to being active politicians themselves. The history and evolution of Italian journalism shows how important these dimensions of elitism and advocacy are: Italian journalists are political actors themselves; they write in a complex and political manner for few other political actors. There is no doubt about this among students and even discerning professionals (Bechelloni 1982, Grossi Mazzoleni 1984, Murialdi 1986, Porter 1983), but nevertheless there is a striking contradiction between a sort of theoretical wisdom diffused among most of the professionals (journalism has to be neutral and detached from power) and real practice (journalists are advocates and close to different social powers).

The elitist dimension of Italian print press is confirmed by the level of the readership. Italy is ranked in one of the lowest positions in the world for newspaper circulation.[2] In 1956 an important Italian journalist, Enzo Forcella, wrote a paper for an academic journal whose title was "Millecinquento lettori" (One thousand five hundred readers), arguing that in those days all journalists, mostly political journalists, knew they were writing for just "One thousand five hundred readers," the small group of people (politicians, business people, army officers, cardinals) who were interested and active in politics. Beyond this group of people there were very few Italians reading daily newspapers. Obviously, today the number is no longer the same, but nevertheless the traditional habit still persists: newspaper readers are very few while the television audience is undoubtedly larger, even if up to few years ago television too had a strong advocacy attitude.

Why do Italian journalists claim to work for the mass audience when, at the same time, they confess that their readership amounts to "one thousand five hundred readers"? Why do they claim to be neutral and objective when they act in a completely different way? Why is there this discrepancy between their real behavior and their self-perception? Why are they unable or unwilling to correctly describe what they do? The explanation lies in the widespread diffusion of what I shall call the "professional model" of journalism, which stresses the necessity of objectivity and neutrality. As previously stated, this has been the only theorized and discussed model throughout the world; in many cases journalists around the world know only this hypothetical, professional model. In any case, confessing to acting contrary to it is seen as an infraction of the dominant model.

But this model is not applicable in all parts of the world, because journalism does not grow in a vacuum: it is the fruit of the interaction between different actors and systems and such differences in social structure and context have to be taken into account even when theorizing models of journalism.

Why is the professional model so diffused?

Different reasons contribute to explaining the diffusion of the "professional" model of journalism. As is well known, many authors have synthetized this mixture of different reasons and motives under the tag of "media imperialism" (Schiller 1976) or "cultural and economic imperialism" or "Americanization" (Schou 1992). Probably, the most complete description of this process lies in Tunstall's book, whose title is highly meaningful: *The Media are American* (Tunstall 1977). Tunstall suggests that at the end of the Second World War different political, economic, and cultural factors combined together for a common goal: the diffusion of values already widespread in US society. From his book, it is possible to underline four different reasons for the attempt to spread these values: (1) the struggle against what was called the "propaganda machine" of the communist countries; (2) the struggle to avoid the return of Fascist and Nazi ideas and structures; (3) the attempt to enlarge and protect the US economy; (4) the availability of scientific and theoretical innovations produced by US universities and research centers, what Tunstall calls the "production of knowledge."

All together these factors have highly contributed to exporting a "professional model of journalism" based on neutrality, autonomy, and detachment from power. A good example of this mixture, of this combination of political and economic goals and scientific theory, is what Margaret Blanchard calls "the free press crusade." It shows how normativism, which was present in such classical textbooks on journalism as *Four Theories of the Press*, which were written at the end of the Second World War, has deteriorated into cultural imperialism, and what Siebert, Peterson and Schramm have stressed as "theories" of the press have become "ideologies" of it (Nerone 1995). One of the risks of normativism is exactly this: very often it theoretically legitimizes a process of professionalization, but also becomes an occasion and a reason for ideological, political, and economic struggle. Losing every possible interpretative strength, from being a theoretical approach, it becomes "ideology." Besides *Four Theories of the Press*, other books have had the same impact on exporting and legitimizing the "professional model of journalism" and, more generally, interpretations on the role of the mass media system: Schramm's book *Mass Media and National Development* became, as Tunstall states, the "UNESCO bible for expanding the media in developing countries" (Tunstall 1977).

The experience of "the free press crusade" clearly shows the mixture of intervening factors. As Blanchard states, efforts of American publishers who, at least at the very beginning, were essentially interested in stopping the competition and the advance of European wire services, together with the State Department, which aimed at contrasting the influence of the communist regimes and at winning the propaganda war against them, put the issue of freedom of the press into the international arena (Blanchard 1986). First the United Nations and then UNESCO debated this issue. The main result was not the approval of any particular document or formula, but the debate about the idea of freedom of the press received wide circulation and discussion. As a matter of fact, while the discussions at the UN and UNESCO slowed down because of procedural accidents and mediation attempts, new media organizations around the world were born and new occasions for discussions, seminars, and conferences were created which reinforced and diffused the professional presuppositions, procedures, and methodologies which lay behind the idea of freedom of the press.

The ideas behind the US model of journalism, whether you call them "liberal" or "socially responsible" or "professional," have therefore spread throughout the entire world, even if in simplified and very ideologically oriented versions. They have come to represent the point for measuring and judging other journalistic behaviors and models; today they represent the ideal norm to which each practitioner is expected to refer. The conclusion Blanchard draws is that "few people had discovered that freedom of the press was culturally based and that no nation could impose its press system on another nation, just as no nation could impose its system of religion or government on another nation" (Blanchard 1986: 402).

Along with Tunstall and Blanchard, several other scholars have pointed out that the diffusion of US wire services, US technology, US movies dealing with stories related to journalism, and US textbooks have contributed to the spreading of ideas and methodologies advancing the professional model of journalism (Altschull 1984, Schiller 1976, Schou 1992). Peter Golding stressed the relationship between market penetration and professionalization of the field. He particularly pointed out how the professions of the media system have spread throughout the Third World following the diffusion of hardwares and technologies. He observes that the BBC, through the organization of specific courses on these matters, has contributed to diffusing the idea of a neutral and objective model of journalism (Golding 1977).

All these interpretations stress one main point: there is no doubt that at the end of the Second World War a process of Americanization took place in most of the European countries. It was moved by economical needs, but its political nature too was clear: there was the attempt to stop the propaganda machine of the communist regime while, at the same time, the Allied forces were struggling against the return of the defeated Nazi and Fascist ideas. To reverse the strict control over a strongly centralized media system, Allied forces encouraged the birth of local press by private owners or institutions (parties and unions) whose ideas were close to those of the Allies. Germany, Denmark, Italy, and France represent good examples of this attempt (Humphreys 1990, Kuhn 1995, Porter and Hasselbach 1991, Schou 1992, Tunstall 1977).

But the diffusion of the professional model was not without problems: in fact, first the Resistance in the occupied countries and then the newborn democracies were developing a press model which was inspired by the ideals of the free press but, at the same time, was an instrument for organizing members and activists and to spread the ideas of the recently established democratic institutions and party organizations. This press model was strongly partisan, resuming the tradition of the party press which had been so diffused in many European countries before the dictatorships and the Second World War.

In this way, the joint attempt of the US government and business enterprises to spread the ideals of the free press met the tradition and the need for political involvement of the media system. The product of this encounter has been, in most cases, a blend of different and contrasting professional models which, in the end, make a striking contradiction between theory and practice. While there was a general, theoretical accordance toward what was becoming the new dominant democratic model (aided by the crusade for it), on the other hand everyday practice was moving in different directions: journalism was becoming one of the main instruments for the political debate which was blossoming in the restored European democracies at the end of the Second World War and, consequently, the professional model was meeting the strong, old tradition of a more literary, comment and advocacy oriented attitude which originally affected the birth of journalism in several European countries (Chalaby 1996).

The free press crusade also contrasted with the fact that the new democratic structures of many European societies were developing differently from those of the US: several social features which made the idea, the structure and the functioning of the free press possible were missing in Europe or were taking different and contrasting directions. The philosophy of welfare state democracy supported a stronger intervention of the state in many social fields, from economics to media, from culture to education. Particularly in the media field, welfare state philosophy was in favor of stronger intervention by the state as regulator and funder of the entire media system, and particularly of the broadcasting system. Market competition itself was strongly affected by state intervention as several news organizations were favored by state subsidies while, in the television field, the monopoly of public service broadcasting did not allow the birth of any sort of market competion.

The intervention of the state went together with a higher level of politicization in many fields. Party structures had become instruments of socialization much more than in the US so that the level of partisanship became very high and stable in many European countries and pervaded several social spheres. In these countries economics was linked to politics and the two fields strongly affected each other; even the media system, like business, frequently overlapped with politics.

Many of the principles which lie behind the "free press crusade" were therefore contradictory to the historical contingencies, the political and cultural traditions of the countries toward which the crusade was addressed. Consequently the ideas of the "professional model of journalism" survived mostly as legitimizing tools and not as real, everyday procedures.

Detached from power?

At least three main features seem to define the "professional model" as has been theorized so far: (1) journalism is supposed to be detached from power; (2) journalism is supposed to be neutral and objective; (3) journalism is supposed to perform functions of vertical communication.

First of all, journalism is supposed to be detached from power, both political and economic. Even if at the very beginning journalism was born essentially as political journalism and was linked to different competing social parts, its subsequent development moved toward larger autonomy, first the press and then the broadcasting system being funded by their own revenues. As is well known, this happened in the US in the first part of the twentieth century with the Penny Press (Schudson 1978) and in the UK with the popular press at the end of the same century (Franklin 1997). This shift from politically committed journalism to neutral, objective journalism has been theorized in most of the texts on journalism. The development toward a market oriented journalism implied: (1) a lowering of the level of partisanship, with the press earning autonomy from the party or other ideologically oriented groups; (2) autonomy from the government of which the press was supposed to become the principal watchdog;

(3) that readers and viewers were becoming the main source of economic independence.

In Italy, as in other European countries, these conditions did not take place and journalism has never detached itself from its economical and ideological leanings, first of all because of its ownership, which has been strongly influenced by the intervention of the state and corporations with economical interests outside of the media system itself: journalism has always represented, and still represents and defends, the interests of the parts to which it is linked.

A clear example of these links is found in the history of a Milan newspaper, *Il Giorno* created in 1956 by Enrico Mattei, general director of the state-owned ENI Corporation. The story of the founding of this daily is told by a privileged witness to it, Piero Ottone, journalist and future director of *Il Corriere della Sera*. Ottone affirms:

> *Il Giorno* was an innovative newspaper which arose with the distinct purpose of renewing Italian journalism and it is only natural that such a man as Mattei was pleased by the idea of innovation; but the real objective of the newspaper, its primary function, was to support in public debate the ideas and the interests of state owned industry, of which ENI was the principal party, against the daily press sustained by private industry.
>
> (Ottone 1985: 78)

As a matter of fact, at the time of the birth of *Il Giorno*, a large part of the other newspapers were the property of private industrial groups that derived their profits from industrial exploits outside the realm of publishing. The new daily, being the voice of state-owned industry, was born to oppose their ideas and outlooks.

This was the objective of a newspaper born in 1956; the situation of the printed press today is not much different and the great majority of newspapers are even now owned by the largest financial and industrial groups in the country whereas, in contrast, the portion of state property has clearly diminished.[3]

The welfare state philosophy, so widespread in European countries, has introduced an element of diversification in comparison to more exceedingly liberal democracies and, in particular, in comparison to the US. The state has intervened substantially in the mass communication system both in print[4] and in broadcasting and thus has also given rise to a journalistic model which is different from the "professional" one. In the case of the printed press, it has intervened as a funder with policies of economic subsidies in support of newspapers in difficulty and, in particular, supporting party publications which may thus continue a long-lived tradition.[5] With the same welfare state logic, the public broadcasting service was born and developed throughout Europe at the end of the Second World War. Depending on various national contexts and historical phases, it instituted strong and stable relations of dependence either with the acting government or with the various parties represented in parliament.[6] Although television in the greater part of Europe was born following the neutral model, or presumed to be so (such as the BBC), in reality such neutrality was not achieved in most of the countries.

Party journalism represents another strong characteristic of many European countries: in Italy it developed with the Socialist and Catholic press at the begininng of the twentieth century (even if it was during the Italian Risorgimento at the middle of the nineteenth century that political journalism made its first appearance) establishing a tradition of advocacy journalism which has gone beyond the party press (Murialdi 1986). Despite attempts to impose or import "professional" forms of journalism of British and especially American origin, the Italian newspapers, after a brief experience of independence, banded with political and industrial groups from which they derived their financial support and whose interests they defended and represented to the public. Of particular significance was the attempt by Albertini at the beginning of the century to bring to the *Corriere della Sera* the presumed neutral objective journalistic model of English origin but Fascism stopped this experience.

The Fascist dictatorship brought about a control and absolute unidirectional use of the press (Cannistraro 1975, Castronovo and Tranfaglia 1976) and then, during the Resistance and immediately afterwards, journalism was used as a means to spread ideas in support of the various factions which were born in opposition to the dictatorship (Farinelli *et al.* 1997, Murialdi 1986). Thus did advocacy journalism become engaged with the literary tradition and was hardly directed toward a large market. Paolo Murialdi, one of the foremost historians of Italian journalism, and a journalist himself, speaks of "literary supremacy" which characterized the origins of Italian journalism, leaving, after a few years, the first literary gazettes open for use by political parties and organizations (Murialdi 1986).

After the 1943 Armistice the activity of the Psychological Warfare Branch (PWB) was very important and contributed in a substantial manner to the rebirth of many newspapers and to the diffusion of the "professional model of journalism." In 1944 PWB approved a "Press Plan for Italy" whose aim was to introduce "correct news and neutrality." This plan was mainly the creature of a British officer Ian Munro, whose political model was the "two-party system" which did not exist in Italy (Pizarroso Quintero 1989). Munro also understimated the old advocacy attitude of the Italian press and the links existing between the newspapers and the groups which were giving life to the resistance. Allied forces were, at the same time, trying to introduce or reinforce the idea of freedom of the press, while they were forced to accept, and even to support the fact that Italian parties involved with the struggle for the liberation of the country had their own papers, whose main aims were those of spreading their ideas and being organizational tools.

In this way, over many years a model of the public sphere developed which is different from the "ideal" liberal one. In this public sphere the means of communication are the voices of organized groups and public television freely offered to them is part of this tradition. One may see this in the "pillarization" in Holland (Brants 1985, McQuail 1992), in the role of "social relevant groups" in German broadcasting (Porter and Hasselbach 1991), and in the logic of "lottizzazione" in Italy by which each of the main competing parties control newspapers and TV channels

In these contexts different groups and their relative subcultures are organized into their own social structures and networks of relations, schools, sports and cultural associations and also newspapers and TV channels. Especially the public broadcasting service, as the whole system of print press, becomes, to a large measure, an arena available to various organized groups to express their own points of view and for dialogue with other groups.

Today this phenomenon has diminished, but nevertheless it still affects the way in which journalism is practiced: the ties with various social powers, with the government on one side and political parties, social groups, politicians, and economists on the other, are all manifested by the strong presence of political themes seen in much of the research (Mancini 1985) and in the accentuated level of advocacy in journalistic information. As regards the journalistic profession itself, this has brought about a confused and weak professional identity and an absence of a consensual code of ethics, despite a professional guild (Ordine dei Giornalisti) to which all journalists must belong.

Objective?

Neutrality and objectivity constitute a second prerogative which characterizes the professional model: the journalist reports the facts in a detached and objective manner and then separately interprets and comments on them. This professional imperative is achieved, as is well known, with the separation of news from commentary, of the news page from the commentary page, and of news reporting from news analysis. Journalism is the combination of the two, but they must be kept completely separate. Objectivity clearly constitutes the main ideological feature of the professional model: a departure from this assumption is a self-evident deviant behavior and implicitly and explicitly rejected. Objectivity, however, has not found a comfortable abode in Italy.

As was well explained by Michael Schudson, objectivity is strictly connected to the necessity to penetrate the reader market. This may be seen with the birth of the Penny Press, which tried to widen the traditional press market up until then essentially based on party or strongly advocate newspapers. With the Penny Press, journalism widens the range of topics covered and it aims at a reader who does not have any particular political leaning (Schudson 1978).

In certain contexts, such as Italy, where, as we have discussed, news organizations are tied to organized interests and political parties, objectivity, the separation of news and commentary, essentially represents a purely external legitimation in keeping with the perceived model of professional canons (often with conscious discomfort) which dominate and beyond which there is no glimpse of alternative models. Indeed, the diffusion of newspapers and television, lined up in defense of political ideals or economic interests, has made it such that one must not necessarily win over an ordinary reader and thus demonstrate unbiased opinion, but rather transmit ideas, protect interests, and organize people who already share the same points of view.

The definition of "missionaire" given by Kocher to German journalists may also apply perfectly to Italian journalists (Kocher 1986). In some cases, objectivity is explicitly rejected, but undoubtedly the common sense of the Italian journalist finds itself in a contradictory and ambiguous situation. The journalist knows that he is practicing a strongly advocate journalism while thinking that his professionalism is essentially legitimated by his being objective and impartial.

The entire history of Italian journalism is the history of advocate and interventionist journalism. The birth of *La Repubblica* in 1976, which became the most widely distributed newspaper in recent years, is a further testimony of this and shows how this attitude has survived up to recently. *La Repubblica*, a newspaper in which the commentary and interpretation pages prevail over the simple informative ones, was born in order to practice interventionist journalism with its own ideas and its own objectives for modernizing of the country. *La Repubblica* is not aligned with existing political or economic groups as much as it represents in itself a "newspaper party," the "Scalfari party" from the name of its founder and at that time its owner, Eugenio Scalfari. *La Repubblica* constitutes a successful model of journalism and is widely followed.[7] Scalfari, the editor of *La Republica*, presented the first issue of his daily paper with these words: "An independent daily, but not neutral. This newspaper is a little different from the others: it is an information newspaper which rather than parading an illusory political neutrality states explicitly it has taken a definitive political choice. This newspaper is written by people who are part of the large field of the Italian left."[8]

Today, the phenomenon of the party newspaper and aligned press has weakened. Nevertheless, the practice, more than the idea, of objectivity is conceived essentially as an empty commonplace, an integral part of a dominant professional model, the refusal of which would be considered deviant behavior.

The schizophrenia between the perceived necessity of being within the canons of the professional model and the everyday practiced objectivity is even more striking if one thinks that a theoretical blow to the concept of objectivity came too from the vast public debate over the role of mass media which took place during most of the 1960s and 1970s following the student revolts and cultural upheaval in that period. That debate too brought to light the weakness and bias of the concept of objectivity and secularized a concept that nevertheless still remains one of the prominent ideas of the professional model of journalism.[9]

There are other reasons for the difficult applicability of the concept of objectivity outside the context in which it was originally developed: it is much easier, as Tunstall points out, to find a position within a two-party system such as that in Britain or the United States: "neither with one or the other," one is detached from both sides (Tunstall 1977). Objectivity is almost impossible within an intricate and fragmented panorama in which a greater number of political forces act and in which even the slightest shades of meaning in a story risk stepping on the positions of one of the forces in the political field.

Moreover, the complexity of the Italian political system includes two other features which go against a possible application of the concept of abstract objectivity. First of all politics, as already stated, pervades many different social fields. Very recently an Italian political scientist, Angelo Panebianco, stated that the First Republic (the period which goes up to the Tangentopoli scandals and the disappearance of the traditional party structures at the beginning of the 1990s) was characterized by a sort of "panpoliticismo" (panpoliticism) by which politics was dominating and influencing many social systems: economics, the judiciary system, and so on.[10] Secondly, the level of political participation is very high, if compared to that of other countries. Political participation can be seen in the level of electoral turnout, in Italy one of the highest in Europe,[11] in the number of political organizations and activists, and so on.[12] In this situation journalists, as most of those who are active in the public arena, cannot be abstracted and detached from the other social powers, as would be required in the professional model.

Vertical communication?

In the classical texts regarding the "professional model" one reads that the principal function of journalism is that, as Seymour-Ure states, of vertical communication, that is, to inform a reader/television viewer who is not up-to-date with the facts about public affairs (Seymour-Ure 1968). The transmission of information from top to bottom is considered the fundamental task of the professional model. This function seems to be particularly useful in those contexts which could be termed "simple," in which there is a limited number of competing parties, in which the number and the structure of intermediate bodies between citizens and power are weak, and therefore mass communication has a predominant role as an intermediary between those in power and citizens.

In other contexts, such as in Italy, such a function appears almost superfluous. It is particularly superfluous in the presence of complex political systems with a large number of parties and competing groups, with a widespread diffusion and ramification of the political party structures and with a limited circulation of mass communication strongly addressed to a sectorial public already politically defined and involved in the electoral debate.

In these contexts, journalistic information generally, but not exclusively, performs a function of horizontal communication allowing the numerous social, political, and economic groups with which the news organizations are aligned to communicate among themselves (Mancini 1990, 1991). The mass media become a fundamental instrument in a form of democracy which assumes structures which are much different from the ones foreseen and in part functioning in the more classical liberal model. Political parties, economic groups (unions, entrepreneurial organizations), and social groups of various types (environmentalists, feminist organizations, cultural organizations, etc.) constitute fundamental intermediaries between the state, government, and citizens. These organizations play important functions of socialization and communication. The diffusion of what Tocqueville would call "civil and political associationism" is routed into the political philosophy which shaped the reconstruction of post-war Italy and which, following some scholars, could be named "anti-authoritarian and pluralist" (Hine 1993) or, using Lijphart typology, "consensual" (Lijphart 1977). Power was dispersed among many bodies and organizations, none of which was able to concentrate enough power, so that each policy decision implies a long process of negotiation among the different social parts. It is also through mass media communications, to which each of these bodies and groups is connected, that they are able to take part in political decision-making: the news organizations represent the petitions and the interests of these groups in their confrontations with the government and with other groups. Each policy decision of any importance is preceded by articles, commentaries, interviews, and in-depth broadcasts in which the leaders of the various organized groups express their opinions, introduce or refuse proposals, and try to establish alliances or break them.

Within this kind of public sphere, some elements of the professional journalism model have no place: objectivity, as has been previously mentioned, becomes an accessory, if not a contradictory, dimension when considering the close ties between news organizations and social demands as well as the high level of political participation. The public sphere is the place where organized groups hold dialogue and mediate their respective positions: the role of the media is not just one of transmitting information but one that makes dialogue possible and develops it.

Limits and transformations of the alternative model

In this model of the public sphere problems and limits are obviously not lacking. The first one has been discussed at length. Because of their history and tradition, and the functions that they carry out, newspapers are directed toward a very limited public: "one thousand five hundred readers." Today, readers are more numerous but, nonetheless, Italy is still ranked among the lowest of industrialized countries in the number of readers. Italian newspapers, with their strong political coverage and partisanship, do not succeed in conquering the mass public, but rather aim at that segment of the public which is already socially conscious of the political problems and is integrated in one way or another in the political debate.

In contrast to the written news, television carries out a more important informational function of the vertical type and its viewing public is obviously greater in number than newspaper readers. Yet, until the beginning of the 1990s, when the political panorama of Italy changed radically with the disappearance of most of the old parties and the arrival of "Forza Italia," even television had played a horizontal communication function, aligning its various channels alongside the major political groups.

Today, the bonds of affiliation have undoubtedly weakened following the commercialization process which the entire system of mass communication has undergone beginning in the 1980s. Still, television keeps its attention fixed on the political universe and, on certain occasions, this interest becomes an occasion to conquer a larger audience. This brings up another important fact in the case of Italy: the high level of political participation and the diffusion and ramification of the party structure have resulted in not only one of the highest voter turnouts in Europe, but also a high degree of involvement, even at the individual level, of the citizens regarding political debate, even if, at the moment, the level of dissaffection toward politics is very high (Ginsborg 1998). Thus, when, at the end of the 1980s, public and commercial television renewed the formats of their current affairs transmissions dedicated to political themes, making them more palatable to viewers, they conquered the evening prime-time TV news ratings and a significant part of the viewing public.[13] Such coverage even produced an excess of political information, advancing the traditional Italian tendency toward abstract debate and political gossip and distracting attention from substantial problems and policy issues.

The commercialization process of the 1980s, along with other changes, has accentuated, in Italy as in all of Europe, a general process of secularization of the entire society and a partial weakening of bonds of political affiliation in the mass communications system. It has redefined the functions between written and televised information, strengthening the latter as a channel of vertical communication and keeping the function of the press essentially, but not exclusively, to horizontal communication. Nevertheless the traditional model of journalism has been transformed only partially; it has kept its attention focused strongly on political themes and its political links have not completely disappeared. Indeed, the major actor of the commercialization process, Berlusconi, strongly used, and still uses, his media empire to support his political activity (Mazzoleni 1995, Statham 1996).

In this situation, the social identity of the journalist appears weak. As previously stated, notwithstanding the existence of a professional guild to which it is necessary to belong,[14] the identity of the journalist often overlaps with a view of himself as the political actor;[15] the codes of ethics are not well established or shared. It is not by chance that in the past few years, with the weakening of the bonds of political affiliation, there has been much debate over the ethics and duty of a profession that now seems to be looking for its own identity. This debate takes place in the context of interactions with the other social systems, and particularly with the political one which seems to push toward a structuring of the profession different from the standard "professional model" though that remains a theoretical point of reference.

Thus, a "Western bias" has come into being: a specific professional model of journalism has become dominant and carried to extremes as the only and absolute one even in those political systems which do not seem to allow this system to work.

Notes

1 The research "Media and democracy" was conducted through questionnaires distributed to a sample of 600 journalists in each of these six countries: USA, Great Britain, Germany, Italy, Sweden, Japan. The questionnaire dealt essentially with role auto-perception and the idea of objectivity (Donsbach and Patterson 1992).

2 In 1995 the first country in newspaper circulation was Norway with 600 copies per 1,000 inhabitants. Italy comes after Spain, Malaysia, Latvia and Ireland with 108 copies per 1,000 inhabitants (Source: World Press Trends 1996).

3 The most widely circulated newspaper, *Il Corriere della Sera*, as well as several other newspapers, is the property of the RCS Group, the majority of whose shares are owned by Fiat which also owns the daily newspaper with the third-largest circulation, *La Stampa*. The daily with the second-largest circulation, *La Repubblica*, is owned by the Cir De Benedetti Group, once owner of Olivetti.

4 Specifically, from the mid-1960s, the Italian national government, through state-owned corporations, has come into possession of numbers of stock shares of various daily newspapers. Under the direction of Eugenio Cefis, Montedison, a state owned chemical industry, owned stock shares in *Il Corriere della Sera* and the majority of stock in *Il Messaggero* and other daily newspapers.

5 Until 1992, all the major Italian political parties owned their own daily newspapers: *Il Popolo* was the Christian Democrat newspaper, *L'Unità* the Communist Party's, *L'Avanti* was the newspaper of the Socialist Party, *L'Umanità* that of the Social Democratic Party, *La Voce Repubblicana* of the Republican Party and the *L'Opinione* of the Liberal Party.

6 In Italy, after a period of subordination by the government in power, the reform of public television (RAI) in 1975 assigned the RAI to the parties represented in parliament. Thus, until 1992 RAI 1, the predominantly viewed channel, was tied to the Christian Democrat Party, RAI 2 to the Socialist Party, and RAI 3 to the major opposition party, the Communist Party.

7 When *La Repubblica* was created it was the property of a group operating just in the journalism sector, the Caracciolo-Espresso Group. Afterwards, this newspaper too was sold to an industrial group, that of De Benedetti, then owner of Olivetti.

8 E. Scalfari, "Un giornale indipendente ma non neutrale," in *la Repubblica*, 14 gennaio 1976.

9 A significant point of this debate is found in the statements contained in *Informazione, Consenso e Disscuso* (Eco et al. 1979).

10 A. Panebianco, "Se la politica," in *Il Corriere della Sera*, November 30 1998.

11 In Europe, Italy has the highest voting turnout after Belgium, Austria, and Sweden. The average European voting abstention is 25.6 percent while Italy has 23.6 percent (Scaramozzino 1998).

12 Following many scholars, the high level of political participation has not avoided a crisis of dissaffection toward politics and the development of different forms of corruption which have ended up in the recent "Manipulite" (clean hands) phenomenon (Ginsborg 1998).

13 This took place essentially during the last two political election campaigns of 1994 and 1996 (Mancini and Mazzoleni 1995, Marini and Roncarolo 1997) and in more recent political events such as the Prodi government crisis in October 1998 in which daily in-depth coverage was broadcast at prime time by the principal networks, RAI and Mediaset, reaching very large audiences.

14 In Italy, in order to become a journalist it is necessary to pass a professional examination organized by the guild of journalists (Ordine dei Giornalisti). This professional examination may be taken only after having been hired and having worked for a news organization for two years or after having attended a school of journalism officially recognized by the guild for two years.

15 The cases of journalists who abandon the profession to begin a political career are extremely numerous. Among the most recent: Giuliano Ferrara, first an activist in the PCI (Italian Communist Party), then a successful journalist, and later a minister in the Berlusconi government; Pietro Badaloni, anchorman for the RAI and later president of the Council of Lazio; Alberto Angelini, also a journalist for the RAI and later member of parliament, and many others.

References

Altschull, H. (1984) *Agents of Power*, New York and London: Longman.

Bechelloni, G. (1982) *Professione giornalista*, Napoli: Liguori.

Blanchard, M. (1986) *Exporting the First Amendment*, New York and London: Longman.

Brants, K. (1985) "Broadcasting and politics in the Netherlands: from pillar to post," in R. Kuhn (ed.) *Broadcasting and Politics in Western Europe*, London: Cass.

Cannistraro, P. (1975) *La fabbrica del consenso*, Bari: Laterza.

Castronovo, V. and Tranfaglia, N. (1976) *La stampa italiana dall'unità al fascismo*, Bari: Laterza.

Chalaby, J. (1996) "Journalism as an Anglo American invention," in *European Journal of Communication*, 11(3): 303–27.

Curran, J. (1991) "Rethinking the media as a public sphere," in P. Dahlgren and C. Sparks (eds.) *Journalism and the Public Sphere in the New Media Age*, London and New York: Routledge.

Donsbach, W. and Patterson, T. (1992) "Journalists' roles and newsroom practices: a cross-national comparison," paper presented at the 42nd Conference of the International Communication Association, Miami, May 21–25.

Eco, U., Livolsi, M. and Panozzo, G. (1979) *Informazione. Consenso e dissenso*, Milano: Il Saggiatore.

Farinelli, G., Paccagnini, E., Santambrogio, G. and Villa, A. I. (1997) *Storia del giornalismo italiano*, Torino: Utet.

Franklin, B. (1997) *Newszak & News Media*, London, New York, Sydney and Auckland: Arnold.

Ginsborg, P. (1998) *L'Italia del tempo presente*, Torino: Einaudi.

Golding, P. (1977) "Media professionalism in the Third World: the transfer of an ideology," in J. Curran, J. M. Gurevitch and W. Janet (eds.) *Mass Communication and Society*, London: Edward Arnold.

Grossi, G. and Mazzoleni, G. (1984) "Per un'interpretazione del rapporto tra Parlamento e sistema informativo: analisi ed indicazione di ricerca," in Camera dei deputati (ed.) *Informazione e Parlamento*, Roma: Camera dei deputati.

Hine, D. (1993) *Governing Italy*, Oxford: Oxford University Press.

Humphreys, P. (1990) *Media and Media Policy in West Germany*, New York, Oxford and Munich: Berg.

Kocher, R. (1986) "Bloodhounds or missionaires: role definitions of German and British journalists," *European Journal of Communication*, 1(1): 43–65.

Kuhn, P. (1995) *The Media in France*, London and New York: Routledge.

Lijphart, A. (1977) *Democracy in Plural Societies*, New Haven and London: Yale University Press.

McQuail, D. (1987) *Mass Communication Theory: An Introduction*, London, Newbury Park, Beverly Hills and New Delhi: Sage.

McQuail, D. (1992) "The Netherlands: freedom and diversity under multichannel conditions," in J. Blumler (ed.) *Television and the Public Interest*, London, Newbury Park and New Delhi: Sage.

Mancini, P. (1985) *Videopolitica*, Torino: Eri.

Mancini, P. (1990) "Tra di noi. Sulla funzione negoziale della comunicazione politica," *Il Mulino*, 328, marzo–aprile: 291–321.

Mancini, P. (1991) "The public sphere and the use of news in a coalition system of government," in P. Dahlgren and C. Sparks (eds.) *Journalism and the Public Sphere in the New Media Age*, London and New York: Routledge.

Mancini, P. and Mazzoleni, G. (1995) *I media scendono in campo*, Roma: Eri.

Marini, R. and Roncarolo, F. (1997) *I media come arena elettorale*, Roma: Eri.

Mazzoleni, G. (1995) "Italian political communication at a turning point," in *European Journal of Communication*, 10(3): 291–321.

Murialdi, P. (1986) *Storia del giornalismo italiano*, Torino: Gutenberg 2000.

Nerone, J. (ed.) (1995) *Last Rights*, Chicago and Urbana: University of Illinois Press.

Ottone, P. (1985) *Il gioco dei potenti*, Milano: Longanesi.

Pizarroso Quintero, A. (1989) *Stampa, radio e propaganda*, Milano: Angeli.

Porter, W. (1983) *The Italian Journalist*, Ann Arbor: University of Michigan Press.

Porter, V. and Hasselbach, S. (1991) *Pluralism, Politics and the Marketplace*, London and New York: Routledge.

Scaramozzino, P. (1998) "Relazione introduttiva," paper at the International Conference of Sise (Società Italiana di Studi Elettorali) on "Le nuove forme di astensionismo," Roma, 21–23 gennaio.

Schiller, H. (1976) *Communication and Cultural Domination*, White Plains: M. E. Sharpe.

Schou, S. (1992) "Postwar Americanisation and the revitalisation of European culture," in M. Skovmand and K. C. Schroder (eds.) *Media Cultures*, London: Routledge.

Schudson, M. (1978) *Discovering the News*, New York: Basic Books.

Seymour-Ure, C. (1968) *The Press, Politics and the Public*, London: Methuen.

Siebert, F., Peterson, T. and Schramm, W. (1963) *Four Theories of the Press*, Urbana and Chicago: University of Illinois Press.

Sreberny-Mohammadi, A. (1991) "The global and the local in international communications," in J. Curran and M. Gurevitch (eds.) *Mass Media and Society*, London, New York, Melbourne and Auckland: Routledge.

Statham, P. (1996) "Berlusconi, the media and the new right in Italy," in *Press Politics* 1(1): 87–106.

Tunstall, J. (1977) *The Media are American*, London: Constable.

19 South African media, 1994–7

Globalizing via political economy

Keyan G. Tomaselli

Trade and economic sanctions against South Africa ended following the demise of legislated apartheid after 1990. International capital had begun by 1994 to acquire interests in local media companies. Domestic black empowerment groups also made major purchases in previously white-owned media corporations. In this chapter I chart the course of these ownership changes and some of the associated ideological shifts. I also examine their significance in terms of democracy and the globalization of black-dominated capital at the end of 1996. The background to these momentous changes will be briefly discussed in terms of:

- opposing historical ideologies—Afrikaner nationalism versus English-derived liberalism;
- oppositional discourses deriving from black and nonracial movements; and
- post-apartheid media trends in terms of the new lexicons of "nation-building" and "empowerment."

I begin by discussing the historical allegiances of different sectors of the South African media. This is necessary to establish the context within which developments between 1990 and 1996 occurred.

Historical background

Movements of South African capital between 1996 and 1997 freed the press from extreme historical ideological and identity positions as either pro- or anti-apartheid. Under apartheid, media had coalesced into various factions between 1948, when the National Party (NP) took power, and 1990 when it unbanned the liberation movements. A coalition Government of National Unity (GNU) took power after the general election of 1994. The African National Congress (ANC) secured a parliamentary majority. Following the transition, media corporations put profit on the agenda as their objective. These post-apartheid ideological shifts were similar to the nineteenth-century experience of the South African English-language press. This press had advocated libertarian values generally, and press freedom in particular. The philosophy had originated in British and European politico-economic developments in which legalization of a political public sphere had liberated the press as a forum for rational–critical debate. This released the pressure on media to take sides ideologically, enabling the early British press to abandon polemics and concentrate on profit opportunities (Habermas 1989: 176).

Up to the late 1980s, ownership of the English-language press was associated with the century-old, largely English–South African-owned, mining industry. This investment had sustained the economic ascendancy of classes associated with British imperial interests. But contradictions emerged early on: liberal editors came to regard apartheid as an irrational and inefficient economic system. In contrast, mining relied on a large workforce whose reproduction of labor power was kept very low through migrant labor and geographical and job segregation (Legassick 1974). Simultaneously, however, the different fractions among resistance movements of the apartheid era resurfaced as interests of media ownership and corporate policy in ways somewhat at odds with the rhetoric of the anti-apartheid struggle.

The early Afrikaans-language press had emerged from the propaganda organs of the Afrikaner-dominated NP. This press opposed English-dominated South African capital and supported Afrikaner capital accumulation. Even after 1948 when the NP introduced apartheid, English industrial capital still constituted the dominant economic fraction. Originally designed to foster and protect the entrenchment of a more agrarian form of *Rentier* capital in the form of insurance and land-bank investments, apartheid tended to marginalize industrial investment. Afrikaner capital had grown around land banking and insurance, activities well suited to Afrikaners' agrarian rather than industrial interests. This created a classical situation in which the culture of risk associated with industrial economies clashed with the conservationist culture of agrarian economics (Kemp 1985). This was the context in which the NP entrenched itself as the ruling political fraction (Muller 1987). The maneuvring necessary for maintaining this uneasy relationship between English and Afrikaner capitals inevitably suppressed black interests.

Analysis of apartheid includes study of how racial discourse "materialized" into political and social practices and state bureaucracies. This was evident, for example, in the language/race-specific radio and TV stations whose footprints coincided almost exactly with the spatial boundaries of each of the legislated racial–ethnic "population" groups—areas known as Bantustans. Each station was administered by bureaucrats coopted from each of the "race" groups, each transmitting "culturally" inflected interpretations and vernacular languages partly machined out of apartheid semantics (R.E. Tomaselli *et al.* 1989). The study of apartheid would thus also examine how racial capitalism (Saul and Gelb 1980) arose out of particular politico–economic, social and psychological conditions fashioned by colonialism, neo-colonialism and fractions of capital within the state. This is the background against which the post-apartheid discourses of diversity, nation-building and empowerment, which characterized the post-1990 scenario, should also be discussed. These terms, as with the ANC's nonracial philosophy, arose out of earlier phases of resistance to apartheid. The main periods are discussed in the next section.

Origins of counter-hegemonic and oppositional movements

Three popular ideologies contested apartheid at different historical conjunctures after 1960. The first was Black Consciousness (BC) up to the early 1970s. The June 1976 Soweto uprising saw a shift toward the formation of the United Democratic Front (UDF) in 1983. The UDF's subsequent alliance with the Congress of SA Trade Unions (COSATU) became known as the Mass Democratic Movement (MDM). The year 1990 and after saw the merging of the internal UDF into the returned ANC. The historical moments of each of these movements remained in the way their adherents related to post-apartheid media. However, earlier resistance needs to be discussed as a background to these developments.

Charterism

The Freedom Charter (1955), drawn up via a process of popular consultation, provided the means to a national unifying consciousness transcending class, ethnicity, tribalism, language, and most political positions (Suttner and Cronin 1986). This was a defining moment in what was to later reemerge as the nonracial policy adopted by the UDF in the 1980s. Nonracialism was also a cornerstone of Nelson Mandela's policy of reconciliation in the 1990s. Nonracialism is problematic because it is a kind of negative conceptualization of a positive social and political ethic. As such, it is a kind of anti-sign, suppressing indicators of racial, ethnic, linguistic, and class differences in the interests of sociopolitical and organizational unity.

Black Consciousness—1970s

During the early 1970s Black Consciousness filled the political and cultural vacuum caused by the banning of the ANC and Pan Africanist Congress (PAC) in 1960. Urbanized black petty bourgeois intellectuals led by Steve Biko, for example, established the Black People's Convention (BPC) in 1972. An indigenous theory of black resistance discursively drew on the American Black Power movement, meshed with the theories of Franz Fanon. Its focus in South Africa was dual: a psychological liberation from racism, and a critique of capitalism. BC produced the first significant move in media mobilization within the corporate press (Raubenheimer 1991).

Many of the BC leaders belonged to the generation of "volunteer cadres" who had sought popular comment on the compilation of the Freedom Charter. Thus the principle of nonracialism enshrined in the Charter informed parallel developments arising out of the same moment of struggle that had given rise to BC. The Charterist moment came to fruition in the formation of the UDF in August 1983. It was at this stage that a range of white center-left and outright socialist or communist groups and organizations sought—and were encouraged—to work under the UDF umbrella.

Mass Democratic Resistance—1983 to February 1990

BC, espoused by the PAC and Azanian Peoples Organisation (AZAPO), which succeeded BPC, argued that race was the determining form of oppression. In contradistinction, the UDF developed a class analysis which located capital as the enemy instead of whites or, specifically, Afrikaners. Apartheid was argued to be a particular form or distortion of capitalism. This resulted in a much more brutal form of economic and class oppression than found in Western capitalist economies. Those states which benefited financially from apartheid, however, were implicated by this analysis in the perpetuation of this system.

The UDF argued that racial oppression was dominant, but that class was determining. In other words, capital, both local and international, was argued to impose a racial capitalism which shifted in response to international pressure on the apartheid regime, and in terms of internal dissent. The objective of capital was to continuously reform apartheid to facilitate the continued extraction of profits in the context of a maturing economy on the one hand, and the growing demands after 1972 for worker and political rights on the other. The cross-racial alliances which resulted from this analysis were often hidden by foreign and local commercial media, which preferred to image conflict in ahistorical racial terms.

This trans-class, trans-race, trans-cultural and trans-linguistic UDF alliance occurred when the apartheid state had belatedly begun to respond to the needs of industrial capital. Prompted by Soweto '76, the state realized that it had to accommodate industrial needs to survive isolation from the wider world economy. The termination of influx control to permit the development of free labor and retail markets, the facilitation of "responsible" trade unionism, and the extension of some political and residential rights to urban blacks, followed in the next decade. Both Afrikaner and English capital negotiated with the state to bring about changes *in* rather than *of* the existing order (Stadler 1987: 3, 6), to revitalize a maturing economy no longer adequately served by illiterate migrant labor.

The NP's attempts at reform, instead of abolishing apartheid, evoked the UDF-led mass-democratic response. The result was an unprecedented crisis for both capital and the state between 1986 and February 1990. This period witnessed a battle for control over the black urban environment, media, and language, and the popular will. The UDF became the national coordinating center of local resistance. Media emerged as a focus for both communication and mobilization, from the local to the national (Tomaselli and Louw 1991).

Open insurrection occurred with the creation of the Tricameral Parliament in 1984. This forum of separate Chambers was elected on racially defined voters' rolls for people of Asian and mixed-race ("colored") origin, but excluding blacks. The state declared a partial emergency in 1985, later extended nationally. By the end of 1986, over 30,000 activists had been detained under emergency regulations (CIRR 1988: 12) and the media was tightly managed via a succession of emergency regulations (Teer-Tomaselli 1993). The Freedom Charter reemerged as a rallying document during this phase, calling on *all* South Africans, no matter their officially designated racial categories, to work toward a democratic future.

From nationalism towards globalism

Gross disparities in wealth, education, living standards, and denial of access to social resources presented daunting barriers to the possibility for a single post-apartheid consciousness (or nationalism) drawing in all South Africa's citizens. Apartheid, more than any other factor, prevented the development of an even minimally homogeneous public sphere or "national culture" as called for by the Freedom Charter.

Apartheid had politicized cultural and linguistic diversity, encouraging a multiplicity of vigorous and frequently antagonistic ethnic consciousnesses. Ideologically, this was apparent from the far-left BC and PAC, through to the reactionary white right. With the possible exception of English, none of the other ten post-apartheid official languages offered themselves as "nationally" unifying sign communities. Added to this was a residual BC antagonism toward transnationalization, especially with regard to perceived Eurocentric values.

The problem of local identity became a prime issue during the transition period. How can local linguistic and ethnic sign communities provide forms of intelligibility within national frames? Can people couple cultural negotiations on these issues with popular access to media? A coherent, if at times momentary, South Africanism did, however, develop out of the strategic management of national symbols, especially those centered on sporting events (Shepperson 1996).

At the very moment that South Africa, and especially black-dominated print media capital, was internationalizing, the popular perception was becoming virulently parochial and alarmingly xenophobic. As technical developments worked toward economic globalization, a parallel development in the ownership and control of both print and broadcast media institutions was apparent. A few major organizations controlled the media and set South African news agendas. The Electronic Media Network (M-Net), a pay-TV channel, for example, was established in 1986 to rescue the Afrikaans press from financial decline after the introduction of advertising to South African Broadcasting Corporation Television (SABC-TV) in 1978 (Collins 1992). Effectively dominated by Afrikaner capital until early 1997, M-Net penetrated markets in Africa, Europe, Scandinavia, the Middle East, and Greece, especially after 1990.

Phases of post-apartheid print media ownership

Two kinds of questions about corporate control are important. The first are "action/power questions." These identify "key allocative controllers" and "operational controllers" who exercise ultimate authority over human and material resources respectively. Second are "structure/determination questions," which identify economic and political determinants constraining both allocative and operational controllers (Murdock 1982: 124).

Strategic movements in mining capital were initiated after 1990 by the Anglo American Corporation (AAC) and Johannesburg Consolidated Investments (JCI). These premier mining houses were interconnected on the Johannesburg Stock Exchange (JSE). Through these equity arrangements, Anglo and JCI owned the bulk of the English-language media. The impending ANC electoral victory required that they act in defense of their broader mining interests, rather than purely those of the press. These movements of finance, discussed below, also reveal the ways in which capital responds to shifts of power within the state.

The media sector toward the end of the 1980s was dominated by SABC, Argus Holdings Ltd, Times Media Ltd (TML), and the Afrikaner-owned Perskor and Nasionale Pers (National Newspapers). The four white-owned press groups together also controlled M-Net. The media environment was thus tightly managed, with closely regulated advertising, printing, and distribution arrangements (Louw 1993: 159–80). Complex relationships thus existed between the media conglomerates of the apartheid era and other South African capital formations.

Argus began restructuring in 1993 as English-dominated business redeployed capital in response to structurally determined local political, and global economic, changes. To achieve this they "unbundled" their companies by selling off constituent parts. Unbundling also indicated a commitment to black empowerment. The crucial understanding from this is that, despite the fact that the media conglomerates chose to undertake selective "unbundling," the result was a redeployment in allocative control as a means of shaping structural processes. I will now chart the different phases of the changing face of South African media allocative control.

Phase I: the Sowetan *for Sowetans*

Argus initiated unbundling by selling 52 percent of the black-targeted the *Sowetan*, the largest daily newspaper, to black-owned Corporate Africa. Its chairman was Dr Ntatho Motlana, leader of the Soweto Committee of Ten during the 1970s, and the Mandelas' personal physician. Argus retained 20 percent of New African Publishers (NAIL)[1] (75 percent of which was owned by Corporate Africa), 42 percent in the *Sowetan* as well as printing, advertising, and management contracts, thus retaining allocative control.

SANLAM, an Afrikaner-owned insurance giant, held 17 percent of Corporate Africa in September 1996. SANLAM, a mutual company, had historically powered *rentier* Afrikaner financial advancement following the British destruction of the Afrikaner agricultural economies between 1889 and 1902. As mentioned earlier, the competition for economic power often results in odd bedfellows. As Robin McGregor (1996) concluded:

> The catalyst throughout the rise of Afrikaner power, to a large degree, has been Sanlam. Black businessmen are demonstrating the same determination, and it is no surprise that the institution which has responded most readily to their need for financial aid has been Sanlam. This is no coincidence. In its early days, Sanlam went through similar, although far less severe, deprivation and exclusion from the mainstream of the economy.

This process of capital interpenetration indicates that people can achieve common purposes within materially objective communities of practice. Identity forged through material struggles tends to bring communities of like experience, even if historically conflicted, into surprising cooperation when broader structural conditions change. Following Union in 1910, English and Afrikaner interests, for example, had buried their class differences to protect white-dominated capital in general. All the while, they continued their ideological struggle—mainly via the media. Afrikaners and English South Africans continued their economic opposition until the NP accepted capitalism in the early 1980s. The value of the anti-apartheid pro-capitalist English press to Anglo during apartheid, thus, was to protect its secondary and tertiary economic interests in the manufacturing and financial sectors, and to prevent nationalization of its mining interests. The nation as the unit of integrated political liberation was achieved after 1990; after that, the terrain of black struggle was for economic empowerment as well.

Phase II: globalization—discursive responses

The impending ANC electoral victory in April 1994 reopened South Africa to foreign reinvestment. Tony O'Reilly's Irish-based multinational Independent Newspapers (IN) identified Argus as a significantly undercultivated asset (*Mercury*, March 13: 6). IN bought 31 percent of Argus from Anglo in January 1994, a stake increased to 58 percent in 1995 and 75 percent by 1999. Argus eventually became the largest company in O'Reilly's international corporation.[2]

By February 1994 the two distinct English presses were Argus and Anglo–JCI's TML, though the latter had minority holdings in the former. In securing effective allocative control over Argus, now separately listed on the JSE as Independent Newspapers, O'Reilly stimulated a second phase in restructuring. This entailed consolidating the new company's majority hold over much of the English-language print media in April 1994 by purchasing TML's holdings in companies previously owned by Argus.

Significantly, only the sale of the *Sowetan* and the consequent formation of NAIL was an unbundling exercise in the strict sense. In passing control of the *Sowetan* to a consortium sympathetic to the ANC, though ironically the paper's staffers were BC leaning, Anglo thereby demonstrated the reactive nature of capitalist business. BC, libertarianism, and the ANC's then mild socialism all found a nexus in the deal. Such is the flexibility and cooptive capacity of capital: it can tolerate, and even capitalize on, opposing discourses within the same company. Ironically, black-dominated political parties and the Black Editors' Forum considered such pluralism to be antithetical to nation-building and cultural unification. Paradoxically, these editors simultaneously called for diversity, new voices, and black empowerment. I return to this issue later.

Phase III: interpenetration of capitals

The purchase of JCI's Johnnic from Anglo American by the National Empowerment Consortium (NEC)[3] in late 1996 signalled a pivotal advance toward the interpenetration of black and white dominated fractions of capital. Johnnic, the R8.5 billion industrial arm of the unbundled JCI, had direct and indirect controlling interests in the Central News Agency chain of retail stores, the recording company Gallo, M-NET and TML (*Sunday Times, Business Times*, June 4, 1995: 1). This bid came after the *Sowetan* had acquired the last of the 1980s progressive–alternative newspapers, *New Nation*, an unashamedly union-supporting socialist weekly. *New Nation* had been the only nationwide socialist weekly under apartheid. From its founding in 1986 until 1994, it had been donor-funded. However, when donors switched their support to the GNU after 1994, the paper could not attract sufficient advertising revenue and ran into financial difficulty. Shortly after its takeover by the *Sowetan*, the paper was shut down (see Mpofu 1995). Before continuing with the restructuring phases of the print media, I will examine the impact of the deal that set up the *Sowetan* as an independent commercial operation.

The history and significance of the Johnnic deal

Anglo had by early 1994 settled on JCI for unbundling following ANC demands for blacks to play a greater role in the economy. NEC was in 1994 a loose association of smaller businesses and unions,[4] including NAIL after January 1996. Although NAIL had the management experience and funds to buy Johnnic on its own, some of the other NEC constituents—as did Anglo—questioned NAIL's commitment to black empowerment. The unions viewed NAIL as a vehicle for black enrichment[5] of an elite group of businessmen rather than facilitating real popular progress (Lunsche 1996: 5). NEC initially bought 20 percent of Johnnic for R1.5 billion at a 7 percent discount, with an option to boost its stake to 35 percent within eighteen months of the conclusion of the deal, at a discount of 5 percent.

The NEC takeover of Johnnic was the biggest cash deal in South African history. Within two years of the 1994 elections, black-dominated capital controlled 10 percent of the JSE. This transaction compares with two acquisitions by Afrikaner capital, in

1964 and 1974, which had thrust Afrikaner ownership through the 7 percent level of JSE market capitalization. Yet the Afrikaner penetration was achieved no less than *twenty-six* years after political control had been won by the NP. In 1964, Anglo American "allowed" Federal Mining Investments to take control of General Mining. Ten years later the Union Corporation takeover by General Mining placed Afrikaner capital on a par with other corporate giants dominated by English-speaking South Africans (McGregor 1996: 5). The benefits of the sale for Anglo were to rid itself of non-core activities, and to coopt the black new class into the national and global economies.

One of Johnnic's companies, Multi-Choice International Holdings (MIH), M-Net's signal provider incidentally, owned 40 percent of Network Holdings, the M-Net cable operator in Europe and Africa. In addition, in late 1996, Pearsons, a British-based publisher, purchased 50 percent of two TML titles, *Financial Mail* and *Business Day*. As a majority shareholder, NEC had allocative control of its core assets. Consequently, it exerted a controlling interest over TML of which it owned 91.4 percent. NEC therefore was represented on the boards of TML and M-Net.

Cyril Ramaphosa, the first chairman of the new Johnnic board of directors, described the Johnnic deal as a step towards greater diversification of the media (*Mercury*, October 28, 1996). Nigel Bruce, former editor of the *Financial Mail*, however, counter-argued that concentration by a particular constituency aligned to the ANC was the result. Although NEC was not involved at the operational level of TML, it was able to implement black empowerment at the allocative level.

Identity and ethnicity of ownership: continuing the restructuring

The Argus restructuring emerged as a significant departure from the pattern of concentrated ownership that historically characterized the South African print media. For the first time ever, mining capital had relinquished newspapers previously regarded as strategically important in ensuring its dominant role in the economy, and the security of capitalism in the face of rising Afrikaner national socialism. However, the later acquisitions by black-dominated capital of TML and the share offerings to black investors by M-Net and Nasionale Pers in 1996 showed a similarly clear break with the practices of Afrikaner capital. Yet this process, the fourth stage of media control restructuring, took place under a quite different set of considerations.[6]

Phase IV: restructuring Naspers and Perskor in the Afrikaans press

Against all predictions (e.g. Louw 1995), the NP-supporting Afrikaans-language press also underwent a sea-change during the early 1990s. Naspers (*Nasionale Pers—National Press*), financed by reformist Cape Afrikaner capital, bought control of the conservative northern Perskor (*Die Perskorporasie—The Press Corporation*) in the early 1980s. This purchase was the outcome of attempts within Afrikanerdom to retain old-style apartheid in the early 1980s (Muller 1987: 146). Naspers in 1996–7 formed new firms and sold shares to companies owned by black business. Its managing director announced that the group was "selling the family silver" to black interest groups for moral and practical reasons (*Sunday Times*, August 11, 1996: 4). Fifty-one percent of the black-targeted *City Press* was earmarked for black investment groups. Naspers also merged its two largest educational publishing concerns, together with its interests in distance education, into a new company and then sold 50 percent to black partners (*Sunday Times*, August 11, 1996: 4).

In particular, the restructuring of Perskor is instructive. At the start of 1996, Perskor owned a number of highly profitable magazines, a stake in M-Net, the *Citizen* daily and a half stake in *Rapport*, a national Sunday paper, among other media. Kagiso Trust, a large NGO, had funded UDF activities during the late 1980s. Empowerment schemes being its objective, Kagiso had previously relied on anti-apartheid funding from oversees donors and contributions from local interest groups. In becoming self-sufficient, Kagiso[7] set up Kagiso Trust Investments (KTI).

KTI's initial media acquisition included a 25.5 percent ownership of two former SABC commercial radio stations and, along with Mail and Guardian Media, applied to the Independent Broadcasting Authority (IBA) for a *new* radio license. In mid-1997 KTI became a joint controlling shareholder of the Perskor Group, but the two parted company in 1998. The deal with KTI was both political and financial. Perskor, which had monopolized NP government printing contracts during the apartheid era, now found itself edged out of the market. The deal was an attempt to help Perskor "shed its verkrampte (reactionary) image and regain some of the government's book printing contracts" (Efrat, *Sunday Times*, November 24, 1996: 10). Similar to the NAIL-Sanlam alliance, the KTI–Perskor cooperation signalled new communities of practice in which the one party sought economic empowerment, and the other political protection, though joint partnerships.

The final result: new political allegiances

The NP's inability to represent big capital in the post-apartheid era and the new-found libertarianism among firms like Naspers and Perskor resulted in some extraordinary shifts of political allegiance during this four-phase transitional period. *Die Burger*, the "mother of Afrikaner Nationalism," had editorially supported the small liberal Democratic Party (DP) while criticizing the NP during the 1994 elections (Uys 1996: 8). Naspers, in what would have been a heresy and politico-economic suicide prior to 1994, even donated funds to the DP, ANC, and NP election campaigns (*Die Burger*, May 11, 1996: 12). Ton Vosloo of Nasionale argued that the company had learned that being too close to a particular party was no longer "expedient" (Uys 1996: 8).

Nationalism and ethnicity: the bridging influence of globalism

All this restructuring was simultaneously a continuation of historical patterns. A "rationalized" public sphere, organized by private, profit-driven organizations and subordinate to the principle of profit-maximization, remained largely closed to wider public participation. The public sphere has thus largely remained under the control of "*property-owning private people*" whose new-found autonomy is rooted in the sphere of commodity exchange (Habermas 1989: 110). It is in this light that charges by President Nelson Mandela in a speech to the International Press Institute (IPI) need to be assessed:

> With the exception of the *Sowetan*, the senior editorial staffs of all South Africa's daily newspapers are cast from the same racial mould … They are white, they are from a middle class background, they tend to share a very similar life experience …

While no one can object in principle to editors with such a profile, what is disturbing is the threat of one-dimensionality this poses for the media. It is clearly inequitable that in a country whose population is overwhelmingly black, the principal players in the media have no knowledge of the life experience of that majority.

(*Star*, February 15, 1994)

Replacing whites with blacks in the corporate press is not really going to solve the problem of structural inequality. Neither will this racial substitution automatically provide increased popular access or diversity of opinion in the media. In fact, as previously "white" newspapers crossed racial readership boundaries, they experienced a commensurate loss in aggregate readership. To bridge class and racial differences through a reverse racial substitution of staffers under the IN or TML ownership structures is one possible solution to creating diversity and reader crossover, but this requires commercial risks. For Ken Owen, former editor of the *Sunday Times* (September 3, 1995: 26), the reproduction of corporate philosophy is the key.

Owen's statement is symptomatic of inherited social structures in the post-apartheid era, but also of Bruce's assumption that newspapers which serve markets will survive, but that those that serve interests will fail (*Natal Witness*, January 6, 1997: 8). What Bruce misunderstands, of course, is that markets under apartheid served racial-capitalist interests. Therefore, the notion of "interests" cannot be easily "separated" from the way "markets" in the era of racial capitalism coalesced. The significant sums of black pension money now invested in TML would have to be protected, not risked (Efrat 1996: 8). In 1998, TML and NAIL therefore agreed that the only way to cross racial divides was to establish a new newspaper, *Sunday World*, launched in March 1999.

These new ventures, no matter the race of the persons who own them, are as likely to bolster capitalist interests as they have in the past, and thus support the continuance of a class-based social formation. The *Sunday Times Business Times* (January 19, 1997: 2), for example, took perverse delight in reporting on Ramaphosa's complaints about the effect of leaks to the press about Johnnic. Or, as journalist and co-owner of Mafube Publishing, Thami Mazwai, himself stated when discussing the Anglo–General Mining deal with reference to the NEC takeover of Johnnic *vis-à-vis* its new shareholders: "To be multiracial is in the logic of business" (*Sunday Independent*, January 19, 1997: 4). And, as the union investment companies ironically argue in defending tactics at variance with union principles: "This is business" (*SA Labour Bulletin* 1996: 37).

An instrumentalist analysis might reveal how capitalists pursue their individual interests (see e.g. Louw 1993). NAIL's acquisitive business operations and practices come into this domain. Analysis on a general level requires investigation of how organizations as a whole operate to advance the collective interests of the capitalist class—including blacks. And here is the conundrum—the new black owners may indeed have facilitated some sort of Africanization of values in the media, but financial survival is determined by readers and advertisers, not intellectuals and cultural commissars claiming "traditional" legitimacy or cultural vision.

The traditionalist Council for African Thought, for example, espouses instrumentalist thinking in assuming that a solely black-controlled press will "mobilize and channel African values and traditions … to bear on public life, and make them influential in moulding and or changing mass behavior and thinking" (*Natal Witness*,

September 11, 1995: 3). This essentialist claim assumes a homogeneity of African societies, denies the existence of different interpretive communities within them, and believes that the media have more influence than they do have. The Council's thinking represents a particular kind of interpenetration of the psyche and the material.[8] This universalizing "traditionalist" discourse is traversing in a different way a similar grid of significations which previously ordered apartheid consciousness. Both incorporate elements of coercion, persuasion and a single world view. Both rest on delegitimizing other discourses, both individual and corporate. "Identity" is semantically slid into the notion of "diversity," which then emerges as the new "totality."

Pluralism is dismissed in an instant: "the media must reflect people's aspirations. It must be a nation reflecting itself. If you read the *Sowetan* and *The Citizen*, it is like living in two countries. As editors, we must break these mindsets" (T. Mazwai, the *Sunday Independent*, January 19, 1994: 4). Mazwai's other words, "diversity in ownership and management," thus offer the opportunity of dialogue, but from the perspective of the new class of media moguls. This is a primarily majoritarian position (Louw 1997), occurring within the communities of practice represented within the terrain of legitimacy mapped out by organizations like the Black Editors Forum. Black journalists helped to bring about changes in political structure; now the site of struggle is occurring at the level of action/power and who gets to obtain allocative control.

Mazwai's allegations against the libertarian discourse of "the public's right to know" were published in the *Sunday Independent*'s opposite editorial pages. He had accused its editor of misconduct in making known the Middle Eastern country which had secured massive South African armaments contracts via Denel, the previous apartheid nuclear company. Mazwai argues that the deal could have been jeopardized, thus negatively impacting the national economy. The *Independent*, in contrast, argued the "public's right to know" and challenged the Supreme Court ruling banning identification of the buyer. These disputes have less to do with "racism" as Mazwai insists, than with differences in ideology.

The above analysis indicates that many media organizations, both print and broadcast including the national broadcaster, have accepted the new discourses of "nation," nonracialism and a South African identity or identities. However, the problems arise in making sense of the effects of the new ownership of Independent Newspapers, TML, and Nasionale Pers. To recapitulate, during apartheid the English press ideologically protected English-dominated capital in general, and mining capital in particular. Now the new ownership cadre simply demands profits in the context of global capital. While IN and TML were making high profits they were, however, unlikely to broaden their readerships in the short term or respond to the kinds of criticisms levelled by Mazwai.

At heart is the competition for political power and the control of instruments which mediate the discourse of that power. The government assumes that a black press will be more supportive of policy than a white-owned press because it will reflect the "black" experience.

Conclusion

My prime argument has been that material changes cannot occur without an accompanying shift in ideology. Since the ANC has accepted free enterprise this process will automatically strengthen the various fractions of capital—local and global, black and white, mixed and interpenetrating—irrespective of demands for a corporate media which reflects the "black" and "traditional" experience. Where English and Afrikaner-dominated capitals were once in antagonistic relations, the new schism may become initially black vs white, although a competitive—and cooperative—interpenetration will be the long-term result.

The media industry is exemplary of similar interpenetration of white and black capitals governed by racially mixed boards of directors in all sectors of the South African economy. By the end of November 1996, 81 percent of the newspaper market remained in South African hands, with the other 18 percent held by O'Reilly. NEC through TML dominated 21 percent, and KTI 5 percent of the 10 percent held by Perskor (Efrat 1996: 8). However, corporate diversity remained elusive. If ideological interests override markets, then the collapse of an opposition press will further reduce what diversity of content currently remains. It makes no difference as to who owns the press. One can still therefore ask: Why did Anglo divest itself of companies that were earning it relatively high returns? Nigel Bruce has an answer. Quite simply, by cheaply selling off Johnnic to ANC-supporting interests, Anglo as an "enduring monopoly" hoped to secure government sanctions of convenience to preserve its diamond monopoly (*Natal Witness*, January 6, 1997: 8). The deal, of course, also draws into the capitalist endeavor the previously most hostile elements of the working class. Anglo therefore protects its mining interests from government as well.

The black-held investment capital came to a significant extent from black union pension and provident funds totalling R20 billion which—almost in waiting as it were—mostly accumulated during the late apartheid era. This could be described as accumulation by default, as unlike early Afrikaner-dominated capital, which had less in reserve on achieving power in 1948, black capital could be put to instant investment opportunity. This immediate impetus hastened the government's privatization program because, for the first time, workers began to see that they had a stake in this process—indeed, they helped bring it about. And herein lie the contradictions: (a) COSATU was opposed to privatization but was nevertheless part of the process; (b) the unions had forgotten the basic principle of class analysis: surplus value can only accrue from labor exploitation. It is their members who generate surplus value. The contradictory consciousness that resulted from the headlong rush by unions into corporate investment resulted in an intelligibility of practice which continued to replicate the class structure, albeit in a more racially inclusive way.

Acknowledgments

This paper draws on Tomaselli (1997) which offers a much more detailed narrative of ownership and control. I am indebted to Arnold Shepperson for his considerable help.

Notes

1 Owned by Motlana, in May 1996, NAIL was valued at R900 million via Corporate Africa on the JSE. Other investors included Sankorp, the investment arm of Afrikaner insurance giant, SANLAM (21.5 percent) and the black consciousness National Council of Trade Unions (13 percent). NAIL's principal investment is 30 percent equity in Metropolitan Life, the country's fifth largest assurance company, bought from SANLAM, in 1992. It also has

a 10 percent interest in MTN, a cellular network, and 21 percent of the African Bank, South Africa's first black owned financial institution. The National Council of Trade Unions, a BC grouping, owns 13 percent of NAIL.

2 I am indebted to Bold *et al.* (1994) for their research into the O'Reilly takeover of Argus.

3 COSATU-affiliated unions, backed by large retirement funds, founded the NEC in early 1995. NEC was made up of fifty black business groups.

4 Unions had become major investors in retailing, stockbroking and radio. In September 1996, the SA Clothing and Textiles Workers Union Investment Company, via its stake in Africa on air, which includes Primedia, gained control of Highveld Stereo and bought 10 percent of Motolink (*Sunday Times Business Times*, November 24, 1996: 14). Union investment companies were supposed to operate separately from the union, an ideal not matched in the practice (*SA Labour Bulletin* 1996: 38).

5 Motlana in particular was singled out for criticism (*Mail and Guardian*, January 8–11, 1996: B1–B3). Thami Mazwai, publisher and editor of *Enterprise*, comments: "As a black journalist encouraging black economic empowerment, people equate me with socialism. I am unashamedly a black capitalist" (*Sunday Independent*, January 19, 1997: 4).

6 Restructuring and mergers flared again in 1998–9, so further phases occurred after this fourth phase, which marks the periodization of this particular study.

7 Kagiso sold insurance giant, Liberty Life, a 25 percent stake in KTI, for R50 million. KTI made its debut in motoring through Kagiso Motors, a joint venture with Imperial Motor Holdings. As part of the New Radio Consortium, Kagiso Trust was awarded Radio Oranje and East Coast Radio, two of the six SABC stations up for sale in 1996 (*Sunday Times Business Times*, November 24, 1996: 14). It also has interests in catering, and a 40 percent stake in Haum Publishing, now called Kagiso Publishers. This purchase was facilitated by a $5 million loan from US Merchant Bank, J.P. Morgan. Haum was previously a very conservative operation. Kagiso is one of the few black groups not involved in the Johnnic deal. Donald Gordon of Liberty serves on the Kagiso board; his father-in-law, Hylton Appelbaum, played a major role in the development of Kagiso (Fallon 1996: 13).

8 Immunologist William Makgoba (1998: 4) even argues the possibility of a genetic or biological basis for "patterns of African thought." This sociobiological idea is not new: it was also argued by Afrikaner nationalists and propagated as justification for apartheid.

References

Bold, L., Bramdaw, N., Gokool, S., Guambe, D., Manhando, S. and Young, D. (1994) "Corporate control and the South African media: the Argus case," unpublished research project, Durban: Centre for Cultural and Media Studies.

CIIR (Catholic Institute for International Relations) (1988) *Now Everyone is Afraid: The Changing Face of Policing in South Africa*, London: CIIR.

Collins, R. (1992) "Broadcasting and telecommunications policy in post-apartheid South Africa," *Critical Arts*, 6(1): 26–51.

Efrat, Z. (1996) "New ownership scramble," *Natal Witness*, November 27: 8.

Habermas, J. (1989) *The Structural Transformation of the Public Sphere*, London: Polity.

Kemp, T. (1985) *Industrialization in Nineteenth Century Europe*, London: Longman.

Legassick, M. (1974) "Legislation, ideology and economy in post-1948 South Africa," *Journal of Southern African Studies*, 1(1): 5–35.

Louw, P.E. (ed.) (1993) *South African Media Policy: Debates of the 1990s*, Johannesburg: Anthropos.

Louw, P. E. (1995) "Shifting patterns in South Africa's press oligopoly," *Media Information Australia*, 77: 73–85.

Louw, P. E. (1997) "Nationalism, modernity and postmodernity: comparing the South African and Australian experiences," *Politikon*, 24(1): 76–105.

Lunsche, S. (1996) "The players who made corporate history," *Sunday Times Business Times*, September 1: 5.

McGregor, R. (1996) "How the guard has changed since Rhodes stormed the SA economy," *Sunday Times Business Times*, December 15: 5.

Makgoba, M. W. (1988) "A basis for the African renaissance," Johannesburg: African Renaissance Conference Programme.

Mpofu, B. (1995) "Corporate monopoly in the South African print media: implications for the alternative press with particular reference to *New Nation*," unpublished MA dissertation, University of Natal, Durban (www.und.ac.za/und/ccms).

Muller, J. (1987) "Press houses at war: a brief history of Nasionale Pers and Perskor," in K. G. Tomaselli, R. E. Tomaselli, and J. Muller (eds.) (1987) *The Press in South Africa*, London: James Currey.

Murdock, G. (1982) "Large corporations and the control of the communications industries," in M. Gurevitch, T. Bennett, J. Curran and J. Woollacott (eds.) *Culture, Society and The Media*, London: Methuen.

Raubenheimer, L. (1991) "From newsroom to the community: struggle in black journalism," in K. G. Tomaselli and P. E. Louw, (eds.) *The Press in South Africa*, London: James Currey.

Saul, J. and Gelb, S. (1980) *The Crisis in South Africa: Class Defense, Class Revolution*, New York: Monthly Review Press.

Shepperson, A. (1996) "AmaBokkebokke! National symbols and the cultural task beyond apartheid," *S—European Journal for Semiotic Studies*, 8/2(3): 395–412.

South African Labour Bulletin (1996) "Union investment, new opportunities, new threats," 2(95): 33–9.

Stadler, A. (1987) *The Political Economy of Modern South Africa*, Cape Town: David Philip.

Suttner, R. and Cronin, J. (1986) *30 years of the Freedom Charter*, Johannesburg: Ravan Press.

Teer-Tomaselli, R. E. (1993) "The politics of discourse and the discourse of politics: images of violence and reform on the South African Broadcasting Corporation's Television News bulletins—July 1985–November 1986," unpublished Ph.D. thesis, University of Natal, Durban.

Tomaselli, K. G. (1997) "Ownership and control in the South African print media: black empowerment after apartheid 1990–1997," *Ecquid Novi*, 18(1): 21–68.

Tomaselli, K. G. and Louw, P. E. (eds.) (1991) *The Alternative Press in South Africa*, London: James Currey.

Tomaselli, K. G., Louw, P. E. and Tomaselli, R. E. (1990) "Language and the crisis of hegemony in South Africa," in S. Thomas (ed.) *Communication and Culture, Vol. 4*, New Jersey: Ablex.

Tomaselli, K. G., Tomaselli, R. E. and Muller, J. (eds.) (1987) *The Press in South Africa*, London: James Currey.

Tomaselli, R. E., Tomaselli, K. G. and Muller, J. (eds.) (1989) *Broadcasting in South Africa*, London: James Currey.

Uys, I. (1996) "A shift in loyalty," *Natal Witness*, May 23: 8.

20 Mediating modernity

Theorizing reception in a non-Western society[1]

Arvind Rajagopal

The career of television in what is known as the developing world has for the most part begun late, relative to the West. Those who write about non-Western television, not only in scholarly volumes but also in the popular media, are usually familiar with it from elsewhere. The appraisals it receives are those of a knowing eye. It is greeted with enthusiasm and with a certain impatience, as something long awaited. The first chapters of its history are already written; the medium comes with a prepared script in a sense that goes beyond the usual arguments of media imperialism. What is missed in those arguments is how the imagination is blunted in apprehending a transplanted technology's distinctive history. We can distinguish two main strands in the response. There is the customary euphoria at mounting another rung on the ladder of progress, at the harbinger of a modernity that is devoutly desired. On the other hand, critics may signal they are wise to the tricks of the tube, to the allure that invariably betrays the medium's promise, as mass consumer culture invades one more domain.

These two lines of response revolve around the figure of the nation. "National culture" becomes the trope through which anxieties about the precise nature of the medium's effects play themselves out. While advancing the cause of "development," television at the same time holds out the promise of defending national tradition, and serving as a line of defense against foreign culture, or against any other elements defined as negative; television culture becomes a key site for discerning symptoms of the national mood.

In theorizing media reception, we are inevitably led to questions of culture: we must either ask or assume what norms and values structure the field under examination. The use of the category of the nation to advance the cause of modernity as well as to defend against its discontents points to a process of displacement: in effect, a sociopolitical agenda is naturalized in terms of a collective identity. An unhistoricized notion of capitalist modernity tends to function as the taken-for-granted context of inquiry in reception studies. A culture of modern, liberal citizenship is assumed as the norm, with certain kinds of political behaviors (e.g. representative democracy, with an informed and well-behaved electorate) and certain divisions between public and private behaviors (e.g. with religious and community culture excluded from the public realm). These are values deriving from a particular interpretation of Western experience. Theory is the rule, and practice the exception, Marx has written, in discussions of civil society.[2] Since the fit between civil society in the West and societies elsewhere is partial, such an approach is doubly unequipped to answer the increasingly complex questions posed by scrambled cultural formations with heterogeneous genealogies.

Modernity in fact offers a contested and contradictory set of values, some of whose key paradoxes crystallize in the concept of the nation. The nation as such is a term that expresses and mediates cultural contradictions of modernity, straddling the historical transition to industrial society by claiming a level of cultural continuity across historical change. The importance of the media in achieving this straddling or, in traditional terms, unifying function, has been noted by several theorists (Anderson 1983, Deutsch 1953, Gellner 1983). Media reception studies thus unavoidably uncover contradictions of lived cultures in non-Western societies. Holding the values of modernity constant when studying them is thus seriously misleading, I argue.

In this chapter, I will illustrate some of the incongruities between the expectations of a modern imagination and the aberrations it is confronted with in the career of television in a non-Western society. I discuss the contradictory characteristics of the nation concept, and argue that the media are a site for the articulation and "resolution" of these contradictions. I suggest that "religion," like "tradition," is a category often used to collect and subsume phenomena inconvenient to modernist inquiry, and is therefore salient for students of non-Western popular culture. I will then go on to discuss some aspects of the recent broadcast and reception of a Hindu epic, which ran as a hugely successful serial on state-run television in India. If the liberal bourgeois public sphere can be said to characterize the norm of modern culture, dominated by narratives of the rational, secular development of individuals, here one is forcefully confronted with deeply embedded premodern narratives of community, narratives whose relevance continues to be felt in a modernizing society.

The media, the nation, and modernity

Nationalism organizes a field of meanings to empower its drive toward modernity; what is undesirable in the course of development is typically defined as exogenous to the authentic, national spirit. The mission of development can then be endorsed without ambivalence, with the nation appearing as the purest expression of this forward movement. The idea of the nation is seen to express the particularity of a culture and at the same time embody a universal ethos, in a paradoxical form. Any contemporary discussion of this paradox must acknowledge Benedict Anderson's influential formulation of the nation as an "imagined community" (1983). Anderson attempts to critique essentialist understandings of the nation, stressing instead its factitious, "imagined" quality. This is a salutary emphasis, and an advance from arguments such as Ernest Gellner's which dismiss nationalisms as spurious precisely because they are imagined and not "real" (Gellner 1983).

Anderson conceives the nation as "a sociological organism moving calendrically through homogeneous, empty time" (Anderson 1983: 31). The focus on "empty time" is related to Weber's notion of disenchantment: humankind soberly faces up to existential realities so far evaded. No longer can communities assume they are "magically alone" (*ibid.*: 35). Here Anderson takes the self-conception of modernity at face value, and so inherits the problems of such a view. Positing a value-free, "empty" modernity relegates the very real values and interests through which it is actualized to the residual category of "tradition," one whose persistence is never satisfactorily addressed. Anderson's argument is persuasive in part because of his silence on the role of the state, which plays no active role in his discussion of nation-ness. The nation comes into its own when state power is achieved, he acknowledges. Indeed, state power is essential to guarantee the virtues of freedom and equality Anderson attributes to the nation. But by rendering the state residual to his account, Anderson imputes a diffuse and voluntary quality to the "imagined community." Ignoring its institutional underpinnings is crucial to his cultural definition of the nation. His account thus idealizes the rhetoric of the liberal democratic state and presents it as a general social condition marking nationhood. Small wonder that, in an age when the crisis of the nation has extended beyond the "Third World" and begun to afflict Europe itself, Anderson's work has been received so enthusiastically. By defining the nation as cohering essentially in the imagination, Anderson sidesteps the delicate issue of its unravelling in reality, and offers reassurance that the *idea* of the nation is still intact.

In most non-Western societies, the institutional bases of national unity have never been a secret, given the relative recency of their political origins. As an ideological state apparatus, in Althusser's (1971) terms, the media can be seen as the sphere *par excellence* in which the representative and unifying claims of the nation are constantly made, challenged, and secured. Images circulate across disparately developed sections of society, articulating with and standing for a highly heterogeneous cultural terrain. To fasten exclusively onto the meanings broadcast and provoked via the media as the means of securing national unity would be an error: society is not held together primarily through consensual values. The coercive and constraining power of social institutions, and the sedimented practices operating across these institutions, help reproduce society and are critical in this process.

Going beyond the gesture of charity

Applying Anderson's argument to "developing nations" highlights the modernist biases contained in his discussion. "Developing nations" are awkwardly situated: they are not quite "there" yet, or not comprehensively at any rate. The fiction that the term "modern" applies equally to them, when it is assumed, is then a gesture of charity rather than one of categorial precision. The inadequacy of the description represents a failure to engage with the specificity of contradictory and uneven development. This is transformed into the failure of reality to live up to the category, a failure tactfully overlooked, or acknowledged in a footnote to the discerning reader. In non-Western societies, the modern is identified with the urban industrial sector, and its presence is acknowledged as partial and uneven. What is the implication for media studies of the partial presence of modernity in its field of study? Treating the remainder as theoretically residual, as "tradition," or as "stagnation," retains modernity as an unspecified norm in the analysis. Yet any serious attention to the field of popular culture, and to the multiple interpretations and forms of resistance provoked by media texts, requires a nonreductive approach to the incompleteness of the modernity evinced in developing countries.

To describe something as "national" does not specify the forces and relations at work so much as it names a field of sovereignty. The culture within this provenance is then not coherent or unitary, least of all in nations characterized by highly polarized and uneven development. What are some terms with which we can consider heterogeneity within the category of the nation itself?

Partha Chatterjee has argued that nationalists in colonial countries derived their political doctrines from the West, but demarcated a sphere of cultural autonomy as the basis for their claim to distinction and sovereignty (Chatterjee 1986). Whereas the West might be conceded to have superiority in the material realm, by virtue of its technology and its dominance in worldly affairs, the distinguishing feature of the colonial nation was an inner, spiritual quality that resisted effacement by mundane forces, and offered resources to challenge domination. Religion might then become a privileged means whereby heterogeneity and difference could be asserted.

In India, the Congress Party, which led the independence movement, proclaimed itself a secular republic, with leaders like Nehru acutely conscious of the danger to minorities in any assertion of a Hindu identity. The official emphasis on secularism was an important achievement, given the strong lobby for a more emphatic response to the co-presence of Pakistan; the latter defined itself as an Islamic rather than a secular state (Gopal 1990). Nevertheless, religion was not something to be shut out so easily from public life. As the rule of the Congress Party became more unstable and its erstwhile secular development became more vulnerable to attack, the "Hindu card" was found to be an effective means of shoring up a declining hegemony. This represented the first explicit use of religion by the ruling party; previously, its use had been relatively low-key and unofficial. With the onset of economic liberalization, and the shift to a more market-driven economy, religious identities became a powerful and effective means of linking the new emphasis on the private sphere with a larger collective vision. The decision to air religious epics on state-run media took place in this context.

A HINDU EPIC GOES PRIME TIME

The success of television in India was announced by the reception, not of *Dallas*, *Dynasty*, or the *Cosby Show*. The show that definitively established the Delhi-centered medium across a large section of the country's diverse population was the serialized version of one of the world's oldest epics, featuring prominent gods and goddesses of the Hindu pantheon.[3] The epic was the *Ramayan*, being an account of the life of the god-king Ram, retold in nearly every region, dialect, and language and often in multiple versions. It drew huge crowds every week. Audience research estimates compiled by market research companies climbed from 40 million to 60 million to 80 million viewers per week over a few months.[4]

For Doordarshan, the state-owned television system, the serial represented a breakthrough in a number of ways. It succeeded in achieving high viewership across linguistically diverse regions, and extended the viewership beyond anything previously achieved. Doodarshan had begun nationwide telecasts only five years previously, on the occasion of the Asian Games held in the capital in 1982. Television had not become a developmental priority for the government until the prestige event of the 1982 Asian Games, when transmission was rapidly upgraded from black and white to color, and imports as well as local television manufacture were promoted by lowering governmental excise rates. The introduction of commercially sponsored, independently produced programming that year was a major development in the highly bureaucratized state TV system, where the routine response to initiatives for change was to neutralize them through marginalization or inaction. In retrospect, the move appears long-delayed and foreordained, given the spread of video, and of satellite broadcasting. In fact, following the failure of the "pro-development soap opera," which sought to blend education with entertainment (but jettisoned the educational component to retain viewers[5]) the mythological soap opera arrived as its successor, rendering the abstract space of the modern nation familiar and intimate, and using Hindu myth to craft parables of development. This was, needless to say, a deeply contradictory exercise.

The *Ramayan* was the first of this genre, beginning on January 17, 1987, only three years after the new regime on Doordarshan, and made Sunday mornings, previously a "soft" spot on the television schedule, into advertising prime time, earning record revenues per week. At the same time, the new medium acquired a legitimacy that had never been envisaged, as a potential source of "moral entertainment." For the first time, there was a show that achieved record audiences in every part of the country, a considerable achievement given the linguistic (and political) divisions in the country.

What was striking about the *Ramayan* was its success in creating deep emotional resonances with its appeal for unconditional submission to patriarchal figures—elder brother, husband, father, king—and its idealization of the warmth and security such submission provides. Mutual loyalty within hierarchy is the basis for order and stability both in the family and in the larger society. No amount of pain and suffering is too much to ensure the happiness of others, in this conception. The epic appeared to be extolling feudal or pre-feudal values at a time when they were seemingly being eclipsed once and for all by market forces.

The English-language press had difficulty in writing about the serial's success. The preferred mode of presenting an epic, for English-educated intellectuals, would have been as a self-consciously historical drama, announcing a high cultural *oeuvre*. The program itself, however, was unreconstructed, low-grade kitsch, and that it should actually be taken so seriously was therefore a matter of embarrassment. This was hardly a suitable manner in which a modern nation should take its bows as it entered the global electronic stage.

One often-quoted explanation was that the show's gimmickry and its melodramatic rendition made it popular. For instance:

> What could possibly have been a sensitive and commanding portrayal ... has instead been put together like an ice cream sundae—with a dollop of values, several scoops of religion, drama and emotion, topped off with educative discourses on duty, love and friendship. ... The gooey mixture, palatable as it is, will be lapped up by eager multitudes.
>
> (Vaid-Fera 1987: 9)

Other explanations delved into Orientalist stereotypes. For example:

> One must understand the importance of mythology to the Indian psyche. The Ramayan and the Mahabharat have from times immemorial [sic], offered the Hindu mind comfortable motifs in an otherwise turbulent universe.
>
> (*Illustrated Weekly of India*, 8 November, p. 11)

The serial's religiosity was in fact an often-cited explanation, raising questions of the political import of the broadcast. Airing a religious serial on state-controlled television raised questions about the government's commitment to secularism. The audience's enthusiasm raised apprehensions about a wave of state-sponsored Hindu chauvinism, with possible repercussions on minorities. In this way, two streams of thought came to converge: those that viewed the inclusion of religion or traditional culture in state-sponsored programs as violating the principle of a secular, modern society, and those that resisted such inclusion on more pragmatic, political grounds.

The following news item, and a prominent public figure's comments on events of a similar nature, point to the uneasy conscience of old-style secularism in this contest:

IRATE FANS STONE POWER HOUSE

JAMMU: July 31 1988 (United News of India dispatch):

Power failure during the popular television serial, "Ramayan" this morning upset the people of the Jewal Chowk area of the city, who damaged a state government bus and stoned the power station. A spokesman for the electricity department said that power supply to some parts of the city was affected due to short circuiting in a portion of the canal power house.

Interviewed about the impact of the *Ramayan*, a prominent lawyer had this to say:

we profess to be a secular country but we don't behave like one. How can you justify people throwing stones at power stations or setting them on fire just because of the electricity failure? Had this sort of reaction come from the same group of people for any other serial when the lights go off? ... India has always been a secular country and we should learn to be tolerant.

(Supreme Court lawyer Gobinda Mukhoty, interviewed in the *National Herald*, August 7, 1988)

There is some confusion here as to whether secularism in India is an "is" or an "ought," between what "we profess" and what "India has always been." The passage clarifies that "India" means *the government* of India, as opposed to "we," the people. Secularism is then an exhortation from the state to "be tolerant." Between secularism as fact and as imperative lies the indeterminate reality of Indian society, persistently refractory to its reformers' efforts. There was no developed civil society, in the modern sense of the term, until the British colonial state began to create one. The factitious and precarious character of the "secularism" so derived is therefore a constant source of anxiety. The anxiety is enough to obscure the precise character of the phenomena that do characterize the society, or to render their accurate apprehension unnecessary.

However, the popular appeal of a "religious" serial like the *Ramayan* cannot be reduced to affirmation of "communal" sentiments. I suggest that the opposition of "communal" and "secular," or their implied referents "nonmodern" and "modern" respectively, is a discursive one, susceptible of mediation between what is otherwise an unyielding polarity. The point is to oppose the kind of cultivated incomprehension secular discourse evinces of the "nonmodern," and to suggest that the sentiments fundamentalists draw on may in fact be accessible to progressive political mobilization.

Viewers talk about the *Ramayan*

My own reaction to the serial was initially negative. The pace of the serial (which, to one used to action-adventure, is slow, sometimes agonizingly so); the cloying manner in which characters spoke to one another; the frequent pauses in the narrative to enable devotees to savor the devotional feelings evoked by incidents; the drawing out of every opportunity for dramatic conflict, often leading to crescendos quite disproportionate to the swiftness and simplicity of their resolution; the seeming suppression of spontaneity and individuality at every turn, in favor of a cheerful and unquestioning submission to the orthodoxy of elders—all these features seemed too objectionable to permit appreciation of the serial.

Among those who talked about the serial, the responses seemed similar to the point of being repetitive, to my ear.[6] One worker told me, "Previously we read about it, and we heard about it. But now we've seen it, so we know it and believe it," suggesting that it was the story's familiarity, and television's apparent authentication of what was familiar, that may have been most attractive. A college teacher told me, "One has lost touch with these epics and with our culture. So it is good that they are showing it on TV. This way, our children can also learn about our culture." If it was not familiar to everyone, then, it ought to be, some felt. Another worker, a young Muslim, said, "Back then, you had Ram Rajya. Look at how things are today." This seemed an important clue; what he said seemed to encapsulate much that I was hearing from others. It was in a conversation with an activist filmmaker some weeks later that the significance of the remark came home to me. Talking about the popularity of the *Ramayan*, he said that the story's appeal was basically that of a lost utopia. His remark was dismissive. As a leftist, he saw the idealization of a religious, feudal past as false and misleading; progressive politics should be oriented to the future, based on a scientific understanding of the world. For me, though, it was like a door opening on all of what I had been dimly intuiting so far. The impossible idealization of family relationships could now be seen as part of the meaning conveyed. By relegating it to a presumed past, both its believability and its unbelievability could be accommodated together in a dynamic contradiction. What had seemed naive credulity on the part of the viewers now appeared more plausible. The Ram Rajya stood as memory, myth, and history simultaneously—hard to dispel, impossible to refute, haunting people with the global alternative possibilities it seemed to offer.

Ram Rajya, the rule of Rama, referred to the golden age of Indian history under the legendary king following his victorious return from battle. Peace, justice, and prosperity prevailed. The king treated his subjects with the same care and love he had for his own family. People, too, loved their king selflessly and would have died for him if necessary. Distinctions of rank may have prevailed, but in that atmosphere of love and sacrifice, they were unimportant. During the nationalist movement, Gandhi used Ram Rajya as a symbol recognizable to peasants and townsfolk alike, of what independent India would be like: that was the freedom they were fighting for. It appeared independently in local struggles as well. Gyan Pandey describes how peasants in Avadh district in the 1920s used "Sita Ram" as a form of greeting and a rallying cry against the British. "Sita Ram" invoked Ram Rajya, and indicated mutual respect, as opposed to the obsequious "Salaam," which emphasized their subalternity (Pandey 1988).

The most important aspect of the response was not only that it was religious, but that it saw the story's values as being fortified by their historicity. This was where the press's criticism of audiences bowing to gimcrack television gods was most misleading. The *Ramayan* was, for them, a story about their past, and like any history, it offered valuable lessons for the present. What seemed like clichés before now became more meaningful.

In today's context, the Ramayan is very important. But in these modern times, people have almost forgotten the Ramayan, or you might say that they have forgotten the ideals of the Ramayan. In this [context], the serial has propagated anew the beliefs in the old ideals.

(Letter PH 29)[7]

In this age, when there is strife all over the world and people are moving towards evil ways, this great poet [Tulsidas] has opened everyone's eyes. ... Today's children, who were forgetting the greatness of Ram's name, you [Ramanand Sagar] have awoken with this great Ramayan.

(Letter DE 132)

As values espoused in a popular television serial, they form an intriguing contrast to what has come to be considered characteristic of television culture in the West. In the US, for instance, an emphasis on private ambition and material success staged against a backdrop of a high-consumption environment fairly dominates programming (Gitlin 1984). How can we theorize the relationship between the modern, bourgeois public sphere and preexisting narratives of community? What are the terms in which we can conceptualize the co-presence of such seemingly different orders of practice?

NARRATIVES OF COMMUNITY: COUNTER-PUBLIC SPHERE IN A TRANSITIONAL SOCIETY

Habermas, in his work on the public sphere, focuses on an immanent critique of the term, contrasting it with its limits in its actual existence and with its decline over time. The political task of the bourgeois public sphere, comprised of the rational–critical discourse of propertied, educated men, became the regulation of civil society, in a relationship of working antagonism with the state.[8] This corresponded to the newly public relevance of the private sphere of society, with the privatization of the economy in the household.[9] The abstraction of the concept corresponds to the character of market exchange: while the public sphere depends on a free market of goods and information, the systematic exclusion of lived experience is critical to its maintenance, as Negt and Kluge have argued.[10] Contestation and debate would inevitably reproduce the terms of the bourgeois world unless they posed the concreteness of subjugated knowledges against these terms. Bourgeois property owners were not interested in the formation of public experience; their prime interest was in the possible countereffects of this public sphere on their private interests. Thus real experience became private and, ultimately, incomprehensible except within the circumscribed terms of market society.

Oskar Negt and Alexander Kluge (1993) offer the notion of a counter-public sphere, resisting the abstraction of the bourgeois public sphere, and posing the immediacy of excluded experience against it.[11] They locate symptoms of the persistent, subterranean awareness of excluded experience in fantasy. Fantasy, by virtue of being private, inarticulate, and unconscious, acts as a "libidinal counterweight" to alienated life and thus constitutes a practical critique of alienation.[12] Although it is usually regarded as remote from the activities and interests of the real world, fantasy's generative impulses lie in the need of individuals to organize their experience, and to make coherent sense out of their lives. However, this need is thwarted by the bourgeois public sphere, which structurally excludes truths that would undermine its existence. Thus the media tend to limit the extent to which audiences' awareness may be raised. Fantasy thus bears the traces of real and powerful requirements, which can be reconstructed to bring out the lineaments of alternative forms of consciousness denied articulation.[13]

Several of the viewers' accounts suggest that such a notion of fantasy was applicable to their experience. Thus for instance:

> Often tears come to my eyes. Then I think that life should be like this, on the basis of ideals.[14]

> Everything in the serial is simply too good. We become so emotional while watching the relationship between Ram and Lakshman, and between Ram and his mother.[15]

> If you analyze it, it seems like a dream that could not have taken place—that there could be so much love between brother and between fathers and sons.[16]

Indeed, the Hindu nationalist movement fashioned itself precisely as a counter-public. Positioning the religio-ritual sphere as the place of excess and otherness, it claims to stand for the truth and the lives of the majority. This truth is, they claim, suppressed by Westernized and corrupt politicians who are dismissive of native traditions and eager to cultivate minority vote banks. Against such a "pseudo-secular" Raj is then posed the self-evident claim of "Hinduness" to reign over the public domain.[17] Counter-publics too have their politics, however. Rather than providing any direct access to shared, excluded life experience, we have instead a unifying net cast by a name, within which jostle diverse fellow travellers who can yet swell the movement. We can find correspondences and similarities among them; it is not these that are decisive. Rather, it is the sense of similitude created by shared names and images that in fact cement the broad-based movement together. A counter-public ideology helps keep the leadership of the party together, and may induce a section of the intelligentsia to join the party's ranks, but a mass base is liable to require methods of mobilization that go beyond strict adherence to a particular ideology.

The kinds of politics that developed under colonial rule, in societies such as India, were unaccompanied by a full-fledged relation to the state, as in Western Europe. If the bourgeois public sphere acquired a discursive, rational–critical character, colonial politics as waged by the colonized was in opposition to the imperial state, rather than in dialogue with it. If Lex Britannica insisted that justice was blind, the situation of colonial subjects, who were denied citizenship, contradicted this claim. Political language hence took shape by emphasizing the uniqueness of indigenous identity, drawing on preexisting narratives of community and the utopian conceptions these harkened to. National identity, even if defined as secular, retains a historic relation to such narratives, as the most powerful means of mobilization available to anti-colonial politics.

Understanding the media in post-colonial societies consists in working through sedimented structures, of an inherited, abstract conception of politics on the one hand, within which the media are placed, and indigenous utopian narratives on the other. Television extends the reach of the prevailing political terrain, bringing to the surface zones of society that might previously have factored into dominant discourses only intermittently. A new kind of intimacy is thus enforced across a split public, introducing a problem or opportunity for political resolution. As I argue elsewhere, the Hindu right attempted to draw on this split as a productive resource, redefining it for their own purposes.

The characteristic failing in media reception studies is that they simplify the mixed and contradictory character of non-Western culture by polarizing it along the familiar axis, traditional–modern. In the case of the *Ramayan* serial, this could result in at least two kinds of treatment. The tele-event, the text together with all the readings and reactions it provoked, could be lumped together as "traditional," and thereby render questions about its existence—why it was made, how it was received, and so on—moot, since it is in the nature of traditions to linger and endure. Alternatively, the tele-event could be described as a blend of traditional and modern, and in this somewhat more ingenious way, again substitute classification for explanation, foregrounding the puzzle of what parts fit the one category, and what the other. Both these approaches utilize an object-centered approach, one that takes entirely for granted what is most interesting and problematic here, namely the context of inquiry. The *Ramayan* serial was broadcast in a "transitional" developing society whose deeply uneven and painful movement toward modernity rendered memories and narratives of premodern pasts variously as idyll and nostalgia, critique and manifesto. Holding the values of modernity constant conceals the very *raison d'être* of such phenomena, which is to question the values of modernity, and to hold out an alternative set for possible refuge or reform. It is important, I suggest, for students of media reception to be critical of the extent to which the universalist notions of modernity have been identified with the particular histories of a few countries. Such a view not only misunderstands the originality of the social experiments being undertaken in large portions of the globe, but also demonstrates the paucity of historical vision applied to the West itself.

Notes

1 This paper is a substantially revised version of an essay written for a special issue of *The Communication Review*, 1(4) (1996) devoted to comparative analysis of the media in Latin America. For a more detailed argument, see Arvind Rajagopal, *Politics after Television: Religious Nationalism and the Reshaping of the Indian Public*, Cambridge: Cambridge University Press (forthcoming).

2 Karl Marx, "On the Jewish Question," in R. C. Tucker (ed.) *The Marx-Engels Reader* (New York: W. W. Norton, 1978), p. 44.

3 In this paper, my discussion pertains to Doordarshan, the state-owned television system, for the period 1987–8. In 1992, state monopoly over television began to erode, with the entry of satellite television. Doordarshan itself introduced a second channel in 1993, DD2 Metro, to provide more entertainment for the urban audience. By linking through satellite the four terrestrial transmitters in the four metros (Bombay, Madras, Delhi, and Calcutta), DD2 Metro was available in forty-two cities; elsewhere a satellite dish was required. Dishes are maintained by local cable operators, and services provided for a monthly fee of between a 100 and 150 rupees. Next to DD2 Metro, the most watched service is the Murdoch-owned STAR TV, which provides four channels: a general entertainment channel called Star Plus, and more specialized interest channels such as Prime Sports, MTV and BBC World Service. ZEE TV, launched by Asia Today Ltd in Hong Kong in 1992, has since also been acquired by STAR, and is one of the leading satellite channels. As of 1993, about 21 percent of TV households had cable TV, in towns with a population of 100,000 and above. About three-quarters of these households had STAR. Star TV Homes Penetration Study, Frank Small and Associates, *Thompson Pocket Reference to Media in India 1993–94*, p. 44.

4 See Indian Market Research Bureau Special Report, *The Ramayan Phenomenon: An Epic Programme* (Bombay 1989). The Sanskrit name for the epic is usually transcribed in English as Ramayana. The modern Hindi name, used in the television serial and by most Hindi speakers, is Ramayan.

5 Both Manohar Shyam Joshi, who wrote the screenplay for *Hum Log*, and S. S. Gill, the Secretary of the Ministry of Information and Broadcasting, who oversaw its production, agree that the experiment was a failure. Personal interviews, New Delhi, August 1989.

6 I interviewed 169 people altogether, in Delhi and in a small town, Kaynagar, some hours away. Most of the interviews were with individuals, but in some cases they were performed with small groups. The interviews lasted anywhere from fifteen minutes to two hours. Ninety were working class, 79 were middle to upper middle class. The names of all interviewees have been changed. All the interviews were performed in Hindi, unless otherwise mentioned, tape-recorded, and transcribed. Unless mentioned, the interviews are with Delhi residents. I also examined letters from Ramayan viewers.

7 In the following letters, the notation "P" refers to those addressed to me personally, in response to a solicitation published in *The Times of India* and in the Hindi language daily *Navbharat Times*, requesting Ramayan viewers to write and describe why they liked the show. "D" refers to those addressed to Doordarshan. "E" and "H" denote the language of the letters, that is, whether they were in English or in Hindi.

8 Habermas 1988: 52.

9 *Ibid.*, p. 19.

10 In her foreword to Negt and Kluge's *The Public Sphere and Experience* (1993), Miriam Hansen discusses some nuances of the word "experience," *Erfahrung*, a term which in the political climate of the 1960s had acquired a critical and oppositional force. She places Negt and Kluge's usage of the term in the context of German critical theory, chiefly the work of Walter Benjamin and Siegfried Kracauer, and suggests that the English and American resonances of its translation ("experience") may be misleadingly empiricist. Hansen suggests that *Erfahrung* is a concept that refers both to unmediated sensation and to the organization of such sensation, i.e. both having and reflecting on experience (pp. xvi–xvii). Thus the exclusion of experience from the concerns of the bourgeois public sphere would simultaneously deprive it of the mediation required to make it intelligible.

11 Miriam Hansen insists, however, that the notion of a counter-public differs from particularized groupings around the notion of "community." A counter-public, she argues, is a specifically modern phenomenon, arising alongside and against the bourgeois public sphere, offering "forms of solidarity and reciprocity that are grounded in a collective experience of marginalization and expropriation, … but no longer rooted in face-to-face relations, and subject to discursive conflict and negotiation" (*ibid.*, p. xxxvi). As opposed to this, she argues, the ideal of community is based on family and kinship relations, holding onto ideals of authenticity, identity and otherness. Such a notion of community is inimical to the articulation of difference within its discursive limits, Hansen states, since its own claim to authenticity is all too literal. Hansen's argument implies a curiously hallowed status for the bourgeois public, one that seems to take its claims at face value. Her apparent idealization of the bourgeois public sphere here contrasts with her position of a few pages earlier: "from its inception, the bourgeois public's claim to represent a general will functions as a powerful mechanism of exclusion … the exclusion of any difference that cannot be assimilated, rationalized and subsumed" (*ibid.*, pp. xxvii–xxviii).

12 Negt and Kluge 1993: 33.

13 Although Negt and Kluge stress the requirement of reconstructing the counter-public sphere, their handling of the epistemological issues involved is at times unsatisfactory. Thus they argue in favor of realist modes of representation as being most likely to engage workers, suggesting for instance that personalization of issues (presumably in heroes or leaders, since they write of "personality cults" (*ibid.*, p. 41)) could be a positive method of communication. They do not centrally tackle the question of representation, i.e. the narratives and tropes through which, unavoidably, articulation of any issues must be carried out.

14 Digamber Singh, Kaynagar, interview.

15 Letter DH 262.

16 Letter PH 12.

17 The Cow Protection movement in Uttar Pradesh, which began in the late 1880s and continued for some years thereafter, provides, I suggest, an example of a kind of indigenous
   counter-public, in which town and country came together. The organization of the movement drew on networks of local support, from village headmen and chiefs, local landlords
   and traders. See J. R. McLane, *Indian Nationalism and the Early Congress* (Princeton, NJ:
   Princeton University Press, 1977), pp. 271–331; G. Pandey, "Rallying round the cow: sectarian strife in the Bhojpuri region, c. 1880–1917," in R. Guha (ed.) *Subaltern Studies II*
   (Delhi: Oxford University Press, 1983); S. B. Freitag, "Sacred symbol as mobilizing idedology:
   the North Indian search for a 'Hindu' community," *Comparative Studies in Society and
   History*, 22(4) (October 1980); A. A. Yang, "Sacred symbol and sacred space in rural India:
   community mobilization in the 'Anti-Cow-Killing' Riot of 1893," *ibid*. See also G. Pandey,
   "Mobilizing the Hindu community," in his *The Construction of Communalism in Colonial
   North India* (New Delhi: Oxford University Press, 1990) pp. 158–200.

References

Althusser, L. (1971) "Ideology and ideological state apparatuses," in *Lenin and Philosophy
   and Other Essays*, trans. B. Brewster, New York: Monthly Review Press.
Anderson, B. (1983) *Imagined Communities: Reflections on the Origin and Spread of Nation-
   alism*, London: Verso.
Chatterjee, P. (1986) *Nationalist Thought in the Colonial World: A Derivative Discourse?*
   London: Zed Books, for the United Nations University.
Deutsch, K. (1953) *Nationalism and Social Communication; An Inquiry into the Foundations
   of Nationality*, Cambridge, MA and New York: MIT Technology Press and Wiley.
Gellner, E. (1983) *Nations and Nationalism*, Ithaca: Cornell University Press.
Gitlin, T. (1984) *Inside Prime Time*, New York: Pantheon Books.
Gopal, S. (1990) *Anatomy of a Conflict: The Babri Masjid–Ramjanmabhumi Dispute*, New
   Delhi: Viking.
Habermas, J. (1988) *The Structural Transformation of the Public Sphere*, trans. T. Burger,
   Cambridge, MA: MIT Press.
Negt, 0. and Kluge, A. (1993) *The Public Sphere and Experience. Toward an Analysis of the
   Bourgeois and Proletarian Public Sphere*, trans. P. Labanyi, J. 0. Daniel and A. Oksiloff,
   Minneapolis: University of Minnesota Press.
Pandey, G. (1988) "Rallying around the cow," in R. Guha, *Subaltern Studies* III, New Delhi:
   Oxford University Press.
Rajagopal, A. (1996) "Communalism and the consuming subject," in *Economic and Political
   Weekly*, 31(6): 341–8.
Vaid-Fera, M. (1987) Imprint, Bombay, p. 9.

21 Performing a dream and its dissolution

A social history of broadcasting in Israel

Tamar Liebes

During the winter of 1998, in celebration of fifty years of national independence, Israel's Public Television produced a documentary series of twenty-four episodes on the history of the state since its inception. At the end of the episode on the Six Day War, my son, who had made a point of watching the episodes covering the first twenty years, remarked: "Now the sad part begins; there is nothing worthwhile left to watch."

In spite of its producers' reflexive, sometimes critical, view, the first two "good decades" shown on TV provided viewers with an uplifting pride and a feeling of witnessing a great, at times heroic, story. These were also the years in which Israel had no television, and Israelis, not knowing what they were missing, collected around one "radio instrument" in the livingroom to listen to the one radio channel, set up in the prime minister's office, politically controlled to the hilt. In the next two decades radio diversified somewhat, but there was only one TV channel, and Israelis, not knowing what they were missing, collected around one "television instrument" in the livingroom, to view the public channel, which was established (now together with radio) as an independent authority. From the beginning of the fifth decade, Israelis split into different rooms to select among an abundance of mostly commercial TV channels—national, transnational, some sectorial. They are told by a government that calls itself "nationalist" that they have too *little* choice, a lack which will be remedied by the law of "open skies" already passed in the Knesset.

I argue here that the changing technological and institutional character of the electronic media, as well as the choice of their formats and contents, is emblematic of the successive stages in the evolution of Israeli society, expressing and bearing witness to the widening cracks within its hegemonic culture. The media provide a reflection of the shifts in this culture—charting its lightspeed route from naive, unreflexive, national solidarity, to an emaciated "consensus" in which government and media operate as a thin façade of a society now segmented into various cultures which openly compete over political domination, with the ethos of the secular Western-style democracy wearing thin.

Looking back at the five decades of Israel's short life, the first two decades seem an era of enthusiastic innocence, in which radio reflects the benevolently paternalistic, taken-for-granted, belief in the instant integration of masses of immigrants (mostly from North Africa) into a secular, Western-style "Israeli culture," a culture which, soon after independence, had become (numerically) a minority culture. Television enters at a moment past the euphoria of the Six Day War, at the onset of an era in which repressed messianic-religious and ethnic-religious forces are gradually unleashed, and a process of the rejuvenation of primordial tribal identities is at work. These are also the years in which the protest over nonconsensual wars takes place, and mainstream Israelis become less committed to the collective. But television, no more self-reflexive than the political establishment it supports, mostly ignores all this, continuing to protect society's sacred institutions, integrating the country round *Dallas* and the *Love Boat*, but also round *The Column of Fire*, a history of Zionism, styled after BBC's *World at War*, and, most memorably, round a number of great historical moments that lifted the national spirit. During the third stage in its evolution, in the 1990s, nationwide media reflect the hegemony of a government which presides over bitterly contesting groups and, knowing that national unity is a dream of the past, chooses to marginalize national television by opening up an enormous choice of "entertainment" channels—providing sex, violence and vulgar talk—in order to neutralize political debate, and thus to contribute to the depoliticization of the public. This process reinforces the entrenchment of separatist cultures in their own enclaves, around their own media, and condemns ordinary Israelis to zapping among indistinguishable transnational channels or turning off their TV sets altogether.

Why "democratic participation" is more complex than it sounds

As historians and social scientists have learned, any story can be turned upside down, and my description of Israeli history as a failed attempt to create a unified nation is no exception. Thus, what for many Israelis, brought up on Herzel's utopia of a secular–liberal community, seems like the shattering of a dream may, from another perspective, be seen as a positive development. This perspective is implied by Dan Hallin (1998) in his critique of the role of broadcasting in fostering "national integration" in new nations. Hallin's juxtaposition of the key concepts of "national unity" and "democratic participation" suggests that he might see the current stage of segmentation in Israeli society and media in a positive rather than negative light. As his arguments are central to my image of what is happening to Israeli democracy and media, I would like to consider them before going into the detailed presentation of the Israeli case, arguing that the terms of the debate are oversimplified, and not necessarily generalizable, as an in-depth analysis within a specific context may demonstrate.

National integration vs. democratic participation

Hallin reexamines the classical studies, conducted in the 1970s, which sought to define the role of the electronic media in the establishment of new nations in what was then labelled "the Third World." The problem with these studies, he argues, is that they hold media's role in "national integration" in high esteem while disregarding their failure to provide a public sphere in which various voices (mostly the less privileged) can be heard. One study states explicitly that certain African countries were not yet ripe for democratic participation, while other studies do so implicitly by equating media with modernity ("progress") in contrast to tradition ("backwardness"), and by emphasizing the importance of media for communicating from the center to the periphery, not vice versa. Katz and Wedell (1977), Hallin notices, do acknowledge the need for preserving native cultural heritage, but he deems their concern too narrowly focused, constituting a romantic gesture rather than an attempt to take seriously the possible contributions of the periphery.

The subtext of these studies, Hallin concludes, is that media democracy may stand in the way of the really important tasks of mobilizing society for economic development. In their zeal to see modernization and economic growth, and in their wish to generalize their findings beyond specific countries, these scholars ignore the political context—failing to consider the implications of media operating, in some cases, in the service of dictatorial regimes, or, in other cases, of neo-populist, corrupt, democracies. In short, these studies should be reprimanded for disregarding the potential of the media in nurturing a pluralistic society. By analyzing the Israeli experience, I would like to point to a number of problems in this critique.

Looking at "national integration" and "democratic participation" in context

In considering Hallin's critique in light of the Israeli experience I want to make three arguments. First, I carry further Hallin's warning that the role of broadcasting in national unity should be looked at within a particular context, adding that in democratic nations this should include empathy for the "natives'" perspective, and to the norms and beliefs of the times. Second, and in line with the first, I argue that democratic participation may be understood in various ways, not all prioritizing the participation of a plurality of voices in the public debate. Third, I argue that the participation of different cultural groups in the public debate does not mean, necessarily, that such participation is "democratic," in the sense of joining a multicultural dialogue.

First, as Hallin notes, the issue of media's role in national integration should be seen in the context of the kind of regime in which it operates. The way of judging the effectiveness of media has to depend on whether one is considering a dictatorship or a corrupt democracy or a society operating according to democratic principles. The media policy of what one considers a bona fide democratic state should be considered, first, within its social and cultural context and from the normative perspective of the ruling elites. Following Geertz's (1983) advice to any outsider who interprets another culture, here too it is useful to form an open-minded understanding about the founders' own perspective of what an enlightened democratic society should be like.

Naturally, in hindsight, fifty years later, one may point to failings and shortsightedness in any policy taken, as long as we remember that our own criticism may look irrelevant or naive fifty years from now. (Theoreticians and scholars are sometimes the first to advocate a change, but by the time the new meanings "take," and their vision is adopted, they may have changed their mind, or regret what was lost, or realize they did not mean it so radically. One should remember how scholars' criticism of the BBC elitism, monopoly, and hegemony quickly turned into mourning for its possible demise, and an adamant defense of the principle of Public Broadcasting.)

Bearing in mind the importance of the "natives'" perspective, let me sketch the cultural (r)evolution of Israeli society, crucial for an understanding of the complex (and formidable) tasks Israeli media had to perform.

The cultural evolution of Israeli society

The roots of the Western-style democracy that characterizes Israel, perhaps not for much longer, can be found within the secular-socialist-Zionist core of Jewish immigrants, mostly from Eastern Europe, who settled in Palestine at the beginning of the century. The pioneer immigration, answering the call of Herzlianic Zionism, which gathered momentum with the British establishment of a National Home for the Jews in Palestine, left behind the traditional Jewish occupations in the various diasporas, to settle and work the land. Israel's central social institutions (such as the Jewish agency, the workers' union, ideological newspapers) were established by the secular-socialist-Zionist leadership at the pre-state period, and were later harnessed to the needs of the state. Shortly following independence, in the beginning of the 1950s, the newly established state of 600,000 Israelis was put to the task of absorbing a mass immigration of Jewish refugees from Asia and Africa, more than twice its own number, who had not gone through processes of secularization and modernization, who suddenly found themselves in an unknown country and culture.

Fifty years later, on a somewhat apocalyptic note, Baruch Kimmerling (1998), an important revisionist sociologist, describes the current state of Israel as "a cracking of the political and cultural hegemony of the Labor party version of secular, Western-style, 'Israeli-ness' [*Yisraeliut*]," which had developed within a secular middle class, now third-generation, who had ostensibly absorbed the oriental immigrants as groups and individuals and the Arabs as individuals and families. This hegemony is threatened by a number of almost autonomous subgroups and cultures—the national-religious settlers, the Orthodox Oriental, the Ultra-orthodox, the Israeli Arabs, and perhaps the new Russians. Whereas in pluralist societies the various cultures accept the universalistic principles according to which the society operates, these cultures seek self-determination for their own brand of religious particularism or wish to replace Israel's Western-style democratic norms with their own. Having reached a critical mass due to high birth rates, immigration, and the acquisition of social and political skills, these "enclaves" have "sharpened existing social boundaries" and created new ones "by recycling and reinforcing histories and collective particularistic memories, [and] retelling the history of the state and ... their place in it, in a different way from the accepted version."

"Democratic participation" may be conceived in different ways

Second, I argue that the concept of "democratic participation" may be conceptualized in different ways, not only in Hallin's terms of "plurality of voices," but also as closely related to "national integration." Seen from the perspective of Israel's founding fathers, "national integration" is directly connected to the idea of "democratizing" the society. Democratic participation, however, was understood not so much in terms of providing a stage for a plurality of voices but in terms of providing equal access to cultural riches. In this the policy of Kol Yisrael—Israel's public radio—was not much different from that of the BBC's early idea of democratic policy, as described by Cardiff and Scannell (1987):

> The policy was democratic not in the sense that it bowed to popular will or sought to cater for the tastes and expectations of the average citizen, but in the sense that it tried to bring within the reach of all those cultural goods which had previously been available only to the privileged.

Democratic access in the Israeli case may have been even more difficult than in the British case. Whereas in Britain broadcasters did not take into account the differences in cultural resources of the various classes (Cardiff and Scannell 1987), in the Israeli case one had to consider not only class and education but a much wider cultural diversity, including various degrees of the mastery of Hebrew, and of distance from the European cultural heritage which was incorporated into Israeli culture. Notwithstanding Israel's image as a self-evidently "Western-style democracy" ("the only democracy in the Middle East"), it is a country in which the majority of the population consists of first-, second- or third-generation refugee immigrants from Asia and Africa, who had to rebuild their lives and learn a new language at the same time that they were expected to start appreciating Mozart.

Regardless of how hegemonic, or over-ambitious, it seems to us, the goal of providing access to cultural goods seemed unquestioningly important then. What today's scholars have lost, in our postmodern, multicultural end of the millennium, is the conviction (or the courage) that allows for deciding that certain cultural goods are inherently enriching, and should be accessible to all members of society. The relativism, which, as Curran (1998) argues, has been reinforced by the academic development of cultural studies, has paralyzed our capacity to judge, inadvertently serving commercial media by making it difficult to call for improvement in quality.

Giving voice to different cultures does not necessarily enhance dialogic pluralism

Beyond the various ways of interpreting "democratic participation" there is the third issue of whether participation necessarily means *democratic* participation. The interpretation according to which a plurality of voices means the creation of dialogue is based on the understanding that these voices accept the rules of the game, and are interested in listening to others and in contributing to the common culture. This interpretation does not take into account that some groups appear on nationwide TV with their own agenda, not necessarily in order to enter their own voice into the dialogue of interacting with others. One has to consider that certain cultures appear in the national arena with the aim of missionizing for their own brands of particularism—fundamentalist religion, for example. Appearing on the national scene helps such groups to reinforce the legitimacy of their own group in the eyes of their members and of potential joiners whom they attempt to recruit.

Thus, "giving voice" to peripheral social groups does not always fulfill the expectation that these groups will start listening to one another. This may be better understood by expanding Katz's scheme (in Gross 1998), according to which minority groups can either talk *to* themselves (say, ultra-orthodox Rabbis in an ultra-orthodox synagogue), *of* themselves (about the content of the weekly Bibilical sequence), *by* themselves (the preaching Rabbi belongs to the community) or they can present themselves to the rest of the society (*of* the minority, *by* the minority, *to* the rest of society) in order to promote better understanding toward their group and to contribute elements of their culture *for* the general reservoir. The possibility not covered in the scheme is the minority talking *to* the majority in order to make gains *for* the minority. In such a case participation becomes a struggle over the principles of the mutual tolerance that strives for, and makes multicultural coexistence possible, leading to a culture war rather than to dialogue. Such interaction may only split the audience into rivals and possible recruits.

In a society based on a large enough majority which supports democratic principles, giving voice to absolutist groups does not constitute a risk to society as a whole. Israel, however, is in a paradoxical situation in which separatist cultures are battling against the Western-style secular democracy, sloganizing about fighting the ruling elite, when this elite has already lost its political power, and is fast becoming a minority numerically. This creates a close race between the fundamentalist religious militant groups who advocate scrapping the principles of equality and democracy, and the individualistic, therefore less organized, Israelis who lack the zeal of the challengers. Taking into account the changing demography, this contest may end with the disappearance of pluralist society. This brings us back to the well known difficulty democratic societies have in defending themselves against antidemocratic rhetoric, which is risky even in more established societies than Israel, with more years of internalized democratic values. This is the dark side of "participation," which serves as a reminder against seeing it only in glowing but oversimplified terms as the road to creating more pluralism.

Having pointed to the problematics inherent in the expectation that "national integration" may be maintained (in an improved, less hegemonic manner) when bringing in the "participation of multiple voices," I return to demonstrate this in greater detail by looking at Israeli society and media in the era of monopoly radio, in the era of the monopoly TV, and in the era of the multiple commercial channels.

Radio days

As a child in Jerusalem in the 1950s I spent hours listening to sounds coming out of our radio, a massive piece of furniture imported from Germany, which occupied the center of the livingroom (Hartley and O'Regan 1992). An avid listener to "the children's corner," I became acquainted with British miners, children in pre-revolutionary Russia, slaves and masters in the American South, and young local heroes who helped to throw the British out, played host to dishevelled, displaced, orphaned refugees from Europe, and unravelled ancient treasures in Palestine's countryside. I remember my alertness when the voice of Moshe Hovav—the grim announcer assigned to rituals and major crises—was heard reading the news, the tears in father's eyes when Adolf Eichman's arrest was announced, the panic aroused by Prime Minister Eshkol, who was heard to "hesitate" in the anxious days leading to the Six Day War, Israel's most brilliant war, and the last in which radio alone was in charge of "us" civilians. And although I missed the live broadcast of the voting in the UN General Assembly on November 29, 1947 on dividing Palestine between the Jews and the Arabs—the most moving media event in the state's history—I have listened to the poor shaky recording many times since.

Hebrew radio was established a decade before the state, under British Mandatory rule, and seen by the Zionists as a vehicle for rallying the community around the revolutionary goal of self-rule. As "Kol Yisrael" ("The Voice of Israel"), Israel's national radio, it continued to perform, single-handed, for the next twenty years (1948 to 1968), the important national missions of creating common ground for the new state—introducing the disparate groups into a new language, shaping the form and content of the society's high holidays and it everyday life, and providing the common agenda. Kol Yisrael kept the public informed and preserved public morale in times of crisis, made Hebrew into the common operative language, and invented and nurtured a common "Israeli culture"—pouring new content into traditional Jewish holidays, shaping the new "civil" holidays (notably the Day of Independence), incorporating everyone in "great moments of history." Radio was the arbitrator of taste, picking songs which would become popular nationwide; commissioned and produced music; gave form to and reinforced the nation's collective memory, and its national myths; and looked after the waves of immigrants—the Russians and Ethiopians are the most recent—by talking to them in their own languages as well as by teaching them the Hebrew language, so they could be incorporated in the general broadcasts. With the arrival of television (at the beginning of the 1970s), radio had to adjust to the loss of its status at society's center stage for collective ritual, building on its technological advantages of immediacy, accessibility, and interactivity to address listeners individually and intimately. Nevertheless, it kept its prioritized place at times of war and lesser crises.

Reporting from the field and keeping up the nation's morale at times of war

Called "The Voice of Jerusalem," the name came as a compromise between the British suggestion of "The Broadcasting Service of Palestine" and that of the Jewish leadership's—"The Broadcasting Service of the Land of Israel" (Caspi and Limor 1992). (In 1998 the Palestinians were broadcasting on "Palestine radio." The Israeli media refer to the Palestinian territory as "The Palestinian Authority".) The service received its highest ratings during the Second World War, in the fifteen-minute weekly commentary on the international situation, aimed at keeping up the morale of the Jewish population and its Jewish-"Palestinian" soldiers serving in the British army, who, in 1942, watched the Nazi army arriving in Alexandria. This role of military interpreter (something between a government propagandist and an independent commentator) became an important institution in wartime. During the Six Day War and, more important, in the anxious period leading toward it, Israelis rallied round the daily radio talks by retired general Haim Herzog, later to become President.

Radio's essential role in wartime has been sustained during the entire period of Israel's existence, even after the establishment of television deprived it of most of its ceremonial and integrative roles. Its accessibility and immediacy, both for reporting from where the action is, and for being heard everywhere (by people at work, in cars, and so on), and the freedom of movement provided by transistors, ensure its continuing centrality in crisis. During wartime (the Yom Kippur War, the Gulf War) the country's radio channels (Kol Yisrael and Galey Zahal—the Army Radio) unite into one channel, both for symbolic reasons and in order to maximize the potential of professional reporting. Though at such times (as in lesser security crises) reporters are torn between their role as citizens and their role as professionals, reporting has generally proved credible (Liebes 1997). Wartime Radio also carries sidelines jobs such as interactive advice programs, soldiers' messages to their families, and even nightime "silent broadcasts" for sleeping citizens, invented during the Gulf War, for the purpose of broadcasting the alarm at time of missile attacks. In war, radio is the most authoritative medium, that is, what in peacetime we would call hegemonic.

Wrongly imagining the audience, and self-consciously inventing "Israeli culture"

Radio, in its first years, was engaged full-time with updating and defining canonic Hebrew, inventing and cultivating "Israeli culture," and, simultaneously, integrating new immigrants into this language and culture. Radio's way of turning immigrants into Israelis had been established during the first years of independence, when the new state received more than twice the number of its original inhabitants. The immigrants were Jewish refugees from Morocco, Yemen, or Iraq who came, following the 1948 war, when their home countries stopped being safe places. In temporary housing in Israel, they joined homeless Jews from Eastern Europe, who had passed through the concentration camps, and had no place to go. The effort of integrating these people into a society which had not yet found its own feet was formidable and, looking back, may have been doomed from the start.

A look at the program scheduled for one weekday in the 1950s shows radio's hierarchical organization of the widely disparate national, religious, ethnic, and cultural groups, living in Israel's 20,000 square kilometers. Kol Yisrael (radio's new name) broadcast on two channels—one nationwide channel, and the second devoted to programs for immigrant groups, by them, and of them, in their own language. This channel broadcast in French (suggestions of sites to visit, a weekly play, news), Yiddish (political commentary, "seeking relatives," "Postbox"—answering listeners' letters, news), Romanian (news, greetings from Israel abroad), Hungarian (news, greetings), Spanish ("with our editor"—talking to the listeners, in the workplace news), Polish (news), Mugrabi ("the government in Israel"—talk, news), and English (news). The same channel also featured Hebrew lessons and "news in easy Hebrew," offering a first step for the immigrant groups to enter the larger society. In terms of our earlier definition, this program broadcast *for* the minority, *by* the majority, *of* the majority. An extended program in Arabic, and a program of church music, titled "a special program for the Christian communities," acknowledged the legitimacy of separate communities, not as targets for incorporation, but as deserving nurturing in their own separate languages and cultures.

The main channel, mostly addressed to mainstream society, opened at 6.30 in the morning with a liturgic singing of psalms, blessing the "tents of Israel," and ended at 11.00 p.m. with the Zionist national anthem (with the unchanged lyrics expressing religious longing from the diaspora), demonstrating how religious rhetoric is ingrained in modern-day secular Israel, entwining the two in a way which would be impossible to disentangle (Kimmerling 1998). As the expression of the desired "Israeli-ness," and a (self) conscious effort to socialize to this culture, radio offered instruction in "everyday Hebrew," talks about local heroes, the teaching of Hebrew songs (titled "sing a new song"), request programs for Hebrew songs, "visits" to sites and settlements, and a prominent time-slot for children and youth programs.

As part of the overall mosaic of very short programs (many lasting only five or ten minutes), within the effort to create a common mainstream language and culture, radio's main channel also provided programs such as "Oriental music" (sometimes in the form of "listeners' requests"), readings from the Bible, and cantorial singing, giving voice to what was perceived as minority cultures, acting as windows for "minority" cultures to present themselves to majority listeners (*of* and *by* the minority, *for* the majority). But the bulk of broadcasting on prime time, and on prestigious days such as Saturdays and holidays, featured classical music (with an effort to incorporate Israeli composers, especially on holidays), radio drama, literature programs (featuring writers and academics who might also discuss Russian or French writers).

Thus, a look at the programs supports the argument that there is a strong sense of hierarchy of cultural expressions to which radio attempts to provide equal access. Even so, programs such as "Oriental music," or "a program for the Yemenite immigrants," demonstrates that broadcasters were not only "integrating" mindless masses into a united whole but were performing a duty to give voice to the "ethnic" cultures of different groups, seeing these as contributing to a ("pluralistic") social dialogue. Indeed, the stars of "Israeli" songs were Yeminite singers, whose music often expressed the (misguided?) attempt of East European composers to create "Oriental" music, in a style that was thought to befit the mosaic of the new country.

Being there when history is in the making

Preceding television in performing secular and religious holidays, and in transporting listeners and viewers to the heart of major ceremonial events, radio's greatest days will be remembered as bringing home, live, the two constitutive events in the birth of the state. The first was the live transmission of the voting in the UN General Assembly (on November 29, 1949) on the division of Palestine into Jewish and Arab states. Captured on newsreel film, at the receiving end, the long-awaited moment is seen in the tense faces of future Israelis, glued to their radio sets, marking down each "yes" and "no" vote, and, at last, hugging and kissing, tears shining in their eyes, when the decision is announced. The second major historical occasion in which Israelis participated thanks to radio, was the assembly of the leadership of the Jewish community in Palestine, in which Ben Gurion, Israel's first Prime Minister, announced the establishment of the state.

During Israel's first twenty years, when television was kept out of bounds, the military parade starred as the high point of the annual Independence celebrations. Ironically just when the right medium for showing off the state's prowess had finally arrived, parades went out of vogue, and were considered vulgar at best. The first broadcast of the new television, some months before it went regularly on air, was a live broadcast of Israel's last parade, after the 1967 war. Independence Day moved out to nature, and later still, into the home, and to the substitutions offered by television (Katz 1998). During the collectivistic years it was radio alone that brought the parade to Israelis who could not get there, making them see the tanks rolling by, and the airplanes demonstrating their acrobatics.

Of the four functions of media in holidays proposed by Katz (1998) Independence Day radio may be said to have supplied the *phatic* function of transporting listeners into the experience (perhaps even creating a more powerful experience by invoking the imagination and, perhaps, by causing listeners to participate more actively than if they had seen the parade on television). Radio also *complemented* the holiday, embellishing it with documentaries, specially written radio dramas, and the singing of Israeli choirs. Radio did not attempt to *substitute* for the event, however. This was not an option in the early days, when people still felt they wanted to share their enthusiasm in person, enough to mingle and dance in the streets on the eve of the holiday, and fight for a place from which to view the parade in the heat. Dusty, sometimes awkward, it was the real thing.

Enter public television

Late for the right reasons?

Television took over the collectivistic role of radio only in 1968. It made its entrance, as its first director tells us, through the back door, and for all the wrong reasons (Katz 1971). What made the Israeli leadership keep television out for twenty years, and what made it change its mind in haste? The serious objections of the political leadership to television, according to Katz, were that it would subvert the effort to renew Hebraic culture, undermine reading, Americanize, and secularize (as argued by religious politicians). There was also fear of the personalization of politics. For twenty years the arguments *for* television, which pointed to its usefulness for nation-building and integration, were not strong enough to overcome these objections.

What finally tilted the balance in favor of television, as in the case of radio, was what the political establishment saw as immediate security needs. In the wake of the Six Day War, the Israeli government, apprehensive about leaving the Palestinians exposed only to Arab TV from the neighboring countries, brought in television in order to safeguard its newly acquired domination. (Ironically, a similar rationale—of safeguarding their rule by venting steam from the Jewish community—led the British to allow the Zionist leadership to establish "The Voice of Jerusalem".)

Defining the role of public television in enhancing integration and multiculturalism

Like radio, then, television broadcasting was introduced for political reasons, but quite opposite to those of radio. Whereas television in the early days embodied the naive hope of heading off a revolutionary movement (in the territories), radio came into being as the voice of a revolutionary movement. But realism prevailed, and by the time regular broadcasting began (in 1968), the pretense of broadcasting to the territories was dropped, and television took its place alongside radio under the aegis of a new (1965) Public Broadcasting Authority, mandated by law. The law demonstrates the lawmakers' belief in the power of the media, as well as in the reconcilability of the values of "national integration" and "multiculturalism." Accordingly, public media are expected by law to reflect "the life of the state, its struggle, its creation, and its achievements," to cultivate good citizenship, to strengthen ties with the Jewish heritage, to reflect the lives and cultural properties of all the "nation's tribes [*sic*!] from the various countries," to broaden knowledge, to reflect the lives of Jews in the diaspora, to advance Israeli and Hebrew culture, to carry broadcasting in Arabic "for the Arab speaking population, and for advancing peace with the neighboring countries," to broadcast to Jews abroad, to provide space for the different opinions and perspectives of the public, and to broadcast credible information. Note that religion is framed in terms of "Jewish heritage" and "values," demonstrating that religion is not considered a threat, or the repression of this threat.

The hierarchical order implicit in the serial mention of Jewish religion, "tribal" culture, and Arab culture is striking. First, broadcasting should act to "strengthen ties" with the Jewish heritage, meaning it should urge incorporation of traditional religious values by the Zionist majority. Next, it should "reflect" the cultures of "all the nation's tribes" in order to provide recognition and status to the minorities in the larger society. Israeli Arabs, lowest on this list, are talked to in their own language, but lawmakers do not include their culture among the cultures of "the tribes" that should be reflected by the broadcasts either for the benefit of society at large or for the enhancement of the minority's status.

The high expectations created by television, and its salience in the public eye, made for harsh criticism and bitter controversy. Radio, which preceded the state, was there from the start, and seemed less threatening, but television was never taken for granted. The debate it had generated twenty years before its establishment continued throughout the years of its operation. It was, and continues to be, attacked politically for toeing the government line; its reporters were, and still are, attacked for being a leftist mafia; it was, and still is, attacked for giving voice only to Western music and culture, or for not giving enough space to Jewish tradition. Also, there was, and still is, a constant debate about the advantages and disadvantages of having more television channels. Incidentally, radio benefited from the fact that television was drawing all the fire, and could be freer to explore more subversive avenues without serious repercussions.

Why did television become the focus for such bitter arguments? First, because of its magical power of transporting viewers to other places, and of making them intimate with real and fictional characters, as if they were in the same room together. (McLuhan should have labelled television as emotionally sweeping and "hot," rather than cognitive and "cold".)

Second, by the time television arrived, everybody—from majoritarian politicians to religious and cultural minority groups—was much more sophisticated about its social centrality and the ways in which it could be used. Thus it immediately became the focus of culture wars. One example is the battle over broadcasting on the Sabbath, which began over the protests of the religious parties; it was decided by an appeal of an individual to the High Court, and considered a victory for the secular majority. Another example is the protest of singers of "Oriental" music (at the beginning of the 1970s) against their supposed discrimination in television's hit parade, and the accusation that producers exercised "racist discrimination" against them. These signs that cultural groups considered themselves outside of the general cultural space seemed peripheral at the time. For most people, however, television did provide a common ground for meeting, in the sense that viewing was accompanied by the knowledge that most other Israelis were also viewing. Television's power to unite was particularly evident on ritual ceremonial occasions, and, daily, on the evening ritual of news.

Gathering Israelis around the "campfire"

The symbol of the power of public television to integrate the nation has been the prime-time evening newscast (Williams 1974), with 70 percent of Israelis tuning in regularly. Israelis did not telephone one another during the news, and viewing was perceived as obligatory in the sense that it was a precondition for joining in conversation the next day. Nevertheless, although television provided a shared agenda for discussion, it did not influence the public's political attitudes, which, from the 1977 election onward, remained split down the middle into "hawks" and "doves" concerning the Arab–Israeli conflict (Liebes 1997).

The centrality of news (and perhaps of other prime-time current affairs programs) shows also in the Katz *et al.* (1997) study, which finds that in the beginning of the 1990s Israelis still regarded television as a medium which served their needs to be informed on current affairs rather than as a medium for entertainment. Radio, with its qualities of immediacy and accessibility, continued to fulfill the collective needs in times of war by mobilizing the reserve units, reporting from the front, instructing the civilian population, keeping up morale, and fighting off rumor (Peled and Katz 1749). War (the Six Day War) brought about the establishment of a popular "open channel," carrying unprogrammed chat and music, always ready for the interruption of breaking news. In between wars, radio's fall from dominance in the era of television brought about its segmentation into a number of channels, cashing in on its qualities of intimacy, informality, and interactivity.

Mobilizing national and group identity in opposition to Dallas

Paradoxically, during the era of the one-channel monopoly, national integration could also be conducted around the viewing of programs such as *Dallas* (Liebes and Katz 1993). Whereas prime-time drama was mostly American, viewing was collective in two senses: first in the viewers' awareness that everybody else is also watching, and in the social and interactive family viewing, which took place mostly round the one television set. Thus, Sue Ellen's morals became a nationwide topic for debate, as heatedly discussed as the pros and cons of retreating from the occupied Palestinian territories. *Dallas* served as a site for debating one's values *vis-à-vis* those of the characters, or, with more sophisticated viewers, *vis-à-vis* those of the producers. A study of the decoding of *Dallas* within different cultural communities demonstrates that certain ethnic groups had early defined their identity particularistically, more in terms of the groups' religion or ethnicity than in terms of individual or of overall national identity. Thus, whereas the news integrated the nation (against the rest of the world), *Dallas* and similar provocations may have contributed to the integration of the specific identity of religious and cultural groups, distinguishing them not only from the capitalist, materialist Americans on the screen but, more significantly, from the Western, non-traditional rest of Israeli society.

Bringing Israelis to participate in history-making moments

The most emotionally uplifting moments in which the viewers felt at one with the collective entity were media events, when television brought history-making into the home (Dayan and Katz 1992). Excepting events such as the Entebbe rescue and Sharansky's landing in Israel, and minor events such as winning international football matches, or coming first in the Eurovision Song Contest, almost all of these media events were highlights in the ordinarily grim narrative of the Arab–Israeli conflict. The emblematic event was the visit of Egypt's President to Jerusalem, to enact the public phase of Israel's peace negotiations with Egypt. This was the case which triggered Dayan and Katz's (1992) insight that leaders who are seeking change may use the power of television to appeal directly to the people over the heads of parliaments and political establishments, circumventing the mediating institutions both on one's own side and the other side. Sensing Israelis' longing for peace, Anwar Sadat had done just that, and had given television its greatest moment. Other moments were less perfect (Liebes and Katz 1997). The signing of the peace with Jordan's King Hussein was less dramatic (as there was prior *de facto* agreement), the signing of the Oslo treaty was more ambivalent on the sides of both leaders, the funeral of Rabin was much more painful. But these, too, were the moments in which television made Israeli citizens into participants, witnesses, sometimes judges, of major events in the country's history.

Television has also invented its own ritual events, notably the celebration of election night, starting with the "television polls" predicting the outcome, staying on to prove that they are correct (once the real results start coming in); the Prime Ministerial debates, in which viewers play judges; and marathon campaigns for good causes. All these are only Israeli versions of what television does elsewhere.

Transfixing Israelis in television-declared disaster marathons

Another unpremeditated live genre, which may have taken the place of the ceremonial events of the 1980s, brings everybody to the set for breaking news. "Disaster marathons" became television's standard format for reporting national traumas during the 1990s, a time in which public television had lost its monopoly to a second competing commercial channel, and to cable and satellite broadcasts. These broadcasts grip the country in the wake of a major news event, mostly following terrorist attacks, but also after the assassination of Prime Minister Rabin, and during the one-day mini-war with the Palestinians following the opening of a tunnel in Jerusalem. On these occasions, television interrupts its schedule, clearing the screen for a disaster marathon which continues long beyond its newsworthiness. This seemingly integrating broadcast may develop into a disruptive rather than a uniting event because of television's need to respond to public feelings by mounting a neo-populist production. At such moments the public returns to the nationwide channels, and television looks for scapegoats to blame, adopting simplified positions, losing the political context, and, with it, infuriating large sections of the population (Liebes 1998). This giving-in to a populist public mood has less to do with journalistic considerations, or with the political convictions of editors, and more with the new capacities of the technology coupled with the demands of cut-throat commercial competition, which affect public broadcasting too .

The era of multiple TV channels

Monopoly public television exploded at the beginning of the 1990s into a multiplicity of channels—with a second over-the-air channel, financed by advertising but supervised by a separate public council, and many cable channels (specializing in sports, children, music, film, and so on). TV's emphasis on news and current affairs shifted more to light entertainment. Talk shows, which have replaced news as the main prime-time public space (Liebes, in press), are fast sinking into sensations, scandals, celebrities, and provocations. At the end of the 1990s these programs dropped all pretense to discuss public issues. The formula for the selection of participants for these programs in 1998 was celebrity, singer, comic, and pretty girls and boys ("hormones," as they are called by one production team). Ironically, the addition of a competing news program has brought down the overall viewership of the news on the two channels to less than what it was when there was only one channel, ending the era in which Israelis felt "obliged" to view the news. A new law of "open skies," already passed by the Knesset, will open Israel to hundreds more channels, completing the transformation of television from a medium that involved Israelis in the political and social agenda to a video shop of identical cheap entertainments, each seeking a maximum number of viewers.

The decollectivization of Israeli society: Can television be blamed?

In the past two decades, two major trends within Israeli society have gradually become apparent. In the 1990s they transformed Israeli society by leading away from a sense of commitment to the polity in two opposite directions. One is the move, within secular mainstream Israelis, away from collectivism, toward individualism. The other is the move of religious and immigrant cultures to separatism or, in some cases, to an attempt to actively substitute for the hegemonic culture. Television cannot be the cause of these trends, but the dynamics of its interaction with various groups in society seems to have contributed to these trends in more than one way.

Television and individualism

The shift in values of mainstream Israeli society from mainly collectivist norms is expressed by the new legitimacy given to hedonistic concerns, engaged more with the present and less with the future, and more with worrying about oneself than about the society and the nation. Katz *et al.* (1997) argue that public television, in its monpolistic era, *slowed up* this process by providing a shared agenda to the whole of the society. On a deeper level, however, a number of less obvious aspects of the message (the patriotism, the constant tension), and of the medium (splitting the audience, personalizing the issues) may have boomeranged, and worked in the opposite direction.

Nor can one ignore the impact of television on the undermining of traditional political institutions (parties, meetings in the town square), shortcutting them as it were by bringing the political leaders directly into the viewers' livingroom. Whereas this new type of public involvement gives access to weaker groups, it contributes to the political passivization of the public (Lazarsfeld and Merton 1948) in that political involvement stays within the livingroom, and does not feed into the public sphere outside. Eventually it may create a feeling of inefficacy and indifference, and reinforce individualism. Television's widely noted effect on the personalization of politics contributed to the direct election for Prime Minister in Israel, and pushed both candidates to the middle of the political spectrum instead of sharpening their ideological differences (Liebes and Peri 1997). Thus, the fears of the medium harbored by the first generation of the political leadership proved right in the long run. The combination of the advances in media technology, and their economic potential, proved strong enough to overcome the initial political intentions of their founders.

In the political climate of the 1990s, the new reality of segmented, entertainment-oriented media fits the political designs of a right-wing government, intent on preventing a serious political debate, by providing Israelis with the voyeuristic visceral pleasures of choosing between Ricky Lane and *Take Off Your Bikini*. To complete this mission the Prime Minister (in his capacity as Minister of Communication) neutralized the public channel by appointing a Director General who hastened to announce that the public is tired of politics, and proceeded to act accordingly. In parallel, the process of marginalizing the public role of media continues by the creation of yet another over-the-air channel to compete with the existing companies that make up the nationwide commercial channel, so that they will no longer be able to afford the fair number of still existing quality programs, including a good news program, and a number of original drama and documentary series.

Television and separate cultures

The second trend away from national integration, which has developed into a real threat to the hegemony of "Israeli-ness" in the 1990s, is the rise of a number of countercultures, mentioned earlier, which are actively working toward changing the state's dominant culture. Strengthened by the decollectivization of the general public, these groups construct their identity *vis-à-vis* the rest of society, some preparing for the struggle of taking over.

The gradual empowerment of these groups is a result of a number of causes (Kimmerling 1998):

1   The inherent difficulty of Zionist nationalism to separate between religion and nation, so that most of the national slogans and symbols are drawn, selectively, from the resevoir of Jewish religion.
2   The unselective mass immigration, mostly from Asia and Africa, in the early 1950s, which had not gone through the process of secularization.
3   The opportunity presented by the Six Day War to the national religious movement for territorial cooptation of the original Land of Israel, as a basis for the creation of a new community according to Halachic Law.
4   The acknowledged autonomy of the Israeli Arab community and the new wave of mass immigration from the former Soviet Union in the 1990s, who, not withstanding their instrumental adaptation to the country, have come to regard themselves as "Israeli persons" who nevertheless hold separate cultural and emotional identities. These societies lead a separate existence in terms of habitation, lifestyles, slang, and so on, and are supported by institutional and sociopolitical systems of their own (such as schools, synagogues, religious and civil beliefs).

How do media enter into the process of empowerment undergone by these groups? First, the technological revolution which made media accessible (first audio and video cassettes, then radio, then time-sharing on satellite TV) could be exploited for integrating separatist communities, and for enticing new followers. The most striking examples of media use for these goals is that of the Ultra-Orthodox-Oriental Shas culture. Quick to realize the effectiveness of electronic media and its compatibility with the group's oral tradition, Shas started with distributing audio-cassettes of populist Rabbis, went on to establish their own, interactive, radio channels, and are now transmitting special satellite broadcasts of the weekly Biblical commentary of their spiritual leader to packed halls of believers.

The use of particularistic, mostly pirate, media channels for recruitment and internal cohesion does not mean that these groups shun nationwide television. Prime-time talk shows have made the representatives of these groups popular, first as curiosities, for their shock value, and later—with the incorporation of Shas, the Ultra-Orthodox and the Russian immigrant party into the new political power elite of right-wing coalition government—for the real threat that they present. From their perspective, these groups take advantage of nationwide television for their needs. All, including the Ultra-Orthodox who ban the viewing of television altogether, appear in advertising spots at election periods. The political leaders of all of these groups give interviews on nationwide television, participate in talk shows, but usually make no concession in the direction of acknowledging universalistic norms in an attempt to be liked by the rest of society. They are there to gain political power by reinforcing their status within their own group, and its sympathizers, soliciting for additional followers. Thus, for example, Ultra-Orthodox politicians make their mark by announcing on nationwide TV that they are not Zionist, that "secular" means "sick," and that their

Talmud-studying sons are serving the country by studying, not by serving in (compulsory) military service the way all non-Ultra-Orthodox are obliged to do. The violation of the principle of equality does not disturb them.

Could the rise of separatism have been brought to public attention earlier? Did public television miss the warning signs? Did it fail in the job of reinforcing national integration by failing to give voice to peripheral groups, and to bring them to the attention of the political establishment? Alternately, did it contribute to the postponement of society's gradual disintegration? Or, perhaps, did it have an indirect effect by undermining the existing political parties, and leaving groups who felt disempowered no other recourse but to start their own separate political institutions? Or are these forces far stronger than anything the political leadership or electronic journalism could be blamed for? In examining the workings of public television we may only speculate on what could have gone amiss.

Reprise: media's role in Israel's evolution from national integration to separatist cultures

In the examination of the role played by Israeli media in regard to national integration and pluralism I proposed that Israel's fifty-year history divides roughly into three periods characterized by their dominant media—national radio in the first two decades, public television in the next two decades, then, during the 1990s, superimposed multiple, mostly transnational TV channels and a parallel system of various versions of religious separatist pirate radio. My main claims are: (1) During the first two decades of Israel's history national radio was in charge of the crucial (and in hindsight probably impossible) task of "national integration," whereas the political debate was carried out in the mostly ideological, party press. (2) Although hegemonic, radio conceived its mission as creating a common ground—on instrumental and ideological levels—among the different ethnic, religious, cultural, and ideological groups, mostly newcomer refugees, from Europe and North Africa, jeopardized by the transition, for many of whom the language was incomprehensible, and idea of democracy new. (3) Radio was the central agent for developing and diffusing a shared "Israeli culture"—based on a Western-style democratic, secular ethos. It was in charge of updating the Hebrew language, defining its "canonic" pronunciation, diffusing existing and new "Hebrew songs." It molded the observance of national (and even traditional) holidays, with contemporary heroes and national myths, drawing on symbols taken from Biblical texts and religious traditions. (4) "National integration," in the first years, mainly offered the various cultural groups access to an odd mixture of the developing "Israeli culture," blending together the riches of Western culture (mainly classical music, world literature and drama) with daily scheduling of liturgic singing, and Bible-reading and commentary, as excerpts of Jewish religion, conceptualized as "heritage." (5) In addition to supplying broadcasts (on a separate channel) for immigrant groups who had not yet mastered the language, radio also made room on the main channel for "ethnic" music and culture. While intended for the minorities themselves, these also gave status to minority cultures and exhibited them to the rest of society (with the idea that mutual acquaintance would eventually breed mutual recognition and respect). (6) On an instrumental level, radio undertook varied missions such as daily morning exercise instruction, a lunchtime program for housewives, tips for farmers, reporting on the daily press, and, in the 1950s, looking for relatives lost in the

Holocaust. (7) Radio brought Israelis into the state's great historical moments, and into national ceremonial events, notably the military parades which marked Israel's independence in its first two decades. (8) In war it was there to report from the front, combat rumor, raise national morale, and tell civilians what measures to take.

Public television, during its monopoly era, displaced radio's role in national integration, albeit in a different form: (1) Whereas radio delineated daily routine, and performed an enormous variety of tasks, television was originally limited to evening broadcasting. Relying on the by-now multichannel radio (broadcasting all day and fast in getting to where the action is), television did what it could do best, leaving radio to take center-stage at times of war, to interact with its listeners, and to provide different channels to cater to (mostly musical) multicultural tastes. (2) With television, the focus of national integration shifted to the shared agenda of the daily evening news, which, during the one-channel era, operated as a "tribal campfire," with most of the country tuning in. (3) Television also took over the performance of traditional and national holidays—in transmitting and supplementing ritual events, inventing its own traditions, often encouraging private, less interactive, modes of celebration by moving Israelis into the home. (4) Ironically, television's form of cultural integration was limited to gathering Israelis to view mostly American programs. As these were watched within the family, and (simultaneously) by most Israelis, they became an important site for struggle over the definition of Israeli-ness. Local drama was missing from the screen, partly because all production efforts went into the unsurpassable drama of the news. (5) Television did "write" the history of Zionism on-screen, and the history of the state of Israel, in two series which gave rise to bitter political–cultural debates, uncovering the internal cleavages. (6) With the technological facilitation of live broadcasting, television adopted the new task of performing national crises alongside preplanned ceremonial events, thus introducing a genre of marathon broadcasting (in times of terrorist attacks, the Gulf War, the Rabin assassination). Such events may also become the focus for unity, but equally often they seem to reveal and egg-on irreconcilable internal conflict. (7) In terms of its impact on political involvement, television undermined political parties by virtually bringing political leaders into the home. What looked like the providing of access to politics, especially for weaker groups, also meant that political involvement started and remained in the private sphere of the home. (8) The ensuing passivization of the public was exacerbated by de-ideologizing and personalizing of politics, itself the product of television.

In the 1990s, when monopoly gave way to numerous, mostly global TV channels, the national integrative function deteriorated and the extent of news viewing declined dramatically. Viewers circulate among channels as they would roam in a video store (Katz 1996). In parallel, the internal integration of separatist groups (for some of whom television is religiously prohibited), and their reaching out for larger audiences, have been reinforced. These ethnic–religious cultures appeal to publics who are increasingly diverted from the general media to their own segmented radio and TV channels. These channels (many illegal) are emerging as the new media of subgroup integration, reinforcing particularistic identities.

Having revealed the end of the story at the beginning, I can only reiterate my admittedly subjective perception that "national integration" and a "pluralist" society in Israel have not lasted "forever," or, worse, have always been an illusion. Looked at from the perspective of the interaction between one society and its media, it may be that the superimposition of the media and of their institutional forms on the parallel social and cultural forces at each stage of the state's development, accelerated the processes of what at first looked like successful "national integration," and later, in a matter of a few years, burst at the seams. Radio may be the most dramatic accelerator, both at the stage of the establishment of cohesion and in the current fragmentation of society into disparate groups.

References

Cardiff, D. and Scannell, P. (1987) "Broadcasting and national unity," in J. Curran, A. Smith and P. Wingate (eds.) *Impacts and Influences*, London and New York: Methuen.

Caspi, D. and Limor, Y. (1992) *The Mediators: The Mass Media in Israel 1948–1990* [Hebrew], Tel-Aviv: Am Oved.

Curran, J. (1998) "Crisis of public communication: a reappraisal," in T. Liebes and J. Curran (eds.) *Media, Ritual and Identity*, London and New York: Routledge.

Dayan, D. and Katz, E. (1992) *Media Events: The Live Broadcasting of History*, Cambridge, MA: Harvard University Press.

Geertz, C. (1983) "From the native's point of view," in *Local Knowledge*, New York: Basic Books.

Gross, L. (1988) "Minorities, majorities and the media," in T. Liebes and J. Curran (eds.) *Media, Ritual and Identity*, London and New York: Routledge.

Hallin, D. (1998) "Broadcasting in the third world: from national development to civil society," in T. Liebes and J. Curran (eds.) *Media, Ritual and Identity*, London and New York: Routledge.

Hartley, J. and O'Regan, T. (1992) *Tele-ology; Studies in Television*, London and New York: Routledge.

Katz, E. (1971) "Television comes to the people of the Book," in I. L. Horowitz (ed.) *The Use and Abuse of Social Science*, New Brunswick: Transaction Books,

Katz, E. (1996) "And deliver us from segmentation," *Annals of the American Academy of Political and Social Science*, 546: 75–92.

Katz, E. (1998) "Broadcasting holidays," *Sociological Inquiry*, 68(2): 230–41.

Katz, E. and Wedell, G. (1977) *Broadcasting in the Third World*, Cambridge: Harvard University Press.

Katz, E., Gurevitch, M. and Haas, H. (1997) "20 years of television in Israel: are there long-run effects on values, social connectedness, and cultural practices?" *Journal of Communication*, 47(2): 3–20.

Kimmerling, B. (1998) "The new Israelis: a multiplicity of cultures without multiculturalism" [Hebrew], *Alpayim*, Tel-Aviv: Am Oved.

Lazarsfeld, P. F. and Merton, R. K. (1948) "Mass communication, popular taste and organized social action," in L. Bryson (ed.) *The Communication of Ideas*, New York: Harper.

Liebes, T. (1997) *Reporting the Arab Israeli Conflict: How Hegemony Works*, London: Routledge.

Liebes, T. (1998) "Television's disaster marathons: a danger for democratic processes?" in T. Liebes and J. Curran (eds.) *Media, Ritual and Identity*, London and New York: Routledge.

Liebes, T. (in press) "Displacing the news: the Israeli talkshow as public space," *Gazette*.

Liebes, T. and Katz, E. (1993) *The Export of Meaning: Cross-cultural Readings of "Dallas,"* Cambridge: Polity.

Liebes, T. and Katz, E. (1997) "Staging peace: televised ceremonies of reconciliation," *Communication Review*, 2(2): 235–57.

Liebes, T. and Peri, Y. (1997) "Electronic journalism in segmented societies," *Political Communication* 15(1): 27–44.

Medzini, M. (1996) "Our political commentator: Moshe Medzini and 'Kol Yerushalaim'," [Hebrew], *Kesher* 20: 82–6.

Pepled, Z. and Katz, E. (1974) "Media functions in wartime: the Israel home front in October 1973," in J. Blumler and E. Katz (eds.) *The Uses of Mass Communication*, Beverly Hills: Sage.

Williams, R. (1974) *Television: Technology and Cultural Form*, New York: Schoken Books.

22 Squaring the circle?

The reconciliation of economic liberalization and cultural values in French television

Raymond Kuhn

France possesses a comprehensive, multilayered media system appropriate to its advanced level of socioeconomic development. During the second half of the twentieth century the structures and functioning of this system underwent significant change. Most obviously, from the 1960s onward television became the most widely used mass medium of information and entertainment, though without fully undermining the specific contributions of the press and radio as print and oral media. Economic liberalization of the broadcasting sector in the 1980s opened up the way for the establishment of new terrestrial television channels. At the same time technological innovation further expanded the potential reach of television through the emergence of additional systems of program delivery such as cable and satellite, which broke the technical straitjacket of television's formative years. In the late 1990s, digitalization pushed the television system further in the direction of multichannel diversity and apparently infinite program choice, while also introducing an element of interactivity into audience usage of the medium. By the end of the century, therefore, the image of one state monopoly channel uniting a nationwide audience in a collective act of passive viewing already seemed a distant memory of a bygone age (Kuhn 1995).

Television's expansion put many issues on the media policy agenda in France. Questions regarding ownership and control, content, financing, and regulation have been at the center of the political debate as policymakers have sought to manage and even anticipate change. Since the early 1980s the television system has moved from one in which state actors played by far the dominant role, to a more differentiated system in which commercial players have become vitally important. This has not led to a simple withdrawal of the state from the field of television policy, but rather to a redrawing of the boundaries between state-led initiatives and the interests of market forces. The state has moved away from an emphasis on top–down control in favor of a role as arbiter and regulator (Barbrook 1995: 148–89). Meanwhile, as French television has become increasingly influenced by supranational and global developments, the state has used regulation to try to protect national cultural values and domestic production industries from external challenges, while also seeking to ensure that French companies are not constrained by excessive domestic ownership restrictions from becoming major players in international media markets.

This changing relationship between state and market provides the organizing framework for this chapter, which is divided into three sections. The first provides an overview of the competitive media system of the late twentieth century, including the press and radio, but with an emphasis on developments in television. The second section investigates the relationship between television ownership, control, and regulation. The third section is concerned with the impact of globalization on French television's cultural role.

France's competitive media system

The growing role played by television in France should be placed within the context of a media system in which competition for audiences and revenue has become ever more intense. Competition has had particularly damaging consequences for the newspaper industry which, whether measured by the number of individual titles or overall circulation figures, has been on the decline since the historic high point of the late 1940s (Albert 1998). Sales of daily newspapers are low by the standards of major European countries such as Britain and Germany, despite a large increase in population and the spread of education since 1945. This is particularly true of those newspapers produced in Paris, which are the only ones which aspire to national status. The biggest-selling newspaper sector consists of provincial dailies, whose comparative success reflects the continuing importance of regional identity even after decades of Jacobin centralist government from Paris. The price to pay for this success, however, has been a considerable depoliticization in content as these papers strive to maximize their local and regional readerships.

In contrast to newspapers, the radio sector has arguably benefited from changes in the media system over the past couple of decades. For much of the post-war era, radio was managed as a state monopoly, with only limited competition from a handful of commercial stations such as Europe 1. The monopoly was definitively abolished in the early 1980s, after which there was a huge expansion in locally based private and community radio stations reflecting a wide range of societal interests. Plagued by financial difficulties, many stations went under because of their inability to raise sufficient advertising revenue, while others recognized "economic reality" and formed themselves into national networks, dominated by a few large companies. As a result, the radio sector moved from state monopoly to unparalleled diversity and then to a commercial oligopoly within the space of a few years. Nonetheless, some of the small-scale community stations continue to broadcast and overall there is a much wider choice of stations than in the days of the monopoly, even if listener choice frequently comes down to selecting from different types of niche-oriented music stations (Hare 1992).

In comparison to the press and radio, television is a relative newcomer to the French media landscape. Though officially established before the Second World War, the medium was slow to make an impact and it was not until the late 1950s that a television set began to be perceived as an essential household item. However, the spread of television in French society was spectacular during the 1960s, with the result that by the end of the decade television viewing had become a routine part of leisure activity. Television's tight grip on the nation's attention has been maintained ever since (Michel 1995).

Television was originally organized as a state monopoly, which grew incrementally (roughly one new channel per decade) to comprise three public channels by the early 1970s. The monopoly was abolished by the Socialist government in 1982 and this opened up the medium to commercial competition. Europe's first terrestrial pay-TV channel, Canal Plus, began transmissions in 1984, while two new privately owned, advertising funded channels started broadcasting in 1986. In the same year the incoming right-wing government took the controversial step of privatizing the main national channel, TF1, which thus became the first public channel in Europe to be hived off to the private sector (Chamard and Kieffer 1992).

As a result, only a few years after the abolition of the state monopoly, the balance in program output between private and public sector channels had shifted significantly to the benefit of the former. During the early 1990s, however, public sector provision in terrestrial television was strengthened while that of the private sector was reduced. In 1992 one of the commercial channels, la Cinq, went into liquidation and in the same year a new Franco-German cultural channel—ARTE—was launched with state support on the terrestrial network vacated by la Cinq. Two years later a public sector educational and training channel, la Cinquième, was established, broadcasting during the day on the same network used by ARTE in the evening.

It was not just in the field of terrestrial television that change was evident. Cable and satellite channels also began to come on stream in the 1980s. The huge potential of fiber optic technology and switched star networks for the provision of a wide range of interactive services persuaded the French state to invest in an ambitious national cable project in the early 1980s (Lunven and Vedel 1993). Simultaneously, the state also provided public resources for the construction and launch of a direct broadcasting satellite (TDF1) to ensure that France would not be left out of what was hoped would be a lucrative hi-tech market for satellite hardware. However, the impact of cable and satellite on the audience was very limited, largely due to the absence of cable networks in many areas and also because of consumer resistance to paying additional costs for television programming at a time when the amount of free television available via terrestrial networks was on the increase. Despite growing private sector involvement in cabling the nation, even by the late 1990s the availabilty of cable across the country was patchy and the hook-up rate of around 10 percent compared very unfavorably with that of Germany and the Benelux countries. Direct broadcasting by satellite was for a long time even less successful than cable in gaining an audience, because of the satellite's limited channel capacity and the perception among viewers that it offered little extension in the way of program choice.

The limited impact of cable and satellite in the transformation of French television in the 1980s is a useful reminder of the need to situate technological developments in media provision within a wider social, political, and economic context. Technological change has undoubtedly had a major influence on the historical evolution of the media in France. To give just one example: new methods of newspaper production and distribution in the late nineteenth century allowed the introduction into the market of mass circulation popular newspapers and ushered in an era of press expansion. However, technology of itself does not determine the form, extent, or pace of change. The introduction of new technology into the newspaper industry in the 1970s and 1980s, for instance, did not have a major influence on the costs of market entry and so did not radically alter existing patterns of newspaper ownership and control (Charon 1991).

More importantly, undue emphasis on technological variables as an explanation for media change can be misleading. The restructuring of the French television system in the 1980s, for instance, was driven more by political than by technological factors. The establishment of a pay-TV channel concentrating on sport and films on the vacant fourth network was a political decision which effectively rejected possible alternatives such as an educational channel or a French-style equivalent of the UK's Channel Four to cater for minority groups and interests in society. The decision to create commercial terrestrial channels was a politically inspired initiative, taken by President Mitterrand in an attempt to present a more modernizing image to his government. Finally, the privatization of TF1 was part of an ideologically driven wide-sweeping economic program undertaken by Prime Minister Chirac's government (1986–88) during a period when conservative forces in France were infused with New Right ideas from the United States. In short, technological developments clearly open up possibilities for change, but political and economic decisions are crucial to an understanding of how that change does (or does not) manifest itself in any given media system.

Ownership, control, and regulation of French television

As the previous section has made clear, a series of public policy decisions by the state resulted in a radical restructuring of the French television landscape during the 1980s. Historically, the state, and in particular the core executive, has been by far the most important political actor in the development of television in France. Indeed for a long period the state appeared almost omnicompetent. Its transmission and programming monopoly meant that until the early 1980s no commercial television channel was allowed to broadcast. Only a very restricted internal market existed from the late 1960s onward in the form of regulated competition between the two main public channels. This was institutionalized after 1974 with the break-up of the unitary state broadcasting corporation and the creation of separate public television companies (Bachmann 1997). In addition to its legal monopoly, the state also interfered directly to structure television's news agenda. For example, during de Gaulle's presidency (1958–69) television news was controlled by the executive to further the interests of the Gaullist regime (Bourdon 1990). For a long time legal monopoly and political control seemed to be two sides of the same coin of state domination of television.

The abolition of the monopoly altered the dynamics of the television system, but without introducing a deregulated, commercial free-for-all which French elites had viewed with some alarm taking place in Italy in the late 1970s. The state continued to control market entry to terrestrial television, with franchises for the new terrestrial commercial networks allocated by state-appointed regulatory authorities. Moreover, in the liberalized television landscape of the post-monopoly era the state introduced regulations designed to prevent concentration of ownership both in the television sector and across different media. This was in response to a situation whereby various press groups were seeking to diversify into television ownership, thus raising questions about the creation of dominant cross-media market positions. Encouraged by the intervention of the Constitutional Council, in 1986 the executive introduced maximum quotas based on market share and potential audience size to govern mono-media and cross-media ownership.

The state also continued to impose rules on television content. During the monopoly era, onerous public service regulations were imposed on state television. Their object was to preserve an educative and informational role for the medium in addition to its entertainment function. Content regulations were not abandoned in the post-monopoly television landscape. However, these were modified to take account of the different status of the outlet, with tougher regulations applied to the public sector terrestrial channels than to pay-TV and thematic channels.

In an attempt to signal an end to the tradition of direct governmental control of television, regulatory authorities were created in the 1980s to supervise the application of the rules and act as a buffer between government and broadcasters (Franceschini

1995). Unsurprisingly, given the tradition of partisan politicization of television, the powers and composition of the regulatory authorities were the object of heated political debate. In fact, between 1982 and 1989 no fewer than three different regulatory authorities succeeded each other: the High Authority (1982–6), the National Commission for Communication and Liberties (1986–9) and the Higher Audiovisual Council (1989–) (Chauveau 1997).

The demise of the first two can be explained by their failure to establish their legitimacy independent of the governments which created them. The High Authority, for instance, was perceived by many on the right to be a tool of the Socialist government, though the evidence for this is hardly overwhelming. The National Commission for Communication and Liberties was reviled by the left for its alleged pro-right sympathies and publicly denounced by President Mitterrand in 1987. Its successor, the Higher Audiovisual Council, has had a longer shelf life than its two predecessors combined and the fact that it was not replaced by Chirac on his accession to the presidency in 1995 perhaps indicates an emerging elite consensus on the Higher Audiovisual Council's performance of its regulatory functions.

With regard to the state's news management activities, government censorship was largely abandoned and direct control relaxed during the presidencies of de Gaulle's successors. In a powerful symbolic move, the Ministry of Information, authoritarian bastion of Gaullist control of state television news, was abolished in 1969. However, the tradition of a close relationship between state and television, especially the public sector channels, has never been wholly relinquished. Appointments to top managerial and editorial posts in public television continue to be made, at least in part, on the basis of political rather than purely professional criteria. More generally, the executive's attempts at media news management are increasingly based on its status as a primary definer. Privileged institutional status and the possession of important news management resources undoubtedly help the executive in its agenda-shaping activities, especially at politically sensitive periods such as the *Rainbow Warrior* scandal and the French military involvement in the Gulf War.

It is clear, therefore, that as far as television is concerned, the state remains an important actor in respect of two of its traditional functions: policymaking and news management. Yet it is also the case that its capacity simply to impose its will in either area has been on the decline over the past two decades. For example, on the question of market entry into the digital television market, the government abandoned the interventionist approach of picking a single national champion and instead allowed three consortia to engage in head-to-head competition. In the field of television news management the capacity of the executive to shape the agenda has been weakened by internal division (such as party-political conflict within the governing coalition or inter-ministerial disputes over policy) and further complicated by the increasingly common experience of cohabitation (1986–8, 1993–5 and 1997–), which institutionalizes a presidential/prime ministerial diarchy at the very heart of the state.

Changes in the relationship between the state and television were accompanied by a growing role for commercial players as the television system became increasingly influenced by market forces. The abolition of the monopoly and the subsequent expansion of television allowed commercial companies to enter a previously barred economic sector of activity. A notable new entrant, for example, was the construction group Bouygues, which despite having no previous experience in the media field took a controlling stake in the privatized TF1 in the late 1980s. Just as significantly, a more competitive television market influenced the behavior of all the main players, whether their status was public or private. The privatization of TF1 changed the balance of the whole television sector, compelling the two remaining public sector channels to compete with their commercial rivals on the latter's terms. The budgetary constraints within which the public sector television channels had to operate had deleterious consequences for the companies' program ouput, audience ratings, and staff morale. Across the system as a whole certain program genres (for example, home-produced fiction and drama) declined, while others (such as variety shows and feature films) increased. Competition for viewers and advertising revenue intensified, with an emphasis on entertainment programming to attract mass audiences. In this new world of French television, the search for advertising funding became crucial for prosperity and even market survival. In these circumstances it appeared that state regulation could not effectively counterbalance the commercial imperative.

Yet it would be misleading to portray the French television system of the 1990s as simply market-led. A more accurate description would be that of a regulated market, in which the interrelationship between regulatory push and market pull in conditioning the behavior of the television channels underpins the functioning of the system. Commercial considerations drive much of the decision-making within television companies, but in the field of terrestrial television generally and most particularly in the case of the public sector companies, the state still exerts an important regulatory influence.

It must be said that it is difficult to make sweeping generalizations about where in practice the balance of influence lies between state regulation and market forces. The case of the demise of la Cinq in 1992 is a case in point. From one perspective the collapse of this commercial terrestrial channel was the result of the company's inability to generate an audience of the requisite size or socioeconomic composition to attract sufficient advertising and thus make itself financially viable—an apparently clear case of market failure. Yet, this analysis needs also to take account of the fact that in terms of its program output the channel was constrained by what its operators regarded as an unnecessarily demanding regulatory regime. Suspicions were voiced that by 1992 the Socialist government was prepared to use regulation to drive a channel out of existence because it considered that the market was oversaturated to the detriment of the terrestrial television system as a whole. In other words, according to this version of events, the channel was regulated out of existence (Perry 1997).

Globalization and national cultural values

Though the changing balance between state and market in French television in the latter part of the twentieth century took place largely within a national context, the interrelationship between them also has to be situated within a changing international media environment. The state and commercial companies may operate predominantly within a domestic television system, but this system is increasingly influenced by European and global developments.

Traditionally the French television system has had solid national roots. The size of the country in terms of both territory and population, combined with its linguistic specificity, ensured that in contrast to several smaller Western European societies, France was able to support a well implanted indigenous television system. Ownership and control of the medium, its output, and regulation were overwhelmingly dominated by national players and domestic considerations. In the 1960s, for example, state television was used by the Gaullists to promote a sense of national consensus around the institutions of the Fifth Republic and their foreign and defense policy, which emphasized French independence and grandeur. Television programs during de Gaulle's presidency were supposed to reflect the best of French values and culture back to the nation, disseminating high cultural artifacts to the growing home audience, even if in practice this lofty objective was not always achieved. The organization of television as a state monopoly limited the sources of program output for French viewers, while the technical constraints of terrestrial transmission ensured that programming from foreign television channels had virtually no impact on large sections of the French audience. To a significant extent, therefore, French television functioned as a closed national system (Thomas 1976).

This is no longer the case. Increasingly, French television is influenced by external developments which have had an impact in areas such as technology, ownership, programming, and regulation. Cable, satellite, and digital technology have undermined the previously largely impregnable national borders in television transmission, allowing output from non-French broadcasters to be easily received within France itself. Foreign media entrepreneurs (such as Berlusconi and Maxwell, though as yet not Murdoch) have for a time held an ownership stake in the liberalized French television system. To fill up the expanding schedules, the amount of imported programming has increased, while domestic variants of foreign programs (such as a French version of *Spitting Image*) have also become part of the staple diet of output. Finally, as a member state of the European Union (EU), France is subject to the regulatory provisions of the EU in television matters, including quotas on European production.

The opening up of France's television borders is, of course, a two-way process. It also allows French companies and product to enter other previously largely closed television markets, notably in other parts of Europe. Some domestic companies have taken advantage of this market enlargement. The most notable success in this regard has been Canal Plus, which within France has successfully pursued a corporate strategy based on vertical integration and in so doing has built up a powerful domestic base in the technological and production sectors (for example in access systems and feature film production) from which to expand into foreign markets. The company has successfully exported its pay-TV format to some other European countries, as well as taking a stake in foreign subscription television ventures. The exploitation of digital technology is currently being used by Canal Plus not just as part of a commercial strategy to increase market share in the domestic market, but also to help position itself as an important transnational player. In similar fashion TF1 has tried to build on its national success as a terrestrial broadcaster to become part of a leading digital consortium in France and also to seek partnership with other leading European broadcasters to be present as a program provider in European markets.

Meanwhile, the French state has tried, albeit with limited success, to use the EU as a forum in which to pursue its own domestically driven television agenda. This has included support for European media initiatives to promote European cultural identities and counter what France regards as the undesirable consequences of American dominance of the global audiovisual market. Such initiatives have included support for subsidies to European independent production companies and quotas on European product to be shown on television channels operating within the EU (Collins 1994).

The state has also taken steps to ensure that French media companies are not disadvantaged by unduly onerous national regulatory constraints on ownership which might prevent them attaining the critical mass considered necessary to compete effectively in international markets. Governments on both right and left have been conscious that few French media companies can really be regarded as major international players. The dilemma faced by government is that the domestic market is not large enough both to sustain a wide range of successful television companies and to provide France with big hitters at the European and global levels. Consequently, regulations currently in force, as well as trying to minimize the extent of foreign shareholdings in French media, allow for significant mono-media holdings and cross-media diversification. The opening up of international television markets has led the French state to prioritize economic and industrial objectives at the expense of an emphasis on domestic pluralism and diversity.

Though for media companies the opening up of markets across Europe may be regarded as a commercial opportunity, globalization has largely been perceived by French political elites as a threat to national cultural values. As a result, much of the state's regulatory thrust in matters of audiovisual content has been dominated by the desire to protect French culture from the allegedly undermining influence of Anglophone media product, notably from the United States. Steps taken in this context include program quotas of home product for French television, the French government's stance during the GATT negotiations in the early 1990s to protect its domestic audiovisual industries, the Toubon law which established a quota on Francophone music output for French radio stations, and the establishment of ARTE as a vehicle for hiqh-quality European cultural television programming.

Certainly strong cultural and economic arguments can be put forward in defense of this approach in terms of promoting national values and protecting indigenous pro-duction industries. Yet some of the underlying rationale for this protectionist approach may be open to question. First, protectionism may featherbed inefficient work prac-tices and provide a subsidy to substandard national product. In the long term this may work against the interests of French production companies competing in an increas-ingly internationalized media economy. Second, if defended on cultural (rather than purely economic) grounds, a protectionist approach may bring the issue of the na-tional origin of product into contradiction with the pursuit of quality in programming. Some programs made outside France may quite simply be better than any of their French equivalents. Third, imported programs such as fiction series and feature films are frequently popular with French viewers. Defense of national product may run up against the exercise of consumer sovereignty in the television marketplace. In short, the policy objectives of greater consumer choice, high-quality output, and the defense of French culture often appear to be in conflict.

More generally, the state's traditional post-war concern that French television should reflect national cultural values is also often at odds with the more liberalized competi-tive system which it has helped bring into being. The growth in the number of channels and the routinization of television viewing have amplified the role of the medium as a vehicle for popular as opposed to high culture. In the 1990s much television output was geared to mass taste, with the viewer regarded as a consumer to be satisfied rather than a citizen to be informed and educated. Game shows, light entertainment pro-grams, soap operas, and films fill the screen. The essential difference between the formative years and the present day is that in a multichannel system there is bound to be more programming catering for popular tastes than in the early elitist years of a single-channel state monopoly. The increasing confinement of high cultural program-ming to specialist channels or the fringes of the public sector networks is the consequence of a market-oriented system replacing a paternalistic, state-dominated one. Regulation may have an influence in program schedules and content, but it is working against the grain of a largely market-driven system.

The state's cultural concern may also reflect a somewhat outdated, Jacobin view of the mass audience. Television has a role to play in reflecting the diversity of contemporary French society. In this respect it has secured some success. For example, young people are better catered for than ever before by television's expansion, with more programs aimed at the 15–34 age group and whole channels geared to youth taste in music, fashion, and video. This development reflects the economic importance of youth in a consumer society. Other social groups have been less well catered for, as television has failed to keep pace with some social changes. For example, while the magazine sector targets women in many of its publications (Bonvoisin and Maignien 1986), television has been slower to adapt to reflect women's growing economic power and diversity of societal roles, even if some women such as Michèle Cotta and Christine Ockrent have provided role models by occupying top positions in French television companies (Ockrent 1997). Perhaps the most glaring failure of French television in the 1990s was its reluctance to reflect the multi-ethnic composition of French society. Whether evaluated in terms of specific programs for ethnic minorities, ethnic minority characters in mainstream fiction output, or positive ethnic minority role models in factual programming (for example, in news presentation), French television largely failed to adjust to the multicultural nature of late twentieth-century society (Hargreaves 1997).

Here a possible contradiction is evident in the approach of the French state to cultural promotion via the audiovisual media. In international forums the French state has emphasized the importance of regulating the global market so as to promote diversity and prevent international cultural homogeneity. Yet regulation has been little utilized to achieve the same objective for different social groups within France itself. Of course it is perfectly legitimate for television to act as a unifying force in society. Television coverage of the national football team's World Cup success in 1998 and of the collective celebration which accompanied it aided a (short-lived?) feeling that whatever their color, gender or class, all French people were part of one society. But television also needs to take account of ethnic, gender and regional pluralism if important social groups are not to be left feeling marginalized by or excluded from the medium.

Conclusion

This chapter has emphasized two key features of the French television system in the late twentieth century. The first is economic liberalization which originated in the 1980s and had important consequences for the relationship between state and market. The state abandoned its monopoly in television ownership and the commercial imperative of audience maximization became the driving force for the functioning of the restructured system. Stung by the costly failure of its government-backed cable and satellite projects in the 1980s, the state also adopted a more market-led approach to the promotion of digital television in the following decade. The era of governmental dominance of French television, particularly marked during the de Gaulle presidency, was over. This was particularly evident in news management activities where the executive could no longer simply impose its agenda on a compliant television newsroom.

Yet this is only part of the picture. Economic liberalization was not synonymous with simple state withdrawal from the field of television policy. The state turned to regulatory levers to influence the operations of the market it had helped create. Regulatory authorities were established to oversee the functioning of the new system and tensions were frequently evident between the channels and the regulators as their different value systems came into conflict.

The role of state regulation was particularly important in the light of the second development emphasized in this chapter: the increasing impact of European and global trends on the domestic television market. While presenting opportunities for French media companies to expand abroad, the permeability of France's previously secure national borders was also perceived by state elites as a challenge and even a threat to national cultural values. Globalization in the media was equated with Anglo-Saxon cultural imperialism, which necessitated a regulatory response from both national and European agencies.

There is a contradiction between economic liberalization and cultural sovereignty which is difficult to resolve. Economic liberalization has made for a more competitive domestic television market in which channels need program product to fill their schedules. Much of this, inevitably, is produced outside France, with the United States as an obvious major external supplier. Cultural sovereignty requires a healthy domestic production industry and, in an era of globalization, an international market for Francophone production. The latter does not compare with the Anglophone or Hispanic market, while the former, though growing, is less developed than its counterpart in Britain. In the newly emerging digital television market it will need all the state's regulatory guile and the domestic market's entrepreneurial skills to allow French media companies to reap the benefits of liberalization at home and abroad while at the same time maintaining a high level of home-produced, good-quality programming.

References

Albert, P. (1998) *La presse française*, Paris: La documentation française.

Bachmann, S. (1997) *L'éclatement de L'ORTF*, Paris: L'Harmattan.

Barbrook, R. (1995) *Media Freedom*, London: Pluto.

Bonvoisin, S.-M. and Maignien, M. (1986) *La presse féminine*, Paris: Presses Universitaires de France.

Bourdon, J. (1990) *Histoire de la télévision sous de Gaulle*, Paris: Anthropos/INA.

Chamard, M.-E. and Kieffer, P. (1992) *La Télé: dix ans d'histoires secrètes*, Paris: Flammarion.

Charon, J.-M. (1991) *La presse en France*, Paris: Seuil.

Chauveau, A. (1997) *L'Audiovisuel en liberté?* Paris: Presses de Sciences Po.

Collins, R. (1994) *Broadcasting and Audio-Visual Policy in the European Single Market*, London: John Libbey.

Franceschini, L. (1995) *La régulation audiovisuelle en France*, Paris: Presses Universitaires de France.

Hare, G. (1992) "The law of the jingle, or a decade of change in French radio," in R. Chapman and N. Hewitt (eds.) *Popular Culture and Mass Communication in Twentieth Century France*, Lampeter: The Edwin Mellen Press.

Hargreaves, A. (1997) "Gatekeepers and gateways: post-colonial minorities and French television" in A. Hargreaves and M. McKinney (eds.) *Post-Colonial Cultures in France*, London: Routledge.

Kuhn, R. (1995) *The Media in France*, London: Routledge.

Lunven, R. and Vedel, T. (1993) *La Télévision de demain*, Paris: Armand Colin.

Michel, H. (1995) *Les grandes dates de la télévision française*, Paris: Presses Universitaires de France.

Ockrent, C. (1997) *La mémoire du coeur*, Paris: Fayard.

Perry, S. (1997) "Television," in S. Perry (ed.) *Aspects of Contemporary France*, London: Routledge.

Thomas, R. (1976) *Broadcasting and Democracy in France*, London: Crosby Lockwood Staples.

Index

Abu-Lughod, L. 75
Adler, Ilya 99
Africa: media in newly independent states
    157–8; rural population disadvantaged 161
Africa Media Investments (AMI) 171
African National Congress (ANC) 279, 280,
    285, 289–90
Al-Ahram (Egypt) 180
Alemán, Miguel 102
Algeria 68, 72
Alisky, M. 100
All-Russia State Television and Radio
    Company *see* VGTRK
Althusser, Louis 295
Ananda Krishnan, T. 143
Anderson, Benedict 294–5
Ang, Ien 7, 147, 148
Anglo American Corporation (AAC) 283,
    285, 286, 290
Appadurai, Arjun 69
Arab Radio and Television (ART) 71
ARABSAT 70
Argentina 54, 55, 56, 58–9
Argus Holdings Ltd 158–9, 283, 284–5, 286
ARTE (Franco-German TV channel) 326,
    331
Asahi (Japan) 192, 193, 196, 199, 200
Associated Newspapers of Zimbabwe
    (ANZ) 170–1
Australia 237–48; Asian culture in 244–6;
    broadcasting in 237, 238, 239–40, 241–4,
    245–7; film in 238, 239, 240–1; Internet
    in 243; media ownership in 240–1,
    243–4; multiculturalism of 244–7; power
    and media in 241–4; press in 237, 240,
    243; television in 239–40, 241–4
Australian Broadcasting Corporation (ABC)
    238, 240, 241, 242, 245–6
authoritarian regimes: and media 4, 15,
    54–6, 124, 124–6; in newly independent
    African states 157, 175–6; pressure to
    democratize in Middle East 69; and
    regionalism in Korea 115

Ayish, Muhammad 70, 75
Azcárraga, Jr., Emilio 101, 102, 103, 105, 108

Bahrain 69, 73, 74
BBC (British Broadcasting Corporation) 71,
    160–1, 162, 181, 227–8, 233, 268, 308
Berezovsky, Boris 87, 88, 89
Berlusconi, Silvio 45, 84, 88, 275, 330
Berry, C. 246
Birch, D. 246
Black Consciousness (BC)(South Africa)
    280, 281, 282, 285
Black Editors' Forum (South Africa) 285,
    289
Blair, Tony 233–4
Blanchard, Margaret 267, 268
Blumler, J. 202
Boland, C. 247
Bolivia 54
Boyd-Barrett, O. 6
Brazil 8, 54, 55, 56, 59
Britain 15, 221–36; auditing practices
    225–6; broadcasting in 227–31, 233;
    gender issues in 226–7, 230; globalization
    and media in 233–4; marketization and
    media in 230–1; news coverage in 230;
    political power in 221–7; press in 231–4;
    privatization in 225; radio in 223, 224;
    satellite broadcasting in 227, 231;
    television in 223, 227–31, 233
Broadcasting Corporation of China
    (BCC)(Taiwan) 127, 129
Bruce, Nigel 286, 288, 290
Brynen, R. 69
BSkyB (British satellite company) 227, 231
Bulgaria 40
Burger, Die (South Africa) 287
Burrell, G. 134
Butler, D. 230
Butler, Nigel and Rhett 168

Cable News/Network Egypt (CNE) 184,
    187

Cable News Network International (CNNI)
184
Callard, S. 65, 73
Canal Plus (French TV channel) 325, 330
capitalism: global 8–10; and racial
oppression in South Africa 281–2;
transition to 41–3, 81–3
Cárdenas Solorzano, Cuautémoc 99, 100,
105
Cardiff, D. 308
Central America 45
Central Daily News (Taiwan) 127, 129,
130, 135
Central Europe 31, 35–49
Central European Media Enterprises Group
(CME) 35, 43–4, 48
Central News Agency (CNA)(Taiwan) 129
Chadwick, P. 237
Chan, J.M. 28
Channel 3 (Britain) 227, 228, 230, 231, 233
Channel 4 (Britain) 227–8, 230, 231, 233
Chatterjee, Partha 295–6
Chavunduka, Mark 170, 172, 173
Chen, Huailin 28
Chernomyrdin, Victor 89
Chiang Ching-kuo 125, 131
Chiang Kai-shek 125, 126
Chile 54
Chimutengwende, Chen 171, 173, 174
China 21–34, 81; active audience in 29–31,
32; advertising in 23, 26, 27; censorship
in 22, 23, 24, 29, 93; and Hong Kong
media 24–5, 30, 31; Internet use in 30,
93; market forces and media in 14, 15,
21–2, 25–7, 32, 45; media practices in
22–3, 26; pay journalism in 23, 26;
popular culture in 29–30, 31; press in 22,
23–4, 30, 31; "reading zones" 29–30;
state control over media in 21, 22, 23, 24,
26–8, 134–5; uneven liberalisation of
media in 23–4, 31
China Times (Taiwan) 127, 135
Chinese Communist Party (CCP) 21, 22, 27
Chomsky, Noam 134, 245
Chosun Ilbo (Korea) 113, 116–17
Choto, Raymond 172
Chronicle (Zimbabwe) 164–5
Chun, Doo-Hwan 113, 114, 115
la Cinq (French TV channel) 326, 329
Clarín and Clarín Group (Argentina) 58–9
clientelism 98, 100, 115–16, 121, 125–8
Clinton, Bill 212, 214, 215; Clintonism
9–10
CNN 70, 184
Colombia 52, 54, 58, 59
colonialism 157–8, 160, 244, 295–6
communism: media after fall of 35–49

Communist Party of the Soviet Union
(CPSU) 81, 85, 97
Confucianism 112, 131
Conservative Party (Britain) 221, 222, 223,
224–5, 230–1, 232, 233
Cook, Timothy 209, 216
Cornford, J. 7
corporatism: liberal corporatism in Britain
221–36; in Sweden 252–3, 255
Corriere della Sera, Il (Italy) 270, 271, 276
COSATU (South Africa) 280, 290, 291
Council for African Thought 288–9
Cow Protection movement (India) 303–4
critical political economy perspective 103–6,
107, 133–4
Crocodile Dundee (film) 239
Cuba 81
cultural globalization 7–8, 10–11
Cunningham, S. 242
Curran, James 124, 148, 265, 309
Czech Independent Television (CNTS) 43
Czech Republic/Czechoslovakia 39, 40, 41,
43, 46

Daily Gazette (Zimbabwe) 167–9, 170
Daily News (Zimbabwe) 170, 171
Dallas (US TV soap) 6; in Israel 316
Dangwai movement (Taiwan) 131
Davies, H. 7
Dayan, D. 316
De Gaulle, Charles 327, 332
Deegan, H. 67
Deng Xiao Ping 24, 27
developing countries 5–6, 67; media and
modernity in 4–5, 293–304
Dong-A Ilbo (Korea) 113, 116–17, 118–19
Dongo, Margaret 176
Donohue, G.A. 128
Doordarshan (Indian TV system) 296–7, 302
Downing, John 3, 32
DPP (Taiwan) 129, 132, 133

East Germany 38, 40, 46
Eastern Europe 14, 15, 31, 35–49, 67
Echeverría, Luis 101, 102
Egypt 14, 15, 178–88, 316; broadcasting in
70, 71, 179, 181–5, 187; cable TV in 184;
censorship in 179, 186; globalization
threat to culture of 185; Internet in 180;
press and publishing in 179–80, 186;
radio in 181–2, 187; satellite broadcasting
in 72, 183–4; state control of media in
179, 181, 186–7; television in 181,
182–5, 187
Egyptian Radio and Television Union
(ERTU) 70, 71, 183–4
Egyptian Satellite Channel (ESC) 183, 184

Egyptian Space Channel 70
Egyptian Television 182
Eko Moskvy (Russian radio station) 87
Electronic Media Network (M-Net)(South Africa) 283, 285, 286, 287
Eliasoph, N. 204
Elliott, Philip 58, 230
Eurnekian, Eduardo 58
Europe after fall of communism 35–49
Excélsior (Mexico) 101, 103–4

Fairfax (Australian media company) 240
Featherstone, M. 133
Feng, Jiansan 133
Financial Gazette (Zimbabwe) 168–9, 172, 177
1st Net (Middle East) 71, 184
Folha de São Paulo (Brazil) 56, 59
Forcella, Enzo 266
Forrester, C. 72
Foster, Frances F. 94
Four Theories of the Press (Siebert *et al.*) 3–4, 36–7, 40–1, 244, 267
France: cable TV in 326; censorship in 327; competitive media system in 325–7; globalization and media in 329–32; media ownership and regulation in 327–9; press in 325, 326; privatization of media in 325–6, 326–7, 328–9; radio in 325; satellite broadcasting in 326; state influence on media 324, 327–9, 332, 333; television in 324–34, 332
Free China (Taiwan) 126, 130
Frith, S. 8
Future (Lebanese satellite channel) 71

Gamson, W.A. 204, 211
García Canclini, Néstor 98
Garnham, N. 124
Geertz, C. 307
Gellner, Ernest 294
German Democratic Republic (GDR) 38, 40, 46
Gibson, Ross 238–9
Giddens, Anthony 6, 7, 11, 234
Giorno, Il (Italy) 270
Glasgow University Media Group 228–9
Globo network (Brazil) 45, 54, 55, 56, 59, 108
Golding, Peter 124, 134, 268
Gorbachev, Mikhail 80–3
GOSTELRADIO (Russia) 85–6, 89
Gouldner, A.W. 131
Guanzhou Daily (China) 22
Gulf War 70, 184, 209, 311
Gurenvitch, M. 315, 318
Gusinsky, Vladimir 87, 88, 89

Habermas, Jürgen 63, 300
Hall, Stuart 6, 206
Hallin, Dan 5, 130, 306–7
Hamilton, Mike 168
Hankyoreh (Korea) 116, 120–1
Hansen, Miriam 303
Hao Bocun 130, 132
Hegel, G.W.F. 46
Herald (Zimbabwe) 165–6, 167, 169
Herman, E. 6, 134
Hindu TV epic in India 296–300, 302–3
Hobsbawm, Eric 11
Hong Kong 21, 24–5, 30, 31, 134–5
Horizon (Zimbabwe) 166–7
Hungary 38–9, 41, 44
Hutton, Will 234

Ibbotson, Peter 163, 164
Illustrated Weekly of India 297
Imevision (Mexican TV network) 105
imperialism, media 5–6, 8, 13, 53
Independent Newspapers 171, 284, 285, 289
Independent Television Commission (ITC) 227, 233
India 13; *Ramayan* Hindu TV series 296–300, 302–3; secularism in 296, 297–8; television in 296–300
Inglehart, R. 203
Instituto Federal Electoral (IFE)(Mexico) 102–3
Inter-American Press Association (IAPA) 51, 100
International Monetary Fund (IMF) 9, 14, 67, 120
Internet 30, 93, 180, 243
Iran 7, 66, 68, 70, 74
Al Isbo'a (Egypt) 180
Islam 66, 69, 73, 74, 178, 183
Israel 15, 70, 72, 305–23; cultural evolution and diversity of 307–8, 308–10, 311–13; democratic participation and media in 306–7, 308–9; news coverage in 315–16, 316–17; radio in 305, 310–13, 315, 320–1, 322; separatism in 309–10, 318–22; Shas culture in 319–20; television in 305–6, 313–20, 321
Italy 15, 45, 265–78; advocacy journalism in 270–2; broadcasting in 271; media ownership in 88, 276; "professional model" of journalism in 265–78; television in 275
ITV (Britain) 227, 228, 230, 231, 233
Iyengar, S. 210
Izvestia (Russia) 83, 84

Jacka, T. 6
Jamrozik, A. 247

Japan 14, 15, 122, 127, 191–201; audience
     ratings 195–6; cable TV in 191–2;
     censorship in 196–7; comics 194;
     journalism in 201; news coverage in
     198–9; press in 192, 193–4, 196–7,
     199–200; radio in 192; satellite
     broadcasting in 191–2; state influence in
     media in 194–6; television in 191–2,
     194–6, 198–9
Japan Socialist Party 198, 199, 200
Al-Jazeera Satellite Channel (Qatar) 71
Johannesburg Consolidated Investments
     (JCI) 283, 285
Johnnic 285–6, 288, 290
Joongang (Korea) 116–17
Jordan 72
Jornada, La (Mexico) 104, 107, 108
Junco de la Vega, Alejandro 104, 107

Kagiso Trust Investments (KTI) 287, 290,
     291
Katz, E. 306, 309, 313, 314, 315, 316, 318
Kavanaugh, D. 202
Khoo, B.T. 141
Kim, Dae-Jung 115, 122
Kimmerling, Baruch 308
Kluge, Alexander 300–1, 303
KMT (Nationalist Party)(Taiwan) 125,
     126–7, 128, 128–9, 130, 133, 135
Kocher, R. 272
Kol Yisrael (Israel) 310, 312
Korea 13–14, 15, 111–23; active audience in
     118–20, 121; advertising in 116;
     alternative media in 119–20, 120–1;
     broadcasting in 113–14, 117, 119; cable
     TV in 117; cultural homogenization in
     118; globalization strengthens state power
     in 122–3; information monopoly in
     117–18; journalism in 113, 114–15,
     118–19; liberal model in 121; news
     coverage in 113; press in 113, 116–18,
     118–19, 120–1; regionalism in 112,
     115–16, 121–2; satellite broadcasting in
     117; state influence on media in 112–16,
     120, 122; Suso corruption scandal 114;
     television in 117
Korea Broadcasting Advertising Corporation
     (KOBACO) 113–14
Korean Broadcasting System (KBS) 119
Kultura (Russia) 86, 87, 90, 94
Kuwait 66, 71, 72
Kuwaiti Investment Properties Co. (KIPCO)
     71
Kwinjeh, Grace 173

Labour Party (Britain) 221, 222, 223–4,
     226, 229, 233–5

Latham, Brian 168
Latin America 14, 15
Lauder, Ronald 35
Lawson, Chappell 105
LBC (Lebanese satellite channel) 71
Lealand, G. 239
Lebanon 71, 73
Lebed, Alexander 89
Leftwich, A. 67
Lenin, Vladimir Ilyich 36, 37–8
Lerner, Daniel 4–5, 64, 146
Li Denghui 130
Liba (Taiwanese cable operator) 133
liberal corporatism in Britain 221–36
liberal democracy in South America 56–9
Liberal Democratic Party (LDP)(Japan) 191,
     194–6, 197, 198, 199
liberal model 3–4, 50–2, 100–3, 106, 107,
     121; media dependency critique 52–4, 56
liberal-pluralism 124, 134
Liberty Times (Taiwan) 129, 130, 135
Lijphart, A. 274
Lin Rongsan 129
Linz, J. 125–6
Lisovsky, Sergei 87, 88, 92
Lo, Ven-hwei 129
Logovaz (Russian media company) 87
Los Angeles riots 205–6
Los Angeles Times 205
Lukács, G. 37
Lukes, S. 204
Lumby, C. 239–40
Luzhkov, Yuri 87, 89

M-Net (South Africa) 283, 285, 286, 287
McChesney, R. 6
McClelland, D. 141
McGregor, Robin 284
McLuhan, Marshall 7
McNair, B. 230
McQuail, D. 244
Mahachi, Moven 172, 173, 174
Mahathir Mohamad 139, 140–2, 143, 145,
     146, 147, 149, 150, 151
Mainichi (Japan) 192, 193, 196, 199
Makgoba, William 291
Malashenko, Igor 88
Malaysia 14, 15, 139–156; Asian values in
     149, 151; audience in 147–9; background
     139–42; economy 140, 141, 150; legal
     controls on media 144–5; Look East
     policy 140, 150; media studies in 147,
     149–50; multiethnic population 139; New
     Economic Policy 140, 141, 144, 150;
     press in 143–5, 146; privatization in
     141–2, 143, 150–1; satellite broadcasting
     in 143; state control of media 142–5,

146–7; television in 142–3, 145, 146; Vision 2020 policy 140, 142, 151
Malaysian Chinese Association (MCA) 144, 150
Malaysian Indian Congress (MIC) 143, 150
Mandaza, Ibbo 173
Mandela, Nelson 176, 281, 287–8
Marx, Karl 293; Marxism 124–5
Mass Democratic Movement (MDM) 280, 281–2
Mass Media Trust (Zimbabwe) 158–60, 170
Mattei, Enrico 270
Mazwai, Thami 288, 289, 291
Mbanga, Wilf 170
MBC television (Middle East) 70–1, 72
MDF (Hungarian Democratic Forum) 41
media dependency paradigm 52–4, 56–7
media imperialism 5–6, 8, 13, 53
Media Institute of Southern Africa (MISA) 175
Media-Most (Russian media company) 86, 87
Mega TV (Malay subscription TV) 143
Mejía Barquera, F. 101–2
Mercurio, El (Chile) 54
MetroVision (Malaysian TV channel) 143
Mexican Academy of Human Rights 105
Mexico 15, 97–110; clientelism in journalism in 100–1; critical political economy perspective 103–6, 107; earthquake 104–5; and liberal model 100–3, 106, 107; market forces and media in 14, 103–6; media ownership in 101; news coverage in 100, 103, 104, 105, 106; "perfect dictatorship" in 98–9; press in 97, 99, 100–1, 103–4, 107, 108; radio stations in 104–5; state and media in 98–103, 103–4; television in 97, 99–100, 101–3, 107–8
Middle East 14, 63–78; censorship in 65, 73, 74, 77; "culturally sensitive programming" in 73–4; democratization of 67–9; gender issues in 68, 74–5, 76–7; as geo-political area 65–6; illiteracy restricts influence of press in 65, 75, 181; market forces and media in 75–6; Middle East and North Africa (MENA) 68, 70; MMDS facilitates state control of media 72, 74; satellite broadcasting in 71, 72; television in 65, 70–7
Middle East News Agency (MENA) 180
Miller, T. 237
Milner, Andrew 238
MMDS (multichannel multipoint distribution system) 72, 74
Modern Daily (Taiwan) 135
modernization: and media in developing

countries 4–5, 64, 293–304; and media imperialism 5–6; in Middle East 66, 67, 77
Modus publications (Zimbabwe) 168, 169
Morgan, G. 134
Morley, D. 148, 151
Morocco 72
Morris, Bill 224
Morris, Meaghan 239
Moskovsky Komsomolets (Russia) 90
Motlana, Ntatho 284, 290, 291
Motoyama, Hikoichi 196
Moyse, Andrew 166
Mozambique 157, 158
Mubarak, Hosni 178, 179, 180, 182–3
Mugabe, Robert 158, 165, 172, 174, 175, 176–7
Mukhoty, Gobinda 298
Mulgan, Geoff 234
Munro, Ian 271
Muradzikwa, Henry 165
Murdoch, Rupert 25, 45, 84, 227, 241, 244; and New Labour 233–4; News Corporation 237, 239–40, 243
Murdock, G. 124, 134, 149, 230
Murialdi, Paolo 271
Murphy, Clive 168, 169
Musarurwa, Willie 165
Muzenda, Simon 164

Namibia 175
Nasionale Pers (Naspers) 283, 286–7, 289
Nasser, Gamal Abdel 178, 179, 182, 186
National Empowerment Consortium (NEC) 285–6, 290, 291
nationalism: and media 203, 294–5, 306–7, 320–1; in post-colonial states 296, 301
Ncube, Trevor 169, 177
Negt, Oskar 300–1, 303
Neilan, E. 129
New African Publishers (NAIL) 284, 285, 288, 290–1
New Nation (South Africa) 285
New Straits Times Press (NSTP)(Malaysia) 144
New York Times 205
News Corporation 237, 239–40, 243
NHK (Japan) 191–2, 194, 195, 197, 199
Nikkei (Japan) 192, 193, 199
NileSat project 183–4
Norte, El (Mexico) 104
North Africa *see* Middle East
North Korea 45, 81; *see also* Korea
Norton, A.R. 69
Nova TV (Czech Republic) 43, 44, 48
NTV (Russia TV channel) 86, 87, 88, 94
Nyarota, Geoffrey 164–5, 169, 170
Nyezavisimaya Gazeta (Russia) 83

Oman 69, 72
Omar, Hanif Mohamad 143
O'Neil, J. 239–40
Oneximbank group (Russia) 84, 87
Orbit (Middle East) 71, 73
O'Regan, Tom 239
O'Reilly, Tony 171, 284, 285, 290
ORT (Russia) 80, 84, 86, 87, 90, 92, 94
Ottone, Piero 270
Al Oula (Orbit programme) 73
Owen, Ken 288

Packer family company 240, 241, 243, 244
Palestine 65, 68, 72, 311, 313
Pandey, Gyan 299
Panebianco, Angelo 273
Parade (Zimbabwe) 166, 167, 170
Park, Chung-Hee 112, 113, 114, 115
Partido Revolutionario Institutional
    (PRI)(Mexico) 97, 98–9, 101, 102, 103,
    105, 106
Patterson, Tom 213–14, 266
Penny Press (United States) 269, 272
Perskor 283, 286, 287, 290
Peru 54, 55–6, 57, 59
Peterson, T. 3–4, 36–7, 40–1, 244, 267
Phoenix Satellite Television Company (Hong
    Kong) 25, 28
PIPSA (Mexico) 100, 104
Poland 38, 39, 41–2, 44
Pool, Ithiel de Sola 5
Poptsov, Oleg 89–90, 91
Porto, M. 108
Pravda (Russia) 83
Premier-SV (Russia) 87, 92
Proceso (Mexico) 104, 105, 107
public sphere concept 63; counter-public
    sphere 300–2, 303–4
Público (Mexico) 104, 107

Qatar 69, 71, 72, 73, 74

Radio Rossiya (Russian radio station) 90
Ramaphosa, Cyril 286, 288
Ramayan (Hindu TV series) 296–300,
    302–3
Rampal, J.C. 131
reception studies of audience 147–8, 151
Reforma (Mexico) 104, 107
Repubblica, La (Italy) 272–3, 276
"reverse colonization" 6
Rhee, Syngman 112, 113
Rhodesian Broadcasting Corporation (RBC)
    162
Robins, Kevin 7, 8
Roh, Tae-woo 114, 115, 116
Romania 38, 40, 44

RTR (Russian TV channel) 86, 87, 89–91,
    94
Rusike, Elias 167, 169
Russia 7, 14–15, 79–94; broadcasting in
    85–91; censorship in 84–5; Gorbachev
    and transition to capitalism 39, 80–3;
    journalism in 91–2; press in 83–5; private
    sector media ownership 87–9; publicly
    owned broadcasting service 89–91;
    satellite broadcasting in 86; scandal
    coverage 84; state interference in media
    89–92; stock market crash (1998) 79,
    92–3; television in 80, 83

Sadat, Anwar el 178, 179, 180, 182, 316
Sagalayev, Eduard 86, 90–1
Saidi, Bill 168
Salinas de Gortari, Carlos 104, 105
Salinas Pliego, Ricardo Benjamín 105
Samper, Ernesto 58
Sánchez Ruiz, Enrique 108
Sankei (Japan) 192, 193
SANLAM (South African company) 284,
    290
Saravision (Saudi Arabia) 74
Saudi Arabia 68, 69, 71, 72, 74, 187
SBS (Korean TV channel) 117
Scalfari, Eugenio 272–3
Scandinavian Broadcasting Systems (SBS)
    43, 44
Scannell, P. 308
Scherer García, Julio 104
Schiller, Herbert 5
Schlesinger, P. 230
Schramm, Wilbur 5, 146; *Four Theories*
    3–4, 36–7, 40–1, 244, 267
Schudson, Michael 3, 103, 131, 272
Sekai (Japan) 200
Serra, Sonia 8
Seymour-Ure, C. 273
Showtime (Middle East) 71, 184
Siebert, F. 3–4, 36–7, 40–1, 244, 267
Siglo 21 (Mexico) 104, 107
Sinclair, J. 6
Singapore 122, 149, 150
Sistema (Russian media channel) 86, 87
Sithole, Tommy 165–6
Sklair, L. 13, 67
Slater, D. 203
Slovakia 41, 43–4
Slovenia 39–40, 43–4
Smith, David 166
Smythe, Dallas 240
social democracy 9–10
Social Democratic Party (SAP)(Sweden)
    252–3, 254
social liberalism 8–9

Socialist Democratic Party (Japan) 198, 199
Solidarity (Polish labour movement) 38, 39
South Africa 67, 176, 279–92; Afrikaans-
language press 280, 286–7; broadcasting
in 280, 283, 289, 291; counter-hegemonic
movements in 280–2; Freedom Charter
281, 282; historical background 279–80;
media ownership in 279, 280, 283–9,
290–1; "national culture" problematic in
282–3; press in 283–90; radio in 291
South African Broadcasting Corporation
(SABC-TV) 162, 283, 287, 291
South America 13, 45, 50–62; audience in
57; authoritarian regimes and media 15,
54–6; censorship in 57; liberal democracy
and media in 56–9; media concentration
in 58–60; media dependency paradigm in
52–4, 56–7; press aspires to liberal model
50–4; state influence on press in 51–2, 56,
57–8, 60; television in 54, 55–6, 58, 59
Sowetan (South Africa) 284, 285, 287, 289
SpaceNet (Egyptian Space Channel) 70
Sparks, C. 3, 31
Special Broadcasting Service (SBS)(Australia)
237, 240, 242, 245–6
Springer Company 44
Sreberny-Mohammadi, A. 6
Staniland, M. 126
Star (South Africa) 173
STAR TV (Hong Kong) 25, 28, 132, 239,
302
Starovoitova, Galina 93
Stent, Michael 171
Straits Times (Malaysia) 144
Strange, S. 69
Sunday Independent (South Africa) 289
Sunday Mail (Zimbabwe) 165
Sunday Standard (Zimbabwe) 170, 172
Sunday Times Business Times (South Africa)
288
Svanidze, Nikolai 91
Sweden 13–14, 15, 251–64; broadcasting in
258; citizenry 254–5, 262–3; immigrant
population 255; media and power
transitions in 256–63; political
background 252–6; press in 256–7,
259–62; radio in 258; scandals exposed
by media 261
Swedish Association of Employers (SAF)
259–60
Swedish International Development
Association (SIDA) 166–7

Taiwan 14, 15, 122, 124–38; broadcasting
in 127–8, 132–3; cable TV in 132–3, 135;
censorship in 126; copyright in 132;
"incorporation" policy 125, 135; press in
126–7, 128–31; state control of media in
125–6, 127–8, 132, 134; television in
127–8, 132–3
Taiwan Daily News 128–9, 135
Tanzania 157, 158
Televisa (Mexican TV company) 45, 97,
99–100, 101–2, 103, 104, 105, 106, 108
Televisión Azteca (Mexico) 105, 106
TF1 (French TV channel) 326, 327, 328–9,
330
Thatcher, Margaret 230–1
Thomson Publications 166
Tichenor, P. 128
Tien, Hung-mao 131
Times Media Ltd (TML) 283, 284, 285,
286, 288, 289, 290
Tumber, H. 230
Tunisia 72
Tunstall, J. 267, 273
Turkey 66, 70
TV Asahi (ANN)(Japan) 192, 198–9
TV-6 satellite channel (Russia) 86
TV-Tsentr (Russian TV channel) 86, 87
TV Tokyo (TN) 192

UAE (United Arab Emirates) 72
Ukraine 44
UMNO (Malaysia) 143, 144, 150
Al-Umran, Hala 73, 74
UNESCO 54, 268
United Daily News (Taiwan) 127, 129, 135
United Democratic Front (UDF)(South
Africa) 280, 281–2
United Nations Development Programme
(UNDP) 67, 68
United States 15, 202–20; "beat system" of
news coverage 209–10; crime and
violence coverage in 205–8;
"infotainment" 214; media imperialism of
5–6, 53; media ownership in 207, 213,
214; political news coverage in 208–18;
political power and media in 204–5; press
in 205–6, 209–14; public consciousness
and media in 214–15; race issues in media
206–7; scandal coverage 212, 214, 215
Utusan Melayu Group (Malaysia) 143, 144

Vaid-Fera, M. 297
Vargas Llosa, Mario 98
VGTRK (Russian TV channel) 86, 89, 90–1,
94
Vietnam 81; Vietnam War 195

Walesa, Lech 41–2
Wang, Jing 27
Wang Tiwu 127
Wang Yongqing 127

Wedell, G. 306
Weiss, Linda 122–3
Wilson, Clive 168–9, 172
World Bank 67, 68, 140

Yeltsin, Boris 82, 84, 85, 86, 88, 89, 90, 91,
    93, 94
Yemen 68
Yomiuri (Japan) 192, 193, 196, 199, 200
Yugoslavia 39–40

Zambia 157, 158, 175
ZANU(PF) (Zimbabwe) 158–60, 164, 165,
    170, 172, 174, 175–6
(PF)ZAPU (Zimbabwe) 165
Zassoursky, I.I. 36, 43, 88
ZIANA news agency (Zimbabwe) 159, 165
Zimbabwe 14, 15, 157–77; BBC task force
in 162; broadcasting in 160–4; censorship
in 173–4; conflicts in Congo 172, 173–4,
176; Ibbotson report 163, 164; news
coverage in 163, 164; press in 158–60,
164–75; radio in 161, 162, 164;
Rhodesian Front regime 158, 161, 162,
168, 176; state control of media in
158–60, 161–3, 172–3, 175–6; television
in 163–4; "Willowgate" scandal 164–5
Zimbabwe Broadcasting Corporation (ZBC)
    159, 160, 161–3, 164
Zimbabwe Independent 169–70, 172, 177
Zimbabwe Mass Media Trust (ZMMT)
    158–60, 170
Zimbabwe Mirror 170, 172, 173
Zimbabwe News 172
Zimpapers company (Zimbabwe) 159, 160,
    165, 168, 169, 170, 171